BEYOND LIBERALISM

IRWIN UNGER

New York University

XEROX COLLEGE PUBLISHING

Waltham, Massachusetts / Toronto

Beyond Liberalism: The New Left Views American History

To TONY and BETSY

Contents

10. Women's Liberation in Perspective

11. The Uses of Violence in America

Introduction

Clearly the most important political development of the 1960s was the emergence of a New Left in the Western nations. In many ways this was a startling phenomenon, seemingly unconnected with what had preceded. Though the Socialists and Communists had made sharp gains immediately following World War II, the traditional Left soon went into eclipse. The Cold War and relative prosperity characterized the latter 1940s and the 1950s, and under the double influence of fear and affluence, Left dissent dwindled or went into hiding. Where strong Marxist parties had existed, as in western Europe, the Left survived, but it became increasingly fossilized and incapable of acting either to precipitate revolution or to effect reform. Where socialism had always been weaker, as in the United States, and where it became the target for vigorous repression, Left opposition virtually disappeared as an active force.

The eclipse was intellectual as well as political. Socialism had been more than a political movement; it had also been a potent analytical tool in the work of philosophers, sociologists, economists, anthropologists, and historians. In each of these fields, Marxist questions, if not Marxist answers, often dominated the dialogues of thinkers and scholars. Even where a non-Marxist orthodoxy predominated, it was often defined in opposition to some alternative Marxist hypotheses.

And in no discipline was the dialogue between the Marxists and their opponents more fruitful and impassioned than in history. Marx himself was a philosopher, an economist, and a sociologist, but at the very heart of his system was a theory of historical development that emphasized the material basis of society and the crucial role of class struggle in generating change. The production and distribution of goods ultimately determined all else in society including art, science, law, religion and even morality. Unfortunately in each society the products of human labor had been unequally allocated. Some men produced wealth, other men enjoyed it, and this great difference set up severe strains that eventually set off revolution and a fundamental change in the class basis of society. Ancient slave society gave way to feudalism; feudalism was followed by bourgeois capitalism; and capitalism in turn, after a desperate struggle that would take the form of imperialism, would be overthrown by socialism. The oppressor classes would disappear and exploitation of the many by the few would finally end for mankind.

This dramatic, secular cosmology intrigued some of the best minds of the nineteenth and twentieth centuries. Marx and his close friend, Frederick Engels, only laid the foundation of what eventually became an elaborate and sophisticated edifice of historical interpretation. Before World War I, men like George Plekhanov and Karl Kautsky helped fill in the outline sketched out by Marx and Engels. In our own century, European Socialists, intellectuals, and scholars such as Albert Mathiez,

Christopher Hill, E. H. Carr, Maurice Dobb, V. Gordon Childs, and others, further developed the Marxist canon, focusing primarily on the great European social revolutions of modern times. With the triumph of the immense Russian and Chinese socialist revolutions of the twentieth century, the Marxist interpretation of history became official dogma in almost one-third of the world.

In the generation extending from about 1910 to 1940, Marxist history also took root in the United States. Some of its practitioners were avowed Socialists or Communists. Algie Simons, Herbert Aptheker, Louis Hacker, Philip Foner, Gustavus Myers, and a small group of authors connected with International Publishers, candidly acknowledged their allegiance to socialism and their adherence to the Marxist historical canon. They wrote studies of American capitalism, of slavery, of the Revolution, of the early national period, and of the Civil War, strongly colored by the Marxist emphasis on class and conflict.

Simultaneously, another conflicting version of American history had begun to emerge, associated with the Progressive impulse of the early twentieth century. The Progressive historians were overtly dedicated to making the past answer questions about the American present. They dissented from the prevailing conservative history, written mostly by easterners and emphasizing the continuities in American life. Native-born midwesterners or southerners, committed to change, these Progressive scholars drew inspiration from an indigenous, American, dissenting, egalitarian tradition. At the same time, however, they were more intensely influenced by Marxist ideas than they were generally willing to admit.

The Marxist and the Progressive interpretations of the American past overlapped at many points. Both views emphasized the prevalence of domestic conflict and social strife; both stressed the economic basis of politics; both discovered hidden social revolutions in the War for Independence and the Civil War; both excoriated imperialism and monopoly capitalism; and both sympathized with the plight of the wage earner. But Marxists and Progressives also disagreed. Where Hacker, Aptheker, and Foner might deplore the most recent manifestations of capitalist excess, they usually respected the constructive work of modernization accomplished by the capitalists in the past. The Progressives were more moralistic and disapproving. To Vernon Parrington, Carl Becker, Fred Shannon, J. Franklin Jamison, Arthur Schlesinger, Sr., and above all, Charles Beard, American capitalism seemed almost evil at every stage of our past. Capitalists had fought against the forces of social and political democratization. Even where their goals and those of the people had coincided, as during the Revolution, the elite had acted selfishly to advance their own interests and to hold back social democracy. The progress made during the Revolution had been followed, in the Critical Period, by the reaction inherent in the conservative Constitution, engineered by the commercial interests. Temporarily checked by the forces of the agrarian South and West, two sections somehow more virtuous than the Northeast, capitalism had triumphed once more with the election of Lincoln. The Civil War that came after Lincoln's election was primarily a revolt of the agrarian South against the threatened domination of the industrial-commercial Northeast. The War was not a struggle for black liberation; it was a triumphal bourgeois revolution, the American equivalent of Europe's great revolutions of 1640 and 1789. And so it went. Each page of the American past was a confrontation between the "masses" and the "classes," with the people invariably duped, defeated, and betrayed. Even such an apparent victory for social democracy as the Homestead Act of 1862, according to David Shannon and Paul Gates, was converted into a vehicle for the engrossing of great chunks of the public domain by speculators.

During the 1920s and the 1930s, the influence of Progressive history was immense. In the earlier decade it suited the debunking mood of the intellectuals who found little to love in the America of Harding and Coolidge. In the thirties, the Progressive mood reinforced the general disillusionment of the intellectuals with American capitalist institutions. With one-fourth the labor force unemployed and the economy stagnating, it required little encouragement for sensitive men to accept the past villainy of the business classes.

World War II and the two decades following witnessed a revulsion against the Progressive historians and also against Marxism, owing to many elements. Men of the Left ascribe it to the needs of the emerging Cold War. The intellectual parallel to the hardening line against the Soviet Union, they say, was a mood of self-congratulation that sought to prettify the American past, and convince Americans that theirs was an unblemished society. Historians who embraced this celebratory approach, many of them erstwhile Progressives and even Marxists, either had been "co-opted" by the attractive blandishments of our affluent society or else had been frightened into conservatism by the witch-hunts of the McCarthy era. Whatever the reason, the historians, like the liberal intellectuals in general, lent themselves to the cause of international reaction and the neo-imperialist role of postwar America.

Whether we accept or reject this interpretation, it is clear that the historians writing in the 1950s and early 1960s did seek to refute the Progressives. In contrast to the vigorous conflict posited by Beard, Becker, Parrington, and the rest, they proposed a broad consensus among the American people, running through almost our entire past. According to Daniel Boorstin, Louis Hartz, Richard Hofstadter, and others, Americans had agreed on the fundamentals of private property and political democracy virtually from the beginning. Conflict had been minimal, or where it was severe, it often involved psychic as opposed to actual economic deprivation, and encouraged fanaticism rather than reasoned and rational opposition. America in this view, was a land that had largely fulfilled its promise and, with the great exception of slavery and the Civil War, had resolved its conflicts with a minimum of disruption and disorder. A different version of this new mood accepted the existence of conflict but rejected the deep dualism implicit in Progressive history. In place of two broad interests battling over fundamentals, a multitude of pressure groups argued over the spoils.

Each of these approaches minimized conflict and emphasized American exceptionalism. At times they seemed to be glorifying America and denying serious national failings. We have had no truly dispossessed classes, if we have had classes at all: we have resolved our difficulties at the ballot box rather than the battlefield; we alone, among great powers, have resisted preying on our neighbors and have managed to avoid extensive imperialist adventures. Obviously there were flaws in this virtuous record. Slavery and the Civil War did produce strife that could not be peacefully resolved. During the earlier phases of industrialization, festering slums appeared, and a restless, discontented working class emerged. During the 1890s, we seized a small empire in the Caribbean and the Far East. But these were the exceptions that proved the rule. We abolished slavery, and finally ended the possibility of future political schism. The slums, and the poor who inhabited them, were a passing phase of the industrialization process. Our imperialist venture was a momentary aberration. The United States no doubt had had its problems, but it solved them more successfully than any other nation on the globe.

Reviewing this national portrait from the vantage of the 1970s, it is easy to see why it came under attack. Its seeming smugness and complacency was apparently belied by the events of the 1960s. In that decade of turmoil, the United States began to look like anything but an unmitigated success. While the country's income grew remarkably, this merely emphasized the persistent poverty of large numbers of our citizens. Blacks were no longer slaves, but legal, social, and economic discrimination were still endemic in the nation. America no longer maintained a formal colonial empire, but it had seemingly become the residual legatee of the colonial empires of the western European nations, and was the main force behind the neocolonial regimes remaining in Europe's former possessions.

Even liberals reviewing the actualities of the sixties have become somewhat skeptical of the positive historical view of consensusites and pluralists. The young men of the Left found it almost totally abhorrent. How could so imperfect a nation have had so perfect a past? Already alienated from the American present, they have come to deplore much of the American past, to doubt the successes, and to focus on the compelling failures. Their outrage against the apologists for present America soon was transformed into anger against the apologists for past America. By 1970 they were well on their way to constructing a version of American history that was influenced by their deep conviction of the country's recent failings.

The beginnings of New Left history can be traced to the work of William Appleman Williams and his students at the University of Wisconsin. At that eminent institution, progressivism had never entirely died. Still at work within the Beardian framework was Fred Harvey Harrington, Merrill Jensen, Howard K. Beale, and William Hesseltine. In 1959, a group of Williams' students began publishing *Studies on the Left,* a scholarly journal dedicated to "the radicalism of disclosure." *Studies* was intended as more than a forum for New Left history and in its later years did devote more space to general Left tactical concerns and to current social and economic problems. But during the first years, the emphasis was historical, and it carried much of the earliest and best New Left history, including articles by Williams, Gabriel Kolko, Lloyd Gardner, Staughton Lynd, and James Weinstein.

Four major historical themes engaged the contributors to *Studies on the Left*: "corporate liberalism," radicalism, imperialism, and ethnic minorities, particularly blacks. In each of these areas, the young Left historians, like their Progressive predecessors, sought to relate the past to the present. Their work on corporate liberalism traced a development from the late nineteenth century through the 1920s that culminated in the post–World War II, corporation-dominated society. Their examination of radicalism looked for precursors to inspire the Left today and provide it with a sense of continuity in America. Their scrutiny of imperialism attempted to disclose the roots of American neocolonialism and to demonstrate the persistence of American expansionism. Their writing on race focused on the long tradition of white bigotry and oppression and the equally long tradition of resistance by blacks.

In 1967, owing to differences among the editors, *Studies on the Left* ceased publication. But by this time, the journal was no longer the principal forum for New Left history. Many of the original contributors had completed their graduate studies. They had entered university teaching, and had begun to write for the traditional professional journals and to publish scholarly monographs. By 1967, they had been joined by many other scholars in their late twenties and thirties who also refused to accept the political and historical orthodoxies of the fifties. The new flood of scholarship reflected the broadening base of the New Left "movement." The original group at *Studies on the Left* had been Socialists. They were scarcely orthodox Marxists and their relations with the old Communist Party were highly ambivalent. They detested the professional anti-Communists, but were themselves capable of devastating criticism of Marxist politics and Marxist history. They were certainly not Communists, but they called themselves Socialists, and Williams himself was an ardent expounder of Marx. Many of the newer scholars were also Socialists, but others were anarchists, black nationalists, and also various sorts of cultural dissenters. The historical themes that concerned them inevitably covered a wider range—women in America, labor and the labor movement, the old South and the Civil War, and antiradical repression.

But despite the expansion of New Left historical scholarship, many of the traditional problems of American history still have not received New Left attention. The New Left has neglected the whole area of the colonial experience. A considerable body of New Left writing now exists on the Revolution and the era of the Confederation; but there is little on the early years under the Constitution or on Jacksonian Democracy. New Left historiography seriously neglects traditional party politics in general, at least those up to the era of the New Deal and Fair Deal. The young Left historians are interested in blacks, and to some extent Jews, but they have not yet written extensively on Indians or European immigrants. They have been occupied with Socialist, abolitionist, and other radical thought, but they have, as yet, neglected cultural history. Urban history has not attracted New Left scholars, nor, except for the work of Eugene Genovese, have they given much attention to economic history. Almost all of their copious writings on American foreign policy have emphasized the period since 1870.

In this collection, therefore, I have not been able to provide a New Left interpretation of every phase of the American past; some traditional and important topics have been omitted entirely. In a number of other cases, I have chosen the only available article in the field, although I have not necessarily felt that it does complete justice to New Left scholarship. Unfortunately, the student does not have a general New Left synthesis to fall back on to fill in the gaps. In 1961, William Appleman Williams published the *Contours of American History,* in which he attempted to provide a complete review of American history from a collectivist and Socialist perspective. It was a work of great originality and force, though marred by careless writing and scholarship and a combative tone. Regrettably, the judgments of men and events in this volume were often highly personal and alien to the mood of the younger New Left scholars. Williams has powerfully influenced the New Left concept of the emerging corporate-liberal state and the nature of American expansionism. But much else in the *Contours* seems eccentric. Williams, for example, has nothing but disdain for the Jacksonians and for the abolitionists. He is, moreover, little concerned with the plight of blacks or other minority groups. Most significant, he readily accepts the view that within certain broad limits there was indeed a consensus in America. Obviously, his is a highly individualistic and idiosyncratic statement.

With these warnings in mind, I hope the reader will find the collection that follows a useful guide to this most recent wave of revisionist history. No doubt students of the American past will find much to disagree with in it. Many of the pronouncements are tentative and incomplete, and will eventually be superseded by more mature work by these same radical scholars or by their successors. Even readers deeply committed to the Left will probably quarrel with some of the conclusions of the authors I have included. Fortunately, within the Left itself, there is still open dialogue on policy, theory, tactics, and history. We must all hope that this continues both for the sake of history and for the health of the nation. At all events, the selections below attest to the enduring vitality of the American past as a matter of concern and interest to thinking people.

One final remark on bibliography is in order. The list of works "for further reading" that precedes each selection contains both New Left items and more traditional pieces. My aim here is to provide the reader with the material for his own assessment. It is not my purpose to indoctrinate or persuade. The authors themselves do that. I hope the dialogue they stimulate, whether external or within the reader's own mind, will amply justify the present anthology.

FOR FURTHER READING:

Jesse Lemisch, "Towards a Democratic History," *Radical Education Project Occasional Paper* (1966); Joan W. Scott and Donald M. Scott, "Toward History: A Reply to Jesse Lemisch," and Jesse Lemisch, "New Left Elitism: A Rejoinder," both in *Radical America* (Sept.–Oct., 1967); Irwin Unger, "The 'New Left' and American History: Some Recent Trends in United States Historiography," *American Historical Review* (July 1967); Jerold S. Auerbach, "New Deal, Old Deal, Or Raw Deal: Some Thoughts on New Left Historiography," *Journal of Southern History* (Feb., 1969); John Higham, "The Cult of the 'American Consensus,' Homogenizing our History," *Commentary* (Feb., 1959). A useful volume of essays written from a New Left perspective is Barton J. Bernstein (ed.), *Towards A New Past: Dissenting Essays in American History,* (Pantheon Books, 1968).

ACKNOWLEDGMENTS

*Footnotes have been omitted except where they are
necessary for an understanding of the text.*

ROBERT L. ALLEN, "Black Nationalism." Reprinted by permission of Doubleday and Company, Inc.
Copyright © 1969 by Robert L. Allen.

BARTON BERNSTEIN, "America in War and Peace: The Test of Liberalism." Reprinted by permission
of Random House, Inc. Copyright © 1969 by Random House, Inc.

PAUL CONKIN, "Origins of a Welfare State." Reprinted by permission of Thomas Y. Crowell
Company, Inc. Copyright © 1968 by Thomas Y. Crowell Company, Inc.

MARTIN DUBERMAN, "The Northern Response to Slavery." Reprinted by permission of Princeton
University Press. Copyright © 1965 by Princeton University Press; Princeton Paperback, 1968.

LLOYD GARDNER, "From New Deal to New Frontiers." Reprinted by permission of The University
of Wisconsin Press. © 1967 by the Regents of the University of Wisconsin.

EUGENE D. GENOVESE, "The Origins of Slavery Expansionism." Reprinted by permission of Pantheon
Books, a Division of Random House, Inc. Copyright © 1961, 1963, 1965 by Eugene Genovese.

DAVID HERRESHOFF, "The Anti-Abolitionists." Reprinted by permission of the Wayne State University Press. Copyright 1967 by the Wayne State University Press.

DAVID HOROWITZ, "The Cold War Begins." Reprinted by permission of Hill and Wang, Inc. and
MacGibbon & Kee, Ltd. Copyright © 1965 by David Horowitz.

PAUL JACOBS AND SAUL LANDAU, "The Movement's Themes; The Movement's Origins." Reprinted
by permission of Random House, Inc. Copyright © 1966 by Paul Jacobs and Saul Landau.

PAUL A. C. KOISTINEN, "The 'Industrial-Military Complex' in Historical Perspective: The Inter War
Years." Reprinted by permission of the *Journal of American History*.

GABRIEL KOLKO, "Conclusion, The Lost Democracy." Reprinted by permission of The Macmillan
Company. © 1963 by The Free Press of Glencoe, a division of The Macmillan Company. "The
United States in Vietnam, 1944-66." Reprinted by permission of Beacon Press. Copyright © 1969
by Gabriel Kolko.

WALTER LaFEBER, "The Economic Formulation." Reprinted by permission of Cornell University
Press. © 1963 by the American Historical Association.

MICHAEL LEBOWITZ, "The Jacksonians: Paradox Lost?" Reprinted by permission of Random House.
Copyright © 1969 by Random House, Inc.

JESSE LEMISCH, "Jack Tar in the Streets: Merchant Seamen in the Politics of Revolutionary America."
Copyright 1968 by Jesse Lemisch. Reprinted by permission.

N. GORDON LEVIN, JR. "War and Revolution, I: Wilsonianism and Leninism, The Ideological Setting
of Conflict." Reprinted by permission of Oxford University Press. Copyright © 1968 by Oxford
University Press, Inc.

GORDON LEWIS, "The Rise of the American Mediterranean." Reprinted by permission of the Agenda
Publishing Company.

STAUGHTON LYND, "A Governing Class on the Defensive: The Case of New York." Reprinted by
permission of *Science and Society*.

RONALD RADOSH, "The Corporate Ideology of American Labor Leaders from Gompers to Hillman."
Reprinted by permission of the Agenda Publishing Company.

JOHN ROSENBERG, "Toward a New Civil War Revisionism." Copyright © 1969 by the United Chapters
of Phi Beta Kappa. Reprinted by permission of the publishers.

DANIEL B. SCHIRMER, "William James and the New Age." Reprinted by permission of *Science and
Society*.

ALLEN SOLGANICK, "The Robber Baron Concept and Its Revisionists." Reprinted by permission of
Science and Society.

ATHAN THEOHARIS, "The Rhetoric of Politics: Foreign Policy, Internal Security, and Domestic Politics
in the Truman Era, 1945–1950." Reprinted by permission of Quadrangle Books. Copyright © 1970
by Quadrangle Books, Inc.

STEPHAN THERNSTROM, "The Process of Mobility." Reprinted by permission of Harvard University, Cambridge, Mass. Copyright 1962, 1964 by the President and Fellows of Harvard College.

CELLESTINE WARE, "Problems of Nineteenth Century Feminism." Reprinted by permission of Tower Publications, Inc. Copyright © 1970 by Tower Publications, Inc.

JAMES WEINSTEIN, "The Scope of American Socialism 1900—1912." Reprinted by permission of Monthly Review Press. Copyright © 1967 by James Weinstein.

WILLIAM APPLEMAN WILLIAMS, "The Transformation of Reality and the Inception of New Ideas." Reprinted by permission of The World Publishing Company. Copyright © 1961 by William Appleman Williams.

HOWARD ZINN, "The New Abolitionists." Reprinted by permission of Beacon Press. Copyright © 1964, 1965 by Howard Zinn. "Violence and Social Change in American History." Reprinted by permission of Howard Zinn. Copyright © 1970 by Howard Zinn.

BEYOND LIBERALISM

1. The Era of the American Revolution

Jack Tar in the Streets: Merchant Seamen in the Politics of Revolutionary America JESSE LEMISCH

For the New Left, American history begins with the American Revolution. In the next few years, as the number of young Left professional historians grows, this will probably change. But as judged by the published work thus far, the New Left does not feel deeply concerned about the period before 1763.

The years surrounding the struggle for independence, however, have seriously engaged them. The reason for this is obvious. Revolutions always interest radicals, though radical scholars have generally devoted more of their attention to the French and Russian revolutions than to our own. One problem with our domestic upheaval is its ambiguity. It is called suggestively both the American Revolution and the War for Independence. Which was it? Was it both? One answer is indirectly provided by Jesse Lemisch, who has devoted his scholarly career to uncovering the lives of the common folk in early America. He has sought, through such studies as the one that follows, to reexamine the "history of the powerless, the inarticulate, the poor. . . ." These, he says, have been neglected, while we have given a disproportionate amount of time to the concerns, opinions, and doings of elite groups.

In his essay below on the merchant seamen of the colonial ports, Professor Lemisch writes the sort of social history he advocates. He also has something interesting to say about the Revolution. The seamen, he declares, were active and often violent patriots, who merged their grievances against impressment with the cause of independence. This does not prove that the Revolution was a proletarian uprising, of course. Nor does it prove that the Revolution was even a serious social upheaval. Elsewhere Lemisch has attempted to demonstrate more directly that the insurgent impulse of these years was egalitarian and democratic; that it was, to use Carl Becker's famous phrase, a struggle not only over "home rule, but who should rule at home." But the present essay does suggest that one part of the colonial working class saw the fight against the crown as an opportunity to improve their own lot. There was, then, a significant social component in the events following 1763 that culminated in independence and the establishment of the American nation.

Source: Jesse Lemisch, "Jack Tar in the Streets: Merchant Seamen in the Politics of Revolutionary America," *William and Mary Quarterly*, 3rd ser. (July 1968), pp. 371–407.

FOR FURTHER READING:

Jackson T. Main, *The Social Structure of Revolutionary America**, (Princeton University Press, 1965); J. Franklin Jameson, *The American Revolution Considered as a Social Movement**, (Princeton University Press, 1940); Richard B. Morris, *The American Revolution Reconsidered**, (Harper Torchbooks, 1967); Richard B. Morris, *Government and Labor in Early America*, (Octagon Books, 1965); Robert E. Brown, *Middle-Class Democracy and the Revolution in Massachusetts 1691–1780**, (Cornell University Press, 1955); James Henretta, "Economic Development and Social Structure in Colonial Boston," *William and Mary Quarterly* (Third Series, January 1965).

Asterisk denotes paperback edition.

Here comes Jack Tar, his bowed legs bracing him as if the very Broadway beneath his feet might begin to pitch and roll. In his dress he is, in the words of a superior, "very nasty and negligent," his black stockings ragged, his long, baggy trousers tarred to make them waterproof. Bred in "that very shambles of language," the merchant marine, he is foul-mouthed, his talk alien and suspect. He is Jolly Jack, a bull in a china shop, always, in his words, "for a Short Life and a Merry one," and, in the concurring words of his superiors, "concerned only for the present . . . incapable of thinking of, or inattentive to, future welfare," "like froward Childeren not knowing how to judge for themselves."

Clothes don't make the man, nor does language; surely we can do better than these stereotypes. Few have tried. Maritime history, as it has been written, has had as little to do with the common seaman as business history has had to do with the laborer. In that *mischianza* of mystique and elitism, "seaman" has meant Sir Francis Drake, not Jack Tar; the focus has been on trade, exploration, the great navigators, but rarely on the men who sailed the ships. Thus we know very little about Jack. Samuel Eliot Morison is one of the few who have tried to portray the common seaman. In an influential anecdote in *The Maritime History of Massachusetts* Morison has described a "frequent occurrence" in early New England. A farmer's boy, called by the smell or the sight of the sea, suddenly runs off; three years later he returns as a man, marries the hired girl, and lives "happily ever after." This experience, Morison tells us, was "typical of the Massachusetts merchant marine," where the "old salt" was almost non-existent and where there never was "a native deep-sea proletariat." The ships were sailed by wave after wave of "adventure-seeking boys," drawn by high wages and *wanderlust*. If they recovered, they took their earnings, married, and bought a farm; if not, these "young, ambitious seamen culled from the most active element of a pushing race" stayed on and rose to become masters in a merchant marine distinguished from its class-ridden European counterparts by easy mobility.

There is much to support Morison's *tableau*. Even if the mystique of the sea has been no more than mystique, still it has existed and exerted a powerful force. Washington, Franklin, and thousands of others did suffer attacks of "sea fever." Seamen were, as Morison says, young men, averaging in one sample slightly over twenty-four, with many like John Paul Jones who went to sea at thirteen and even some who went at eight. Many of them "hove in hard at the Hause-hole" and became masters of their own vessels; later, while their sons and grandsons added to their wealth, they retired, perhaps to their farms, and wrote proud histories of their successes. Some, like Nicholas Biddle, found the navy a better outlet for their ambitions than the merchant service. Others, following Morison's pattern, quit the sea early and turned to farming. For many there was mobility between generations and between trades. Seamen and landsmen might be distinct classes in Europe, but in America, men such as Albert Gallatin who knew both the Old World and the New found no "material distinction." So Jack Tar seems to have been simply the landsman gone to sea, indistinguishable from his fellows ashore, and, together with them, on his way to prosperity.

If the seaman was a clean young farm-boy on the make—and likely to succeed— why was Josiah Franklin so apprehensive lest young Benjamin "break loose and go to sea"? Why did Josiah fight his son's "strong inclination to go to sea" by frantically trying to make of him a joiner, a bricklayer, a turner, a brazier, a tallow-chandler, a cutler, a printer—anything, so long as it would keep him on land? Why did Washington's uncle suggest that young George would better become a planter or even an apprentice to a tinker, while explicitly urging that he not become a seaman?

"All masters of vessels are warned not to harbor, conceal, or employ him, as they will answer for it, as the law directs." To a fleeing apprentice, dissatisfied with the "bondage" of work ashore, to a runaway slave, the sea might appear the only real shelter. Men with no experience at sea tried to pass for seaman and before long discovered that they had indeed become seamen. Others *were* seamen, apprenticed in one vessel and fled to another. Still others, deserted soldiers, bail-jumpers, thieves, and murderers, had gotten into trouble with the law. And others went to sea entirely unwillingly, originally impressed—perhaps from jail—into the navy, or tricked into the merchant service by crimps. These were the floaters who drifted and slipped their moorings, the suicides, the men whose wives—if they had wives—ran off with other men; the beneficiaries in their wills—when they left wills—were innkeepers. Hitherto, argued a proponent of a United States navy in 1782, the merchant marine had been "the resource of necessity, accident or indulgence."

The merchant marine was a place full of forces beyond the seaman's control: death and disease, storms, and fluctuations in employment. Indeed, the lack of "old salts" in Morison's merchant marine might reflect a sombre irony: was the average seaman young because mobility rapidly brought him to another trade or because seamen died young? A man in jail, said Dr. Johnson, was at least safe from drowning, and he had more room, better food, and better company. The Quaker John Woolman was one of the few sensitive enough to see that if the "poor bewildered sailors" drank and cursed, the fault lay not so much in themselves as in the harsh environment and the greed of employers. Nor was the road up through the hawse-hole so easy as Morison asserts. That the few succeeded tells us nothing of the many; only the successful left autobiographies. Perhaps the sons of merchants and ship-masters made it, along with the captain's brother-in-law and those who attended schools of navigation, but what of the "poor lads bound apprentice" who troubled Woolman, those whose wages went to their masters? What of the seamen in Morison's own Boston who died too poor to pay taxes and who were a part of what James Henretta has called " the bottom" of Boston society? What of those who went bankrupt with such frequency in Rhode Island? Why, at the other end of the colonies, did Washington's uncle warn that it would be "very difficult" to become master of a Virginia vessel and not worth trying?

The presence of such men, fugitives and floaters, powerless in a tough environment, makes *wanderlust* appear an ironic parody of the motives which made at least some men go to sea. Catch the seaman when he is not pandering to your romanticism, said former seaman Frederick Law Olmsted a century later, and he will tell you that he hates the sight of blue water, he hates his ship, his officers, and his messmates—and he despises himself. Melville's Ishmael went to sea when he felt grim, hostile, and suicidal: "It is a way I have of driving off the spleen." No matter what we make of Ishmael, we cannot possibly make him into one of Morison's "adventure-seeking boys." Others, perhaps, but not Ishmael. The feelings of eighteenth-century Americans toward seafaring and seamen, and what evidence we have of the reasons men had for going to sea indicate that there were many like Ishmael in the colonial period, too, who left the land in flight and fear, outcasts, men with little hope of success ashore. These were the dissenters from the American mood. Their goals differed from their fellows ashore; these were the rebels, the men who stayed on to become old salts.

Admiralty law treated seamen in a special way, as "wards." Carl Ubbelohde says that seamen favored the colonial Vice Admiralty Courts as "particular tribunals in case of trouble," and Charles M. Andrews and Richard B. Morris agreed that these courts were "guardians of the rights of the seamen." The benefits of being classified as a "ward" are dubious, but, regardless of the quality of treatment which admiralty law accorded to seamen, it certainly does not follow that, all in all, the colonial seaman was well treated by the law. Indeed, if we broaden our scope to include colonial law generally, we find an extraordinarily harsh collection of laws, all justifiying Olmsted's later claim that American seamen "are more wretched, and are governed more by threats of force than any other civilized laborers of the world." There are laws providing for the whipping of disobedient seamen and in one case for their punishment as "seditious"; laws prohibiting seamen in port from leaving their vessels after sundown and from travelling on land without certificates of discharge from their last job; laws empowering "every free white person" to catch runaway seamen. We find other laws, less harsh, some seeming to protect the seaman: laws against extending credit to seamen and against arresting them for debt, and against entertaining them in taverns for more than one hour per day; laws against selling them liquor and prohibiting them from playing with cards or dice; laws waiving imprisonment for seamen convicted of cursing; laws requiring masters to give discharge certificates to their seamen and laws prohibiting hiring without such certificates. Finally, there are laws which clearly do help the seaman: laws requiring masters to provide "good and sufficient diet and accommodation" and providing for redress if the master refused; laws providing punishment for masters who "immoderately beat, wound, or maim" their seamen; laws providing that seamen's contracts be written.

These harsh or at best paternalistic laws add up to a structure whose purpose is to assure a ready supply of cheap, docile labor. Obedience, both at sea and ashore, is the keystone. Charles Beard at his most rigidly mechanistic would doubtless have found the Constitution merely mild stuff alongside this blatantly one-sided class legislation. Today's historians of the classless society would do well to examine the preambles of these laws, written in a more candid age, by legislatures for which, even by Robert Brown's evidence, most seamen could not vote. Again and again these laws aim to inhibit acts of seamen which may do "prejudice to masters and owners of vessels" or constitute a "manifest detriment of . . . trade." The seamen's interests are sacrificed to the merchants', and even the laws which seem friendly to the seaman benefit the master. Laws against giving credit, arresting, and suing aim to keep the seaman available rather than involved in a lawsuit or imprisoned; the certificates and written contracts seek to prevent desertion and to protect the master against what would today be called a "strike"; the laws protecting seamen against immoderate punishment and requiring adequate food and accommodation are implicitly weak in that they require that dependents make open complaint against their superiors. Sometimes this limitation is made explicit, as in a South Carolina law of 1751 whose stated purpose is "TO DISCOURAGE FRIVOLOUS AND VEXATIOUS ACTIONS AT LAW BEING BROUGHT BY SEAMEN AGAINST MASTERS AND COMMANDERS."

Thus if we think of Jack Tar as jolly, childlike, irresponsible, and in many ways surprisingly like the Negro stereotype, it is because he was treated so much like a child, a servant, and a slave. What the employer saw as the necessities of an authoritarian profession were written into law and culture: the society that wanted Jack dependent made him that way and then concluded that that was the way he really was.

II

Constantly plagued by short complements, the Royal Navy attempted to solve its manning problems in America, as in England, by impressment. Neil Stout has recently attributed these shortages to "death, illness, crime, and desertion" which were in turn caused largely by rum and by the deliberate enticements of American merchants. Rum and inveiglement certainly took a high toll, but to focus on these two causes of shortages is unfairly to shift the blame for impressment onto its victims. The navy itself caused shortages. Impressment, said Thomas Hutchinson, caused desertion, rather than the other way around. Jack Tar had good reasons for avoiding the navy. It would, a young Virginian was warned, "cut him and staple him and use him like a Negro, or rather, like a dog"; James Otis grieved at the loss of the "flower" of Massachusetts's youth "by ten thousands" to a service which treated them little better than "hewers of wood and drawers of water." Discipline was harsh and sometimes irrational, and punishments were cruel. Water poured into sailors' beds, they went mad, and died of fevers and scurvy. Sickness, Benjamin Franklin noted, was more common in the navy than in the merchant service and more frequently fatal. In a fruitless attempt to prevent desertion, wages were withheld and men shunted about from ship to ship without being paid. But the accumulation of even three or four years' back wages could not keep a man from running. And why should it have? Privateering paid better in wartime, and wages were higher in the merchant service; even laborers ashore were better paid. Thus Stout's claim that the navy was "forced" to press is only as accurate as the claim that the South was forced to enslave Negroes. Those whose sympathies lie with the thousands of victims of this barbaric practice—rather than with naval administrators—will see that the navy pressed because to be in the navy was in some sense to be a slave, and for this we must blame the slave owners rather than the slaves.

Impressment angered and frightened the seamen, but it pervaded and disrupted all society, giving other classes and groups cause to share a common grievance with the press-gang's more direct victims: just about everyone had a relative at sea. Whole cities were crippled. A night-time operation in New York in 1757 took in eight hundred men, the equivalent of more than one-quarter of the city's adult male population. Impressment and the attendant shortage of men may have been a critical factor in the stagnancy of "the once cherished now depressed, once flourishing now sinking Town of Boston. "H.M.S. *Shirley's* log lists at least ninety-two men pressed off Boston in five months of 1745-1746; *Gramont* received seventy-three pressed men in New York in three days in 1758; *Arethusa* took thirty-one in two days off Virginia in 1771. Binges such as these left the communities where they occurred seriously harmed. Preachers' congregations took flight, and merchants complained loudly about the "many Thousands of Pounds of Damage." "Kiss my arse, you dog," shouted the captain as he made off with their men, leaving vessels with their fires still burning, unmanned, finally to be wrecked. They took legislators and slaves, fishermen and servants. Seamen took to the woods or fled town altogether, dreading the appearance of a man-of-war's boat—in the words of one—as a flock of sheep dreaded a wolf's appearance. If they offered to work at all, they demanded inflated wages and refused to sail to ports where there was danger of impressment. "New York and Boston," Benjamin Franklin commented during the French and Indian War, "have so often found the Inconvenience of . . . Station Ships that they are very indifferent about having them: The Pressing of their Men and thereby disappointing Voyages, often hurting their Trade more than the Enemy hurts it." Even a ferryboat operator complained as people shunned the city during a press; food and fuel grew short and their prices rose.

From the very beginning the history of impressment in America is a tale of venality, deceit, and vindictiveness. Captains kept deserters and dead men on ships' books, pocketing their provision allowances. In 1706 a captain pressed men and literally sold them to short-handed vessels; his midshipman learned the business so well that after his dismissal he became a veritable entrepreneur of impressment, setting up shop in a private sloop. Another commander waited until New York's governor was away to break a no-press agreement and when the governor returned he seriously considered firing on the Queen's ship. In Boston in 1702 the lieutenant-governor *did* fire, responding to merchants' complaints. "Fire and be damn'd," shouted the impressing captain as the shots whistled through his sails. The merchants had complained that the press was illegal under 1697 instructions which required captains and commanders to apply to colonial governors for permission to press. These instructions, a response to complaints of "irregular proceedings of the captains of some of our ships of war in the impressing of seamen," had clearly not put an end to irregularities. In 1708 a Parliament fearful of the disruptive effect of impressment on trade forbade the practice in America. In the sixty-seven years until the repeal in 1775 of this "Act for the Encouragement of the Trade to America" there was great disagreement as to its meaning and indeed as to its very existence. Did the Sixth of Anne, as the act was called, merely prohibit the navy from impressing and leave governors free to do so? At least one governor, feeling "pinioned" under the law, continued impressing while calling it "borrowing." Was the act simply a wartime measure, which expired with the return of peace in 1713? Regardless of the dispute, impressment continued, routine in its regularity, but often spectacular in its effects.

Boston was especially hard-hit by impressment in the 1740's, with frequent incidents throughout the decade and major explosions in 1745 and 1747. Again and again the town meeting and the House of Representatives protested, drumming away at the same themes: impressment was harmful to maritime commerce and to the economic life of the city in general and illegal if not properly authorized. In all this the seaman himself becomes all but invisible. The attitude towards him in the protests is at best neutral and often sharply antagonistic. In 1747 the House of Representatives condemned the violent response of hundreds of seamen to a large-scale press as "a tumultuous riotous assembling of armed Seamen, Servants, Negroes, and others . . . tending to the Destruction of all Government and Order." While acknowledging that the people had reason to protest, the House chose to level *its* protest against "the most audacious Insult" to the governor, Council, and House. And the town meeting, that stronghold of democracy, offered its support to those who took "orderly" steps while expressing its "Abhorence of such Illegal Criminal Proceedings" as those undertaken by the seamen "and other persons of mean and Vile Condition."

Protests such as these reflect at the same time both unity and division in colonial society. All kinds of Americans—both merchants and seamen—opposed impressment, but the town meeting and the House spoke for the merchant, not the seaman. They opposed impressment not for its effect on the seaman but for its effect on commerce. Thus their protests express antagonism to British policy at the same time that they express class division. These two themes continue and develop in American opposition to impressment in the three decades between the Knowles Riots of 1747 and the Declaration of Independence.

During the French and Indian War the navy competed with privateers for seamen. Boston again protested against impressment, and then considered authorizing the governor to press, "provided said Men be impressed from inward-bound Vessels from Foreign Parts only, and that none of them be Inhabitants of this Province." In 1760 New York's mayor had a naval captain arrested on the complaint of two shipmasters who claimed that he had welched on a deal to exchange two men he had pressed for two others they were willing to furnish. With the return of peace in 1763 admirals and Americans alike had reason to suppose that there would be no more impressment. But the Admiralty's plans for a large new American fleet required otherwise, and impressment began again in the spring of 1764 in New York, where a seven-week hot press was brought to a partial stop by the arrest of one of the two offending captains. In the spring and summer a hunt for men between Maine and Virginia by four naval vessels brought violent responses, including the killing of a marine at New York; another fort, at Newport, fired on another naval vessel.

Along with the divisions there was a certain amount of unity. Seamen who fled after violently resisting impressment could not be found—probably because others sheltered them—and juries would not indict them. Captains were prevented from impressing by the threat of prosecution. And in 1769 lawyer John Adams used the threat of displaying the statute book containing the Sixth of Anne to frighten a special court of Admiralty into declaring the killing of an impressing lieutenant justifiable homicide in necessary self-defense.

There were two kinds of impressment incidents: those in which there was immediate self-defense against impressment, usually at sea, and those in which crowds ashore, consisting in large part of seamen, demonstrated generalized opposition to impressment. This is what the first kind of incident sounded like: a volley of musketry and the air full of langrage, grapeshot, round shot, hammered shot, double-headed shot, even rocks. "Come into the boat and be damned, you Sorry

Son of a Whore or else Ile breake your head, and hold your tongue." Small arms, swords and cutlasses, blunderbusses, clubs and pistols, axes, harpoons, fishgigs, twelve-pounders, six-pounders, half-pounders. "You are a parsill of Raskills." Fired five shots to bring to a snow from North Carolina, pressed four. "You have no right to impress me . . . If you step over that line . . . by the eternal God of Heaven, you are a dead man." "Aye, my lad, I have seen many a brave fellow before now."

Here is hostility and bloodshed, a tradition of antagonism. From the beginning, impressment's most direct victims—the seamen—were its most active opponents. Bernard Bailyn's contention that "not a single murder resulted from the activities of the Revolutionary mobs in America" does not hold up if extended to cover resistance to impressment; there were murders on both sides. Perhaps the great bulk of incidents of this sort must remain forever invisible to the historian, for they often took place out of sight of friendly observers, and the only witness, the navy, kept records which are demonstrably biased and faulty, omitting the taking of thousands of men. But even the visible records provide a great deal of information. This much we know without doubt: seamen did not go peacefully. Their violence was purposeful, and sometimes they were articulate. "I know who you are," said one, as reported by John Adams and supported by Thomas Hutchinson. "You are the lieutenant of a man-of-war, come with a press-gang to deprive me of my liberty. You have no right to impress me. I have retreated from you as far as I can. I can go no farther. I and my companions are determined to stand upon our defence. Stand off." (It was difficult for Englishmen to fail to see impressment in such terms—even a sailor *doing* the pressing could feel shame over "fighting with honest sailors, to deprive them of their liberty.")

Ashore, seamen and others demonstrated their opposition to impressment with the only weapon which the unrepresentative politics of the day offered them—riot. In Boston several thousand people responded to a nighttime impressment sweep of the harbor and docks with three days of rioting beginning in the early hours of November 17, 1747. Thomas Hutchinson reported that "the lower class were beyond measure enraged." Negroes, servants, and hundreds of seamen seized a naval lieutenant, assaulted a sheriff and put his deputy in the stocks, surrounded the governor's house, and stormed the Town House where the General Court was sitting. The rioters demanded the seizure of the impressing officers, the release of the men they had pressed, and execution of a death sentence which had been levied against a member of an earlier press-gang who had been convicted of murder. When the governor fled to Castle William—some called it "abdication"—Commodore Knowles threatened to put down what he called "arrant rebellion" by bombarding the town. The governor, who, for his part, thought the rioting a secret plot of the upper class, was happily surprised when the town meeting expressed its "Abhorence" of the seamen's riot.

After the French and Indian War press riots increased in frequency. Armed mobs of whites and Negroes repeatedly manhandled captains, officers, and crews, threatened their lives, and held them hostage for the men they pressed. Mobs fired at pressing vessels and tried to board them; they threatened to burn one, and they regularly dragged ships' boats to the center of town for ceremonial bonfires. In Newport in June 1765, five hundred seamen, boys, and Negroes rioted after five weeks of impressment. "Sensible" Newporters opposed impressment but nonetheless condemned this "Rabble." In Norfolk in 1767 Captain Jeremiah Morgan retreated, sword in hand, before a mob of armed whites and Negroes. "Good God," he wrote to the governor, "was your Honour and I to prosecute all the Rioters that attacked us belonging to Norfolk there would not be twenty left unhang'd belonging to the Toun." According to Thomas Hutchinson, the *Liberty* Riot in Boston in 1768 may have been as much against impressment as against the seizure of Hancock's sloop: *Romney* had pressed before June 10, and on that day three officers were forced by an angry crowd "arm'd with Stones" to release a man newly pressed from the Boston packet. *Romney* pressed another man, and on June 14, after warding off "many wild and violent proposals," the town meeting petitioned the governor against both the seizure and impressment; the instructions to their representatives (written by John Adams) quoted the Sixth of Anne at length. On June 18 two councillors pleaded with the governor to procure the release of a man pressed by *Romney* "as the peace of the Town seems in a great measure to depend upon it."

There were other impressment riots at New York in July of 1764 and July of 1765; at Newport in July of 1764; at Casco Bay, Maine, in December 1764. Incidents continued during the decade following, and impressment flowered on the very eve of the Revolution. Early in 1775 the practice began to be used in a frankly vindictive and political way—because a town had inconvenienced an admiral, or because a town supported the Continental Congress. Impresses were ordered and took place from Maine to Virginia. In September a bundle of press warrants arrived from the Admiralty, along with word of the repeal of the Sixth of Anne. What had been dubious was now legal. Up and down the coast, officers rejoiced and went to work.

Long before 1765 Americans had developed beliefs about impressment, and they had expressed those beliefs in words and deeds. Impressment was bad for trade and it was illegal. As such, it was, in the words of the Massachusetts House in 1720, "a great Breach on the Rights of His Majesties Subjects." In 1747 it was a violation of "the common Liberty of the Subject," and in 1754 "inconsistent with Civil Liberty, and the Natural Rights of Mankind." Some felt in 1757 that it was even "abhorrent to the English Constitution." In fact, the claim that impressment was unconstitutional was wrong. (Even *Magna Charta* was no protection. *Nullus liber homo capiatur* did not apply to seamen.) Instead impressment indicated to Benjamin Franklin "that the constitution is yet imperfect, since in so general a case it doth not secure liberty, but destroys it." "If impressing seamen is of right by common law in Britain," he also remarked, "slavery is then of right by common law there; there being no slavery worse than that sailors are subjected to."

For Franklin, impressment was a symptom of injustice built into the British Constitution. In *Common Sense* Tom Paine saw in impressment a reason for rejecting monarchy. In the Declaration of Independence Thomas Jefferson included impressment among the "Oppressions" of George III; later he likened the practice to the capture of Africans for slavery. Both "reduced [the victim] to . . . bondage by force, in flagrant violation of his own consent, and of his natural right in his own person."

Despite all this, and all that went before, we have thought little of impressment as an element in explaining the conduct of the common man in the American Revolution. Contemporaries knew better. John Adams felt that a tactical mistake by Thomas Hutchinson on the question of impressment in 1769 would have "accelerated the revolution. . . . It would have spread a wider flame than Otis's ever did, or could have done." Ten years later American seamen were being impressed by *American* officers. The United States Navy had no better solution for "public Necessities" than had the Royal Navy. Joseph Reed, President of Pennsylvania, complained to Congress of "Oppressions" and in so doing offered testimony to the role of *British* impressment in bringing on revolution. "We cannot help observing how similar this Conduct is to that of the British Officers during our Subjection to Great Britain and are persuaded it will have the same unhappy effects viz., an estrangement of the Affections of the People from the Authority under which they act which by an easy Progression will proceed to open Opposition to the immediate Actors and Bloodshed." Impressment had played a role in the estrangement of the American people from the British government. It had produced "Odium" against the navy, and even six-year-olds had not been too young to have learned to detest it. The anger of thousands of victims did not vanish. Almost four decades after the Declaration of Independence an orator could still arouse his audience by tapping a folk-memory of impressment by the same "haughty, cruel, and gasconading nation" which was once again trying to enslave free Americans.

III

The seamen's conduct in the 1760's and 1770's makes more sense in the light of previous and continued impressment. What may have seemed irrational violence can now be seen as purposeful and radical. The pattern of rioting as political expression, established as a response to impressment, was now adapted and broadened as a response to the Stamp Act. In New York General Gage described the "insurrection" of October 31, 1765, and following as "composed of great numbers of Sailors." The seamen, he said, were "the only People who may be properly Stiled Mob," and estimates indicate that between a fifth and a fourth of New York's rioters were seamen. The disturbances began among the seamen—especially former privateersmen—on October 31. On November 1 they had marched, led primarily by their former captains; later they rioted, led by no one but themselves. Why? Because they had been duped by merchants, or, if not by merchants, then certainly by lawyers. So British officials believed—aroused by these men who meant to use them, the seamen themselves had nothing more than plunder on their minds. In fact, at that point in New York's rioting when the leaders lost control, the seamen, who were then in the center of town, in an area rich for plunder, chose instead to march in an orderly and disciplined way clear across town to do violence to the home and possessions of an English major whose provocative conduct had made him the obvious political enemy. Thus the "rioting" was actually very discriminating.

Seamen and non-seamen alike joined to oppose the Stamp Act for many reasons, but the seamen had two special grievances: impressment and the effect of England's new attitude toward colonial trade. To those discharged by the navy at the end of the war and others thrown out of work by the death of privateering were added perhaps twenty thousand more seamen and fishermen who were thought to be the direct victims of the post-1763 trade regulations. This problem came to the fore in the weeks following November 1, 1765, when the Stamp Act went into effect. The strategy of opposition chosen by the colonial leadership was to cease all activities which required the use of stamps. Thus maritime trade came to a halt in the cities. Some said that this was a cowardly strategy. If the Americans opposed the Stamp Act, let them go on with business as usual, refusing outright to use the stamps. The leaders' strategy was especially harmful to the seamen, and the latter took the more radical position—otherwise the ships would not sail. And this time the seamen's radicalism triumphed over both colonial leadership and British officials. Within little more than a month the act had been largely nullified. Customs officers were allowing ships to sail without stamps, offering as the reason the fear that the seamen, "who are the people that are most dangerous on these occasions, as their whole dependance for a subsistence is upon Trade," would certainly "commit some terrible Mischief." Philadelphia's customs officers feared that the seamen would soon "compel" them to let ships pass without stamps. Customs officers at New York yielded when they heard that the seamen were about to have a meeting.

Customs officers had worse luck on other days. Seamen battled them throughout the 1760's and 1770's. In October 1769 a Philadelphia customs officer was attacked by a mob of seamen who also tarred, feathered, and nearly drowned a man who had furnished him with information about illegally imported goods. A year later a New Jersey customs officer who approached an incoming vessel in Delaware Bay had *his* boat boarded by armed seamen who threatened to murder him and came close to doing so. When the officer's son came to Philadelphla, he was similarly treated by a mob of seamen; there were one thousand seamen in Philadelphia at the time, and according to the customs collector there, they were "always ready" to do such "mischief." This old antagonism had been further politicized in 1768 when, under the American Board of Customs Commissioners, searchers began to break into sea chests and confiscate those items not covered by cockets, thus breaking an old custom of the sea which allowed seamen to import small items for their own profit. Oliver M. Dickerson has described this new "Invasion of Seamen's Rights" as part of "customs racketeering" and a cause of animosity between seamen and customs officers.

Many of these animosities flared in the Boston Massacre. What John Adams described as "a motley rabble of saucy boys, negroes and mulattoes, Irish teagues and outlandish jack tarrs," including twenty or thirty of the latter, armed with clubs and sticks, did battle with the soldiers. Their leader was Crispus Attucks, a mulatto seaman; he was shot to death in front of the Custom House. One of the seamen's reasons for being there has been too little explored. The Massacre grew out of a fight between workers and off-duty soldiers at a ropewalk two days before. That fight, in turn, grew out of the long-standing practice in the British army of allowing off-duty soldiers to take civilian employment. They did so, in Boston and elsewhere, often at wages which undercut those offered to Americans—including unemployed seaman who sought work ashore—by as much as 50 per cent. In hard times this led to intense competition for work, and the Boston Massacre was in part a product of this competition. Less well known is the Battle of Golden Hill, which arose from similar causes and took place in New York six weeks before. In January 1770 a gang of seamen went from house to house and from dock to dock, using clubs to drive away the soldiers employed there and threatening anyone who might rehire them. In the days of rioting which followed and which came to be called the Battle of Golden Hill, the only fatality was a seaman, although many other seamen were wounded in the attempt to take vengeance for the killing. The antipathy between soldiers and seamen was so great, said John Adams, "that they fight as naturally when they meet as the elephant and Rhinoceros."

IV

To wealthy Loyalist Judge Peter Oliver of Massachusetts, the common people were only "Rabble"—like the "Mobility of all Countries, perfect Machines, wound up by any Hand who might first take the Winch." The people were "duped," "deceived," and "deluded" by cynical leaders who could "turn the Minds of the great Vulgar." Had they been less ignorant, Americans would have spurned their leaders, and there would have been no Revolution. I have tested this generalization and found it unacceptable, at least in its application to colonial seamen. Obviously the seamen did not cause the American Revolution. But neither were they simply irrational fellows who moved only when others manipulated them. I have attempted to show that the seaman had a mind of his own and genuine reasons to act, and that he did act—purposefully. The final test of this purposefulness must be the Revolution itself. Here we find situations in which the seamen are separated from those who might manipulate them and thrown into great physical danger; if they were manipulated or duped into rebellion, on their own we might expect them to show little understanding of or enthusiasm for the war.

To a surprising extent American seamen remained Americans during the Revolution. Beaumarchais heard from an American in 1775 that seamen, fishermen, and harbor workers had become an "army of furious men, whose actions are all animated by a spirit of vengeance and hatred" against the English, who had destroyed their livelihood "and the liberty of their country." The recent study of loyalist claimants by Wallace Brown confirms Oliver Dickerson's earlier contention that "the volumes dealing with loyalists and their claims discloses an amazing absence of names" of seamen. From a total of 2786 loyalist claimants whose occupations are known Brown found only 39, 1.4 per cent, who were seamen (or pilots). (It is possible to exclude fishermen and masters but not pilots from his figures.) In contrast, farmers numbered 49.1 per cent, artisans 9.8 per cent, merchants and shopkeepers 18.6 per cent, professionals 9.1 per cent, and officeholders 10.1 per cent. Although as Brown states, the poor may be underrepresented among the claimants, "the large number of claims by poor people, and even Negroes, suggests that this is not necessarily true."

An especially revealing way of examining the seamen's loyalties under pressure is to follow them into British prisons. Thousands of them were imprisoned in such places as the ship *Jersey,* anchored in New York harbor, and Mill and Forton prisons in England. Conditions were abominable. Administration was corrupt, and in America disease was rife and thousands died. If physical discomfort was less in the English prisons than in *Jersey,* the totality of misery may have been as great, with prisoners more distant from the war and worse informed about the progress of the American cause. Lost in a no-man's land between British refusal to consider them prisoners of war and Washington's unwillingness in America to trade trained soldiers for captured seamen, these men had limited opportunities for exchange. Trapped in this very desperate situation, the men were offered a choice: they could defect and join the Royal Navy. To a striking extent the prisoners remained patriots, and very self-consciously so. "Like brave men, they resisted, and swore that they would never lift a hand to do any thing on board of King George's ships." The many who stayed understood the political significance of their choice as well as the few who went. "What business had he to sell his Country, and go to the worst of Enemies?" Instead of defecting they engaged in an active resistance movement. Although inexperienced in self-government and segregated from their captains, on their own these men experienced no great difficulties in organizing themselves into disciplined groups. "Notwithstanding they were located within the absolute dominions of his Britanic majesty," commented one, the men "adventured to form themselves into a republic, framed a constitution and enacted wholesome laws, with suitable penalties." Organized, they resisted, celebrating the Fourth of July under British bayonets, burning their prisons, and escaping. Under these intolerable conditions, seamen from all over the colonies discovered that they shared a common conception of the cause for which they fought.

At the Constitutional Convention Benjamin Franklin spoke for the seamen:

> It is of great consequence that we shd. not depress the virtue and public spirit of our common people; of which they displayed a great deal during the war, and which contributed principally to the favorable issue of it. He related the honorable refusal of the American seamen who were carried in great numbers into the British prisons during the war, to redeem themselves from misery or to seek their fortunes, by entering on board of the Ships of the Enemies to their Country; contrasting their patriotism with a contemporary instance in which the British seamen made prisoners by the Americans, readily entered on the ships of the latter on being promised a share of the prizes that might be made out of their own Country.

Franklin spoke *against limiting* the franchise, not *for broadening* it: he praised the seamen, but with a hint of condescension, suggesting that it would be prudent to grant them a few privileges. A decade later a French traveller noticed that "except the laborer in ports, and the common sailor, everyone calls himself, and is called by others, a *gentleman*." Government was still gentleman's government: more people were defined as gentlemen, but Jack Tar was not yet among them.

V

Bernard Bailyn has recently added needed illumination to our understanding of pre-Revolutionary crowd action. Bailyn has disagreed with Peter Oliver and with modern historians who have concurred in describing pre-Revolutionary rioters as mindless, passive, and manipulated: "far from being empty vessels," rioters in the decade before the outbreak of fighting were "politically effective" and "shared actively the attitudes and fears" of their leaders; theirs was a " 'fully-fledged political movement' " Thus it would seem that Bailyn has freed himself from the influential grasp of Gustave Le Bon. But Bailyn stopped short of total rejection. Only in 1765, he says, was the colonial crowd "transformed" into a political phenomenon. Before then it was "conservative"—like crowds in seventeenth- and eighteenth-century England, aiming neither at social revolution nor at social reform, but only at immediate revenge. Impressment riots and other "demonstrations by transient sailors and dock workers," Bailyn says, expressed no "deep-lying social distress" but only a "diffuse and indeliberate antiauthoritarianism"; they were "ideologically inert."

Other historians have seen the colonial seamen—and the rest of the lower class—as mindless and manipulated, both before and after 1765. The seeming implication behind this is that the seamen who demonstrated in colonial streets did so as much out of simple vindictiveness or undisciplined violence as out of love of liberty. Certainly such motivation would blend well with the traditional picture of the seaman as rough and ready. For along with the stereotype of Jolly Jack—and in part belying that stereotype—is bold and reckless Jack, the exotic and violent. Jack *was* violent; the conditions of his existence were violent. Was his violence non-political? Sometimes. The mob of seventy to eighty yelling, club-swinging, out-of-town seamen who tried to break up a Philadelphia election in 1742 had no interest in the election; they had been bought off with money and liquor.

Other violence is not so clear-cut. Edward Thompson has seen the fighting out of significant social conflict in eighteenth-century England "in terms of Tyburn, the hulks and the Bridewells on the one hand; and crime, riot, and mob action on the other." Crime and violence among eighteenth-century American seamen needs reexamination from such a perspective. Does "mutiny" adequately describe the act of the crew which seized *Black Prince,* re-named it *Liberty,* and chose their course and a new captain by voting? What shall we call the conduct of 150 seamen who demanded higher wages by marching along the streets of Philadelphia with clubs, unrigging vessels, and forcing workmen ashore? If "mutiny" is often the captain's name for what we have come to call a "strike," perhaps we might also detect some significance broader than mere criminality in the seamen's frequent assaults on captains and thefts from them. Is it not in some sense a political act for a seaman to tear off the mast a copy of a law which says that disobedient seamen will be punished as "seditious"?

Impressment meant the loss of freedom, both personal and economic, and, sometimes, the loss of life itself. The seaman who defended himself against impressment felt that he was fighting to defend his "liberty," and he justified his resistance on grounds of "right." It is in the concern for liberty and right that the seaman rises from vindictiveness to a somewhat more complex awareness that certain values larger than himself exist and that he is the victim not only of cruelty and hardship but also, in the light of those values, of injustice. The riots ashore, whether they be against impressment, the Stamp Act, or competition for work express that same sense of injustice. And here, thousands of men took positive and effective steps to demonstrate their opposition to both acts and policies.

Two of England's most exciting historians have immensely broadened our knowledge of past and present by examining phenomena strikingly like the conduct and thought of the seamen in America. These historians have described such manifestations as "sub-political" or "pre-political," and one of them has urged that such movements be "seriously considered not simply as an unconnected series of individual curiosities, as footnotes to history, but as a phenomenon of general importance and considerable weight in modern history." When Jack Tar went to sea in the American Revolution, he fought, as he had for many years before, quite literally, to protect his life, liberty, and property. It might be extravagant to call the seamen's conduct and the sense of injustice which underlay it in any fully developed sense ideological or political; on the other hand, it makes little sense to describe their ideological content as zero. There are many worlds and much of human history in that vast area between ideology and inertness.

A Governing Class on the Defensive:
The Case of New York STAUGHTON LYND

The question of class in America is important to the New Left historians. They feel that the "establishment" historians have grossly exaggerated the absence of class divisions and class conflict in our past. The preceding selection by Lemisch, accepts class as an implicit fact of our history. The essay of Staughton Lynd's that follows is quite explicitly concerned with analyzing the class dimension of the struggle over the Constitution in New York State.

Lynd is one of the most able and prolific of the New Left historians. The son of the prominent sociologists Robert and Helen Lynd, he devoted his early scholarly attention to examining the basis for politics in Dutchess County, New York, from the later colonial years through the Revolution and into the Confederation period. He was, as he says elsewhere, anxious to demonstrate the validity of the Beard-Becker-Jamison view of the existence of a serious class struggle during the Revolutionary era. This struggle, Lynd claims, culminated in a conservative victory with the adoption of the Federal Constitution. With that rare courage and honesty he has so often exhibited in his political activities, Lynd would later admit that the case of Dutchess County, where there was a large tenant class, was probably not typical of America, and that the choice of the Hudson Valley county biased his conclusions.

But Lynd has moved beyond his first efforts. In the essay below he takes up one of the jarring facts of the dispute over the Constitution—the strong support of the new frame of government by the mechanics of New York City. Obviously, in his simple dichotomy of rich and powerful Federalists and poor and weak anti-Federalists, Beard was wrong, Lynd declares. But he was certainly not wrong when he detected class forces at work through American history, or when he asserted that the work that men did and the economic interests they sought to protect helped to determine the political positions they took.

FOR FURTHER READING:

Charles A. Beard, *An Economic Interpretation of the Constitution**, (Free Press, 1935); Forrest MacDonald, *We the People: The Economic Origins of the Constitution**, (University of Chicago Press, 1963); Merrill Jensen, *The New Nation**, (Vintage Books, 1965); Carl Becker, *The History of Political Parties in the Province of New York 1760–1776**, (University of Wisconsin Press, 1960); Robert E. Brown, *Charles Beard and the Constitution: A Critical Analysis of "An Economic Interpretation of the Constitution of the United States"**, (Princeton University Press, 1956); Alfred Young, *The Democratic Republicans of New York, The Origins 1763–1797*, (University of North Carolina Press, 1967).

Asterisk denotes paperback edition.

New York Antifederalists were for the most part "new men" of plebeian origin, striving for equal access to economic opportunity, social acceptance, and political leadership. But they were not merely self-interested: for, resenting the pervasive

Source: Staughton Lynd, *Class Conflict, Slavery and the United States Constitution* (Indianapolis: The Bobbs-Merrill Company, Inc., 1967), chap. v, "A Governing Class on the Defensive: The Case of New York," pp. 109–132.

domination of farm and forum by men of wealth and rank, they also genuinely sought to enlarge the number of people involved in the political process.

The Federalists of New York exemplify even more dramatically the two-sided, ambiguous nature of the Revolutionary movement. Their brilliant leaders—Hamilton, Schuyler, Robert R. Livingston, Governeur Morris, Duane and Jay—*were* conservatives, and not merely in the revisionist sense that what they sought to conserve was liberal. They took it for granted that society was a hierarchy of ranks, with a wealthy and leisured elite at its head and "the lower orders" and "the peasants" under their rule. They were conservative also in the very modern sense of resisting fiercely government intrusions on free enterprise. Yet they were *also* deeply public-spirited men, critical of any tendency in each other to put private concerns before devotion to country and firmly committed to republican government.

The following pages will document and attempt to clarify these paradoxes in the politics of New York ratification. To Beard it seemed obvious, by analogy to the robber barons of his own day, that if the Founding Fathers were substantial capitalists, concerned to fashion a society in which men of wealth and good family would have a decisive voice, then their professed devotion to popular government was hypocritical, and resistance to their rule by the mass of common men inevitable. It seemed obvious, but, as I hope to demonstrate, it was not true.

I

Power in the State of New York before the American Revolution lodged in the hands of a small group of families whose income derived both from commerce and land. This was a ruling class, not merely in the sense that its members had similar interests, but also in the sense that they were bound together by close family ties (thus Hamilton married into the Schuylers, and Duane and Jay into the Manor Livingstons), shared a common ethos of *noblesse oblige,* and, at least in crises, tended to act together as a political unit. Beard's famous mistake (corrected in the 1935 reprinting of his *Economic Interpretation*) of supposing that the Hudson Valley landlords opposed the Constitution, sprang from his over-narrow conception of economic interest, and in particular, from his artificial distinction between "realty" and "personality." To which group did James Duane, proprietor of Duanesburg, kin to Livingstons, and Mayor of New York in the Critical Period, belong? Obviously to both. Chancellor Robert R. Livingston declared in 1780 that "I have no personal property," as his father had lamented eighteen years earlier that "my personall Estate is no more, and we ought to take care of the Reall." Alexander Hamilton, in contrast, was the principal spokesman of the nation's investors in fluid capital. Yet Livingston and Hamilton found common cause in the proposed United States Constitution and were the two principal Federalist speakers at the state ratifying convention.

What was at stake, in 1788, for both up-river landlords and metropolitan merchants, was aptly expressed in an exchange of letters between Alexander Hamilton and Robert Livingston, Jr. (the aged Lord of Livingston Manor) on the eve of the New York elections of 1785. "The situation of the state at this time is so critical," Hamilton wrote

> that it is become a serious object of attention to those who are concerned for the *security of property* or the prosperity of government, to endeavor to put men in the

Legislature whose principles are not of the *levelling kind* [italics in original]. . . .
All men of respectability, in the city, of whatever party, who have been witnesses
of the despotism and iniquity of the Legislature, are convinced, that the principal
people in the community must for their own defence, unite to overset the party I
have alluded to. I wish you to be persuaded Sir, that I would not take the liberty to
trouble you with these remarks with a view to serving any particular turn; but, from
a thorough conviction, that the safety of all those who have anything to lose calls
upon them to take care that the power of government is intrusted to proper hands.

After the election, Livingston replied:

In this last election, by Compleating the necessary Junction previous to the day of
Election [which] we have so often desired & Endeavourd for; by uniting the interests
of the Rensselaer, Schuyler, & our family, with other Gentm. of property in the
County in one Interest . . . we Carryed this last Election to a man.

"I trust," concluded the Third Lord, "we Shall always have the like Success provided we Stick Close to Each other."

In this illuminating exchange, property spoke to property, power to power, and
the barriers separating proud great families and dividing city from country were
overcome. The link between Hamilton and Livingston, as revealed by these letters,
was surely basically economic: the political convictions on which they stood
stemmed from a struggle for power between contending economic groups, and the
power they sought meant economic security and dominion for their kind of people.
Note that this is not economic interest in Beard's restricted sense of "advantages
which the beneficiaries expected would accrue to themselves first" or an immediate
interest in "personal possessions." That is what economic interest may mean in a
stable society wherein legislation centers on the allocation of a pork barrel of
discrete economic advantages among competing claimants. But the Constitution
was the settlement of a revolution. What was at stake for Hamilton, Livingston, and
their opponents, was more than speculative windfalls in securities: it was the
question, what kind of society would emerge from revolution when the dust had
settled, and on which class the political center of gravity would come to rest.

In1788, in the State of New York, it was not at all certain which class would rule.
However it may have been in other states, it was not true in New York that "leadership at the close of the [Revolutionary] era belonged substantially to the same segment of the society as it did at the beginning"; nor was it the case "that the social
conventions governing the employment of the colonial franchise survived the Revolution without serious impairment." It was not true in Dutchess County, where
landlords dropped out of politics after 1777, and not a single member of the old
ruling families held important elective or appointive office until after 1788. It was
not true in New York City, where the artisans fought bitterly in 1785 and 1786 for
artisans in the legislature, and sought to make elective all important municipal offices
from the mayoralty down. Nor was it true in New York State as a whole, governed
throughout this period by a man whose "family and connections," in the words of his
defeated opponent, did "not entitle him to so distinguished a predominance." Philip
Schuyler, who said this about George Clinton, had boasted before the election of
1777, "they may chuse who they will I will command them all." It did not work
out quite this way. Late in the war, Schuyler's son-in-law tactfully commented
that the great man, then serving in the New York Senate, was "exposed to the

mortification of seeing important measures patronised by him frequently miscarry."

A strong anti-aristocratic spirit was at work among the common people of the state during the years 1777–1788, and in state politics the little group of conservative nationalists was consistently on the defensive. When, in the spring of 1784, Robert R. Livingston acquired Oliver Delancey's "large square pew" at St. Paul's church, one might have thought the Revolution had been a personal success for him; but the triumph was tainted by the fact that in 1785, as in 1777, the Chancellor had to withdraw from the race for Governor "on account of the prejudices against his family name." Livingston himself was able to respond flexibly to the new times. Others were more impatient. On the eve of the Army–Congress plot of 1783, Morris wrote to John Jay (a passage omitted by Sparks from his version of the letter in his *Life of Morris*):

> You and I, my friend, know by Experience, that when a few Men of Sense and Spirit get together, and declare that they are the Authority, such few as are of a different Opinion may easily be convinced of their mistake by that powerful Argument the Halter.

The political challenge to conservative power in New York came from aspiring new men like George Clinton, Abraham Yates, and Melancton Smith, figures who in many cases had begun their careers as stewards and surveyors for the great landed magnates whose power they now began to contest. In the first election under the new state constitution, in 1777, the old Son of Liberty John Morin Scott ran for governor along with Schuyler and Clinton, "rail[ed] at an *Aristocratic Faction* which he pretends has formed and organized the new government," and blamed his failure to obtain high office on Duer, Duane, Robert R. Livingston, Philip Livingston, and Gouverneur Morris, "whom he described as a faction & tends [*sic*] to a family interest." Defeated in the gubernatorial election, Scott used his Senate seat to introduce legislation for price-fixing and land confiscation. Gouverneur Morris commented on this radical program: "It was hardly possible to embitter [the] bitter Draught these Laws had prepared, yet it was effected by the manner of enforcing them. Men of old approved Character who respected their Neighbours and were respected would not descend to it. The Executors of these new Laws therefore were Men who like the Laws themselves were new." The Clintonian tax program, Hamilton agreed, was put into the hands of local assessors who used their power to punish Tories.

It was only as the New York conservatives lost control of state government to their upstart opponents, that the thought of the conservatives turned clearly in a centralist direction. At first, they were by no means the centralizing nationalists which they later became. "I am resolved," Edward Rutledge wrote John Jay on the eve of the Declaration of Independence, "to vest the Congress with no more Power than that [which] is absolutely necessary, and to use a familiar Expression, to keep the Staff in our own Hands." This mood lasted just so long as the conservatives retained their confidence in controlling what Robert R. Livingston called the "torrent" of democratic sentiment in the states. When that confidence failed, when in 1779–1780 the conservatives turned to Congress to effect their program, they turned to it as "a refuge against majority rule." Hamilton wrote in July 1781 that "it would be the extreme of vanity in us not to be sensible, that we began this revolution with very vague and confined notions of the practical business of government."

The remark applied as much to the future authors of *The Federalist* as to anyone else.

Among the vague and confined notions which New York conservatives had to unlearn, was their visceral opposition to government intervention in the economy. Early in the war it was radicals, not conservatives, who favored a managed economy. Marinus Willett, for instance, wrote to John Jay in 1777 that he approved New York's embargo on the export of flour. "I am not unaware," Willett explained, "of that common argument that trade will regulate itself [but] a virtuous private trader appears to me as rare in this day as the Phoenix; trade is got into the hands of I don't know who: but am sure it is not in the hands of men of public virtue." Gouverneur Morris was an outstanding exponent of the "common argument" mentioned by Willett. Morris, like Adam Smith, believed that "the Principle of self Interest is like the Power of Gravity to Fluids, which brings them to a level, merely by the Mutability of their component Parts." Writing to Livingston, Morris declared that "Restrictions of Commerce injure the State without serving the general Cause and undue Exertions of Government like the Convulsions of Delirium exhaust the Patient in unproductive Efforts." In the midst of the financial crisis of 1779, when the Continental currency dropped from a ratio of 8:1 to specie to a ratio of something like 40:1, and when (in the words of General Washington) it took a wagonload of money to buy a wagonload of provisions, Morris could write:

> Nothing therefore is requisite than that the People should be actuated by that Regard to private Interest which has been ineffectually written and preached and prayed against from the Fall of Adam to the present Hour.

Gouverneur Morris' unblushing advocacy of laissez-faire was typical of the New York conservative leaders. Although they sometimes voted for price-fixing or confiscation bills for reasons of expediency, the New York conservatives unanimously condemned them in their private correspondence. Egbert Benson of Dutchess, for example, voted for price regulation although in private he declared:

> A regulating scheme has not been attempted anywhere in the State except at Albany. . . . It is amazing that people should still pursue a system so evidently futile and absurd. I sincerely wish the *limitation* may be *limited* to the City of Albany. I possibly am in the opposite extreme and so far from reducing prices agreeable to this plan, I think the Embargo Act ought immediately to be repealed and our farmers indulged with an opportunity of carrying their produce to the highest market.

How did these vigorous proponents of free enterprise come to adopt the mercantilist program of currency devaluation, national impost, central bank, and stronger Federal government? The catalyst seems to have been the financial crisis of 1779–1780, which persuaded even Morris of the need for a "regular Plan." This crisis was as significant in shaping the outlook of the Federalist leaders as was the depression of 1785–1786 (to be discussed presently) in fixing the sentiments of the Federalist voters. Once converted, the New York conservatives played a key role in pushing through Congress the first steps of the new national program. The little group decided collectively how to distribute themselves between the state legislature and the national Congress. In Congress, James Duane was particularly conspicuous, "no other member," as he wrote to Livingston, "having knowledge of our money matters sufficiently comprehensive." Three years later, when that "intriguing industrious body" (as his friend Morris called him) had successfully lobbied through Congress the currency devaluation of March 1780, and, in February 1781, the proposal for a Federal impost and the appointment of Robert Morris as Financier, Duane referred to the latter as a plan "on which I hazarded my political Reputation."

Hamilton expounded the changed conservative attitude in his "Continentalist" essays of 1781–1782.

> There are some, who maintain, [he wrote] that trade will regulate itself, and is not to be benefitted by the encouragements, or restraints of government. Such persons will imagine, that there is no need of a common directing power. This is one of those wild speculative paradoxes, which have grown into credit among us, contrary to the uniform practice and sense of the most enlightened nations.

"Unless," Hamilton concluded, "we can overcome this narrow disposition and learn to estimate measures, by their general tendency, we shall never be a great or a happy people, if we remain a people at all." Public banks, for example, were "like all other good things . . . subject to abuse and when abused, become pernicious. . . . But no wise statesman will reject the good from an apprehension of the ill."

Well before the end of the war, the Federalist leadership had evolved the program and the ideology which they would champion in 1787–1788. In the process, these powerful New Yorkers had moved beyond the circle of state affairs. By 1783 they were working intimately and continuously with other middle-state conservatives to strengthen the federal government. Thus, as New York Receiver of Taxes for Robert Morris toward the end of the war, Alexander Hamilton also served as lobbyist for Morris' plans to repeal the legal tender and punitive features of state paper-money laws. In July 1782, Hamilton and Schuyler saw through the New York legislature resolutions calling for a national convention to strengthen the Confederation (the last nationalist act of that body for half a decade); in the same month, a meeting of public creditors in Philadelphia called for stronger federal powers; in September 1782, New York answered Pennsylvania with a convention of creditors at Albany, chaired by Schuyler, which planned an abortive state convention for November. The same handful of men founded the banks in New York City and Philadelphia which were rallying points for investors in the Critical Period. Hamilton's brother-in-law, John B. Church, was a leading stockholder of both institutions. New Yorker Robert R. Livingston suggested the Philadelphia Bank of North America in 1780, while in 1783 Gouverneur Morris, by then a Philadelphia resident, proposed to Alexander Hamilton a Bank of New York. "A consolidated group whose interests knew no state boundaries and were truly national in their scope" was taking shape. Nothing illustrated it better than a letter Robert Morris wrote to Philip Schuyler shortly after becoming Financier, early in 1781. "I need," the Financier told the Patroon, "one thousand barrels of flour for the new campaign; I assume your credit as a private gentleman is good for this amount; proceed accordingly, and bill me." By thus harnessing the energies of private enterprise to the national need, supplies were obtained for the triumph of Yorktown.

II

By 1783, the cause of stronger Federal government had a brilliant galaxy of leaders in New York; what the cause needed was popular support.

Twice during the war the Federalist leaders had seriously considered strengthening Congress by dictatorial means. The first occasion was the crisis of 1780. In May, Schuyler wrote to Duane that it was necessary to "lodge dictatorial powers" either in the Commander-in-Chief, or in him, together with a small committee; Schuyler went on to suggest names for the committee. In November 1780, Schuyler suggested a dictatorial central committee for New York as well. Hamilton stated in September that Congress had been too liberal in observing the letter of its instructions: "They should have considered themselves as vested with full power *to preserve the republic from harm.*" That same year Robert R. Livingston, as chairman of a committee of Congress for increasing its powers, used identical language in calling on that body to assume all necessary powers "by the authority which the nature of the trust reposed in them vests with them."

Such thoughts, during the troubled eighteen months between the fall of Charleston and the surrender at Yorktown, are no proof of conspiratorial intent. Tom Paine, the voice of the Revolution, quite agreed with the New York conservatives that the financial crisis of 1779-1780 called for centralized government in the hands of businessmen. As late as March 1781, Robert R. Livingston wrote Philip Schuyler: "Have you devised any plan to extricate us from our present difficulties? or are we still to blunder on without object and without system?" When the two principal New York conservatives expressed bewilderment, lesser men could hardly have had a surer sense of purpose.

In the spring of 1783, however, Gouverneur Morris and Hamilton, at least, were involved in conspiratorial designs much less creditable. With peace at hand, they made their desperate bid to utilize the army's demand for pay in forcing through Congress the nationalist program. Morris, as quoted earlier, spoke at this time of the persuasion of the halter, while Hamilton wrote to the reluctant Washington: "I confess could force avail I should almost wish to see it employed."

This seems to be all the evidence for unrepublican intentions on the part of the New York Federalist leaders. After 1783, they settled down to search for a constituency. The Federalists found their strongest popular support among the artisans of New York City.

The genuineness of artisan support for the Constitution is beyond question. The election for delegates to the New York ratifying convention was (as in no other state) by secret ballot and open to all adult males, and the New York City Federalist margin was twenty-to-one: since the artisans were a good half of the city's adult male population, they must have voted overwhelmingly for ratification. Moreover, as in all other large cities, the city mechanics capped their ballots with a victory parade in which craft after craft marched under its banners.

Jackson Main has pointed up the theoretical significance of the artisans' Federalism. "The most serious of all objections to an interpretation based exclusively on an alignment along class lines," Main wrote, "is the complete absence of a division of opinion in the towns. Where there should have been the most feeling, the least existed." How shall we account for the artisans' enthusiasm for a document which, according to Beard, was the reactionary and antidemocratic product of a ruling class?

The answer must go right back to John Fiske. The Federalist *leaders* knew what they wanted before 1783, but the New York City artisans, who would become Federalist *voters*, were preoccupied in 1783 and 1784 with a belligerent, class-conscious attempt to rewin a foothold in the city from which the war had exiled them seven years. The depression of the mid-1780's transformed their outlook. The spring of 1785 saw a general uneasiness about trade stagnation suddenly grow acute and urgent. Then, as John Jay remarked, Federal ideas began to thrive; the early summer of 1785 produced in every major American city a merchant-mechanic alliance on behalf of stronger Federal government.

The objects of the merchant-mechanic committees formed in Boston, New York, Philadelphia, Baltimore and Charleston in 1785 were, first, to press for stronger Federal power to regulate trade, and second, to reinforce legislation—as in Non-Importation days—by the moral sentiment and direct action of local communities. The first concern is illustrated by a petition from "Artificers, Tradesmen and Mechanics" of New York City to the Continental Congress, early in 1785, which stated that "we sincerely hope our Representatives will coincide with the other States, in augmenting your power to every exigency of the Union." The second concern is exemplified by the resolve of the Philadelphia shoemakers not to buy, sell, repair, let be repaired by an employer, or work for employers who bought, sold or repaired, imported European boots or shoes.

Imported manufactures brought the menace of British economic power directly home to the New York City artisans. Thirty thousand hats and 97,000 pairs of shoes, for example, poured into the city during the three years 1784–1786. Here again was an echo of "the ever-memorable period of the Stamp Act": after, as before, the Revolution, the encouragement of native manufactures seemed a part of the struggle for independence. "When the minds of the people of America were really virtuous," wrote a newspaper correspondent in 1785, "at the beginning of the late contest, every man was convinced of the necessity of our encouraging manufactures, and employing our own people, that we might be truly independent." The General Society of Mechanics and Tradesmen struck the same note. European imports, the Society told its Boston counterpart, "are not only highly unfavorable to every mechanical improvement, but . . . nourish a spirit of dependence which tends in some degree to defeat the purpose of our late revolution."

Men of all classes rejoiced that, toward the end of the eighties, articles such as nails, oil, linens and glass were more cheaply manufactured in America than abroad. Robert Boyd, chairman of the General Society of Mechanics and Tradesmen, and Peter Curtenius, bitter Antifederalist merchant, joined with conservatives John Jay, Alexander Hamilton, Richard Varick, and Robert Troup, in promoting the all-important iron industry. By 1787, Curtenius' Air Furnace could offer iron articles ranging from tea kettles to the heavy pots and rollers used in sugar-refineries and slitting-mills, "equal to any imported from Europe, and the Price less."

To the artisans, the campaign for the Constitution seemed a direct continuation of the independence struggle. It was symbolic that in Boston, a meeting of tradesmen and artisans at the old Revolutionary meeting-place, the Green Dragon tavern, chaired by Paul Revere, rousingly supported the Constitution and allegedly swayed Samuel Adams to vote for ratification. In New York, politicians of all persuasions shared with the artisans a fear that England, by dumping goods on the American market, closing the West Indies, and other harassments, could destroy de facto the independence it had granted de jure. "What most immediately and deeply impresses me," John Morin Scott had written to James Duane even before the evacuation of New York City, "is the apprehension that a Treaty of Amity and Concord may be consorted with Great Britain, which may ultimately sap and overturn the independence of these United States." Reciprocity, Scott concluded, would not be real equality. The Lord of Livingston Manor believed that unless the British allowed Americans "to trade to their West Indian Islands on the Same footing as we did formerly, to enable us to make remittances & Supply ourselves with Salt Rum Sugar molasses etc. in our own bottoms," American trade would soon dwindle "to little or nothing." John Jay, now Secretary of State, agreed that the British insistence on repayment of old debts, while forbidding Americans to obtain means of payment from the West Indian trade, had placed merchants of the newly-independent nation in an intolerable vise. In that same summer of 1785 when American merchants and mechanics were combining to protect themselves, John Adams, America's representative in England, wrote that "the [English] *disigns of ruining, if they can our carrying Trade, and annihilating all our Navigation, and Seaman is* [sic] *too apparent."* He who had fought for the Massachusetts cod in the peace negotiations of 1782 was in no yielding mood.

> If the English will persevere in excluding our Ships from their West India Islands, Canada, Nova Scotia, and Newfoundland . . . we must adopt in all the States the Regulations which were once made in England. . . . I should be sorry to adopt a Monopoly. But, driven to the necessity of it, I would not do Business by the Halves. . . . We must not, my Friend, be the Bubbles of our own Liberal Sentiments. If we cannot obtain reciprocal Liberality, We must adopt reciprocal Prohibitions, Exclusions, Monopolies, and Imposts.

Tom Paine, the former stay-maker, as usual caught the national feeling in a phrase when he wrote that a stronger Federal government would be "our anchor in the world of empires."

New York publications were quick to transfer the old anti-Tory sentiment to the new Federalist cause. When the Chamber of Commerce appointed a committee to deal with the trade depression, it was presented to the public as a step "to break the fetters and restraints which we have tamely suffered the British to fix on our trade." A newspaper writer asked: "Is it any breach of charity to suppose, that those men who oppose the increase of the power of Congress for regulating our commerce—or who oppose laws for imposing duties on British goods—are under the influence of British principles or connections?" By thus fusing the old radical anti-British sentiment with the conservative interest in a stronger Federal government, the merchants destroyed whatever hope there might have been for Antifederalism in New York City.

Throughout the pregnant summer of 1785, newspaper correspondents addressed themselves directly to the need to bury old class antagonisms and cement a merchant-mechanic alliance. Merchants and mechanics, one writer said, must sink "all old causes of difference in eternal oblivion." "A Friend to the Community" expressed the same sentiment forcibly.

> The present unsettled state of our trade and commerce is truly alarming [he began], and much depends on the exertions of the merchants and mechanics among us. . . . However secure either may feel with respect to their own strength and consequence—however determined they may be to abide by the resolutions formed by their own particular class, unless the merchants and mechanics *mutually* request and obtain the assistance of each other, their attempts to subvert the machinations of our enemies will prove entirely futile and abortive. . . . Thus . . . we shall see the mechanic look with pleasure on the prosperity of the merchant, and the merchant will view with a smile of approbation the system which shall be adopted to promote the interest of the honest mechanic.

Farmer, merchant, and mechanic, said another statement, had united in '76 to withstand their common foes; they must do so again.

And they did. When the New York legislature rejected a Federal impost in the spring of 1785, a committee was set up by the Chamber of Commerce to protest the legislature's action and to correspond with the counties. The committee included former merchant Sons of Liberty Isaac Sears, John Broome, Isaac Ledyard and William Malcolm, conservative businessmen William Duer and William Constable, and mechanic-manufacturer White Matlack. Believing that "no partial or limited determination upon such questions could produce substantial Effects," the committee enlarged itself to include three prominent mechanics—silversmith William Gilbert, carpenter Anthony Post, and ropemaker Thomas Ivers—together with some new faces from the old Sons of Liberty: Jacobus Van Zandt and Nathaniel Hazard. The committee proceeded to memorialize the rest of the state, requesting that their memorial be laid "before the inhabitants of the several districts in your county, and that you will unite in giving pointed instructions to your representatives." In March 1786, when the Federal impost again hung in the balance in the New York legislature, a general meeting of city inhabitants unanimously approved the impost, and left copies of a petition at three taverns for signature.

Well before the ratification debate of 1787–1788, the Federalists had won to their cause not only most of the old radical leaders of New York City, but much of the mechanic rank-and-file. In 1785, Hugh Hughes observed that a "coalition" had been formed between all parties in the city, although a few mechanics still hung back.

The city Antifederalist leaders became generals without an army. Melancton Smith was not supported by the Mechanics' Committee when he sought an Assembly seat in 1785, and was rejected again when he and David Gelston ran for the Senate in 1787. On the eve of elections for the ratifying convention in 1788, Marinus Willett was said to have "become a proselyte, declaring it [the proposed Constitution] might be right—since it appears to be the sense of a vast majority"; while at the same time Hamilton observed that the city Antifederalists, fearing that New York City would secede from the state, did not advocate outright rejection of the Constitution. Thus, before the famous drama at Poughkeepsie had begun, the issue was in some sense already settled. Those debates on which so much attention has been lavished were, so far as New York City is concerned, the froth cast up by a wave which had already done its work.

As the artisan population of the city, three or four thousand strong, marched down Broadway on July 23, 1788, to celebrate adoption of the Constitution by the requisite nine states, their floats and slogans testified to their enthusiasm. A "federal loaf," 10 feet long, 27 inches in breadth, and 8 inches in height, was carried by the Bakers, together with "a flag, representing the declension of trade under the old Confederation." "Americans, encourage your manufactures!" proclaimed the Skinners, Breeches Makers, and Glovers, while the Peruke Makers and Hairdressers rejoined, "May we succeed in our trade and the union protect us." The Blacksmiths chanted, "Forge me strong, finish me neat, I soon shall moor a Federal fleet," as sturdy members of the trade, riding the float, hammered away at an anchor. On they came—the Ship Joiners, with their motto: "This federal ship will our commerce revive, And merchants and shipwrights and joiners shall thrive"; the humble Cartmen saying: "To every craft she gives employ, Sure Cartmen have their share of joy"; the Brush Makers, who proclaimed: "May love and unity support our trade,

And keep out those who would our rights invade." And after these there came several dozen more trades, including the Cordwainers, Carpenters (the largest trade, with 392 marchers), Hatters, Cabinet Makers, Sail Makers, Gold Smiths, Tobacconists, Paper Stainers, Artificial Florists, and last but not least the Tailors, with their magnificent slogan: "And they sewed fig leaves together."

III

Thus the United States Constitution, sponsored in New York as elsewhere in the nation by patricians such as Philip Schuyler and the Livingstons, was ardently supported, in New York as elsewhere, by those "restless mechanics" who regarded the patricians as their traditional enemies. Does this disprove the thesis that the Constitution was the instrument whereby a governing class on the defensive recovered its traditional power?

Not at all. To begin with, scholars on both sides of the question agree that New York's well-to-do supplied the Federalist *leadership*. "It seems clear," writes Jackson Main, "that most of the wealthy landowners and merchants, in and out of the [state ratifying] convention, were Federalists and that the Antifederalists, while drawing some of their leaders from this class, were on the whole men of lesser means."

The financial crisis of 1779–1780 crystallized the mercantilist, nationalist program of these Federalist leaders. The depression of 1785–1786 swung the artisan voters behind this program. Both groups felt an economic interest in the Constitution. To the Federalist leaders it offered a check on interference with property by the states. To the artisans it offered jobs and markets. But for each group, in addition, strengthening the Federal government seemed a way to promote the Revolution. In the eyes of the artisans in the mid-1780's, as in those of the well-to-do leaders of the "counter-revolutions" of 1780–1781 and 1787–1788, no contradiction existed between immediate, personal economic interests and the patriotic goal of sustaining the national economy and preserving national independence.

That ratification attracted many voters from the urban poor proves only that the Antifederalists failed to voice the aspirations of much of that humble constituency to which their rhetoric was addressed, and that, for the moment, other things were more important to the artisans than the struggle over who should rule at home. But only for the moment. The alliance between merchants and mechanics was, as Walsh says of Charleston, "not completely natural." When Hamilton, once in power, catered to the needs of importing merchants rather than to mechanic demands for protection against British manufactures, the artisans deserted him. As early as the fall of 1788 a spokesman for New York City's "middling or lower class of people" reopened the controversy, asserting that if this group "had any regard to their independence and liberty, parties must be formed, and a contention arise between the different classes."

2. The Early Nation

The Jacksonians: Paradox Lost? MICHAEL LEBOWITZ

From the Confederation period to the Jackson Era is a long leap. It would be possible to fill some of the gap with the scholarship of Alfred Young of Northern Illinois University, whose massive work, *The Democratic Republicans of New York,* employs a modified class interpretation of the Federalist-Jeffersonian Republican "First Party System." But Young's interesting book is diffuse and difficult to excerpt. William Appleman Williams' *Contours of American History* covers the whole sweep of American history and deals, inevitably, with the early years of the Republic. The reader will find a selection from *The Contours* touching on the Reconstruction period in this collection. Aside from these two works, however, the overall fact is clear: New Left spadework for the years from 1790 to 1828 still remains to be done.

The Jackson period has attracted somewhat more attention from the Left. Williams pictures the Jacksonians as strict laissez-faire-ists who, compared with those benevolent paternalists, the Whigs, surrendered human values for the sake of economic progress. His view of the Jacksonians owes much to Richard Hofstadter, a fact readily explained by Hofstadter's own dissent from the liberal tradition in his earlier work. But in this case, at least, it seems likely that Williams has expressed a rather idiosyncratic opinion, not generally accepted by most of the New Left scholars.

In the selection below by Michael Lebowitz, Jackson is largely restored to Left favor. Lebowitz does not turn him into a heroic tribune of the people, but he does suggest that Jacksonian democracy was an authentic vehicle for expressing discontent, and that there was more to Jackson and the Jacksonian coalition than a radical individualism oriented toward profits.

FOR FURTHER READING:

Arthur Schlesinger, Jr., *The Age of Jackson**, (Little, Brown and Co., 1945); Edward Pessen, *Jacksonian America: Society, Personality and Politics**, (Dorsey Press, 1969); Lee Benson, *The Concept of Jacksonian Democracy: New York as a Test Case**, (Princeton University Press, 1961); Frederick J. Turner, *The United States 1830–1850**, (Norton, 1965); John Ward, *Andrew Jackson, Symbol for an Age**, (Galaxy Books, 1962); Richard McCormick,

Source: Michael Lebowitz, "The Jacksonians: Paradox Lost?" in *Towards a New Past: Dissenting Essays in American History,* ed. Barton Bernstein (New York: Pantheon Books, 1968), pp. 65–89.

The Second American Party System: Party Formation in the Jacksonian Era*, (University of North Carolina Press, 1966); Marvin Meyers, *Jacksonian Persuasion: Politics and Belief**, (Stanford University Press, 1957).

Asterisk denotes paperback edition.

While conflicting evidence and interpretations may produce truth, they may also generate anxiety. And those who survey the Jacksonians will find in the gaggle of contradictory interpretations, in the parade of urban proletariat, rising middle classes, agrarian goodfolk, classical economists, and others, ample reason for anxiety. It is possible, of course, to react to this dilemma by suppressing contradictory evidence or, alternatively, by solemnly declaring all interpretations correct *in part* and then proceeding about one's own business. Yet the most satisfactory method of reducing anxiety is by reconciling the discordant themes, and this impulse may account for the attractiveness of the device of paradox as applied to the Jacksonians. In the limbo of paradox, all is possible. Notwithstanding its therapeutic value, however, the employment of a paradox interpretation may be no more than a mechanism by which the confusion of present historians is projected back to the actors of the period. It all bears looking into.

Although the contrary position often is argued implicitly, an interpretation of the Jacksonian movement should begin at the beginning. Here we have Jackson, the hero of New Orleans, a man who projects himself back into the public eye with his resolute actions in the Seminole Campaign and who receives from congressional criticism and ultimate acquittal an extension of public attention. The "Old Hero," man of action and defender of America against its enemies, triumphantly tours the Eastern cities in 1819 as the country enters a new crisis. The country next discovers Jackson, the proposed presidential candidate, as a local conservative Tennessee political faction advances his name in order to regain advantages on a state level. Support spreads rapidly—despite the limited objectives of his local backers. Jacksonian sentiment emerges in Alabama, Mississippi, North Carolina, and in Northern cities.

In the locus of that initial support is its essence. A Calhoun lieutenant attributes Jackson's popularity early in 1823 in Pennsylvania to "the grog shop politicians of villages and the rabble of Philadelphia and Pittsburgh." At a Cincinnati Clinton meeting, an attempt is made to reverse the organizers' proposal and to support Jackson for President and Clinton for Vice-President. William Green, who jumped into the Clay camp after the derailment of Clinton's candidacy, describes that meeting (a meeting presumably swelled because of unemployment resulting from a fire at the large steam mill):

> A powerful excitement in favour of Jackson among some men and more boys, seemed to threaten a dissolution of the meeting . . . the noise on the occasion referred was characteristic of the cause it was attempted to promote. The cries of "The Hero of New Orleans," "Hurra for the 8th of January," were calculated to inflame the passions of an ignorant multitude, and did so. . . . Better that N. Orleans had been lost. . . .

Elsewhere, the early Jackson support is described simply as "the people." The people, the rabble, the ignorant multitude declare themselves early for the Old Hero, the man of action and defender of America against its enemies. Who could compare with him?

Yet the "people" were soon joined by politicians and political factions with ears to the ground and ends to be served. In Ohio, local political leaders and a rural political organization shifted to Jackson as the Clinton campaign dissolved. In Pennsylvania, opposing parties vied to lead the fight for Jackson, and in the process the Calhoun campaign was shelved. In Maryland and New Jersey, displaced Federalist and disappointed Calhoun politicians chose Jackson as the man to lead them to their deserved rewards. The election of 1824 gave Jackson a plurality of electoral votes; yet the forbidding John Quincy Adams was selected to be President in the House of Representatives. The Jackson movement now had at its head the man of action, the choice of the people and the victim of the corrupt bargain of base and dishonest politicians.

Once in office, the Adams administration displayed the strong nationalistic tendencies of its President and Secretary of State and generated, in the process, a congressional opposition which consisted of Jackson and Calhoun men and the Old Republican supporters of Crawford. The Calhoun men, united by ties of ambition and then by opposition to the national policies, were the first to merge with the Jackson cause; subsequently, the Crawford men led by Van Buren came over, convinced that Jackson was more likely than Adams to support a Jeffersonian program of limited central government. Jackson was not the first choice of politicians, with or without programs, but he was available.

Now the Jackson coalition prepared for the next election. Newspapers were established around the country to spread the party line. Correspondence and vigilance committees emerged to guide and coordinate local activities. Legislative bills were tailored to increase support from doubtful regions. And the people were provided with songs, slogans, and talismans to reinforce their faith. Jackson was the candidate of the people, and the people were urged to support him against their enemies. It was a successful campaign, with Jackson receiving an overwhelming majority of electoral votes. The Jackson machine had elected a president, and the people gloried in their triumph.[1]

The Hero in office, believing himself to be the champion of the people, did not disappoint his most enthusiastic followers. He defeated in battle nationalizing tendencies in his Maysville Road Veto, defended the integrity of the nation in the nullification controversy, and entered into conflict with the greatest of all monsters and enemies of the Republic, the Second Bank of the United States. In return, the people reelected Jackson and then gave support to his chosen successor. Van Buren, in his turn, punctured the little monsters, the state banks, which had puffed themselves up and feasted at the leavings of their old master.

Not all of Jackson's original backers, however, were pleased. There were defections. Advocates of national public works and protective tariffs, upholders of Southern states' rights, supporters of the national bank and then of the state banks in turn left the Democratic party. Men of wealth, alarmed at what they considered a spirit of anarchy, shifted into the opposition—though they left behind some who were not prepared to move.[2] The Whig party, a party composed of old opponents of the Jackson men plus recent defectors, a party blatantly united only in its opposition to the Democratic party, took the field against a party which itself had been united largely only in its opposition to the Adams administration. In 1840 the Whigs, with a Western military hero, a well-organized campaign of ballyhoo, and a depression on their side, were given their turn—by the people.

From scattered support to semiorganized movement to machine to victory, one dominant theme comes through, and that is coalition—coalition for power, coalition for political and social ends, coalition against common enemies. In particular, the extent to which the "presidential issue" was used, on a state and national level, by ambitious politicians justifies the description of the Jackson machine as a "loose, opportunistic, all-inclusive and eclectic" coalition. It similarly devaluates those analyses of the Jacksonians which concentrate on the cross-sectional characteristics of the politicians. For when the Jacksonian movement is considered as an unfolding process, it becomes clear that the movement must be traced to the earlier periods, to the original support for Jackson which surprised and discomforted the state politicians. The shock of Jackson's own Tennessee backers, the dismay of Calhoun and Crawford men—all this was the product of a movement which caught fire without the manipulations of established politicians. Once the support for the Old Hero had been demonstrated, only the blind, the entrenched, or the unambitious among politicians could ignore it. The politicians followed the "people"; unfortunately, many historians have followed the politicians.

But, then, who were the "people"? In the 1828 election when Jackson received 178 electoral votes to 83 for Adams, he carried only 56 percent of the popular vote. (Nor did the proportion change significantly in subsequent elections.) And since it is doubtful that the "enemies of the people" constituted almost half of the population, it is apparent that many of "the humble members of society— the farmers, mechanics, and laborers" did not vote for Jackson. Nevertheless, neither the closeness of votes nor the employment of leaders drawn from a common stock implies the identity of the two parties. For the Jacksonians deployed a unique rhetoric, a rhetoric chosen for a purpose—and people believed it.

In states where the Jacksonians campaigned actively and called upon the people "to come forth in their own strength and majesty," they came. Voting participation rates climbed—with special gains in those Middle and Western states which had been the main target of the Jackson campaign.[3] This was a rhetoric consistent both with the early appeal of Jackson and with Old Republican dogma: a call against aristocracy, privilege, and government interference with a providential order; a call for the simple, the natural, the just. These were clever appeals, but that in no way detracts from the fact that they struck a responsive chord. It was easy enough to call the people out against their enemies, but what determined their enemies? Clearly, both the appeals and the nature of those to whom the appeals were directed must be central in an examination of the Jacksonians.

In *Andrew Jackson*: *Symbol for an Age*, John W. Ward explored the symbolic use of Jackson by contemporaries as a way of revealing the values of the period. It was an age, he found, which emphasized the role of nature, which rested its faith in a providential order, which stressed the role of man's will. It was an age which believed that the man who strove, who exerted his will to conquer nature, would receive his just rewards. An age in which Nature and Providence united to provide the man of will with the opportunity to create his own destiny, it was an age in which every success was further proof of the beneficence of the order. And for a time which stressed such values, Andrew Jackson, orphan and self-made man, man of action and man of iron will, was a fitting vessel.

Many of the same themes appear in Marvin Meyers' examination of Jacksonian values. Here again the emphasis is upon steady work, upon an industry honest and simple. It is the view of an order in which industry, economy, and useful toil are certain to be rewarded in an ideal world; a world in which the industrious stand in opposition to the idle and speculative. In such a scheme, where the artificial and unnatural were equated with evil, the place of government was a logical one: the ideal government was one which removed itself from interference with the natural order. In a world of bliss, there was no place for the legislation of bliss.[4]

In this context, the main Jacksonian policies—opposition to special corporate charters, hostility toward paper money, suspicion of public enterprise and public debt—fall into place; all involve resistance to an interference with a natural and just order. Meyers interprets these policies and the accompanying appeals as reflecting the desire of Jacksonians to maintain or restore the virtues of an earlier and simpler age. They were, he argues, appeals to a generation which sought a return to an old agrarian republic, to a paradise lost.

Yet Meyers is obsessed by facts. He knows that this was a period of rapid economic change, and he is familiar with Hofstadter's treatment of the age as one of emerging liberal capitalism and of acquisitiveness. Thus Meyers takes his Old Republican man, blends him with the New Acquisitive man, and discovers the schizophrenic Jacksonian, the man who looks backward while plunging forward. And with this dualistic man, Meyers explains the Jacksonian paradox, that a movement which idealized the past cleared the way for the future. He explains the paradox by personifying it.

It is difficult to avoid the suspicion that paradox, irony, and hybrid interpretations of the Jacksonians are the result of the tendency to think in terms of an archetypical Jacksonian. If we recall the coalitional aspects of the Jackson movement, if we move away from a composite Jacksonian, can we understand better to whom this imagery and rhetoric appealed?[5]

Clearly, the men whose values and status should be examined first (both in order and in importance) were the farmers. They were, after all, a significant majority of the population. However, despite their numbers, despite the description of Jacksonian rhetoric as agrarian rhetoric, despite speculations that the Jacksonians wished to return to an earlier agrarian republic, farmers get little attention from historians of the Jacksonians. The lack of emphasis is striking. There are analyses of party workers, bankers, manufacturers, trade union activists—of any individuals who succeeded in detaching themselves from the mass. Yet the farmers, unorganized, anonymous, and collectively most important, are largely ignored.

When the farmer's political behavior is considered, it becomes readily apparent that although much Jacksonian rhetoric was directed toward the farmer, the most noble of all men, he did not direct all of his collective favor toward the Jacksonian party. Why? Was the type of appeal made by the Democrats more attractive to a particular type of farmer? Can one, in fact, talk accurately about *the* farmer or were differences among farmers great enough to make this a misleading category? Were the differences within the category of farmers greater than differences between farmers and other categories?

The picture of the farmer during this period is generally that of a new settler taking land, either clearing it himself or purchasing it from a person who cleared it. With the aid of the major transportation changes of the period, he finds he is able to produce for distant markets. His land value rises; he invests in more land or improves his land. Often he becomes more interested in the speculative value of his land than in production. He is the rising entrepreneur in farming: he is the expectant agricultural capitalist. For him, transportation-changes, banks, and other advances are tools which provide the opportunity for higher returns.

Yet this is not the only farmer of the period. The very changes benefitting the first farmer tend to add to another farmer's problems. While improved river transport and new canals aided both the Western farmer and the consumers, "western wheat demoralized farmers in the older communities, who were already struggling with declining fertility, low yields, parasitic infestations, increasing costs, and declining prices." These latter farmers, the victims of regional specialization effects of transport changes, might tend to center in the older regions of the Middle States, in New England, in parts of the South. Some might respond simply by moving, others by shifting into different agricultural products in which they had a comparative advantage, and others by working their land even harder. There were two farmers in this period, and one had good reason to be discontent.

But how could nature's nobleman, the hardy farmer, the member of the steady honest class, reconcile the disappointment of his goals with his vision of a world in which men received just returns for honest labor? His vision provided him with an answer: one could expect to receive one's reward only if self-seeking men had not upset the natural balance by obtaining special privileges and other obstructions to justice from government. Here, then, was a farmer to whom the Democratic party could appeal—an embattled farmer, a disappointed farmer, a declining farmer.[6]

Of course, if the embattled and declining farmers were the Democratic farmers, the Jacksonian paradox as applied to farmers would be somewhat weakened. One would not be able to argue that these farmers were looking back to a simple old republic while advancing in a new order. Those Democratic farmers who feared the new order would be those who were *injured* by it, those for whom a solid old world was crumbling. In their efforts to find reasons, rather than questioning a providential design or focusing upon the real causes, they tended to emphasize the most obvious artificial aspects of the new order: banks, bank paper, and the paper aristocracy. It was banking which altered the normal relationship between prices and costs; it was banking, both in expansion and contraction, which "disturbed the equality of society," which was "a two-edged sword in the hands of the enemy." And theirs could not be a negative concept of government, for government action was necessary to undo the evil which had been done. The "independent silence of the farmer, who ask[ed] nothing from his government but equal laws, and nothing of heaven, but rain and sunshine" was replaced by the demand, "Get out of my sunlight." [7]

By combining, then, our knowledge of the nature of Jacksonian appeals and of the changes in the fortunes of farmers in the period, it is possible to suggest the hypothesis that farmers in relatively declining regions were more likely to vote for the Democrats than those in relatively rising regions. It should be emphasized that we are not arguing that all Western farmers were rising farmers or that rising farmers had no reason to vote Democratic. Rather our suggestion is twofold: that declining farmers were more likely to vote Democratic than were rising farmers in any region (because of the nature of Jacksonian appeals), and that the proportion of declining farmers was likely to be higher in the older or bypassed areas than in the emerging ones.[8]

One of the most significant attempts to examine a hypothesis of this nature and to employ the type of information required for a test occurs in Lee Benson's *The Concept of Jacksonian Democracy*. Utilizing county and township data for New York State, Benson examines the argument that the Whigs were "the prosperous farmers living on better soils or along good transportation routes" and the Democrats, "the poor or less-well-to-do farmers." He concludes, after looking at figures on voting and housing assessments, that there is no basis for this traditional claim; on the contrary, "the Democrats tended to find their strongest support in eastern New York among groups living in long-settled areas and enjoying considerable prosperity." [9]

Benson's conclusions may appear to disprove the hypothesis we have suggested above; but if so, it is only because he is not entirely precise in the interpretation of his observations. Whereas the hypothesis relating declining farmers to the Democrats is a dynamic statement which requires information on *changes* in economic status, Benson examines a static proposition relating wealth to voting affinity. In his hypothesis and in the variables considered, there is no place for change or for the responses to change. And, as Jacksonian appeals reveal, it was change which was central to the period.

A conclusion that the Democrats received their strongest support from farmers in the wealthiest regions is not necessarily inconsistent with the suggestion that the Democrats were supported by farmers in declining regions. A relatively wealthy Eastern farmer *could* be the farmer whose economic position was declining. Yet would it be his wealth or his declining status which attracted him to the Democratic position? In several places, Benson indicates that the prosperity of Eastern farmers was due not to their enterprise but primarily to their "headstart." "Yorker families," he notes, "had decades, often centuries to pick out the best sites, accumulate wealth (and status) and pass it on to their descendants." Of course, the best sites of decades and centuries ago were obviously not the best sites of this period—and accumulated wealth and status were not necessarily *accumulating* wealth and status. In this light, what did it mean to be "enjoying considerable prosperity"?

Actually, it is even questionable whether Benson correctly identifies "prosperous" economic units. His variable for wealth, the average value of dwelling unit per family, tells us more about previous investment in housing than it does about prosperous *farming* units, and it is supported only by "impressionistic" evidence about the relative position of towns within counties. The image of grand old houses constructed in the bloom of eastern New York and now presiding over declining and marginal farmland is a powerful one.

The significant sectional differences and the identification of older ("wealthier") regions with rural Democratic strength in New York revealed in Benson's study are entirely consistent with the argument relating declining farmers to the Jacksonian persuasion. And as Benson notes in his own discussion, New York may not be an exceptional case. (The correspondence between areas of *long-time* Democratic support and areas of low land value has often been noted.) The hypothesis is not challenged; neither, though, has it been properly tested.[10]

Were there any other groups (or segments of groups) besides farmers which had reason to resent the economic changes of the Jacksonian period? Among the other "humble members of society," mechanics and laborers, employment and price fluctuations or economic dislocation could easily be a source of discontent. The same transportation improvements, for example, which aided Western farmers and demoralized Eastern farmers were logically such as to disrupt the activities of those Western mechanics who had previously functioned behind the natural tariff wall of high transportation costs; and if these mechanics searched, they could certainly find a scapegoat in the presence of a bank which facilitated the import of Eastern merchandise.[11] Yet there were more far-reaching changes than these, which increased the insecurity of many members of the remaining two humble classes.

The Jacksonian period was one in which master mechanics found themselves threatened by the emergence of the merchant-capitalists. "With easy access to credit," this new group "began to invade the mechanical trades and to establish small-scale factories." For masters who found themselves undersold by quantity production, an obvious response was an attack on what they considered the source of their problem: the banks, which made possible the engrossing activities of their favored competitors and which thus increased the difficulties of those who earned their living by labor. Another response for a master, though, was the attempt to emulate the merchant-capitalist by shifting to a greater use of apprentices as a source of cheap labor in place of more costly journeymen. This reaction, shifting the pressure to the journeymen, produced trade union activity on the part of the journeymen with the intent of preventing the downgrading of craft skills and status. Innovations in the organization of industry during this period clearly were the cause of discontent for some mechanics.

Overriding all concerns in the 1830s, though, for the journeyman and the master (and other small businessmen) was the enormous price increase from 1834 to 1837. For the small businessman, the contractor, the grocer, price changes upset the normal relations between costs and prices; for the wage earner, both journeyman mechanic and unskilled laborer, gains in money wages lagged significantly behind price rises. "Wage-workers, already concerned over their loss in status, became desperately alarmed over money-earnings, which exchanged for less and less food and shelter."

For those injured by declining real wages, there were two resorts: an attempt to increase money wages at least proportionately to price rises, and/or an attack on the source of inflationary tendencies. Generally, that source was identified as the banking system—and in particular, the small notes generated by the banks. In the Loco Foco claim "as the currency expands, the loaf contracts" was typified the belief that bank notes operated as a tax upon the laboring people. Therefore, the participation of wage earners in trade union activity to raise money wages and in political coalition to attack the banking system were in no way inconsistent.[12]

Both in trade union activity and in the struggle against the inflationary tendencies of the banking system, there was a common assumption that wage earners suffered from a weak position relative to the power of other groups within the society. And central to this weakness was their inability to combine—both for legal reasons and also because of the nature of their productive activity. In relationship to trade union activity, this issue was often raised; unions were defended as a countervailing force against the combinations of others. Thus Frederick Robinson argued: "the capitalists, monopolists, judges, lawyers, doctors and priests . . . know that the secret of their own power and wealth consists in the strictest concert of action. . . . Unions among themselves have always enabled the few to rule and ride the people." Or, as John Greenleaf Whittier complained:

The merchants may agree upon their prices; the lawyers upon their fees; the physicians upon their charges; the manufacturers upon the wages given to their operatives; but the *laborer* shall not consult his interest and fix the price of his toil and skill. If this be the *law*, it is unjust, oppressive and wicked.

Although it was less obvious, the same weakness characterized the position of wage earners in respect to rising prices. "The laboring part of the community (farmers and laborers) are the last in society who can bring up their services to the standard of a depreciated currency," noted William Carroll in 1823. "Wages are the first to be affected by a depreciated medium, and the last to adapt themselves to it. The poor are therefore the first victims of overissues," argued Theodore Sedgewick, Jr., in 1835. The vulnerability of wage earners, however, was not the result of chance factors; it too had its roots in their relative weakness, in their relationship to the productive process. Rhetorically asking if wages rose proportionately to prices, the *Weekly Ohio Statesman* replied:

> *They do not*, and from the circumstances of the case, *they can not*. And the reason is obvious.—The bankers who cause the expansion, and consequent depreciation of paper, (or *increase* of prices, just as you choose—the meaning is the same) are incorporated—connected—concentrated. They act simultaneously and immediately. But mechanics and laborers are simply individuals—unincorporated—unconnected —pursuing different occupations, and frequently waging opposite pursuits.

Nor was it only the bankers who were able to swim with the tide of bank money. "There is a privity of interest and feeling between these banks and the merchants and speculators dependent upon them. The latter *anticipate* the expansion. They expand with it. They govern their dealings by it. But the mechanic and the laborer are only aware of it when everything they consume is cracked up 100 or 200 per cent. upon their hands." A belief in their relative weakness (attributed often to unequal legislation), an acceptance of the quantity theory of money, and the experience of falling real wages: all of this made logical an attack by wage earners upon the banks, which gave artificial and fictitious value to all things, which disturbed the equality of society, which were a two-edged sword in the hands of the enemies of the people.[13]

Rather than simply the cupidity of expectant capitalists, among urban mechanics and laborers there were attitudes and reactions identifiable as those of people *injured* by change—as opposed to those of people impatient with it. The expectant capitalist argument is an attractive one; but before concluding that it was a dominant attitude among wage earners, it is necessary to show that wage earners acted and supported positions during this period which were not in their interest *as wage earners* to take. While on many issues the interests of wage earners were not inconsistent with those of small businessmen, for some wage earners this coincidence was probably no more than that. Unskilled laborers, for example, were the least well off of all workingmen, the most subject to seasonal and cyclical unemployment and the most helpless in dealing with uncurrent paper money; they were probably also the least likely to allow illusions of expectant capitalism to dominate their concern over their immediate position.

If the hypothesis relating the relatively declining farmers to the Democrats has an urban counterpart, it is that the laborers and mechanics least subject to illusions of expectant capitalism, most helpless in the face of movements of an economy which they did not understand, were more likely to vote Democratic. (Once again, this is a statement of a general tendency—not all rising mechanics would be Whigs.) In this light, Benson's identification of New York lumbering towns as generally Democratic is worthy of note. Unable to find any "economic" reason for this pattern, Benson suggests that lumbering may have generated antipuritanical behavior and that antipuritans may have tended to vote Democratic.[14] However, before concluding that frequenters of grog shops were more likely to vote Democratic (and confusing a symptom with a cause), it may be suggested that Jacksonian positions on paper money and privilege were particularly attractive to low-skill and unskilled workers with limited horizons. And this same attraction may go a long way towards explaining the initial adherence of unskilled immigrant Irish Catholics to the Democratic party.[15]

The opposition of workingmen's parties to Democratic candidates has often been cited as an indication of a gap between the Jacksonians and labor.[16] Yet the dominant tone of that opposition (where it in fact occurred) was that of the vehemence of reformers to betrayers of the faith. Workies and Loco Focos, "methodists of democracy," sought to bring the Democrats back from where they had been led astray by entrepreneurial elements in the party; and when the Democrats responded by absorbing parts of the workingmen's program, support for the latter groups dwindled. In this sense, the workingmen's parties may be viewed as a wing of a general movement which centered in the Democratic party. As Pessen concluded, the existence of workingmen's parties reveals that "an important minority in the Jacksonian Era were disenchanted with their society and its institutions." And much of this disenchantment was the disenchantment of the injured and declining rather than that of the rising.

Thus, consideration of economic changes during the Jacksonian era indicates that not all groups within the society had reason to praise the changes which were occurring. Some in this period found their positions and status under attack or deteriorating; and they were likely to respond to Jacksonian (or more extreme) attacks on government—granted privileges, public spending, and paper money. In this sense, it may be argued that the Jacksonians represented, partly, declining groups. An association of the Jacksonian persuasion with declining groups is a natural one; Meyers himself notes that the political analysis of Jacksonian Democracy would be simpler and clearer "if the Jacksonians could in fact be taken for innocent—still better, struggling—victims of external social changes." Impressed, though, by the economic changes of the period and the apparent role of Jacksonians in creating them, Meyers rejects this possibility and creates in its stead the paradoxical Jacksonian, the man who backed into the future. The Jacksonians need not be viewed as only the losers of the period; it is sufficient to suggest that a significant portion of them, however, were.

Where does this leave the expectant capitalists, the rising merchants and manufacturers, the frontier achievers who have generally been identified with the Jackson party? And what of programs in Jacksonian and workingmen's platforms which were designed to appeal to men on the make, men who supported reforms in order to rise? Obviously, there were many of these men among the Jacksonians—more than can be accounted for by the availability of patronage and favors from a successful party. The Jacksonians were a coalition of rising and declining men; but on what basis were they able to unite?

For people unsatisfied with the status quo, the belief in a beneficent natural order provided an obvious scapegoat to explain the failure of goals—man-made disasters. The unhappy rising master mechanic and the declining farmer could easily agree that it was the existence of artificial privileges which was the bane of all. Thus, the attack on artificial interferences with the natural order was a logical recourse for those who failed to receive their just rewards (as defined by themselves). This was clearly the argument of men on the rise, who found themselves confronted by special privileges; yet it was similarly the cry of injured men. Whereas historians have heard in the Jacksonian appeals the voice of the rising middle classes, they have largely turned a deaf ear to the supporting chorus from men who were the victims of economic change.[17]

As the discussion has developed, the issue which has come increasingly to the fore is that of banking. And this is as it should be. The battle over privilege in the Jacksonian period was primarily one over the privilege of banking. Banking dominated both national and state politics in all regions, and it is not unimportant that both parties attempted to pin the "bank party" label on the other. For banks were the monsters, the unnatural things, and those associated with the banks were the enemies of the people. Thus, it is both necessary and appropriate that the peculiar Jacksonian coalition be examined in relation to banking.

In political and economic life, banking occupied a position more central than it was subsequently to hold. Banks had two essential functions: as providers of currency at a time when the demand for money for transaction purposes was rapidly increasing, and as providers of credit facilities at a time when the opportunities for investment were outrunning the resources of private accumulation.[18] Individuals, accordingly, confronted banks in two roles: as credit seekers and as currency takers. Often one role was dominant.

On the credit side, access to banking facilities meant an ability to command resources. Yet since only banks chartered by governments were able to function freely under normal circumstances (and charters were limited), the holders of existing bank charters were in a position to dominate and to exclude. The merchant or manufacturer from a distant (deprived) town or region suffered from discrimination when he sought accommodation from a bank; the small, unestablished merchant or mechanic found the limited resources of existing banks in his own town channeled to his more respectable competitors; and boosters and entrepreneurs in new industries saw older, more traditional callings favored by banks dominated by representatives of the latter. Limitation of bank charters meant that established groups, established industries, established regions were in a position to gain and maintain undue influence and power.

For the excluded credit seekers, the further extension of banks, in both newer regions and older regions, was a first demand. Where efforts to achieve this were unsuccessful, however, the solution was either a removal of *all* privileges or a removal of all controls over the extension of these privileges. Eliminate artificial privileges which produce injustice and unnatural power or extend these privileges sufficiently to remove any suggestion of power and monopoly: this was the program of rising men, of rising sections, of rising industries.[19] The dominant tone was that of men who expected to rise once unnatural and discriminatory constructs were removed. And there appears to be no reason to associate such men more with the Democrats than with the Whigs. While Democrats (particularly in older regions) often fell into this category, Whig supporters, especially of the Anti-Masonic variety, were as likely to attack monopoly and privilege from this perspective.

For those individuals whose primary relationship to banks was that of currency takers, banking was also the central issue of the period. Both because of the bank notes which circulated below face value and because of rising prices (which contemporaries attributed to bank-note issues), the power of banking was judged by such men as the power to tax. It was a power to tax which was condemned by men who received uncurrent money or who found their returns rising less rapidly than their costs, by men who were struggling or declining.[20] And such men were hard-money Democrats.

Clearly, an entrepreneurial demand for more banks or for the removal of legislative control over banks and a currency taker's demand either for *no* banks or for the removal of bank control over the currency were inconsistent—once the issues were drawn distinctly. *As long, however, as the conflict was one between defenders of existing banks and those disturbed by the status quo, rising and declining groups could unite under the same banner.* All could agree: the banks were a source of power for a selected few, were the product of discriminatory legislation which upset the natural balance, and were the enemy of the people. What was uncertain, though, was whether banks per se were all these things.[21]

One way of examining the differences between those Democrats who represented declining elements and those who fit the stereotype of rising men may be to investigate the distinction between hard-money Democrats and those more "moderate" on the bank issue. It should be possible to study state legislative debates on the question and to explore the economic characteristics of the sections represented on each side of the debate. From legislative votes, there is some indication that on this issue the difference between the two types of Democrats was greater than that between "moderate" Democrats and Whigs.[22] If subsequent study does reveal such a pattern, then one suggested conclusion is that the rising man, the man on the make, the expectant capitalist was in no way uniquely related to the Jacksonians; rather, the declining or embattled man who struggled against change would appear the more unique Jacksonian.[23] And this conclusion would conform not only to the image appropriate to the Jacksonian persuasion, but also to the identities discovered by those historians who have studied the rising men in each party.

However, if the Jacksonians included both rising men and declining men, with the declining men representing the unique element in the party, then why have the Jacksonians been identified as rising men? In part, it may be due to the tendencies to study dominant and emerging individuals or to ignore declining elements in the period.[24] Yet a more deceptive tendency may be operative. Since there have been no systematic studies of the characteristics of the Jacksonians, one is inclined to conclude that the identification of the Jacksonians as rising men has been made because the period of Jacksonian national political dominance coincided with a period of rapid economic growth—and that, implicitly, historians have assumed that the policies pursued by the Jacksonians produced (and were intended to produce) the economic changes of the period.

But why assume that Jacksonian policies had anything (significant) to do with the economic growth of the Jacksonian Era? The Jacksonians had little to do with the flow of capital from Europe (which also made its way to Canada and Australia). In fact, the Whigs were often more enthusiastic advocates of public projects, which generated the securities for foreign investors. Nor does the argument emphasizing the assault on the Bank of the United States and the subsequent flood of state banks provide much support for the view that the Jacksonians changed the course of development. Even assuming that the expansion in the number of state banks had a positive effect on economic growth, it began *before* Jackson's veto. In New York State, for example, the expansion followed the passage of the Safety Fund Act in 1829, which broke a long impasse over the chartering of banks. And in Ohio, banks which had failed were re-established and banks previously authorized were placed in operation—beginning in early 1831. The expansion of state banks occurred as the demand for banks rose; and this was a function of the expansion in general economic activity. It was an expansion in the number of banks which occurred via specific state charters—not via laissez-faire policies. Here, too, contemporary records suggest that a large proportion of state bankers were Whigs.

The Jacksonian paradox, the idea that Jacksonians, though opposing economic progress, in fact cleared the path for it, has as its base the assumption that the Jacksonians actually *did* foster economic change. This is an unsubstantiated assumption, and without it the paradox disappears. Attempts to explain the paradox by arguing from the general to the particular, by creating hybrid, Janus-like, confused, paradoxical Jacksonians, are marred by the neglect of injured and declining men in this age of rising men, by the failure to recognize that not everyone benefits, in the short run, from economic advance. The suggestion here has been that it was these "victims," these farmers, laborers, and mechanics, who gave Jacksonian Democracy its dominant tone.[25] But this would imply that the "campaign claptrap" meant something, that studies of leading men in each party are misleading, and that speculations based upon a consideration of rhetoric and ideology may be a better guide than an implicit vulgar economic determinism which substitutes, for the study of economic problems, genuflection to indices of past economic growth.

NOTES

1. See Robert Remini, *The Election of Andrew Jackson* (Philadelphia, 1963) for a fine discussion of events from 1824 to 1828 and the creation of the Democratic election machine. By beginning his account in 1824, however, Remini de-emphasizes the origins and appeal of the early Jacksonian movement and thus may place undue emphasis on the activities of politicians in his chosen period.

2. In his paper "Money and Party in Jacksonian America" (presented to the American Historical Association in December 1966), Frank Gatell notes both that 84 percent of the men of wealth in New York City were Whigs in 1844 and that one third of the original wealthy Democrats bolted the party.

3. Statistics on voting participation rates, a significant additional tool for analysis, are the work of Richard P. McCormick in his "New Perspectives on Jacksonian Politics," *American Historical Review* (January 1960) and later, his *The Second American Party System: Party Formation in the Jacksonian Era* (Chapel Hill, N.C., 1966). McCormick uses decennial federal census data, and then, by "interpolation," estimates the number eligible to vote at the time of national elections. Unfortunately, he does not explain his interpolation procedure—nor does he justify adequately his restriction to federal data. Thus, his voting participation rates for Ohio in the elections of 1824 and 1828 are 35 percent and 76 percent respectively. Calculation of voting participation, however, from Ohio's official count of eligible voters (collected on a county basis and published in the official state newspaper) indicates voting participation of 40 percent and 90 percent respectively. McCormick, by his method, overstates the number of eligible voters by 15 percent in 1824 and 19 percent in 1828. (McCormick's Ohio 1840 estimate of 84.5 percent is less impressive when compared with earlier official estimates.) Several questions are in order: To what extent did McCormick's method for interpolation take into account business cycles? Are waves of migration considered and was there a lag between migration and

eligibility? (*Any* lag!) To what extent does an 1840 voting participation rate (calculated from actual population and coming at a point when westward migration and immigration are lessened) contain less of a downward bias than those for preceding elections? McCormick explains that he avoided the available state data in order to maintain consistency. Was this data used, however, to improve his method of extrapolation and his estimates of the number eligible to vote? These questions, which are important, should not have to be asked. For McCormick's methodology, see *ibid.*, p. 379. For figures on eligible Ohio voters, see *Ohio State Journal,* January 9, 1828; for figures on voting, see *Ohio State Journal,* November 11, 1828.

4. John Kenneth Galbraith, *American Capitalism: The Concept of Countervailing Power* (Boston, 1956), p. 28: "In a state of bliss, there is no need for a Ministry of Bliss."

5. As Lynn Marshall noted in his discussion of Jackson's Bank Veto message, it is necessary to move beyond talk of the Jacksonian appeal and to an "investigation of the general values and aspirations of the people to whom it was addressed." "The Authorship of Jackson's Bank Veto Message," *Mississippi Valley Historical Review* (1963–64), p. 466.

6. Charles G. Sellers' description of ferment in Tennessee as that of the "disquietude of an agrarian people, nurtured on Jeffersonian precepts" is quite consistent with the general argument here: "Banking and Politics in Jackson's Tennessee," *Mississippi Valley Historical Review* (June 1954).

7. James Kirke Paulding, *Letters from the South* (New York, 1817), p. 73.

   It is significant to note the similarity of Jacksonian themes to the arguments of Adam Smith (all quotations are from the Modern Library edition of *Wealth of Nations*):
   "Projectors disturb nature in the course of her operations in human affairs; and it requires no more than to let her alone, and give her fair play in the pursuit of her ends that she may establish her own designs." (p. xliii)
   "All systems either of preference or of restraint, therefore, being thus completely taken away, the obvious and simple system of natural liberty establishes itself of its own accord." (p. 651)
   "In the political body, however, the wisdom of nature has fortunately made ample provision for remedying many of the bad effects of the folly and injustice of man." (p. 638)

8. The existence of the Anti-Masonic party, initially organized on noneconomic issues, and strong in rural areas, introduces definite complications. In particular, Anti-Masonic opposition to the Democrats in New England appears contrary to the suggested hypothesis. However, in New England rank-and-file members of the Anti-Masonic parties did not generally follow their leaders into the Whig coalition—unlike the experience in the Middle States. Was differing behavior due to the characteristics of the various areas? Were declining farmers less likely to follow their Anti-Masonic leaders into the Whigs? For purposes of testing the hypothesis, areas in which Anti-Masonic support shifted to the Democrats could be classified as Democratic regions. For Anti-Masonic shifts, see McCormick, *Second American Party System,* p. 49, p. 75, p. 84, p. 121, p. 146.

9. *Ibid.*, p. 150. Benson, as his readers know, does not himself adopt the inverse of this "traditional claim." Instead, he argues that there was "no significant relationship between *wealth* and voting in 1844" and suggests that any relationship which *appears* to exist is, in fact, the product of ethnic and behavioral variables. Yet Benson's methods in this case (as in others) are quite dubious. He is descriptive rather than analytical and uses this license to slip from examination of county voting behavior to examination of deviant town behavior within counties. In both cases, too, he fails to distinguish between ethnic and sectional conflict—a distinction crucial because of the tendency of ethnic immigrant groups to settle closely together. Despite Benson's interest in the behavior of Germans, Dutch, Old British, and the like, his failure to explain Yankee voting behavior gives the game away. Yankees, an estimated 65 percent of New York's population, tended to vote Whig in western New York and Democratic in eastern New York; in large sections of eastern New York, adjoining rural counties voted Democratic—whether they were Yankee or Dutch. So, rather than attributing Democratic votes in predominantly Dutch counties to piety, tradition, and the belief in witchcraft, the regional variation in Yankee voting should act as a control against an erroneous conclusion. For a discussion of some other errors, see the writer's review essay, "The Significance of Claptrap in American History," *Studies on the Left,* Vol. III, No. 2 (1963).

10. Materials for such a test are available from state and federal records. Data which might be used are, with all their faults, real property assessments per improved acre, assessed personal property per capita, *changes* in the above variables over a given period, the proportion of gainfully employed men in agriculture, and material on product mix and yield per acre. Such information might be employed to attempt to explain voting behavior or changes in voting behavior for counties or townships on a national or state level, respectively. And ethnic variables could be subsequently introduced to see if

they add significant explanatory power. A serious test of the determinants of voting behavior requires the use of multiple correlation procedures. The promised land cannot be reached by selecting high and low units in each county—despite the economy of such an approach. (See the supplementary note on method for the paperback edition of *The Concept of Jacksonian Democracy*.)

11. "In 1826 Drake and Mansfield noticed that Cincinnatians were complaining of the influx of foreign manufactured goods. This complaint was joined with a criticism of the Bank of the United States which mobilized eastern credit to encourage the sale of eastern manufactures in the West," Harold E. Davis, "The Economic Basis of Ohio Politics, 1820–1840," *Ohio State Archaeological and Historical Quarterly*, XLVII (1938), 288.

12. Obviously, there was far more involved in the struggle over banks than simply the desire "to create better business conditions and remove panics." See Joseph Dorfman, "The Jackson Wage-Earner Thesis," reprinted in *The Economic Mind in American Civilization* (New York, 1966), Vol. II.

13. It is interesting to note the argument in the *Ohio Statesman* begins with the initial assumption that "the scale prices for mechanic labor is exactly proportioned to the ordinary cost of provision, rent, fuel, *etc.*" Disaster follows a decision made "in the secret councils of the Banks."

14. Benson estimates that 75 percent of men engaged in lumbering in New York State voted Democratic. *Concept of Jacksonian Democracy*, p. 205.

15. Benson estimates that 95 percent of the Catholic Irish in New York State voted Democratic in 1844. *Ibid.*, p. 171, p. 185.

16. The workingmen's parties, of course, included among the leaders and members many who were neither mechanics nor laborers. They too were coalitions, and even the mechanics among them may not have been a representative sample of labor. Mechanics, for example, as a group were more likely to respond favorably to the tariff issue than common laborers.

17. See, for example, Hofstadter: "This is the philosophy of a rising middle class; its aim is not to throttle but to liberate business, to open every possible pathway for the creative enterprise of the people." *American Political Tradition*, p. 62. Much of the confusion over the battle against privilege in this period has been the result of a failure to distinguish clearly between those in the coalition who opposed the existence of specific privileges and those who were opposed only to their exclusiveness.

18. The Turner-Hammond conflict over the frontier demand for banks rests on this dual function. For a discussion emphasizing the importance of the growing public demand for banknotes, see the writer's "The Role of Banks in Developing Regions . . ." presented to the Canadian Political Science Association in June, 1967.

19. Specific evidence concerning New York State supporting many of these general points appears in the writer's "In the Absence of Free Banks, What?" in the *Bulletin* of the Canadian Association for American Studies, Winter, 1967.

20. This "tax" was not one which fell only upon labor: "Banks are, in fact, legally authorized banditti, levying contributions and indirect taxation from every honest business." Byrdsall, *History of the Loco-Foco*, p. 111.

21. A definite effort has been made to avoid the particular issue of the Second Bank of the United States and to concentrate instead on the general issue of banking. On one level, the Second Bank may be viewed as a Philadelphia bank, attempting to control a hinterland that was slipping away from it, as a bank equipped with a capital and an institutional form which were inflexible and which came into conflict with a national (Western) bourgeoisie and competing (imperial) metropoli. However, most of those who cheered and voted for Jackson in the Great Struggle fought the symbol rather than the reality of the Bank.

22. In Ohio Assembly debates in 1837, for example, a series of proposals aimed at curbing banks received the consistent, support of over 20 Democrats (out of 36) and a handful of Whigs (out of 30). "Moderate" Democrats and Whigs combined to defeat these measures.

23. Apropos, Meyers notes at one point that there is some evidence that "the Jacksonians were relatively weak among the most successful, ambitious, enterprising groups." He finds the evidence inconclusive—it is most damaging to his thesis—and returns to his split Jacksonian. It may be suggested that not only were the Jacksonians relatively weak among such groups, but that the Jacksonians of this ilk were, as a group, the major source of defectors to the Whigs. Meyers, *Jacksonian Persuasion*, p. 138.

24. Although Meyers summarizes Taylor's discussion of economic changes (in the above-cited work) and at several points notes the effect of transportation innovation upon the "intersectional division of labor," he does not appear to recognize that the "sequence of

economic adaptations of the largest consequence" meant disappointment and decline for some. Adaptation is not the hope of every man, and "a view of economic processes" which sees only the good side of adaptation is perhaps not the best one with which to understand the Jacksonians (many of whom saw only the bad side). *Ibid.,* pp. 116–20.

25. The generalization that the Whigs spoke to the hopes of Americans, and the Jacksonians to their fears and resentments, would appear not only to be true but also to be logical. Cf. Meyers, *ibid.,* p. 13, and Glydon G. Van Deusen, "Some Aspects of Whig Thought and Theory in the Jacksonian Period," *American Historical Review* (Jan. 1958).

The Anti-Abolitionists   DAVID HERRESHOFF

The extent and the depth of the indigenous American radical tradition is one of the most important concerns of New Left historians. As we shall see below, various native political movements have been nominated by Left scholars as genuinely radical in their analysis and in their programs. They have spent less time analyzing the influences of foreign radical ideology on American political and social thought.

The reason for this is probably related to conservative assertions about radical activities in America. Conservative historians often emphasize the alien nature of radical movements in this country. These have been alien, they say, not merely in the strict sense of being inspired by European thinkers, but also in being ill-suited to American actualities. In a country without a proletariat and without serious class conflict, ideas originating in European circumstances, they insist, simply were irrelevant. The ineffectuality of these movements and their failure to win a large following in America clearly confirms this fact.

David Herreshoff's essay below examines the thought of one American radical intellectual strongly influenced by such European thinkers as Pierre Joseph Proudhon, Robert Owen, Claude Henri de Saint-Simon, and Charles Fourier. He notes the difficulties and dilemmas that the social lot of American workingmen before 1860 caused for an American radical intellectual who sought to apply European ideas to his own society.

FOR FURTHER READING:

Arthur Schlesinger, Jr., *The Age of Jackson**, (Little, Brown and Co., 1945); Arthur Schlesinger, Jr., *Orestes Brownson**, (Little, Brown and Co., 1966): Everett Webber, *Escape to Utopia: The Communal Movement in America,* (Hastings, 1958); Martin Duberman, *James Russell Lowell**, (Beacon Press, 1966).

Asterisk denotes paperback edition.

Inspired by the distress of workers under capitalism in the 1820's and 1830's, Orestes Brownson anticipated much in later American leftism, especially since 1917. If human suffering made Brownson radical, a political dilemma vitiated his radicalism. The dilemma arose from the antagonism between the North's system of wage labor and the South's slavery. Brownson, and all radicals of his generation,

---

Source: David Herreshoff, *American Disciples of Marx: From the Age of Jackson to the Progressive Era* (Detroit: Wayne State University Press, 1967), chap. ii, "The Anti-Abolitionists," pp. 31–48.

had to decide whether the wage system was the worse of the two labor systems, whether it was a lesser evil than slavery and therefore a system he could temporarily accept, or whether to avoid the issue by preferring self-cultivation to politics. In the early 1830's Brownson tried self-culture and would have agreed with Thoreau that "it is hard to have a Southern overseer; it is worse to have a Northern one; but worst of all when you are the slave-driver of yourself." But for most of his years as a radical, Brownson was a strong advocate of political action and sought solutions for the problems of his age in the struggles of parties and classes. He increasingly felt that the American situation was forcing him to choose between unappealing alternatives. This feeling induced exhausting tensions which led him to abandon radicalism in the 1840's. Brownson's career as a labor radical, with its abrupt ending, established an American pattern; since Brownson many American labor radicals have been gored by the dilemma of the lesser evil: how to deal with the enemies of their enemies. Perennially, this dilemma has fragmented American radical movements.

For Brownson politics and religion were always inseparable. He came to radicalism from rural Protestant beginnings. Born in 1803 in Stockbridge, Vermont, Brownson, while a farm boy, was largely self-educated. An earnest seeker for the true faith, he joined the Presbyterian Church in 1822, became a Universalist two years later, and was ordained a Universalist minister in 1826. With his turn from Presbyterianism to religious liberalism, Brownson was attracted to the nascent American labor movement and its first experiments with independent labor politics. Workers' organizations federated in several cities in the late 1820's, and the resulting central labor bodies produced workingmen's parties in Pennsylvania, New York, and New England. When the Workingmen's party of New York was formed in 1828, Brownson (then twenty-five years old) joined it and became a supporter of a comparatively moderate faction in the party headed by Robert Dale Owen and Frances Wright. With Owen and Wright, Brownson opposed a more extreme faction in the Workingmen headed by Thomas Skidmore. The Skidmore faction stood for abolition of the right of inheritance as the means of making a permanent social revolution. Owen and his followers, on the other hand, sought to elevate the workers by establishing free compulsory education. They believed that knowledge, rather than property, is power. Brownson thought they shared the belief of "the whole non-Catholic world . . . in the power of education to redeem society." Both factions of the "Workies," as members of the Workingmen's party were called, viewed themselves as representatives of the "producing classes"—a category taking in farmers and self-employed manufacturers, as well as wage workers. They saw a sharp cleavage in society between producers and accumulators of wealth; the latter class consisted mostly, in their scheme, of merchants and bankers. The Workies tried to make American party lines conform to that cleavage.

Brownson's formal membership in the Workingmen's party lapsed when the organization split during its first year leaving New York laborers with a choice among three groups bearing the Workingmen's label. Brownson, in any case, felt ill-suited by temperament to be a party regular. "The truth is," he explained in his autobiography, "I never was and never could be a party man, or work in the traces of a party." He kept in touch with the Workingmen's movements during the years of Jackson's presidency when some Workies, including Brownson's friend Isaac T. Hecker, tried to keep alive the idea of a labor party independent of the Democrats.

These men called themselves the "genuine Democracy" to distinguish themselves from the official Democrats. "Tammany Hall undertook to absorb us when we had grown too powerful to be ignored," relates Hecker. "They nominated a legislative ticket made up half of their men and half of ours. This move was to a great extent successful, but many of us who were purists refused to compromise . . ."

Brownson gave such efforts sympathy without active support. He had lost enthusiasm for independent workingclass parties and had come to the conclusion that independent labor politics in the United States was doomed to fail because the workingmen

> are neither numerous nor strong enough to get or to wield the political power of the State. . . . The movement we commenced could only excite a war of man against money, and all history and all reasoning in the case prove that in such a war money carries it over man. Money commands the supplies, and can hold out longer than they who have nothing but their manhood. It can starve them into submission.

Giving up the project of a distinct class party, Brownson looked about for a way of inducing "all classes to cooperate for the workingmen's cause." He lost interest at this time in the Owenite proposal for compulsory education as the means of workingclass emancipation, and took up Channing's ideas of personal regeneration through individual effort. His friend Hecker testifies that in the middle 1830's Brownson was "the American Proudhon" and that he gave Saint-Simonian lectures to the Workingmen, "the object being the amelioration of the condition of the most numerous classes of society in the speediest manner." But in the years when he was giving such lectures, a Massachusetts leader of the Workingmen chided Brownson for his indifference to political action.

The cause of the workers kept Brownson's sympathies through the 1830's, although he was sometimes disappointed in the meagerness of the workers' demands. The thought of striking for a ten-hour day, for instance, appalled him. "We never supported the ten-hour system," he explained in 1838,

> but if the mechanics had struck for six hours, instead of ten, we would have supported them to the best of our ability. Six hours is enough for any man to labor in one day, enough for his health, and enough, in a state of society at all approaching a just one, for his worldly prosperity. Man has a mind as well as a body, and should have time to think as well as exercise his limbs.

Brownson's strong sense of the injustice of the workers' lot impelled him to try once more to find in political action the path to a better society. This time he came to politics as a transcendentalist, but he came aware of the panic of 1837 and the misery it spelled for workers. The Workingmen's reform through universal education, and the self-improvement doctrine of Channing, now seemed equally to him to be mockeries. Economic reform, he now believed, was the precondition to a meaningful pursuit of the aims of Owen and Channing. "Give your starving boy a breakfast before you send him to school," he demanded, in effect, of the Owenites; and he advised the advocates of self-culture to offer "your beggar a cloak before you attempt his moral and intellectual elevation." The latter suggestion, addressed to the followers of Channing, was to be seconded by Thoreau when he began his pursuit of the higher laws in *Walden* with an analysis of man's need for food, shelter, clothing, and fuel: "not till we have secured these are we prepared to entertain the true problems of life with freedom and a prospect of success."

Brownson's sense of the practical was infused with the transcendental insight that "society is for man, not man for society," but his was no longer the individualist transcendentalism, for he now urged that "the perfection of the social state is the means" to individual perfection. The time had "come for all predominance of class to end; for Man, the People to rule." Only then would the work of the friends of man "cease to be the melioration of society, and become the perfecting of the individuals of each successive generation. . . . This done and the wish of the workingmen is fulfilled; the visions of the prophets are realized." Inherent in his language is the messianic spirit of Brownson's labor radicalism. Side by side with visionary enthusiasm there was in Brownson a willingness to stare dispassionately at American realities.

Even in a depression the condition of the American workers could not be convincingly evoked by allusions to empty bellies and ragged clothing. Brownson therefore acknowledged a "general increase in wealth throughout the civilized world for the last forty or fifty years." Productivity of labor and the production of goods had "so multiplied as to baffle all efforts at calculation." The standard of living of the workers was obviously higher than that of their fathers and grandfathers at the time of the American Revolution. However, the immiseration of the proletariat was real, Brownson thought, and the need for labor radicalism in the United States genuine:

> The laboring classes most certainly account many things necessaries of life now, which they then accounted its luxuries. But they are not now less poor. Poverty and wealth are merely relative terms. The only true method of judging this matter is to ascertain whether the position of the producer, relatively to that of the accumulator, be higher or lower, than it was at the epoch of the Revolution . . . it is altogether more difficult for the common laborer to maintain the same social position now, than it was fifty years ago. The general style of living has more than kept pace with the increase of wealth.

Brownson hoped that American workers would grow increasingly restive even as they received benefits from the growth of the productive forces. He expected labor radicalism to persist because the movement of society toward affluence would not keep pace with the rising expectations of the workers, who would take more and more things as necessities that their parents had as luxuries. In the long run such a class would not be bribed into conservatism; struggling to embrace the ever elusive, dazzling American style of life, the working class would again and again reach beyond the necessities of the moment.

Such was Brownson's defense of the theory of impoverishment of the workers in a land of plenty. It was a more compelling defense than any which would ignore or deny the reality of rising living standards. At this time, the 1830's, Brownson saw the working class as an embodiment of his transcendental faith in man's ability to prevail over his environment. That ability, he believed, was about to be demonstrated in the United States: "This too is the country in which the noble ideas of man and society, which French and German scholars strike out in their speculations, are first to be applied to practice, realized in institutions." It would have to be here rather than in Europe, because there Europeans

> have old institutions to combat; old prejudices to overcome; old castles and churches to clear away . . . and armed soldiery are ready to repulse them. But here is a virgin soil, an open field, a new people, full of the future, with an unbounded

faith in ideas, and most ample freedom. Here, if anywhere on earth, may the philosopher experiment on human nature, and demonstrate what man has it in him to be when and where he has the freedom to be himself.

The ideas of Kant and Hegel, refined by the French socialists, were now to shape an imminent social revolution in the United States.

What would the revolution accomplish? Brownson did not give details about the structure of the new society. "I have no plan of a world-reform for you to adopt," he wrote in 1840, "for I have not yet found one that I could adopt myself." None of the schemes for utopia, from Plato to Robert Owen and Fourier, seemed to him "of any great value." Like Marx, Brownson was long on analysis of present society and short on description of future society. Yet Brownson, like Marx, had the principles of the new society firmly in mind. It would be a classless society; it would be bountifully productive; it would humanize the work process by overcoming the opposition between work and play and between head and hand labor; it would not seek to return to a pre-industrial economy but would make use of modern technology; it would not rest on common property, but would not regard private property as inviolable; its ideal worker would not be the yeoman toiling in solitude, but the man engaged in collective labor and enjoying the "encouragement of warm-hearted and enlightened companionship"; and it would establish marriage on the mutual love of social equals, not on property and the subordination of women as in the past.

The new society, Brownson reasoned, would come about through the political struggle of social classes. Having discarded the method of self-culture, he proposed to engage in the politics of the day, keeping "ever in view" the revolutionary goal and judging "the wisdom of every political or legislative measure . . . by its tendency to carry us towards it, or to remove us from it." The immediate task, thought Brownson, was to defend the American Union from the businessmen whose conduct during the depression of 1837 was "threatening the very existence of the republic by its general baseness." The way to defend the Union was to attack economic institutions and policies which served mercantile and manufacturing interests to the detriment of agricultural interests. Translated into party terms this meant that the workers should support the Jacksonian Democracy against the Whigs in order to put themselves in a better position to fight for their own aims. As Brownson saw the class alignment of American politics in 1840,

> the interests of landed property combined with those of labor are now arrayed against the banks generally; but if they are successful, it will not be because the interests of labor count for anything; but because the farming and planting interests are stronger than the mercantile and manufacturing interests. The proletaries, though voters in this contest, serve merely to swell the forces of one or the other party . . . they will gain, however, if the landed interests triumph. . . .

In Brownson's expectation, the bloc of three classes in the Democratic party—the workers, farmers, and planters—would not survive the final triumph of Jacksonianism over the business community. That triumph would prepare the North for a new revolution in which wage workers, small farmers, and self-employed businessmen would be ranged against all employers of labor, whether rural or urban. There would then be "a deeper question at issue than is commonly imagined; a question which is but remotely touched in your controversies about United States Banks and

Sub-Treasuries, . . . free trade and corporations." Their opportunity having been made ready for them by the Jacksonians, the workers would in due course overwhelm their adversaries. "In any contest they will be as two to one, because the large class of proprietors who are not employers, but laborers on their own lands or in their own shops will make common cause with them." The capitalists, having been previously curbed—though not destroyed—by the Jacksonians would go under in the revolution. America was pregnant with a new society, Brownson believed, because of polarization of wealth and poverty. The frontier, he said, was of dwindling value as a safety-valve for the aggrieved poor since unemployed proletarians lacked the means to migrate westward from the eastern cities to set themselves up as farmers. Besides—this he predicted in 1840!—the unsettled lands would all be taken up by 1890. Sanctioned by the gospel of Christ, though opposed by organized religion, the revolution would make America's political democracy more meaningful by realizing social democracy.

A social democracy, in Brownson's conception, would know neither capitalists nor wage workers. Every man would incorporate the functions of both, and America would thus become a nation of individuals who possess themselves, of citizens who exploit no one and are exploited by no one. One great legislative measure would establish social democracy and bar the way to a return to power of a privileged class: the abolition of the inheritance of property. This measure, which Brownson had opposed in 1828 when he was in the Workingmen's party, would assure each generation of Americans an equal start in life. The final sweeping away of inequality and privilege would be accomplished by the Locofocos, the left wing of the Democratic party.

While Brownson was working out his revolutionary program for the left-wing Jacksonians, he began to experience a pull toward moderation, gradualism, acceptance of the status quo which was entirely at odds with that program. The rightward pull was a consequence of his Democratic politics. He had announced his affiliation to the Democratic party in 1839 in an article devoted to "Democracy and Reform," the thesis of which was that the Democrats, as the movement party in America, were destined to emancipate wage laborers, women, and the slaves once they had torn down the system of class privilege and federal power upheld by the Whigs, the stand-pat party in the country. Since the Democratic Party would ultimately serve the interests of all the egalitarian movements, Brownson reasoned, it was only logical that the radical laborites, the feminists, and the abolitionists should immediately support the Democrats against the Whigs. But, however logical, Brownson's tactic was unacceptable to the abolitionists; for them to enter the Jacksonian Party would have required accommodating themselves to slavery, deferring the struggle for abolition. Opposition to antislavery agitation was the unavoidable price paid by northerners for political alliance with the southern planters. Brownson's involvement with the Democrats therefore thrust him painfully but inevitably into choosing between the abolitionists and the planters.

At the height of his radicalism, Brownson recognized the universality of the egalitarian principle. "We can," he acknowledged in 1838, "legitimate our own right to freedom only by arguments which prove also the negro's right to be free." But in the next breath he went on to argue against the abolitionists' efforts to make the Negro free. The abolitionists, he complained, are impractical, out of step with the times; they did not understand what it means to be politic:

> The question for to-day is the currency question,—not the most interesting question in itself surely, nor a question of the first magnitude; but it is first in the order of time. . . . What will be the question for to-morrow we ask not.

To be a consistent Jacksonian Democrat twenty years before the Civil War, Brownson had to maintain that slavery was not a politically relevant issue in the United States. It was the social make-up of the Jacksonian coalition, far more than the urgency of Jacksonian fiscal policy, which made Brownson oppose the abolitionists. In taking his stand Brownson was the prisoner of his allies. Anyone wishing to coexist in a coalition with the pro-slavery interest had, at the very least, to regard abolition agitation as untimely and impolitic. Pained by the requirements of the planter-farmer-labor bloc, Brownson uttered the *cri de coeur* of a man who represses his instinct for justice in the name of political calculation:

> There is something exceedingly unpleasant in being, even in appearance, opposed to the advocates of freedom. . . . Our own love of excitement, of new things, to say nothing of certain dreams we indulge concerning a golden age that is to be, strongly dispose us to join with the abolitionists, and to rush on in the career they open up to a bold and energetic spirit. There is something, too, in the very idea of freeing two or three millions of slaves, which, in these mechanical and money-getting times is quite refreshing and capable of dazzling the imagination. . . . There is something almost intoxicating in going forth as a bold knight in the cause of humanity, to plead for the wronged and the outraged, to speak for the dumb, and to do battle for the weak and defenseless.

It was what Brownson thought to be a necessary alliance with the planters which kept him out of the "refreshing," "dazzling," "almost intoxicating" antislavery movement. He resisted the abolitionists out of loyalty to the northern wage workers who, he was convinced, could make no headway against their employers without the powerful aid of the planters. Allying himself with the planters, the enemies of labor's enemies, he attacked the abolitionists vehemently and, in attacking them, sensed he was denying his own deepest inclinations. He consoled himself with the reflection that self-denial was "one of the first laws of morality." Much later he rued the practicality of his politics. "Perhaps," he wrote of the abolitionists during the Civil War, "if we who have so long sneered at them as fanatics, had studied less to be wise and politic, and had been more living men . . . more truly heroic . . . instead of merely prudent and expedient, their fanaticism would have revolted us less."

But during the period of his labor radicalism, Brownson found relief from his qualms about his response to the abolitionists in cataloguing them among the enemies of American liberty:

> The money power is seeking to bind the nation's free spirit with chains of gold, and mistaken philanthropy is fast rending it in twain; associations, sectarian and moral espionage are fast swallowing up individual freedom, and making the individual man but a mere appendage to a huge social machine.

In the American republic, as here represented, capitalists were strengthening the centralist and authoritarian trend in the government and the economy while the abolitionists were trying to tear the Union apart, and Fourierist, temperance, health-food, Sabbath, and other reformers devoured personal freedom. Missing from the catalogue of evildoers is the slave owner, for this is a radical Jacksonian's account of the menaces besetting American liberty. Fixing this aberrant image of America's social ills in his mind, Brownson tried for a time to avoid the dilemma which the coexistence of the wage system and slavery posed for his generation of radicals. But finally, in "The Laboring Classes," the greatest of his radical essays, Brownson faced the political question in the rivalry of two systems of exploitation.

It is better to be a wage worker than a slave, Brownson acknowledged, because the wage worker's "rights as a man are legally recognized, though not in fact enjoyed; for he is nearer the day of his complete enfranchisement, and has greater moral force and more instruments with which to effect it." If it were not for the fact that it is an easier condition from which to escape than chattel slavery, and if Americans had no alternative to the two systems, he would give "preference to the slave system over that of labor at wages." The "pro-slavery" anti-capitalism of Brownson is close to the view expressed by Friedrich Engels in his *Condition of the Workingclass in England.* Writing in 1844, young Engels saw the proletarian "placed in the most revolting, inhuman position conceivable for a human being. The slave is assured of a bare livelihood, the serf has at least a scrap of land on which to live; each has at worst a guarantee for life itself. But the proletarian must depend on himself alone." His intense reaction to the heinousness of capitalism and the misery of the proletariat might have led Engels, as it did Brownson in America and Lassalle in Germany, to seek allies for the workers among the landed opponents of the business community. But the labor radicalism of the Marxists, unlike the varieties associated with Brownson and Lassalle, developed a conditionally positive attitude toward the bourgeoisie and eschewed alliances with junkers and plantation owners. For the sake of the future, the Marxists were willing to support the present against the past; not so Brownson. He would accept neither the capitalist present nor the feudalist past, even provisionally. "We . . . oppose with all our might both systems," he thundered. "We would have neither slave nor proletary." That was his wish; his practice was to support the Democrats.

That practice was a cause of the growing tension between labor radicalism and abolitionism. Among American radicals only Albert Brisbane, Charles Fourier's apostle to the new world, saw a possible way to bring the laborites and the anti-slavery people together. "It would be a noble step, it strikes me," Brisbane suggested in 1845,

> if the advance guard of the Abolitionists would include in their movement a reform of the present wretched organization of labor, called the wage system. It would add to their power by interesting the producing classes . . . and would prepare a better state for the slaves when emancipated, than the servitude to capital, to which they now seem destined.

But Brownson's hostility to the abolitionists, and the usual indifference of anti-slavery men to the plight of the wage workers, kept the movement which aimed to revolutionize the South at odds with the one which aimed to revolutionize the North. "Why is it," Brownson asked, "that so few of the real workingmen here are abolitionists?" He himself answered the question, and in answering it disclosed a fatal weakness of the labor radicalism of his time: "It is because they feel that they themselves are virtually slaves, while mocked with the name of freeman, and that the movements in behalf of freedom should best be directed towards their emancipation."

Though bitter and narrow, this answer of Brownson's had some reason in it. As Brownson saw it, social change in the United States would proceed region by region, not nationally. The labor radicals, he believed, could make a social revolution against capital in the North while chattel slavery remained intact in the South. In effect, this was a theory of socialism in one region based on the "law" of uneven development. Moving from the premise that social change occurs at even tempos in all regions (albeit from different starting points), he observed that wage workers are closer to genuine freedom than slaves, and he concluded that the wage workers would achieve freedom before the slaves. This was not a bad syllogism, although it overlooked the possibility that the existence of slavery might arrest the progress of the wage workers and that the slaves might have to win legal emancipation before the wage workers could arrive at "complete enfranchisement."

Brownson's theory of regional revolution was an integral part of his labor radical politics. In developing it, he explored the significance of the American states' rights doctrine for his policy of allying the workers, farmers, and planters. Brownson saw that the national Democratic party was a combination of democrats and anti-democrats and that its make-up prevented its becoming an agency of social change. Nationally, the Democratic party would tend to be neutral on great social issues; only on the state or regional level could it have a coherent social policy. Making a virtue out of this reality, Brownson argued that the federal government ought to be neutral on social issues. With the Democrats at the helm, the federal government would be neutral, but when the Whigs were in power, the federal authority would be used exclusively in the interests of the capitalists. It was therefore in the interest of the labor radicals to keep the Democrats in power in Washington; only then could a labor revolution be carried on in the North without the likelihood of federal counter-revolutionary interference.

If it were to work, the Brownson tactic of using the Jacksonians to abet labor-radical ends needed the mutual loyalty of the allies in the national coalition. On one side, the planter would have to uphold strict construction of the Constitution and oppose the economic policies of the business community. On the other, the wage workers would be required to uphold strict construction while opposing abolitionist subversion of the South's peculiar institution. A lapse on the part of either the planters or the workers would wreck the alliance and might provoke retaliation.

Indeed, the partners in the Jacksonian alliance performed with less than perfect loyalty to one another in the presidential election of 1840. Van Buren and the Democrats lost to Harrison and the Whigs by a margin of almost 150,000 in a popular vote of almost 2,500,000. The Whigs seduced many Jacksonians with the aid of their hard cider and log cabin demagogy, and the result jolted Brownson's faith in the readiness of the working class for enlightened political action. Discouraged by the "maddened and maddening hurrahs of the drunken mob which went for 'Tippecanoe and Tyler too,' " Brownson nevertheless thought that workers who voted for Harrison had not meant to repudiate the Jacksonian program but only to express loss of confidence in the men who had administered it. He was sure that if the Whigs in power attempted to undo the accomplishments of the Jacksonians, the workers would turn the Whigs out at the next election. But Brownson took a far sterner view of southern disloyalty to the Jacksonian alliance. He found no excuses for the planters who had voted Whig, and he threatened the South with the specter of a labor-abolitionist alliance:

If you desert us, if you side with the business population of the other sections of the country, and aid them in establishing a National Bank, in laying a protective tariff, and assuming directly or indirectly the State Debts, . . . you may rest assured that the Democracy in one solid phalanx will go against your institutions. . . . They feel that you have been neither true to them, nor to yourselves . . . and unless you go *en masse* for the Constitution, you must not be surprised if they go *en masse* against slavery.

Brownson himself was not quick to back up this threat. He did go against slavery in the Civil War, but his immediate response to the collapse of his hope that the Jacksonians would create the opportunity for a labor revolution in the North was to abandon labor radicalism. The American scene was characterized for him by a hateful capitalism, an easily cajoled, helpless working class, and a conservative agrarian South which now appeared to be the only serious counter-force to capitalism. As the conservative and constitutionalist elements in Brownson's political thought came to the fore, he abandoned religious liberalism and sought sanction for his new politics in the Catholic church. "I became henceforth a conservative in politics," he later explained, "instead of an impractical radical, and through political conservation I advanced rapidly toward religious conservatism."

What happened to Brownson thereafter has little relevance for the development of Marxism in America, except for his response to secession and the Civil War. There is a curious parallel, as well as a contrast, between Brownson's response to the Civil War and Marx's. Brownson, a Calhoun supporter at the beginning of his conservative period in 1844, was for Lincoln in the 1860 presidential campaign. In the first year of the war he began to urge immediate emancipation as a means to victory over the Confederacy. Deeming Lincoln's conduct of the war lacking in energy, Brownson supported the radical John C. Frémont for the Republican nomination in 1864. If this looks like capricious behavior in an old admirer of Calhoun and a professed enemy of social radicalism, it is not. Brownson's militant support of the North during the Civil War was calculated to make the United States safe for conservatism. In his radical period Brownson had seen the southern slave-holders as a force which could keep the northern capitalists from using the federal power for their own ends and so provide opportunity for a labor revolution in the North.

Having himself become a conservative, Brownson now saw that the South's rulers might play an entirely different role in national politics. It now appeared to him that the South ought to be kept in the Union to weigh against northern radicalism, not for it. If, as Brownson expected, no radical reconstruction of southern society took place after the defeat of the Confederacy, the South would exercise a conservative influence on the nation. As early as 1865 he spelled out this prediction of the trend of American politics in *The American Republic:*

In the states that seceded socialism has never had a foothold, and will not gain it, for it is resisted by all the sentiments, convictions, and habits of the southern people, and the southern people will not be exterminated nor swamped by migrations from the North or from Europe. They are and always will be an agricultural people, and agricultural people are and always will be opposed to socialistic dreams, unless unwittingly led for a moment to favor it. . . .

He denounced the idea of "hanging, exiling, or disfranchising the wealthy landholders of the South, in order to bring up the poor and depressed whites," but was sure that

"that policy will never be carried out." As for the Negroes, if "enfranchised, they will always vote with the wealthy landholding class, and aid them in resisting socialistic tendencies." In 1865 Brownson was the prophet of the Dixiecrat coalition which was to endure for generations as a bulwark against leftward change in America.

Marx, of course, was also a supporter of the Union in the Civil War, but for different reasons than Brownson. Like Brownson, he was sometimes critical of what seemed to him Lincoln's indecisiveness. In arguing the case for speedy emancipation, Marx even quoted Brownson, but he did not go to Brownson's extreme of advocating the replacement of Lincoln by Frémont in 1864. Marx hoped that destruction of the slave system through victory for the Union would bring the American people to grips with the labor question. "Every independent movement of the workers was paralyzed so long as slavery disfigured part of the Republic," he wrote in *Capital* in 1867, and he implied that an aftermath of the war would be the rise of a strong American labor movement which could make capitalism versus socialism a practical issue in the United States. The crisis of secession and reunion, however, was resolved in a manner more to Brownson's liking than to Marx's. Twelve years after the war the party of northern business made a deal with the party of southern planters.

The Compromise of 1877, which gave Hayes the Presidency and the white supremacists the South, "scotched," in the words of C. Vann Woodward, "any tendency of the South to combine forces with the internal enemies of the new economy—laborites, Western agrarians, reformers." It also generally confirmed for a long time the vision of Brownson and disappointed the vision of Marx. There are times in history when brilliant cynicism provides a clearer outlook on the future than does generous hope. Marx knew that there could be no socialism in the United States without the fraternal unity of black and white workers, that "labour cannot emancipate itself in the white skin where in the black it is branded," but in 1867 he mistakenly assumed that the brand was removed from the blacks, that the Civil War had truly freed the Negro. Even before it ended Brownson had a clearer idea of what the Civil War might accomplish. "You will never," he told the abolitionists in the third year of the war, "make the mass of the white people look upon the blacks as their equals." And he understood that race prejudice would bolster the conservative principle of hierarchy in American society. "We talk no more of elevating the laboring classes," said this ex-radical. "All cannot stand at the top of society, for if all were at the top there would be no bottom and society would be the bottomless pit." However he felt little need to worry about the possibility of the triumph of hellish social equality in America. Brownson knew that abolition would encourage attempts to gain full equality for the Negro, to establish the rights of women, and to abolish private property. But egalitarian radicals, he predicted, would not advance far along the road to socialism in America. He cheerfully affirmed in 1865 that with the abolition of slavery, "there is no social grievance of magnitude enough to enlist any considerable number of people . . . in a movement to redress it." He recalled that the abolitionists "could not and never did carry the nation, even in the question of slavery itself" before the war. Now, after the war, "the exclusion of negro suffrage can never be made to appear to the American people as anything like so great a grievance as was slavery." It was to be a long time before this analysis would begin to be outdated.

It is small wonder that the energies of Brownson and his generation of American radicals were expended at cross-purposes. Class struggle in America before the Civil War could not develop along simple capital-versus-labor lines. The complexities of interclass alliances and antagonisms made it hard for the radicals to know what to do next; they consequently had many causes but no unifying cause. Brownson had tried to change the situation by subordinating all other radical causes to that of the wage workers. It had seemed reasonable to him not to try to attack all injustices simultaneously, and to ask the slaves and the women to give precedence to the workers. The antislavery men and the feminists never saw the point. "The genuine Yankee," Brownson once complained, "is never satisfied with doing one thing at a time. He is really in his glory only when he has a dozen or more irons in the fire at once." Trying to avoid what struck him as the futile multifariousness of Yankee radical activity, Brownson became a prototype of the American labor radical. Scouting abolition and ignoring other non-labor reform movements, Brownson, on joining the Jacksonians, found himself compelled to center his attention on issues—such as banking—having little bearing on the largest issue to face his generation: the slavery question. Abolitionists and other radicals tended to respond in kind with indifference or hostility to the cause of labor.

After the war a new selection of labor radicals appeared. Older men like Wendell Phillips, Stephen Pearl Andrews, and William West were links between the old radicalism and the new. But the continuity they supplied was too thin to naturalize the alien radicalism of the Germans who shaped socialism in America between the Civil War and the rise of the De Leon and Debs movements. Brownson himself symbolizes the discontinuity between the first American labor radicals and their successors. His radicalism perished from a dilemma he could not grapple with, avoid, or wish out of existence.

The Northern Response to
Slavery MARTIN DUBERMAN

One movement of fine radical, as well as impeccably native, credentials was abolitionism. Though the American antislavery movement borrowed from its British counterpart, after 1833—when Britain abolished slavery in her empire—the problem of slavery remained American and Americans thereafter contributed disproportionately to its solution.

Abolition, among radical movements, has a special claim on the attention of Left historians. We must remember the role of the Civil Rights Movement of the early 1960s in inspiring and enspiriting the entire New Left Movement. The sense of identification with Black Liberation among the young activists has been quite

Source: Martin Duberman, "The Northern Response to Slavery," in *The Antislavery Vanguard: New Essays on the Abolitionists,* ed. Martin Duberman (Princeton: Princeton University Press, 1965), pp. 395–413.

strong, and remains strong today, even though white radicals no longer find themselves able to participate in it very effectively. Out of this unflagging concern grows a continuing interest in the antislavery movement of the period before the Civil War.

In the essay below, one of the most talented young historians of the Left, Martin Duberman, deals with some of the problems surrounding pre-Civil War antislavery in the United States. He is concerned at the outset with the ambiguous Free Soil movement. He asks why Americans in the North were unwilling to accept the need for a radical abolitionist solution, even after they had come to see the dangers of an expansionist slave power. In his answer, he exhibits an unusual sensitivity to the force of accepted values, and is not entirely critical of those who were willing to accept the continued existence of slavery in the South in exchange for restricting its geographical spread. Yet at the same time, he remains more sympathetic to the abolitionists, the antislavery radicals whose views the Left finds ultimately more congenial. He defends these men against their detractors, both contemporary and recent, and seeks particularly to acquit them of the charge that their radicalism grew out of a neurotic striving for status or self-aggrandizement.

FOR FURTHER READING:

Martin Duberman (ed.), *The Antislavery Vanguard: New Essays on the Abolitionists**, (Princeton University Press, 1965); Gilbert Hobbes Barnes, *The Anti-Slavery Impulse 1830–1844*, (Peter Smith, 1957); Louis Filler, *The Crusade Against Slavery 1830–1860**, (Harper Torchbook, 1960); Dwight L. Dumond, *Anti-Slavery: The Crusade for Freedom in America**, (Norton, 1966); Aileen Kraditor, *Means and Ends in American Abolition: Garrison and His Critics on Strategy and Tactics 1834–1850*, (Pantheon Books, 1969); James B. Stewart, "The Aims and Impact of Garrisonian Abolitionism 1840–1860," *Civil War History*, (September, 1969).

Asterisk denotes paperback edition.

The abolitionist movement never became the major channel of Northern antislavery sentiment. It remained in 1860 what it had been in 1830: the small but not still voice of radical reform. An important analytical problem thus arises: why did most Northerners who disapproved of slavery become "nonextensionists" rather than abolitionists? Why did they prefer to attack slavery indirectly, by limiting its spread, rather than directly, by seeking to destroy it wherever it existed?

On a broad level, the answer involves certain traits in the national character. In our society of abundance, prosperity has been the actual condition—or the plausible aspiration—of the majority. Most Americans have been too absorbed in the enjoyment or pursuit of possessions to take much notice of the exactions of the system. Even when inequalities have become too pronounced or too inclusive any longer to be comfortably ignored, efforts at relief have usually been of a partial and half-hearted kind. Any radical attack on social problems would compromise the national optimism; it would suggest fundamental defects, rather than occasional malfunctions. And so the majority has generally found it necessary to label "extreme" any measures which call for large-scale readjustment. No one reasonably contented welcomes extensive dislocation; what seems peculiarly American is the disbelief, under *all* circumstances, in the necessity of such dislocation.

Our traditional recoil from "extremism" can be defended. Complex problems, it might be said, require complex solutions; or, to be more precise, complex problems have no solutions—at best, they can be but partially adjusted. If even this much is to be possible, the approach must be flexible, piecemeal, pragmatic. The clear-cut blueprint for reform, with its utopian demand for total solution, intensifies rather than ameliorates disorder.

There is much to be said for this defense of the American way—in the abstract. The trouble is that the theory of gradualism and the practice of it have not been the same. Too often Americans have used the gradualist argument as a technique of evasion rather than as a tool for change, not as a way of dealing with difficult problems slowly and carefully, but as an excuse for not dealing with them at all. We do not want time for working out our problems—we do not want problems, and we will use the argument of time as a way of not facing them. As a chosen people, we are meant only to have problems which are self-liquidating. All of which is symptomatic of our conviction that history is the story of inevitable progress, that every day in every way we *will* get better and better even though we make no positive efforts towards that end.

Before 1845, the Northern attitude toward slavery rested on this comfortable belief in the benevolence of history. Earlier, during the 1830's, the abolitionists had managed to excite a certain amount of uneasiness about the institution by invoking the authority of the Bible and the Declaration of Independence against it. Alarm spread still further when mobs began to prevent abolitionists from speaking their minds or publishing their opinions, and when the national government interfered with the mails and the right of petition. Was it possible, men began to ask, that the abolitionists were right in contending that slavery, if left alone, would not die out but expand, would become more not less vital to the country's interests? Was it possible that slavery might even end by infecting free institutions themselves?

The apathetic majority was shaken, but not yet profoundly aroused: the groundwork for widespread antislavery protest was laid, but its flowering awaited further developments. The real watershed came in 1845, when Texas was annexed to the Union, and war with Mexico followed. The prospect now loomed of a whole series of new slave states. It finally seemed clear that the mere passage of time would not bring a solution; if slavery was ever to be destroyed, more active resistance would be necessary. For the first time large numbers of Northerners prepared to challenge the dogma that slavery was a local matter in which the free states had no concern. A new era of widespread, positive resistance to slavery had opened.

Yet such new resolve as had been found was not channeled into a heightened demand for the abolition of the institution, but only into a demand that its further extension be prevented. By 1845 Northerners may have lost partial, but not total confidence in "Natural Benevolence"; they were now wiser Americans perhaps, but Americans nonetheless. More positive action against slavery, they seemed to be saying, was indeed required, but nothing too positive. Containing the institution would, in the long run, be tantamount to destroying it; a more direct assault was unnecessary. In this sense, the doctrine of nonextension was but a more sophisticated version of the standard faith in "time." [1]

One need not question the sincerity of those who believed that nonextension would ultimately destroy slavery, in order to recognize that such a belief partook of wishful thinking. Even if slavery was contained, there remained large areas in the Southern states into which the institution could still expand; even without further expansion, there was no guarantee that slavery would cease to be profitable; and finally, even should slavery cease to be profitable, there was no certainty that the South, psychologically, would feel able to abandon it. Nonextension, in short, was hardly a foolproof formula. Yet many Northerners chose to so regard it. And thus the question remains: why did not an aroused antislavery conscience turn to more certain measures and demand more unequivocal action?

To have adopted the path of direct abolition, first of all, might have meant risking individual respectability. The unsavory reputation of those already associated with abolitionism was not likely to encourage converts to it. Still, if that doctrine had been really appealing, the disrepute of its earlier adherents could not alone have kept men from embracing it. Association with the "fanatics" could have been smoothed simply by rehabilitating their reputations; their notoriety, it could have been said, had earlier been exaggerated—it had been the convenient invention of an apathetic majority to justify its own indifference to slavery. When, after 1861, public opinion did finally demand a new image of the abolitionists, it was readily enough produced. The mere reputation of abolitionism, therefore, would not have been sufficient to repel men from joining its ranks. Hostility to the movement had to be grounded in a deeper source—fear of the doctrine of "immediatism" itself.

Immediatism challenged the Northern hierarchy of values. To many, a direct assault on slavery meant a direct assault on private property and the Union as well. Fear for these values clearly inhibited antislavery fervor (though possibly a reverse trend operated as well—concern for property and Union may have been stressed in order to justify the convenience of "going slow" on slavery).

As devout Lockians, Americans did believe that the sanctity of private property constituted the essential cornerstone for all other liberties. If property could not be protected in a nation, neither could life nor liberty. And the Constitution, so many felt, had upheld the legitimacy of holding property in men. True, the Constitution had not mentioned slavery by name, and had not overtly declared in its favor, but in giving the institution certain indirect guarantees (the three-fifths clause; non-interference for twenty-one years with the slave trade; the fugitive slave proviso), the Constitution had seemed to sanction it. At any rate no one could be sure. The intentions of the Founding Father [sic] remained uncertain, and one of the standing debates of the antebellum generation was whether the Constitution had been meant by them to be a pro- or an antislavery document.[2] Since the issue was unresolved, Northerners remained uneasy, uncertain how far they could go in attacking slavery without at the same time attacking property.

Fear for property rights was underscored by fear for the Union. The South had many times warned that if her rights and interests were not heeded, she would leave the Union and form a separate confederation. The tocsin had been sounded with enough regularity so that to some it had begun to sound like hollow bluster. But there was always the chance that if the South felt sufficiently provoked she might yet carry out the threat.

It is difficult today fully to appreciate the horror with which most Northerners regarded the potential breakup of the Union. The mystical qualities which surrounded "Union" were no less real for being in part irrational. Lincoln struck a deep chord for his generation when he spoke of the Union as the "last best hope of earth"; that the American experiment was thought the "best" hope may have been arrogant, a hope at all, naïve, but such it was to the average American, convinced of his own superiority and the possibility of the world learning by example. Today, more concerned with survival than improvement, we are bemused (when we are not cynical) about "standing examples for mankind," and having seen the ghastly deeds done in the name of patriotism, we are impatient at signs of national fervor. But 100 years ago, the world saw less danger in nationalism, and Americans, enamored with their own extraordinary success story, were especially prone to look on love of country as one of the noblest of human sentiments. Even those Southerners who had ceased to love the Union had not ceased to love the idea of nationhood; they merely wished to transfer allegiance to a more worthy object.

Those who wanted to preserve the old Union acted from a variety of motives: the Lincolns, who seem primarily to have valued its spiritual potential, were joined by those more concerned with maintaining its power potential; the Union was symbol of man's quest for a benevolent society—and for dominion. But if Northerners valued their government for differing reasons, they generally agreed on the necessity for preserving it. Even so, their devotion to the Union had its oscillations. In 1861 Lincoln and his party, in rejecting the Crittenden Compromise, seemed willing to jeopardize Union rather than risk the further expansion of slavery (perhaps because they never believed secession would really follow, though this complacency, in turn, might only have been a way of convincing themselves that a strong antislavery stand would not necessarily destroy the Union). After war broke out the value stress once more shifted: Lincoln's party now loudly insisted that the war was indeed being fought to preserve the Union, not to free the slaves. Thus did the co-existing values of Union and antislavery tear the Northern mind and confuse its allegiance.

The tension was compounded by the North's ambivalent attitude toward the Negro. The Northern majority, unlike most of the abolitionists, did not believe in the equality of races. The Bible (and the new science of anthropology) seemed to suggest that the Negro had been a separate, inferior creation meant for a position of servitude.[3] Where there was doubt on the doctrine of racial equality, its advocacy by the distrusted abolitionists helped to settle the matter in the negative.

It was possible, of course, to disbelieve in Negro equality, and yet disapprove of Negro slavery. Negroes were obviously men, even if an inferior sort, and as men they could not in conscience (the Christian-Democratic version) be denied the right to control their own souls and bodies. But if anti-Negro and antislavery sentiments were not actually incompatible, they were not mutually supportive either. Doubt of the Negro's capacity for citizenship continually blunted the edge of antislavery fervor. If God had intended the Negro for some subordinate role in society, perhaps a kind of benevolent slavery was, after all, the most suitable arrangement; so long as there was uncertainty, it might be better to await the slow unfolding of His intentions in His good time.

And so the average Northerner, even after he came actively to disapprove of slavery, continued to be hamstrung in his opposition to it by the competitive pull of other values. Should prime consideration be given to freeing the slaves, even though in the process the rights of property and the preservation of the Union were threatened? Should the future of the superior race be endangered in order to improve the lot of a people seemingly marked by Nature for a degraded station? Ideally, the North would have liked to satisfy its conscience about slavery and at the same time preserve the rest of its value system intact—to free the Negro and yet do so without threatening property rights or dislocating the Union. This struggle to achieve the best of all possible worlds runs like a forlorn hope throughout the ante-bellum period—the sad, almost plaintive quest by the American Adam for the perfect world he considered his birthright.

The formula of nonextension did seem, for a time, the perfect device for balancing these multiple needs. Non-extension would put slavery in the course of ultimate extinction without producing excessive dislocation; since slavery would not be attacked directly, nor its existence immediately threatened, the South would not be unduly fearful for her property rights, the Union would not be needlessly jeopardized, and a mass of free Negroes would not be precipitously thrust upon an unprepared public. Nonextension, in short, seemed a panaca, a formula which promised in time to do everything while for the present risking nothing. But like all panaceas, it ignored certain hard realities: would containment really lead to the extinction of slavery? would the South accept even a gradual dissolution of her peculiar institution? would it be right to sacrifice two or three more generations of Negroes in the name of uncertain future possibilities? Alas for the American Adam, so soon to be expelled from Eden.

The abolitionists, unlike most Northerners, were not willing to rely on future intangibles. Though often called impractical romantics, they were in some ways the most tough-minded of Americans. They had no easy faith in the benevolent workings of time or in the inevitable triumphs of gradualism. If change was to come, they argued, it would be the result of man's effort to produce it; patience and inactivity had never yet helped the world's ills. Persistently, sometimes harshly, the abolitionists denounced delay and those who advocated it; they were tired, they said, of men using the councils of moderation to perpetuate injustice.

In their own day, and ever since, the abolitionists have faced a hostile majority; their policies have been ridiculed, their personalities reviled. Yet ridicule, like its opposite, adoration, is usually not the result of analysis but a substitute for it. Historians have for so long been absorbed in denouncing the abolitionists, that they have had scant energy left over for understanding them. The result is that we still know surprisingly little about the movement, and certainly not enough to warrant the general assumptions so long current in the historical profession.

Historians have assumed that the abolitionists were unified in their advocacy of certain broad policies—immediate emancipation, without compensation—and also unified in refusing to spell out details for implementing these policies. To some extent this traditional view is warranted. The abolitionists did agree almost unanimously (Gerrit Smith was one of the few exceptions) that slaveholders must not be compensated. One does not pay a man, they argued, for ceasing to commit a sin. Besides, the slaveholder had already been paid many times over in labor for which he had never given wages. Defensible though this position may have been in logic or morals, the abolitionists should perhaps have realized that public opinion would never support the confiscation of property, and should have modified their stand accordingly. But they saw themselves as prophets, not politicians; they were concerned with what was "right," not with what was possible, though they hoped that if men were once made aware of the right, they would find some practical way of implementing it.[4]

The abolitionists were far less united on the doctrine of immediate emancipation —at least in the 1830's, before Southern intransigence and British experience in the West Indies, convinced almost all of them that gradualism was hopeless. But during the 1830's, there was a considerable spectrum of opinion as to when and how to emancipate the slave. Contrary to common myth, some of the abolitionists did advocate a period of prior education and training before the granting of full freedom. Men like Weld, Birney, and the Tappans, stressing the debasing experience of slavery, insisted only that gradual emancipation be immediately begun, not that emancipation itself be at once achieved.[5] This range of opinion has never been fully appreciated. It has been convenient, then and now, to believe that all abolitionists always advocated instantaneous freedom, for it thus became possible to denounce any call for emancipation as "patently impractical."

By 1840, however, most abolitionists had become immediatists, and that position, "practical" or not, did have a compelling moral urgency. Men learned how to be free, the immediatists argued, only by being free; slavery, no matter how attenuated, was by its very nature incapable of preparing men for those independent decisions necessary to adult responsibility. Besides, they insisted, the Negro, though perhaps debased by slavery, was no more incapacitated for citizenship than were many poor whites, whose rights no one seriously suggested curtailing.

The immediatist position was not free of contradiction. If slavery had been as horrendous as the abolitionists claimed, it was logical to expect that its victims would bear deep personality scars—greater than any disabilities borne by a poor white, no matter how degraded his position. Either slavery had not been this deadly, or, if it had, those recently freed from its toils could not be expected to move at once into the responsibilities of freedom. This contradiction was apparent to some immediatists, but there was reason for refusing to resolve it. Ordinarily, they said, a system of apprenticeship might be desirable, but if conditions to emancipation were once established, they could be used as a standing rational for postponement; the Negro could be kept in a condition of semislavery by the self-perpetuating argument that he was not yet ready for his freedom.[6]

Moreover, any intermediary stage before full freedom would require the spelling out of precise "plans," and these would give the enemies of emancipation an opportunity to pick away at the impracticality of this or that detail. They would have an excuse for disavowing the broader policy under the guise of disagreeing with the specific means for achieving it. Better to concentrate on the larger issue and force men to take sides on that alone, the abolitionists argued, than to give them a chance to hide their opposition behind some supposed disapproval of detail.[7] Wendell Phillips, for one, saw the abolitionists' role as exclusively that of agitating the broader question. Their primary job, Phillips insisted, was to arouse the country's conscience rather than to spell out to it precise plans and formulas. *After* that conscience had been aroused, it would be time to talk of specific proposals; let the moral urgency of the problem be recognized, let the country be brought to a determination to rid itself of slavery, and ways and means to accomplish that purpose would be readily enough found.[8]

No tactical position could really have saved the abolitionists from the denunciation of those hostile to their basic goal. If the abolitionists spelled out a program for emancipation, their enemies would have a chance to pick at details; if they did not spell out a program, they could then be accused of vagueness and impracticality. Hostility can always find its own justification.[9]

A second mode of attack on the abolitionists has centered on their personalities rather than their policies. The stereotype which has long had currency sees the abolitionist as a disturbed fanatic, a man self-righteous and self-deceived, motivated not by concern for the Negro, as he may have believed, but by an unconscious drive to gratify certain needs of his own. Seeking to discharge either individual anxieties or those frustrations which came from membership in a "displaced élite," his anti-slavery protest was, in any case, a mere disguise for personal anguish.[10]

A broad assumption underlies this analysis which has never been made explicit—namely, that strong protest by an individual against social injustice is ipso facto proof of his disturbance. Injustice itself, in this view, is apparently never sufficient to arouse unusual ire in "normal" men, for normal men, so goes the canon, are always cautious, discreet, circumspect. Those who hold to this model of human behavior seem rarely to suspect that it may tell us more about their hierarchy of values than about the reform impulse it pretends to describe. Argued in another context, the inadequacies of the stereotype become more apparent: if normal people do not protest "excessively" against injustice, then we should be forced to condemn as neurotic all those who protested with passion against the Nazi persecution of the Jews.

Some of the abolitionists, it is true, *were* palpable neurotics, men who were not comfortable within themselves and therefore not comfortable with others, men whose "reality-testing" was poor, whose life styles were pronouncedly compulsive, whose relationships were unusual compounds of demand and phantasy. Such neurotics *were* in the abolitionist movement—the Parker Pillsburys, Stephen Fosters, Abby Folsoms. Yet even here we must be cautious, for our diagnostic accuracy can be blurred if the life style under evaluation is sharply different from our own. Many of the traits of the abolitionists which today "put us off" were not peculiar to them, but rather to their age—the declamatory style, the abstraction and idealization of issues, the tone of righteous certainty. the religious context of argumentation. Thus the evangelical rhetoric of the movement, with its thunderous emphasis on sin and retribution, can sound downright "queer" (and thus "neurotic") to the 20th century skeptic, though in its day common enough to abolitionists and nonabolitionists alike.

Then, too, even when dealing with the "obvious" neurotics, we must be careful in the link we establish between their pathology and their protest activity. It is one thing to demonstrate an individual's "disturbance" and quite another then to explain all of his behavior in terms of it. Let us suppose, for example, that Mr. Jones is a reformer; he is also demonstrably "insecure." It does not necessarily follow that he is a reformer *because* he is insecure. The two may seem logically related (that is, if one's mind automatically links "protest" with "neurosis"), but we all know that many things can be logical without being true.

Even if we establish the neurotic behavior of certain members of a group, we have not, thereby, established the neurotic behavior of *all* members of that group. The tendency to leap from the particular to the general is always tempting, but because we have caught one benighted monsignor with a boy scout does not mean we have conclusively proved that all priests are pederasts. Some members of every group are disturbed; put the local police force, the Medal of Honor winners, or the faculty of a university under the Freudian microscope, and the number of cases of "palpable disturbance" would probably be disconcertingly high. But what *precisely* does their disturbance tell us about the common activities of the group to which they belong—let alone about the activities of the disturbed individuals themselves?

Actually, behavioral patterns for many abolitionists do *not* seem notably eccentric. Men like Birney, Weld, Lowell, Quincy—abolitionists all—formed good relationships, saw themselves in perspective, played and worked with zest and spontaneity, developed their talents, were aware of worlds beyond their own private horizons. They all had their tics and their traumas—as who does not—but the evidence of health is abundant and predominant. Yet most historians have preferred to ignore such men when discussing the abolitionist movement. And the reason, I believe, is that such men conform less well than do the Garrisons to the assumption that those who become deeply involved in social protest are necessarily those who are deeply disturbed.

To evaluate this assumption further, some effort must be made to understand current findings in the theory of human motivation. This is difficult terrain for the historian, not made more inviting by the sharp disagreements which exist among psychologists themselves (though these disagreements do help to make us aware of the complexities involved). Recent motivational research, though not conclusive, throws some useful new perspectives on "reformers." [11]

A reaction has currently set in among psychologists against the older behaviorist model of human conduct. The behaviorists told us that men's actions were determined by the nature of the stimulus exerted upon them, and that their actions always pointed towards the goal of "tension reduction." There was little room in behaviorist theory for freedom of choice, for rationality, or for complex motives involving abstract ideas as well as instinctive drives.

Without denying the tension-reducing motives of certain kinds of human behavior, a number of psychologists are now insisting on making room for another order of motivation, involving more than the mere "restoration of equilibrium." Mature people, they believe—that is, those who have a realistic sense of self—*can* act with deliberation and *can* exercise control over their actions. This new view presumes an active intellect, an intellect capable of interpreting sensory data in a purposive way. The power of reflection, of self-objectification, makes possible a dynamic as opposed to a merely instinctive life. Men, in short, need not be wholly driven by habit and reflex; they need not be mere automatons who respond in predictable ways to given stimuli. Rather, they can be reasoning organisms capable of decision and choice. Among the rational choices mature men may make is to commit themselves to a certain set of ethical values. They are not necessarily forced to such a commitment by personal or social tensions (of which they are usually unaware), but may come to that commitment deliberately, after reflective consideration.

The new psychology goes even one step further. It suggests that the very definition of maturity may be the ability to commit oneself to abstract ideals, to get beyond the selfish, egocentric world of children. This does not mean that every man who reaches outward does so from mature motives; external involvement may also be a way of acting out sick phantasies. The point is only that "commitment" need not be a symptom of personality disturbance. It is just as likely to be a symptom of maturity and health.

It does not follow, of course, that all abolitionists protested against slavery out of mature motives; some may have been, indeed were, "childish neurotics." But if we agree that slavery was a fearful injustice, and if motivational theory now suggests that injustice will bring forth protest from mature men, it seems reasonable to conclude that at least some of those who protested strongly against slavery must have done so from "healthy" motives.

The hostile critic will say that the abolitionists protested *too* strongly to have been maturely motivated. But when is a protest *too* strong? For a defender of the status quo, the answer (though never stated in these terms) would be: when it succeeds. For those not dedicated to the current status, the answer is likely to be: a protest is too strong when it is out of all proportion to the injustice it indicts. Could any verbal protest have been too strong against holding fellow human beings as property? From a moral point of view, certainly not, though from a practical point of view, perhaps. That is, the abolitionist protest might have been *too* strong if it somehow jeopardized the very goal it sought to achieve—the destruction of human slavery. But no one has yet shown this to have been the case.[12]

At any rate, current findings in motivational theory suggest that at the very least we must cease dealing in blanket indictments, in simple-minded categorizing and elementary stereotyping. Such exercises may satisfy our present-day hostility to "reformers," but they do not satisfy the complex demands of historical truth. We need an awareness of the wide variety of human beings who became involved in the abolitionist movement, and an awareness of the complexity of human motivation sufficient to save us from summing up men and movements in two or three unexamined adjectives.

Surely there is now evidence enough to suggest that commitment and concern need not be aberrations; they may represent the profoundest elements of our humanity. Surely there are grounds for believing that those who protested strongly against slavery were not all misguided fanatics or frustrated neurotics—though by so believing it becomes easier to ignore the injustice against which they protested. Perhaps it is time to ask whether the abolitionists, in insisting that slavery be ended, were indeed those men of their generation furthest removed from reality, or whether that description should be reserved for those Northerners who remained indifferent to the institution, and those Southerners who defended it as a "positive good." From the point of view of these men, the abolitionists were indeed mad, but it is time we questioned the sanity of the point of view.

Those Northerners who were not indifferent to slavery—a large number after 1845—were nonetheless prone to view the abolitionist protest as "excessive," for it threatened the cherished values of private property and Union. The average Northerner may have found slavery disturbing, but convinced as he was that the Negro was an inferior, he did not find slavery monstrous. Certainly he did not think it an evil sufficiently profound to risk, by "precipitous action," the nation's present wealth or its future power. The abolitionists were willing to risk both. They thought it tragic that men should weigh human lives in the *same* scale as material possessions and abstractions of government. It is no less tragic that we continue to do so.

NOTES

1. Arresting slavery's further spread, Lincoln said, would "place it where the public mind shall rest in the belief that it is in course of ultimate extinction . . ." ("House Divided" speech, June 16, 1858, Roy P. Basler, ed. *The Collected Works of Abraham Lincoln,* New Brunswick, 1953, II, 461.)

2. For a sample pamphlet exchange, see Lysander Spooner, *Unconstitutionality of Slavery* (Boston, 1845), and Wendell Phillips, *Review of Lysander Spooner's Essays on the Unconstitutionality of Slavery* (Boston, 1845).

3. On this point see W. S. Jenkins, *Pro-Slavery Thought in the Old South* (Chapel Hill, 1935), and William Stanton, *The Leopard's Spots* (Chicago, 1960).

4. See, for example, L. Maria Child, *The Right Way the Safe Way* (New York, 1860). After the Civil War began, the abolitionists modified their stand on compensation—thus showing that "pragmatic flexibility" of which they were supposedly devoid. In the winter of 1861, Garrison got up a petition to compensate loyal slaveholders, and in 1862, most abolitionists gave enthusiastic approval to plans for compensated emancipation in the District of Columbia.

5. For sample abolitionist writings advocating gradual freedom, after apprenticeship, see L. Maria Child, *Anti-Slavery Catechism* (Newburyport, 1836), pp. 18–19; J. A. Thome and J. W. Alvord to T. Weld, February 9, 1836, *Letters of Theodore Dwight Weld, Angelina Grimké Weld, and Sarah Grimké, 1822–1844*, eds. G. H. Barnes and D. L. Dumond (New York, 1934), I, 257; C. K. Whipple, "The Abolitionists' Plan," *The Liberty Bell* (1845). Even Garrison was at first willing to hold newly freed slaves in "the benevolent restraint of guardianship" (*Thoughts on African Colonization* [Boston, 1832], pp. 79–80). Donald Mathews has pointed out to me that Benjamin Lundy in *The Genius of Universal Emancipation* printed many plans for gradual freedom (e.g., in the issues of September 5, 12, 15, 1825), but, discouraged by the lack of response, Lundy finally discontinued doing so. Thus it might be well to ask whether the abolitionists, in moving steadily toward "immediatism" (a shift largely completed by 1840), had not been driven to that position by the intransigence of their society in the preceding decade, rather than by any inherent "extremism" in their own temperaments.

6. See, for example, James A. Thome and J. Horace Kimball, *Emancipation in the West Indies* (New York, 1838), pp. 83, 85, 108.

7. For sample awareness of the dilemma inherent in "plans," see William Jay, *An Inquiry into . . . the American Colonization, and Anti-Slavery Societies* (New York, 1835), p. 197; "Instructions of the American Anti-Slavery Society to Theodore Weld," February 20, 1834, in Barnes and Dumond, *Weld-Grimké Letters,* I, 126.

8. See, for example, his speech "Daniel O'Connell" in Wendell Phillips, *Speeches, Lectures, and Letters* (Boston, 1891), Second Series, pp. 384–420.

9. I am not suggesting that all those who opposed immediatism were necessarily opposed to emancipation; no doubt some of those in opposition objected only to the means, not the end. I know of no way, though, to measure accurately the proportionate strength of the two groups, nor, more complicated still, the degree to which each actually understood its position.

10. In pointing out what seems to me certain inadequacies in this stereotype, I do not mean to imply that no psychological or sociological explanation of the abolitionists is possible. Wide personality variations among individual abolitionists is not incompatible with their sharing a few traits in common—these traits being the crucial ones in explaining their "reform motivation." But if so, these common traits have not, in my view, yet been delineated. Which is not to say that they did not exist, nor that they may not be successfully isolated in the future. There could, for example, be some point in examining the "sociological truism" that "when family integration weakens, the individual becomes more available for participation in some kinds of collective behavior" (Leonard Broom and Philip Selznick, *Sociology,* New York, 1957, p. 406), or the suggestion by Seward Hiltner that "the person who is vociferous and diligent on behalf of minority groups may be impelled by unsolved authority problems" ("Psychology and Morality," *Princeton Alumni Weekly,* September 22, 1964). Then there is the possibility, first suggested to me in conversation with Silvan Tomkins, of a connection between "being good to others" and an unfulfilled (because frightening) need to get close to people; by expressing concern for the unfortunate it becomes possible to discharge safely (because impersonally), some of the pent-up need for warmth and affection. Needless to say, all the cautions I try to outline in this essay against current psycho-social interpretations of the abolitionists, would apply to any future interpretations as well.

11. For recent discussions, see R. S. Peters, *The Concept of Motivation* (London, 1958); Gardner Lindzey, ed. *Assessment of Human Motives* (New York, 1958); Robert C. Birney and Richard C. Teevan, eds. *Measuring Human Motivation* (New York, 1962); Erich Fromm, "The Revolutionary Character" in *The Dogma of Christ* (New York, 1963).

12. In this regard, there has been a persistent confusion of two separate indictments against the abolitionists: first, that they disrupted the peace, and second (in the classic formulation given by Daniel Webster), that they "bound more firmly than before" the bonds

of the slave. It is undeniably true that the abolitionists contributed to the polarization of public opinion, and to that extent, to the "disturbance of the peace" (which is not the same as war). But it does not follow that because they stirred up passions, they made freeing the slaves more difficult. This would be true only if it could be shown that the slaves could have been freed *without* first arousing and polarizing opinion. The evidence does not seem to support such a position. In all the long years before the abolitionists began their campaign, the North had managed to remain indifferent to the institution, and the South had done almost nothing, even in the most gradual way, toward ameliorating it. Had the abolitionists not aroused public debate on slavery, there is no guarantee that anyone else would have; and without such a debate it seems unlikely that measures against the institution would have been taken. The fact that the debate became heated, moreover, cannot wholly be explained by the terms in which the abolitionists raised it; what must also be taken into account is the fact that the South, with some possible exceptions in the border area, reacted intransigently to *any* criticism of the institution, however mild the tone or gradual the suggestions.

3. The Civil War Era

The Origins of Slavery Expansionism   EUGENE D. GENOVESE

To New Left historians the Civil War represents the final triumph of the new forces of industrialism. It was the American equivalent of the French Revolution, and it was less concerned with slavery than with the locus of power in America. At the same time it destroyed slavery, an undeniable fact that causes some difficulties for the New Left.

The quandary stems from the Left's simultaneous skepticism of the new era following 1865 and of its corporate leadership, and its deep antipathy to the slave regime. The same capitalists who ended slavery, by this interpretation, also seized control of the national government and bent it to their selfish ends. Either the capitalist exploiters had considerable redeeming qualities, or the precapitalist slave South did. Either alternative is not easy to accept.

The Progressives, particularly Beard, found the dilemma less knotty to deal with, and indeed scarcely saw it as a problem at all. Beard was not notably a sympathizer with either the abolitionists or the slaves, and he admired the slave South more than the aggressive, capitalist North. This insensitivity to social justice has been noted by Staughton Lynd among others, and has led Lynd to criticize the man whom he otherwise deeply esteems.

In the end Lynd tries to resolve this predicament by borrowing from the Marxist historian Barrington Moore, Jr. Moore refuses to romanticize either Southern slave-holders or Northern antislavery men, and it is somewhat suprising that Lynd finds his views acceptable. A more succinct version of this unsentimental analysis is the following essay of Eugene Genovese. Unlike many of the New Left, Genovese, like Moore, is a committed Marxist. While he is obviously sympathetic to the black man's striving for social justice, he is not a neo-abolitionist. As a good Marxist, he tends to believe that there is no point in attacking men—or praising men—for following their class interests. He also feels, as the essay below suggests, that it was an expansionist South rather than a militant North that was the aggressor in the events that led to the Civil War.

An important part of his argument depends on the efficiency of slave labor. If that labor was effective only when applied to new lands, Genovese's hypothesis

Source: Eugene D. Genovese, *The Political Economy of Slavery: Studies in the Economy and Society of the Slave South* (New York: Pantheon Books, 1965), chap. x, "The Origins of Slavery Expansionism," pp. 243–274.

becomes more plausible. In this essay, Genovese seeks to demonstrate that slavery was indeed an inefficient system of extracting wealth from the soil, a view that has recently come under serious attack from a group of economic historians, notably Alfred Conrad and John Meyer. The piece that follows is both an ingenious re-statement of the economic failings of slavery and an interesting analysis of Civil War origins.

FOR FURTHER READING:

Eugene Genovese, *The Political Economy of Slavery: Studies in the Economy and Society of the Slave South**, (Pantheon Books, 1965); Barrington Moore, Jr., "The American Civil War: The Last Capitalist Revolution," in *Social Origins of Dictatorship and Democracy**, (Beacon Press, 1966); Charles and Mary Beard, *The Rise of American Civilization*, Volume II, Chapters XVII, XVIII, XX, Revised Edition, (The Macmillan Company, 1933); James G. Randall and David Donald, *The Civil War and Reconstruction*, (D. C. Heath, 1961); Avery Craven, *The Coming of the Civil War**, 2nd Edition, (University of Chicago Press, 1957); Alfred Conrad and John Meyer, "The Economics of Slavery in the Ante-Bellum South," *Journal of Political Economy*, (April, 1958); Staughton Lynd, "On Turner, Beard and Slavery," *Journal of Negro History*, (October, 1963).

Asterisk denotes paperback edition.

Once upon a time in the happy and innocent days of the nineteenth century, men believed that Negro slavery had raised an expansionist slaveocracy to power in the American South. Today we know better. The revisionists have denied that slavery was expansionist and have virtually driven their opponents from the field. Their arguments, as distinct from their faith in the possibilities of resolving antagonisms peacefully, rest on two formidable essays. In 1926, Avery O. Craven published his *Soil Exhaustion as a Factor in the Agricultural History of Maryland and Virginia*, which sought to prove that the slave economy could reform itself, and three years later Charles William Ramsdell published his famous article on "The Natural Limits of Slavery Expansion," which constituted a frontal attack on the "irrepressible conflict" school.

I propose to restate the traditional view, but in such a way as to avoid the simplistic and mechanistic notions of Cairnes and his followers and to account for the data that has emerged from the conscientious and often splendid researches of the revisionist historians. Specifically, I propose to show that economics, politics, social life, ideology, and psychology converged to thrust the system outward and that beneath each factor lay the exigencies of the slaveholding class. Each dictated expansion if the men who made up the ruling class of the South were to continue to rule.

Roots and Taproot

Antebellum Southern economic history reinforces rather than overturns the nineteenth-century notion of an expansionist slaveocracy. That notion undoubtedly suffered from grave defects and considerable crudeness, for it insisted on the lack of versatility of slave labor and the steady deterioration of the soil without appreciat-ing the partially effective attempts to reform the slave economy. Yet the revisionist work of the Craven school, which has contributed so much toward an understanding of the economic complexities, has not added up to a successful refutation.

We may recapitulate briefly the main points of the preceding studies, which lead to the economic root of slavery expansionism. At the beginning we encounter the low productivity of slave labor, defined not accordingly to some absolute or purely economic standard, but according to the political exigencies of the slaveholders. The slaves worked well enough in the cotton and sugar fields, when organized in gangs, but the old criticism of labor given grudgingly retains its force.

Slave labor lacked that degree and kind of versatility which would have permitted general agricultural diversification. Slaves could and did work in a variety of pursuits, including industrial, but under circumstances not easily created within the economy as a whole. Division of labor on the plantations and in society proceeded slowly and under great handicaps. The level of technology, especially on the plantations, was kept low by the quality and size of the labor force. Mules and oxen, for example, replaced faster horses principally because they could more easily withstand rough and perhaps vengeful handling. Negro laborers had been disciplined to sustained agricultural labor before being brought to the Americas. Their low productivity arose from the human and technological conditions under which they worked, and these arose from the slave system.

An analysis of Southern livestock and the attempts to improve it reveals the complex and debilitating interrelationships within the slave economy. The South had more than enough animals to feed its population but had to import meat. A shortage of liquid capital made acquisition of better breeds difficult, and the poor treatment of the animals by the slaves made maintenance of any reasonable standards close to impossible. As a further complication, the lack of urban markets inhibited attention to livestock by depriving planters of outlets for potential surpluses. The South boasted an enormous number of animals but suffered from their wretched quality.

Slavery provided a sufficient although not a necessary cause of soil exhaustion. It dictated one-crop production beyond the limits of commercial advantage and in opposition to the political safety of the slaveholders. Planters could not easily rotate crops under the existing credit structure, with a difficult labor force, and without those markets which could only accompany industrial and urban advance. The sheer size of the plantations discouraged fertilization. Barnyard manure was scarce, commercial fertilizers too expensive, and the care necessary for advantageous application unavailable. The shortage of good implements complicated the operation, for manures are easily wasted when not applied properly.

Craven insists that the existence of a moving frontier, north and south, brought about the same result, but as we have seen, the special force of slavery cannot so easily be brushed aside. The North confronted the devastating effects of soil exhaustion and built a diversified economy in the older areas as the frontier pushed westward. The South, faced with the debilitating effects of slavery long after the frontier had passed, had to struggle against hopeless odds.

These direct effects of slavery received enormous reinforcement from such indirect effects as the shortage of capital and entrepreneurship and the weakness of the market. Capital investments in slaves and a notable tendency toward aristocratic consumption had their economic advantages but inhibited the rise of new industries.

The Southern market consisted primarily of the plantations and could not support more than a limited industrial advance. The restricted purchasing power of the rural whites, of the urban lower classes, and indirectly of the slaves hemmed in Southern manufacturers and put them at a severe competitive disadvantage relative to Northerners, who had had a head start and who had much wider markets in the free states to sustain production on an increasing scale. The barriers to industrialization also blocked urbanization and thereby undermined the market for foodstuffs.

Southern industrialization proceeded within the narrow limits set by the social milieu as well as by the market. The slaveholders controlled the state legislatures and the police power; they granted charters, set taxes, and ultimately controlled the lives of regional industries. So long as industry remained within safe limits the slaveholders offered no firm resistance, or at least no united front. Those limits included guarantees against the rise of a hostile and independent bourgeoisie and excessive concentrations of white workers of doubtful loyalty. Since the big slaveholders provided much of the capital for industry and since the plantations provided much of the regional market, the risks remained small, for even the nonslaveholding industrialists necessarily bound themselves to the rural regime and tried to do good business within the established limits. Industry made some progress; industrialization, understood as a self-propelling process, did not.

The South made one form of agricultural adjustment while slavery remained. The great agricultural revival in the Upper South overcame the most serious effects of slavery by reducing the size of slaveholdings, converting surplus slaves into cash, and investing the funds in the supervision, fertilization, and reconversion of smaller estates. This process threatened the economic and ideological solidity of the slaveholders' regime and had other drawbacks, but the most important, it broke on an immanent contradiction. The sale of surplus slaves depended on markets further south, which necessarily depended on virgin lands on which to apply the old, wasteful methods of farming. Reform in one region implied exhaustive agriculture in another. Thus, the process of agricultural reform had narrow limits in a closed slave system and had to be reversed when it pressed against them. No solution emerged from within the system, but one beckoned from without. The steady acquisition of new land could alone guarantee the maintenance of that interregional slave trade which held the system together.

This economic root of slavery expansionism was only one of several roots, but itself grew strong enough to produce an ugly organism. If we begin with the economic process it is because the external threat to the slaveholders mounted so clearly, objectively and in their consciousness, with each new census report on the material conditions of the contending forces. The slaveholders might, of course, have resigned themselves to Lincoln's victory, accepted the essentials of the Wilmot Proviso, faced the impending crisis of their system, and prepared to convert to some form of free labor. Anything is possible where men retain the power to reason. Such a choice would have spelled their death as a ruling class and would have constituted moral and political suicide. Many contemporaries and many historians ever since have thought that they should have agreed to do themselves in. With this view I do not wish to argue. Neither did they.

The economic process propelling the slave South along expansionist paths had its political and social parallels, the most obvious being the need to re-establish parity in the Senate or at least to guarantee enough voting strength in Washington to protect Southern interests. In an immediate political sense the demand for more slave-state Congressmen was among the important roots of expansionism, but in a deeper sense it was merely a symptom of something more fundamental. Had the South not had a distinct social system to preserve and a distinct and powerful ruling class at its helm, a decline of its political and economic power would have caused no greater alarm than it did in New England.

A second political root was the need to protect slavery where it was profitable by establishing buffer areas where it might not be. Just as the British had to spend money to secure ascendancy in Tibet so that they could make money in India, the South had to establish political control over areas with dubious potentialities as slave states in order to protect existing slave states. The success of the Texas cause removed the fear of Mexican tampering with slaves in Louisiana, much as annexation removed potential British-inspired tampering. "Texas must be a slave country," wrote Stephen F. Austin to his sister. "The interest of Louisiana requires that it should be; a population of fanatical abolitionists in Texas would have a very pernicious and dangerous influence on the overgrown population of the state." In 1835, when a large Mexican force was reported near the Brazos River, the slaves apparently did attempt to rise. One hundred Negroes were severely punished, some executed.

John A. Quitman, former governor of Mississippi, tried to organize a filibustering expedition to Cuba during 1853–1855, particularly because he feared that abolition there would present dangers to the South. Samuel R. Walker and Albert W. Ely, among others, warned that Britain and France would force a weak Spain to sacrifice Cuban slavery and thereby isolate the South as a slaveholding country. Many far-sighted Southerners understood the danger of permitting the isolation of Southern slavery. They desired Cuba in order to secure political control of the Caribbean, as well as for economic reasons.

Beyond Cuba and the Caribbean lay Brazil, the other great slaveholding country. "These two great valleys of the Amazon and the Mississippi," declared the *Richmond Enquirer* in 1854, "are now possessed by two governments of the earth most deeply interested in African slavery—Brazil and the United States . . . The whole intermediate countries between these two great valleys . . . is a region under the plastic hand of a beneficent Providence . . . How is it to be developed?" [*sic*] With black labor and white skill. Cuba and Santo Domingo, it continued, were potentially the bases for the control of the whole Caribbean. Such a political complex would cause the whole world to "fall back upon African labor."

The warning of the Louisville *Daily Courier* in 1860 that Kentucky could afford to remain in the Union but that the Lower South could not touched the central issue. Suppose, it asked, Kentucky sold its slaves south. "And then what? Antislavery will not be content to rest. . . . The war will be transferred to the Cotton States."

The need to push forward in order to ward off concentrations of hostile power arose from the anachronistic nature of the slave regime. By 1850, if not much earlier, world opinion could no longer tolerate chattel slavery, and British opposition in particular was both formidable and implacable. The transformation of the Caribbean into a slaveholders' lake and an alliance or understanding with Brazil held out the only hope of preventing a dangerous and tightening containment.

Slaveholders also sought additional territory to reduce the danger of internal convulsion. Lieutenant Matthew F. Maury, who helped bring about the American exploration of the Amazon Valley in the 1850s, discussed the eventual absorption of much of Latin America by the United States:

> I cannot be blind to what I see going on here. It is becoming a matter of *faith*—I use a strong word—yes a matter of faith among leading Southern men, that the time is coming, nay that it is rapidly approaching when in order to prevent this war of the races and all its horrors, they will in self-defense be compelled to conquer parts of Mexico and Central America, and make slave territory of that—and that is now free.

Representative Thomas L. Clingman of North Carolina told the House that Northerners were "too intelligent to believe that humanity, either to the slave or the master, requires that they should be pent up within a territory which after a time will be insufficient for their subsistence, and where they must perish from want, or from collision that would occur between the races." Southerners always kept the West Indian experience in front of them when they discussed the racial proportions of the population.

Probably, steady infusions of new land were also needed to placate the nonslaveholders, but we know little about slaveholder-nonslaveholder relationships as yet and little can be said with certainty.

The psychological dimension of slavery expansionism has been the subject of various essays and has, for example, emerged from interpretations of Southern frustration and resultant aggression. We need not pursue esoteric lines of inquiry, especially with formulas so broad as to be able to encompass almost every society in any age, to appreciate that a psychological dimension did exist. As Southerners came to regard slavery as a positive good and as they came to value the civilization it made possible as the world's finest, they could hardly accept limits on its expansion. To agree to containment meant to agree that slavery constituted an evil, however necessary for the benefit of the savage Africans. That sense of mission so characteristic of the United States as a whole had its Southern manifestation in the mission of slavery. If slavery was making possible the finest society the world had ever known, the objections to its expansion were intolerable. The free-soil argument struck at the foundations of the slaveholder's pride and belief in himself.

It is difficult but unnecessary to assess the relative strength of the roots of slavery expansionism. Each supported and fed the taproot—the exigencies of slaveholder hegemony in a South that fought against comparative disadvantages in the world market and that found itself increasingly isolated morally and politically. From another point of view, each was a manifestation of those exigencies. Although some appear to be objective, or matters of social process, whereas others appear to be subjective, or matters of psychological reaction to possibly imaginary dangers, the difference becomes unimportant when each is related to the fundamental position of the slaveholders in Southern society. The existence of a threatening economic process, such as has been described, would have been enough to generate fear and suspicion, even without the undeniable hostility arising in the North on political and moral grounds.

The "Natural Limits" Thesis

With these observations on the origins of slavery expansionism aside, we may consider the revisionists' objections. Since Ramsdell's article, "The Natural Limits of Slavery Expansion," most cogently presents the opposing view, let us summarize it as much as possible in his own words:

1. Slavery in the territories was the most persistent issue of the 1840s and 1850s. "It seems safe to say that had the question been eliminated or settled amicably there would have been no secession and no Civil War."

2. Free-soilers demanded that slave labor and the plantation system should be excluded from the Western plains to guarantee the predominance there of the free farmer and to prevent any extension of the political power of the slaveholders. Southerners sought to uphold their constitutional rights in the territories and to maintain sufficient political strength to repulse "hostile and ruinous legislation."

3. Slavery expanded "in response to economic stimuli." No conspiracy or political program brought about expansion; in fact, Southerners were too individualistic ever to have agreed on such a program.

4. By 1849–1850, "The westward march of the cotton plantations was evidently slowing down." Only in Texas was the Cotton Belt advancing; elsewhere it stopped at given geographic lines.

5. Even in Texas there were geographical limits. "Therefore, in the early fifties, the cotton plantations tended to cluster in the river counties in the eastern and southern parts of the state." Elsewhere, small farmers and herdsmen were establishing a free-labor economy, for slavery was unprofitable and could not take root.

6. Railroads, if capital could have been raised, would have guided cotton westward up to the black-land prairies of central Texas or the semi-arid plains of western Texas. Beyond that cotton could not go. Woodlands were lacking, and fencing was impossible until the invention of barbed wire in the late 1870s. Here, then, was a temporary barrier.

7. Beyond it lay a permanent barrier. "The history of the argricultural development of the Texas plains region since 1880 affords abundant evidence that it would never become suitable for plantation slave labor." Twenty years of experimentation with windmills, dry farming, and drought-resistant food crops were required before cotton farmers could conquer the plains. The experimental period involved much capital and great risks of a type hard to associate with the plantation system. Labor-saving machinery, not gang labor, was needed.

8. Even in the 1850s, Mexican labor was cheaper than Negro slave labor, and the Germans of southwestern Texas had an antipathy to slavery.

9. Slavery had less chance beyond Texas. "Possibly, southern California could have sustained slavery, but California had already decided that question for itself. . . . As to New Mexico, the census of 1860, ten years after the territory had been thrown open to slavery, showed not a single slave . . ."

10. In Kansas-Nebraska, slavery at best would have come to dominate the hemp regions of eastern Kansas, "but the infiltration of slaves would have been a slow process."

11. "To say that the individual slaveowner would disregard his own economic interest and carry valuable property where it would entail loss merely for the sake of

a doubtful political advantage seems a palpable absurdity." Southerners knew that slavery would not take root in the Southwest but considered establishment of the principle necessary to a defense against abolitionist attacks on the institution itself.

12. "The one side fought rancorously for what it was bound to get without fighting; the other, with equal rancor, contended for what in the nature of things it could never use."

13. On expansion into Latin America: there were mixed motives for desiring more annexations, most of them having nothing to do with slavery. In particular, Scroggs has shown that "had [William] Walker succeeded, those pro-slavery expansionists who had applauded him would most certainly have been sorely disappointed in him." Walker sought a private empire, not annexation by the United States.

14. The proposal to reopen the slave trade, which was often linked to expansion, failed to arouse necessary support even in the South.

15. Ramsdell concludes by suggesting that without such expansion slavery slowly would have declined in profitability and would have given way to an alternative system. The great obstacle to peaceful reform would have been the problem of the place of the free Negro in Southern society.

With due respect for Ramsdell's scholarship and with full appreciation for the workmanlike manner in which he presented the essentials of the revisionist argument, I submit that the thesis is self-contradictory, that it confuses slavery expansionism with the prospects for cotton expansion, and that it rests on the untenable assumption that slaveholders were merely ordinary capitalists who happened to have money in slaves but who might have come to see the advantage of investing differently—the assumption, that is, that no deep identification was made by the slaveholders of slavery with civilization, that slave ownership imbued the master class with no special set of values and interests incapable of being compromised.

The Contradictory Nature of the "Natural Limits" Thesis

The "natural limits" thesis is self-contradictory—and, in one important sense, irrelevant—for it simultaneously asserts that slavery was nonexpansionist and that it would have perished without room to expand. The only way to avoid judging the thesis to be self-contradictory is to read it so as to state that slavery needed room to expand but that, first, it needed room only in the long run and, second, that it had no room. This reading removes the contradiction but destroys the thesis.

If the slave states would eventually need room to expand, they had to set aside new territory when they could get it or face a disaster in a few years or decades. Hence, wisdom dictated a fight for the right to take slaves into the territories, for ultimately that right would be transformed from an abstraction into a matter of life and death. W. Burwell of Virginia wrote in 1856 that the South needed no more territory at the moment and faced no immediate danger of a redundant slave population. "Yet statesmen," he concluded, "like provident farmers, look to the prospective demands of those who rely upon their forethought for protection and employment. Though, therefore, there may be no need of Southern territory for many years, yet it is important to provide for its acquisition when needed . . ."

To establish that slavery had no room to expand is not to refute the theory of slavery expansionism. If it could be firmly established that slavery needed room to expand but had none, then we should have described a society entering a period of internal convulsion. The decision of most slaveholders to stake everything on a desperate gamble for a political independence that would have freed them to push their system southward emerges as a rational, if dangerous, course of action.

The Territorial Question

One of the most puzzling features of Ramsdell's essay is the virtual equation of cotton and slavery. Only occasionally and never carefully does he glance at the prospects for using slave labor outside the cotton fields. To identify any social system with a single commodity is indefensible, and in any case, Southern slavery had much greater flexibility. Ramsdell's essay is puzzling with respect to these general considerations but even more so with respect to his specific contention that contemporary Southerners viewed the territorial question as a cotton question. They did not.

When the more intelligent and informed Southerners demanded the West for slavery they often, perhaps most often, spoke of minerals, not cotton or even hemp. Slavery, from ancient times to modern, had proved itself splendidly adaptable to mining. Mining constituted one of the more important industries of the Negroes of preconquest Africa, and slave labor had a long history there. The Berbers, for example, used Negro slaves in West Africa, where the salt mines provided one of the great impetuses to the development of commercial, as opposed to traditional and patriarchal, forms of slavery. Closer in time and place to the South, Brazil afforded an impressive example of the successful use of slave labor in mining. In the middle of the eighteenth century diamond mining supplemented gold mining in Minas Gerais and accounted for a massive transfer of masters and slaves from the northeastern sugar region. Southern leaders knew a good deal about this experience. "The mines of Brazil," reported *De Bow's Review* in 1848, "are most prolific of iron, gold, and diamonds . . . . The operation is performed by negroes . . . 30,000 negroes have been so employed." The eastern slave states had had experience with gold mining, and although the results were mixed, the potentialities of slave labor had been demonstrated. Planters in the Southwestern states expressed interest in gold mines in Arkansas and hopefully looked further west. "If mines of such temporary value should, as they may, be found in the territories, and slaves could be excluded from these," wrote A. F. Hopkins of Mobile in 1860, "it would present a case of monstrous injustice."

During the Congressional debates of 1850, Representative Jacob Thompson of Mississippi, later to become Secretary of the Interior under Buchanan, expressed great concern over the fate of the public domain of California if she were to be hastily admitted to the Union and expressed special concern over the fate of the gold mines. Ten years later, after a decade of similar warnings, pleas, hopes, and threats, S. D. Moore of Alabama wrote that the South was "excluded from California, not pretendedly even by 'isothermal lines,' or want of employment for slave labor, for in regard to climate and mining purposes the country was admirably adapted to the institution of African slavery." Had it not been for the antislavery agitation, Representative Clingman told the House in 1850, Southerners would have used slaves in the mines of California and transformed it into a slave state. Albert Gallatin Brown, one of the most fiery and belligerent of the proslavery extremists, wrote his constituents that slave labor was admirably suited to mining and that California could and should be made into a slave state. Even as a free state California demonstrated the usefulness of slave labor. In 1852 the state legislature passed a mischievous fugitive slave law that could be and was interpreted to allow slaveholders to bring slaves into the state to work in the mines and then send them home.

Similarly, a Texan wrote in 1852 that a Mississippi and Pacific railroad would secure the New Mexico territory for the South by opening the mining districts to slave labor. During the War for Southern Independence, Jefferson Davis received a communication from his Southwestern field commander that a successful drive to California would add "the most valuable agriculture and grazing lands, and the richest mineral region in the world."

Southerners had long cast eyes toward Mexico and looked forward to additional annexations. "I want Cuba," roared Albert Gallatin Brown. "I want Tamaulipas, Potosí, and one or two other Mexican states; and I want them all for the same reason—for the planting or spreading of slavery." Throughout the 1850s, *De Bow's Review* printed articles about Mexico and particularly about Mexican mines. In 1846, Joel R. Poinsett reviewed Waddy Thompson's *Reflexions on Mexico* and noted the extensive mineral wealth in an article that struck no bellicose note. During the same year Gustavus Schmidt, in a humane, nonracist, nonchauvinist account, wrote of Mexico's "inexhaustible deposits of gold and silver." In 1850, Brantz Mayer of Baltimore estimated that one-fifth of Mexican territory contained excellent mineral resources. Covetous eyes and bellicose projects appeared soon enough.

> The mineral resources of Mexico are unquestionably immense.... The moment Mexico falls into the hands of the Anglo-Saxon race, every inch of her territory will be explored.... The mines of Mexico, which have now been worked near three hundred years, are inexhaustible; and they only need the protection of a good government and the skill of an intelligent and industrious people, to render them productive of the most astonishing quantities of the precious metals.

George Frederick Holmes, in a long, rambling article on gold and silver mines, wrote glowingly of Chile as well as Mexico. H. Yoakum ended an article on Mexico with the warning, *"You must make progress, or you will be absorbed by a more energetic race."* Southerners and Mexicans took these designs seriously. Confederate troops marched into New Mexico with the intention of proceeding to Tucson and then swinging south to take Sonora, Chihuahua, Durango, and Tamaulipas. The Confederate government tried to deal with Santiago Vidaurri, the strong man of Coahuila and Nuevo León, to bring northern Mexico into the Confederacy, and Juárez was so alarmed that he was ready to go to great lengths to help the Union put down the rebellion.

It is one thing to note that Southerners sought to expand slavery into Mexico's mining districts or that they lamented the political barriers to the expansion of slavery into New Mexico's; it is another for us to conclude that their hopes and desires were more than wishful thinking. Allan Nevins has presented a formidable case to suggest that slavery had little room even in the mining districts of the Southwest and Mexico. He shows that even in the Gadsden Purchase the economic exigencies of mining brought about the quick suppression of the enterprising individual by the corporation. Western mining, as well as transportation, lumbering, and some forms of agriculture, required much capital and became fields for big business. High labor costs led to a rising demand for labor-saving machinery, but Nevins does not consider that this very condition might, under certain circumstances, have spurred the introduction of slave labor. He writes:

> For three salient facts stood out in any survey of the Far West. First, this land of plain and peak was natural soil for a free-spirited and highly competitive society, demanding of every resident skill and intelligence. It was, therefore, even in that Gadsden Purchase country which had been bought at the behest of the slave states, a country naturally inhospitable to slavery. Second, when so much energy was steadily flowing into western expansion, and such wide outlets for more effort existed there, it was impossible to think of the country turning to Caribbean areas for a heavy thrust southward. Its main forces moved naturally toward the sunset, where rich opportunities were hardly yet sampled. The cotton kingdom, which realized that the West gave little scope for its peculiar culture, might plan grandiose Latin American adventures; but it would get little support from other regions. And in the third place, conditions in the West demanded capital and organization on a broad scale; if it was a land for individualists, it was even more a land for corporate enterprise—a land for the businessman. Those who pondered these three facts could see that they held an ominous meaning for the South. The nearer Northwest had already done much to upset the old sectional balance, and the Far West, as it filled up, would do still more.

On economic grounds Nevins' analysis has much to offer, but his remarks on the competitive struggle in the Southwest and on the inability of Southerners to get national support for Caribbean adventures do not prove nearly so much as he thinks. At most, they suggest that the North was strong enough to block slavery expansionism into the Southwest and frustrate Southern ambitions elsewhere. If so, the case for secession, from the proslavery viewpoint, was unanswerable.

Nevins' remarks illustrate the wisdom of other Southern arguments—that the South had to secure new land politically, not by economic advance, and that the South had to have guarantees of positive federal protection for slavery in the territories.[1] The *Charleston Mercury,* climaxing a decade of Southern complaints, insisted in 1860 that slavery would have triumphed in California's gold-mining areas if Southerners had had assurances of protection for their property. It singled out the mineral wealth of New Mexico as beckoning the South and even saw possibilities for slave-worked mining in Kansas. With fewer exaggerations De Bow, a decade earlier, had pointed to the political aspect of the problem: "Such is the strength and power of the Northern opposition that property, which is ever timid, and will seek no hazards, is excluded from the country in the person of the slave, and Southerners are forced, willingly or not, to remain at home. Emigrants, meanwhile, crowd from the North." During the bitter debate in Congress over the admission of California, Senator Jeremiah Clemens of Alabama replied heatedly to Clay in words similar to those used by De Bow. Free-soil agitation, he said, had kept slavery from the territories. "Property is proverbially timid.

The slaveholder would not carry his property there with a threat hanging over him that it was to be taken away by operation of law the moment he landed." Representative Joseph M. Root of Ohio, Whig and later Republican, commented on such charges by boasting that if the Wilmot Proviso had accomplished nothing more than to create a political climate inimical to slavery expansion, it had accomplished its purpose.

The Southern demand for federal guarantees made sense, but even that did not go far enough. Ultimately, the South needed not equal protection for slave property but complete political control. If a given territory could be organized by a proslavery party, then slaveholders would feel free to migrate. Time would be needed to allow the slave population to catch up; meanwhile, free-soil farmers had to be kept out in favor of men who looked forward to becoming slaveholders. Under such circumstances the territory's population might grow very slowly, and the exploitation of its resources might lag far behind that of the free territories. Nothing essential would be lost to the South by underdevelopment; the South as a whole was underdeveloped. In short, the question of political power necessarily had priority over the strictly economic questions.

Even if the South had looked forward to extending the cotton kingdom, the political question would have had to take priority. Douglass C. North has incisively described the rhythm of such extensions:

> Long swings in the price of cotton were the result of periods of excess capacity with a consequent elastic supply curve of cotton over a substantial range of output. Once demand had shifted to the right sufficiently to use all available cotton land, the supply curve became rather inelastic. A rise in cotton prices precipitated another move into new lands of the Southwest by planters and their slaves. Funds from the Northeast and England financed the transfer of slaves, purchase of land, and working capital during the period of clearing the land, preparing the soil and raising a cotton crop. There was a lag of approximately four or five years between the initial surge and the resulting large increase in output which caused a tremendous shift to the right in the supply curve and the beginning of another lengthy period of digesting the increased capacity.

Under such circumstances the political safety of slavery, especially during the difficult interlude North describes, always had to be assured before any significant economic advance could occur. Significantly, even the long-range possibility of irrigating the Southwest was noted in *De Bow's Review* as early as 1848.

Slavery certainly would have had a difficult time in Kansas, although as Nevins has shown, greater possibilities existed than Stephen Douglas or many historians since have been prepared to admit. The proslavery leaders there, Atchison and Stringfellow, fully appreciated the importance of the prior establishment of political power, as their rough tactics and ingenious scheme to monopolize the timber and water resources showed. Nevins, on the other hand, questions the ability of the South to provide settlers. We shall return to this objection.

For the moment let us consider Kansas as solely and inevitably a wheat state. Large slave plantations have not proved well adapted to wheat growing, but small plantations were doing well in the Virginia tidewater. In open competition with Northwestern farmers the slaveholders probably would have been hurt badly. They knew as much. When, for example, Percy Roberts of Mississippi maintained that

Negro slavery could thrive in the Northwest grain belt, he simultaneously maintained that the African slave trade would have to be reopened to drive down the cost of labor and put the slaveholders in a favorable competitive position. Historians like Nevins and Paul W. Gates have expressed confidence that slavery could not have triumphed in Kansas even if it had been allowed a foothold. They may be right, but only if one assumes that the South remained in the Union. Slavery expansionism required fastening proslavery regimes in such territories, but ultimately it required secession to protect the gains. Had Kansas joined a Southern Confederacy as a slave state, its wheat-growing slaveholders could have secured the same internal advantages as the sugar planters of Louisiana, and Union wheat could effectively have been placed at a competitive disadvantage in the Southern market.

Ramsdell's dismissal of Southern interest in Cuba and Central America, however necessary for his argument, does not bear examination. Southern sugar planters, who might have been expected to fear the glutting of the sugar market should Cuba enter the Union, spoke out for annexation. They seem to have been convinced that suspension of the Africa slave trade to Cuba would raise the cost of production there to American levels and that they would be able to buy Cuban slaves cheaply. Besides, as Basil Rauch points out, Louisiana sugar planters were moving to Cuba during the 1850s and looking forward to extending their fortunes. Southerners, like Northerners, often spoke of annexation in nationalist terms and sometimes went to great lengths to avoid the slavery question. J. J. Ampère heard that Cuba had been detached from the mainland by the Gulf Stream and rightfully belonged to the United States. He recommended that France reclaim Britain on the same grounds. He also heard that Cuba had to be annexed to provide a rest home for American consumptives. J. C. Reynolds, writing in *De Bow's Review* in 1850, described appalling losses in the illegal slave trade to Cuba and urged annexation to bring American law enforcement there and to end the terrible treatment of the Negroes. More sweepingly, some argued that without more territory the Negroes of the United States would be extinguished by overpopulation and attendant famine. All for the poor Negroes! Others, like Soulé and Albert Gallatin Brown, bluntly demanded Cuba and Central America to strengthen and defend slavery.

As for William Walker, he said enough to refute the Scroggs-Ramsdell interpretation. His *War in Nicaragua* makes clear that American politics made it necessary for him to appear to renounce annexation and that he was biding his time. No matter. His purpose there, as he boldly proclaimed, was to expand slavery as a system.

Opposition to territorial expansion by many Southerners has led some historians to deny the existence of an "aggressive slaveocracy" or to assert, with Ramsdell, that Southerners were too individualistic to be mobilized for such political adventures, which were often contrary to their private interests. No conspiracy theory is required. That there were many Southern leaders who sensed the need for more territory and fought for it is indisputable. That individual Southerners were not always willing to move when the interests of their class and system required them to merely indicates one of the ways in which slavery expansionism proved a contradictory process. Southerners opposed expansion for a variety of reasons, but mostly because they feared more free states. Expansion southward had the great advantage of not being cotton expansion, and the economic argument against it was weak. On the other hand, many feared that the annexation of Cuba would provide an excuse for the annexation of Canada or that the annexation of Mexico would repeat the experience of California. This opposition should be understood essentially as a preference for delaying expansion until secession had been effected, although there were, of course, many who opposed both.

The Anguish of Contradiction

If the slave South had to expand to survive, it paradoxically could not do so when given the opportunity. Unsettled political conditions prevented the immigration of slave property, much as the threat of nationalization or of a left-wing or nationalist coup prevents the flow of American capital to some underdeveloped countries to which it is invited.

"Where," asks Allan Nevins when discussing Kansas, "were proslavery settlers to come from? Arkansas, Texas, and New Mexico were all calling for slaveholding immigrants, and the two first were more attractive to Southerners than Kansas." Slave property necessarily moved cautiously and slowly. So long as it had to move at the pace set by Northern farmers, it would be defeated. The mere fact of competition discouraged the movement of slaveholders, and if they were willing to move, they could not hope to carry enough whites to win.

An area could be safely absorbed by the slave regime only by preventing Northern free-soilers from entering. Danhof has demonstrated that farm making was an expensive business.[2] Northern farmers had a hard time; Southern farmers, without slaves or minimal savings, found it much harder. Traditionally, the more energetic nonslaveholders moved into new land first and cleared it; the planters followed much later. If those early settlers had to secure the territory against free-soilism before the planters and slaveholders moved in, the struggle could not ordinarily be won. Many Southern nonslaveholders could be and were converted to the antislavery banner once they found themselves away from the power and influence of the slaveholders. Charles Robinson bitterly criticized John Brown for his inability to appreciate the possibilities of persuasion: "While our free state colonies were trying to convert the whites from the South and make them sound free-state men, John Brown thought it better to murder them."

Missouri and Kansas, therefore, were worlds apart. W. A. Seay, in an article entitled "Missouri Safe for the South," dismissed suggestions that Missouri would abolish slavery. The nonslaveholding counties, he noted, lay in the southern part of the state and were inhabited by men from other parts of the South who owned no slaves only because they were as yet too poor. Their allegiance to the system rested ultimately on the ability of the slaveholders to retain political power and social and ideological leadership and to prevent these men of the lower classes from seeing an alternative way of life. Yet, by 1860 even Missouri had become a battleground because of its special geographic position and Northern and foreign immigration. Kansas could never be secured for slavery unless the slaveholders had political control and the migrating Southern farmers were isolated from corrupting influences. As it was, Northerners, according to Representative William Barksdale of Mississippi, went as families, whereas Southerners often went as young adventurers who had no intention of remaining once the excitement was over.

The South's anguish arose from having to expand and being unable to meet the test of expansion set by life in mid-nineteenth-century America. Like T. S. Eliot's Hollow Men, it found that

> *Between the desire*
> *And the spasm*
> *Between the potency*
> *And the existence*
> *Between the essence*
> *And the descent*
> *Falls the shadow*

Only if a territory shut out free-soil immigration, quickly established the political hegemony of the slaveholders, and prepared for a much slower development than Northerners might give it, could it be secured for slavery. These conditions negated slavery expansionism, but only so long as the South remained in the Union.

Invitation to a (Self-Inflicted) Beheading

The South had to expand, and its leaders knew it. "There is not a slaveholder in this House or out of it," Judge Warner of Georgia declared in the House of Representatives in 1856, "but who knows perfectly well that whenever slavery is confined within certain specified limits, its future existence is doomed." The Republican party, said an editorial in *The Plantation* in 1860, denies that it wants to war on slavery, but it admits that it wants to surround it with free states. To do so would be to crush slavery where it now exists. Percy L. Rainwater's study of sentiment in Mississippi in the 1850s shows how firmly convinced slaveholders were that the system had to expand or die. Lincoln made the same point in his own way. He opposed any compromise on slavery expansion in 1860 because he feared new and bolder expansionist schemes and because he wished to contain slavery in order to guarantee its ultimate extinction.

Nevins' discussion of Lincoln's view illuminates one of the most tenacious and dubious assumptions on which many historians have based their interpretations of the origins of the war:

> In view of all the trends of nineteenth century civilization, the terrible problem of slavery could be given a final solution only upon the principle . . . of gradual emancipation. . . . The first step was to stop the expansion of slavery, and to confine the institution within the fifteen states it already possessed. Such a decision would be equivalent to a decree that slavery was marked for gradual evolution into a higher labor system. Slavery confined would be slavery under sentence of slow death. The second step would be the termination of slavery in the border states. Missouri by 1859 stood near the verge of emancipation . . .

The assumption on which these notions rest is that the South, faced with containment, could have accepted its consequences. On the further assumption that men may agree to commit suicide, the assumption is plausible.

If instead of speaking of the South or of the system of slavery, we speak of the slaveholders who ruled both, the assumption is less plausible. The extinction of slavery would have broken the power of the slaveholders in general and the planters in particular. Ideologically, these men had committed themselves to slaveholding and the plantation regime as the proper foundations of civilization.

Politically, the preservation of their power depended on the preservation of its economic base. Economically, the plantation system would have tottered under free labor conditions and would have existed under some intermediary form like sharecropping only at the expense of the old ruling class. The "higher" forms depended on the introduction of commercial relations that would have gradually undermined the planters and guaranteed the penetration of outside capital. We have the postbellum experience to cite here, although it took place at a time when the planters had suffered hard blows, but slaveholders saw the dangers before the war and before the blows. "Python," in a series of brilliant articles in *De Bow's Review* in 1860, warned that emancipation, even with some form of "apprenticeship" for the Negroes, would open the way for Northern capital to command the productive power of the South. Once Negro labor is linked to capital in the open market, he argued, rather than through the patriarchal system of plantation slavery, it will fall prey to a predatory, soulless, Northern capitalism. There will be no place left for the old master class, which will be crushed by the superior force of Northern capital and enterprise or absorbed into them. "Of what advantage is it to the South," he asked, "to be destroyed by Mr. Douglas through territorial sovereignty to the exclusion of Southern institutions, rather than by Mr. Seward through Congressional sovereignty to the same end? What difference is there to the South whether they are forcibly led to immolation by Seward, or accorded, in the alternative, the Roman privilege of selecting their own mode of death, by Douglas? Die they must in either event."

These words demonstrate that the probable effect of a "higher labor system" on the fortunes of the slaveholding class was not beyond the appreciation of its intellectual leaders. We need not try to prove that so specific an appreciation was general. The slaveholders knew their own power and could not help being suspicious of sweeping changes in their way of life, no matter how persuasively advanced. Their slaveholding psychology, habit of command, race pride, rural lordship, aristocratic pretensions, political domination, and economic strength militated in defense of the status quo. Under such circumstances an occasional voice warning that a conversion to tenantry or sharecropping carried serious dangers to their material interests sufficed to stiffen their resistance.

No demagogy or dogmatic speculation produced "Python's" fears. Even modest compensation—paid for by whom?—would have left the planters in a precarious position. At best, it would have extended their life as a class a little while longer than postbellum conditions permitted, but Northern capital could not long be kept from establishing direct relationships with tenants and sharecroppers. The planters would have steadily been reduced to middlemen of doubtful economic value or would have merged imperceptibly into a national business class. The change would have required, and eventually did require under disorderly postbellum conditions, extensive advances to laborers in the form of additional implements, fertilizer, household utensils, even food, and innumerable incidentals. This process guaranteed the disintegration of the old landowning class, however good an adjustment many of its members might have made to the new order.

Those who, like Max Weber, Ramsdell, even Phillips, and countless others, assume that the South could have accepted a peaceful transition to free labor gravely misjudge the character of its ruling class. The question of such a judgment is precisely what is at issue. As noted in the Introduction to this volume, a revisionist historian might accept the empirical findings reported here and even the specific interpretations of their economic significance and still draw different conclusions on the larger issues. The final set of conclusions, and the notion of a general crisis itself, eventually must rest on agreement that the slaveholders constituted a ruling class and that they displayed an ideology and psychology such as has merely been suggested in these studies.

The slaveholders, not the South, held the power to accede or resist. To these men slaves were a source of power, pride, and prestige, a duty and a responsibility, a privilege and a trust; slavery was the foundation of a special civilization imprinted with their own character. The defense of slavery, to them, meant the defense of their honor and dignity, which they saw as the essence of life. They could never agree to renounce the foundation of their power and moral sensibility and to undergo a metamorphosis into a class the nature and values of which were an inversion of their own. Slavery represented the cornerstone of their way of life, and life to them meant an honor and dignity associated with the power of command. When the slaveholders rose in insurrection, they knew what they were about: in the fullest sense, they were fighting for their lives.

NOTES

1 I find it strange that Nevins attacks this late antebellum demand as an abstraction; his own evidence indicates that it was of central importance to the slavery cause.

2 Clarence H. Danhof, "Farm-making Costs and the 'Safety Valve,'" *JPE, XLIX* (June 1941), 317–59. *Cf.* Nevins, *Emergence of Lincoln,* I, 159, on Kansas in the 1850s. Thomas Le Duc has argued that many farmers could and did squat in squalor while slowly building a farm: "Public Policy, Private Investment and Land Use in American Agriculture, 1825–1875, *Agr. Hist.,* XXXVII (Jan. 1963), 3–9. Even with this qualification, capital and resources were a big factor, and the competitive advantage of Northern farmers over Southern is beyond doubt. Only when circumstances permitted the massive movement of planters and slaves could the result be different.

Toward a New Civil War Revisionism JOHN ROSENBERG

The Marxist wing of the New Left regards the Civil War as an essential stage in the march of history. The less ideological New Left, like many of the liberals, has generally seen it as an equally necessary step in the destruction of slavery. Each group for its own reason, cheers for the Union and applauds its victory, for the Union cause was the progressive one.

Source: John Rosenberg, "Toward a New Civil War Revisionism," *American Scholar,* vol. 38, no. 2 (Spring 1969), pp. 250–272.

A newer mood has now begun to appear among some of the youngest radical scholars. This mood reflects the attitude, increasingly prevalent among black militants, that the War accomplished little for the black man. True, it granted him technical freedom, but as we can see when we look around us in modern America, that freedom is largely a sham. The black man is everywhere in de facto bondage, whatever the legal fiction may be. All that the Civil War accomplished was to free white Americans of guilt and enable them ultimately to avoid dealing with the fundamental racism of white society. Moreover, by making freedom, whether real or apparent, a gift of the white man, the Civil War denied the black man the opportunity to free himself. The myth of white liberation accordingly serves to deprive blacks of any sense of their own courage and autonomy, at the same time allowing whites to assume a moral credit they do not deserve.

Much of the New Left is strongly influenced by this new black militancy. Civil rights leadership, originally composed of young white radicals, is now drawn from the blacks themselves, and in other areas of radical concern, blacks have become the pacesetters. The article below, by a young white scholar, reflects this new tone. Though a white man, John Rosenberg in this piece clearly thinks black.

FOR FURTHER READING:

Herbert Aptheker, *American Negro Slave Revolts*, (Columbia University Press, 1943); Herbert Aptheker, *The Negro in the Civil War*, (International Publishing Company, 1938); Benjamin Quarles, *The Negro in the Civil War**, (Little, Brown and Company, 1969); Bell Wiley, *Southern Negroes, 1861–1865**, (Yale University Press, 1965); John Hope Franklin, *The Emancipation Proclamation**, (Doubleday and Company, 1963); Dudley T. Cornish, *Sable Arm: Negro Troops in the Union Army 1861–1865**, (Norton, 1966); Thomas Pressly, *Americans Interpret Their Civil War**, (Free Press, 1965); Arthur Schlesinger, Jr., "The Causes of the Civil War," *Partisan Review*, (October, 1949).

Asterisk denotes paperback edition.

"The Civil War," Robert Penn Warren has written, "is our only 'felt' history— history lived in the national imagination." In a fundamental sense it was not the "Second American Revolution" as Charles Beard maintained, it was the first; "we became a nation," as Warren stated, "only with the Civil War." It is our Civil War, not our war of separation from Great Britain, which has proved more durable as the source of our national identity; it is really Lincoln the savior, not Washington the founder, who personifies America. It is not surprising, then, that the way each generation has viewed our national epic has been inextricably bound up with the way it viewed the nation. Consequently, each generation has felt impelled to reinterpret the Civil War to itself and for itself.

Two of the major influences in this continual reinterpretation have been the issues of race and war; the manner in which not only professional historians but also the public at large have viewed these twin themes has had a great deal to do with the way they understood and evaluated the Civil War. Thus, two of the major interpretations of this century were profoundly affected by contemporary attitudes toward the Negro and toward American participation in the two world wars. One was written by a generation whose outlook was heavily influenced by the war of 1917 and its aftermath and which was largely indifferent to the problems of American Negroes; the other was written by the following generation, which had learned a different lesson from its experiences with World War II and the cold war and which showed greater concern for the conditions of Negroes in this country. Since the war in Vietnam and the domestic racial crisis are having a major impact on the outlook of a new generation, it would be surprising if another interpretation of the Civil War did not emerge. It is my intention to suggest the form such a new interpretation might take.

The interpretation that came to be known as "revisionist" challenged the popular Beardian view that the Civil War resulted from an irreconcilable economic clash, and it also rejected the earlier nationalist view that the war was an inevitable conflict between slavery and freedom. The leading advocates of the revisionist position, Avery O. Craven and James G. Randall, both shared in the widespread disillusionment with war that followed World War I. "Just as Americans beginning about 1935 executed something like an about face in their interpretation of the World War," wrote Randall in 1940, "so the retelling of the Civil War is a matter of changed and changing viewpoints. In the present troubled age," he continued, "it may be of more than academic interest to re-examine the human beings of that war generation with less thought of the 'splendor of battle flags' and with more of the sophisticated and unsentimental searchlight of reality."

Randall's writing reveals a profound disgust for war. "For the very word 'war,'" he claimed, "the realist would have to substitute some such term as 'organized murder' or 'human slaughterhouse.'" He criticized most writings about war because in them "the war is offstage in that its stench and hideousness do not appear." Although he was not as outspoken on this issue as Randall, Craven agreed that war was seldom justified. "Those who force the settlement of human problems by war," he wrote, "can expect only an unsympathetic hearing from the future. Mere desire to do 'right' is no defense at the bar of history."

The revisionists criticized the previous interpretations for assuming that the differences between the sections were irreconcilable and hence that man was incapable of avoiding the catastrophe of war. Thus, Randall's concern with "the human beings" of the war generation and Craven's criticism of "those who forced" the antagonism to the point of war reflected their belief that the war was caused by people and not by an irreconcilable conflict over basic issues. In his first major article, Craven charged that "differences—economic, social, and political—did not then [in 1825] or afterwards portend an 'irrepressible conflict' between North and South, to be settled only by bloodshed. The War Between the States in 1861–65 did not come simply because one section was agricultural and the other industrial; because one exploited free labor and the other slaves; or because a sectional majority refused to respect the constitutional rights of a minority!" Unlike Randall, Craven did believe that the sections were divided by economic interests, but he did not believe that these differences alone could have produced war.

For the revisionists to make their case that the differences between the sections were not basic enough to cause war, it was necessary for them to challenge the centrality of slavery. Randall did this by pointing out that the principal disputes were over runaway slaves and the extension of slavery into the territories. He thought that the numbers involved were too insignificant to lead to war (the census of 1860 listed eight hundred and three runaway slaves and two slaves in the Kansas territory) and that the whole question "was magnified into an issue altogether out of scale with its importance." Craven drew a distinction between slavery as a reality and slavery as a symbol. Of these two quite different slaveries, the first was economic and the second was psychological. And it was the psychological one that caused the trouble: "The first could be almost ignored in our study of sectional conflict had it not become the symbol of all sectional differences; the second leaves few pages of history from 1830 to 1860 untouched."

"Slavery," Craven thought, "was not a major economic fact in Southern life" or even the controlling factor in the life of the Negro. "The fact of his status as a slave may, in the main, be ignored. He should be thought of, first, only as a different racial element in the society. . . . " Slavery offered both advantages and disadvantages; there was little unusual about it. "What owning and being owned added to the usual relationship between employer and employee, it is difficult to say." In addition to his physical freedom and the right to drift aimlessly, Craven wrote, the slave was deprived of such things as "the dignity of responsibility and the stimulation of worry." His life partner was often chosen for him, which made his plight in that respect "as bad as that of European royalty but only a trifle worse than that of the rural whites. . . ." Slavery as a reality, then, was not really so bad and hence could not have produced a sectional conflict.

It is important to recognize the subtle but significant difference between Randall's and Craven's approach to the problem of slavery. As Professor David Potter has noted, "where Craven discounted the significance of slavery as an institution, Randall minimized its significance as an issue. One of his [Randall's] most effective arguments was his contention that, while the broad issue of freedom versus slavery may be worth a war, the issue as defined by the opposing forces in 1861 was not that broad, and was not worth a war in the form in which they defined it; for the Republicans in 1861 did not propose to emancipate the slaves, they even agreed in 1861 to guarantee slavery in the existing slave states and to return fugitive slaves to slavery."

In short, the revisionists did not believe that the war was caused by slavery or any other irreconcilable differences between the sections. Craven concluded that the conflict was made of "emotions, cultivated hostilities, and ultimately of hatred between the sections." This hatred was produced not by the wounds, which were slight, but by the salt of controversy poured on them: "Differences were but the materials with which passions worked. . . . The conflict was the work of politicians and pious cranks! The people knew little of each other as realities. They were both fighting mythical devils." Thus Craven traced the outbreak of hostilities to inept political leaders and fanatics who magnified what real divisions there were out of all proportion. "The move for an independent South which came to a climax in 1861 did not arise from permanent physical and social conditions," Craven wrote in 1939. "It sprang rather from temporary factors cultivated both without and within the section." Randall went so far as to claim that wars were never caused by basic issues. "One of the most colossal of misconceptions," he argued, "is the theory that fundamental motives produce war. The glaring and obvious fact is the artificiality of war-making agitation."

Where previous interpretations had explained the increase of emotionalism and the appearance of extremists as the result of the sectional conflict, of the historical situation itself, Craven and Randall viewed them as the cause of the conflict. The fatal crime the revisionists attributed to these "fanatics" and "demagogic politicians" was that they transformed real and concrete issues into abstractions, and hence presumably into the unreal. "What were but normal differences in the beginning of the period thus gradually became principle." Throughout revisionism runs the theme that principles, morals and abstractions were the wrench the fanatics threw into the works of democracy; the democratic process, so well equipped to handle "real" issues, was torn asunder when the dangerous and unnecessary questions of right and wrong were forced upon it. Thus, a "needless war" resulted when the "blundering generation" allowed "their short-sighted politicians, their over-zealous editors, and their pious reformers to emotionalize real and potential differences and to conjure up distorted impressions of those who dwelt in other parts of the nation." They turned "normal American conflicts" into "a struggle of civilizations."

Although the revisionists were nominally critical of the extremists in both sections, they usually reserved their most bitter condemnation for those in the North. The South is generally pictured as responding to external attack, its extremists spawned by those of the North. Craven, for example, was consistently more critical of the reformers than of the evils they were trying to correct. Claiming that the abolitionist movement "arose out of the apprehensions engendered by changes going on in the immediate environment of the reformers," he noted that historians were becoming "less inclined to grant unstinted praise to the fanatic and [are] not certain about the value of his contribution." In fact, Craven went so far as to wonder "if the developments of history might not have been more sound without him." Randall, too, seemed to single out the abolitionists, noting that their "avenging force of puritanism in politics" was "a major cause of the conflict." But in assessing guilt for the cardinal sin of substituting abstractions for realities, Craven employed a double standard. While he believed the abolitionists guilty of introducing questions of morality into politics and converting concrete issues into principles, Craven had a warm spot in his heart for Robert E. Lee, who, we are told, "chose to yield deeply held convictions regarding immediate concrete issues in order to stand by those intangible, yet more profound values which had to do with honor, with self-respect, and with duty."

From the 1930's onward revisionism enjoyed wide acceptance in the historical profession and society at large. It partially resulted from and appealed to a general disillusionment with war, and it also reflected a disappointment and loss of faith in the United States that was prevalent among intellectuals in the depressed thirties. Many believed that the immediate results of the Civil War, and even the society they lived in, did not justify the terrible sacrifices that had been necessary to achieve them. Randall spoke of "the hateful results of the war" and claimed that "the triumph of the Union was spoiled by the manner in which victory was used." Craven looked around at the United States in 1939 and saw "Workers talking of 'wage slavery,' capitalists piling fortunes high while poverty and starvation stalk the streets. . . . To such ends did three decades of quarreling and four years of bitter warfare make substantial contributions."

As late as 1950, Kenneth Stampp, an historian who seemed to share some of the revisionists' assumptions about war, closed his study of the secession crisis with the strong implication that the Civil War had been a disaster unmitigated by the bestowal of formal freedom on the slaves. According to Stampp, the conflict had ended "with the rich richer and the slaves only half free. Nationalists," he concluded bitterly, "might rejoice that the Union was preserved. But what the Yankees achieved—for their generation at least—was a triumph not of middle-class ideals but of middle-class vices. The most striking products of their crusade were the shoddy aristocracy of the North and the ragged children of the South. Among the masses of Americans there were no victors, only the vanquished." But despite this pessimistic conclusion, Stampp maintained that "Unless the concept of 'national interest' is reevaluated, their [that of the generation of 1861] decision, their choice of war rather than peace, must be accepted as just and right."

In 1950, when Stampp wrote, there was no sign that Americans were about to reevaluate the concept, or the sanctity, of their national interest. Americans tend to view themselves as the polar opposites of their enemies. Consequently, the experience of opposition both to the total evil of Nazi Germany and to the current cold war with another system of total evil, Stalinist Russia, tended to confirm the view that the American nation, whatever its minor flaws, was the embodiment of all the noble Western values. Perhaps America was not perfect, but it was certainly better than any alternative that had appeared. Fired by the hot war against Hitler and tempered by the cold one against Stalin, a new generation came to hold attitudes about America and about war that were strikingly at odds with those held by the generation of the thirties. Thus, the Civil War came to be celebrated as a necessary step on the way to a more perfect democracy and a more powerful nation. It was now assumed without question that the very existence of the country must be protected at all costs, by any means. A generation that had sanctioned the use of atomic weapons to speed the already certain defeat of the Japanese was not likely to quarrel with the use of war as a legitimate means of securing national objectives, and certainly not as a means of preserving the nation itself.

This resurgence of patriotism and renewed acceptance of war inevitably came to be reflected in the historical profession. In his presidential address to the American Historical Association in 1951, Samuel Eliot Morison commented favorably on this shift of attitudes. "There is," he said, "a decided change of attitude toward our past, a friendly, almost affectionate attitude. . . ." He had harsh words for those historians who, "caught in the disillusion that followed World War I, ignored wars, belittled wars, taught that no war was necessary and no war did any good, even to the victor." Instead of criticizing war, Morison urged, historians should point out that "war does accomplish something, that war is better than servitude, that war has been an inescapable aspect of the human story."

These post-World War II historians, whom Professor Thomas Pressly has called the "new nationalists," had themselves supported and participated in America's involvement in what they considered a just war. Believing from their own experience that wars were caused by very real ideological conflicts, they rejected the revisionist contention that "artificial agitation" was always the primary cause. Criticizing the revisionists for ignoring moral confrontation in history, these historians stressed the necessity for moral choice, both on the part of historical actors and historians themselves. Since the intractability of evil in the world made conflict a moral necessity, those so-called "moderates" who tried to effect compromises were nothing more than appeasers. As Arthur Schlesinger, Jr., the most articulate of the new nationalists, stated the problem of conflict and compromise: "The issue here posed —what policy would have averted war—goes down to the question we formulate today [1947] in terms of appeasement or resistance." Predictably, the new nationalists vigorously denounced the Crittenden Compromise, the last major effort at sectional conciliation.

Senator Crittenden of Kentucky had proposed a series of unamendable Constitutional amendments to protect slavery in the states where it existed and in the District of Columbia, to guarantee it beneath the line of 36° 30′, and to exclude it above that line. According to Professor Harold Hyman, "kudos for Crittenden's formula calls for conviction that any peace is better than any war." This "ignominious capitulation" could not be preferred over the Republicans' policy of firmness "unless prejudgement exists that anything is preferable to confrontation." Schlesinger similarly rules out compromise: "A society closed in defense of evil institutions," he wrote, "creates moral differences far too profound to be solved by compromise." The revisionists, he claimed, did not face the "hard fact" that "closed and authoritarian social systems tend to create a compulsive intransigence in their own ruling groups and that these groups may respond much more to a firmness which wakens them to some sense of actuality than to a forbearance which is never great enough and always to be discounted." One is tempted to conclude that Schlesinger and Hyman share a prejudgment that, where profound moral differences exist, any war is better than any peace.

In an influential article published in *Partisan Review* in 1949, Schlesinger mounted a sustained attack against revisionism. He argued that historians need moral sensitivity as much as objectivity to understand the past. "By denying themselves insight into the moral dimension of the slavery crisis," he contended, "the revisionists denied themselves a historical understanding of the intensities that caused the slavery crisis." By failing to recognize the significance of moral outrage, in other words, the revisionists were led to false conclusions about the war's causation. "Because the revisionists felt no moral outrage themselves, they deplored as fanatics those who did feel it, or brushed aside their feelings as the artificial product of emotion and propaganda."

Reintroducing moral outrage into the historical process, Schlesinger made a persuasive argument that indignation and emotion are no more "artificial" than anything else. Since "sometimes there is no escape from the implacabilities of moral decision," the abolitionist could not refrain—and hence should not be blamed for not refraining—from vehemently attacking slavery. "If revisionism has based itself on the conviction that things would have been different if only there had been no abolitionists, it has forgotten that abolitionism was as definite and irrevocable a factor in the historical situation as was slavery itself." Revealing the influence of his own experiences, he concluded that "To say that there 'should' have been no abolitionists in America before the Civil War is about as sensible as to say that there 'should' have been no anti-Nazis in the nineteen-thirties or that there 'should' be no anti-Communists today."

But Schlesinger did more than defend the abolitionists. In addition to defending their antislavery feelings, and the actions based on them, he justified the war they helped to produce. For the revisionists, the war was "needless" and "repressible" because the sectional conflict was not fundamental or necessary but was instead the artificial product of agitation by irrational extremists and a "blundering generation" of politicians. For Schlesinger, the war was an inevitable conflict between Good and Evil. Where the revisionists claimed that the debate over slavery in the territories was an "unreal" or "magnified" one about an imaginary slave in an impossible place, Schlesinger and the new nationalists compared the territories to Poland and the South to Germany. Schlesinger, for example, argued that, "The democracies could not challenge fascism inside Germany any more than opponents of slavery could challenge slavery inside the South, but the extension of slavery, like the extension of fascism, was an act of aggression which made a moral choice inescapable." And since resistance was preferable to appeasement, war was the only moral choice: the Civil War was "an 'irrepressible conflict,'" Schlesinger wrote, "and hence a justified one."

The new nationalists substituted a commitment to the moral necessity of war for the revisionists' disillusionment with it, and they heaped praise on the abolitionists' vigorous opposition to evil in place of the revisionists' criticism of their irrational extremism. Consequently, it is not unfair to say that the new nationalists, unlike the revisionists, believed, in words made famous by Senator Goldwater in another context, that "moderation in pursuit of justice is no virtue, and extremism in defense of liberty is no vice." Or, as Oscar Handlin put it, "There surely is a difference between a fanatic for freedom and a fanatic for slavery."

Schlesinger's interpretation reflected the outlook of liberal veterans of World War II and the cold war, but a new generation that has rejected so much of the affectionate attitude toward our past noted by Morison is likely to find this liberal version of our Civil War increasingly inadequate. As we move into the second century of the post-Civil War era, the lingering plight of American Negroes and the destructive impact of American nationalism on the rest of the world seriously challenge the justification of the Civil War—that it freed the slaves and preserved the nation—and calls for a new revisionism.

This new revisionism, it must be pointed out, is not really history at all; it is a new way of *evaluating* the Civil War, not of explaining it. Most historians are not willing to engage themselves in this kind of thinking. They are willing to explore the question of whether those who participated in the war or those who lived after the war but before the present felt it was justified, but they generally are reluctant to consider whether the war was justified or unjustified on the basis of what they think of America in 1969. Even if this were acceptable behavior on the part of professional historians, ordinary citizens surely need not recognize the scholarly injunction to refrain from personally judging and evaluating the past. Especially now, when an increasing number of young people are deeply concerned with the problem of justifying war, it is worthwhile to examine the justifiability of a war nearly all Americans regard as just.

Indeed, few historians themselves recognize their own injunction not to evaluate the past; the only difference is that their evaluations are usually unconscious. As the philosopher William Dray has pointed out, the historians' debate about the inevitability of the war has really been a debate about its justifiability. The core of these disputes has not been whether the war *could* have been avoided, but whether it *should* have been. "What they are quarreling about is surely the stand to be taken on a moral issue," Dray writes. "That issue is whether war with one's fellow countrymen is a greater moral evil than acquiescence in political and economic domination, or in the continuance of an institution like chattel slavery"—or, one might add, than peaceful separation.

The former revisionists, believing as they did that the war was unjustified, purported to show that it could have been avoided, and hence they blamed the entire generation for not avoiding it. A new revisionism, however, would not attempt a new historical explanation of the war; instead, it would openly be concerned with the manner in which Americans today view it. It would not blame the men of

1861 for a catastrophe that was probably beyond their capacity to avoid. Their problem was not that they were "blundering," but that they were normal; to have avoided war under the circumstances would have been heroic. A new revisionism, then, would challenge the prevalent assumption that that catastrophe was a worthwhile and justifiable sacrifice. Thus, a new revisionism would be concerned with current attitudes and not with the old question of historical inevitability. It is one thing to recognize that historical actors in many situations cannot reasonably be expected to have acted other than they did, but it is quite another to celebrate their actions as the new nationalists do. One may differ with the revisionists and *excuse* the men of 1861 without accepting the attempt of the new nationalists to *justify* their decision. One may empathize with them—a generation hopelessly entangled in a web of nationalism and slavery—and still severely criticize those historians who today view the war as a Good Thing. One may believe, as I do, that the Civil War —or more accurately, a civil war—was unavoidable and still believe that it was a tragedy that cannot be justified either by contemporary war aims or by the results it achieved. A new revisionism, then, would not deduce justifiability from inevitability as Schlesinger does.

Since a new revisionism would be openly presentist, would be concerned with evaluation from hindsight, the issue is not whether civil war in principle is a greater moral evil than slavery or secession, but whether the actual Civil War that occurred should be justified because of what it prevented or achieved. The two issues involved were slavery and union. The new nationalists claim that the Civil War was justified to abolish one and preserve the other; a new revisionism would argue that it was not. It would argue, first, that the mere preservation of the American nation against the will of a large number of its inhabitants does not justify any sacrifices, and, second, that the limited improvement in the status of the Negro in this country was not worth the expenditure in lives required to make that improvement possible.

Generally, those who justify the Civil War do so on the grounds that it freed the slaves, not that it saved the Union. If the war had ended "prematurely," and thus left slavery intact, presumably they would not now justify it. This was the position taken by most abolitionists, a number of whom, in fact, did fear that the war would end before the slaves were freed. But there were also a number of abolitionists who remained pacifists despite their hatred of slavery, or who were not pacifists but still would not support a war for the preservation of the Union on the mere possibility that the slaves would be freed in the process. Consequently, I think the crucial question the Civil War presents today to all who are not simple nationalists is whether its results have vindicated the many abolitionists who supported it or the few who did not.

Those today who justify the war predictably claim the results have vindicated its supporters. Despite their recognition that the official war aim was merely the preservation of the Union, those abolitionists who supported the war, such as William Lloyd Garrison and Wendell Phillips, did so because of their assumption, which proved correct, that winning the war would require emancipation. Despite their previous advocacy of disunion, they did an abrupt about-face when Fort Sumter was fired on. A pacifist until the war broke out, Garrison announced after Sumter: "All my sympathies and wishes are with the government, because it is entirely in the right, and acting strictly in self-defense and for self-preservation." Accused of inconsistency, he replied, "Well, ladies and gentlemen, when I said I would not sustain the Constitution because it was 'a covenant with death and an agreement with hell,' I had no idea I would live to see death and hell secede. Hence it is that I am now with the government to enable it to constitutionally stop the further ravages of death, and to extinguish the ravishes of hell." The North, cleansed of all its corruption and left virtuous by the South's secession, was thus engaged in a noble crusade.

These abolitionists knew that the government's only purpose was to save the Union, and their abandonment of disunion was not based exclusively on regard for the Negro's welfare; after Sumter they shared in the general surge of patriotic fervor that swept the North. Thus, in his famous speech announcing support for the war, Wendell Phillips stated that he believed "in the possibility of justice, in the certainty of Union." The American flag, which he said had previously represented slavery and oppression, had come to represent "sovereignty and justice," presumably in that order. Phillips, no longer thinking there was a conflict between union and freedom, became a staunch unionist. "Do you suppose I am not Yankee enough to buy Union when I can have it at a fair price?" he asked those who accused him of compromising his principles.

There were some abolitionists, however, who either were not Yankee enough or who did not think the price of war was fair, and a new revisionism would support their position. Lydia Maria Child, one of the most sensitive and perceptive people in this group, felt there was little "of either right principle, or good feeling, at the foundation of this unanimous Union sentiment." In addition to being upset because her husband had been almost mobbed at a Union meeting for suggesting that the government should help the slaves, she was dismayed at Lincoln's stated intention of not interfering with slavery where it existed and with General Butler's offer to use his Massachusetts troops to put down any slave rebellion in Maryland. "In view of these things," she wrote, "the Union-shouts, and hurrahs for the U. S. flag, sound like fiendish mockery in my ears." George Bassett, an Illinois abolitionist, could not support the war because "It is not a war for Negro liberty, but for national despotism." In a similar vein, an ex-Garrisonian at Yale was disturbed that "Abolitionists and Disunionists of thirty years' standing should now be found lending pen and voice to uphold and urge on a war waged solely and avowedly to preserve and perpetuate the Union. . . . Is anyone so blind as to fancy that the capitalists, who last winter were mobbing Mr. Phillips, have now struck hands with him for a crusade against slavery . . . ?"

The disillusionment and despair of these abolitionists were heightened by the fact that many of their former colleagues seemed to become themselves more interested in saving the Union than in freeing the slaves. Moncure Conway, whom some Eastern abolitionists had sent to England to represent their position, learned of the swelling nationalism among his colleagues the hard way. When it was learned that he had naïvely informed the Confederate envoy that the abolitionists would withdraw their support from the war if the Confederacy would free the slaves, he was soundly denounced in the North. Repudiating their envoy, the Boston *Commonwealth* and the *National Anti-Slavery Standard* announced that "the anti-slavery men will not sanction any proposal that included a recognition of the Confederacy." Conway was so crushed when he learned that many former abolitionists would prosecute the war even if slavery were not an issue that he abandoned not only the war but the United States itself and decided to stay in England. "It never entered my mind," he wrote his wife, "that any leading anti-slavery man wd question the principle involved—wd in any way support the war simply for conquest or Union whether Liberty were or were not involved. The wholesale slaughter of men is vile enough anyway; but to slaughter them except for the holiest cause is *worse* than treason to any government that does it."

In short, there were abolitionists who thought the North's cause was less than holy. Certainly at the time there was much to support their position, for there can be no doubt that the official purpose of the war, at least initially, was exclusively to save the Union. Even the New York *Tribune* declared that "this war is in truth a war for the preservation of the Union, not for the destruction of slavery. . . . We believe that slavery has nothing to fear from a Union triumph." Lincoln stated repeatedly that he had no intention of interfering with slavery, and the widely respected Springfield (Mass.) *Republican* wrote that "If there is one point of honor upon which more than another this administration will stick, it is its pledge not to interfere with slavery in the states." As late as August, 1862, Lincoln was precise and unequivocal as to his purpose. In his famous reply to Horace Greeley's advocacy of emancipation, the President who would be known as the Great Emancipator wrote: "My paramount obective in this struggle is to save the Union, and is not either to save or destroy slavery. If I could save the Union without freeing any slaves I would do it, and if I could save it by freeing all the slaves I would do it; and if I could save it by freeing some and leaving others alone I would also do that."

But, as we all know and as the pro-war abolitionists had predicted, Lincoln did decide that he had to free the slaves, or rather some of them, in order to save the Union (indeed, his letter to Greeley was written exactly one month after he wrote the first draft of the Emancipation Proclamation).[1] Even so, in retrospect it appears that those abolitionists who refused to follow Garrison and Phillips into active support of the war showed the greater wisdom, for the motives behind abolition and the Reconstruction amendments had serious effects on the quality of freedom thereby bestowed. It was obvious to many that freedom granted purely for the purpose of military necessity would be severely limited. As Lydia Maria Child accurately predicted in 1862, before the Emancipation Proclamation had been proclaimed, "Even should [the slaves] be emancipated, merely as a 'war necessity,' everything *must* go wrong, if there is no heart or conscience on the subject."

Just as there was no conscience in emancipation, so there was little in the Reconstruction legislation. The First Reconstruction Act, as C. Vann Woodward has recently written, "was not primarily devised for the protection of Negro rights and the provision of Negro equality. Its primary purpose, however awkwardly and poorly implemented, was to put the Southern States under the control of men loyal to the Union. . . ."

Indeed, as Woodward indicates, there is a great deal of evidence to suggest that the primary concern of most Reconstruction legislators was with whites in the North, not blacks in the South. It was feared that unless the freedom of the ex-slaves was secured in the South they would swarm over the North in search of it. There is even evidence that suggests that those who drafted the Fifteenth Amendment were more concerned with securing Republican majorities in the North (where most states still refused to enfranchise Negroes) than civil rights for Negroes in the South. This is not to deny that there was some sincere support for Negro rights, but, as Woodward points out, "it was not the antislavery idealists who shaped the Fifteenth

Amendment and guided it through Congress. The effective leaders of legislative action were moderates with practical political considerations in mind—particularly that thin margin of difference in partisan voting strength in certain Northern states." The Fifteenth Amendment has often been seen as the crowning success of idealistic Northern war aims. But read more carefully, as Woodward concludes, it "reveals more deviousness than clarity of purpose, more partisan needs than idealistic aims, more timidity than boldness." Thus, if we are to justify the Civil War because it led to Reconstruction, our justification must be based on the legal possibilities Reconstruction created for future generations, not what it actually achieved or even tried to achieve for the slaves, whom it only partially freed.

What little progress Negroes have been allowed to achieve has occurred almost exclusively in the past fifteen years. There is no doubt that the achievements of what Woodward calls the Second Reconstruction would have been a great deal more difficult without those of the First, but are those achievements enough to justify the ravages of our Civil War? The question is not whether Negroes are better off today than they would have been had there been no war. We may assume that they are. The question is whether the quantity and quality of freedom our society has been willing to grant is valuable enough to justify the death of one man for every six slaves who were freed. Everyone must work out his own equation for the moral calculus of war, his own formula to match ends with means. It is worth pointing out, however, that liberals generally object to sacrificing one generation for the possible benefit of the next, at least when other societies do it. It is no secret that real freedom for the Negro remained much more of a promise, or a hope, than a reality for nearly a century after the Civil War. Since Arthur Schlesinger, Jr., justified the war primarily as a noble fight for freedom, it is difficult to understand how he could have been so optimistic about the results in 1949 when he wrote his article in *Partisan Review*. One wonders what examples of Negro freedom, what applications and affirmations of the Fourteenth Amendment, so inspired him that he was able to look with favor on a war that had sacrificed six hundred thousand lives on the altar of that freedom.

I have no illusions about the Negroes' fate had they not been freed by the war, and it could reasonably be argued that I would not question the efficacy or the morality of the war if I were black. Perhaps. But certainly there are many black militants today who feel no gratitude toward their emancipators, nor should they. They argue quite effectively that it would have been much better for all concerned if the slaves had seized their freedom rather than receive it in bits and pieces as a result of quarrels among their oppressors. Our image of the "Sambo personality" and the happy, docile slave reinforces our skepticism that a successful slave revolt could have occurred, but no one can be sure of what might have been. As Eugene Genovese has pointed out, slaves in Saint Domingue were described in the same fashion as Southern Sambos, until, that is, they rose up in the greatest slave revolt in history. If, as Genovese suggests, the French Jacobins had taken power in 1790 instead of 1794 and the slaves had been freed "as the result of the vicissitudes of Jacobin-Girondist factionalism," there would now be Haitian scholars attempting to explain the black's docility in the face of oppression.

This is not, of course, to suggest that there would have been a slave rebellion, but it does suggest that we are foolish if we assume that "it couldn't happen here." Even if slavery or some modified form of oppression (but what have we had if not modified oppression?) had lasted well into the twentieth century, there is no reason to assume that it would have lasted forever. The blacks would certainly have shared in the wave of anticolonial feelings that has swept up other oppressed peoples in this century. Indeed, they are sharing in it even though supposedly freed. Even if an independent South resembled South Africa (which is unlikely since there has been cultural interdependence between the races in the South), there is room to question whether the difference between the conditions of Negro life in America and South Africa is so great as to justify over half a million deaths. Are we so accustomed to organized violence that we automatically accept without question the conclusion that the Civil War was justified even though it merely loosened the shackles of slavery? Can we be so sure that the privilege of moving from the plantation to the ghetto is worth the death and destruction of a brutal war?

It could be argued that even though emancipation has not been complete, it nevertheless was a necessary preliminary to any future progress. It is true, of course, that history will not end this year, but this bit of knowledge is of limited value in evaluating the war. The argument of future progress—that the results of emancipation are not yet known—requires an optimism about the future that America's treatment of the blacks in the past and present does not support. Moreover, the further into the future one projects this potential progress, the more difficult it becomes to argue that such progress would have been impossible but for emancipation in 1865.

Another argument against a new revisionism is that the Civil War can be justified by what it prevented, if not by what it achieved. But one need not argue that Negroes are no better off because of the war; the question is whether there has been enough real, as opposed to merely legal, improvement to justify the terrible sacrifices required to achieve it. Even admitting that the Negroes' plight has lessened, however, it is hard to say how much of that improvement is simply the seepage of industrial development and our involvement in two world wars. And it is highly unlikely that the spread of slavery into the territories or the South's peaceful secession would have thwarted forever the development of industrialism and technology. It is possible that emancipation in 1865 speeded up the process, but that is a far different matter from saying that improvement in the Negroes' condition would have been impossible without the Civil War. It is certainly possible to imagine other paths to the present and future (or another present and future) which, although they may have been worse than the one we have followed, would not have been enough worse to make up for the many who involuntarily paid for the difference with their lives.

The only other justification for the Civil War, that it preserved the American Union, is less difficult to deal with. Ever since the Puritans attempted to build their City on a Hill, Americans have assumed that their country was morally set off from Europe; commentators on our national character have all pointed to the qualities of innocence and virtuousness, of freedom from the guilt and corruption of the Old World, in Americans' conceptions of themselves.

Robert Penn Warren has argued that this feeling of moral superiority, the "Treasury of Virtue," as he calls it, derived in large part from the experience of freeing the slaves in the Civil War. Despite the overwhelming evidence that emancipation was merely a by-product of the war, not its purpose, the doctrine of the Treasury of Virtue views the war as a purposeful crusade so full of righteousness that there was enough left over to make up for whatever small failings subsequently occurred. "From the start," Warren wrote, "America had had adequate baggage of self-righteousness and phariseeism, but with the Civil War came grace abounding. . . . From the start, Americans had a strong tendency to think of their land as the galahad among nations, and the Civil War, with its happy marriage of victory and virtue, converted this tendency into an article of faith nearly as sacrosanct as the Declaration of Independence." This assumption of American virtue, of American grace in a sinful world, was reinforced by the experience of opposition to the tyrannies of Hitler and Stalin and was reflected in much of the new nationalist historiography.

There is a great paradox in this contemporary liberal view of our history. It is well known that this hardheaded, tough-minded, pragmatic liberalism, the liberalism exemplified by Arthur Schlesinger, Jr., is rooted in the moral and philosophical assumptions associated with Reinhold Niebuhr. But along with their pessimistic view of man and tragic view of history, derived from Niebuhr, these liberals incongruously link a highly sanguine and favorable view of the United States. According to Niebuhr, it is all but impossible for societies to act morally, but according to this liberal version of our history the United States has nearly always done so. Where the Niebuhrian universe is filled with fallible men, insoluble moral problems, and complex societies where good and evil (but mostly evil) are woven inextricably together, Schlesinger's liberalism seems to see a history that reveals a virtuous, perfectible America opposing various enemies—the South, Germany, Russia—that are totally evil.

It should be pointed out that Niebuhr's disciples did not depart from his position any more than he did himself. In *Moral Man and Immoral Society* he had written that nations become even more hypocritical than usual in time of war. "In the imagination of the simple patriot the nation is not society but Society. Though its values are relative they appear . . . to be absolute. The religious instinct for the absolute is no less potent in patriotic religion than any other. The nation is always endowed with the aura of the sacred. . . . " Niebuhr is no simple patriot, but the impact of war, hot and cold, did bring him under the influence of patriotic religion. As Christopher Lasch has pointed out, Niebuhr, like many others, believed the cold war forced an ultimate choice between "Marxist despotism" and the "open society" of the West. As the leader of the "Free World," America, in short, became "Society," its values absolute, its existence sacred.

Thus, the tough-minded liberal view of the Civil War was informed by an assumption that the hard reality of evil made conflict necessary and by a commitment to the preservation of the United States at all costs. Schlesinger accused the revisionists of being "sentimentalists" who attempted to "escape from the severe demands of moral decision," who believed that "evil will be 'outmoded' by progress and that politics consequently does not impose on us the necessity for decision and for struggle." But this "realism" now seems equally sentimental for believing that total war can be moral and that America is exempt from the fallibility, self-interest, and collective egoism that Niebuhr's outlook attributes to other nations. If the revisionists were sentimentalists for putting their faith in Progress, certainly Niebuhrian liberals are equally sentimental for putting theirs in the United States. If the revisionists were optimistic for believing that the Civil War could be avoided,

Schlesinger and his sympathizers are equally optimistic for believing that the forward march of American progress justifies all the sacrifices along the way.

For despite the participants in the American Celebration, the recent behavior of the United States does not inspire certainty that its preservation was worth whatever sacrifices other generations were called on to make. Arguments that nearly any amount of death and suffering one hundred years ago were justified to preserve the United States because of its moral attributes can no longer be maintained, if, indeed, they ever could. It has become clear that we are a nation like all nations, that as a Great Power we are behaving no more morally than have other Great Powers.

Since the Civil War, if not before, the pursuit of national policy has required the abandonment of many national ideals. Born on the proposition that legitimate government requires the consent of the governed, the United States nevertheless found it necessary to retain the allegiance of a substantial part of its population by force. Some of the more doctrinaire radicals of the time could not support this effort. "The same principle that has always made me an uncompromising abolitionist," said George Bassett, "now makes me an uncompromising secessionist. It is the great natural and sacred right of self-government." The radicalism of his contemporaries, however, had been replaced by an uncompromising nationalism. There is a revealing parallel between the Northern position in the Civil War and recent American interventions in other civil wars. In both cases there is a professed commitment to the principle of self-determination, but in both cases some attribute of those determining themselves invalidates the principle. In the case of the South, it was the presence of slavery; in our recent interventions, it was the presence of Communists, supposed or real, on one side of the conflict.

Niebuhr has noted the irony involved in this compromising of ideals by both the Communists and the United States, although he thinks the Communists have jettisoned their earlier values far more willingly and completely than has the United States. "Insofar as communism tries to cover the ironic contrast beween its original dreams of justice and virtue and its present realities by more and more desperate efforts to prove its tyranny to be 'democracy' and its imperialism to be the achievement of universal peace, it has already dissolved irony into pure evil."

The tyranny of our ghettoes and a "freedom" for Negroes that allows them an equal opportunity only to be killed in a cruel and unjust war have gone a long way toward dissolving America's own irony. For those who are no longer communicants in our patriotic religion, the Civil War begins to appear as a tragedy unjustified by its results. In addition to realizing that war itself is at least as evil as any human or ideological enemy, many Americans have come to deemphasize the significance of merely legal reforms, which have only a limited effect on the quality of most people's lives. Since the former revisionists were not overly concerned with the plight of the Negro, they held that a war over his status was irrational and unnecessary. The new nationalists, on the other hand, were keenly sensitive to the immorality of chattel slavery, and they were willing to justify nearly any extreme to eradicate it. But after more than a hundred years of emancipation, over a decade since the Brown decision, and several civil rights laws, it is now apparent that much more than legal change is required to constitute real progress. How naïve it now seems to justify the slaughter of six hundred thousand men for the slim reward of a formalistic and incomplete emancipation. Lydia Maria Child was right: because the nation has not demonstrated much "heart or conscience" on the subject of freedom for the ex-slaves, everything has gone wrong.

It will be apparent that a new revisionism such as the one outlined above would, like all previous interpretations of the Civil War, be firmly rooted in its own time. Consequently, it may be invalidated (indeed, one hopes it will be invalidated) by future developments: if significant gains are made by Negroes, and those gains are seen as dependent upon emancipation in 1865, then perhaps the sacrifices of the war should be regarded as justified. Thus the new revisionism may become as naïve as the new nationalists' interpretation now seems, but unfortunately it does seem appropriate for our own time. Even Lincoln can be called upon to support this view. At Gettysburg, he solemnly requested his audience to join him in resolving ". . . that these dead shall not have died in vain; that this nation, under God, shall have a new birth of freedom; and that this government of the people, by the people, for the people, shall not perish from the earth." This government did not perish from the earth, but that new birth of freedom never occurred. Sadly, we must conclude that those dead did die in vain.

NOTES

1. The Proclamation applied only to those areas in the South still at war with the United States, not to those under federal control. It was said at the time that Lincoln freed the slaves only where he did not have power to do so. As the London *Spectator* dryly observed, the underlying principle was "not that a human being cannot justly own another, but that he cannot own him unless he is loyal to the United States."

The Transformation of Reality and the Inception of New Ideas   WILLIAM APPLEMAN WILLIAMS

As we have noted above, William A. Williams, though one of the fathers of New Left American history, is an intense individualist and cannot be easily placed in any niche. It is no surprise that his interpretation of Radical Reconstruction is in some ways unique. While he accepts the predictable view that the Radicals represented the industrial interest, and their program for the South was intended to protect and nurture that interest, he is unwilling to ignore the real complexity of events. He observes, for example, that the business groups were not completely united. They often had conflicting views of national policy and differed considerably among themselves on such matters as financial policy and the tariff. Much of Williams' explanation, moreover, is informed by his thesis regarding the differences that run through our history between the mercantilists and the laissez-faire-ists.

Source: William Appleman Williams, *The Contours of American History* (Chicago: Quadrangle Books, 1966), "The Transformation of Reality and the Inception of New Ideas," pp. 300–319.

Yet the basic elements of the New Left perspective of Reconstruction are all here too: the failure to give land to the freedmen owing to the Radicals' inability to see beyond the sanctity of private property; the class element in race relations in the South; and, of course, the close association between expanding industrial horizons and the political and social arrangements constructed for the South by the Radicals. All of these, skillfully interwoven with much of the social and economic history of the generation following Appomattox, mark this selection as a fine, succinct summary of what the New Left believes Reconstruction was all about.

FOR FURTHER READING:

Kenneth Stampp, *The Era of Reconstruction, 1865–1877**, (Alfred A. Knopf, 1965); John Hope Franklin, *Reconstruction After the Civil War**, (University of Chicago Press, 1961); James S. Allen, *Reconstruction: The Battle for Democracy**, (International Publishing Company, 1937); Howard K. Beale, *The Critical Year: A Study of Andrew Johnson and Reconstruction*, (Ungar, 1958); James McPherson, *The Struggle for Equality: Abolitionists and the Negro in the Civil War and Reconstruction**, (Princeton University Press, 1964); W.E.B. DuBois, *Black Reconstruction in America**, (Russell, 1956); Irwin Unger, *The Greenback Era: A Social and Political History of American Finance 1865–1879**, (Princeton University Press, 1968).

Asterisk denotes paperback edition.

Reconstruction as a National Phenomenon

In some important ways . . . the Civil War did not produce an unconditional defeat of the south as is so often assumed. The south was beaten in the field, occupied and ruled in surrender, and in some respects treated as a colony. But counterattacking with the Negro problem and with the subversive weapon of economic opportunity, it found weak spots in the north's main line. For if there was an era of reconstruction in the south presided over by the north, there was just as certainly an era of reconstruction in the north that was not really presided over by anybody; it was a bitter and violent struggle among the major elements of the new industrialism, the older entrepreneurs and bourgeoisie, and the agrarians and laborers. The old sectional alignments and economic structure were disrupted by the railroads, the rising financiers, the factory, and the institution of the corporation.

Hence the conservative and radical wings of the revolutionary laissez-faire coalition that supplied the dynamic power of the Civil War found themselves not only at odds with each other and the south, but beset by new opponents within the north. As in all revolutions, the hard core of radicals offered the most nearly integrated set of attitudes and policies. Thoroughgoing advocates of classic individualistic and entrepreneurial laissez-faire capitalism, men like Benjamin F. Wade of Ohio, Benjamin F. Butler of Massachusetts, William D. (Pig Iron) Kelley and Thaddeus Stevens of Pennsylvania, and John A. Griswold of New York, had four primary objectives.

They wanted to establish the long-term predominance of the Republican Party throughout the south and the north, with themselves in control of it. To that end, and also because they were willing and even anxious to apply the principles of pure laissez faire across the board *at home,* they wished to free the Negro and then establish him as an element in the political economy. While not all the radicals accepted it as a program, the cry of "40 acres and a mule" for the Negro caught the spirit of this approach. Entrenched in power and having humbled the south, they could enact legislation that would establish the framework for their kind of capitalism.

"Get the rebel States into a territorial condition," Stevens advised, "and it can easily be managed." To acquire and hold the necessary voting strength, the radicals offered a high tariff for manufacturing, free land for dirt farmers, land and other subsidies to the railroads, soft (or inflationary) money for all expanding entrepreneurs, jobs or land to workers and immigrants, control of the cotton market and domestic trade to New Englanders, and the south as a new frontier to northern entrepreneurs and politicians. With this strategy in mind, the radicals badgered Lincoln incessantly for an edict of emancipation, fought him on other issues, and used the northern army to control the south while they sought to remake it in their image of laissez faire.

But the radicals lacked the power to transform their vision of the true laissez-faire society into reality. Hence, though the Civil War was brought on by a revolutionary coalition, it did not become a truly revolutionary war. In the language of the French Revolution, the Thermidorian reaction proceeded concurrently with the revolution itself. The result was a society trying to deal with the circumstances of maturing institutional industrialism by using the ideas and the ethic of individualist laissez faire.

Property rights and anti-Negro prejudice were the reefs that ripped open the frigate Revolution. In a fundamental sense, of course, the conflict between property rights and a laissez-faire revolution was built into the *Weltanschauung*, just as was a similar dilemma into the mercantilist's outlook. For private property was (and is) the cornerstone of the laissez-faire system, and hence revolutionaries who proposed to act on the principle of domestic confiscation of property in order to establish the prerequisites of the system put their hand on the lid of Karl Marx's Box.

The trap was apparent: if it was permissible to take private property in order to establish or maintain laissez faire, then no sophistry could deny the equal right to take it in order to construct socialism. Only a few of the radical leaders—Wendell Phillips was one of them—proved willing to follow their ideals and their logic to a candid realization that socialism rather than capitalism would provide the kind of society that they wanted. Most radicals saw the danger and drew back. Conservatives never considered the idea. Nothing illustrates the triumph of property rights more clearly than the subsequent practice of pinning the label "communist" on even those merchants and wholly bourgeois dirt farmers who in the 1870s, and later, wanted to regulate the railroads in order to restore competition in the market place. And on the Negro issue, the problem of property rights was further reinforced by general economic and social considerations. As it was in the beginning, so did the antislavery coalition remained predominantly anti-Negro.

Lincoln grasped the troubles of a laissez-faire revolution that was caught, on the one hand, in the contradictions of its theory and, on the other, between those ideas and the reality of the changes that were taking place. "The dogmas of the quiet past are inadequate to the stormy present," he flatly announced in his intense argument of 1862 for compensated emancipation. "We must think anew and act anew. We must disenthrall ourselves, and then we shall save the country." But neither Lincoln nor anyone else made this vital breakthrough. Hence the soul of laissez faire went marching on into a world of vastly different substance and proportions. This dichotomy provides the fundamental insight into American history after Fort Sumter.

Lincoln's failure to present a postwar program meant that he simply did not have one. But admittedly it was difficult to develop policies that combined antislavery and prowhite attitudes without at the same time classifying the Civil War as a traditional political and economic conflict. Liberal historians have been trying ever since to square this circle. Lincoln's own approach to reconstruction in the south pointed toward the kind of compromise that was ultimately made between 1874 and 1880. Lincoln's death opened the way for the radicals, but they lacked the power to execute fully even that part of their program based on honoring private property. They were never more than a bare plurality in the north even at the height of their influence, southerners proved masters of political guerrilla warfare, and the dynamic development of the north during and after the war so mangled the old political economy that the radicals could not muster a new coalition on any grounds.

These northern developments gave the southern conservatives the opportunity to reassert their power. They did so, however, in a society where industry, and especially the railroad corporation, was playing an increasingly important role. The Civil War was not the first modern or industrial war. It was the last merchant-agrarian war. It produced an industrial system rather than being fought with one. While there is a basic timelessness, for example, about the situation and the human crisis in Stephen Crane's *The Red Badge of Courage,* no one who has known combat in a modern war would seriously maintain that the story delineates the problem of bravery, or even captures the sense of what Crane's protagonist called "the great death," in the context of modern war where machines define men as wiggles in a line on a radarscope.

As railroads played an increasing role in northern logistics and troop movements, they also announced the coming of a new order. They extended and integrated the market place and so made it possible to specialize and consequently accelerate other economic activities. This was a tremendous boost for cities, and by the 1870s the pattern of industrial urbanism was firmly established. Railroads symbolized the steady rise of the corporation as a form and way of organizing economic activity, and revealed the depersonalizing of labor that went with this institution. By the 1870s, for example, 520 of 10,395 businesses in Massachusetts were incorporated. But the 520 held $131,182,090 of the $135,892,712 total capital, and employed 101,337 of the 166,588 workers.

The accumulation of capital for such corporations being a major task, the financier became more important both as an active entrepreneur and as a supplier of commercial services. Railroads not only developed close connections with such investment firms, but generally reintroduced the idea of thinking about the economic life of the country as a system. Yet they did so, not as public leaders as in the days of mercantilism, but as private leaders of one of the functional groups and institutions that were becoming the competing units of laissez faire. Hence the individual began losing his effective power and sense of relevance at an increasing rate. Yet at the same time the wide powers of private leaders began to create a kind of harmony in the system which tended to reinforce the ideology of laissez faire even though it ultimately became irrelevant to the reality of the system.

Clearly enough, these aspects of the railroad did not mature immediately. It is vital to recognize, however, that they did have an immediate impact. Given a national transportation system, for example, general advertising became feasible. A New York firm promptly responded and in 1879 began making market analyses and supplying plans, writers, and artists for advertising campaigns. Functional groups —such as the American National Steel Manufacturers, the Iron Founders Association, the National Board of Trade—formed their own organizations. The basic pattern is well exemplified in the American Bar Association, organized in 1878.

In the narrow sense, the lawyers staunchly upheld individualism, private property, and laissez faire. "The great curse of the world," they declared, "is too much government." But they also accepted the individual's shift to corporate organization and the concurrent restriction of the market place. Defending monopoly as "often a necessity and an advantage," they justified trusts as "a defensive weapon of property interests against the communistic trend." And some members were even then, like Samuel J. Tilden, corporation lawyers who had gone into politics with this more inclusive and systematic view of political economy. Such men personified the beginnings of a new gentry composed of economic giants and professional politicians who would ultimately assert their power over national life.

But the combination of Lincoln's death and the determined and traditional agrarian conservatism of President Johnson gave the radicals an opportunity to extend and consolidate their power. Johnson might have effected a moderate compromise with the south, for there was considerable sympathy, both active and latent, for such a reconciliation, but his unyielding position played into the hands of men like Stevens and Sumner, and William Pitt Fessenden of Maine. Rallying support by calling up the specter of a southern victory-in-defeat, and stressing the survival of the Republican Party and the new industrialism, the radicals effectively defeated the President. Their effort to impeach him failed, but it was in all essential respects an unnecessary attempt. In dramatizing the power of the legislature as against the executive it provided a classic manifestation of the spirit of laissez faire.

The more important failure of the extreme radicals (or revolutionaries) was their inability to handle the issue of providing the Negro with property. Once that objective was abandoned, the radical program consisted of three contradictory pairs of policies and attitudes: high tariffs and low land costs; great malice and little restraint; soft money and hard politics. Hence the radicals were successful only as long as they could sustain wartime and political emotions, as long as westerners were primarily concerned with real estate, until southern whites reasserted their power, and until a new combination of financiers, merchants, and farmers established itself as a competing alliance in the north.

Crosscurrents of Reconstruction

Having passed the tariff of 1864, given the farmer the Homestead Act of 1862 (along with formal representation in the government and educational aid), and subsidized the railroads, the radicals occupied the south and jammed through the 13th, 14th, and 15th Amendments which ostensibly ended slavery, defined the Negro as a citizen and asserted his right to vote. Though they were not in any sense guiding a mass movement to liberate the Negro and remake the south, the radicals had considerable support for their program. In the negative sense, which may have been the most important, many Americans were preoccupied with the exploiting of their own opportunities and simply acquiesced. Yet as indicated by the frequency with which various individuals and groups in the north used the term "imperialism" to describe their own operations as well as those of their competitors, a good many participated actively in the reconstruction program. And a surprising number of westerners, like the wool growers and others who hoped to industrialize the upper Mississippi Valley at a faster rate, even supported the tariff.

Financial leaders, on the other hand, were less enthusiastic about the radical policy of soft money. Bankers did not like having the government in the money business, and had opposed the National Banking Act of 1862. Their gains from inflation were small. Along with a good many of the rising corporation industrialists, such financial spokesmen were likewise cool to any wholesale equality for the Negro; the other side of that attitude was a desire, particularly strong among New York merchants, to restore their prewar economic connections with the south. And in addition to the merchants, who were always inclined toward low tariffs or free trade, some manufacturers and politicians were shifting away from high rates. Some of them had been frightened by the Panic of 1857 or had supported increases as a war measure. But others began to argue that the new industrial system would need foreign markets for its surpluses; hence high tariffs would only invite retaliation abroad. In the first years after the war, however, these various elements were too weak to disrupt the radical program once it was put into operation.

Radical difficulties began with the collapse of the alliance between Pennsylvania entrepreneurs and New England textile and manufacturing interests. Originally the product of a happy union between laissez-faire idealism and self-interest, the coalition agreed on support for the iron industry and a project involving the organization of the Negro to produce cotton on Gargantuan plantations managed by the Freedman's Bureau. Cotton would then be taxed if exported. The anticipated result, in conjunction with the Bureau's political and educational projects, was cheap cotton for New England, general business control of the south, and a solid Republican vote from the Negro. But southern devastation, poor weather in the year of the crucial crop, and Britain's ability to find cotton elsewhere combined to defeat the plan.

Boston bounced back with a low-tariff strategy designed to win western support and replace New York as the financial and mercantile center of the country. In a completely logical way, therefore, the radical coalition was disrupted by the loyalty of its members to the laissez-faire axiom of following their own particular interests. New England stressed trade and textiles while Pennsylvania emphasized iron and steel. Boston's switch was important, but the radicals were also weakened by the south's increasing ability to resist outside control, by other divisions in the north, and by a fortuitous food shortage in Europe.

Western manufacturers like Cyrus McCormick responded favorably to the New England return to low tariffs. McCormick concluded that he would reap more profits indirectly through expanded foreign markets for the farmers' crops than he would by being protected against imported machinery. Farmers wanted the overseas sales, and also remembered the south as an old customer and political ally with whom they might again do business. And western merchants and other businessmen were anxious to restore their prewar trade with the south, or to enter it for the first time. The merchants took the lead. "Commerce must bear the burden of taxation and businessmen are the best judges of their own wants, and what will most conduce to their prosperity," they declared at a national meeting in Detroit in 1865, adding that it "behooves them to take a deeper interest in governmental affairs."

After organizing the National Board of Trade in 1868, the merchant alliance then obtained a direct import law (1870) that made it possible to ship goods directly to inland cities before paying customs. This effectively by-passed New York in many transactions and gave Boston and the western merchants a strong competitive position in the southern and territorial markets. Coinciding with the south's lack of capital with which to regenerate and diversify its economy, and with the Negro's difficulty in finding employment at anything but agricultural labor, this northern businessmen's coalition consolidated the new economic slavery of tenant farming, sharecropping, and the planter store. Shackled to the cotton crop, the Negro (and his white counterpart) became perennial debtors to their new overseers. While it exaggerates the reality, there is a significant measure of truth in the idea that the Civil War gave more freedom —at least in the short run—to the white upper class of the south than it did to the slave. Both were liberated, but the one group far more effectively.

As should be apparent, the merchant-planter-store system involved the railroads and the monetary system in every transaction. Consequently one group of businessmen and farmers joined the financial interests in favoring a deflationary money policy; they concluded that inflation hurt them more than it helped. A similar coalition, led by radicals like Stevens, and generally based on the expanding iron and steel industry, preferred to keep the wartime greenback paper-money system and even to expand it. They argued vigorously that contraction would retard economic development ("Businessmen are hungry for money."), operate unfairly against everyone except bondholders, and hurt domestic manufacturers by undercutting the tariff. Since the per-capita money supply had declined from $30.35 in 1865 to $17.51 in 1876, the argument had considerable relevance. But the vote in the Congress on contraction revealed that the west was almost evenly divided (36 yes to 35 no), and the combination of a good harvest and foreign-crop failures temporarily damped the farmer's insurgency.

Thus sustained, the alliance between eastern and western businessmen, including farmers, turned away from the money issue to the question of railroad abuses. As much opposed in their own way to railroad policies as the western farmers, the merchants not only helped to initiate the attack on the lines in both sections of the north, but the New York group joined forces with their Boston and Chicago competitors on the issue. Anger against the roads had appeared as early as 1863, and the House of Representatives had passed regulatory laws in 1874 and 1878 only to have them ignored by the Senate.

Regulation as an Essential Feature of Laissez Faire

Though a first impression might indicate otherwise, the farmers, and merchants, remained within the framework of laissez faire in making their attack on the railroads. They wanted to become more effective (and profitable) entrepreneurs within the system, they did not want to change it. Their logic followed that of the master himself. For as Adam Smith reiterated *ad nauseam*, the key element in laissez-faire theory was the market place. As long as it expanded, and as long as individuals had free access to it, unrestrained competition produced both individual freedom and the general welfare. When some part of it ceased to expand, however, Smith explicitly called for regulation to preserve competition.

Not only were the railroads by their very nature part of the structure of the whole *system's* market place, but they demanded such tremendous investments that the market place in which they could be constructed (i.e., the railroad industry per se) was very small. Entrance into it was anything but free. Furthermore, the market place for railroads had a saturation point beyond which it was irrational and unprofitable to build any more. On all these counts, but especially that concerning the railroads as a structural part of the system's general market place, the first principles of laissez faire justified regulation, even demanded it. The market place had to remain neutral, or as nearly so as possible, so that the various interests would be afforded the famous "open field" for competition. A monopoly of the market place itself was simply indefensible under laissez faire.

Quite rightly, therefore, the farmers demanded that the structure of the market place be stabilized so that competition could continue to their greater benefit. To this end they concentrated on establishing rules and limits for the railroads and on initiating co-operative enterprises to produce or buy certain necessities. Thus, though it started as a fraternal society generally but vaguely interested in benefits for agriculture, the Grange movement began in 1869 to concern itself more directly with the state of the political economy.

It shifted its approach for two reasons: the farmer found it impossible to sublimate his real difficulties in social functions and lecture meetings, and other farm organizations came forward with more vigorous economic and political proposals. Grangers in Iowa organized co-operatives as early as 1872 in order to harvest the benefits of mass purchasing and insurance programs. Two years later they were manufacturing their own harvesters and selling them at about half the market price. Californians even started their own banks. Such enterprises failed because of the lack of sufficient capital, prices that were too low, litigation and price-cutting by their competition, a lack of the co-operative spirit among the farmers themselves, or because the agrarians became manufacturers (and raised their prices).

Collaboration with the merchants in an antirailroad campaign proved more effective. Nor were the merchants slow to see the advantages of an economic liaison with the large agrarian market. Montgomery Ward and Co. was founded in 1872 as the direct result of discussions between the Grange and urban businessmen. Spearheaded in Illinois by the Chicago Board of Trade as well as by farmers, the alliance produced on the political side a warehousing law of 1867 that required railroads to load grain from nonrailway elevators, pushed through a constitutional amendment authorizing regulation in 1870, and fixed maximum freight and passenger rates in 1871. A similar coalition in New York effected the famous Hepburn Investigation of 1879. Other states followed all such examples. Attacking excessive rates, discrimination in charges between short and long hauls, personal favoritism, and the general arrogance and corruption of the system, the assault put the railroads temporarily on the defensive.

Less encouraging was the revelation that outsiders lacked the experience and knowledge to dig out the full story of corporation affairs so that the general public could help to formulate and then choose between alternate plans for enforcing equitable and responsible business conduct. Georgia and California reacted to this serious problem in 1879 by establishing permanent commissions staffed by experts to keep a running check on the lines. This was the beginning of an approach that gained national acceptance and application in later years. In two major cases, meanwhile, the Supreme Court upheld the axiom of public accountability in a way that revealed the paradox of an uncompleted revolution.

By way of validating an Illinois regulatory law in the case of *Munn.* v. *Illinois* (1877), Chief Justice Morrison R. Waite explicitly invoked mercantilist precedents. Citing the English common law as enunciated by Lord Chief Justice Hale during the period of Shaftesbury's influence in the 1670s, and examples taken from the era of Madison and Monroe, Waite reasserted the principle that "property does become clothed with a public interest when used in a manner to make it of public consequence, and affect the community at large." He also reiterated a cardinal principle that had been vigorously defended by Madison and Marshall. "For protection against abuses by legislatures, the people must resort to the polls, not to the courts."

Waite thus reopened the issue that had plagued the mercantilists: how can the public welfare be advanced and protected if private property is allowed to stand above other values? He boldly asserted that it could not, and also reaffirmed the principle that the courts were bound to respect the judgment of the people in such fundamental questions. But while his reference to English common law of the mercantilist era was valid in the broad sense, his use of Lord Hale's judgments was open to serious criticism. For that law concerned property which had been endowed with public interest by law. Technically, at any rate, the railroads stood outside this category. Hence his decision (as he probably realized) rested on shaky ground.

The state laws also begged a second important part of the railroad question. As the connecting links in a national system, veritably the nervous system of Adam Smith's expanding market place, the railroads could not be broken into arbitrary fragments along political boundaries without causing serious consequences. Though their underlying purpose was both equitable and relevant within the *Weltanschauung* of laissez faire, in operation such particularistic regulations were both illogical and inefficient. This was especially the case so long as the central question concerning private property was not resolved; such laws could not only disrupt service, they could actually cause serious economic dislocations.

Waite and his court knew this was a touchy issue. For in upholding the law of a postwar Louisiana legislature that regulated the place and circumstances of slaughtering for public consumption, the majority placed considerable emphasis on the point that any butcher could use the facilities. They thus revealed the basic ambivalence and dilemma of the entire war and reconstruction era: on the one hand, the ideology of the revolution was laissez faire for private property; on the other, considerations of public welfare and the changes in the economy created the necessity for a corporate outlook that would place equal stress on social property.

But the Louisiana law does clarify one vital issue: the exercise of northern power in the south was by no means wholly absurd or selfish. Therein lies the real tragedy of reconstruction in the south. For it was the north's inability to resolve the conflict between its antislavery ideals and its commitment to private property that subverted the originally revolutionary objectives. That failure made it much easier for the Ku Klux Klan and the Red Shirts to succeed as the advance guards of a counter-revolution based on self-interest, on personal, rather than social, property rights, and on race hatred. Yet even the southern whites paid a backhanded tribute to the greater ideal by presenting themselves as men who would restore the paternalism of the region's lost gentry.

Paradoxes of Southern Rehabilitation

Supported by the power of the Congress and the Presidency and backed by the Union Army, the freed Negro dominated the early phases of reconstruction. The Negroes were in themselves half the issue, and their legislative program was the other half. They were poor, and they had a vague image of the north as the good society. Hence they demanded relief acts, educational programs, basic public investments and improvements, and political reforms. Both the victorious northerners and the new southern leadership, which was industrial rather than planter, had to operate within this context.

Too often lumped together under the title Carpetbagger and described as corrupt politicians and economic grave diggers, the northerners who went south actually composed a varied contingent. It included a sizable quick-profit brigade, dedicated revolutionaries trying to make the south "identical [with the north] in thought, sentiment, growth, and development," and honest politicians who reformed where they could and did a great deal to encourage southern recovery and improvement. A good many others, perhaps the plurality, were simply men who found southern reconstruction an underground railway along which to escape from their wives, the law, or poor pickings in the north. But consciously or unconsciously, all of them saw reconstruction as what some Wisconsin veterans called the new frontier. To many, at any rate, it seemed to offer more opportunities with less labor and risk than the forbidding prairie, the western mountains and desert, or the business market place.

As it did in the north, reconstruction produced waste, debts, and corruption in the south. But not only is it factually wrong to blame the Negro for all the weaknesses and failures, but the indictment is a double-edged sword. After all, the Negro in the postwar era was the product of American civilization, and his northern and southern masters were reaping their own harvest. In reality, the Negro did amazingly well. To cite but one example, the Negro-based reconstruction governments in South Carolina provided public schooling for 500 per cent more children.

Southern whites initially divided on how to cope with the rise of the Negro. Upper-class leaders either joined the Republicans (and won the epithet Scalawag), or tried to organize new parties based on the Negro vote. Despite their race prejudice, they were willing to trade a significant measure of equality for political and economic leadership. "Go in for the niggers," exclaimed one of them bluntly, meaning buy the Negro vote by letting them hold office and relaxing some social taboos. Many changed their strategy when confronted with the taxes required to finance the Negro legislative program. Some were willing to let "every office in the State [of Louisiana], from Governor to the most insignificant constable, [be] filled by a negro" in return for lower taxes. But the northern white could always outbid them in that game, and lower-class white southerners withheld their support.

Though the racial attitudes of the poor whites probably played the largest part in their opposition to collaboration with the freed Negro, it is misleading to discount economic and class considerations. Such collaboration did after all occur a relatively short time later. During the immediate postwar period, however, a good many poor whites clearly viewed the Negro as a lower-class citizen who was leap-frogging over himself—a competitor enjoying special and unfair advantages. Hence it seems far more likely that economic, class, and racial antagonisms reinforced each other. Joining their upper-class rulers, the poor whites formed a political and extra-legal alliance that ultimately defeated the Negroes and the Republicans.

But once again in keeping with northern reconstruction, the southern white party was pro-industrial and fundamentally conservative. Hence the irony of the disputed election of 1876. As the prewar defender of the individual entrepreneur, the Democratic Party nominated in Samuel J. Tilden a corporation lawyer who symbolized the cutting edge of the new industrialism. And the Republicans, coming more and more to be dominated by giants of the new society like Roscoe Conkling, selected in Rutherford B. Hayes a personification of the older capitalism. Neither candidate was particularly solicitous for the Negro. The compromise that put Hayes into the White House was based on a common ground; had the two parties differed on fundamentals, the deal would have been impossible.

Depression and Crisis in the North

In the broader sense, however, the compromise has to be understood as part of laissez-faire capitalism's reaction to the onset of grave economic troubles in 1873. It was a closing of ranks against the general difficulties of the system, against the agitation of farmers and laborers, and against a general increase in lawlessness and dissatisfaction. Far from being the culminating embrace of reconstruction (that came in the routine election of 1880), the compromise of 1876 was only the first scene of the final act. The real climax came with the great railroad strike and associated industrial disorders between 1876 and 1878. Having destroyed the old planter aristocracy and come to terms with its industrial successor, the leaders of northern laissez faire had to consolidate their power within their own coalition.

For despite its extensive contributions to the victory, the labor movement never fully overcame a skepticism about the purposes and consequences of the war. Draft riots in New York revealed that underlying resistance and at the same time typified, and were in part caused by, anger over inflation and unemployment. Labor also fought the Contract Labor Law of 1864 which increased the influx of cheap and manageable immigrant labor, the repression of strikes, and the attack on the apprenticeship system. It also maintained a campaign for the eight-hour day; and some groups still agitated for land and monetary reforms that would enable the worker to save enough to become an entrepreneur.

While it declared for all these objectives, the National Labor Union's noble and egalitarian willingness to admit women and Negroes and to organize the unskilled along with trade craftsmen only compounded its other difficulties. The trouble was not so much that the Union's reform goals contradicted its more narrowly economic objectives, but rather that its *Weltanschauung* of laissez faire made it extremely hard to pursue both in any integrated fashion. While ostensibly against the wage system, and therefore concerned to establish co-operative production units, the Union also wanted small capitalists to expand and thereby hire more workers, fought for more rigorous apprenticeship regulations, and favored arbitration over strikes.

As with the farmers who turned to co-operatives, the labor approach to such organizations did not signify any fundamental break with capitalism and private property in favor of socialism. However unrealistic it may seem a century later, labor's conception of a co-operative was entirely within the logic of laissez faire: it was the idea of an association of petty capitalists joined in a legitimate trust. The object was to restore and extend their competitive power in a more balanced and equitable market place. Although disrupted by economic and racial opposition to the Negro, and by the narrow conception of self-interest held by the leaders of the movement to emancipate women (who were willing to serve as strikebreakers), the National Labor Union was basically divided and perplexed over how to cope with the new industrialism. It disintegrated into groups that concentrated on functional or local issues, or joined various political movements such as the Greenback campaign for an inflationary money policy. Negroes formed their own union in 1869, and women, after their brief regression into heterosexual alliance, climbed back onto the high road of emancipation to a position of separate and unequal standing.

During the depression's worst years, therefore, the labor movement declined to approximately 50,000 members (about 1 in 100 workers). But that figure is misleading on two counts: among those in the labor group were the iron, steel, and railroad workers, who were organized and militant, and the seemingly small number was supplemented by large numbers of unemployed adults and aimless youths. With new jobs almost nonexistent and wages in 1875 down to $1.50 for a ten-hour day, the crisis had become the most general breakdown of capitalism in American history. A major riot erupted in New York in 1874. Elsewhere great numbers of parvenu tramps roamed the country. Boston leaders compared the situation to "some great fire or more serious calamity." But even when measured against the Chicago fire, the depression was far worse both in its immediate impact and the time it took to rebuild the community. A sizable number of upper-class leaders throughout the country sensed that they were threatened with a fundamental challenge to the existing order.

"I won't call employers despots, I won't call them tyrants," remarked one steelworker, "but the term capitalist is sort of synonymous and will do as well." Even the Governor of Massachusetts admitted in 1874 that the state's textile workers were "becoming exhausted, . . . growing prematurely old, and . . . losing the vitality requisite to a healthy enjoyment of social opportunities." Coal miners struck in 1875 only to be defeated and lose their union as well as 20 per cent of their wages. Other employers were from one to four months tardy in paying wages. And a major strike at the Cambria Iron Works in Pennsylvania, which had integrated its operations from ore to blast furnaces and a company town for its workers, failed with pathetic human consequences.

Then in a move that could hardly have been more remarkably symbolic, railroad workers refused in 1877 to take a further pay cut and touched off an industrial war in West Virginia that soon spread to other states. "It's a question of bread or blood," explained a Pennsylvania Railroad worker, "and we're going to resist." Blood it was. Ordered into Pittsburgh by President Hayes, federal troops confronted an unorganized alliance of railroad strikers, unemployed steelworkers, and juvenile and adult delinquents. Stones from the kids provoked rifle fire from the adults and that begot carnage and arson by everyone. Parts of the city became a shambles.

Other outbreaks followed in Baltimore, Chicago, and St. Louis. But lacking any clear leadership, even from the tiny group of socialists and communists who belatedly discovered the crisis, the riots passed away in what might be called a euphoria of bourgeois second thoughts.

Though labor won some immediate gains (the railroads gradually restored the pay cuts), the long-range results are more difficult to estimate. Erupting out of agitation against Chinese labor imported for railroad construction, riots in San Francisco led to the formation of the Sand Lot Party which enjoyed considerable influence in California for a few years. But as that episode suggests, labor's vision was certainly limited and clearly inclined to be bigoted. Most of its rising leaders, like Samuel Gompers and Adolph Strasser of the cigar workers, turned away from any program that envisioned a different and better system outside the confines of laissez faire to concentrate on strengthening labor's position in the existing order. And although it polled over a million votes in the election of 1878, and advocated other reforms as well as monetary inflation, the Greenback campaign soon lost its verve and support.

In the broader sense, the conservative response to the crisis of 1877 was accepted by a plurality of Americans. Chaos and violence crystallized the existing anxiety of the middle class that it was being squeezed between those who would destroy the rights of property and others who abused them. But forced to choose, its members clearly preferred the chance to exploit the liberties of the entrepreneur. And upper-class leaders became even more determined to consolidate their control over the system. A federal judge named Walter Gresham who followed Tilden into the Democratic Party was a bit more extreme and outspoken than most, but he nevertheless typified the general attitude of his stratum of society. "Democracy is now the enemy of law and order and society itself," he concluded, "and as such should be denounced." Gresham's private attitude was given public exposure by a young middle-class entrepreneur from Indiana named John Hay, who had been one of Lincoln's secretaries and who aspired to leadership for himself. Hay's book, *The Breadwinners,* was a fictional polemic against labor. As a novel it was feeble art, but it outsold by a wide margin a rival interpretation of the crisis of 1877, Henry F. Keenan's *The Money Makers.*

Secretary of State Seward and the Adaptation of the Frontier Thesis to Industrialism

Hay and Gresham also came to personify a developing bipartisan consensus on foreign policy. Both saw overseas economic expansion as the long-range solution to such dangerous unrest and the malfunctioning of the system that caused it; Gresham's performance later as Secretary of State under President Grover Cleveland, and Hay's actions in the same post under President William McKinley were to show this outlook in its matured form. Though they were not in a position to deliver the dramatic results produced by Gresham and Hay, the same basic approach guided key foreign-policy leaders during the postwar era.

Expansionists of the reconstruction period faced several handicaps. Seward explained the most important of them very simply, remarking that the public "refuses to dismiss" the issues of readjustment in order to pursue world power. This attitude magnified the impact of the overt opposition. Such critics were afraid that more expansion would reopen the question of slavery or that it would undercut the political and economic functioning of the laissez-faire system. Carl Schurz neatly combined all such arguments in his opposition to taking any Caribbean islands. "Have we not enough with one South? Can we afford to buy another one?" But the expansionist coalition was only checked; it was not disrupted, nor was it replaced by a new alliance of anti-expansionists.

"I chant the new empire, grander than before. I chant commerce opening," sang Walt Whitman in praise of the American who "colonizes the Pacific." William Gilpin, a friend of President Jackson who had supported the Mexican War with great enthusiasm, returned to the campaign by reissuing (1873) his treatise on *The Mission of the North American People.* "The *untransacted* destiny of the American people," he cried, ". . . is to . . . rush . . . to the Pacific Ocean . . . to establish a new order in human affairs . . . to regenerate the superannuated nations." Businessmen joined in with petitions "to establish and maintain our ascendancy in Asia," and to *"manage it so that the whole world would be tributary to us."* And in his annual message of 1868, President Andrew Johnson curtly dismissed the old argument "that our political system cannot be applied to an area more extended than our continent." The principle and the system were "of sufficient strength and breadth to comprehend within their sphere and influence the civilized nations of the world."

Although he was an expansionist, Johnson's remarks plainly bore the imprint of Secretary of State Seward. Still concerned to construct "such empire as the world has never before seen," Seward understood the need to change the nature and purposes of territorial expansion as the economy became more industrial. While retaining some of his earlier belief that Latin-American countries would eventually apply for statehood, and speaking openly of "our" Panama isthmus, he clearly realized that commercial expansion was the key to making America "the master of the world." Instead of needing territory for colonization, the new kind of economic expansion required key land bases for the projection, development, and protection of trade and investment.

Internal improvements were needed to insure "diminished cost[s] of production," and wars should be avoided because the United States was "*sure* to be aggrandized by peace" because it would control world commerce. As Lenin was to argue more than two generations later, Seward maintained as early as 1853 that the key to overcoming British supremacy was to be found in Asia. "France, and England, and Russia," were the rivals: "Watch them with jealousy, and baffle their designs against you." "You are already the great continental power of America. But does that content you? I trust it does not. You want the commerce of the world. This is to be looked for . . . on the Pacific. . . . The nation that draws most from the earth and fabricates most, and sells the most to foreign nations, must be and will be the great power of the earth."

Seward's accomplishments fell shy of his desires. France was already on the way out of Mexico when he intervened, and his fullhanded shove only accelerated the retreat. He failed to acquire either the Danish West Indies or Hawaii. But in the 1960s there was to be no need to belabor the significance of his Alaskan success; even at the time, some Americans understood its role in outflanking the British in North America and in giving the United States a strategic bridge across the top of the Pacific basin. "It seems inevitable," commented *The New York Times,* "that all that commerce should be American." And today Seward's vigorous effort to penetrate the Asian mainland by establishing a foothold in Korea seems eerily prescient. Seward confounds the view that America had world power "thrust upon it" by external force of circumstance.

Much the same is to be said of President Ulysses S. Grant, whose desire to push overseas expansion was a central theme of his two terms in the White House. Grant was persistently concerned for "new markets for the products of our farms, shops, and manufactories." Indeed, one of his strong reasons for seeking the nomination for a third term was to help American investors expand their overseas operations. With the tutoring that he and Seward provided, other industrial nations recognizing that a new competitor had entered the world arena. Britain astutely realized that the turn of the trade balance in 1877, when America began regularly to export more than it imported, was more important than the violence in Pittsburgh. The evidence was irrefutable, explained the London *Times,* because American tools and machinery were cutting into the market in England itself, as well as in Australia and Canada.

For that matter, England had already provided in 1871 the single most dramatic symbol of America's rise to world power. Worried about Bismarck's unification of Germany through the defeat of France, and concerned about Russia's renewed push into the Black Sea region, Great Britain apologized for having allowed its shipbuilders to aid the Confederacy. It formally expressed, "in a friendly spirit, the regret felt by Her Majesty's Government." Buoyed up by that candid recognition of their power, and having checked the laborers and the agrarians, the leaders of America's Age of Laissez Nous Faire moved on to the fulfillment of their self-interests and the maturation of the system's contradictions.

4. The Gilded Age and Progressivism

The Robber Baron Concept and Its Revisionists   ALLEN SOLGANICK

Though many New Left historians are willing to acknowledge the creative side of capitalism, others are not. Observing the excesses of business enterprise in our own era, they find it difficult to accept the forward-looking nature of the business leaders of the past. Their strictures on the Rockefellers and the Carnegies are strongly reminiscent of the attitudes of their Progressive predecessors.

In part, the New Left response is influenced by the recent attempt of the consensus historians to rehabilitate the Robber Barons. Men like Allan Nevins, Louis Hacker, Edward Chase Kirkland, and Thomas Cochran, writing largely in the 1950s, celebrated the great post–Civil War captains of industry and sought to turn them into industrial statesmen. Though they were no doubt aggressive and sometimes brutally direct men, the business leaders of the late nineteenth century helped make America rich. Ultimately, their creative efforts benefited all parts of the population. As for their unscrupulousness, much of it can be ascribed to the uncertainties of existing law. Many practices that are now illegal were not against the law before 1900, and we cannot judge the business magnates of the period by the values of our own day.

Such an approach, however valid, is understandably offensive to the New Left. It epitomizes the smugness of the conservative decade that preceded the 1960s. It turns one of the more vulnerable aspects of the American past into an occasion for self-congratulation. Several New Left historians have taken issue with this "revisionist" view of the Robber Barons. One of the best dissenting statements is the essay below by Allen Solganick.

FOR FURTHER READING:

Matthew Josephson, *The Robber Barons,* (Harcourt, Brace and Company, 1934); Allan Nevins, *A Study in Power: John D. Rockefeller, Industrialist and Philanthropist,* (Scribner's, 1953); Edward C. Kirkland, *Dream and Thought in the American Business Community 1860–1900**, (Quadrangle, 1964); Gustavus Myers, *History of the Great American Fortunes,* (Modern Library, 1963); Gustavus Myers, *The Ending of Hereditary American Fortunes,* (Julian Messner, 1939); Gabriel Kolko, "The Premises of Business Revisionism," *Business History Review,* (Fall, 1959).

Asterisk denotes paperback edition.

Source: Allen Solganick, "The Robber Baron Concept and Its Revisionists," *Science and Society,* vol. 29, no. 3 (Summer 1965), pp. 257–269.

Concomitant with the development of the Cold War has been the rise of a self-proclaimed school of revisionist historians who purport to improve our understanding of American economic history in the period between the Civil War and the turn of the century. Specifically, they feel that the Robber Baron concept of business enterprise is in need of substantial revision. The individual historians in this school hold diverse opinions as to several aspects of the Robber Barons' activities, but are unanimous in agreeing that big businessmen played a creative role in the development of the American economy. Indeed, this creativity is the unifying theme of the revisionist school. H. Wayne Morgan states the revisionist argument thusly: "Suffice it to say that the stereotype of the Robber Baron is much overdrawn. It must be balanced with a fuller picture, showing the new technology he often brought to his industry, the wealth and resources he developed for the economy in general, the social good he sometimes did with his money offsetting the bitter fact that he paid little taxes."

This "stereotype" of which Morgan speaks had been developed by men like Gustavus Myers, Thorstein Veblen, and Matthew Josephson. Chronicling the careers of men of wealth in the United States, Myers showed the use of government and extra-legal methods in the accumulation of private fortunes. His work was largely ignored until Josephson resurrected it in the 1930's when business came under general attack. Josephson drew not only on the work of Myers and the "muckrakers," but also on the theoretical contributions of Veblen who asserted that although some capitalists had played a creative role with respect to technology and economic growth prior to 1860, after that time they became a drag on development, administering "a salutary running margin of sabotage in production, at the cost of the underlying population."

The present paper is both a rebuttal of recent revisionist work and a revindication of Veblen's view. The first part discusses attempts by the revisionists to discredit the critics of monopoly, and the attempts to portray the era as one during which everyone was satisfied. The second section deals with the question of monopoly. Finally, the matter of whether the Robber Barons were in fact creative with respect to technology and economic growth is handled in the third section.

I. The Robber Barons, the Critics and Discontent

As one basis for the need for a fresh look at American capitalism, the revisionists have attempted to discredit various critics of monopoly. Thus, one writer bewails the "anti-capitalist bias" of American historians. Another entitled his article "The Anatomy of Prejudice: Origins of the Robber Baron Legend." Still another concluded that the Robber Baron concept was "born apparently of a desire for denunciation rather than objective analysis." And, "no recent student approached the era with more bias than did Matthew Josephson, three of whose works have remained standard interpretations of the period for a generation." One is prompted to ask how Josephson's work managed such general acceptance if he was so evidently biased? However, a more important question is what evidence of "bias," "prejudice," and "non-objectivity" have the above quoted authors brought forth? The answer, of course, is none; the sole basis of their charges is not that the facts were dishonestly reported, but rather that the critics were guilty of misinterpreting those facts. This assertion by the revisionists is in turn based on their assumption that the Robber Barons were creative, a matter to be dealt with later.

Professor Kirkland, on the other hand, actually claims to have discovered distortion of evidence by Henry Demarest Lloyd, author of the famous *Wealth Against Commonwealth*. Dubbing it a "utopian fantasy," Kirkland goes on to state that charges in Lloyd's book "had the paraphernalia of documentation and footnote reference," but "the handling of evidence is not persuasive." The only example of distortion which is given by Kirkland is a misinterpretation of the connection between Standard Oil and the Rothschilds. Yet, Professor C. M. Destler, writing fifteen years prior to the publication of Kirkland's book, found that in checking 420 of Lloyd's 648 references to source material only 10 inaccuracies in statement occurred, and these in ways "not of great import." Of 241 important undocumented statements, 229 were verified completely, 8 partially, and only 4 were incorrect. Destler was forced to conclude that "when all allowances are made, Lloyd's pioneering report of the methods by which the oil monopoly was established and maintained remains substantially unaltered. . . ." Hence, Professor Kirkland can be the only scholar to whom Lloyd's evidence is "not persuasive." The attempts to discredit these Robber Baron historians as being irrational, compulsive denouncers (Bridges), most biased (Morgan), pseudo-scientific and unscholarly (Kirkland), turns out to be based on assertion only. That is, it is entirely unsubstantiated. The Robber Baron school of historians bases its criticisms of big business on solid documentation of the facts. This leaves the revisionists with only one criticism left. Namely, that the Robber Baron school presented only one side of the picture, leaving out the positive contribution made by the big businessmen. As will be shown later, this criticism is also based on assertion only.

However, the revisionists do not depend solely on discrediting critics of monopoly. They claim that this era was one of general satisfaction among the populace. Kirkland argues that if business were indeed greedy, without social purpose, dishonest, and exploitative, the "Republican Party, the party of big business," would not have "enjoyed almost uninterrupted political success. . . . Perhaps it is simpler to believe that the performance of the economy during this era was not as bad as pictured and in general won popular endorsement." Furthermore, he contends that the statement that the rich got richer and the poor poorer is "completely inaccurate."

These arguments are quite incorrect. Simon Kuznets found increasing inequality of income occurring during the period between 1870 and 1900, primarily due to the trust movement which resulted in substantial capital gains to those who were already rich. Kirkland is right if he is speaking of absolute income levels. However, it would be correct to say that during this period the rich were getting richer and the poor relatively poorer. As many economists have shown, relative rather than absolute income is more important for the individual's comparisons with other people. Marx pointed out that "although the enjoyments of the worker have risen, the social satisfaction that they give has fallen in comparison with the increased enjoyments of the capitalists, which are inaccessible to the worker, in comparison with the state of development of society in general."

In reply to the argument that the recurrent election of Republicans indicated a general contentment with business, it should be noted that both parties were "parties of big business." Corruption was quite widespread, and as two of Kirkland's fellow revisionists have pointed out, whenever discontented groups fought for reforms "they met the disciplined representatives of the ruling cliques, who had sufficient resources to beat almost any candidate, platform plank, or bill they disliked. The improvised organizations of the protestants could not compete with the major parties. . . . Mute testimony to the failure of groups outside the ruling interests lies in the Republican and Democratic platforms; the record of Republican and Democratic administrations tells that failure aloud." Many factors are necessary to explain the Republican ascendancy, and to claim a lack of discontent as the primary reason is clearly untrue.

There are no indexes available showing the rise and fall of popular discontent, but if one could be constructed it would undoubtedly exhibit a steadily upward trend during the Gilded Age. This was an era which witnessed the birth of the Grangers, Greenbackers, Populists, National Labor Union, A.F.L., and numerous other groups of discontented citizens. Indeed, it was the farmers of Kansas who first used the term "Robber Baron" to describe railroad leaders in an anti-monopoly pamphlet written in 1880. One populist song of the period spoke of "monopolies banded together to beat a poor hayseed like me," while labor added to the refrain that "those mean monopolizers had the cheek to take the stand, and ask to get protection from the honest working man."

The famous incidents of discontent, like Homestead and Pullman, are reflected in the high level of aggregate strike activity during this period. Work stoppages which, for the five-year period 1881–1885, averaged 528 per year and involved an annual average of 176,000 workers, increased with fluctuations so that the corresponding figures for the period 1896–1900 were 1390 and 386,000. During a period characterized by a high degree of instability, with major downturns in 1872, 1882, and 1892, discontent should be expected. The percentage decline in output of consumer durables for the cycles of 1872, 1882, and 1892 were respectively 33, 25, and 34. Of the total of 35 years between 1865 and 1900, 16 were depression years. One author estimated average unemployment in the period 1889–1898 to be twelve per cent of the total labor force. However, even when they were employed, workers had reason for discontent. The number of deaths and injuries of employees on railroads for the 1890's was enormous. In 1900 there were 1,018,000 railroad workers employed of whom 2,550 were killed and 39,643 injured that year. By contrast, in 1957 with a work force almost exactly the same size, the number of deaths and injuries on the job declined to 195 and 12,245 respectively. Thus, working conditions must have been very hazardous if railroad conditions are any indication.

Professor Kirkland's argument that discontent was infrequent has no basis in fact. The Robber Baron, John D. Rockefeller, was certainly not speaking of a docile working class when he wrote in 1907 that "these stories about my wealth. They have a bad effect on a class of people with whom it is becoming difficult to deal . . . the stress which is laid in those stories arouses hatred and envy not against the individual only but against organized society. . . . It is the general trend I have in mind, which is arraying the masses against the classes."

II. The Robber Barons and Monopoly

The concentration movement in American industry after the Civil War is a well-known fact. Alfred Chandler found that when continued production at full capacity threatened to drop prices to the detriment of profits, "many small manufacturers in the leather, sugar, salt, distilling and other corn products, linseed and cotton oil, biscuit, petroleum, fertilizer, and rubber boot and glove industries joined in large horizontal combinations. In most of these industries, combination was followed by consolidation and vertical integration, and the pattern was comparatively consistent." However, the revisionists deny that this meant monopoly was spreading. For instance, Kirkland states that "though combinations were often bewailed by critics as likely to lead to the imposition of 'extortionate' and 'monopoly' rates, the large corporations were precisely those which were most enterprising in the adoption of cost saving devices."

Whether the large corporations were in fact "the most enterprising" in technological innovation will be the subject of the next section. The question here is, to the extent that costs were lowered by large corporations, how much of this meant higher monopoly profits and how much benefit did the consumer experience? The simple fact of an adoption of cost-saving equipment tells us nothing about who were the beneficiaries. Nor can the citation of price reductions tell us whether or not monopoly power was exerted, for this period witnessed about a 25 per cent decline in the general level of prices.

On the other hand, much evidence exists which confirms the generally accepted view that this was a period when monopoly became a major element in the economic and political life of the nation. One noted economist has succintly stated why combinations occurred at this time: "Competition is profit-destroying and monopoly is profit preserving. Consequently profit-motivated economic units attempt to establish monopolies whenever possible." That this maxim applied to the Robber Barons has been confirmed several times.

The Hepburn Committee in 1879 found that 90 per cent to 95 per cent of all the refiners in the country acted in harmony with Standard Oil and in 1892 the Supreme Court of Ohio declared that the object of the Standard Oil Company was "to establish a virtual monopoly of the business of producing petroleum, and of manufacturing, refining and dealing in it and all its products throughout the entire country, and by which it might not merely control the production, but the price, at its pleasure."

The example of Standard Oil is multiplied in the aggregate. It was the belief of the Industrial Commission in 1902, after a most exhaustive study, "that in most cases the combination has exerted an appreciable power over prices and in practically all cases it has increased the margin between raw materials and finished products. Since there is reason to believe that the cost of production over a period of years has lessened, the conclusion is inevitable that the combinations have been able to increase their profits." In addition, while monopolies had presumably been banned under the common law, 27 states and territories by the close of 1890 had seen fit to pass laws intended to prevent or destroy them.

The most important study of the relationship of the Robber Baron to monopoly was done by Professor C. M. Destler, who studied 43 notable capitalists of this era. He found that 16 had milked their corporations for their own profit; 23 charged exorbitant rates when a monopoly position made it possible; 13 profited from control and manipulation of the press; at least 13 practiced political corruption; 16 exhibited marked hostility to the labor movement; and railroad favors in rates or services were important for 11. He was forced to conclude that "monopoly, partially or wholly, temporarily or more permanently achieved, was a significant or dominant feature of the entrepreneurial activity of at least thirty-six of the forty-three."

Destler was convinced by his study that "for the bulk of the entrepreneurs studied and for many other contemporary business leaders, there is justification [for the term] 'the robber barons,' or Howard Mumford Jones' analogy with the Renaissance despot. . . ." His view is shared by two more recent writers who, while still clinging to the belief that the Robber Barons played a creative role, nevertheless condemn their more piratical aspects. Thus, Tipple states that "if big businessmen like John D. Rockefeller were attacked as Robber Barons, it was because they were correctly identified as destroyers." And Miller asserts that "the Progressive indictment survives in the general history books because it is a true bill." All of the available evidence points up the fact that this era witnessed the emergence of large-scale monopoly, and no facts have been advanced which would modify this view.

III. The Robber Barons' Alleged Creativity

The theme which unifies the revisionist school is that, regardless of any cupidity, no one can deny the fact that the Robber Barons played *the* creative role in the economic development of the country. For example, a recent textbook asserts that "without business leadership, no amounts of capital, natural resources, or labor could have brought the United States into its position of industrial predominance." Another author notes a "striking growth of output." Still another states that the system at this time "added immensely to both natural and human wealth." A much used source book on this period speaks of "decades of prodigious expansion," and Professor Kirkland claims that the talent for business enterprise was "the source of abundance." The progressive Professor Tipple states that this was "an age when the corporation made unprecedented achievements in production." And finally, even William Appleman Williams, who otherwise is in no way connected with the revisionists, speaks of a "tremendous surge of industrial strength" which is "the undeniable achievement of the laissez-faire entrepreneur. . . ."

The use of words such as "striking," "immensely," "prodigious," "abundance," "unprecedented," and "tremendous" would lead one to believe that the record of growth was noteworthy, to say the least. However, the facts do not warrant such a conclusion, whether we compare the performance of the economy with previous performance, with the performance of other capitalist economies either during the same period or at a later date, or with the performance of the socialist economies. Indeed, as will be shown below, "the depression of 1893–1896 was the culmination of more than two decades of unsatisfactory performance of the American economy."

Since investment in fixed capital is an important determinant of growth, we would expect a very high growth rate in the post-Civil War era. Instead, we find that the average decennial rate of growth of fixed capital was much higher during the period 1839–1859 than it was in 1869–1899. Thus, in comparison with earlier achievements in the growth of fixed capital, the United States witnessed a decline, not a "surge."

Another indicator in judging growth is the output of commodities. Since services were not a very significant factor during this period, the commodity output figures are a close approximation to total income. Not only was the average decennial rate of change of value added in agriculture, mining, and construction lower in the post-Civil War period, but this was also true of manufacturing, supposedly the area where "fantastic" and "prodigious" rates of growth were to be found. It is difficult to reconcile the assertions of the revisionists with the actual facts. The evidence shows that the United States developed more slowly during the era of the Robber Barons than it had before these "creators" arrived on the scene.

Not only does the United States during this period exhibit an unspectacular record with regard to its own past, but also three other countries, Sweden, Denmark, and Canada, were experiencing the same rate of growth of per capita income.

And, of course, many capitalist countries have displayed higher growth rates than this in the twentieth century. Finally, when we compare the United States' record of about four per cent a year increase in Gross National Product with the nine per cent a year figure which is a conservative estimate of China's growth, the record does not seem so "striking."

Relating to this "surge" of output is the revisionist contention that America's industrial capitalists "were enterprisers, adventurers, and innovators, for the great forward strides of technology were possible only as a result of their risk-taking." However, it was precisely the Robber Barons' role with respect to technology which led Veblen to term them saboteurs. The evidence that is available, scantly as it is, tends to support Veblen's view. The actual picture of the forward strides in technology reveals an extremely cautious exploitation of almost riskless opportunities.

Destler in his study of 43 capitalists found that at least 15 of the 38 nonbanking capitalists were alert to the advantage that adopting the latest technical improvements would give them in competition. Only three of those studied were inventors themselves, while another two used research technicians. As one major example, Standard Oil contributed nothing to the improvement of the basic technology of petroleum before the turn of the century. Destler concluded that "within the field of risks borne . . . the analysis indicates considerable success in exploitation of business opportunities involving little or no risk. Monopoly risk [i.e., no risk] was enjoyed by 21 in the group. Nine others profited from government subsidies or railroad-construction contracts, or both, that minimized the risks for the entrepreneurs involved."

Another relevant study was done by W. Paul Strassman, who examined four industries: iron and steel, textiles, machine tools, and electric power. His conclusions are radically different from those which revisionists would have us believe. He found that "the vast majority of innovations which seemed hazardous to people at the time were not, in fact, risky and that for most sweeping changes in manufacturing methods the process of innovation was already a safe and even predictable routine." This was due to the interrelatedness of innovations in key industries, so that change became mutually reinforcing. However, the pace of technological development "was not as rapid as might have been feasible on the basis of technology alone." Old methods of production managed to survive for decades after they became partially obsolete. For instance, in the textile industry ring spindles were a commercial success by 1845, but the number of mule spindles continued to increase until around 1900. Furthermore, more than ten years elapsed before the Northrop automatic loom appreciably reduced the sales of other looms. The same thing happened in the iron and steel industry: forges and bloomeries kept expanding after the introduction of puddling and rolling; charcoal smelting expanded until around 1890; the number of puddling furnaces reached a maximum 25 years after Bessemer steel was successfully made in 1867; and crucible steel production increased for some 39 years after the first successful open hearth of 1870. Strassman finds "conspicuous caution" as a major characteristic of entrepreneurs during this period.

IV. Conclusion

We see, then, that the final revisionist assertion, namely, that the Robber Barons were "adventurers" and risk-takers, falls under the weight of the facts. It has been shown that the revisionist arguments as to the critics, the state of popular discontent, the development of monopoly, and the creativity of the Robber Barons are all mere assertions, unsubstantiated by an examination of the available evidence. Matthew Josephson's terse description of the period still holds true: "The expanding America of the post-Civil War era was the paradise of freebooting capitalists, untrammeled and untaxed. . . . Theirs is the story of a well-nigh irresistible drive toward monopoly, which the plain citizens, Congresses, and Presidents opposed —seemingly in vain."

It is clear that the performance of the economy during the Gilded Age was poor. Yet, the revisionists are immune to facts. Thus, in the future we can expect to see more literature expounding the virtues of this or that capitalist, as the demand for such literature increases. And as the shortcomings of capitalism become more apparent, the demand for more and more baseless apologies will undoubtedly increase.

The Process of Mobility STEPHAN THERNSTROM

Marx and his disciples believed that capitalism inevitably impoverished the working class. Whether it came early or late, in the end, the standard of living of the wage earners was destined to fall to subsistence levels leaving the proletariat constantly in misery and at the edge of starvation. At the same time, those who started in the middle class, with the exception of a small group, would be pushed down to the level of the workers. The final result would be a great mass of the exploited poor and a tiny minority of great capitalists.

Obviously this description of capitalism does not allow much room for the steadily improving conditions among the laborers and for mobility from this group into the ranks of the middle class. The New Left, of course, is not bound tightly by the theories of Marx, but on the other hand, it is interested in the working classes and it is concerned with the experience of the workingman in America.

The conservative view of the American workingman, as one would expect, emphasizes the degree to which he has found it possible to move up the social ladder. Consensus historians point to this mobility to explain the relative absence of class strife in the United States. The American proletariat was slow to form unions and hesitant to join class-conscious political parties because they recognized that their

---

Source: Stephan Thernstrom, *Poverty and Progress: Social Mobility in a Nineteenth Century City* (Cambridge, Mass.: Harvard University Press, 1964), chap. vi, "The Process of Mobility," pp. 138–165.

stay in the wage-earner class was at most temporary. This country, they knew, rewarded the economic virtues of hard work, frugality, and sobriety, and they felt that they could rely on their own efforts to improve their lot.

This picture is very attractive, and obviously fits the conservative view of the American success story, but how mobile a society did exist in the United States? In the essay that follows Stephan Thernstrom examines social mobility between 1850 and 1880 in the city of Newburyport, Massachusetts. Though a man of the left, and unwilling to accept the conservative formula, Thernstrom voluntarily risks the most exacting statistical analysis. His results are not dogmatic or strident, but they do not support the exaggerated conservative view of mobility in 19th century America.

FOR FURTHER READING:

Stephan Thernstrom, *Poverty and Progress: Social Mobility in a Nineteenth Century City**, (Harvard University Press, 1964); Irvin G. Wylie, *The Self Made Man in America: The Myth of Rags to Riches**, (Free Press, 1966); Seymour M. Lipset and Reinhard Bendix, *Social Mobility in Industrial Society**, (University of California Press, 1959); Norman Ware, *The Industrial Worker 1840–1860: The Reaction of American Revolution Industrial Society to the Advance of the Industrial Revolution**, (Quadrangle, 1964); Gerald Grob, *Workers and Utopia: A Study of Ideological Conflict in the American Labor Movement**, (Quadrangle, 1969); David Montgomery, *Beyond Equality, Labor and the Radical Republicans, 1862–1872*, (Alfred A. Knopf, 1967).

Asterisk denotes paperback edition.

The laborers of Newburyport have so far been observed from two angles of vision. Hundreds of unskilled workmen and their sons were viewed first in their occupational role; and then in terms of the frequency with which they managed to accumulate savings and to purchase real estate. It was necessary to isolate these two dimensions of social mobility and to consider each separately, but that simplifying device can now be abandoned in order to deal with some of the key relationships between advances in the occupational and property spheres. First, characteristic patterns of working class family mobility will be identified by surveying some representative cases from the 287 families studied. Then the critical question of whether upwardly mobile fathers customarily succeeded in passing on their gains to their children will be systematically explored. That will lead to an interpretative review of the major findings concerning working class social mobility in the 1850–1880 period.

Patterns of Family Mobility

A rough classification of Newburyport's laboring families into high mobility, intermediate mobility, and static categories will make it easier to discern typical patterns of family mobility. The high mobility category, which includes a sixth of the 287 families studied, encompasses every family at least one of whose members entered a nonmanual occupation during these three decades. Those families whose male members were all confined to unskilled and semiskilled jobs, and who never came into possession of as much as $300 in property during these years are classed static. The intermediate mobility category covers the range of cases between these two poles.

■ **High Mobility Families.** Forty-seven of the 287 laboring families who resided in Newburyport a decade or more between 1850 and 1880 were highly mobile. Twenty-two of these cases involved the mobility of adult laborers into nonmanual occupations; in the other twenty-five it was the son of the original laborer who first crossed over into the middle class occupational universe.

The most important avenue of high mobility open to the older generation was, surprisingly, not small business but agriculture. A New England manufacturing city seems an unlikely setting for the fulfillment of Jeffersonian dreams, but sixteen of the twenty-two highly mobile fathers became farm owners, and a good many other laborers did some farming on the side.

Newburyport residents in this period were within reach of a large supply of arable land. Six miles long but only half a mile wide, the city hugged the banks of the Merrimack River; open fields formed its western border. A workman like Thomas Ronan was alert to the possibilities that lay at his doorstep. In 1855, having scraped together a few hundred dollars from his wages, Ronan bought a small house on the western edge of town, and moved his wife and eight children from their cramped working class dwelling on Beck Street. Ronan reported his occupation as "farmer" on the 1860 Census, though he was not yet assessed as the owner of farm equipment or livestock. In 1864 he paid taxes on $900 in real estate, $200 in livestock, and a $100 wagon. By 1867 he had acquired a second house and two more farm lots, and his real property holdings had reached $1600. The Census of 1870 listed Ronan as the owner of $2000 in real estate and $1500 in personal property.

Ronan became more affluent than most of his fellow laborers who became farm owners—Dan Creedon's $1400, William Eustis' $1800, Ichabod Little's $1300 were more typical estate values—but the pattern of his ascent was characteristic of the group. The key step was the setting aside of enough money to purchase a lot on the outskirts of the city. Once land had been acquired, the process of becoming a full-fledged farmer was often slow. Ronan claimed his new status very quickly; other laborers continued to live in rented dwellings for years, working as day laborers and farming their plots in their spare time. In many cases it was impossible to distinguish a laborer who owned farm property from a farmer; census and city directory occupational listings for such men were frequently inconsistent. The sixteen farmers placed in the high mobility class here represent a minimum estimate. Some two dozen others who still reported themselves as laborers on the Census of 1880 owned small amounts of arable land and livestock, and undoubtedly derived some part of their income from agriculture.

About two thirds of the common laborers in Newburyport at this time were born in rural Ireland, while a good many others were migrants from the farms of Maine, New Hampshire, and Vermont. They were, in short, no strangers to the soil. It was significant that life in the industrial city did not invariably require a total break from the rural environment to which these men were accustomed. This was the case in Newburyport, and there is evidence that it was true to some degree in even the larger urban centers of the period. A select minority from the laboring class succeeded in becoming full-fledged farmers, and many others became yeomen part-time.

To rank farm ownership and operation a nonmanual occupation is a sociological convention; actually the farmer performed heavy manual labor. The farm owner is classed with the businessman and the professional because he was a proprietor—because he commanded capital, made decisions as to what he would produce, and sold at least part of his product for a profit. The laborers who became farm owners in Newburyport appear to have customarily produced little more than enough to satisfy the wants of their family and to have rarely become significantly involved in farming for the market. Even the exceptionally prosperous Thomas Ronan estimated the value of his produce at only $550 on the Census of 1870; most of these men supplied no detailed crop information on the agricultural schedules of the census because they produced less than the $500 minimum specified by the Census Bureau.

The fact that farm work was little different from ordinary labor, and that farms held by mobile laborers were not operated as businesses suggests that the environment in which the children of these mobile laborers grew up was not particularly conducive to success in the middle class world. The career patterns of the sons of the sixteen farm owners confirm this interpretation. Only two youths from this group entered a white collar, professional, or business calling: one became a clerk, and eventually an independent grocer; another began his career as a school teacher. Several simply stayed home and labored on their fathers' farms; some of these presumably would someday become independent farmers by inheritance. The majority, however, gravitated to simple manual occupations, becoming fishermen, mill operatives, butchers, masons.

Farming was much more accessible to the older generation in our sample than the other nonmanual callings. None of these workmen was able to enter a profession, of course, but it is surprising that only six of the entire group ventured into small business. The security of the farm and the familiarity of its task drew most of these successful laborers, including those with the largest stocks of capital. The few business owners were very small operators: Freeman Greenough's investment as a "provisioner" was a mere $300; William O'Neal's house, the front room of which served as a tavern and liquor store, was valued at $1000. Whether from insufficiency of capital, incompetence, or bad luck, these small businessmen were much less prosperous than their brethren who purchased farms.

Business pursuits, on the other hand, gave the children of mobile laborers an environment somewhat more favorable to attainment of high status positions. The experience of the Freeman Greenough family suggests some of the possibilities. The Greenoughs came to the city from Maine sometime in the forties, and the father found work as a day laborer. Freeman and one of his sons were classified as laborers in the Census of 1850, while two more of his boys were mill operatives. A few years later, with his small savings, he opened a "provisions" shop at his place of residence. The business returned very little profit, judging from his tax assessments, but Greenough was able to keep it going until his death in 1881. Three of his sons left Newburyport while still youths, one of them with some employment experience as a clerk. A fourth, Joseph, began his career as a hostler. In 1870, at 34, he was still in a humble calling, a driver with no taxable property. His account at the Institution for Savings must already have contained a substantial capital reserve, however, for in the next decade his rise was meteoric. The 1873 assessments show him with five horses and two carriages, worth $900; in 1876 it was twelve horses, five carriages, four hacks, a stable, and a house, a total investment of $4800. By 1880 Joseph's livery stable was valued at $11,000, by 1883, $15,000.

Joseph's oldest boy was registered in the Latin preparatory section of the high school in 1880; it is very likely that with this much education he entered a non-manual calling after graduating. Freeman Greenough's fifth son, Henry, had a more erratic career. He was a mill operative as a youth, later a confectioner, then a clerk in a provisions shop. By 1870 he had returned to the mill, and in 1880 he was recorded as a hack driver, probably working for his successful brother. Two of Henry Greenough's sons, however, found white collar jobs.

In all, twenty-two Newburyport families were ranked in the high mobility category because of the intra-generational mobility of an unskilled manual laborer; another twenty-five families entered that category by virtue of the social advances of their children. The composition of these two groups present sharp contrasts. Three quarters of the older generation achieved high status by the purchase of a farm; none of the second generation high mobility cases moved into agriculture. Half of these mobile sons found white collar jobs, a category of occupation entered by none of the older generation of laborers. The other 50 percent of these sons, as opposed to one quarter of the fathers, became independent small businessmen. Many of these youths had brief experience as factory operatives, but not one made his ascent within the corporate hierarchy. The humble mill hand who struggles to become foreman and ends up chairman of the board, it was shown earlier, was rarely portrayed in the success literature of this period; he was a later creation. In this small way, at least, the mid-nineteenth century mobility ideology accurately mirrored social reality.

The businesses opened by the sons of Newburyport laborers were precarious ventures. They were neighborhood affairs, requiring only enough capital to buy a small inventory of goods and to pay the rent—five of these sons became retail grocers, three of them were ice dealers, two were fish sellers. Low capital requirements allowed easy entry; members of this group typically worked in some manual job for a few years in order to accumulate savings on which to operate. Profits, not surprisingly, were minimal. Only Stephen Fowle and Joseph Greenough reported a rapid and sustained increase in wealth over the period. The threat of bankruptcy was not negligible. One youth opened a grocery with $500 in 1860 and lost everything in five years; he was forced to find work in a hat factory, where he was still employed in 1880. Had this study been carried past 1880, other instances of downward mobility would have been recorded; several of these tiny enterprises were no longer listed in the 1886 city directory. For fathers and sons alike, then, business ownership was not an unrealizable goal; neither, on the other hand, was it a guarantee of secure prosperity once attained.

A new development was the small white collar elite group—fourteen clerks, a bookkeeper, and a clerk lawyer—which had come into existence by 1880. Only two of the members of this group had ever worked in a manual occupation. Boys did not begin their careers as laborers or operatives and later edge their way up into white collar positions. The white collar and laboring worlds were clearly separated. One entered the white collar group only after having received considerable schooling, and one entered it directly. The immense growth of the white collar occupations, just beginning throughout America during this period, was to make the distinction between inter-generational and intra-generational mobility opportunities increasingly sharp; the type of mobility represented by these white collar workers was to become the chief means of social ascent.

Since the white collar worker was necessarily an educated man, the family which produced him had to be in a position to forgo the immediate economic benefits of child labor long enough to allow him to attend school longer than his working class peers, who customarily began work in their early teens. It is not surprising, therefore, that the fourteen families whose sons became clerks and professionals were markedly more prosperous than the families of sons who ventured into business for themselves. Four fifths of the fathers of the latter group remained propertyless unskilled laborers; fully two thirds of the fathers of the former group became property owners, and several were occupationally mobile as well. The case of John G. Buckley was representative. Indistinguishable from a hundred other destitute laborers in 1860, Buckley made a respected place for himself in Newburyport during the following two decades, though remaining a laborer. By 1880 Buckley had become the owner of four houses, worth $2200, and had been appointed a night watchman on the police force. (His younger brother Cornelius accumulated $2900 in real estate over the same period.) Sending his two sons to school was not an impossible drain on the John Buckley's resources: one attended a seminary and became a priest, the second took a position as a clerk after graduating from high school.

If white collar workers usually came from families which were able to give special advantages to them, other members of the family should have shared some of the gains. The career patterns of the brothers of these white collar youths fitted this expectation. The brothers of the laborers mobile into business callings usually found unskilled and semiskilled manual jobs; the siblings of the laborers mobile into white collar occupations tended to enter skilled or nonmanual occupations. A few took white collar jobs themselves, and about half chose skilled callings. Thus Pat Moylan's eldest son became a blacksmith, the other two sons obtained clerkships; John Carnes became a barber, James Carnes a clerk; Jeremiah McDonald became a clerk, his younger brother an office boy. The youngest children, as we might expect, were most likely to achieve the highest status; it was often the increment to family income produced by the employment of their elder brothers that paid for their education.

■ Intermediate Mobility Families.   The category "intermediate mobility" designates families whose members remained entirely with the working class occupational world between 1850 and 1880, but who succeeded in elevating themselves *within* the working class during this period. The forty-seven families in the high mobility class accounted for all the dramatic interclass mobility achieved by unskilled manual laborers in Newburyport at this time. But the other 240 laboring families included in the survey cannot be indiscriminately characterized as static. Within the broad penumbra of the manual laboring class there were important variations in occupational status and in economic position. Two types of intermediate mobility were distinguished here. A family was placed in this category either if one of its members rose into a skilled occupation, or if it acquired a significant amount of property.

Only one fifth of the 145 families in the intermediate mobility class achieved occupational mobility into a skilled craft. Thirteen of the older generation of our sample entered skilled positions between 1850 and 1880. They included four carpenters, three masons, a painter, a tailor, a ropemaker, and an engineer. Wage levels in the skilled trades were well above the prevailing rate for unskilled labor; all but two of the thirteen came into possession of property worth $500 or more.

New security of employment, the relative ease of home ownership and saving, and pride of craft all gave grounds for a feeling of status improvement.

In one important respect, however, the gains of these men were limited. An essential element of the superior status of the traditional artisan was that he was able to transmit craft status to his children. The son of the skilled tradesman was expected to serve an apprenticeship himself, and then to enter a craft, often that of his father. Only two of the twenty sons of these mobile laborers followed this course; fourteen became factory operatives or seamen, and another four became casual laborers. To the extent to which the ability to pass on social and economic advantages to one's children is a criterion of success, the success of these laborers was distinctly qualified.

The skilled trades were a somewhat more important avenue of mobility for the younger generation. In our analysis only sixteen families appear to boast a son in a skilled occupation, but the figure is misleading low. To classify families according to the attainments of their most successful member obscures the extent of intermediate mobility of this kind; many of the brothers of youths in white collar jobs held skilled positions themselves. . . . laborers' sons who had learned a trade were still a fairly select minority in 1880, but skilled positions were definitely more accessible to them than to their fathers.

Much the largest portion of the intermediate mobility group consisted of families whose members remained in the low-skill, low-pay occupational universe throughout these decades, but who were able to accumulate significant property holdings. The wealth of the 116 occupationally static families in the intermediate mobility category is indicated in Table 1. The variation was wide. A small elite, twenty-one

TABLE 1. Maximum property holdings of occupationally static laboring families[a]

Size of holding	Number of families	Percentage of group
$300–599	27	23%
$600–899	37	32
$900–1199	22	19
$1200–1499	9	8
$1500 and over	21	18
Total	116	100

[a] Families are categorized here according to the maximum figure listed in census schedules and assessor's valuation books, 1850–1880.

families, reached the $1500 mark; a few of these went well above that figure. Jeremiah Long, for instance, already owned a $700 house in 1850. Two of his sons were employed as mariners. Their wages plus the rent paid by four boarders gave Long an unusually large income. In 1856 he bought another house, increasing his real property holdings to $1300; in 1860 he paid taxes on property worth $1700; and by 1870 the Census listed him as the owner of $3000 in real estate and $2000 in personal property.

A more typical figure from the wealthier stratum of propertied laborers was Tim Marooney. Marooney had scraped together $400 by 1867, when he invested it in a shack on the edge of the city. With two cows, a few chickens, and no rent to pay, Marooney found it possible to save a substantial portion of his wages. By 1870 he paid taxes on $500 in personal property as well as $500 in real estate;

during the seventies, with the aid of four mortgages, he built a second house on Railroad Street and a third one on Auburn Street. Marooney was worth $1900 in 1880. The family of James Barrett eventually arrived at about this economic level too, but its success came in the second generation. Barrett himself, a common laborer on four successive censuses, never acquired any taxable property. Both of his sons took semiskilled positions while in their early teens. One left Newburyport during the Civil War and never returned; the other was at various times a mill operative, a mariner, and a comb factory employee. The 1882 city directory listed the second as a day laborer like his father, yet by this time he had become the owner of two houses valued at $1800.

These twenty-one relatively wealthy families represented but a small fraction of the total laboring group, of course. The average property-owning laborer in Newburyport accumulated holdings of less than a thousand dollars. The modest progress of the Norton family was characteristic of the dozens of small property holders. The native-born father was a laborer in 1850 and 1860, then a watchman. He saved nothing during those years, so far as can be determined. Three of his four sons as teen-agers worked in the mills. One son moved away in the late sixties. A second became a teamster; he possessed no taxable property by 1880, but did hold an account at the Institution for Savings. The third Norton boy became an operative in a comb factory and was able to purchase a $600 house after two decades of employment there. The fourth, a fisherman, claimed $200 in personal property on the Census of 1870 and was a savings bank depositor; despite the fact that three of his young children were employed in 1880, however, as yet he owned no real estate. Not much of a success story, surely, but not a condition of absolute stagnation either. As the Nortons might have viewed it, one member of the family had definitely advanced into the ranks of the respectable, home-owning citizenry, while two others had taken at least a short step in that direction by setting aside some savings.

■ Static Families.   Two thirds of the laboring families in Newburyport had advanced themselves at least as much as the Nortons by 1880. The remaining third, ninety-five families, were unable to rise out of the most depressed, impoverished segment of the manual laboring class. A man like John Martin, for instance, was a casual laborer in 1860; he later became a laborer at the local gas works, living with his family in a small building owned by the gas company. An Irish immigrant, Martin was illiterate, and his children saw more of the factory than they did of the schoolhouse. Martin's daughters worked in the cotton mills until marriage; one son became a fisherman, the second an operative in a rope factory. Dennis Sughrue was still an ordinary laborer in 1880; his fourteen-year-old boy was a mill hand, while his older son had graduated to the brickyard. Neither family payed any property taxes at all during this period. The Martins, the Sughrues, and the Lowrys had their names in the newspaper occasionally, when one of them was arrested for drunkenness; heavy drinking on a common laborer's wages was a nearly foolproof way of keeping one's family in dismal poverty. About this substantial segment of the Newburyport working class little more can be said. These men were failures according to the values of the competitive society in which they lived, and the early careers of their children suggested that the habit of failure could easily develop in this environment.

The statement that as many as a third of the laboring families resident in

Newburyport at this time achieved neither occupational mobility nor property mobility, however, is in one respect highly misleading. Families which lived in the community for only ten years during the period studied were obviously less likely to accumulate property or climb in the occupational hierarchy than families more firmly rooted in Newburyport. Table 2, which classifies families according to length of residence in the city, shows this clearly. Over 40 percent of the families in Newburyport for ten years remained at the very bottom of the social ladder; only 5 percent of the laboring families who lived there throughout the 1850–1880 period are found in the static category. And, similarly, the proportion of families in the high mobility and intermediate mobility categories rose steadily with increased length of residence in the city. Table 2 provides a simple overview

TABLE 2.   Mobility of laboring families according to length of residence

	Ten years	Twenty years	Thirty years
Number in sample	145	101	41
High mobility	8%	21%	32%
Intermediate mobility:			
Occupational skill	8	7	27
Property			
$1000 or more	16	19	12
$300–999	26	22	24
Static	43	32	5

of the cumulative significance of several social processes—selective geographical mobility, occupational mobility, and property mobility—which affected the status of the unskilled laboring families of Newburyport. It reinforces the broad conclusion that the great majority of families who settled in the community for very long were able to make at least a modest social advance.

From Generation to Generation: Social Mobility as a Cumulative Process

An important aspect of the social mobility patterns of working class families in nineteenth century Newburyport has only been touched on so far. Was social mobility usually a cumulative process? Was the son of an upwardly mobile laborer likely to emulate his father and continue to climb upward, or were his career prospects no better than those of a youth whose father remained a propertyless unskilled workman?

In Table 3 the occupational achievements of these working class youths are classified according to the highest occupation attained by their father in the 1850–1880 period, and the results are rather surprising. No consistent positive relationship between the occupational mobility of fathers and sons is revealed. The children of laborers mobile into a semiskilled occupation were more successful than the sons of static laborers in both the semiskilled and skilled callings, as we would expect. But workmen who climbed into a skilled trade were unable to transfer higher status to their children; their sons found skilled jobs less often than the sons of semiskilled men, and were the least successful of all the groups at penetrating the nonmanual occupations. And the sons of the small elite of laborers who rose into a nonmanual occupation during this period, paradoxically, clustered in unskilled laboring jobs more heavily than the sons of men still at the

Son's occupation at the last census on which he was listed in the 1850–1880 period	Father's highest occupation in the 1850–1880 period			
	Unskilled	Semi-skilled	Skilled	Non-manual
Number in sample	234	38	23	24
Unskilled	26%	3%	9%	29%
Semiskilled	54	63	70	29
Skilled	13	24	17	8
Nonmanual	8	10	4	33

bottom of the occupational scale. The children of these highly mobile fathers, it is true, obtained nonmanual positions more often than did men in the other groups. But even so, only a third of them attained middle class occupational status, and this is a liberal estimate, since it includes youths working on a farm owned by their father as nonmanual employees. Table 3 provides no support for the belief that occupationally mobile men imparted exceptionally high mobility aspirations to their children, nor for the hypothesis that a mobile father was able to ease his sons' entry into a higher status occupation.

If the occupational mobility of working class fathers did little to further their children's career prospects, perhaps property mobility had a more positive effect. Common sense suggests that youths from the thrifty, respectable, home-owning segment of the working class would develop higher ambitions than the children of laborers living at the bare subsistence level, and that they would possess superior resources in the contest for better jobs. The evidence, however, does not confirm this plausible hypothesis. Property mobility and inter-generational occupational mobility were not necessarily complementary forms of social mobility; indeed, Table 4 indicates that in some instances they were mutually exclusive. The sons

TABLE 4. Occupational status attained by laborers' sons according to the property holdings of their fathers

Son's occupation at the last census on which he was listed in the 1850–1880 period	Father's maximum property holding in the 1850–1880 period		
	Less than $300	$300–899	$900 or more
Number in sample[a]	121	65	48
Unskilled	24%	22%	35%
Semiskilled	59	57	38
Skilled	7	18	21
Nonmanual	11	3	6

[a] The numbers here are smaller than on Table 3, because property data was analyzed only for families resident in Newburyport for a decade or more during the period.

of property-owning workmen entered skilled manual callings more often than the sons of propertyless laborers, but they remained disproportionately concentrated in unskilled positions and, most surprising, somewhat underrepresented in non-manual occupations.

This striking discovery recalls an aspect of working class property mobility about which the prophets of the mobility ideology were understandably silent. The ordinary workman of nineteenth century Newburyport could rarely build up a savings account and purchase a home without making severe sacrifices. To cut family consumption expenditures to the bone was one such sacrifice. To withdraw the children from school and to put them to work at the age of ten or twelve was another. As Table 13 shows, the sons of exceptionally prosperous laborers did *not* enjoy generally superior career opportunities; the sacrifice of their education and the constriction of their occupational opportunities, in fact, was often a prime cause of the family's property mobility.

This pattern was particularly characteristic of Irish working class families in Newburyport. It was shown in Chapter Four that immigrants and their children moved upwards on the occupational scale with greater difficulty than their Yankee counterparts. When we consider property mobility, however, the roles of the two groups are reversed. In Table 5, which reveals ethnic differences in family mobility

TABLE 5.   Mobility of native-born and foreign-born laboring families by length of residence

	Ten years		Twenty years		Thirty years	
	Native	*Foreign*	*Native*	*Foreign*	*Native*	*Foreign*
Number in sample	36	109	27	74	16	25
High mobility	8%	8%	30%	18%	31%	32%
Intermediate mobility:						
Occupational skill	8	7	15	4	38	20
Property						
$1000 or more	8	18	4	24	6	16
$300–999	17	28	19	23	13	32
Static	58	38	33	31	13	0

patterns, the occupational advantages of the native are again evident. But within the large group of laboring families whose members remained in unskilled and semiskilled jobs, the immigrants were notably more successful in accumulating property. Of those who had been in Newburyport for ten years nearly 60 percent of the native families but less than 40 percent of the foreign families failed to accumulate significant property holdings. Thirteen percent of the native families in residence for thirty years but none of the foreign families in this group were completely immobile in both the property and occupational hierarchies. In each of the three groups close to 50 percent of the immigrant families obtained a property stake in the community while remaining near the bottom of the occupational ladder; the comparable figure for native families was only half that.

That Irish working class families were especially successful in accumulating property but especially unsuccessful in climbing out of the low-status manual occupations was hardly a coincidence. The immigrant laborer received wages no higher than those of the Yankee workman, but he had a greater determination to save and to own. Perhaps the land hunger displayed by the Irish laborers of Newburyport was a manifestation of older peasant values. In any case, it was a hunger which could be satisfied to a remarkable extent by even the lowliest laborer —but only at a price. The price was not only ruthless economy; equally necessary was the employment of every able-bodied member of the family at the earliest possible age. The cotton mill or the shoe factory was not to provide the teen-agers of the second generation with the education made increasingly necessary by a rapidly industrializing economy, as the exceptionally low mobility of Irish youths into nonmanual occupations so plainly reveals.

For the working class families of nineteenth century Newburyport, therefore, social mobility was not a cumulative process. The varying kinds of social advances made by laboring families were not complementary aspects of a smooth natural progression out of the working class occupational world. Property mobility did not usually facilitate inter-generational occupational mobility; often it was achieved by sacrificing the education of the younger generation. Nor did the movement of a laboring father into a higher-status occupation seem to improve the career prospects of his children very much. The upward advances of these ordinary laboring families remain impressive, but the facile assumption of progress from generation to generation must be abandoned.

The Meaning of Mobility: A Trial Balance

If nineteenth century Newburyport was to develop a permanent proletarian class, the families dealt with in this study should have formed it. These unskilled workmen began at the very bottom of the community occupational ladder in the 1850–1880 period. Their situation seemed anything but promising. They lacked both vocational skills and financial resources. Many were illiterate, and few had the means to see that their children received more than a primitive education. Most were relative strangers in the city, migrants from New England farms or Irish villages. Few inhabitants of Newburyport at mid-century were more likely candidates for membership in a permanently depressed caste.

That these working class families did not remain in a uniformly degraded social position throughout the 1850–1880 period is by now abundantly clear. If the Newburyport laboring class gave birth to no self-made millionaires during these years, the social advances registered by many of its members were nonetheless impressive. A brief review of the findings on geographical, occupational, and property mobility will clarify the significance of these social gains and provide a fresh perspective on social stratification in the nineteenth century city.

By 1880 the undifferentiated mass of poverty-stricken laboring families, the "lack-alls" who seemed at mid-century to be forming a permanent class, had separated into three layers. On top was a small but significant elite of laboring families who had gained a foothold in the lower fringes of the middle class occupational world. Below them was the large body of families who had attained property mobility while remaining in manual occupations, most often of the unskilled or semiskilled variety; these families constituted the stable, respectable, home-owning stratum of the Newburyport working class. At the very bottom of the social ladder was the impoverished, floating lower class, large in number but so transient as to be formless and powerless.

The composition of the Newburyport manual labor force in the latter half of the nineteenth century, we have seen, was extraordinarily volatile. A minority of the laboring families who came to the city in those years settled for as long as a decade. Most did not, and it was these floating families whose depressed position most resembled the classic European proletariat. Recurrently unemployed, often on relief, they rarely accumulated property or advanced themselves occupationally. Substantial numbers of these impoverished unskilled workmen, men who "had no interest in the country except the interest of breathing," were always to be found in Newburyport during this period, but this stratum had remarkably little continuity of membership. Members of this floating group naturally had no capacity to act in concert against an employer or to assert themselves politically; stable organization based on a consciousness of common grievances was obviously impossible. The pressure to migrate operated selectively to remove the least successful from the community; a mere 5 percent of the laboring families present in Newburyport throughout this entire thirty-year period found both occupational mobility and property mobility beyond their grasp.

The floating laborers who made up this large, ever renewed transient class occupied the lowest social stratum in nineteenth century Newburyport. A notch above it was the settled, property-owning sector of the working class; above that was the lower middle class, the highest social level attained by members of any of these laboring families. To obtain middle class status required entry into a nonmanual occupation and the adoption of a new style of life; this was an uncommon feat for either unskilled laborers or their children. Five sixths of the laboring families resident in Newburyport for a decade or more during this period found the middle class occupational world completely closed to them. And among the remaining sixth, the high mobility families, were many which remained partially dependent on manual employment for their support. It is doubtful that many of the elite high mobility families developed the attitudes and behavior patterns associated with the middle class style of life. This seems particularly unlikely in the case of laborers who became the operators of small farms, whose sons rarely entered middle class occupations. Nor did a marginal business or a menial clerkship necessarily provide the economic security and inspire the commitment to education needed to insure the transmission of middle class status to the next generation. The importance of the small group of laborers and laborers' sons who purchased shops and farms or found white collar jobs should not be minimized: these men did provide proof to their less successful brethren that class barriers could be hurdled by men of talent, however lowly their origin. But it should be emphasized that many of these upwardly mobile workmen obtained only a precarious hold on middle class status, and that their social milieu often differed little from the milieu of the propertied sector of the working class.

By far the most common form of social advance for members of laboring families in Newburyport in this period was upward movement *within* the working class, mobility into the stratum between the lower middle class and the floating group of destitute unskilled families. A few men from these intermediate mobility families became skilled craftsmen; this was extremely rare for the older generation but less unusual as an inter-generational move. Most often, however, these families advanced themselves by accumulating significant amounts of property while remaining in unskilled or semiskilled occupations. Here were men who offered the market little more than two hands and a strong back, but who succeeded in becoming respectable home owners and savings bank depositors.

What was the social significance of these modest advances? Nineteenth century propagandists took a simple view. The property-owning laborer was "a capitalist." If there was a working class in America, as soon as "a man has saved something he ceases to belong to this class"; "the laborers have become the capitalists in this new world." Accumulated funds, however small, were capital, and the possession of capital determined the psychological orientation of the workman. It was the nature of capital to multiply itself; he who possessed capital necessarily hungered for further expansion of his holdings. To save and to invest was the first step in the process of mobility; investment inspired a risk-taking, speculative mentality conducive to further mobility. The distinction between the "petty capitalist" workman and the rich merchant was one of degree. To move from the former status to the latter was natural; it happened "every day." Similar assumptions lie behind the still-popular view that "the typical American worker" has been "an expectant entrepreneur."

This was sheer fantasy. A mere handful of the property-owning laborers of Newburyport ventured into business for themselves. More surprising, the property mobility of a laboring man did not even heighten his children's prospects for mobility into a business or professional calling. Indeed, the working class family which abided by the injunction "spend less than you earn" could usually do so only by sacrificing the children's education for an extra paycheck, and thereby restricting their opportunities for inter-generational occupational mobility.

Furthermore, the use these laborers made of their savings testifies to their search for maximum security rather than for mobility out of the working class. An economically rational investor in nineteenth century Newburyport would not have let his precious stock of capital languish in a savings bank for long, and he certainly would not have tied it up in the kind of real estate purchased by these laborers. The social environment of the middle class American encouraged such investment for rising profits, but the working class social milieu did not. The earning capacity of the merchant, professional, or entrepreneur rose steadily as his career unfolded—the very term "career" connotes this. The middle class family head was ordinarily its sole source of support, and the family was able both to accumulate wealth and to improve its standard of living out of normal increments in the salary (or net profits) accruing to him over the years.

Ordinary workmen did not have "careers" in this sense. Their earning capacity did not increase with age; in unskilled and semiskilled occupations a forty-year-old man was paid no more than a boy of 17. Substantial saving by a working class family thus tended to be confined to the years when the children were old enough to bring in a supplementary income but too young to have married and established households of their own.

The tiny lots, the humble homes, and the painfully accumulated savings accounts were the fruits of those years. They gave a man dignity, and a slender margin of security against unpredictable, uncontrollable economic forces which could deprive him of his job at any time. Once the mortgage was finally discharged, home ownership reduced the family's necessary expenses by $60 to $100 a year, and a few hundred dollars in the savings bank meant some protection against illness, old age, or a sluggish labor market. A cynical observer would have noted the possibility that home ownership served also to confine the workman to the local labor market and to strengthen the hand of local employers, who were thus assured of a docile permanent work force, but few laborers of nineteenth century Newburyport were disposed to think in these terms.

Families belonging to the propertied stratum of the working class, in short, were socially mobile in the sense that they had climbed a rung higher on the social ladder, and had established themselves as decent, respectable, hard-working, churchgoing members of the community. They had not, however, set their feet upon an escalator which was to draw them up into the class of merchants, professionals, and entrepreneurs.

The contrast between the literal claims of the rags-to-riches mythology and the actual social experience of these families thus appears glaring. A few dozen farmers, small shopkeepers, and clerks, a large body of home-owning families unable to escape a grinding regimen of manual labor: this was the sum of the social mobility achieved by Newburyport's unskilled laborers by 1880. Could men like these have felt that the mobility ideology was at all relevant to their lives?

I think so. True, many of the optimistic assertions of popular writers and speakers were demonstrably false. Class differences in opportunities were deep and pervasive; a large majority of the unskilled laborers in Newburyport and a large majority of their sons remained in the working class throughout the 1850–1880 period. Not one rose from rags to genuine riches. Whoever seeks a Newburyport version of Andrew Carnegie must settle for Joseph Greenough, keeper of a livery stable worth $15,000, and Stephen Fowle, proprietor of a small newsstand. But we err if we take the mobility creed too literally. The rapt attention nineteenth century Americans gave Russell Conwell did not mean that his listeners literally believed that they soon would acquire riches equivalent to "an acre of diamonds." One ingredient of the appeal of mobility literature and oratory was that pleasant fantasies of sudden wealth and a vicarious sharing in the spectacular successes of other ordinary men provided a means of escaping the tedious realities of daily existence. Fantasies of this sort are not likely to flourish among men who have no hope at all of individual economic or social betterment. And indeed the laborers of Newburyport had abundant evidence that self-improvement was possible. To practice the virtues exalted by the mobility creed rarely brought middle class status to the laborer, or even to his children. But hard work and incessant economy did bring tangible rewards—money in the bank, a house to call his own, a new sense of security and dignity. "The man who owns the roof that is over his head and the earth under his dwelling can't help thinking that he's more of a man than though he had nothing, with poverty upon his back and want at home; and if he don't think so, other people will."

The ordinary workmen of Newburyport, in short, could view America as a land of opportunity despite the fact that the class realities which governed their life chances confined most of them to the working class. These newcomers to urban life arrived with a low horizon of expectations, it seems likely. If it is true that "in the last analysis the status of the worker is not a physical but a mental one, and is affected as much by comparisons with past conditions and with the status of other groups in the community as by the facts in themselves," the typical unskilled laborer who settled in Newburyport could feel proud of his achievements and optimistic about the future. Most of the social gains registered by laborers and their sons during these years were decidedly modest—a move one notch up the occupational scale, the acquisition of a small amount of property. Yet *in their eyes* these accomplishments must have loomed large. The contradiction between an ideology of limitless opportunity and the realities of working class existence is unlikely to have dismayed men whose aspirations and expectations were shaped in the Irish village or the New England subsistence farm. The "dream of success" certainly affected these laboring families, but the personal measure of success was modest. By this measure, the great majority of them had indeed "gotten ahead."

William James and the New Age DANIEL B. SCHIRMER

In general, the New Left is more critical of progressivism than of populism. They consider populism authentic, grass-roots native radicalism; progressivism, a movement of the middle class with a strong business contingent among its supporters, seems less genuinely insurgent.

There is much to be said, surely, for the idea that the Progressives were middle-class reformers, opposed to fundamental change in the property relations of the country. Few consensus historians would assert otherwise. But there are some paradoxes in the Left's skepticism of the Progressives. If they reject Progressive policies, they embrace Progressive intellectuals. We have already seen how much the New Left historians are indebted to Charles Beard. Indeed, Beard, one of the outstanding Progressive thinkers, is the godfather of New Left scholarship, and a number of young radical scholars have emphatically acknowledged their debt to him. Even Lynd, who deplores Beard's indifference to the black man, and rejects his oversimple formulations regarding the American Revolution and the Constitutional struggle, explicitly accepts his general class approach and his emphasis on the economic dimension of American history.

In the selection below, a young New Left scholar praises still another Progressive thinker, William James. James was not a radical, yet his new approach to knowledge, pragmatism, was a powerful solvent of the conventional wisdom, and for James himself, and to a still greater degree for his disciple, John Dewey, it led to a friendly attitude toward socialism and a cooperative society. Equally important to Daniel Schirmer was James' hostility to imperialism, a sentiment that makes him congenial to the New Left of today.

FOR FURTHER READING:

Morton White, *Social Thought in America: The Revolt Against Formalism**, (Beacon Press, 1957); Ralph D. Perry, *The Thought and Character of William James,* (Little, Brown and Company, 1935); Gay Wilson Allen, *William James: A Biography**, (Viking Press, 1969); Daniel Aaron, *Men of Good Hope: A Story of American Progressives**, (Galaxy, 1961).

Asterisk denotes paperback edition.

A highly perceptive young man of Spanish descent, George Santayana was a colleague of William James in the Philosophy Department at Harvard. Later in life

Source: Daniel B. Schirmer, "William James and the New Age," *Science and Society,* vol. 33, no. 4 (Fall–Winter 1969), pp. 434–445.

Santayana remembered a conversation James and he had with a senior member of the department, George Herbert Palmer.

> One afternoon in the autumn of 1898 we were standing in Palmer's library after a brief business meeting, and conversation turned on the terms of peace imposed by the United States on Spain after the Cuban war. James was terribly distressed. Addressing himself rather to Palmer, who was evidently enjoying the pleasant rays of the setting sun on his back, and the general spacious comfort of his library . . . James said he felt he had lost his country. Intervention in Cuba might be defended on account of the perpetual bad government there and the sufferings of the natives. But the annexation of the Philippines, what could excuse that? What could be a more shameless betrayal of American principles? What could be a plainer symptom of greed, ambition, corruption, and imperialism? [Santayana, *The Middle Span*, p. 167.]

There was reason for James' display of distress. In all his life the political issue which moved him most deeply was imperialism (R. B. Perry, *The Thought and Character of William James,* p. 245). For him the American plunge into the vortex of world imperialism was a deeply disturbing experience. In the years around the turn of the century his private conversation and correspondence flashed with anger and indignation at the turn in American affairs. He spoke out publicly on this matter in a way he did on no other. Between 1895 and 1904 he wrote eight letters to the press highly critical of United States foreign policy. In 1903 he gave an address to the annual meeting of the New England branch of the Anti-Imperialist League and in 1904 he was elected a vice president of that organization, joining his friend and fellow-member of the Harvard faculty, Charles Eliot Norton, in that capacity. If Americans of the present day have come to look upon James as one of the most distinguished intellectuals of his time, his contemporaries knew him as one of the most outspoken in opposition to the imperialist policies of the government.

Opposition to the Spanish-American War centered in Boston and gave rise to the New England Anti-Imperialist League in the fall of 1898. This organization then carried on a most active and nationwide campaign to halt the war against the Philippine independence movement. The Anti-Imperialist League was initiated by a group of Brahmin reformers, such as Gamaliel Bradford, Moorfield Storey, Edward Atkinson, and Erving Winslow. Although ministers, trade unionists, and men from various ranks and callings gave their adherence to the Anti-Imperialist League, the key leadership was always provided by this core of Boston men who came from families of established wealth and social position, of Revolutionary and Puritan ancestry.

William James took a place in the leadership of the anti-imperialist movement in Massachusetts, but perhaps more as an ally than otherwise. He was *with* the Boston anti-imperialists, but not *of* them in the strictest sense. Like many of these men, he came from a family of inherited wealth. Like them he had a cultivated contempt for commercial rapacity and greed, and for the philistine worship of "the bitch-goddess, Success." He had been a Mugwump and deserted the Republicans for the Democrats in 1884, hoping at the time for the emergence of a more intelligent and reform-minded political leadership. He too had come to maturity during the Civil War years, and while he had not worn a uniform because of frail health, his father had been an ardent Union patriot and both his younger brothers had served as officers in Negro regiments. His address at the Shaw memorial exercises was testimony that the Civil War and all it stood for was as important to him as it was to Edward Atkinson, Moorfield Storey, and George Boutwell.

However, the grandfather of William James, who had amassed the family fortune, had been an Irish immigrant and he had settled in Albany, New York. James therefore was Albany Irish, not Boston Yankee. It is true that his philosopher father had been a good friend of Ralph Waldo Emerson and his circle. But in the face of Boston society's awesome genealogies, William James, like his father before him, remained a little an outlander, though much appreciated and cultivated by the Brahmins. Moreover, James was an intellectual before all else, and an intellectual with even a touch of the Bohemian, as shown in his fondness for bright ties, striped shirts, Norfolk jackets, and, more seriously, in his reckless generosity and warmth of spirit. On the other hand, most of the Boston anti-imperialists were business or professional men who were at the same time men of some cultivation and intellectual stature. Where most of the Boston anti-imperialists tended toward social conservatism, not so James. He was not only democratic in his political outlook, but in his social attitudes as well. Some of his friends despaired of him for his apparent lack of social discrimination. In their eyes he took up every crank that came along. He carried this egalitarian leaning somewhat vaguely into the realm of theory as well; he spoke of the need for a redistribution of wealth and declared a devout belief "in the gradual advent of some sort of socialistic equilibrium" (Perry, p. 237).

Then again, James differed in his approach to the problem of imperialism from the leaders of anti-imperialism in New England. Men like Atkinson, Storey, and Winslow quite clearly gave an importance to economic motivation (the desire for foreign trade, markets, investment opportunities) in the drive behind United States imperialism. James approached the question of imperialism as a psychologist with definite leanings toward philosophical idealism, that is to say, less objectively, with more attention to subjective motivation and interplay, and with a high degree of abstraction. In June 1898 James analyzed the origin of the imperialist war aims of the United States:

> ...when, in its ultimatum to Spain, Congress denied any project of conquest in Cuba, it genuinely meant every word it said. But here comes in the psychologic factor: once the excitement of action gets loose, the taxes levied, the victories achieved, etc., the old human instincts which our nation has will set up new demands. We shall never take Cuba.... But Porto Rico, and even the Philippines, are not so sure. We had supposed ourselves...a better nation morally than the rest, safe at home, and without the old savage ambition, destined to exert great international influence by throwing in our "moral weight," etc. Dreams! Human nature is everywhere the same; and at the least temptation all the old military passions rise, and sweep everything before them. [*Letters of William James, Vol. II*, p. 74.]

James saw the root of imperialism as a more or less absolute tendency of the human race toward aggression and violence, as something quite independent of specific historical development or circumstance. Six years later, in talking to a Boston gathering for international peace he drove home the point: "Our permanent enemy is the rooted bellicosity of human nature" (William James, *Memories and Studies*, pp. 300–301).

Both James and the more typical Boston anti-imperialists shared a common vantage point in their thinking that imperialist policy was a betrayal of the best traditions of the American past. Here the more typical anti-imperialist leaders seemed to stop in their thinking (no matter how effective their practical politics), as if to imply that a return to the past was a solution. James attempted to move forward with the times, in a manner that further bespoke his subjective and idealist orientation.

If James saw a somewhat abstract and absolute tendency toward aggression in human nature as the root of imperialism, he saw a similar abstract and absolute counterforce in a human tendency toward reason and sanity, which he came to personify in the liberal intellectuals as a group. These, the forces of reason, were the antidote to imperialism. It is just here that James struck a new note, a note of internationalism, which he felt to be in keeping with the times. This was a note which the more typical anti-imperialists, in their subliminal longing for a return to the past, did not give forth. James in effect said: well then, the United States has thrown over her old ways of international righteousness in favor of imperialism. So be it. This simply means that men of reason in America now face the same problems as have their counterparts in imperial Europe. Therefore, those Americans must make common cause with their allies the world over; that is the only way out.

It is possible that James' strong internationalist leanings were fostered by his thought and practice as a scientist, by the internationalism of science, if you will. He had wide connections with psychologists and philosophers in France, Switzerland, Germany, England, etc.; he followed the meetings of international scientific bodies and carried on an extensive international correspondence which touched on world politics as well as science.

In his correspondence with the Swiss psychologist Flournoy, for example, he discussed the Dreyfus case and the role of the French intellectuals in fighting for the vindication of Dreyfus. He identified the chauvinist elements behind the persecution of Dreyfus with the proponents of military conquest in the United States, and the Americans who spoke up for the independence of the Philippines with the French liberal intelligentsia who fought for Dreyfus' vindication, calling them, in fact, "les intellectuels." It is thus quite likely that the international ties of friendship and science which James enjoyed helped him to see the need and the possibility for anti-imperialist activity on a world scale; helped him to see the American anti-imperialist movement as part of an international political tendency.

One of the first times James gave expression to this was in a letter to W. D. Howells, written in Rome on November 16, 1900. Writing of the Philippine "war of conquest," James said, "To me it simply means the death of the old American soul. . . . I think 'les intellectuels' of every country ought to band themselves into a league for the purpose of fighting the curse of savagery that is pouring over the world" (letter in Houghton Library, Cambridge, Mass.). He wrote Charles Eliot Norton from England in the spring of 1901 in much the same vein:

> Don't feel too bad about the country. We've thrown away our old privileged position among the nations, but it only showed that we were less sincere about it than we thought we were. The eternal fight of liberalism has now to be fought by us on much the same terms as in the older countries. We have still the better chance in our freedom from all the corrupting influences from on top which they now suffer. [Letter in Houghton Library, Cambridge, Mass.]

Talking to students of the Graduate School at Harvard in 1902, he posed in the sharpest manner the confrontation of forces he saw involved in the contemporary political reality: "Speaking broadly, there are never more than two fundamental parties in the nation: the party of red blood, as it calls itself, and that of pale reflection; the party of animal instinct, of jingoism, fun, excitement, bigness; and that of reason, forecast, order gained by growth, and spiritual methods—briefly put, the party of force and the party of education" (R. B. Perry, *The Thought and Character of William James*, p. 240). Here it is clearly evident that James tended to sublimate and cast into ideal form the concrete political and economic realities of the imperialist situation.

James, who had been one of the most articulate and distinguished of the voices associated with the anti-imperialist movement, was asked to make the main address at the annual meeting of the New England Anti-Imperialist League in 1903. In this speech he rounded out and summed up the conclusions he had so far reached on the question of imperialism, at the same time indicating his differences with the anti-imperialist leadership, especially in what he regarded as the lack of realism in their outlook:

To the ordinary citizen the word anti-imperialist suggests a thin-haired being just waked up from the day before yesterday, brandishing the Declaration of Independence excitedly, and shrieking after a railroad train thundering toward its destination to turn upon its tracks and come back.... As a group of citizens calling to our country to return to the principles which it was suckled in, I believe that we Anti-Imperialists are already a back number.... The country has once for all regurgitated the Declaration of Independence and the Farewell Address, and it won't swallow again immediately what it is so happy to have vomited up. It has come to a hiatus. It has deliberately pushed itself into the circle of international hatreds, and joined the common pack of wolves. It relishes the attitude. We have thrown off our swaddling clothes, it thinks, and attained our majority. We are objects of fear to other lands. This makes of the old liberalism and the new liberalism of our country two discontinuous things. The older liberalism was in office, the new is in opposition. Inwardly it is the same spirit, but outwardly the tactics, the questions, the reasons, and the phrases have to change. American memories no longer serve as catchwords. The great international and cosmopolitan liberal party, the party of conscience and intelligence the world over has, in short, absorbed us; we are only its American section, carrying on the war against the powers of darkness here, playing our part in the long, long campaign for truth and fair dealing which must go on in all countries until the end of time. [From the Report of the Fifth Annual Meeting of the New England Anti-Imperialist League, 1903.]

Burdened by social conservatism, and fundamentally men of affairs rather than intellectuals, the Boston anti-imperialist leadership shied away from the search in theory for new solutions to new problems. James criticized them for their failure, and for his part made an effort to think things out in his own way.

James made his appreciation of the international character of the struggle against contemporary imperialism a part of his criticism of the anti-imperialist leadership for their parochial and one-sided emphasis upon the moral position of the United States in world affairs both past and present: "Angelic impulses and predatory lusts divide our heart exactly as they divide the hearts of other countries. It is good to rid ourselves of cant and humbug, and to know the truth about ourselves. Political virtue does not follow geographical divisions" (Report of the Fifth Annual Meeting of the New England Anti-Imperialist League, 1903).

James was clearly not altogether abstract in his analysis of imperialism; the firm ground of concrete reality was after all the taking off point for his ascent into the realm of ideality and subjectivism. Thus James gave weight to the specific condition of inter-imperialist rivalry as a motive force in United States policy: "The country has deliberately pushed itself into the circle of international hatreds and joined the common pack of wolves." It was at his point of appreciation of the concrete reality of the imperialist condition in a decisive aspect, the mutual rivalry of the powers, that James reached toward a new concept, a new solution—a gathering of anti-imperialist forces on a world scale to stem the tide of war and savagery.

James did not rest at this point, however, in his attempt to think through the problems of the new age brought on by the United States' assumption of a more active, more dominant role in the arena of world power politics. The first manifestations of this new stage in American foreign policy would come to an end: the Spanish war would close, the Philippines be subdued, and Theodore Roosevelt, after the Panama Canal episode, would move on to place the United States at the center of the world stage in his mediation of the Russo-Japanese war.

James expressed sympathy for the Japanese in this war, indicating as the source of his sympathy impatience with the imperialist attitude of racial arrogance: . . . "the insolence of the white race in Asia ought to receive a check" (*Letters WJ and TF,* p. 158). It was against the background of the Russo-Japanese war that James delivered an address to the International Peace Congress held in Boston in November, 1904. Once again he deplored humanity's powerful and irrational drive toward violence that he saw as the root of war. But in re-emphasizing his concern for solutions and checks to this problem of compulsive psychological forces, as he saw it, he hinted at a new theme he would later develop more fully: in order to prevent the outbreak of war it is necessary to "foster rival excitements, and invent new outlets for heroic energy" (*Memories and Studies,* pp. 305–306).

Nothing more clearly illustrates James' preoccupation with what he called the "full-inwardness" of the problems of imperialism, militarism, peace, and war than does the fact that in these, the last years of his life, he began to read military biographies and to otherwise collect material for a study which he intended to write and call either *A Psychology of Jingoism* or *Varieties of Military Experience.* This work he never completed.

On the whole, in his writings and speeches on imperialism and war, James tended to turn reality inside out: to maximize the role of the subjective, the state of mind, and to minimize the role of the objective, the circumstance of fact. Saying this may help to explain a certain drift away from reality in his consideration of these issues, but it does not deny his flashing insights, the continual forward thrust of his thought, and its essential democratic intent.

The farthest reaches of James' thinking on international politics are revealed in all their disparate but interconnected facets in his last piece on the subject, *The Moral Equivalent of War,* written in 1910, the year of his death. In this essay, James put forward a scheme of universal peacetime conscription which would harness the youth of the nation, rich and poor alike, for a certain number of years to battle with nature for production and human livelihood:

To coal and iron mines, to freight trains, to fishing fleets in December, to dishwashing, to road-building and tunnel-making, to foundries and stoke holes, to the frames of skyscrapers would our gilded youth be drafted off, according to their choice, to get the childishness knocked out of them, to come back into society with healthier sympathies and soberer ideas. [*Memories and Studies*, p. 291.]

So would James provide society with a peaceful substitute for the excitements and challenges of war, and reform the rich in the bargain.

As he elaborated on this proposal, James threw out an observation which brilliantly illuminated the whole proceeding and raised it to a new level of reality. James laid his finger on the key feature of the international situation in the year 1910: the critical tension between the imperial powers, the mounting arms race, the threatening presence of general war:

The military instincts and ideals are as strong as ever, but are confronted by reflective criticisms which sorely curb their ancient freedom. . . . Pure loot and mastery seem no longer morally avowable motives, and pretexts must be found for attributing them solely to the enemy. England and we, our army and navy authorities repeat without ceasing, arm solely for "peace," Germany and Japan it is who are bent on loot and glory. "Peace" in military mouths today is a synonym for "war expected." The word has become a pure provocative, and no government wishing peace sincerely should allow it ever to be printed in a newspaper. Every up-to-date dictionary should say that "peace" and "war" mean the same thing, now *in posse,* now *in actu.* It may even reasonably be said that the intensely sharp competitive *preparation* for war by nations *is the real war,* permanent, unceasing; and that the battles are only a sort of public verification of mastery gained during the "peace"-interval. [*Memories and Studies,* p. 275.]

Set against this grim background, James' well-meaning proposal for anti-war reform with a "moral equivalent" seems a rather frail means of exorcising pervasive dangers. World War I was only four years away. Historical hindsight makes the disparity between the real problem James quickly sketched in and the idealized solution he developed at length quite apparent.

As the antagonisms mounted which would lead to catastrophe, however, James maintained his earlier position of cool-headed internationalism, refusing to take at face value the peaceful protestations of "his own" militarists, and seeing a common striving for mastery on both sides, a mutual rivalry, of which peace and war were but discontinuous forms of one continuous process.

When the last holdouts of Boston anti-imperialism were still concentrating their attention in matters of foreign policy on a devoted but narrow focus on the demand for Philippine independence, James, with his sensitivity to the new, was casting a sharp glance at the decisive split between the major powers and the dangers of war which this suggested. The main thrust of his anti-imperialist concern had shifted from the question of Philippine independence to that of world peace.

The radical restlessness of James' mind had moved him further away from his anti-imperialist friends in another regard: he had become socialist in his convictions. (Sympathies for the underdog, for labor, for the unorthodox, for democratic social and economic reform doubtless provided background for this development as well.) In a letter to his brother Henry, written in 1908 after reading G. Lowes Dickinson's *Justice and Liberty,* James said:

Stroke upon stroke, from pens of genius, the competitive regime, so idolized 75 years ago, seems to be getting wounded to death. What will follow will be something better, but I never saw so clearly the slow effect of [the] accumulation of the influence of successive individuals in changing prevalent ideals. Wells and Dickinson will undoubtedly make the greatest steps of change. [*Letters II,* pp. 317–318.]

It was especially the writings of H. G. Wells which led James to the acceptance of socialism of a Fabian sort. It was characteristic of him to be over-sanguine about the effect of the ideas of men like Wells in doing away with "the competitive regime." In fact, it was against "the more or less socialistic future towards which mankind seems drifting" that he especially saw the need for an institution like universal conscription in the battle with nature to preserve in a new form the virtues of supreme effort and self-sacrifice which he identified with the old war-dominated and competitive way of life, for him already doomed. It was more with this interest and less as a means of checking war's outbreak that James at this point put forward the idea of the moral equivalent. It was the preservation of the military virtues in the ideal construct of a world at peace, more than the portentous arms race in the actual world of fact, to which James gave weight in this essay. So did, to the last, the abstract and idealist elements in James' thinking swing him erratically away from the concrete reality he, at the same time, saw with such acute insight.

James' thought on imperialism, nonetheless, showed continuous movement and development. He never gave up the effort to see new problems in a new way. He demonstrated this to good advantage in a few paragraphs from *The Moral Equivalent of War*, where he made what amounted to a confession of political faith. Here he linked world peace and socialism together. Where in the past he had seen the drive to war as a permanent and unchanging absolute, now he saw it as conditional, relative to time and place, indeed, subject to supersession. Where he had seen the ideals of rationality, or at most men of rationality, as the sole check to imperial drives, now he saw as well a new system of social organization, socialism, as a part of this process. With foresight he posited the monstrous growth of military technique as one of the main deterrents to war. He rejected the then-prevalent "yellow-peril" theories inspired by the awakening of Japanese imperialism, and saw instead a system of world peace which would embrace the peoples of Asia as well as those of Europe. But let James speak for himself:

> . . . I will now confess my own utopia. I devoutly believe in the reign of peace and in the gradual advent of some sort of socialistic equilibrium. The fatalistic view of the war-function is to me nonsense, for I know that war-making is due to prudential checks and reasonable criticisms, just like any other form of enterprise. And when whole nations are armies, and the science of destruction vies in intellectual refinement with the sciences of production, I see that war becomes absurd and impossible from its own monstrosity. Extravagant ambitions will have to be replaced with reasonable claims, and nations must make common cause against them. I see no reason at all why this should not apply to yellow as well as to white countries, and I look forward to a future when acts of war shall be formally outlawed as between civilized peoples. [*Memories and Studies,* pp. 286–87.]

William James ran ahead of his fellow anti-imperialists in Boston in his general thinking on imperialism and its attendant problems. But however much further his mind carried him along the way, he displayed an integrity of character that was quite typical of the best of the other anti-imperialists. Like Storey, Bradford, Atkinson and others, he suited the deed to the word, the act to the thought. He, too, was an activist. James had democratic and anti-imperialist ideals; he joined the anti-imperialist movement of his time and spoke out. He saw the need of world peace; he wrote and spoke on its behalf.

Did the old heritage, the moral toughness of the Puritans, the Revolutionaries, and the Abolitionists find new expression in the Boston anti-imperialists and their articulate friend, William James? It seemed so when James sounded the battle-call: "I do not believe it to be healthy-minded to nurse the notion that ideals are self-sufficient and require no actualization to make us content. . . . Ideals ought to aim at the *transformation of reality*" (*Letters II*, p. 270).

It may be objected that his thinking did not always tend to inspire in others that activity which James saw as desirable. It may be said that in the early stages of his thought James saw the forces of imperialism so absolute as to make their curbing nearly hopeless, and that in the last stages of his thought he saw the drift to a system of world socialism and peace so powerful as to make a struggle against war nearly unnecessary. All this may well be. The passage of time, the accumulation of historical experience, may have afforded the generations after James a more steady insight into the problems of world peace. Whether we match his ardor and passion for its realization depends on us.

Conclusion, "The Lost Democracy" GABRIEL KOLKO

One of the harshest critics of the Progressives is Gabriel Kolko, a radical scholar of great range and energy, who has written on poverty, foreign affairs, and railroad regulation, as well as progressivism. Professor Kolko's view of the Progressives was anticipated by a number of earlier historians. In the 1930s, John Chamberlain asserted that "all the economic reforms" that had been "undertaken in the spirit of Bryan, of La Follette, of Wilson" had "worked in a way precisely against the grain of Progressive or neo-democratic hopes. . . ." Regulatory legislation had often been passed at the behest of the industries to be regulated, and had succeeded scarcely at all in subordinating the corporations to the public interest. William A. Williams also anticipated Kolko's ideas by a number of years in his *Contours of American History*. Almost simultaneously, James Weinstein, former editor of *Studies on the Left*, suggested a similar concept of progressivism as a self-conscious alternative to socialism.

Nevertheless Kolko's is the clearest, best-developed argument for the corporate and conservative origin of political progressivism. In developing his theme, Kolko

Source: Gabriel Kolko, *The Triumph of Conservatism: A Reinterpretation of American History, 1900–1916* (Chicago: Quadrangle Books, 1967), "Conclusion, 'The Lost Democracy,'" pp. 279–287, 301–305.

rejects both the Progressive and Old Left historical canon. He insists that business in the last years of the nineteenth century was not becoming less competitive. Quite the contrary: Business was confronted by an ever growing problem of raids, price cuts, and general "industrial war." The merger and "trust" movement in the 1890s was one effort to blunt the edge of this threat, but it proved insufficient and left business as unstable and risky as before. Government intervention seemed the only logical recourse at this point. Fearful of the effects of destructive competition, businessmen sought to use government to regulate industry, but the regulation they and their Progressive allies advocated and got was scarcely radical. Progressivism, whatever its rhetoric, was little more than window-dressing that helped preserve the inequalities of wealth and power in the United States.

FOR FURTHER READING:

Gabriel Kolko, *The Triumph of Conservatism: A Reinterpretation of American History, 1900–1916**, (Quadrangle, 1967); Gabriel Kolko, *Railroads and Regulation, 1877–1916**, (Princeton University Press, 1970); James Weinstein, *The Corporate Ideal in the Liberal State 1900–1918,* (Beacon Press, 1968); Robert Wiebe, *Businessmen and Reform: A Study of the Progressive Movement**, (Quadrangle, 1968); John Chamberlain, *Farewell to Reform,* (John Day, 1932); George Mowry, *Theodore Roosevelt and the Progressive Movement**, (Hill and Wang, 1960); Marvin Gettleman, "Charity and Social Classes in the United States 1874–1900," *American Journal of Economics and Sociology,* (April and July 1963).

Asterisk denotes paperback edition.

The American political experience during the Progressive Era was conservative, and this conservatism profoundly influenced American society's response to the problems of industrialism. The nature of the economic process in the United States, and the peculiar cast within which industrialism was molded, can only be understood by examining the political structure. Progressive politics is complex when studied in all of its aspects, but its dominant tendency on the federal level was to functionally create, in a piecemeal and haphazard way that was later made more comprehensive, the synthesis of politics and economics I have labeled "political capitalism."

The varieties of rhetoric associated with progressivism were as diverse as its followers, and one form of this rhetoric involved attacks on businessmen—attacks that were often framed in a fashion that has been misunderstood by historians as being radical. But at no point did any major political tendency dealing with the problem of big business in modern society ever try to go beyond the level of high generalization and translate theory into concrete economic programs that would conflict in a fundamental way with business supremacy over the control of wealth. It was not a coincidence that the results of progressivism were precisely what many major business interests desired.

Ultimately businessmen defined the limits of political intervention, and specified its major form and thrust. They were able to do so not merely because they were among the major initiators of federal intervention in the economy, but primarily because no politically significant group during the Progressive Era really challenged their conception of political intervention. The basic fact of the Progressive Era was the large area of consensus and unity among key business leaders and most political factions on the role of the federal government in the economy. There were disagreements, of course, but not on fundamentals. The overwhelming majorities on votes for basic progressive legislation is testimony to the near unanimity in Congress on basic issues.

Indeed, an evaluation of the Progressive Era must concede a much larger importance to the role of Congress than has hitherto been granted by historians who have focused primarily on the more dramatic Presidents. Congress was the pivot of agitation for banking reform while Roosevelt tried to evade the issue, and it was considering trade commissions well before Wilson was elected. Meat and pure food agitation concentrated on Congress, and most of the various reform proposals originated there. More often than not, the various Presidents evaded a serious consideration of issues until Congressional initiatives forced them to articulate a position. And businessmen seeking reforms often found a sympathetic response among the members of the House and Senate long before Presidents would listen to them. This was particularly true of Roosevelt, who would have done much less than he did were it not for the prodding of Congress. Presidents are preoccupied with patronage to an extent unappreciated by anyone who has not read their letters.

The Presidents, considered—as they must be—as actors rather than ideologists, hardly threatened to undermine the existing controllers of economic power. With the possible exception of Taft's Wickersham, none of the major appointees to key executive posts dealing with economic affairs were men likely to frustrate business in its desire to use the federal government to strengthen its economic position. Garfield, Root, Knox, Straus—these men were important and sympathetic pipelines to the President, and gave additional security to businessmen who did not misread what Roosevelt was trying to say in his public utterances. Taft, of course, broke the continuity between the Roosevelt and Wilson Administrations because of political decisions that had nothing to do with his acceptance of the same economic theory that Roosevelt believed in. The elaborate relationship between business and the Executive created under Roosevelt was unintentionally destroyed because of Taft's desire to control the Republican Party. Wilson's appointees were quite as satisfactory as Roosevelt's, so far as big business was concerned, and in his concrete implementation of the fruits of their political agitation—the Federal Reserve Act and the Federal Trade Commission Act—Wilson proved himself to be perhaps the most responsive and desirable to business of the three Presidents. Certainly it must be concluded that historians have overemphasized the basic differences between the Presidents of the Progressive Era, and ignored their much more important similarities. In 1912 the specific utterances and programs of all three were identical on fundamentals, and party platforms reflected this common agreement.

This essential unanimity extended to the area of ideologies and values, where differences between the Presidents were largely of the sort contrived by politicians in search of votes, or seeking to create useful images. None of the Presidents had a distinct consciousness of any fundamental conflict between their political goals and those of business. Roosevelt and Wilson especially appreciated the significant support business gave to their reforms, but it was left to Wilson to culminate the decade or more of agitation by providing precise direction to the administration of political capitalism's most important consequences in the Progressive Era. Wilson had a small but articulate band of followers who seriously desired to reverse the process of industrial centralization—Bryan and the Midwestern agrarians reflected this tradition more than any other group. Yet ultimately he relegated such dissidents to a secondary position—indeed, Wilson himself represented the triumph of Eastern Democracy over Bryanism—and they were able to influence only a clause or amendment, here and there, in the basic legislative structure of political capitalism.

But even had they been more powerful, it is debatable how different Bryanism would have been. Bryan saw the incompatibility between giant corporate capitalism and political democracy, but he sought to save democracy by saving, or restoring, a sort of idealized competitive capitalist economy which was by this time incapable of realization or restoration, and was in any event not advocated by capitalists or political leaders with more power than the agrarians could marshal. Brandeis, for his part, was bound by enigmas in this period. Big Business, to him, was something to be ultimately rejected or justified on the basis of efficiency rather than power accumulation. He tried to apply such technical criteria where none was really relevant, and he overlooked the fact that even where efficient or competitive, business could still pose irreconcilable challenges to the political and social fabric of a democratic community. Indeed, he failed to appreciate the extent to which it was competition that was leading to business agitation for federal regulation, and finally he was unable to do much more than sanction Wilson's actions as they were defined and directed by others.

There was no conspiracy during the Progressive Era. It is, of course, a fact that people and agencies acted out of public sight, and that official statements frequently had little to do with operational realities. But the imputation of a conspiracy would sidetrack a serious consideration of progressivism. There was a basic consensus among political and business leaders as to what was the public good, and no one had to be cajoled in a sinister manner. If détentes, private understandings, and the like were not publicly proclaimed it was merely because such agreements were exceptional and, generally known, could not have been denied to other business interests also desiring the security they provided. Such activities required a delicate sense of public relations, since there was always a public ready to oppose preferential treatment for special businesses, if not the basic assumptions behind such arrangements.

Certainly there was nothing surreptitious about the desire of certain businessmen for reforms, a desire that was frequently and publicly proclaimed, although the motives behind it were not appreciated by historians and although most contemporaries were unaware of how reforms were implemented after they were enacted. The fact that federal regulation of the economy was conservative in its effect in preserving existing power and economic relations in society should not obscure the fact that federal intervention in the economy was conservative in purpose as well. This ambition was publicly proclaimed by the interested business forces, and was hardly conspiratorial.

It is the intent of crucial business groups, and the structural circumstances within the economy that motivated them, that were the truly significant and unique aspects of the Progressive Era. The effects of the legislation were only the logical conclusion of the intentions behind it. The ideological consensus among key business and political leaders fed into a stream of common action, action that was sometimes stimulated by different specific goals but which nevertheless achieved the same results. Political leaders, such as Roosevelt, Wilson, and their key appointees, held that it was proper for an industry to have a decisive voice or veto over the regulatory process within its sphere of interest, and such assumptions filled many key businessmen with confidence in the essential reliability of the federal political mechanism, especially when it was contrasted to the unpredictability of state legislatures.

Business opposition to various federal legislative proposals and measures did exist, of course, especially if one focuses on opposition to particular clauses in specific bills. Such opposition, as in the case of the Federal Reserve Bill, was frequently designed to obtain special concessions. It should not be allowed to obscure the more important fact that the essential purpose and goal of any measure of importance in the Progressive Era was not merely endorsed by key representatives of businesses involved; rather such bills were first proposed by them.

One can always find some businessman, of course, who opposed federal regulation at any point, including within his own industry. Historians have relished in detailing such opposition, and, indeed, their larger analysis of the period has encouraged such revelations. But the finding of division in the ranks of business can be significant only if one makes the false assumption of a monolithic common interest among all capitalists, but, worse yet, assumes that there is no power center among capitalists, and that small-town bankers or hardware dealers can be equated with the leaders of the top industrial, financial, and railroad corporations. They can be equated, of course, if all one studies is the bulk of printed words. But in the political as well as in the economic competition between small and big business, the larger interests always managed to prevail in any specific contest. The rise of the National Association of Manufacturers in the Progressive Era is due to its antilabor position, and not to its opposition to federal regulation, which it voiced only after the First World War. In fact, crucial big business support could be found for every major federal regulatory movement, and frequent small business support could be found for any variety of proposals to their benefit, such as price-fixing and legalized trade associations. Progressivism was not the triumph of small business over the trusts, as has often been suggested, but the victory of big businesses in achieving the rationalization of the economy that only the federal government could provide.

Still, the rise of the N.A.M. among businessmen in both pro- and anti-regulation camps only reinforces the fact that the relationship of capitalists to the remainder of society was essentially unaltered by their divisions on federal intervention in the economy. In terms of the basic class structure, and the conditions of interclass relationships, big and small business alike were hostile to a labor movement interested in something more than paternalism and inequality. In this respect, and in their opposition or indifference to the very minimal social welfare reforms of the Progressive Era (nearly all of which were enacted in the states), American capitalism in the Progressive Era acted in the conservative fashion traditionally ascribed to it. The result was federal regulation in the context of a class society. Indeed, because the national political leadership of the Progressive Period shared this *noblesse oblige* and conservatism toward workers and farmers, it can be really said that there was federal regulation because there *was* a class society, and political leaders identified with the values and supremacy of business.

This identification of political and key business leaders with the same set of social values—ultimately class values—was hardly accidental, for had such a consensus not existed the creation of political capitalism would have been most unlikely. Political capitalism was based on the functional unity of major political and business leaders. The business and political elites knew each other, went to the same schools, belonged to the same clubs, married into the same families, shared the same values —in reality, formed that phenomenon which has lately been dubbed The Establishment. Garfield and Stetson met at Williams alumni functions, Rockefeller, Jr. married Aldrich's daughter, the Harvard clubmen always found the White House door open to them when Roosevelt was there, and so on. Indeed, no one who reads Jonathan Daniels' remarkable autobiography, *The End of Innocence,* can fail to realize the significance of an interlocking social, economic, and political elite in American history in this century.

The existence of an Establishment during the Progressive Era was convenient, even essential, to the functional attainment of political capitalism, but it certainly was not altogether new in American history, and certainly had antecedents in the 1890's. The basic causal factor behind national progressivism was the needs of business and financial elements. To some extent, however, the more benign character of many leading business leaders, especially those with safe fortunes, was due to the more secure, mellowed characteristics and paternalism frequently associated with the social elite. Any number of successful capitalists had long family traditions of social graces and refinement which they privately doubted were fully compatible with their role as capitalists. The desire for a stabilized, rationalized political capitalism was fed by this current in big business ideology, and gave many businessmen that air of responsibility and conservatism so admired by Roosevelt and Wilson. And, from a practical viewpoint, the cruder economic conditions could also lead to substantial losses. Men who were making fortunes with existing shares of the market preferred holding on to what they had rather than establishing control over an industry, or risking much of what they already possessed. Political stabilization seemed proper for this reason as well. It allowed men to relax, to hope that crises might be avoided, to enjoy the bountiful fortunes they had already made.

Not only were economic losses possible in an unregulated capitalism, but political destruction also appeared quite possible. There were disturbing gropings ever since the end of the Civil War: agrarian discontent, violence and strikes, a Populist movement, the rise of a Socialist Party that seemed, for a time, to have an unlimited growth potential. Above all, there was a labor movement seriously divided as to its proper course, and threatening to follow in the seemingly radical footsteps of European labor. The political capitalism of the Progressive Era was designed to meet these potential threats, as well as the immediate expressions of democratic discontent in the states. National progressivism was able to short-circuit state progressivism, to hold nascent radicalism in check by feeding the illusions of its leaders—leaders who could not tell the difference between federal regulation *of* business and federal regulation *for* business.

Political capitalism in America redirected the radical potential of mass grievances and aspirations—of genuine progressivism—and to a limited extent colored much of the intellectual ferment of the period, even though the amorphous nature of mass aspirations frequently made the goals of business and the rest of the public nearly synonymous. Many well-intentioned writers and academicians worked for the same legislative goals as businessmen, but their innocence did not alter the fact that such measures were frequently designed by businessmen to serve business ends, and that business ultimately reaped the harvest of positive results. Such innocence was possible because of a naive, axiomatic view that government economic regulation, per se, was desirable, and also because many ignored crucial business support for such measures by focusing on the less important business opposition that existed. The fetish of government regulation of the economy as a positive social good was one that sidetracked a substantial portion of European socialism as well, and was not unique to the American experience. Such axiomatic and simplistic assumptions of what federal regulation would bring did not take into account problems of democratic control and participation, and in effect assumed that the power of government was neutral and socially beneficent. Yet many of the leading muck-rakers and academics of the period were more than naive but ultimately conservative in their intentions as well. They sought the paternalism and stability which they expected political capitalism to bring, since only in this way could the basic virtues of capitalism be maintained. The betrayal of liberalism that has preoccupied some intellectual historians did not result from irrelevant utopianism or philosophical pragmatism, but from the lack of a truly radical, articulated alternative economic and political program capable of synthesizing political democracy with industrial reality. Such a program was never formulated in this period either in America or Europe.

Historians have continually tried to explain the seemingly sudden collapse of progressivism after the First World War, and have offered reasons that varied from moral exhaustion to the repression of nonconformity. On the whole, all explanations suffer because they really fail to examine progressivism beyond the favorable conventional interpretation. Progressive goals, on the concrete, legislative level, were articulated by various business interests. These goals were, for the most part, achieved, and no one formulated others that big business was also interested in attaining. Yet a synthesis of business and politics on the federal level was created during the war, in various administrative and emergency agencies, that continued throughout the following decade. Indeed, the war period represents the triumph of business in the most emphatic manner possible. With the exception of a brief interlude in the history of the Federal Trade Commission, big business gained total support from the various regulatory agencies and the Executive. It was during the war that effective, working oligopoly and price and market agreements became operational in the dominant sectors of the American economy. The rapid diffusion of power in the economy and relatively easy entry virtually ceased. Despite the cessation of important new legislative enactments, the unity of business and the federal government continued throughout the 1920's and thereafter, using the foundations laid in the Progressive Era to stabilize and consolidate conditions within various industries. And, on the same progressive foundations and exploiting the experience with the war agencies, Herbert Hoover and Franklin Roosevelt later formulated programs for saving American capitalism. The principle of utilizing the federal government to stabilize the economy, established in the context of modern industrialism during the Progressive Era, became the basis of political capitalism in its many later ramifications.

In this sense progressivism did not die in the 1920's, but became a part of the basic fabric of American society. The different shapes political capitalism has taken since 1916 deserve a separate treatment, but suffice it to say that even Calvin

Coolidge did not mind evoking the heritage of Theodore Roosevelt, and Hoover was, if anything, deeply devoted to the Wilsonian tradition in which Franklin Roosevelt gained his first political experience.

*   *   *

. . . Any reasonable generalization on the phenomenon of progressivism must necessarily take into account the economic realities and problems of the period, and the responses that were set in motion. Yet the crucial factor in the American experience was the nature of economic power which required political tools to rationalize the economic process, and that resulted in a synthesis of politics and economics. This integration is the dominant fact of American society in the twentieth century, although once political capitalism is created a dissection of causes and effects becomes extraordinarily difficult. The economy had its own problems, dictated by technological innovation, underconsumption, crises, and competition. But these difficulties were increasingly controlled by political means to the extent that the consideration of economic problems outside their political context is meaningless. The "laws of capitalist development" were not self-contained imperatives in the technological, economic, or political sphere, but an inseparable unification of all three elements.

The object of such a combination was not merely capital accumulation, although it was that as well, but a desire to defend and exercise power through new media more appropriate to the structural conditions of the new century: the destructive potential of growing competition and the dangerous possibilities of a formal political democracy that might lead to a radical alteration of the distribution of wealth or even its total expropriation. Politics and the state become the means of attaining order in the economic sphere and security in the political arena. And they were accessible tools because the major political parties and leaders of the period were also conservative in the sense that they believed in the basic value of capitalist social relations—of some variation of the status quo. The resilience of capitalism, under these circumstances, becomes something that cannot be evaluated in isolated economic terms. Behind the economy, resting on new foundations in which effective collusion and price stability is now the rule, stands the organized power of the national government. The stability and future of the economy is grounded, in the last analysis, on the power of the state to act to preserve it. Such support does not end crises, nor does it eliminate antagonisms inherent in the very nature of the economy, but it does assure the ability of the existing social order to overcome, or survive, the consequences of its own deficiencies. The theory of the national government as a neutral intermediary in its intervention into the economic process is a convenient ideological myth, but such a contention will not survive a serious inquiry into the origins and consequences of such intervention. The rhetoric of reform is invariably different than its structural results. Such mythology is based on the assumption that those who control the state will not use it for their own welfare.

It is important to stress that under conditions of political capitalism the form of the industrialization process, and of the political machinery of society, take on those characteristics necessary to fulfill the peculiar values, attributes, and goals of the ascendant class of that society. The rationalized, dominated, and essentially totalitarian decision-making process is not a consequence of forces inherent in industrialism, but in political capitalism in all its components. The organization of industry is based on the decisions of men whose motives have nothing whatsoever to do with inexorable destiny. Mergers, the scale of effective production, the nature of the production itself, and the direction given to the fruits of technology—all these were decisions made by men whose motives, interests, and weaknesses were peculiar to the basic capitalist assumptions upon which they operated. Their errors were many, as were the possibilities for their failure; but the national government stood behind them so that the consequences of their mistakes would not be calamitous. Perhaps industrialization would not have permitted democratic control and direct participation in the work process under any cimcumstances. All one can do is point to the large extent to which the concentration of industry in this period had nothing to do with considerations of efficient technology, and suggest that no effort whatsoever was ever made to democratize the work situation and industrial control, much less consider the desirability of reducing technological efficiency, if necessary, in such a way as to make decentralization or workers' control possible.

Nor is there any evidence to suggest that the bureaucratization of the political machinery of society, to the extent it took place, was as inevitable as the concentration of industry. It was perfectly logical for men who had spent years solving their economic problems or making their fortunes through political means to also welcome the intervention of a centralized state power to meet problems they could not solve themselves. Social forces, dynamic institutional factors, were the cause of bureaucratic developments in the form of new political agencies and the strengthening of many of the older ones. American capitalism was not merely interested in having law that operated like a piece of machinery, as Weber suggested, but in utilizing the state on terms and conditions which made bureaucratic functions class functions. Bureaucracy, in itself, needed a power base in order to operate in a roughly continuous, systematic fashion. Since it had no economic power itself, it had to support, and hence be supported by, powerful economic groups. This was especially true in a situation where the conditions of political activity were defined by political parties which in turn reflected economic interests, or where the idea of the bureaucracy originated with those operating in the very area in which the bureaucracy was to function.

The skeptical reader may ask whether political capitalism changed after 1916, or perhaps whether capitalism was made more socially responsible by virtue of the stability and rationalization it attained through political means. The question is a moot one, and would take at least one more volume to answer properly. All one can do is point to the continuity in the nature of the political parties and their key leaders, but, more important, to the perpetuation of the same distribution of wealth and the same social relations over the larger part of this century. The solution of economic problems has continued to take place in the political sphere, and the strength of the status quo is based ultimately on the synthesis of politics and economics. Crises have been overcome, or frozen, as much by the power of the state as by internal economic resources applied by business in isolation.

The question remains: Could the American political experience, and the nature of our economic institutions, have been radically different than they are today? It is possible to answer affirmatively, although only in a hypothetical, unreal manner, for there was nothing inevitable or predetermined in the peculiar character given to industrialism in America. And, abstractly regarding all of the extraneous and artificial measures that provided shape and direction to American political and economic life, and their ultimate class function, it would be possible to make a case for a positive reply to the question. Yet ultimately the answer must be a reluctant "No."

There can be no alternatives so long as none are seriously proposed, and to propose a relevant measure of fundamental opposition one must understand what is going on in society, and the relationship of present actions to desired goals. To have been successful, a movement of fundamental change would have had to develop a specific diagnosis of existing social dynamics and, in particular, the variable nature and consequences of political intervention in the economy. It would have, in short, required a set of operating premises radically different than any that were fomulated in the Progressive Era or later. Populism rejected, on the whole, the values of business even as it was unable to articulate a viable alternative. Intellectually it left a vacuum, and, more important, the movement was dead by 1900. The Socialist Party suffered from the fetishistic belief in the necessity of centralization that has characterized all socialist groups that interpreted Marx too literally, and it had a totally inaccurate estimate of the nature of progressivism, eventually losing most of its followers to the Democrats. The two major political parties, as always, differed on politically unimportant and frequently contrived details, but both were firmly wedded to the status quo, and the workers were generally their captives or accomplices. No socially or politically significant group tried to articulate an alternative means of organizing industrial technology in a fashion that permitted democratic control over centralized power, or participation in routine, much less crucial, decisions in the industrial process. No party tried to develop a program that suggested democracy could be created only by continuous mass involvement in the decisions that affected their lives, if the concentration of actual power in the hands of an elite was to be avoided. In brief, the Progressive Era was characterized by a paucity of alternatives to the status quo, a vacuum that permitted political capitalism to direct the growth of industrialism in America, to shape its politics, to determine the ground rules for American civilization in the twentieth century, and to set the stage for what was to follow.

The Scope of American Socialism, 1900-1912   JAMES WEINSTEIN

The same years that witnessed the rise of "corporate liberalism" also saw the growth of American socialism. Socialist ideas, as we have seen, first appeared in the United States before the Civil War. These were derived largely from the Utopian Socialists rather than from Marx, however, and it was not until the 1860s and 1870s that Marxism began to influence American social thinkers and American labor leaders. In those decades the National Labor Union sought to establish ties with the Marxist International Workingmen's Association, while other labor groups,

Source: James Weinstein, *The Decline of Socialism in America 1912–1925* (New York: Monthly Review Press, 1967), chap. i, "The Scope of American Socialism, 1900–1912," pp. 1–26. See source for footnote.

many of them German, organized American "sections" of the First International. In 1872, the International, already enfeebled, was actually transferred to New York from London. In 1876, it officially died and was, as it were, interred in the United States.

But Americans continued to be interested in socialism, and in the next twenty years the movement grew among laboring men and intellectuals. The number of organizations inspired by Marx, Ferdinand Lasalle, and the anarchist, Bakunin, is bewildering, but their multitude suggests that the Socialist vision of a better world truly appealed to Americans. In 1876, a number of socialist bodies coalesced into the Workingmen's Party of the United States. The next year it changed its name to the Socialist Labor Party and under that label it continues to exist.

Between this time and the end of the century, the SLP was the dominant Socialist body in the United States. Under the brilliant, but acerbic and contentious leadership of Daniel DeLeon, the party maintained a precarious existence against the fierce opposition of the conservative press, a conservative citizenry, and a conservative trade union movement. Much of its strength, like that of other Socialist and anarchist groups, came from the foreign-born, a fact that seemed to confirm the inappropriateness of socialism for the United States.

With the formation of the Socialist Party of America in 1901, American socialism began to become less marginal. As James Weinstein shows, the SPA, led by Eugene V. Debs, prospered remarkably and come close to becoming a mass party capable of substantially affecting the course of American political life. This little-known fact helps to establish the credentials of socialism in America and suggests that the Socialist failure was accidental rather than inherent in the nature of either America or socialism.

FOR FURTHER READING:

James Weinstein, *The Decline of Socialism in America 1912–1925**, (Vintage, 1969); H. Wayne Morgan, *Eugene V. Debs, Socialist for President*, (Syracuse University Press, 1962); Ray Ginger, *Eugene V. Debs: A Biography**, (Collier Books, 1962); David Sherman, *The Socialist Party of America**, (Quadrangle, 1967); Ira Kipnis, *The American Socialist Movement 1897–1912*, (Greenwood, 1968).

Asterisk denotes paperback edition.

I

Unlike the "movement" today, when radicals cluster around ever-changing combinations and permutations of committees, societies, sects, and parties, radicalism in the years before 1920 focused in one organization: the Socialist Party of America. Some anticapitalist radicals remained outside the Party and organized separately or as rivals, but these groups were marginal. The Socialist Labor Party, which has maintained its identity from its founding in 1877 to the present, was the Socialist Party's major competitor; after the split in 1899 that led to the formation of the Socialist Party, the SLP remained static and isolated. The Industrial Workers of the World likewise rejected the Socialist Party, although at its founding in 1905 it had close ties with such leading Socialists as Eugene V. Debs and Algie M. Simons. As timed passed, the IWW moved further from political action and became more intolerant of Socialist attitudes toward the trade union movement. In the course of this development, it also attracted many radical intellectuals—Max Eastman, John Reed, Floyd Dell, Arturo Giovanetti—as sympathizers; the result of this association has been a mythology that places the IWW at the center of early twentieth-century American radicalism. But while the romantic appeal of the Wobblies has triumphed in literature and history, as a social force the IWW did not approach the Socialist Party in its impact on contemporary American life.

The organization of the Socialist Party of America in 1901 was the result of a confluence of the major socialist and radical tendencies in the United States and marked the coming of age of the movement. The Party was far from homogeneous or orthodox in the present sense of that word, but it grew rapidly in the years from 1901 to 1912, and retained its basic character and strength until 1919. Spreading its roots widely, American socialism reached into many parts of the country and into areas of American life never since affected by openly socialist ideas. This was possible in large part because of the Party's internal diversity and its democratic and open structure. Unlike radical movements of the last four decades, the old Socialist Party permitted and benefited from a wide range of doctrinal and ideological views and tendencies within its ranks. Since the early 1920's, debates between socialists of different tendencies have increasingly become disputes between parties; before 1920 such differences were generally accepted as normal and desirable aspects of the process of developing a viable mass party.

The character of American radicalism since 1925 has obscured the nature of pre-World War I socialism in the United States. Historians of American socialism have been led to the obsession of New Deal and post-New Deal radicals with the ideological disputes between Stalinist and Trotskyist (in which many of them were enmeshed) to assume that the old movement was equally narrow and isolated—that it never succeeded in introducing the ideas of socialism into the consciousness of large numbers of Americans. The prevailing tendency is to assume that socialism was, as it now seems to be, alien to the United States. Daniel Bell, for example, points to the failure of Marxian socialism during the Great Depression and the New Deal and, correctly in my opinion, goes on to seek the reason for this failure in the nature of the movement, rather than in general social or political conditions in the 1930's. But, in common with most other historians of American socialism, Bell views the pre-1920 movement as politically and ideologically consistent with that of the Depression decade, and so misses much about the nature of the earlier movement.

Bell's treatment conforms well with the myths and traditions of post-1920 radicalism, as well as with the predispositions of other historians. This projection of the characteristics of the Socialist and Communist Parties of the 1930's back into the prewar period leaves us with a view of the Old Party as narrow and marginal, and also as divided into hostile sects whose spectrum from right to left was analogous to the divisions in European socialism during the First World War.

Such a view serves better to obscure than to clarify the American socialist past; yet a tradition has grown up that treats "Left" versus "Right" in the old Socialist Party as a conflict of worker against petty bourgeois, industrial unionist against craft unionist, fighter for equality against racist, antiwar versus pro-war. In short, "Left" is equated with fidelity, or at least adherence, to "Marxist" principles, and "Right" with opportunism. However, few such polarities existed in the Socialist

Party before 1920—though of course the problem of determining when an innovation is principled and when opportunist is always present in politics.

It is true that factionalism existed in the early movement and that there was a superficial, or rhetorical, continuity. In the Socialist Party of America the categories of Left, Right, and Center were more useful in defining attitudes toward others than as guides to how a group would line up on any given issue; yet there were four clearly discernible groupings within the Party, each relating to these categories. Party members were conscious of divisions between Left and Right. They thought in these terms; and the Left, Center, and Right groupings had their own publications and often competed for leadership in city, state, and national structures of the Party. Hulet Wells, a left winger in Seattle, Washington, believed that the "real line of demarcation" was always acceptance or rejection of the "class philosophy of Marx." In Washington, the right-wing neo-populists in the Party hoped to "appeal to all classes," Wells explains, whereas the trade unionists and the IWW's based their policies on the working class. But another contemporary Socialist, Jesse Wallace Hughan, believed that the Socialist Party was "divided neither into two opposing camps nor into a number of warring factions." This was demonstrated, she wrote, by the "unanimity with which all groups cooperate in such enterprises as the party press, a contest for free speech, or labor conict." Still, she recognized "a gradual shading" from "revolutionists on the left to constructivists on the right," with groups in between whose characteristics were "seldom exact and always changing," and "whose members indulge in mutual criticism."

Hughan's view comes nearer the mark. There were differences in tactical approaches among the several tendencies. Some looked to a coalition of workers with farmers or other middle-class radicals, while some frowned on such an alliance. Defining the working class was also a source of difficulty. The IWW-oriented Left tended to regard only the unskilled and migratory workers as genuine proletarians, while the Right and Center emphasized the importance of the organized industrial workers in such unions as the United Mine Workers, The International Association of Machinists, The United Brewery Workers, the Western Federation of Miners, and the Railroad Brotherhoods. These differences within Socialist ranks, along with others, led some contemporary observers and later historians to describe the right-wing Socialists as merely the left wing of progressivism. But this approach underestimates the unifying strength of the Socialists' anticapitalist perspective. In terms of their ultimate commitment to thoroughgoing social transformation, both wings of the Party, or, rather, all groups, were "revolutionary." In terms of their ability to adjust their tactics to the needs of their constituencies, all groups were "constructivists." How principled each group was, was rarely tested; when it was, as on the question of racism and opposition to American participation in the First World War, the divisions did not follow Left-Right lines, as we shall see.

II

Each of the four discernible tendencies within the Party had a leader of nationwide renown whose ideas and attitudes roughly characterized the grouping he led. On the Right was Victor Berger, German-born schoolteacher, printer, editor, and professional politician, who represented the "constructive" wing of the movement.

Berger was the most successful of American Socialists in building a stable political organization based upon the trade unions. In Milwaukee, the great majority of union locals were Socialist, and the Socialist organs spoke for the unions. Berger's newspaper, *The Milwaukee Leader,* proclaimed its status as the official paper of both the Federated Trades Council of Milwaukee and the Wisconsin State Federation of Labor, and the unions served as the hard core of Berger's political base.

From the day in 1893 that he became editor of the *Wisconsin Vorwaerts,* daily organ of the Socialist Labor Party, Berger was the undisputed leader of Milwaukee socialism. Like most early Socialists, his initial experience was in the Socialist Labor Party, but his devotion to the adaptation of "scientific socialism" to the American environment quickly led to a break with the doctrinaire organization. Soon after he began editing the *Vorwaerts,* Berger broke with the Socialist Labor Party, founded the Social Democratic Society, and forged a three-way alliance with the local People's Party and the Federated Trade Council. In 1896, however, he lost hope in populism; and soon after Eugene V. Debs announced his conversion to socialism in January 1897 (Berger had brought Debs a copy of *Das Kapital* to his cell in the Woodstock jail), he and Debs helped form the Social Democracy of America. It was this organization that joined a dissident group of Socialist Laborites to form the Socialist Party of America in 1901.

In the Socialist Party, Berger constantly asserted the need to make socialism relevant to the existing problems of American workers. He saw no immediate prospects for the transition to socialism in the United States, or in any other part of the world. In this respect, as in many others, Berger shared the orthodox Marxist view that the revolution would come first in the most advanced capitalist countries. "In the trust system," he believed, "capitalism has just stepped into a new phase," the duration of which was "unlimited according to our present light." At the same time, Berger observed, capitalism was no longer a civilizing force, but had "already become a menace to civilization"—and this created the possibility of achieving socialism in the foreseeable future, "if the working class understands its mission." Meanwhile, it was the task of the Socialists to educate workers and to struggle to improve their lot "economically, morally, and physically."

Some people viewed this concern for social reform as an identification of socialism and progressivism, but Berger insisted that "every success in this direction will naturally compel us to make new demands and attain new benefits for the proletariat which will weaken the capitalist system." Only through such a process could the Socialists hope to bring the working class to consciousness of its strength and its "mission."

Socialism was the next epoch of civilization into which the world was evolving. Neither feudalism nor capitalism had arisen or disappeared at a given date; nor would socialism replace capitalism on the world scene "at one stroke." The period of transition, Berger often wrote, would be gradual and would require two conditions in each country: the winning of a majority of the population by the Socialist Party, and a concentration of industry sufficient to make it "ripe for collective production." As with all Marxists in the days before the Russian Revolution, the idea of a successful revolution in an underdeveloped country was beyond Berger's imagination. Even in the United States, Berger was unsure that the second condition had been met. The trusts were already matured, he observed, but other industries, including farming, were not yet ready to be worked collectively and so should be left in private hands.

Berger argued strongly against those Socialists who were constantly speaking of revolution, which he interpreted to mean a "catastrophe," as the path to socialism. He recognized and partially accepted Marx's statement that "force is the midwife at the birth of every new epoch," but saw in this "no cause for rejoicing." Looking for "another way out," Berger found it in the ballot, backed up by an armed people. The proletariat "outnumbered the capitalist class most effectively," and thus had the "fate of every country in its hands," if it could "come to terms with the farmers." There was, of course, the danger that the capitalists would not recognize a working-class victory; but if the American people were fully armed, a peaceful transition would be assured. "An armed people," he frequently repeated, "is always a free people."

The difference between Berger and left-wing Party members was indicated in an interview he and Debs granted Lincoln Steffens in 1908. At one point Steffens asked Debs what he would do with the trusts. "Take them," Debs replied. This greatly agitated Berger. "No," he said, "I answer that we would offer to pay." This, he explained was not essentially a matter of justice, but of "tactics," and the tactic on this question had already been decided by the Party as a whole.

To justify his position, Berger explained that the Socialists were "the inheritors of civilization and all that is good in it." Art, music, buildings, public works, the sense of right and wrong—"not one of these shall be lost, and violence like that would lose us much." As an analogy, Berger pointed to the Civil War. Before that carnage some "tried to avert it by proposing to pay for the slaves," but "the fanatics on both sides refused." The result was four years of war at a cost of ten billion dollars and hundreds of thousands of lives. "We ought to learn from history," Berger concluded. "We will offer compensation" because "it seems just to present-day thought and will prove the easiest, cheapest way in the end."

As a politician, Berger was unsurpassed in the Socialist Party. First elected to Congress in 1910, he was re-elected in 1918 but was refused a seat because of his antiwar activity. In a special election to fill the vacancy left by his unseating, Berger won again in 1919. Again he was unseated, and this time he failed of re-election until 1922, after which he remained in Congress until 1927. Editor of the *Milwaukee Leader*, Berger presided over the Milwaukee Socialists and guided them to their victories in 1910, 1916, and in the years that followed. An active trade unionist, he was president of his local of the Typographical Union and a perennial delegate to AFL conventions. Berger's belief that the Socialists could win control of the AFL if they worked within that organization made him a consistent foe of the IWW and of dual unionism. But his loyalty to the AFL did not keep him from opposing Samuel Gompers. He was convinced that the "American labor movement will remain reactionary as long as [Gompers] has any influence." At the same time, Berger shared some of Gompers' more reactionary attitudes on the race question and on the immigration of Orientals.

Sometimes associated with Berger, but more often characterized as a leader of the "Center," Morris Hillquit represented the pre-World War I orthodox Marxist tradition. A Russian immigrant, born in Riga, Hillquit grew to maturity on New York City's Lower East Side, where he spent his early radical years as an organizer and journalist for the United Hebrew Trades, a forerunner of the International Ladies Garment Workers Union.

When he was 18, he joined the Socialist Labor Party, and as an outstanding young labor lawyer rose rapidly in party ranks. But Hillquit and Daniel De Leon soon differed over tactics, and a long and bitter fight began. By 1896, Hillquit found himself solidly opposed to the Party leader, especially on the question of the organization of the Socialist Trade and Labor Alliance as a rival to the AFL. He was chosen to head the opposition to De Leon within the Party. Then, in 1899, along with Max Hayes and Ben Hanford (both leaders of the International Typographical Union), and followed by a majority of the membership, Hillquit seceded and organized a rival party. It was this "Rochester" Socialist Labor Party that fused with Berger's Social Democrats of Milwaukee and with Debs in 1901 to form the Socialist Party.

As a leader of the Center tendencies in the Party, Hillquit often played the role of arbitrator in disputes between Left and Right, attempting frequently and often successfully to reconcile the positions of the contending groups. His efforts, however, were sometimes resented, especially by the Left, not so much because of differences in principle between Hillquit and the more militant Party members, but because his rhetoric was alien to their radical traditions. Ironically, Hillquit was fond of thinking of himself as an Americanizer of Marx, but his mild expositions of socialist principles were most infuriating to the indigenous left wingers of the Southwest and the Northwest. These native old-Americans had been reared in the rhetoric of class warfare, which they favored even when (as in the case of the ex-populists) the programs they advocated were no more radical than those put forward by Hillquit. On one occasion, for example, Hillquit commented that the workers alone, "especially the workers in the narrower sense of the term," were "neither numerous nor strong enough to successfully accomplish the Socialist revolution." They needed "the cooperation of persons from other classes, and," Hillquit believed, "that cooperation can be obtained." In their election campaigns, especially where, as in many municipal contests, victory was possible, all Socialists except the followers of William D. Haywood acted on these assumptions and shaped their tactics accordingly. But only rarely would a left winger admit this in public.

Even Eugene V. Debs, who seldom involved himself in personal disputes, attacked Hillquit on occasion. When Hillquit debated Samuel Gompers on socialism and the labor movement, Debs charged him with exhibiting all "the cleverness of a pettifogging lawyer" who had sparred "all around the class struggle without touching it." Debs observed that Hillquit could have made a much stronger case had he not been restrained by "the fear of offending the American Federation of Labor." In matters of principle, however, Hillquit's position rarely differed from that of Debs. Both advocated industrial unionism; both opposed dual unionism, sabotage, and violence; both actively opposed American participation in the First World War; and, as we shall see, both maintained the same attitude toward the Russian Revolution and the Third International.

The principles Eugene Debs and Hillquit held in common have led some historians to place them together as moderates. But Debs' rejection of Socialist participation in the AFL and his rapport with the spirit of Western radicals qualify him as a left winger. Unlike any other Socialist leader, Debs was part of a central experience in American labor history. He came to socialism via the Woodstock jail and the ruins of his American Railway Union after the defeat of the great Pullman strike in 1894. A former Democratic member of the Indiana Assembly, a strong supporter of populism, and then of Bryan in 1896, Debs always retained a firm belief in political action. But his participation in politics as a Socialist was not based on a desire for office. "If there were any chance of my election," he once told Lincoln Steffens, "I wouldn't run. The party wouldn't let me." What Debs sought was a "majority of Socialists, not of votes," because "there would be no use getting into power with a people that did not understand, with a lot of office-holders undisciplined by service in the party, unpurged by personal sacrifice of the selfish spirit of the present system." Debs ran for President, he explained, "to teach social consciousness." When socialism was "on the verge of success," the Party would nominate "an able executive and a clear-minded administrator; not—not Debs."

Debs opposed capitalism because "It's wrong. It's inherently unjust, inhuman, unintelligent, and—it cannot last." Graft, corruption, poverty, crime and cruelty were "evidences of its weaknesses and failure; the signs that it is breaking down."

"Why not wait, then, for it to break down?" Steffens asked.

"Because we have minds," Debs replied, "human intelligence is a force of nature. It could assist the process of evolution by searching intelligently for the root of all evils as they arise."

Debs was more than the perennial standard bearer of the Party and its leading editorial writer. Aggressively class conscious, consistent champion of the oppressed, and implacable foe of the inequities of modern industrial capitalism, he personally embodied the unity of Populist, Christian, Marxist, and militant trade union traditions that fused to form the Socialist Party in 1901. To most Americans, Debs was the hero and the symbol of the movement, though he chose never to play a role in the Party organization commensurate with his popularity, preferring instead to remain above the organizational disputes. Not until his release from prison in 1922, when the Socialist Party was weaker than it had been when it was organized, did Debs take a seat on the National Executive Committee of the Party. This self-abnegation created an unfortunate situation in the prewar years, for Debs represented and expressed the mood of the largest sections of the Party. His absence from its organizational center at times created a discordance between the spirit (and the tactics) of the national leadership and the Party membership.

William D. Haywood represented the fourth and most distinct tendency within the Social Party. A one-time secretary-treasurer of the Western Federation of Miners, and general organizer of the IWW, Haywood, like Debs, had come to socialism through his experience as an industrial unionist. Unlike Debs, however, Haywood had no background of political activity in his early years in the mines and never developed any regard for its educational value. Haywood's concept of socialism and the manner in which it would come about was even more vague than that of Berger, Hillquit, and Debs. He was concerned almost entirely with fighting labor's immediate battles and with organizing the unorganized. His attitude toward political action flowed directly from this concern. Haywood urged "every working-man to use the ballot at every opportunity," and was himself a candidate for governor of Colorado in 1906. The real value of the ballot, in Haywood's eyes, however, was in the opportunity it offered to win administrative control of local government so as to "use the powers of the police to protect the strikers."

Haywood's political theories were a composite of socialist and syndicalist ideas. He shared with the syndicalists a vision of society reorganized around the factories, mines, and other places of production—to be realized through a general strike. During a period of transition, however, Haywood believed it "absolutely necessary" that the workers also control the governmental machinery, which would be used to "inspire confidence and compel the wheels of industry to move in spite of the devices and stumbling blocks of the capitalists." Haywood and his comrades in the IWW defined their theories as industrialism, rather than syndicalism. The syndicalists, or at least the Syndicalist League of North American, concurred.

Unlike Haywood and the IWW, which it opposed, the Syndicalist League rejected and "bitterly" opposed the "international Socialist Party," insisting that the labor unions alone represented the interests of the working class. At the same time, the Syndicalist League opposed the dual unionism of the IWW, and sought to divert the mainstream of the American labor movement leftward by participating in the American Federation of Labor as a "militant minority."

Haywood urged the worker to use the ballot, but he spoke to virtually disfranchised groups—nonferrous metal miners in the remote camps of the mountain states, lumber workers of northern Louisiana and the Northwest, migratory agricultural workers, and immigrant industrial workers. Unlike Debs, whose roots were strongest among the workers in the older, more settled industries, Haywood's constituents existed on the edges of society. The demands of his followers were more elemental than those of other Party members because the conditions under which they lived were more barbarous, and his hostility to reform followed largely from a belief that few reforms could effect the conditions under which the membership of the IWW existed.

Similarly, Haywood did not share with Berger, Hillquit, or Debs the view that capitalism might survive for a considerable time. His was an apocalyptic vision of the revolution. Believing that it could occur at any time, he did not see the need to develop long-term strategy.

These differences and the dual unionism of the IWW were the real sources of the antagonism between Haywood and the center and the right-wing groupings of the Party. Haywood rarely, if ever, advocated the use of violence during strikes. His leadership of the Lawrence textile strike was marked by the quiet discipline he instilled in the strikers, and a policy of passive resistance was followed wherever possible. In Akron, Ohio, in 1913, Haywood advised striking rubber workers that their "greatest weapon" was "to keep your hands in your pockets," and "let there be no violence . . . not the destruction of one cent's worth of property, not one cross word." But he did take delight in proposing sabotage at speeches in New York City, the heartland of Hillquit's influence. At Cooper Union in early 1912, Haywood affirmed his hatred for the law and annouced that he was "not a law-abiding citizen." A few months later he boasted, "I believe in sabotage, that much misunderstood word."

These antics did not endear Haywood to the leaders in New York, but the IWW raids on locals of the Western Federation of Miners and the United Mine

Workers did more to antagonize such Socialist trade unionists as Max Hayes, Berger, John H. Walker, and Adolph Germer. Since the Socialist Party did not officially enter union disputes, it would have been difficult to attack Haywood directly on this basis. Instead, at the convention in 1912, the Right and Center sponsored a successful amendment to the Party constitution which banned the advocacy of crime, sabotage, or other methods of violence—and in 1913 had Haywood recalled from his position as a member of the Party's National Executive Committee for violating the ban at a public meeting.

Haywood himself ceased being active in the Socialist Party after his recall from the National Executive Committee in 1913, but those who shared his views continued to exercise some strength in Minnesota, Washington, and in scattered areas throughout the West. They failed to achieve a more influential position in the Party because Debs agreed with Hillquit and Berger that tactics which involved "stealth, secrecy, intrigue and necessitate individual acts of violence for their execution" were unacceptable to the American working class, and because Debs opposed the IWW after 1908. The adoption of the "anti-sabotage clause," Article II, section 6, of the Party constitution at the convention of 1912 marked the beginning of the decline of syndicalist influence in the Party. Yet many Haywood supporters retained both their membership and a smoldering hostility to Hillquit and Berger for their role in eliminating Haywood from the leadership. In 1919 this long-dormant resentment would break forth again and exacerbate the differences among American Socialists.

III

No brief summary, such as that above, can begin to present an accurate picture of the heterogeneity of early twentieth-century socialism in the United States. In addition to the major tendencies from Left to Right, there were several other groupings, less familiar to historians, which swelled the ranks of the movement. The Populists, for example, were an important source of Socialist Party membership, in some states imparting a special flavor to the organization. In Texas, Oklahoma, Alabama, Louisiana, and Missouri, many former Populists found their way to socialism. A Texas Populist editor complained to Tom Watson in 1907 that while the older Populists were still all right, the younger men were "sliding into the Socialist party or what they think is such, but which is really an aggravated case of Populism." In Texas, both older and younger Populists transferred their allegiance to the new movement. Clarence Nugent, whose father was the Populist candidate for governor in 1892, was an active Socialist. In 1915 the young Nugent addressed the first meeting of Negro Socialists in Fort Worth, thus carrying on the Populist tradition of cooperation with the Colorado Farmers' Alliance. Similarly, the publisher of the Halletsville *Rebel,* the major Socialist paper in Texas, was the son of the veteran Alliance and Populist leader, former judge E. O. Meitzen of Halletsville. Both father and son were Socialist converts. The younger Meitzen, a member of both the typographical and farmer unions, was Socialist candidate for governor in 1914.

In Oklahoma, too, where the Populists had not merged with the Democrats in support of Bryan in 1896, they contributed heavily to Socialist strength. Many local Socialist agitators and speakers were "ex-middle-of-the-road Populists" of old American stock. The one large contributor to Oklahoma's first Socialist newspaper, Steuben deKalb Wham, was a well-to-do farmer and a founder of the Populist Party.

Many other leading Socialists were former supporters of populism. James H. Maurer of Pennsylvania, Victor Berger, and Charles Morrill, the long-term Socialist state representative in Massachusetts, had supported the People's Party in 1892 and after. Populism, however, did not mold their characters; they were already Socialists or Single-Taxers when the People's Party was organized. In several of the Southern states, on the other hand, the entire socialist movement sprang out of populism and was flavored by it.

The Texas and Oklahoma Socialists were strong supporters of the Party's left wingers. They, and farmers like them on the hot plains of New Mexico, Arkansas, Kansas, and Missouri, came by the thousands to hear "Gene" Debs, Kate Richards O'Hare, Caroline Lowe, Arthur Le Sueur of North Dakota, and other Socialist spellbinders exhort them to fight for the cooperative commonwealth. At these meetings the farmers spent their days reading socialist literature, eating barbecued beeves, and singing old populist songs with new socialist words. These farmers also admired Haywood; when he was recalled from the National Executive Committee in 1913, Texas voted more heavily against the move than any other state. On the Negro question, too, the Oklahoma Socialists were closer to the positions of Debs and Haywood than to the racism of Victor Berger. Like Haywood, Tad Cumbie, a leader of the Oklahoma "intransigents," always took pleasure in flaunting his radicalism. At Party conventions Cumbie always wore a flaming red shirt. When Victor Berger likened the militant leftists at the Party convention in 1912 to the Hebrews, who carried bundles of hay on their journeys so as not to have to sleep on land contaminated by Gentiles, Cumbie responded by appearing the next day with a tiny bundle of hay pinned to his shirt.

But if these Texas and Oklahoma Socialists were leftists, their stance often conflicted with orthodox Left positions. On the land question, for example, their program met the demands of the tenant farmers who constituted the bulk of their support—but contradicted traditional Marxism. To prevent speculation in land, and eliminate tenancy, the Oklahoma and Texas Socialists demanded that farm land not cultivated by the owners be taxed at its full rental value and that actual use and occupancy be the only basis of title to land. Land in the possession of the state, or later to be acquired, would be rented to landless farmers by the board of agriculture at prevailing rates of share rent. Payment was to cease when the total paid in equaled the value of the land. Thereafter, the tenant was to acquire for himself and his family in perpetuity the right of occupancy, with the land reverting to the state when it was no longer worked. Land for this purpose was to come from the public domain, enlarged through purchase and reclamation of arid land and land sold for taxes, and by the appropriation of segregated and unallotted Indian lands.

In attacking this program at the 1910 Party congress, Victor Berger pointed out that there was nothing socialistic either in government encouragement of family farms or in leasing land. At best, Berger declared, such a program encouraged "State Socialism." Somewhat condescendingly, he referred to the program as Georgian, an accusation to which the Texas Socialists happily pleaded guilty. Stressing their debt to Henry George, Texas Socialists even conducted a minor campaign to reconcile the Party with his spirit. Hostility to the single tax, wrote the *Rebel*, was not based on principle, but on George's denunciation of the Socialist Labor Party at the Syracuse convention of the United Labor Party of New York, in 1887.

Texas-Oklahoma Socialists often took positions at odds with traditional doctrine. Unlike many left wingers, they shared with the "opportunists" a concern with reconciling Christianity and socialism—and with bringing ministers into the party. In common with other left wingers, however, the Texans were astringently hostile to the "bureaucrats" in Chicago and to Morris Hillquit. They considered decentralization "the old Landmark and firm foundation" of Party organization. In short, the ex-Populists were considered left wingers largely because of their hostility to the national organization; it would be impossible and pointless to place them firmly in any of the traditional ideological categories.

The Christian Socialists, likewise, are not easily categorized. They were not close to the Haywood-IWW group or to the orthodox Marxists; and though they were warmly sympathetic to Debs, his views and theirs did not always coincide. Before the World War, two active Christian Socialist organizations existed: the interdenominational Christian Socialist Fellowship organized in Louisville, Kentucky in 1906, and the Church Socialist League, an Episcopal group formed in 1911. Neither affiliated directly with the Socialist Party, but many of their adherents were active Party members.

The smaller of them, the Church Socialist League, had an estimated 600 or 700 members in 1917, of which about 100 held Socialist Party cards. For eleven years, from 1914 to 1924, the League published a quarterly journal, *The Social Preparation*, at Utica and Geneva, New York; while the Fellowship published a sometime weekly, sometime monthly, newspaper, the *Christian Socialist,* in Chicago.

The roots of Christian socialism in the United States went back into the 1870's and 1880's, and were intertwined with the National Socialist movement inspired by Edward Bellamy's *Looking Backward*. The general secretary of the Christian Socialist Fellowship, the Reverend Edward E. Carr, had traveled the Bellamy route to socialism and had been a founding member of the Socialist Party. Not all leading Christian Socialists were Party members. The Reverend Walter Rauschenbusch never joined the Party, though he shared the outlook of his fellows and became a Special Contributor to the *Christian Socialist* in 1914. As the editors of that journal wrote, those joining the Fellowship, whether in the Party or not, did so "for one great specific purpose, 'to permeate the churches and other religious organizations with the social message of Jesus, which in an age of machine production means Socialism, and nothing else.'" The paper frequently urged its readers to join the Socialist Party and to be active in its affairs.

In spirit the *Christian Socialist* was close to Debs and to E. R. Meitzen and his *Rebel* group; although an atheist, Debs' moral tone was close to that of these Protestants. In a "comment on Christ's words," Debs wrote that "Jesus taught that the air and the sea and the sky and all the beauty and fullness thereof were for all the children of men; that they should all equally enjoy the riches of nature and dwell together in peace, and bear one another's burdens and love one another, and that is what socialism teaches and why the rich thieves who have laid hold of the earth and its bounties would crucify the Socialists as those robbers of the poor crucified Jesus two thousands years ago.

During the many bloody strike battles of the prewar years, the *Christian Socialist* exhibited a militant loyalty to the working class. After the Ludlow massacre, in which the Colorado militia shot up and then burned a strikers' tent colony (killing seventeen miners and their families, many of whom suffocated or were burned to death), the paper placed the blame squarely on John D. Rockefeller. Rockefeller controlled the Colorado Coal Company, against which the strike had been conducted, and financed the militia. "Contemptible as Rockefeller is," wrote Irwin St. John Tucker, the paper's managing editor, "he acts strictly in accordance with capitalist morality." The dead women and children of Ludlow were but "human sacrifices laid at the altar of his worship; he chants a hymn to capital as they die among the flames." Rockefeller had been widely condemned for his responsibility in the affair and had conducted his own investigation of it, after which he announced his innocence. Tucker commented: "His conscience is determined by his pocketbook; and since his pocketbook prospers, his 'conscience acquits him.'" To Rockefeller, Tucker concluded, "deaths of the women and children in Ludlow are their own fault. They got in the way of his god; and his god crushed them."

Like Debs (but also like Hillquit and Berger), Christian Socialists advocated industrial unionism, opposed the IWW, and insisted on the primacy of political action. During a copper strike in Calumet, Michigan, someone (the strikers charged that it was a Citizens' Alliance man) called "Fire" while the strikers' children were having a Christmas party in the union hall. As the crowd rushed down the stairs to the doorway, deputy policemen blocked the exit and seventy-two strikers' wives and children were crushed to death or suffocated. "Great is the patience of the poor," commented the editors. "Too great we often think." Yet, "their anger must be enlightened and directed toward political action, not insurrectionary violence. Workers who do not know enough to vote for their class on election day, will never be able to obtain their freedom any other way."

On the Negro question the Christian Socialist Fellowship was somewhat in advance of the Party in general, and far ahead of Berger, Robert Hunter, and others close to the AFL. The Fellowship had many active Negro members and a special organization for work among Negro church groups. Its Secretary to the Colored Race was a Negro minister from Iowa, the Reverend George W. Slater, who wrote frequently for the *Christian Socialist*, and for Negro journals, which accepted articles about socialism from him. Yet some ministers in the Fellowship took anti-Oriental positions, as did the Reverend J. Stitt Wilson, a contributing editor of the *Christian Socialist*, mayor of Berkeley, California, and a member of the Party's National Executive Committee. With many other California Socialists and trade unionists, Wilson supported the exclusion of Japanese and Chinese from the United States at the Socialist congress of 1910 and at the convention of 1912.

Christian Socialists came to socialism through a belief that life on earth could approach the Kingdom of God—and by way of a search for means to make Christianity more meaningful to American workers. This "practical" socialism implied a commitment to seek amelioration of present inequities, but it did not mean only the improvement of material conditions; social morality was equally important. In 1901, Walter Rauschenbusch observed that some Socialists did not rally around ideals, but solely around narrow class interests. If this view prevailed, he warned, "if you can establish it that it is purely a matter of selfishness, and that the sense of justice, the ideal of brotherhood, the longing for a truer and nobler life count for nothing, you have cut the heart out of the social movement." Debs, of course, understood this and always spoke in moral terms, of justice and brotherhood. It is probably for this reason that the Christian Socialists felt such a close kinship with him.

Before the World War, American socialism was diffuse geographically as well as in its tendencies. Until 1918 the greatest relative voting strength of the movement lay west of the Mississippi River, in the states where mining, lumbering, and tenant farming prevailed. New York, since 1917 the bastion of socialism in the United States, placed twenty-ninth and twenty-fourth in the percentage of Socialist votes in 1912 and 1916. Even in New York, the Party's greatest strength was upstate. Until 1917, Schenectady was the Socialist stronghold, electing the Reverend George R. Lunn as mayor in 1911 and 1915, and sending a Socialist to the state assembly in 1911. The states with the greatest percentages of Socialist voters in the prewar years were Oklahoma, Nevada, Montana, Washington, California, Idaho, Florida, Arizona, Wisconsin, and Texas. In that order, all appeared among the top dozen states in the Presidential elections of both 1912 and 1916. Oklahoma had the largest and most complete organization: 12,000 Party members in 961 locals, 38,000 subscribers to the *Appeal to Reason*, 53,000 Socialist voters in the state in 1914. In that year, five Socialists were elected to the Oklahoma assembly and one to the state senate, along with more than 130 Socialist county and township officers.

In other Western states, Socialists were less organized, but they more than held their own in relation to the East. From 1910 to 1918, the majority of Socialist state legislators were elected in Kansas, Nevada, Montana, California, Minnesota, Utah, New Mexico, Idaho, Washington, and Wisconsin.

As in other American political parties, the geographic distribution of the membership of the Socialist Party corresponded to its political variations. The basic strength of Haywood and the Syndicalists came from timber workers in the Northwest, in upper Michigan and Minnesota, and from dissident groups in the Western Federation of Miners, spread out from Arizona to Butte, Montana. The former Populist tenant farmers, as has been noted, had their greatest impact on the Socialist movements in Kansas, Texas, and Oklahoma, with some influence in Washington, Missouri, and North Dakota. The Christian Socialists seemed to have had most of their following in Illinois, Iowa, Utah, Northern California, and upstate New York. On the other hand, the "constructive" Socialists, the followers of Berger and Hillquit, were strongest in the larger cities such as New York, Philadelphia, Milwaukee, Los Angeles, Boston, and Chicago, where success was more dependent upon stable organization and good working relations with the central labor councils of the AFL than it was in many of the smaller cities and towns where Socialists were active.

Geographical diversity contributed to the polarity in the minds of contemporary Socialists between "revolutionists" and "constructivists." But even here different self-images did not always mean different attitudes toward organization or program. Those who succeeded in building a stable electoral base, as did the Milwaukee

Socialists under Victor Berger's leadership, the New Yorkers who followed Hillquit, and the left wingers in Texas and Oklahoma, given direction by Tom Hickey, E. R. Meitzen and others, emphasized programs of immediate relevance to their constituents and concentrated on precinct organization. Those with less stable constituents (among migratory workers or immigrant women and children in the textile industry) often deprecated "practical" programs and emphasized apocalyptic, or "revolutionary" appeals. Yet the "revolutionists" made practical demands: higher wages, shorter hours of work, improved conditions—in short, those related directly to job conditions and directed against the employer. The "constructive" demands tended to be more political in that they were made against the state: maximum legal interest rates; state grain elevators; municipal ice, electric, and water plants. There was nothing incompatible in these two sets of demands, and in some places both were made; but since different constituencies were often involved, there was competition within the Party over which should be emphasized.

These differences were exacerbated by the parochial character of most Party leaders. Eugene V. Debs, because of the range of his experience, was the only truly national leader the Socialist Party ever developed. He was almost equally popular among railroad workers spread out along the network of repair and maintenance shops in the Midwest and Southwest, among coal and metal miners, Christian Socialists, ex-Populists, IWW Socialists, and even among the brewery workers and garment workers who formed the backbone of Berger's support in Milwaukee and Hillquit's in New York. But since Debs evinced little interest in the organizational affairs of the Party, and since neither the Christian Socialists nor the ex-Populists were capable of winning national office, control of the Party organization fell into the hands of Berger, Hillquit, and their supporters. They were aided by their strategic location in the larger cities, where the national and many of the state offices were located (the national office was in Chicago). In addition, well-known writers or public figures, such as John Spargo, A. M. Simons, Robert Hunter, J. Stitt Wilson, often were the "constructivist" candidates for the National Executive Committee and this helped consolidate control by the Center and Right. Of those on the Left who ran for national positions, only Bill Haywood and Kate Richards O'Hare were well known throughout the Party. Thus Hillquit and Berger came to exercise a disproportionate influence over the Party organization.

5. Expansionism and The First World War

The Economic Formulation   WALTER LaFEBER

The New Left believes that the United States has always been an expansionist nation; that from the colonial period on we have cajoled, coerced, and cheated the Indians, and taken their lands; that from 1812 onward, we have also lusted after the territory of our continental neighbors, Canada and Mexico, and have ripped large chunks of it from the latter. Beginning in the post–Civil War era, their history continues, we began to look overseas for "new frontiers" to replace those that in former years we found in the Indian-occupied West. In the following half-century we involved ourselves in a war with Spain and acquired a small empire in the process. Thereafter, we avoided further territorial annexations, but we continued, through trade penetration and through "gunboat diplomacy," to exploit and control weaker powers to serve our interests.

Consensus historians have generally insisted that American expansionism was both benevolent and short-lived; that it grew either out of a desire to emulate the other great powers, or out of a sincere urge to bring freedom to oppressed peoples under Spanish yoke. At all events it was supposedly a temporary aberration that ended, at the latest, with our granting the Philippines complete independence after 1945.

In the essay below, Walter LaFeber examines the roots of America's late-nineteenth-century outward thrust. In this selection from his brilliant book *The New Empire,* he focuses on the business community and emphasizes the economic component of expansionism. Elsewhere, he also assigns significance to other factors, but throughout the book he stresses the close connection between business pressures and the response of the American government towards the weaker states and the decrepit empires that came within our sphere.

FOR FURTHER READING:

Richard Van Alstyne, *The Rising American Empire**, (Quadrangle, 1965); Ernest May, *Imperial Democracy: The Emergence of America as a Great Power,* (Harcourt, Brace and World, 1961); Ernest May, *American Imperialism,* (Atheneum, 1968); Julius Pratt, *Expansionists of 1898**, (Quadrangle, 1964); David Pletcher, *The Awkward Years: American Foreign*

Source: Walter LaFeber, *The New Empire: An Interpretation of American Expansion, 1860–1898* (Ithaca, N. Y.: Cornell University Press, 1963), chap. iv, "The Economic Formulation," pp. 176–196.

Relations Under Garfield and Arthur, (University of Missouri Press, 1962); William Appleman Williams, *The Roots of the American Empire*, (Random House, 1969); H. Wayne Morgan, *America's Road to Empire: The War With Spain and American Expansion**, (Wiley, 1965).

Asterisk denotes paperback edition.

The American Business Community: Analysis

Social upheavals and labor violence intensified as the depression entered its most critical period during the last months of 1894 and the first half of 1895. By the end of 1895, however, the American business community had reached a consensus on the causes of and solutions for the depression. Spokesmen for this community displayed special concern with two immediate problems: stopping the outflow of gold and halting the inflow of American securities from Europe. These problems were, in turn, subsumed in the larger challenge of increasing exports so that plants could dispose of their surplus goods and resume full productivity and regular employment. The administration demonstrated its agreement with this analysis when Secretary of the Treasury, John G. Carlisle, submitted a remarkable annual report in 1894 which held that American exports were the chief hope of restoring economic prosperity in the United States.

Halting the outflow of gold and the inflow of American securities from Europe were two sides of the same problem. Much of the gold that left the New York subtreasuries went into the pockets of panicky European investors. Business and political experts soon viewed exports of merchandise as the solution for both problems. Merchandise exports would stop gold exports by bringing so much money to the United States that the flow inward would overbalance the gold flow outward. Exports would also solve the foreign investment dilemma: first, they would invigorate American industries and so make the system attractive to foreign investors; second, the exports would provide the capital to replace any foreign investment which refused to take another plunge into American securities.

This last point became a particularly fascinating feature of the mid-1890's. In his message requesting the repeal of the Sherman Silver Purchase Act, Cleveland expressed the hope that repeal would revive interest in American investments and increase the amount of money available. But after the repeal, European money could not be found in any quantity. Instead, assistance came from an unexpected source—American banking houses. Capital, scarce in early summer of 1893, became so plentiful during the latter part of the year that loan rates dropped to very low levels. Some of this money bought out European investors and put American firms, especially railroads, into American banking hands.

The growing power of American bankers also affected United States relations with other countries. The nation became steadily more independent of foreign capital. Some American investors, moreover, found the home market too narrow and unprofitable. By 1896 their capital was moving into Caribbean and South and Central American money markets. Financial spokesmen also began noticing the relation of exports to investment capital. In the few years before 1893, exports had managed to balance the nation's international debts, but had failed to help the country's economy expand, since withdrawals of European investments more than offset the export gains. To maintain an expanding industrial economy, these amounts of exports were not enough. Either exports had to be increased or European capital found; otherwise the industrial expansion which had occurred since 1865 could not be maintained. When Europeans neglected the American investment market from 1893 to 1896, business spokesmen expected exports to be important means of obtaining needed capital. In other words, the United States would have to sell enough merchandise on the international market so that the nation could balance the debt it owed to that same market and have sufficient capital left over to finance the expansion of home industry.

This presented a gargantuan task. The dimensions of the problem became strikingly evident in mid-1894, when business journals noted that during the 1894 fiscal year exports exceeded imports by $259,567,000, yet gold had left the country in increasing amounts since January 1. Statistics for the 1894 calendar year told the same story. Although exports of merchandise, gold, and silver reached an enormous sum of $250,000,000, the *Commercial and Financial Chronicle* lamented, "Yet even at this moment the outflow of gold is still in progress." *Bradstreet's* paradoxically termed such an enormous export surplus as "Our Disappointing Foreign Trade." The gold exports halted in mid-1895 because of the manipulations of the Morgan-Belmont bond syndicate, which was helping the Treasury maintain its reserve by buying gold abroad. Business circles harbored no illusions, however. They frankly admitted that the syndicate had "certain limits" in supplying "the deficiency in natural media of exchange."

Businessmen believed their chief hope lay in autumn crop exports taking up where the syndicate left off. There were still fond memories of the 1891 and 1892 export years. But, as one business journal warned, if these exports failed to materialize there would probably result "unfortunate consequences which some of our contemporaries [the silverites] apparently delight to describe." By November, 1895, it became obvious that exports were not sufficient to handle the job. The New York correspondent for the *Economist* outlined the situation in detail. Over $7,300,000 had left the Treasury's gold reserve during the week of November 23, and "most . . . has gone to pay our debts." If exports of cotton, wheat, provisions, and other staples could continue in large amounts, gold would return to the country. But when these exports could not match the import of foreign goods and American securities returned by European investors, "it is inevitable that gold will leave this country."

As gold continued to flow outward, business circles cried that they would have "to continue to suffer this sort of financial nightmare every time our international trade statistics indicate an unfavourable trade balance." One authority publicly prescribed the cure which many businessmen were considering. A. S. Heidelbach, the senior member of a large international banking firm in New York, declared that in order to end the gold out-flow, the balance of trade in merchandise would have to reach "at least" $350,000,000 a year. Some disputed his figures, but few disputed his solution.

The selling of American securities not only endangered the gold reserve but also threatened to stunt the growth of the industrial economy through financial starvation. Reports issued by *Banker's Magazine* and Worthington C. Ford, Chief of the Bureau of Statistics, clearly explained the relationship between foreign funds and American economic strength. The irony of this situation lay in the fact that surplus money glutted American banks. Secretary Carlisle noted in his 1895 report that money had been hoarded "until it nearly reached the proportions of a panic." Business magazines concurred with this view. Much of this money abjured depression-ridden domestic securities and moved into foreign markets. Americans actually increased their investments abroad by almost $250,000,000 during the depression. Most of this money went to Canada and Latin America. Not only did this movement of capital leave American industries in their stagnant condition, but it greatly aggravated the balance of payments by enlarging the American demand for foreign exchange.

Industrialists began to realize a harsh fact. As *Bradstreet's* commented, money would flow into American factories only when there would be "developments of commercial activity and legitimate business in lines which, up to the moment, cannot be clearly foreseen." This journal added that "if business becomes active," European investors would also "at once come back to the market." *Bankers' Magazine* agreed with this analysis. To restore this commercial activity, however, demand had to be found.

By late 1895 the business community and the Cleveland administration agreed that exports provided one solution for the economic problems. In the business community no one summarized this agreement better than Henry W. Cannon, President of the Chase National Bank. Writing in February, 1895, Cannon stated that in order to prove to European investors that the United States could maintain gold payments, "it is necessary . . . that we should compete in the markets of the world with our goods and commodities, and also reconstruct our currency system." The New York reporter for the *Economist* stated the proposition tersely in September, 1895: "Either goods or gold must go abroad to pay for our purchases there, and thus far this autumn our shipments . . . have not equalled expectations."

The most significant and influential statement of this sort, however, came from Secretary Carlisle in his annual report of 1894. He noted at the outset that the United States had been kept "almost constantly in the position of debtors." Then in a striking analysis of what he considered to be the American system's dynamic, Carlisle observed that the nation's "prosperity . . . depends largely upon [its] ability to sell [its] surplus products in foreign markets at remunerative prices" in order to pay off loans and interest and to secure credit abroad. The American economy, Carlisle warned, could survive the selling of securities by foreign investors in only two ways: "One is for our people to export and sell their commodities in foreign markets to a sufficient amount to create a balance of credit in their favor equal to the amount to be withdrawn, and the other is to ship gold, that being the only money recognized in the settlement of international balances." The latter course had been resorted to since 1893, and the results had been disastrous. The Secretary's either/or alternative appeared to be the only escape out of the depression.

With recovery defined in such terms, the responsibility upon American exporters was great. Unfortunately, this responsibility came at a time when they could ill bear the burden. Exports for the 1894 fiscal year had been surpassed only twice before in American history, but ominously, the four leading staples—breadstuffs, provisions, cotton, and petroleum—had fallen off in value almost six million dollars. In order to find outlets, their producers had to accept very low prices, "in some cases," one journal declared, "the lowest ever made." The *Commercial and Financial Chronicle* and the *Economist* agreed with *Bankers' Magazine* that "there has been a natural cause" for the worsening depression; "small exports and agricultural depression, are . . . now the chief remaining obstacles to a return of general prosperity." Unlike 1891 and 1892, cotton and wheat exports could not restore normal conditions.

Amid this gloom, Worthington C. Ford published an article, "The Turning of the Tide," in the summer of 1895. He entitled it thus although exports had declined $75,651,000, although the export balance had greatly decreased in comparison with 1894, and although the export staples, especially wheat and cotton, had suffered disastrous setbacks in the 1895 fiscal year. But Ford was correct in terming it a "Turn," for the figures in the export tables of fiscal 1895 marked not only a turn in the depression but a pivotal point in American commercial history. These figures indicated that, although farm exports had slumped, industrial exports had reached all-time highs. Iron and steel had especially topped their previous high levels of 1894 by nearly a million dollars. Ford emphasized this change further by noting that the nation imported less food in 1895, but that "more raw materials for domestic industries, more partly manufactured articles and more manufactures for consumption" arrived.

In making this analysis, Ford simply repeated what some business journals had been proclaiming since early 1894. *Bankers' Magazine* and the *Commercial and Financial Chronicle* echoed *Bradstreet's* conclusion that the agricultural depression formed "the worst obstacle to our general business recovery." Another journal observed that because of newly opened wheat lands in Latin America and Russia "it is practically impossible for the United States to compete with foreign exports of wheat." Out of this analysis arose a new evaluation of international trade. Several articles printed in *Bankers' Magazine* during the fall of 1894 best illustrate the new conclusions formed by these business spokesmen.

These articles postulated that a "great revolution in prices" had occurred which made impossible a return to former price levels. Now "the cheapest" country would "win in the great National, and International race for the commerce of its own people [and] for that of the world." The journal lamented that the nation's agriculture, "hitherto regarded as the source of our National prosperity," would have to be sacrificed in this race. But clearly, the American farmer could no longer compete in world markets. He could perform an even more vital function, however, for the cheapness of foodstuffs, "together with cheaper raw materials," would provide "the foundation . . . of our future manufacturing supremacy over Europe." Upon this new industrial base "we must soon depend for our nation's prosperity, instead of upon her producers of food, feed, and raw materials." The visions arising from this premise were grandiose. There would be no more boom times followed by depression, but "slow and steady improvement . . . and our surplus manufacturing capacity turned to the production of goods we may be able to export hereafter, at reduced cost and thus keep all our industries permanently employed, as England does, having the world's markets in which to unload any accumulation."

Corroborating this reasoning, industrial goods slowly edged upward on the export charts, accounting for 15.61 per cent of the total exports in the fiscal year 1892, 19.02 per cent in 1893, 21.14 per cent in 1894, and jumping to 23.14 per cent in 1895. This, plus the announcement in mid-1895 that a large shipment of United States steel was to go abroad to compete in the highly competitive European market, "attracted considerable attention," in the words of *Literary Digest.* Examining these events, the New York *Journal of Commerce,* the New

York *Herald,* and the antijingoist Louisville *Courier-Journal* had their views well summed up by the London *Iron and Coal Trades Review:* "The Americans themselves argue . . . that they must continue to increase the export of their manufactured goods, since their exports of food and other raw products must inevitably decline."

Businessmen saw foreign markets as vitally important for their economic welfare, but they also clearly saw and feared the social consequences which would follow should their programs of commercial expansion fail to restore prosperity. Nowhere was this stated better than in *Bankers' Magazine* of February, 1894. This article is certainly one of the most interesting printed during the 1890's in business or popular journals. Written during the time when Populism was reaching its peak and labor uprisings threatened, the article re-evaluated American society along the classic lines of James Madison's *The Federalist,* No. 10.

The article opened by noting that business was severely depressed, and that destitute tramps symbolized the United States of 1894. It then asked bluntly whether the American political system had reached the end of its usefulness. The United States had become sectionalized not only politically, but even more dangerously, "on business and economic questions." These "sectional differences are growing greater" as the people's interests grow more diversified. The article searched for the source of this trouble: "Have we grown too fast to consolidate our strength; or, are the interests of new communities naturally antagonistic to those of older ones?" The political economist would answer that "the greater the general good and prosperity, the greater that of the individual." But "neither the economics, nor the ethics of our times are founded upon Humanitarianism," but "upon the cornerstone of self, self-interest, self-aggrandizement, power and wealth, at the expense of everybody else."

These selfish interests have "become irreconcilable, by becoming so diversified" and so "have brought our National Government into its present impotency." The journal did not believe that Americans would admit that "we have grown too great, to hold our wide Empire intact, by the bond of commonweal." But after all, the Roman Empire had disintegrated when it failed to govern well a vast expanse of territory. The lesson was plain. If the depression and its attendant economic discontent continued to clog the political machine erected by the Founding Fathers, only two possible alternatives presented themselves: follow the British Empire and allow more local autonomy, or centralize to a great extent so that the majority may govern without hindrance. This was an analysis of a crisis. It rested on the hope that improved economic conditions would end Populist and labor unrest and enable the machine of 1787 to continue with few repairs. But the importance of the article lay in the fact that the spokesman for a vital segment of the business community realized that the political penalty would be severe if the American economy continued to appear bankrupt.

The American Business Community: Solutions

Worthington C. Ford's article, "The Turning of the Tide," not only observed the slow change from foodstuffs to manufactured products in American exports, but calculated that such a change would switch the focus of the nation's commercial interest. Ford noted that "the political consequences" of the change were displayed in the increasing trade with underindustrialized areas such as South America, Oceania, and Africa and a corresponding decrease of trade with Europe. Again, Ford only summarized what American business and political circles had realized for some time.

This did not mean that American manufacturers refused to compete in European markets. In 1895 the entry of United States iron ore and steel in British and continental markets excited Wall Street. American paper products invaded established European markets. Even United States investment capital began flowing to Europe in increased amounts. But challenging European manufacturers in their own backyards was risky business. South America and Central America, on the other hand, not only provided a natural outlet for manufactures, but possessed geographical advantages and also came under the political protection of the Monroe Doctrine. True, American trade with the nations to the south approximated only one-seventh of the entire trade which the Latin-American nations carried on, but this fact merely strengthened American desires to obtain this market. Latin America appeared to be a virgin prize well located for an easy seduction. United States interest in Asian markets also increased after 1895, but this movement would not influence State Department policy makers in an important way until 1897.

American financiers and manufacturers moved into Latin America with a conscious, concerted effort. As the *Bankers' Magazine* insisted in early 1894, if "we could wrest the South American markets from Germany and England and permanently hold them, this would be indeed a conquest worth perhaps a heavy sacrifice." The "sacrifice" this journal had in mind was probably the American farmer. In any case, increasing numbers of investors moved into the Latin-American area to make this conquest after 1893. In early 1894 a New York steamship company opened a regular trade route between New York and the Pacific coast of South America. By 1896 business had grown so profitable that the line increased its fleet, and a rival American company entered the field. A group of Chicago railroad capitalists signed a contract in 1895 to construct an important railway in Mexico. Several Denver financiers completed an important Costa Rican railway line in 1895. In Colombia a company composed entirely of Americans built and operated a railway along the Atlantic coast. It purchased its locomotives and cars in the United States. Another American-financed railway was under construction in Guatemala. One railroad official noted the American interest in Mexico when he remarked in early 1895 that "there are fully three times as many Americans in Mexico this winter looking up lands as were there last winter."

A group of New York City bankers obtained a dominant share of Santo Domingo's finances in 1893 when they purchased the nation's debt from a Dutch company. Receiving the right to collect all customs revenues, this syndicate could exert a powerful influence on the Santo Domingo government. American capitalists controlled a Salvadoran company which obtained a government monopoly over the Bay of Jiquilisco and built a new port (El Triunfo) in 1894–1895. The port soon exacted the trade of the entire region, and by early 1896 coffee exports were nearly doubling each month. United States capital in Mexico, Cuba, and the Caribbean area alone amounted to $350,000,000 by 1898.

The investor moved southward with a minimum of fanfare. The merchant and manufacturer, however, invaded Latin America with the cheers of commercial manifest destiny ringing in his ears. In 1889 James G. Blaine had led, and the businessmen had willingly followed. But after 1893 the businessmen played at least an equal role in focusing attention southward and in some instances blazed paths which the State Department followed in formulating Latin-American policies. *The Age of Steel* echoed Brooks Adams by declaring in 1895 that "there is no fixedness in commercial supremacy. It has come and gone from one nation to another." *Bankers' Magazine* added, "There is no reason why our manufactures should not find an enlarged market in the southern half of this hemisphere." *Bradstreet's* noted that the industrialists were responding with an aroused interest in Latin America by late 1894. This interest took many forms—renewed demands for an Isthmian canal, increased attention given to reciprocity, the enthusiasm displayed by cotton and woolen textile manufacturers in developing Latin-American markets, the growth of and interest in industrial expositions held in the southern United States, the development of commercial museums, and, finally, the formation and growth of the National Association of Manufacturers.

Bradstreet's mirrored much business opinion when it wrote that the Clayton-Bulwer Treaty should be formally abrogated as soon as possible, though this should be done "within the bounds of international courtesy." The *Economist's* New York correspondent observed that "considerable interest is taken in the outlook for the construction of the Nicaragua Canal," and then added an anti-British note that became more prominent as the depression progressed, "and particularly because of the attention directed to the control of that canal in recent British publications." *Bradstreet's* published a long summary of a paper by Emory R. Johnson, which emphasized the commercial, not the strategic, advantages of such a passageway. A canal, Johnson reported, would give the United States "a decided advantage over other nations" in "the future development of the South American and Oriental countries."

A renewed interest in reciprocity appeared in early 1895 just as the Wilson-Gorman tariff went into operation. Three key business organizations especially displayed some inquisitiveness in the possibility of renewing the reciprocity amendment of 1890. The newly organized National Association of Manufacturers and the National Board of Trade expressed particular interest in negotiating reciprocity pacts with Mexico, Central America and South America, and the Spanish-American colonies. Andrew Carnegie published an article in which he termed reciprocity "the best step" in obtaining foreign trade otherwise unobtainable.

Cotton and woolen textile manufacturers displayed intense interest in southern markets. Worthington C. Ford noted that the cotton industry was moving into the southern United States not only for cheaper labor, but because "geographically the South is nearer what are considered the natural markets of the United States— Central and South America." Ford further observed that in the past twenty years (1874–1894), the output of American cotton mills had jumped in volume five times. The greatest increase in exports had gone to South America and Asia, and this trade had expanded in spite of stiff competition from British and German agents. Meanwhile, the Boston *Commercial Bulletin* reported that woolen manufacturers worried about the "falling off of the export demand" which set the mills to "manufacturing for the home rather than the foreign market." These industrialists regretted especially the abrogation of reciprocity. Their exports were 11,000,000 yards less than in the previous several years, and 8,000,000 yards of this had formerly gone under reciprocity treaties to Cuba, Santo Domingo, and Brazil.

Southern businessmen hoped to alleviate the depression in their section by developing Latin-American markets. Believing it to be "only a question of time when the United States will hold a practical monopoly of the trade of South America," the Chattanooga *Tradesman* urged that if "the South shall push her advantages . . . her ports will soon have a monopoly of many lines of trade" with Central America and South America. Good reasons for such optimism could be found in several industrial expositions held in the South during the mid-1890's. The largest and most publicized of these was the Atlanta Exposition of 1895. President Cleveland and several members of his cabinet found time to visit this affair. In inviting Secretary of State Richard Olney, Chairman J. W. Avery commented, "The foreign trade idea is the basic and uppermost feature of the Exposition, both with our own people and the foreigners." Earlier, Avery had been sent to Latin America by the Atlanta business community to drum up interest in the exposition. Secretary of State Gresham, Olney's predecessor, assisted Avery's expedition by writing letters of introduction for the agent to all the United States ministers in South America. The letters instructed the ministers "to cooperate in his purposes." Commercial ties between Atlanta businessmen and groups in Costa Rica, Guatemala, and Mexico soon appeared.

American commercial museums provided another approach to obtaining more Latin-American trade. Stimulated by the exhibits at the Chicago World's Fair in 1893, the full bloom of this movement appeared in the flowering of the Philadelphia Commercial Museum in the 1894–1897 period. Secretaries of State Gresham and Olney displayed active interest in this undertaking. William Pepper, the President of the museum, wrote Olney in 1895 that he had "been surprised and gratified at the rapid spread of interests" shown by American manufacturers for the project. Speaking at the museum's national opening in June, 1897, Olney outlined the inevitability of Western Hemispheric economic solidarity. "Trade does not of course go, like kissing, by favor," the Secretary declared. "Its sure and only basis is selfish interest." "Intimate commercial intercourse" between North and South America, he insisted, was "inevitable." New York City soon followed Philadelphia's example and constructed its own commercial museum.

Perhaps the most publicized and concerted movement for the extension of foreign markets and control of Latin-American trade began with the formation of the National Association of Manufacturers in January, 1895. The depression operated as a direct cause of this movement. As one student of the organization has written, "it was apparent to the manufacturers who had struggled through the depression years of 1893 and 1894 that some positive action was necessary to enlarge domestic and foreign markets." The opportunity for such positive action came in the fall of 1894 when a southern trade paper, *Dixie,* threw out a suggestion to manufacturers to display their wares in a Mexico City industrial exhibition. *Dixie* was deluged with letters. The response so overwhelmed the journal's owners that they suggested that interested manufacturers band together and "have a meeting . . . in some central city." Several southern and several Cincinnati firms planned a convention for January, 1895. The invitations outlined a basic seven-point program, with three of these points directly related to foreign trade: a thorough development of foreign commerce including exhibition warehouses, a merchant marine, and reciprocity.

When the convention opened in Cincinnati, Warner Miller, former Senator and President of the Nicaragua Canal Company, set the tone by noting that the panic of 1893 and the ensuing depression had created much interest in new markets outside the United States. The featured speaker of the convention, Governor William McKinley of Ohio, brought the delegates to their feet with a trade pronouncement which embodied nearly everything the nascent organization desired.

We want our own markets for our manufactures and agricultural products; we want a tariff for our surplus products which will not surrender our markets and will not degrade our labor to hold our markets. We want a reciprocity which will give us foreign markets for our surplus products and in turn that will open our markets to foreigners for those products which they produce and which we do not.

Charles Heber Clarke, Secretary of the Manufacturers' Club of Philadelphia, followed McKinley and localized the new organization's interest. Devoting his speech almost exclusively to Latin America, he concluded that this area "ought to belong to us in a commercial sense." He highlighted his speech by asking for an international money order system to replace the payments which now went through London. This statement was significant, for it implied that the United States now believed that it had sufficient economic power to assume control of international payments from Great Britain. Clarke also asked for bimetallism, for he believed that the gold standard drove up the prices of American manufactured goods in South American silver areas.

M. E. Ingalls, President of the "Big Four" railroad system, stressed another point at the convention, a point that has been noted earlier in this chapter. Since the American farmer was losing the European market, Ingalls explained, outlets for industrial goods would have to be found in Latin America and the Far East. Ingalls proposed raising the tariff so high that American manufacturers would be able to dump their surplus at rock-bottom prices in foreign markets. This, in effect, repeated the *Bankers' Magazine*'s idea that the nation's farmers would have to be sacrificed on the altar of American industry.

Several general themes emerged as the convention proceeded. One emphasized the need for foreign and especially Latin-American markets. A second motif was a strong anti-British feeling. Pointed references were made to Britain's control of international trade and finance. The N.A.M. asked the federal government for assistance which would enable American industries to compete on more equal terms with the British. A third theme appeared as the organization also requested other extensive favors from the national government. *Iron Age* later criticized the convention for "relying solely upon extraneous help." A pro-N.A.M. journal sarcastically informed *Iron Age* that, after all, the government *was* "the servant of the people." These three themes were embodied in the preamble to the N.A.M. Constitution. Every objective in this preamble looked to the government to improve market conditions and trade, as it asked for reciprocity, a "judicious system of subsidies" to build a merchant fleet, a Nicaraguan canal, and the rebuilding of internal waterways.

After the convention, a series of circulars were sent to influential industrialists and politicians. The first circular outlined the association's "Purposes." It listed fourteen of these, eight of them directly connected with foreign trade. One large section stressed the importance of "The Promotion of Spanish-American Trade." This part noted, "The trade centres of Central and South America are natural markets for American products," and the development of this trade "promises to be one of the most effective and most valuable lines of work undertaken by the National Association of Manufacturers." In early 1896 the N.A.M. sponsored a "party of representative American business men" who visited Argentina, Uruguay, and Brazil. The visitors hoped to learn more of the "resources of the countries" and "to indicate the means by which the trade between the nations interested can be enlarged and extended." Venezuela attracted special attention as the N.A.M. erected its first sample warehouse in Caracas. This occurred during and immediately after the United States settlement of the Venezuelan boundary dispute with England.

The purposes of the N.A.M. were not lost on the business world. The St. Louis *Age of Steel* and the Pittsburgh *American Manufacturer* believed this organization to be "the beginning of an intelligent, organized effort to extend our foreign trade in manufactures . . . with the neighboring nations of Spanish America." The Chattanooga *Tradesman,* however, pointedly remarked that several of the leading exporting interests—cotton and woolen manufacturers, coal mine owners, and lumbermen—had not attended the N.A.M. meeting. By omitting these three interests, the *Tradesman* commented, the discussion at Cincinnati "was not as wise as it might have been."

Great Britain watched these movements with unconcealed fear. The London *Chamber of Commerce Journal* noted that even in British colonies American goods were becoming dominant; everywhere "the markets are flooded with all descriptions of American manufactures" which endeavor to drive out British goods with "what amounts to quite an alarming promise of success." This journal could have especially pointed to the changes which had only recently occurred in Honduras' trade. American commercial influence had grown so large in that British colony that Honduras adopted the United States gold dollar as its monetary unit in 1894. Among the several British papers which noted the revival of the Monroe Doctrine fetish in America during the summer and fall of 1895, the *British Trade Journal* observed that "it is all very well to ignore and ridicule America's Monroe Doctrine in its purely political aspects," but there is "surely an unwritten Monroeism working like yeast in the commercial world of America," and this "we must combat—or take the consequences of our fatuity." French observers also noted the growth of this "unwritten Monroeism."

American newspapers quickly replied in kind to such remarks. The New York *Tribune* proclaimed that, while the United States had depended on "a phrase" in the Monroe Doctrine, Europeans had moved into South America and converted these nations "into commercial dependencies." The Atlanta *Constitution* warned that the United States had to draw the line or "suffer imperialism to overrun Central and South America." But vastly more important, the Cleveland administration formulated a foreign policy which attempted to obtain and protect the objectives that the American business community's spokesmen had delineated. This policy climaxed in the Venezuelan crisis of 1895.

The Rise of the American Mediterranean GORDON LEWIS

The Caribbean was the overseas area where America's power was most blatantly exercised. Here, amid some of the most magnificent scenery and the most majestic beaches in the world were found weak and disorderly successor states and the remains of seventeenth and eighteenth century empires. The region so close to the United States and to the shipping routes to the West Coast had immense strategic importance and at the same time represented a potential source of exploitable resources. By the last half of the nineteenth century it was also a power vacuum that Americans felt called on to fill.

With the important exception of Puerto Rico and the Virgin Islands the United States did not actually occupy territory in the Caribbean region. Our tactical need to protect our southern flank and the Panama Canal could be satisfied by naval bases such as those we acquired in Cuba and the British possessions; we could gain our economic ends through investments; the power vacuum could be filled by establishing virtual protectorates over Haiti, Cuba, and the mainland republics of Central America, and by putting other nations on notice that we did not intend tolerating their intervention.

The way the United States justified and rationalized its effort to turn the Caribbean into an American lake, and the response of Latin Americans to our penetration southward, is examined in Gordon Lewis' essay below. It is a temperate but earnest indictment of the hypocrisy of imperialism, and a plea for a change of heart. It is also a warning about the impossibility of continuing our previous policies.

FOR FURTHER READING:

Dexter Perkins, *The History of the Monroe Doctrine*, (Little, Brown and Company, 1955); Dexter Perkins, *The United States and Latin America*, (Louisiana State University Press, 1961); Scott Nearing and Joseph Freeman, *Dollar Diplomacy: A Study in American Imperialism**, (Monthly Review Press, 1966); Howard C. Hill, *Roosevelt and the Caribbean*, (Russell, 1965); Rayford Logan, *The Diplomatic Relations of the United States with Haiti 1776–1891*, (University of North Carolina Press, 1941); James F. Rippy, *The United States and Mexico*, (Reprint House International); William Appleman Williams, *The United States, Cuba and Castro*, (Monthly Review, 1962).

Asterisk denotes paperback edition.

The roots of American interest in the Caribbean go back, historically, to the very foundation of the Republic. Modern scholarship has amply documented the important role of the West Indian trade in the commercial life of the American colonies, and the economic importance of the region was emphasized more than a century later by the status of the Panama Canal as the key to the commercial expansion of the Pacific. That economic basis of American interest was reinforced, of course,

Source: Gordon Lewis, "The Rise of the American Mediterranean," *Studies on the Left*, vol. 2, no. 2 (1961), pp. 42–58.

by strategic considerations. From the infancy of the American experiment, its leading statesmen lived in constant apprehension of the encroachments of the European powers in the hemisphere. The apprehension does not seem unfounded when it is remembered that for the best part of a century after 1787 the Republic had to face the icy hostility of all the European chancelleries, so that as late as the Civil War period it was possible for a British political leader as liberal as Gladstone to be making speeches in support of the cause of the Confederacy. British policies in Canada, the Oregon controversy, the quixotic adventure of the Second Empire in Mexico, the fear of European diplomatic influence in the independent state of Texas after 1836, all contributed to buttress the American qualms about the dangers of European expansionism in the hemisphere. There was no particular fear about Spanish aggression designed to regain the lost American colonies, for Spain was clearly on the decline and, indeed, many of the later American attitudes toward Puerto Rico can only be properly understood if they are seen as offshoots of an earlier contempt for Spanish decadence in the region; it was not too difficult to extend Mr. Dooley's Chicago-Irish lampooning of the Spaniard to the Cuban and the Puerto Rican. The real fear of every American Secretary of State from Jefferson to Bryan was that the hemispheric territories in the vicinity of the United States would be torn from Spain and fall into the more aggressive clutch of Britain or France or, later, of Germany. The fear received its definitive theoretical expression, naturally, in the Monroe Doctrine of 1823, which was based upon the New World isolationism of Washington and Jefferson. Its practical application was mapped out in the form of American policies within the field of Caribbean international relationships, beginning with the audacious Louisiana procurement of 1803 and ending with what essentially became, after the war of 1898, the organization of an American sphere of influence more and more insulated against European penetration and controlled by application to the Caribbean of the dogma of Manifest Destiny.

The details of that development are well known. Before 1898 they were part of a larger American national expansionism on the immediate national frontiers—the acquisition of Florida, the Texan War, the control of the Pacific coast. After 1898, they came to constitute a more aggressive policy in the more immediate Caribbean area—the seizure of Cuba and Puerto Rico, the establishment of the Panama Republic as an instrument for the American control of the isthmian canal, the growth of "dollar diplomacy" in Haiti and the Dominican Republic, military intervention in the Central American states, strategic imperialism in the form of acquired naval bases and an effort, somewhat less successful, to set up American influence in the states of the South American continental littoral. It should be noted that there has been, throughout, a remarkable consistency of policy on the part of successive American national administrations. Both of the major political parties have espoused the Caribbean expansionist program. The Grant administration, it is true, failed to obtain congressional consent to its proposal to annex Santo Domingo by treaty, but a generation later no influential voice was raised against the annexation of the Spanish islands. Seward and Blaine, as Republican Secretaries of State, were matched in their zeal for the policy of annexation by Democratic Secretaries like Olney. And once popular disapprobation of overseas expansion began to decline sometime after 1893, every President from McKinley to Coolidge, and every Secretary of State from Hay to Kellogg, whatever his party affiliation and whatever the tone of his utterances on American relations with the Latin American-Caribbean world, was impelled to much the same sort of decision when confronted with the responsibility of solving one of the perennial Caribbean crises. A record of anti-imperialist sentiment did not prevent Bryan, in his brief occupancy of the State Department, from propagating a scheme for obtaining a controlling influence in the affairs of the Central American republics by means of an American insurance of their bond issues on the world financial market. Both of the liberal Presidents Cleveland and Wilson entertained high ideas of international morality with indisputable sincerity. But the one approved the Olney dispatch of 1895, on the Venezuelan dispute, which became one of the best-known statements of the new expansionism in its assertion that "the United States is practically sovereign on this continent, and its fiat is law upon the subjects to which it confines its interposition;" while the other's real sense of shame over the first Mexican War of 1846 as a ruthless predatory enterprise did not prevent him from adopting a policy of active, albeit reluctant, interference in the affairs of revolutionary Mexico after 1913; nor did it deter him from a policy of paternal despotism in the Central American and Caribbean areas that included the Crowder mission of "preventative intervention" in Cuba and the military occupation of Haiti and Santo Domingo by United States Marines.

The sole distinction between Republican and Democratic action was, at best, one of degree rather than kind. Both agreed with the new nationalism. Both supported the type of sentiment contained in the observation of the Assistant Secretary of State in 1904 that "it seems plain that no picture of our future is complete which does not contemplate and comprehend the United States as the dominant power in the Caribbean." The power of the isolationist tradition in the national life, of course, had not forever disappeared under the bewitching influence of such sentiments on the larger world canvas, as the withdrawal from the League of Nations experiment decisively showed. What is of suggestive interest, however, is that withdrawal from Europe was never coupled with any idea of withdrawal from the Caribbean. Even the concept of an isolationist America, like that of a "fortress America" a generation later, subsumed an exclusive American sovereignty within the region. By the end of the First World War, that had become a settled element of national foreign policy, both Democratic and Republican. The earlier dream of a virtuous farmer's Republic abjuring imperialist habits—described, for example, in the statement of Representative Rhea in 1811 that he would not be in favor of annexing West Indian territory unless "it would please the Almighty Maker of worlds to move the foundations of the West Indian islands and place them alongside of the United States"—had by that time become irrevocably lost with the departed springtime innocence of the American people.

The factors that went into the making of this American imperialism were naturally miscellaneous. There was the growing popularity, in the Nineties, of the cult of sea-power, made fashionable by the writings of Mahan. There was the occasional influence of the American filibuster, like Walker in his Nicaraguan escapade and General Cazneau in Santo Domingo, as well as that of such European counterparts as the quixotic Danish Captain Christmas, who played a sort of Rafael Sabatini hero role in the extended negotiations that led up to the sale of the Danish West Indies to the United States in 1917. There was even, at times, the temptation to use external adventure as a means of assuaging domestic discontents, as evidenced in Seward's *Thoughts for the Consideration of the President,* composed at a moment of Union difficulties during the Civil War. There was the influence, always formidable in American life, of the popular press, and American historical scholarship has fully demonstrated the contribution of the Hearst and Pulitzer "yellow press" towards the generation of a popular war sentiment in the period immediately preceding the outbreak of war in 1898. Along with these there was the semi-militaristic feeling that outside adventure was "healthy" for a nation, a feeling publicized not only by American conservative writers, but also hinted at by liberals like Herbert Croly.

All of these elements, however, were ancillary causes only, not to be compared in their importance with the twin major factors of economic interest and continental defense strategy. With regard to that first factor, the relationship between the state-power and organized business interests in the growth of overseas expansionism in the American case has not always been easy to decipher, for there was present no separate class, like the "nabobs" of British India or the "West India interest" in the eighteenth century English House of Commons, whose sole interest lay in overseas economic imperialism, nor were the interests of American capitalism so sharply divided between the groups operating in the domestic field and those specializing in the foreign field. Nor is it intellectually a sound enterprise to portray the nationalist-expansionist program as a self-conscious and evil manipulation of the political process by "big business," for so to do—as is the tendency in a book like *Dollar Diplomacy,* written by Scott Nearing and Joseph Freeman in 1925— is to undertake the thoroughly un-Marxist procedure of attributing motives to the imperialists instead of recognizing their behavior as a simple and logical consequence of the system they in part represent. Having made that point, however, it is indubitably true that however passive a role American business played in the initial impetus towards expansion, it did not long delay in seizing firm hold of the commercial opportunities opened up by the military men and the politicians. Within a generation or even less after the Treaty of Paris, the large American sugar corporations had taken over the bulk of cane-production in Cuba, Santo Domingo and Puerto Rico, replacing the *colono* system of cultivation with the bureaucratized impersonalism of the huge and heavily capitalized *central.* By 1925, with the exception of a few Italian-owned concerns, the principal sugar estates in Santo Domingo were American-owned; by 1933, the year of the first Batista *coup d'état,* American sugar investment had become the basis of the Cuban economy, supported by incorporation into the American import quota system; while by 1935, on the eve of the local agrarian reform movement, nearly fifty per cent of all lands operated by sugar companies in Puerto Rico were under the control of the four big American-owned concerns. A similar process occurred in the world of oil. The fabulously rich Maracaibo oilfields of Venezuela, opened up in 1918, were taken over by the international oil cartels, with a dominant American interest, with the result that by 1955, American companies occupied a predominant position in the industry's gross investment, to the extent of some 61%, as compared with the figure of 47% in the case of the Middle East and 54% in that of Canada. By that time, too, the South American country had become, in the words of Romulo Betancourt's book title, a "petroleum factory" controlled by an alliance of American oilmen and native militarists.

The semi-feudal empires of sugar and oil, in their turn, were reinforced by the financial and mercantile Americanization of the Caribbean and Middle American countries. With the aid of the State Department, the New York banking houses became the guarantors of the bonded indebtedness of one country after another. The favorite device to procure that end was a compulsory American customs receivership, frequently guaranteed by treaty arrangement, as, for example, in the 1907 Convention forced upon Santo Domingo. The device had the double effect of, first, directing the flotation of loans to the New York finance market and, second, creating a practically airtight monopoly for the intrusion of American business concessions in the fields of public works, mining, fruit cultivation, electricity and railroad services, steamship communications and lumber exploitation. The outcome, for most of the small countries concerned, was a system in which government, politics, economic activity, the very texture of social life itself were shaped by the *diktat* of the major foreign trading concerns. "His country," wrote a well known American journalist, at the turn of the century, about the average Caribbean citizen, "no matter what her name may be, is ruled by a firm of coffee merchants in New York City, or by a German railroad corporation, or by a line of coasting steamers, or by a great trading house, with headquarters in Berlin, or London, or Bordeaux. . . . You find this condition of affairs all through Central America, and you are not long in a Republic before you learn which merchant or which bank or which railroad corporation controls it, and you soon grow to look upon a mule loaded with boxes bearing the trademark of a certain business house with more respect than upon a soldier who wears the linen ribbon of the Government." The only change that had taken place a generation later was that American enterprise had become relatively more powerful as the economic meaning of the Monroe Doctrine conferred upon the American banker, in alliance with the American Government, the exclusive prerogative of enforcing the terms of the commercial relationship upon the Caribbean consumer. A series of case-studies by American scholars—Dr. Jenks' *Our Cuban Colony,* Dr. Knight's *The Americans in Santo Domingo,* Professor Rippy's *The Capitalists and Colombia*—has described what this process fully involved. By 1930 the region had indeed become the American Mediterranean.

The second leading factor in the development of American imperialism in the Caribbean was national defense. From the very start, when Balboa forced his way across the Darien isthmus to reach the Pacific, the international existence of the Caribbean sea has whirled around the weighty strategic importance of the Panama-Nicaragua canal project. It engaged the attention of early Spanish historians of the New World like Herrera, and of such men as Humboldt, Franklin, and Goethe. The most famous of all Latin American emancipators saw the vast political implications of the location of the isthmus: "If the world," Bolivar wrote, "were to select a spot for its capital, it would seem that the Isthmus of Panama must needs be chosen for this august destiny, situated as it is at the center of the world, looking in one direction towards Asia, and in the other towards Africa and Europe, and equidistant from America's two extremities." Characteristically, however, as its Canal diplomacy unfolded, the American leviathan-power was concerned less with the cultural than with the commercial, and even more the strategic, promise of the isthmian passage (Panama City, today, is hardly a Paris or a Rio de Janeiro). Control of the passage would mean a connecting link between the American east and west coasts; it would facilitate hemispheric defense, a need graphically illustrated by the naval dispositions of the 1898 war; and it would finally establish American interest as paramount in the whole area. All this came to require, from the viewpoint of the American nationalist, both a unilateral American regulation of the Canal region and a right to fortify the immediate environment; and it is interesting to observe how those demands were slowly advanced to abrogate, finally, the promise of a neutralized and non-militarized canal written into the clauses of the early Clayton-Bulwer Treaty of 1850. That meant, too, the final sacrifice of both the commercial interests of Great Britain in the canal—surely as real as American interests—and of the collective interest of the international community to the single interest of the American nation. Senator Morgan's extravagant claim that the construction of the canal should be seen as "the proud mission of our Government and people, under a providence that is as peculiar to them as the founding of the kingdom of the Messiah was to the seed of Abraham" has been the sort of braggadoccio, as much as any real defense needs, that has driven Washington, increasingly, into a policy of going beyond the canal area to construct naval and air bases throughout the land screen that faces it: Roosevelt Roads, Guantanamo, Chaguaramas.

Perhaps, indeed, the argument of defense has been exaggerated. At least an American authority noted as far back as 1929 that an elaborate system of Caribbean naval stations east of the canal did not seem necessary as a defense against Japanese attack from the west of it, and that the progress of aviation was rapidly bringing nearer the day when Japanese aviators would be able to reach the American continent without going near the canal or its Caribbean defenses; and the Pearl Harbor attack twelve years later would appear to have vindicated the accuracy of the analysis. The chief motive behind the purchase of the Danish West Indies in 1917, again, was the desire to prevent Germany from securing a naval base at St. Thomas or St. John. But, as later events turned out, the only threat of an enemy beachhead being established in the archipelago came from the possibility that Britain or France, in their efforts to appease the Axis powers after 1935, might have been willing to hand over the islands of either Trinidad or Martinique, respectively, to Hitlerite Germany. But that contingency was met by President Roosevelt's readiness to have the U. S. Fleet seize the islands in case the threat were to materialize. The secret power exercised by military cliques on the foreign policies of European nations is an old story. What is surprising, in the American case, is that the anti-militarist bias of the democratic creed did not prevent a similar secret power from growing up in Washington after the eighteen nineties. Indeed, it is not without some significance that some of the most industrious architects in the shaping of the Caribbean as an American lake were naval men like Mahan and military men like General Wood; and that they were members of the neo-Hamiltonian movement centered around an important group of men—Henry Cabot Lodge, Elihu Root, Herbert Croly, Albert J. Beveridge and the two Adams brothers—that attempted, between 1890 and 1920, to reinstate the ethic of military professionalism in a society given over too much, as they saw it, to the corroding values of a business pacifism. Their effort failed with the return to "normalcy" in 1920. But it did not fail before they had succeeded in persuading national opinion that the Caribbean, at least, was henceforth to be regarded and retained as an American sphere of influence.

Two elements in the pattern of "Manifest Destiny" deserve some extended annotation. The first is the armory of methods utilized by the United States in its practical application of the theory. It has been one of the myths of the American democracy that it was above employing the methods that had been used by a quasi-feudal Europe in the search for world power. Yet the history of American enterprise in the Caribbean reveals not merely a readiness to emulate those methods, but also a genius to improve upon them. There was the method of armed intervention to protect American propertied interests, as in Cuba in 1906 and Haiti in 1915. There was the method of the "financial protectorate," imposed, as in Haiti and Santo Domingo, by formal treaty and, in Cuba, by measures such as the famous Platt Amendment of 1902, conferring, as the latter did, a right of continuous American intervention in the local fiscal sovereignty. There was the tactic of forcing an "undesirable" political leader out of office by withdrawing or withholding diplomatic recognition—as was the case with the Huerta regime in Mexico in 1913— although the fact that Latin American *politicos* had used terrorist methods as evil as those of General Huerta in order to gain power did not elsewhere deter Washington from recognition. Nor was there any real aversion to the method of military intervention for the purpose of promoting revolutions favorable to the American interest, the most famous and the least excusable of such adventures being President Theodore Roosevelt's provocative encouragement of the revolution in the province of Panama in 1903, engineered by the French international adventurer Bunau-Varilla as the occasion for the final capitulation of the helpless Colombian Government and Congress to the American scheme for obtaining a unilaterally-controlled zone in the Panama district. Outright occupation of a country, of course, was repugnant, genuinely so, to American governments. But the sentiment did not prevent the transformation of a Central American nation like Nicaragua into what was, bluntly, a "client state" run by American-appointed officials; nor did it deter the McKinley administration from the brutal suppression of the Aguinaldo patriotic insurrection against the American occupants of Luzon in the Philippine Islands after 1898.

Patently, the Achilles heel of all imperialist enterprise—its reliance, in the last resort, upon naked force—made itself apparent in the American case just as it did in the British and the French. Certainly, it was nothing less than a gesture of poetic justice that, in 1897, the Spanish Minister of State replied to American protests against Spanish brutality in Cuba with the pertinent reminder that the Spanish army in that island had done nothing more than what Sheridan had done in his wartime invasion of the Shenandoah Valley or what Sherman had done in his terrible march through Georgia or what, finally, the confederate Government had perpetrated in its huge prison camp at Andersonville. The brutality of Marines in Hispaniola, if less spectacular, was equally real. The general situation was further compromised by the fact that in the absence of any tradition of American colonial administration, the men who were appointed by Washington to be ministers or special executive agents or financial receivers in the Caribbean and mid-American countries were hardly of the best calibre. They were appointed, in the main, on the basis of the "spoils system," not on that of merit or of record. Secretary of State Bryan's letter of 1913, addressed to the General Receiver of Customs in Santo Domingo and requesting knowledge of any likely appointments that might be put to use as rewards for "deserving Democrats," is well known. The unhappy result, only too often, was the appointment of men like Magoon in Cuba and James Mark Sullivan in the Dominican Republic.

The second aspect of "Manifest Destiny" to be noted is the impressive catalogue of intellectual rationalizations to which it gave birth as Americans sought to square their new-found imperialism with their democratic and egalitarian tradition. In this respect, America did not differ from other nations, although it is possible that the Puritan background of the tradition, as in the case of England, too, made the search for a moral foundation more urgent than it was in other nations. In any case, the collection of theories whereby Americans have justified to themselves the pursuit of empire is varied and astonishing. Dr. Weinberg's definitive analysis has listed them with a remarkable anthropological exhaustiveness. The justification, at times, has taken the form that it is a "law of nature" for a people to expand, sometimes the form that if expansion ceases, death supervenes. Or it has been the argument of natural right, used to justify expansion by geographical propinquity, expansion for national security, or even expansion to prevent the possible accession of a dangerous neighbor. Or outward growth may be justified by a theory of predestined geographical use, so that the superior ability of the American to "use" the territory he has coveted becomes, as in the case of the American Indian, a sufficient rationalization of forced expropriation. Nor is the doctrine of the "white man's burden" neglected, so that it becomes the moral duty of America to civilize the "backward" peoples, to spread Christianity, to prevent (a special glossary on the text) the sacrifice of native peoples to Catholic "barbarism," such as that of Spain in the Philippines. The religious argument was a powerful one with the American Protestant missionaries who used their Calvinist economic virtues to found the first dynasty of wealthy expatriate clans in the Hawaiian islands after 1820. The decline of Christian faith has made it obsolete and old-fashioned in a later century; but it is worth noting that the universe of reference of the "quiet American" in the contemporary world overseas is really much the same sort of thing merely stripped of its religious verbiage.

As far as the particular Caribbean expansionism is concerned, two other ingenious systematizations of policy were invoked. One was the thesis that the American nation is justified in territorial seizure where the present occupying country hinders the interests of "collective civilization" by its refusal or tardiness to cultivate the potential of the region under its jurisdiction. That was the official justification for President Roosevelt's actions in relation to the Panama Canal. According to this thesis, the United States held a vague mandate from world civilization to coerce a nation which, by its "selfish" actions (in the Canal issue, Colombia), stood in the way of measures that would benefit the world as a whole. It was a thesis anticipated as early as 1826 in Representative Cambreling's observation, with reference to Cuba, that "the right of Spain once extinguished, from the nature of our position and our peculiar and various associations with that Island, our right becomes supreme; it resists the European right of purchase; it is even paramount to the Mexican and Colombian right of war." The thesis, moreover, applied, apparently, not only to the exploitation of virgin lands, but also to the economic and technical development of already established economies. Thus, President Taft could speak of the necessity of remembering, when thinking of the Caribbean, that "it is essential that the countries within that sphere shall be removed from the jeopardy involved by heavy foreign debt, and chaotic national finances, and from the ever-present danger of international complications due to disorder at home. Hence, the United States has been glad to encourage and support American bankers who were willing to lend a hand to the financial rehabilitation of such countries."

The other thesis particularly used with reference to Caribbean action, along with this concept of America as a trustee of international interests, involved the self-image that Americans have always tended to have of themselves as the greatest exponents of "democracy" the world has seen. Whatever the historical and ideological roots of the idea—the "new world" ideology, the impact of the frontier on American thought, natural law theories—its spokesmen have seen democracy not merely as a system of government, but also as a moral condition; and they have seen the exportation of democracy to other nations as the peculiar duty of American leadership. The truth does not seem to have made itself evident to that leadership that representative institutions of the Western liberal type have been the outcome of a special collection of social and cultural conditions in the advanced industrializing societies of the nineteenth century and not of a universal and absolute law of social nature. It is revealing that even as sophisticated a mind as Woodrow Wilson was able to combine a theoretical recognition of that truth with a passionate belief in the obligation of America to push "good" government upon less fortunate peoples. His remark to Sir William Tyrrel, "I propose to teach the South American Republics to elect good men," meant, in effect, American intervention in the affairs of those countries and American sponsorship of local candidates who measured up to American standards of "goodness." That was the case, at least, with President Guerrero in Panama in 1904 and with President Jimenez in Santo Domingo in 1914. Sponsorship could not help but mean a more or less permanent intervention in order to keep the favored candidate in office. For the entire theory of "democracy," in its American sense, required the presence of far too many factors that were conspicuously absent in the societies to the south. Politics, in Mexico or Nicaragua, or Cuba or Haiti, careered around the representative type of politician who combined strong personal ability with a complete absence of scruple with respect to the methods he pursued in satisfying his ambition. The idea of popular consent was thus even more of an antiquated fiction than it was in the United States. Nor was it sufficiently appreciated that a politician who owed his office to the good will of the U. S. State Department, often backed by a show of open force, could not hope to play any genuinely "democratic" role in the governing of his society because his main obligation was to the foreign authority and the main thing desired of him was the effective maintenance of "order" so that the outside propertied and strategic interests might not be placed in peril. Finally, the spirit no less than the method of compulsory democracy was illiberal, for it was accompanied by an attitude of self-righteous condescension to those supposed to benefit from it. The worst example, of course, was the spectacle of the opprobrious epithets hurled by President Roosevelt against the Bogota politicians who, naturally enough, were reluctant to yield to the "big stick" tactics of Washington during the canal crisis of 1902–1903. Yet even when a cultured man, such as Root, was in charge at the State Department, that sort of arrogant contempt was replaced, not by a sense of equality, but by a secret patronizing tone. The Secretary's remark that the people of Central America "are perfectly willing to sit at the feet of Gamaliel if Gamaliel won't kick them or bat them on the head" was, after all, hardly a complimentary remark. Franklin Roosevelt, it is true, repudiated the idea, behind all of this, that the United States had a right, by means of the doctrine of paramount interest, to act alone as the policeman of the hemisphere. He insisted that "when the failure of orderly processes affects the other nations of the continent . . . it becomes the joint concern of a whole continent in which we are all neighbors." But that was in 1933, before the new President had had a chance to invent institutional methods that would be appropriate to a foreign policy of friendly collaboration.

The ideology of "democracy for export" permeates much of the apologetic literature on American activities in the Caribbean. The American citizen has been told that American rule or influence has brought enormous benefits to the Caribbean peoples by way of stamping out diseases, improving sanitation and communications, building schoolhouses and establishing honest and efficient methods of public administration. Much of all this is true, for it would demand a complete absence of any sense of proportion not to admit that there are areas of Caribbean life, in education, in irrigation, in medicine, in which the devoted zeal of American officials has been worthy of all honor, within the limits that conditions have permitted. As a surgeon of the U. S. Army, General Wood's interest in health improvement and sanitation in Cuba after 1898 became a famous chapter ῾ι the history of the world's fight against tropical diseases. It required a quite obsessional hatred of Americans to believe—as did the Puerto Rican Nationalist Party in an unfortunate episode in 1932—that American doctors could undertake a deliberate scheme of exterminating native populations under the guise of treating them for tropical illnesses. Apart, however, from the consideration as to whether even genuine progress that is imposed upon a politically subordinate society can be regarded as "democratic" in any real sense of the word, there is the distinct consideration that the details of the progress have been incidental rather than central purposes of American action. They were not elements of a deliberately conceived imperial policy, nor did they correspond in any way to grand outlines of imperial intent worked out by officials with care and foresight, as had been the case, for example, with British officials ever since Macaulay in India. American officials never anticipated a permanent stay for their rule in occupied countries, because the national administrations preferred, if possible, to seek their ends by indirect rather than direct rule. Thus, no Administration in Washington ever considered, as some American private citizens interested in the Caribbean at times suggested, the issuance of a proclamation establishing a fifty years tenure in an occupied country for the purpose of helping to replace that habit of *caudillismo* in politics with that of parliamentary responsibility after the Western fashion. This attitude became even stronger once the period of direct military intervention was replaced, after 1930 or so, by a period of indirect political and diplomatic influence. The result was that the improvement measures introduced by American officials were of a transient character only, lacking a base in the form of any long-term planning for social and economic rehabilitation. Even more important, they lacked the base of a popular support in the countries concerned, an absolute necessity were they to become permanent. Indeed, the measures carried through often had the consequence, if not the planned purpose, of streamlining political and administrative machinery for the better exploitation by outside interests of the Caribbean resources; the new road system developed in Puerto Rico after 1900, for example, primarily catered to the transportation needs of the new American sugar companies.

Individual American officials often managed to create a sense of genuine partnership with their local counterparts. But that was the exception, not the rule. It was extremely rare for Washington, when it made its diplomatic appointments in the region, deliberately to set out to court Caribbean approval by the appointment of a colored ambassador or minister. A notable exception was the appointment of the Negro Frederick Douglass to the Port-au-Prince post in 1889, and it is worth recording that during his two years' stay in the island he completed the writing of an introduction to the first English version of the life of Toussaint l'Ouverture written by the great French Senator, Victor Schoelcher, who had been mainly responsible for the French slavery emancipation measure of 1848. Nor, indeed, was the record of American administrative officials always impeccable. Perhaps the best-known example of their irresponsibility is that of the U. S. Commissioner in Santo Domingo, J. H. Hollander, one-time President of Johns Hopkins University, whose acceptance of a handsome private fee from the Dominican Government was unearthed by a House of Representatives subcommittee in 1911 and subsequently aired for the Caribbean audience by the prominent Dominican intellectual Fabio Fiallo, whose imprisonment a decade later by the American military Government became one of the *causes celêbres* of Latin American freedom.

In sum, American activity in the Caribbean, like all colonial activity anywhere, must be finally judged by its essences and not by its accidents. Democratic altruism and its offshoots were throughout subordinate to strategic and commercial considerations. That can be seen in the gradual transformation of the Monroe Doctrine, during the century after its promulgation, from a limited doctrine of non-intervention into a doctrine justifying open intervention on the part of the United States in the internal affairs of the hemisphere as a whole. The change was justified on the ground that the United States, by virtue of its geographical position and political power, enjoyed a natural right as the special guardian of hemispheric liberties. The effective guarantee against the possible abuse of that right was assumed to reside in America's eminent moral distinction as a free society. The guarantee assumed a sort of neo-Grecian theory of "civilization" versus "barbarity." As the constitutional theorist Burgess phrased it, it was "the manifest mission of the Teutonic nations, that interference in the affairs of populations not wholly barbaric, which have made some progress in state organization, but which manifest incapacity to solve the problem of political civilization with any degree of completeness, is a justifiable policy." The guarantee, obviously enough, was a nebulous one. By the time that the first President Roosevelt issued his famous Corollary to the Monroe Doctrine in 1904, the theory of guardianship had in truth become a wide-ranging theory of hemispheric police-power, which could be used whenever the United States decided that its vague criteria had been violated. What had been in its origin a prohibition of European imperialist adventure in the hemisphere became transformed, in fact, into a mandate for American imperialism. The Doctrine had become, in Alberdi's phrase, a doctrine of intervention against intervention. It is hardly a matter of surprise, then, that whereas President Monroe's original declaration had been received with almost unanimous approval, even relief, by the newly-formed Latin-American republics, its later metamorphosis into an imperialist idea dampened the original enthusiasm. Bolivar's fears, at an early stage, are well known. They became more widespread as the American power took on more and more the habits of European powers. They gave rise, increasingly after the Panama Congress of 1826, to a search for Pan-American institutions that could serve as resistants to the growth of American political tutelage over the region. The search was accompanied by political concepts such as Pan-Hispanism and Pan-Caribbeanism, designed to offset the cultural permeation of the region by American ideas. Hence, too, a growing literature on the part of the Latin-American intelligentsia to emphasize the historical dignity of their cultural heritage against the strident tones of the "Yankee" democracy. The search for institutions led ultimately to the creation of bodies like the Pan-American Union and the Organization of American States, always with the confederationist bias initially given to the search by Bolivarian political thought. For always the grand purpose of this search was to clothe with some institutional apparatus the proud boast of the 1826 Congress that "a hundred centuries hence, posterity, searching for the origin of our public law and recalling the compacts that solidified its destiny, will finger with respect the protocols of the Isthmus."

The intellectual counterpart to this growth of institutions based on the needs—social, economic and strategic—of the Latin-American and Caribbean peoples also became more assertive, especially after the turn of the century. It is to be seen in the work of José Enrique Rodó, in the poetry of Rubén Darío, in the scholarship of Garcia Calderón, in the famous essay of Manuel Ugarte on *The Destiny of a Continent*. It is true that the note of too much of the literature was that of a shrill and shallow vituperation, often curiously ill-informed about the realities of American life. The observation of the Colombian novelist Vargas Vila, that "wherever the Englishman goes, a village is born; wherever the Yankee goes, a race dies," indicated that, only too often, the Latin American publicist went beyond a spirit of anger, warranted by the facts, to a spirit of ugly hatred. It thus became only too easy for Americans to discount the entire criticism as the fruit of spleen or envy. It could be dismissed as just another expression of the clamorous and exaggerated rhetoric of the "Latin temperament." But the original sin, nevertheless, lay with the Americans. Nor were Americans, as a people, helped towards a more understanding attitude by their leaders. As late in the day as 1928—to take examples from the Caribbean only—President Coolidge could blandly notify Puerto Ricans that "the United States has made no promise to the people of Porto Rico that has not been more than fulfilled;" and, following him, President Hoover could leave a lasting wound with the people of the U. S. Virgin Islands by his inopportune remark that those American possessions were "an effective poorhouse." The "Open Door" policy, on a larger scale, made it plain, after 1899, that the full weight of American officialdom would be thrown behind the economic expansion of American business overseas; nor did the "good neighbor" policy of the New Deal, a generation later, fundamentally alter that end.

The general upshot of all this was a disastrous neglect of any sustained effort to court Latin susceptibilities, to meet Latin prides and prejudices halfway. In one way, possibly, the unpopularity of the United States was unavoidable. For there is no record in history of an empire that in the long run has not had to pay the price of the antagonism of its subjects. The unpopularity, nevertheless, was needlessly exacerbated by the general American character traits: the almost boyish passion of the American to be liked, the general American contempt for the past, the tendency of the American people to reduce the culturally strange to the status of the "backward" or the "picturesque," and their conviction that other people can solve their problems only by copying the American Way. All this was immeasurably strengthened by the general fact that, alien to each other in language, race, habitual practices and thought-patterns, each civilization, North American and South American, entertained an abiding assurance of its own innate superiority and a tendency to boastfulness almost so deeply imbedded as to seem, in both cases, a dominant national trait. There had been no real clash between the two opposites for the best part of their respective histories, with the exception of the Mexican War; for while the North American drive had been towards the virgin west, the South American drive had been towards the consolidation of a national independence in the southern hemisphere frequently applauded and supported by liberal and democratic sentiment within the United States. After the Spanish-American war, that ceased to be. The hitherto divergent paths crossed as the American democracy embraced the ambitions of a hemispheric leader. That involved overseas territorial acquisition—what Professor Bemis has styled the "great national aberration." It was the peculiar fate of Puerto Rico that she was to become, thereafter, a *locus* and a testing-ground of the conflicts that were thereby unleashed.

Nor should sight be lost of the fact that the American presence in the region since the turn of the century has brought with it the spirit and practices of American racial prejudice. Segregation made its appearance at the American naval and military bases; all the public institutions of the Panama Canal Zone were based on Jim Crow policies, for example, a practice supported by the AFL "lily white" unions until the CIO organizers moved into the reservation after 1947. The American military mind, no more than elsewhere, was hardly liberal in these matters, so that, to take one example only, much of the Haitian attitude to Americans springs from the period of the U.S. military occupation after 1915, when Marine Corps officers and NCO's were permitted to become veritable potentates in their administrative districts, one of whom later composed a book on his experiences with the suggestive title of *The White King of La Cenave*. Americans, both residents and wealthy tourists, have combined, along with British colonial officialdom, to keep the islands of the Bahamas a white ghetto up to this very day. Nor does this sort of thing depend only upon American military adventures and strategic imperialism. Its further growth, indeed, is more likely to proceed through the twin developments of Caribbean tourism and Caribbean industrialization. For both of these developments, of necessity, involve the growing "Americanisation" of the region. Tourism means American wealth alienating tropical beaches, setting up, in effect, segregated hotel strips as on the Jamaican north coast, even the establishment, as in the Mill Reef colony in Antigua, of exclusive wealthy communities of rich American businessmen and their families living in luxurious isolation away from the "natives." Industrialisation, in its turn, especially if under American capital sponsorship, as in Puerto Rico, is certain to sharpen race attitudes as a new competitiveness enters the local economic and social life. The Puerto Rican informant who told Mr. Christopher Rand that "on the mainland, there has always been a lot of social mobility and a lot of color discrimination, here there has been little social mobility and little color discrimination," quite properly emphasized a connection between the two phenomena that is sure to increase in its effects as the most Americanised island-society in the region follows more and more the model of American state capitalism. It is true that Caribbean society suffers, here, from its own special brand of indirect, discreet "shade" discrimination for which Americans are not responsible. But its replacement with the more open "black-white" discrimination of the North American pattern can only produce new and uglier tensions and hostilities which the Caribbean multi-racial society will find difficult to accept.

All this constitutes the historical background to the emergent Caribbean Revolution of the mid-century period. It is symptomatic of the persistency of the region as an American "sphere of influence" that, sixty years after, it would not be misleading to apply the portrait of 1900 to the facts of 1960. The Monroe Doctrine is still invoked to justify U. S. intervention and to deny non-U. S. intervention in the affairs of other hemispheric nations; there is less open arrogance, perhaps, but the Guatemala affair of 1954, and the American support, quietly offered to the British Government of 1953 of the Churchillian repression of the British Guiana constitution in that year were not in essence different from the Panama affair of 1903. There is the same tradition of equating the Caribbean with metropolitan naval bases and military outposts. The bases-destroyers deal of 1941 used British embarrassments to further American strategic imperialism, and it is worth noting that the recent West Indies-United States agreement still denies to the new West Indian Federation its rightful claim to the Chaguramas naval base in Trinidad as the proposed capital of the Federation. The advent of "commonwealth status" for Puerto Rico has not done anything to lessen that island's position as the nerve-center of the U. S. Caribbean defense-system, with the local political will denied any participation in the federal legislative process which determines military expenditures in the island. There has been, it is true, the growth of bodies, like the Caribbean Commission and the Organization of American States, that seems to offer new institutional expressions of Cordell Hull's dream of replacing American unilateral leadership with a system of "collective trusteeship" exercised by all the American Republics. But of the first of those bodies it must be said that its transference from Port-of-Spain to San Juan in 1960 has only served to increase the fears of Caribbean creole leaders like Aime Césaire that the United States influence in the Commission's policies will thereby be increased; while of the second body it has to be noted that, as the embodiment of the so-called "Inter-American System," it constitutes, in the mild language of the now historic letter of the Chilean university students to President Eisenhower, the most complete of the many hemispheric international arrangements in which the United States takes part, and the one in which the United States obtains most advantages, while acquiring fewest obligations in respect to its associates.

American liberalism frequently asserts that all this changed with the advent of the second Roosevelt's "good neighbor" policy. The persistent support of the ugly Caribbean dictatorships of Batista, Trujillo and Somoza belies the assertion. Franklin Roosevelt, indeed, no more released his mind from the American gentleman's assumption that he and his class were the natural leaders of the Americas than did Woodrow Wilson. His penchant for retired naval and military gentlemen played havoc with the Puerto Rican governorship, for example, as he appointed grave misfits like General Blanton Winship and Admiral Leahy to the Governor's Palace in San Juan. He could use colonial appointments as astutely as any Colonial Office regime for imperial ends. Thus, to take an example only, Jim Farley has related how in 1940, Henry Woodring was ousted from the War Department because of his reluctance to approve the sale or transfer of U. S. Army planes to beleaguered Britain and was offered the Puerto Rican governorship as an obvious consolation for his wounded feelings. Nor was the Rooseveltian mind above the temptation to think of the Caribbean peoples in race terms; and there is a well-known passage of the 1940–41 secret negotiations with London in which the President wondered, to Hull, why, "if we can get our naval bases," we should "buy with them two million headaches, consisting of that number of human beings who would be a definite economic drag on this country, and who would stir up questions of racial stocks by virtue of their new status as American citizens." This is the sentiment which in the sixties, still denies statehood to Puerto Rico and still seeks to raise barriers against the Puerto Rican influx into New York. Nor does the Kennedy liberalism—the announced heir to the Roosevelt tradition—look, at the moment, as if it will improve upon that record. The appointment of a Puerto Rican to the position of Assistant Secretary for Latin-American affairs is far from being the widespread use of Puerto Ricans and Latin Americans in consular and ambassadorial posts promised by the Kennedy forces during the 1960 political campaign. Mr. Kennedy's now famous *gaffe* on the incitement of civil war within the Cuban Revolution has not given way to a more friendly attitude towards Havana. And the 1961 Latin-American aid program has yet to prove that it promises a fundamental breakaway from the governing postulates of American investment in the Latin-American area, the first of which has been the deployment of capital investment for the production of goods for export rather than for Latin home consumption, and the second of which has been the alliance between the bureaucracy of the technical-assistance programs and the traditionalist governing *élites* of the receiving countries. There is nothing to suggest, so far, that expanded aid to Latin America will not produce the gross mistakes of the older aid-programs elsewhere: in particular, the export of American capitalist production techniques without an appreciation that those techniques require, for their fullest expansion, a radical socio-economic revolution that can only come about through the destruction of the governing *élites* of semi-feudalistic societies. Real agrarian reform in Latin-America, this is to say, means the full acceptance of the Mexican-Cuban method.

In the long run, the American people will have to accept the fact that the Caribbean like the rest of Latin America, can no longer be regarded as the American Mediterranean lake. That means a number of things. It means the effective internationalization of the Panama Canal Zone. It means, perhaps, the political independence of Puerto Rico. It means an attempt on the part of Americans to understand the simple cultural truth that modern revolutions cannot be seen simply through the prism of the American Revolution of the eighteenth century. By geographical law and historical necessity there is a real American interest in the region. But it must be ensured by means of a genuine partnership with other Caribbean-Mid-American countries; it cannot continue through the medium of a Monroe Doctrine which has been made obsolete as the geographical isolation of the New World from the Old has disappeared with the advent of an international technology. No student of the area is unaware of the politics of the Washington sugar quota, for example, that is used in order to build up friends for American policies, and few things have been more distressing than the undignified lobbyings of the area's "sugar island" governments for a share in the increased quota allocations created by the abrogation of the U.S.-Cuba trade agreements. The politics of the imperial Uncle Sam create, in response, the politics of the creole Uncle Tom; much of Caribbean history has been the history of the variations on that theme. Above all, America, including liberal America, will have to accept West Indians as equal persons, not only theoretically, but emotionally as well. "It is so rare to hear or read," a Puerto Rican playwright-*independentista* has recently declared in a fine *cri de coeur* that sums up that general truth, "a personal report on Puerto Ricans coming from an American visitor who is neither a public relations official on Government payroll, a smiling Congressman, a New York politician, a 'good will' visitor on a well paid tropical vacation, or a 'generous friend of Puerto Rico' with thousands of dollars at stake on the island. Honest Puerto Ricans are simply fed up with so much praise and flattery, so much sugar and honey, so much superficiality, so much outrageous demagogy coming from so many patronizing *amigos*." For the West Indian and the Latin American to ask for an end to that sort of cultural condescension, after all, is to ask for nothing more than what the American people, after 1787, requested from the European.

War and Revolution, I: Wilsonianism and Leninism, The Ideological Setting of Conflict N. GORDON LEVIN, JR.

The First World War was a traumatic event for the Old Left. In Europe it destroyed the Second International, the organization that had brought some unity of purpose and tactics to the worldwide Socialist movement. In the United States, the declaration of war in April 1917 similarly tore apart the Socialist Party of America. As in Europe some Socialists endorsed the war; more opposed it as imperialist and nationalist, and in America, unlike Europe, the party organization officially denounced the country's involvement. The Party's stand soon brought it under severe attack both by the government and by vigilantes, culminating in the arrest for sedition of Eugene V. Debs, the Party's leader and perennial candidate for President.

Since 1918, Socialists and Progressives have almost invariably regarded the Great War as a calamity. It was a confrontation between rival capitalist states in which the working classes had no real stake, and for which they gave their lives by the millions. Two consequences of the war are more problematical for the Left, however: the Bolshevik Revolution of 1917, and the peace settlement at Versailles. Both of these are the subjects of N. Gordon Levin's essay below. Levin is not interested in evaluating bolshevism. He is concerned, rather, with the way the Communist Revolution affected President Woodrow Wilson's foreign policy and the Wilsonian vision of a future world order. For a man of the Left he is quite generous to Wilson, though he makes no bones about the degree to which fear of Communist world revolution influenced the President's thought and the peace settlement of 1919.

Source: N. Gordon Levin, Jr., *Woodrow Wilson and World Politics: America's Response to War and Revolution* (New York: Oxford University Press, 1968), chap. i, "War and Revolution, I: Wilsonianism and Leninism, The Ideological Setting of Conflict," pp. 13–49.

FOR FURTHER READING:

Thomas A. Bailey, *Woodrow Wilson and the Lost Peace**, (Quadrangle, 1963); Thomas A. Bailey, *Woodrow Wilson and the Great Betrayal,* (Quadrangle, 1963); William Appleman Williams, *American-Russian Relations 1781–1947,* (Rinehart, 1952); Arno Mayer, *Politics and Diplomacy of Peacemaking: Containment and Counter Revolution at Versailles 1918–1919,* (Alfred A. Knopf, 1968); Daniel Smith, *The Great Departure: The United States and World War One 1914–1920,* (Wiley, 1965); Daniel M. Smith, *American Intervention 1917: Sentiment, Self-Interest or Ideals**, (Houghton Mifflin, 1966); Martin J. Sklar, "Woodrow Wilson and the Political Economy of Modern United States Liberalism," *Studies on the Left,* (Fall 1960).

Asterisk denotes paperback edition.

The world views of both Woodrow Wilson and Vladimir I. Lenin, like those of most messianic political thinkers, were centered on a dominant faith or myth. At the core of Wilson's political creed was a conception of American exceptionalism and of the nation's chosen mission to enlighten mankind with the principles of its unique liberal heritage. In Lenin's case, the central myth concerned the imminent liberation of mankind from liberalism, capitalism, and imperialism through the means of a proletarian revolution led by a knowledgeable socialist vanguard. From this basis, Leninist ideology would challenge not only Wilson's ultimate goal of a capitalist-international system of free trade and liberal order, but also the President's final decision to achieve this aim by fighting a liberal war against Germany in the interests of universaling self-determination and democracy throughout Europe. In 1917, these two mutually exclusive visions of world history came directly into conflict when Lenin and Wilson both became, almost simultaneously, major historical actors.

1. Liberal and Revolutionary Socialist Critiques of Imperialism

Woodrow Wilson's vision of a liberal world order of free trade and international harmony did not oppose but rather complemented his conception of the national interests of American capitalism. By the turn of the century it was clear to Wilson that the growth of the American economy, especially in heavy industry, meant that America would soon be competing for the markets of the world with the other major industrialized powers. The future President also correctly saw that the Spanish-American War and the subsequent annexation of the Philippines marked the realization by the nation that the next frontier to be conquered consisted of the fertile export market of Asia. Indeed, this new frontier had to be conquered lest the United States burst with the goods its new industrial system was capable of creating. On the eve of his first presidential campaign, Wilson told the Virginia General Assembly that "we are making more manufactured goods than we can consume ourselves . . . and now, if we are not going to stifle economically, we have got to find our way out into the great international exchanges of the world."

A constant *leitmotif* in Wilson's speeches both before and during his campaign for the presidency in 1912 was the concern that recession and stagnation might overtake the American economy if exports were not drastically increased. Wilson also insisted that, in order to achieve the commercial expansion necessary for American prosperity, it would be necessary to remove certain structural defects in the American economy. In this connection, he emphasized the inadequate credit facilities provided by American banking institutions for export expansion and also stressed his opinion that the merchant marine was inferior to those of America's competitors in international trade. Wilson also attacked the high protective tariff because, among other reasons, its rates brought retaliation against American goods by other countries. The essence of trade was reciprocity, and one could not sell unless one was also willing to buy. Wilson had no doubt that technological efficiency guaranteed American success in international commercial competition, and that, given a chance, "the skill of American workmen would dominate the markets of all the globe."

Wilson's Secretary of the Treasury, William G. McAdoo, was no less convinced than the President that American economic stability was dependent on the movement of surplus products into the mainstream of foreign commerce. He championed, therefore, all Wilson's efforts to remedy the defects in American capitalism which were inhibiting our export expansion. In the same vein, McAdoo worked tirelessly throughout most of Wilson's first term for the passage of an act to create government-supported merchant marine to prevent foreign competitors from shutting the United States out of world markets by discriminatory freight rates. McAdoo also understood that reciprocity was basic to any effort to avoid depression by a policy of export expansion and that for this reason, among others, Wilsonian efforts to lower the tariff were wise. Finally, McAdoo was fully aware of the relationship of banking reform to the growth of America's commercial role in the world. Writing in the summer of 1915, McAdoo said of the Federal Reserve Act that "this great piece of financial legislation has put this country in position to become the dominant financial power of the world."

In this general area of commercial expansion, it is also significant that, under Wilson, Chairman Joseph E. Davies and Vice Chairman Edward N. Hurley of the Federal Trade Commission conceived of the role of the FTC, in part, as one of coordinating joint government-business efforts to make American capitalism rational, co-operative, and efficient. Davies and Hurley hoped thereby both to enhance the stability of the American economy and to increase its competitive potential in world trade. In late 1915, Davies proudly announced at an exporters' convention that it was the purpose of the Federal Trade Commission to aid "in the development of the power and greatness of this nation as an industrial, commercial and financial nation in the world." In a similar vein, Secretary of State William Jennings Bryan told the first National Foreign Trade Convention, meeting in Washington in the spring of 1914, that the Wilson Administration was "earnestly desirous of increasing American foreign commerce and of widening the field of American enterprise." Bryan also emphasized that the State Department would work to "obtain for Americans equality of opportunity in the development of the resources of foreign countries and in the markets of the world."

It is little wonder that Wilson's speeches and letters in 1916 radiated pride in what his first Administration had done to promote American trade abroad. Time and again Wilson stressed the aid given by the Federal Reserve Act, the Federal Trade Commission, and the Commerce Department to American exporters, and called on the nation's business leaders to rise to their global opportunities. It should be noted, however, that the Wilsonian program of commercial expansion did not go uncriticized domestically. On the Right, some Republican and Progressive nationalist spokesmen, such as Theodore Roosevelt, Albert Beveridge, George Perkins, and Henry Cabot Lodge, were not willing to see tariffs lowered as a means of increasing exports, and they were not averse to having exports expanded by the alternate method of international economic rivalry backed by naval preparedness. On the Left, socialists questioned the very concept of trade expansion itself, arguing that there was no real surplus to export, but only those goods which the lower classes were not able to consume at existing price and income levels. Beyond the question of under consumption, socialists and some radical liberals also saw a danger of navalism, imperialism, and war in any vigorous program of export expansion. In the Center, however, the Wilsonian position implicitly held, against both conservative and radical critics, that it was possible to have economic expansion and yet to avoid such traditional imperialistic practices as protection, economic warfare, and navalism. Yet, in order fully to understand how Wilson could ideologically fuse commercial expansionism with a form of anti-imperialism, it is now important to grasp that, for the President, export was the necessary material aspect of a national mission to spread the values of American liberalism abroad in the interests of world peace and international liberal-capitalist order.

In essence, Wilson approached the question of America's export trade from the perspective of the Puritan sense of "a calling." Like the Puritans, who placed earthly vocations, or callings, in a larger context of service to God and man, Wilson saw the enlargement of foreign commerce in terms of a duty in the service of humanity. During the early years of the war, and American neutrality, the President coupled his exhortations to American businessmen of commercial expansion with a messianic conception of the service which America was able to provide to a suffering world whose productive facilities had been upset by the struggle. "The war," he claimed, "has made it necessary that the United States should mobilize its resources in the most effective way possible and make her credit and her usefulness good for the service of the whole world." In this sense, the competitive advantage in world trade which America possessed due to her technological and productive efficiency was, for Wilson, not a threat to other nations, but rather a godsend. The peaceful triumph of America in the markets of the world was, therefore, to be both a service and a lesson for a suffering humanity. In Wilson's terms:

> America has stood in the years past for that sort of political understanding among men which would let every man feel that his rights were the same as those of another and as good as those of another, and the mission of America in the field of the world's commerce is to be the same: that when an American comes into that competition he comes without any arms that would enable him to conquer by force, but only with those peaceful influences of intelligence, a desire to serve, a knowledge of what he is about, before which everything softens and yields, and renders itself subject. That is the mission of America, and my interest, so far as my small part in American affairs is concerned, is to lend every bit of intelligence I have to this interesting, this vital, this all-important matter of releasing the intelligence of America for the service of mankind.

The fusion which Wilson made here of America's economic and political missions reveals the roots of the President's combined vision of moral and material expansion. The commercial health of America was, for Wilson, the visible evidence of underlying political and moral strength. Having ideologically unified liberalism, capitalism, and missionary-nationalism, Wilson never doubted that "all the multitude of men who have developed the peaceful industries of America were planted under this free polity in order that they might look out upon the service of mankind and perform it." For the President, the extension of American trade around the world was inseparable from the export of American liberalism. In his eyes the national purpose was one of seeking "to enrich the commerce of our own states and of the world with the products of our mines, our farms, and our factories, with the creations of our thought and the fruits of our character." Toward the end of his first term, Wilson addressed a Salesmanship Congress in Detroit in words that speak volumes as to the unity of his world view of liberal-capitalist expansionism:

> This, then, my friends, is the simple message that I bring you. Lift your eyes to the horizons of business; do not look too close at the little processes with which you are concerned, but let your thoughts and your imaginations run abroad throughout the whole world, and with the inspiration of the thought that you are Americans and are meant to carry liberty and justice and the principles of humanity wherever you go, go out and sell goods that will make the world more comfortable and more happy, and convert them to the principles of America.

New Freedom foreign policy in regard to China and Latin America, during Wilson's first term, exemplified the relation of the President's ideology of moral and material export to his liberal anti-imperialism. In the Far East, Wilsonian concern for the territorial integrity, stability, and political independence of China was not an abstract anti-imperialist position arrived at in an economic and social vacuum. Actually, Wilson's opposition to the traditional policies of spheres of influence and territorial annexation in China was inextricably bound up with his concept of the type of liberal world order of commercial freedom within which the genius of American capitalism could best win its rightful place in the markets of the world. Since Wilson never questioned his basic assumption that American commercial and moral expansion into China contributed to the welfare of the Chinese people, there was a unity in his mind of both his allegiance to the export of American surplus products and his opposition to traditional imperialism in China. In this connection, the Wilson Administration refused to continue the Taft policy of encouraging an American banking group to participate in a projected financial consortium of six major powers for China. The President took the position that the terms of the planned Six-Power Consortium threatened the political and economic independence of China, and that large segments of the American banking community had been refused admittance to the program. In opposing United States participation in the Consortium, Wilson was not however, opposing the principle of the expansion of American capitalism into underdeveloped areas. On the contrary, the Administration felt that, once free of the restraints of the Consortium, the American banking and business community as a whole could do a better job of serving the Chinese with the aid of the Departments of State and Commerce.

In Latin America, Wilsonian policy sought to relate American economic expansion to the creation of an hemispheric system of free trade and liberal-capitalist order to be led by the United States. Wilson, McAdoo, and Commerce Secretary William C. Redfield were all anxious to promote the extension of American financial and commercial activity in South America, and they emphasized government support to this end. Adding his voice, Secretary of the Navy Josephus Daniels argued that since America had to sell her surplus products abroad in order to maintain domestic prosperity, American businessmen had best learn how to conquer the markets to the South.

Yet, if Wilsonians envisioned a commercial hemispheric harmony transcending power politics, it is also true that in the sensitive Caribbean area the Wilsonian urge to export liberialism and protect America's commercial and strategic interests from any European encroachments led to armed interventions to maintain stability. In late 1915 House recorded:

> He [Lansing] laid some memoranda before me concerning the Caribbean countries which he thought needed attention. He believes that we should give more intimate direction to their affairs than we would feel warranted in doing to other South American states. He puts them in the same category with Santo Domingo and Haiti and believes we should take the same measures to bring about order, both financial and civil, as we are taking in those countries. I approved this policy and promised to express this opinion to the President.

As regards Mexico, however, Wilson successfully resisted pressure to apply the traditional interventionist and conservative solutions of Republican nationalism to the problems created by the Mexican Revolution. Instead, he slowly developed a policy of aid to the Mexican Constitutionalists to the end that Mexican feudalism would be destroyed and broad-based land ownership established. Wilson hoped that these changes, coupled with education, would create the prerequisites for liberalism, capitalism, and stability in Mexico.

In the light of coming events in Russia and the future confrontation of Wilson and Lenin, it is important to understand at this juncture that the revolution which Wilson came to support in Mexico was conceived by him to be basically liberal-capitalist rather than socialist in intent. There is no evidence that the President ever changed his mind about a statement that he made in 1913 to the British diplomat Sir William Tyrrell: "the United States Government intends not merely to force Huerta from power, but also to exert every influence it can to secure Mexico a better government under which all contracts and business concessions will be safer than they have ever been." In short, Wilson held that the avoidance of crude economic exploitation and of traditional imperialist practices in Mexico and Latin America would lead both to increased legitimate American investment to the South and to a just liberal-capitalist hemispheric order. In this fashion both the material and moral missions of American liberal-expansionism could be fulfilled.

Wilson and House hoped to cap their vision of an American-inspired and American-led liberal order in the Western Hemisphere with a Pan-American Pact providing for mutual guarantees as to arbitration, disarmament, and territorial integrity. Even though the pact was not actualized, Colonel House recorded some thoughts concerning it which serve to illustrate the universal scope of the Wilsonian non-socialist critique of existing world politics. "It was my idea," wrote House, "to formulate a plan, to be agreed upon by the republics of the two continents, which in itself would serve as a model for the European nations when peace is at last brought about." Indeed, the hope that somehow America could supply the answer to the problems of war-torn Europe became a major element in Wilsonian foreign policy from 1914 to 1917. In the President's eyes, it should be remembered, the vast wartime expansion of America's export trade was a means of American aid to mankind. In defense of his policy of neutrality, Wilson argued that "we can help better by keeping out of the war, by giving our financial resources to the use of the injured world, by giving our cotton and our woolen stuffs to clothe the world." This missionary ideology of foreign aid through export also extended to a vision of the role which America might play as the reconstructor of devastated Europe in the postwar period. In a statement capturing his conception of the redemptive power of business and international trade, Wilson affirmed early in 1916 that:

> Somebody must keep the great stable foundations of the life of nations untouched and undisturbed. Somebody must keep the great economic processes of the world of business alive. Somebody must see to it that we stand ready to repair the enormous damage and the incalculable losses which will ensue from this war.

This Wilsonian vision of a role for the United States in European reconstruction was intimately related to the President's awareness that the export trade of 1914–16 had made America the major financial power in the world. This development had necessarily greatly enlarged the potential influence of American capitalism on the international commercial and political scene. "We have become not the debtors but the creditors of the world," Wilson told an audience at Shadow Lawn on the day before the 1916 election, adding, "We can determine to a large extent who is to be financed and who is not to be financed . . . we are in the great drift of humanity which is to determine the politics of every country in the world." The President's realization that the United States was "becoming by the force of circumstances the mediating nation of the world in respect of its finances" was clearly a major element in his confident assertion that "we shall someday have to assist in reconstructing the processes of peace." The fact that the aggregate resources of the national banks of the United States exceeded by three billion dollars the aggregate resources of the Bank of England, the Bank of France, the Bank of Russia, the Reichsbank of Berlin, the Bank of Netherlands, the Bank of Switzerland, and the Bank of Japan, helped to give Wilson confidence that America was better prepared than ever before to "lead the way along the paths of light." The ultimate Wilsonian hope was to use America's expanding commercial and political influence to establish on a world-wide scale the type of liberal-capitalist order of commercial freedom which had been the goal of his concern for American moral and material expansion in China and Latin America. To this end, the President, in close co-operation with Colonel House, opted for the role of mediator in the World War. Indeed, House's missions to Europe as Wilson's emissary during the 1914–16 period may be seen as efforts to convince the European powers that their best interests would be served by a negotiated peace to be made lasting by their mutual co-operation with the United States in the creation of a new political and economic world system in which the seas would be free, territorial integrity mutually guaranteed, and financial expansion into underdeveloped areas handled in a co-operative atmosphere. In such a world, traditional imperialism would be obsolete and American liberal-expansionism could prosper in an atmosphere of peaceful international-capitalism.

In 1912 Colonel House wrote a utopian novel entitled *Philip Dru: Administrator,* whose protagonist, upon becoming dictator of America, succeeds in bringing Germany into an Anglo-American inspired world order "of peace and commercial freedom," within which "disarmaments were to be made to an appreciable degree, customs barriers were to be torn down, zones of influence clearly defined, and an era of friendly commercial rivalry established." During his actual trips to Europe, between 1914 and 1916, House used all his diplomatic skills in an effort to re-integrate Germany into a harmonious international-capitalist concert of Western powers led by England and the United States. In the spring and early summer of 1914, on the eve of war, House sought unsuccessfully to bring about an Anglo-German *rapprochement* around the principles of concert of power, naval disarmament, and peaceful commercial rivalry. In his Diary, House recorded his conception of the best way to approach the Kaiser in the interests of a rational world system of economic and political order:

> My purpose is to try to show the Emperor that if he will consent to take the initiative in the matter I have in mind, it will rebound greatly to Germany's commercial and material welfare. It is not in my mind to suggest to him to lessen at all his military organization or to disturb his Continental relations. It is only to try to show him that an understanding with Great Britain and the United States will place him in a position to curtail his naval program and open up a wider field for German commerce, besides insuring the peace of the world.

The Colonel's desire to reintegrate Germany into a stable Western international structure was intensified by the outbreak of war in August 1914. Writing to James W. Gerard, the American Ambassador in Germany, House expressed the hope that the Kaiser would consider a peace based on mutual disarmament and territorial guarantees. "With Europe disarmed and with treaties guaranteeing one another's territorial integrity," the Colonel reasoned, "she [Germany] might go forward with every assurance of industrial expansion and permanent peace." On his second peace mission to Europe, in early 1915, House sought to fuse America's export-oriented concern for freedom of trade and neutral rights with an appeal to Germany's leaders to exchange their traditional reliance on national power for an Anglo-German *détente* based on freedom of the seas and peaceful commercial expansion. In the fall of 1915, House sought to present his position to Count Bernstorff, the German Ambassador to America:

> During the conversation we spoke of peace overtures, and of when and how they might begin. I impressed upon him my belief that no peace parlays could be started until Germany was willing to consent to abolish militarism and Great Britain to abolish navalism. I enlarged upon Germany's splendid opportunity for industrial advancement with the freedom of the seas assured, and I made it clear that the one thought uppermost in the mind of the Western Allies was a peace free from the menace of another such war.

At the core of House's vision of Western unity was a program through which the bitterly competitive process of financial and commercial expansion by the advanced nations into the undeveloped world could be restructured in a rational and co-operative manner. In the Colonel's conception, the American desire to maintain the Open Door in colonial areas for the export of American surplus products was joined to the liberal impulse to end a major cause of imperialist conflict by reforming world politics from within. As House explained it to British leaders in early summer 1914:

> My plan is that if England, the United States, Germany and France will come to an understanding concerning investments by their citizens in undeveloped countries,

much good and profit will come to their citizens as well as to the countries needing development. Stability would be brought about, investments would become safe, and low rates of interest might be established.

Co-operative management of the world's backward areas also provided, in House's mind, further means of bringing Germany into a peaceful international-capitalist world system. In his *Philip Dru: Administrator,* House had already sketched out a program in which Germany would be allowed commercial expansion in Latin America, the Balkans, and the Near East. On his actual peace missions, the Colonel often urged upon Allied and German leaders the possibility of sublimating Germany's expansive energies into less aggressive channels by giving her financial opportunities in the undeveloped areas.

In the light of House's efforts to place the "backward" peoples into the context of a harmonious liberal world order, a dimension was added to Wilson's own desire to use American mediation and financial power to reconstruct and reunify the Western world. Wilson tended to view American neutrality and peace-making as a duty due to the system of world leadership by the great "white" nations of the West, a position which would be reinforced by the imminent challenge of Bolshevism to that system from the Left. Secretary of State Robert Lansing records a significant comment of Wilson's made just after the German declaration of unlimited submarine warfare in February 1917, in which the President made explicit his vision of world liberal peace based on unified Western commercial and political leadership:

> The President, though deeply incensed at Germany's insolent notice, said that he was not yet sure what course we must pursue and must think it over; that he had been more and more impressed that "white civilization" and its domination over the world rested largely on our ability to keep this country intact as we would have to build up the nations ravaged by the war.

On close analysis, then, Wilsonian liberal anti-imperialism emerges as a limited form of international reformism. That is to say, Wilson opposed traditional exploitive imperialism involving territorial annexations, armed force, protectionism, and war. The President did not, however, question either the structural inequitability of the commercial and financial relationships between the agrarian and the industrialized areas of the world or the correlative economic and political world predominance of the West. Wilson's basic concern, inspired both by the expansive needs of American capitalism and by his own liberal-internationalist ideology, was to make more rational and humane the existing world economic and social relationships. The mandate system, which he was to advocate at Paris, was a classic example of his paternalistic orientation. In essence, Wilson and House were reformers with a faith that there was a potential for peace and justice latent in the international-capitalist system which would develop once it was liberated from imperialist irrationality. This Wilsonian position was, of course, to the Left of the views of many Republican and Progressive nationalist *vis à vis* America's role in the world, but it did not go far enough in its anti-imperialism for many socialists, who insisted that capitalism per se was the root cause of imperialism and war. In this connection, Wilson's world view was not unlike that of such English non-socialist anti-imperialists as Norman Angell, E. D. Morel, and J. A. Hobson, who also offered a rational and democratic critique of protectionism, navalism, secret diplomacy, and colonialism. Along with Wilson and House, these liberals argued that Britain and Europe would prosper best under a commercial and political concert of power which would guarantee free trade, international-capitalist stability, and peace.

Undoubtedly the most complete expression of the Wilsonian anti-imperialism of liberal order may be found in the conceptions of formal international co-operation which Wilson and House developed in the 1915–16 period. By 1916 Wilson hoped to associate America in a postwar union with other leading powers, including Germany, to achieve disarmament, freedom of the seas, mutual territorial guarantees, and international arbitrations. Writing to House on the eve of the Colonel's departure for his third peace mission to Europe, Wilson succinctly expressed his vision of a co-operative international order of commercial freedom:

> I agree with you that we have nothing to do with local settlements,—territorial questions, indemnities, and the like—but are concerned only in the future peace of the world and the guarantees to be given for that. The only possible guarantees, that is, the only possible guarantees that any rational man could accept, are (a) military and naval disarmament and (b) a league of nations to secure each nation against aggression and maintain the absolute freedom of the seas.

The emphasis here on the freedom of the seas recalls again the intimate connection in Wilsonian ideology between the needs of an expanding American capitalism and the goals of international liberalism and anti-imperialism. In accepting his renomination for the presidency in September 1916, Wilson made this connection clear by affirming:

> We have already formulated and agreed upon a policy of law which will explicitly remove the ban now supposed to rest upon co-operation amongst our exporters in seeking and securing their proper place in the markets of the world. The field will be free, the instrumentalities at hand. It will only remain for the masters of enterprise amongst us to act in energetic concert, and for the Government of the United States to insist upon the maintenance throughout the world of those conditions of fairness and of even-handed justice in the commercial dealings of the nations with one another upon which, after all, in the last analysis, the peace and ordered life of the world must ultimately depend.

An exchange of memoranda between Lansing and Wilson in early 1917 also shows that concern for commercial freedom and an international Open Door were basic elements in the President's hopes for a liberal postwar order. By the latter half of 1916, Wilson's speeches, which were full of the mission of American capitalism to reconstruct a war-torn world, also affirmed the closely related duty of America to join a future concert of powers in the maintenance of international peace and justice. Beyond war there hopefully lay a liberal-internationalist community of civilized powers, inspired by the moral and material expansion of America, which would guarantee world peace, international law, and freedom for commercial expansion. As the President told an audience in Indianapolis during the campaign of 1916:

> I have said, and shall say again, that when the great present war is over it will be the duty of America to join with the other nations of the world in some kind of league for the maintenance of peace. Now, America was not a party to this war, and the only terms upon which we will be admitted to a league, almost all the other powerful

members of which were engaged in the war and made infinite sacrifices when we apparently made none, are the only terms which we desire, namely, that America shall not stand for national aggression, but shall stand for the just conceptions and bases of peace, for the competition of merit alone, and for the generous rivalry of liberty.

At the very time, however, that Wilson was formulating his vision of a liberal future, a Russian political exile in Switzerland was developing an ideological assault not only on traditional imperialism but on liberal-capitalist anti-imperialism as well.

The efforts of Wilson and House to reform world politics within a context of international-capitalism fitted the world view of the German socialist theorist Karl Kautsky, but not that of Lenin. It is for this reason that the Lenin-Kautsky controversy concerning socialism's reaction to imperialism, a controversy raised above mere sectarianism by the Russian Revolution is vital to an understanding of the Wilson-Lenin confrontation itself.

In a series of articles written during the early years of World War I, Kautsky developed his theory that military and territorial imperialism were not inevitable phenomena in the behavior of capitalist nation-states. Kautsky felt that imperialism, in the classic sense of the term, was a *policy* pursued by capitalist powers, rather than being an inevitable *phase* or stage of capitalist development. This distinction, which may at first glance seem to be merely an effort to split hairs, is crucial, for it allowed Kautsky to suggest that there were other methods or policies through which the advanced industrial capitalist states of the West might expand into the undeveloped agrarian areas of the world besides navalism, militarism, territorial colonialism, and protectionism. Kautsky believed that he saw tendencies in international-capitalist behavior which suggested that sophisticated bourgeois statesmen would soon realize that war and militarism were irrational and upsetting to the orderly processes of world finance and trade. Indeed, Kautsky saw the possibility of enlightened and cartel-oriented capitalists opting for a world-wide policy of peace, free trade, disarmament and co-operative development of backward areas. The term given by Kautsky to this possible bourgeois policy of world peace was ultra-imperialism. Clearly, Colonel House, whose peace missions to Europe we have seen to have been in large part efforts to reconstruct a unified and liberalized international-capitalist community led by the Western powers, provides a classic example of what Kautsky meant by the ultra-imperialist statesman.

Yet if Kautsky, like all social democrats, was both encouraged and discouraged by progressive tendencies he perceived in bourgeois circles, Lenin was not. Kautsky's formulation of the possibility of a peaceful change from a system of militarism and war to one of rational ultra-imperialism was a direct threat to Lenin's revolutionary socialist position. For, whatever his intentions, Kautsky had buttressed the axiom of reformist liberalism that the progressive tendencies inherent in capitalism and liberalism were not yet exhausted. Lenin's writings in the 1915–17 period are full of efforts to counter both Kautskyism and liberal anti-imperialism by claiming that imperialism and war were not mere policies which an enlightened liberal-capitalism might discard. Instead, Lenin insisted that imperialism was an essential part of the final stage of capitalist development, and could be ended only by socialist revolution.

Lenin's theory of imperialism emphasized that the mutual need of all monopoly-capitalist nations to find outlets for their surplus capital, created by domestic underconsumption, led to an inevitable economic and political division of the undeveloped world among the powers. Yet no such division of the colonial areas of the world could be permanent and stable, according to Lenin, since the balance of power among the competing capitalist states would shift with the passage of time, necessitating a redivision of spheres of influence by force of arms. It was therefore the "contradictions" inherent in the process of capitalist expansion which militated against Kautskyite and liberal hopes for the peaceful evolution of international capitalism. Lenin asked socialists, in addition, to compare "the extreme disparity in the rate of development of the various countries and the violent struggles of the imperialist states, with Kautsky's silly little fable about ultra-imperialisms." So far as Lenin was concerned, the concept of the unity of international-capitalism was conceivable of realization in only one of two forms: either as a temporary union of many capitalist states in military and commercial alliance against one or two others, or as a union of major capitalist powers for the purpose of destroying a revolutionary-socialist state. Clearly, then, the Bolshevik view of the League of Nations was previewed in Lenin's writings well before 1917.

For Lenin, Kautsky's major sin lay in his (Kautsky's) tendency to blunt the revolutionary spirit of the masses by drawing off their discontent into what the Bolsheviks conceived to be, verbal and harmless assaults on imperialism from the tame perspective of bourgeois pacifism. Lenin scorned all liberal anti-imperialist notions of disarmament, arbitration, and free trade arguing that such Kautskyite solutions were mere utopian palliatives in the era of monopoly-capitalist imperialism from which only socialist revolution could rescue mankind. Lenin was quick to condemn Wilson's peace initiatives in the winter of 1916–17, seeing them as part of a moderate socialist and liberal movement to create a non-revolutionary peace of compromise among the imperialist powers, which peace would then be covered with the rhetoric of bourgeois pacifism. In this connection, Lenin was often at pains to claim that no democratic or anti-imperialist peace was possible under capitalism, and, therefore, to speak, as did Kautsky, of the possibility of the attainment of a more just international order without revolution was to accept the utopian abstractions of bourgeois pacifism. Obviously, Lenin's form of anti-imperialism was far removed from the Wilsonian liberal-internationalist concern for a peace of accommodation among the powers. It should be noted, as well, that Lenin also opposed the efforts of moderate socialist elements to hold a conference at Stockholm during the war in the interests of agitation for a speedy compromise peace. The German Sparticists and the Russian Bolsheviks attacked the Stockholm Conference as an exercise in imperialist peace-making covered by a gloss of reformist rhetoric.

Lenin's opposition to what he conceived to be any form of a peace through a capitalist accommodation is perhaps best exemplified by his attitude on the self-determination question. The Leninist position on self-determination was more universal in its scope than that of Wilson, in that it insisted on socialists' working for the independence of all subject peoples, whether in Russia, the Dual Monarchy, Asia, or Africa, and not simply those controlled by the Central Powers. Lenin's assumption was that socialist support for the breakup of all empires might encourage bourgeois nationalism in the short run, but that in the end the triumph of socialism in the newly freed states would lead to the voluntary amalgamation of free revolutionary states into large and economically viable socialist units. From this revolutionary perspective on the national question, Lenin opposed all liberal- and moderate-socialist peace proposals which sought to return international politics to a modified *status quo ante bellum*. For Lenin, the Stockholm slogan of peace without annexations or indemnities was too moderate in that it did not call for a revolutionary effort to free peoples subjugated or annexed by the major powers prior to 1914. While other socialist theorists on the far Left, such as Rosa Luxemburg, were scornful of nationalism in Asia, Africa, and Eastern Europe because they feared bourgeois domination, Lenin was willing to risk co-operation with bourgeois nationalism in wars of national liberation in order to strike a revolutionary blow at what he conceived to be the system of world domination by the capitalist West. Indeed, Lenin's stress upon the revolutionary-socialist implications of self-determination in Asia proved to be a major cause of early British opposition to Bolshevism. In the final analysis, Lenin's implacable hostility to the influence of the West in the underdeveloped areas of the world, coupled with his insistence on a revolutionary-socialist peace, helped to form the ideological gulf separating the Leninist world view from that of Wilsonian liberal anti-imperialism.

2. Democracy, Autocracy, and Bolshevism

Wilson's conception of the origin of the world war was a basic component of his American exceptionalist ideology, and his conception was closely related as well to his desire to use the moral and economic strength of America to establish a liberal world order. In Cincinnati, late in the 1916 campaign, Wilson addressed himself to the causes of the European holocaust:

> Nothing in particular started it, but everything in general. There had been growing up in Europe a mutual suspicion, an interchange of conjecture about what this Government and that Government was going to do, an interlacing of alliances and understandings, a complex web of intrigue and spying, that presently was sure to entangle the whole of the family on that side of the water in its meshes.

Several things should be noted in relation to this statement. First of all, by placing the locus of responsibility for the war on "European" phenomena, such as secret diplomacy and entangling alliances, Wilson remained consistently within the ideological pattern formed by his fusion of liberal anti-imperialism and American exceptionalism. While Lenin saw the war as the inevitable result of competition among imperialist nations in an era of monopoly capitalism, Wilson blamed atavistic and irrational patterns of European national behavior and retained a faith in the peaceful and orderly potential of international capitalism in general and of American moral-commercial expansionism in particular. Nonetheless, despite the great differences between the liberal-capitalist and the revolutionary-socialist critiques of the war, the two ideologies had one thing in common. From the particular levels of abstraction which each afforded, it was possible to transcend views of the war held by the partisans of the nations involved and to see the conflict critically and objectively as a historical experience emerging from a particular set of political and economic institutions. This was true even if the definition of those institutions offered by Wilsonians and Leninists differed greatly. Indeed, many American radicals and socialists retained positions of critical objectivity *vis à vis* the war during the 1914–18 period, which positions could be placed on an ideological continuum at varying points between the poles of liberal and socialist anti-imperialism. The problem becomes further complicated, however, by the fact that by April 1917 the President had moved from his position of liberal objectivity toward the war to a position advocating liberal war against Germany in association with the Entente. The point was that the very missionary liberal nationalism which gave Wilson his neutral and critical objectivity toward the war was also paradoxically capable of supplying an ideological basis for American participation in a war against German autocratic imperialism. To understand fully the Wilsonian transition from liberal mediation to liberal war, it is necessary to consider both the problem of German submarine warfare and the presence within the Wilsonian anti-imperialist mind of certain latent ideological tendencies which would help to motivate an American liberal war against Germany.

The submarine warfare used by Germany during the war could not help but be threatening to Wilson, whose vision, both of America's expansionist mission and of a liberal world order, was so deeply related to a concern for freedom of the seas and the maintenance of international law. The President sought to make his position on the necessity to defend American rights on the seas clear to an audience in Topeka, Kansas, early in 1916:

> There are perfectly clearly marked rights guaranteed by international law which every American is entitled to enjoy, and America is not going to abide the habitual or continued neglect of those rights. Perhaps not being as near the ports as some other Americans, you do not travel as much and you do not realize the infinite number of legitimate errands upon which Americans travel—errands of commerce, errands of relief, errands of business for the Government, errands of every sort which make America useful to the world. Americans do not travel to disturb the world; they travel to quicken the processes of the interchange of life and of goods in the world, and their travel ought not to be impeded by a reckless disregard of international obligation.

This conviction, that Americans were justified in traveling to serve the world commercially, was often affirmed by the President during his speaking tour of the Mid-West on behalf of his military preparedness program in the early weeks of 1916. In this connection, it should be kept in mind that by the end of 1915 American exports to the Allies had grown to such proportions that the recession which plagued the country early in Wilson's first term had been overcome by the effects of the immense war trade. Related to the material issue, however, was the fact that, for Wilson, the very process of defending the nation's rights on the seas became an important aspect of America's unique liberal service to mankind. If it was the exceptional destiny of the United States to feed, clothe, and morally instruct the world, it was also its duty to maintain the rule of law on the high seas for the benefit of all neutral trading nations. As the chief representative and trustee of neutral rights, Wilson was convinced that the mission of the United States was "to assert the principles of law in a world in which the principles of law have broken down." In defending America's neutral rights, then, the President was as certain as always that there was complete unity between the national interest of the United States and the values of liberal-internationalism. This was the uniqueness of America, a nation which since its inception had "undertaken to be the champions of humanity and the rights of men. Without that ideal there would be nothing that would distinguish America from her predecessors in the history of nations."

It must be emphasized that Wilson and his leading advisers made a clear moral distinction between British naval encroachments on commerce alone and the German submarine threat to both trade and lives. After the torpedoing of the *Lusitania,* it was clear that Wilson was prepared, if pressed, to go to war with Germany on an issue which he saw as involving basic principles of neutral rights and international law. Convinced that unrestricted submarine warfare posed a total challenge to the liberal world order which it was America's duty to foster, the President told his audiences on the preparedness tour that the armed forces of the United States were ready to defend those American rights which were identical with universal human rights, and that the defense of basic principles by force was preferable to ignoble compromise. Speaking in Washington in late February 1916, Wilson expressed succinctly his willingness to take America to war, if that were necessary to defend her most cherished ideals:

> America ought to keep out of this war. She ought to keep out of this war at the sacrifice of everything except this single thing upon which her character and history are founded, her sense of humanity and justice. If she sacrifices that, she has ceased to be America; she has ceased to entertain and to love the traditions which have made us proud to be Americans, and when we go about seeking safety at the expense of humanity, then I for one will believe that I have always been mistaken in what I have conceived to be the spirit of American history. . . . I would be just as much ashamed to be rash as I would to be a coward. Valor is self-respecting. Valor is circumspect. Valor strikes only when it is right to strike. Valor withholds itself from all small implications and entanglements and waits for the great opportunity when the sword will flash as if it carried the light of heaven upon its blade.

The President also felt that the armed defense of American and neutral rights would not be at odds with but would rather complement his conception of America's responsibility to join a post-war community of powers in the maintenance of international peace and justice. In short, Wilson's response to German submarine warfare proved that a propensity for war in defense of the particular and universal values of American liberal-nationalism was latent in his thought well before the actual entry into the war.

Nevertheless, the President hoped to be able to defend his principles and to keep the United States at peace. The Wilson-House vision of a reunified Western world functioning with liberal-capitalist harmony has already been discussed at length. Indeed, the President's conception of America's duty to pacify Europe and reconstruct a liberal world order seemed often to assert itself most strongly in his thought at those times when the submarine issue seemed about to force a final break between the United States and Germany. The climatic Wilsonian peace effort of the winter of 1916–17 reflected both Wilson's desire to co-opt Germany into a liberal concert of powers and a fear on the President's part that an imminent resumption of unrestricted submarine warfare by Germany might force the United States to enter the war. The evidence also suggests that, until February 1917, Colonel House never fully gave up the hope that a German-American conflict could be avoided through the voluntary acceptance of the Wilsonian vision of Western commercial and political unity by Germany's leaders.

Wilson and House were both concerned with the consequences of a total Allied victory over the Central Powers. Should German power be crushed, it was possible that Tsarist imperialism would menace the West. Then too, both the President and

House were disturbed lest high-handed actions by the British navy and Allied plans for postwar economic competition indicate that British-naval- and protectionist-oriented Toryism might overcome British liberalism and constitute a serious postwar threat to freedom of the seas and the international commercial Open Door. Such apprehensions as to the possibilities latent in total Entente victory served to counter-balance the Wilsonian urge toward war with Germany over the use of submarines, and to reinforce the Wilson-House conviction that only a compromise peace without victory could provide the foundation necessary for international liberal stability.

Because Wilson has such a strong urge to re-establish Western liberal-capitalist unity under American guidance, another ideological element was needed to justify fully war with Germany to the President. This element was supplied to the Administration by House and Lansing in the form of the theory that the World War was a conflict between aggressive German autocracy and defensive Allied democracy. This theory was capable of neutralizing Wilson's counter tendencies to view the war, from the perspective of liberal American exceptionalism, as having emerged from a welter of universal "European" institutions such as alliances, secret diplomacy, and militarism. The autocracy vs. democracy concept also gave an ethical finality to the schism in Western unity which Wilson was hesitant to accept irrevocably until March 1917, when the resumption of German unrestricted submarine warfare led the President finally to believe that Imperial Germany could not be peacefully re-integrated into a liberal-capitalist international community. Wilson's eventual full acceptance of the autocracy vs. democracy concept also, as we shall see, widened the gulf between him and Lenin.

In Colonel House's wish-fulfillment fantasy, *Philip Dru: Administrator,* the American dictator Dru appeals to the British people over the head of their anti-American conservative government, thereby achieving its replacement by a liberal regime with whom Dru co-operates in creating an Anglo-American-sponsored program designed to uphold "the peace and commercial freedom of the world." House himself, despite his desire to include Germany in a postwar commercial and political community of the powers, did place his greatest hopes for the future on what he conceived to be the enlightened liberalism of such British leaders as Sir Edward Grey, a man, according to the Colonel, of "unselfish outlook, broad vision and high character." By the end of 1915, House had come to believe that Grey shared with Wilson the vision of the maintenance of postwar stability and international freedom of trade through a league of major Western powers. This faith in the possibility of a future Anglo-American partnership in the maintenance of liberal world order was the basis of the moderately pro-Allied character of House's mediation efforts during 1915 and 1916. Given the commanding position of Germany on the war map in the early stages of the war, his concern for a liberal compromise peace would alone have been enough to bring the Colonel's sympathy to the beleaguered Allied cause in the interests of maintaining a balance of power as the basis for negotiation. When one adds the submarine issue and pronounced liberal Anglophilia to the formula, however, it is even easier to see why the Colonel's mediation efforts operated on the assumption that all peace proposals had to have prior Allied approval and should in no way interfere with necessary Entente military activity. House felt that, even if the Entente ought not to achieve total victory, it must not lose.

In a larger sense, moreover, the evidence suggests that, although House's over-all aim as a mediator was to bring about the peaceful reintegration of Germany into a liberal-capitalist world order, by early 1915 the Colonel had in reality grave doubts about the willingness of autocratic Germany to enter a Wilsonian international community. These doubts were much stronger than similar fears House had as to the future intentions of reactionary elements in the Entente. Indeed, there ran through the Colonel's correspondence and diary a stream of concern, broken by momentary periods of optimism as to German developments, to the effect that an aggressive Germany, dominated by the military, constituted a future threat to America, and that Germany would try to place a diplomatic wedge between the United States and the Allies in order to win an imperialist peace based on the German-dominated war map. As he came to see the German autocracy as the principal threat to his and Wilson's vision of a liberal world order, House felt increasing solidarity with the Allies as the defenders of democratic values. The Colonel wrote to Wilson early in 1916 that were Germany to win a victory "the war lords will reign supreme and democratic governments will be imperilled throughout the world." Earlier, House had theorized that English power was not objectionably exercised due to the existence of British democracy, and that only a democratic Germany could be a "satisfactory member of the society of nations." By early 1916, through negotiating the House-Grey Memorandum, the Colonel succeeded in making explicit his conception that the United States should co-operate with the Allies, peacefully if possible but with force if necessary, in ending the war and creating a new international order on Wilsonian terms. House's goal remained the same as it had been on his first trip to Europe in early summer of 1914, namely, to foster a new and rational concert of liberal-capitalist powers. By 1916, however, the Colonel had well advanced the ideological process through which, with the impetus of German submarine warfare, this goal would no longer be sought by the diplomacy of mediation and would become a Wilsonian war aim.

Secretary of State Lansing was far more committed than the somewhat ambivalent House to the theory that Imperial Germany could not be an acceptable partner in a liberal world community. By the summer of 1915, Lansing was convinced both that German submarine warfare was symptomatic of a total threat to democracy posed by German absolutism throughout the world, and that the United States should be prepared to take part in the war, if necessary, to prevent the Central Powers from either winning or breaking even. During 1916 and early 1917, Lansing was worried by Wilson's and House's efforts in the area of mediation and was also concerned by the President's periodic efforts to prod the British on the question of neutral rights. The Secretary felt that such policies might result at best in a compromise peace with German imperialism, and at worst in an irrevocable split between the United States and the Allies, leading to a German victory. Convinced that only democracies were fit partners for a peace league, Lansing opposed any plan to include the Central Powers in a projected postwar concert of nations. With the German declaration of resumption of unrestricted submarine warfare in February 1917, Lansing pressed unrelentingly for war. Angered by Wilson's hesitation to make the final decision to enter the conflict that as President he had tried so long to end, Lansing repeatedly emphasized the necessity for a liberal crusade to defeat German absolutism and thereby lay the foundation for permanent peace in universal democracy. Writing to a close friend in late February 1917, Lansing affirmed his view "that modern civilization is threatened by military Absolutism and that the only hope of a permanent peace lies in the triumph of the principle of Democracy." We shall see that

Lansing's militant commitment to liberalism proved important not only as a basis for Administration opposition to German autocracy but because it later became a basis for the hostile Wilsonian response to the Bolshevik challenge to the values of liberal-capitalism.

It is not surprising, then, that neither House nor Lansing opposed the subtle but steady process through which Sir Edward Grey, while appearing to encourage Wilsonian mediation efforts, was in reality working to enlist American influence and power behind the achievement of Allied war aims. Of course, this British policy was in no sense predetermined to succeed. Had Germany's leaders been willing to give up their hopes for a total victory, to abandon submarine warfare and accept their defeat on the seas, and to use their military superiority on the land to sue openly for an honest compromise peace in late 1916, there is no doubt that they could have seriously undermined the Wilson Administration's ties with the Allies. This was true because whatever political, ideological, and economic ties were growing between the Wilson Administration and the embattled Allies in the 1914–16 period, there always remained, especially in the President's mind, an element of suspicion of Allied imperialism and a continued irritation with Britain's wartime naval and blockade policies. Moreover, until the Germans made their final decision to try for total victory through unlimited submarine warfare, Wilson remained more committed than House, and especially more committed than Lansing, to the vision of an American-inspired liberal world order to be built on the foundations of a true compromise peace without victory for either side.

Wilson himself proved far less prepared to accept completely the autocracy vs. democracy theory of the war than either of his two principal foreign policy advisers. It is true, of course, that at times Wilson seemed to reveal a latent moral commitment to the Allied cause; one evening in the fall of 1915 he confided to House that "he had never been sure that we ought not to take part in the conflict and if it seemed evident that Germany and her militaristic ideas were to win, the obligation upon us was greater than ever." Nonetheless, despite his latent tendency to make an identification between the cause of the Entente and the values of American missionary liberalism, the main thrust of Wilson's thought and action in the 1914–17 period was in the direction of critical and objective neutrality toward the war coupled with an effort to end the conflict by mediation and the re-establishment of international commercial and political stability. In this connection, Wilson looked upon the House-Grey negotiations of early 1916, which implied extremely close Anglo-American co-operation, as part of the mediation process and in no sense a commitment to go to war in alliance with the Entente. In fact, Wilson's anger both with Allied reluctance to ask him to move for peace and with British infringements on American neutral rights was instrumental in his decision to act publicly for peace in December 1916 despite Allied objections. In the end, it took not only the resumption of unrestricted German submarine warfare in February 1917 but also the liberal March Revolution in Russia to bring the President to accept the war on the terms of a conflict between autocracy and democracy.

The presence of the Tsarist regime among the Allies, in addition to British recalcitrance on neutral rights, had been of concern to Colonel House as he tended more and more to see in the Entente the nucleus for a liberal postwar world. The Colonel was convinced of the possibility that a separate peace could be arranged between Russia and German reactionaries, for, as he told Wilson, "there is no doubt that the Russian bureaucracy and the German militarists have some understanding and will work together so far as the Russian and German people will permit." This fear of relationship between German and Russian reaction was, of course, evidence that House saw the war as a potential liberal crusade even prior to American entry. The news of the March Revolution thrilled House, who had "been fearful lest bureaucratic Russia and autocratic Germany would link fortunes and make trouble for the democracies of the world"; and he urged Wilson, as the great liberal of modern times, to recognize the new Russian Government as soon as England and France did so.

The significance of the March Revolution was also grasped by Lansing, who sought to convince Wilson that "the Russian Government founded on its hatred of absolutism and therefore of the German Government would be materially benefitted by feeling that this republic was arrayed against the same enemy of liberalism." Actually, the reactions of House and Lansing were typical of those of many liberals in the United States and the Allied countries, who responded to the March Revolution by claiming that it had purified the Entente cause of the stigma of Tsarist reaction, and thereby removed the last barrier to seeing the war ideologically in terms of a contest between autocracy and democracy. Wilson himself, in the Cabinet meeting of March 20, 1917, "spoke of the glorious act of the Russians, which in a way had changed conditions," but added the doubt that he could "give that as reason for war." By April 2, when he asked Congress for a declaration of war, however, Wilson had clearly resolved the question of Russia in his mind and had adopted the House-Lansing view of the significance of the March Revolution both to the Allied cause and to America's war aims:

> Does not every American feel that assurance has been added to our hope for the future peace of the world by the wonderful and heartening things that have been happening within the last few weeks in Russia? Russia was known by those who knew it best to have been always in fact democratic at heart, in all the vital habits of her thought. . . . The autocracy that crowned the summit of her political structure, long as it had stood and terrible as was the reality of its power, was not in fact Russian in origin, character, or purpose; and now it has been shaken off and the great, generous Russian people have been added in all their naïve majesty and might to the forces that are fighting for freedom in the world, for justice, and for peace. Here is a fit partner for a League of Honor.

For the next three years Wilson would seek to defend this vision of a liberal Russia against the threats posed both by German imperialism on the Right and by Bolshevism on the Left.

The ideological implications of the President's final conversion to the autocracy vs. democracy theory of the war also extended beyond the Russian question, however. We have seen that Wilson and House sought to end the split in the Western community of nations through mediation, and that the President took his mission as world reconstructor and peace-maker with great conviction. If, however, the Entente alliance could be transformed by the Russian Revolution and Wilsonian participation into the nucleus of postwar liberal world system, then America could enter the war without doing violence to Wilson's overriding desire to create a liberal-capitalist community of Western powers. The unchanged goal of reintegrating Germany into a reunified West could eventually be accomplished in a postwar climate of universal democracy, despite the momentary unwillingness of Germany's existing rulers to accept a peaceful role in a liberal world order. Assuming that a Germany liberalized by war would be generously treated by a democratic Entente at the eventual peace conference, the President saw no necessary contradiction between his desire on the one hand for a liberal war against German imperialism and his hope on the other for a compromise peace to form the basis of a new commercial and political world harmony. Indeed, Wilson told Congress in his war message that "only free peoples can hold their purpose and their honour steady to a common end and prefer the interests of mankind to any narrower interest of their own." Then too, once it was accepted that the war was caused by German militarism, rather than by general "European" imperialistic practices, as Wilson had originally held, it was possible for Wilsonians to handle their American exceptionalist distrust of possible Entente imperialism by emphasizing a belief in the peaceful proclivities of liberal states. What was basically needed, according to Wilson, was the remaking of a peaceful liberal-capitalist Germany which could act with international restraint and responsibility. Until then, German imperialism had to be fought militarily.

In a larger sense, it could be said that the decision to bring the United States into the war solved the problem of finding a method of actualizing the President's world view by firmly wedding American military strength to Wilson's missionary liberal-internationalism. Actually, Colonel House had been urging this seemingly contradictory fusion of national power and international-liberalism on the President since 1914. On the one hand, the Colonel insisted that Wilson's voice could carry prestige abroad only if American dignity were maintained in Mexico and if the United States embarked on an impressive program of military and naval preparedness. House was also convinced that American firmness in regard to German submarine warfare was essential to the retention of the respect of the Allies and their willingness to co-operate with the United States in building a postwar world. On the other hand, the Colonel often declared that it was his and Wilson's purpose to eliminate militarism and navalism, and that the President, in working for peace and a new world order, should seek to "rally the liberals of the world" even possibly in opposition to conservative elements in the Entente. It should be stressed, however, that House did not feel that he was inconsistent in trying to join nationalism with liberal anti-imperialism. As if to reassure Wilson on this point, the Colonel wrote in the spring of 1916 that "your desire to stop the war and your willingness to help maintain the peace of the world afterwards would not be inconsistent with a demand for a navy commensurate with these purposes."

In reality, Wilson seemed as able as House to combine the exercise of national power with an appeal to international liberalism. The President's willingness to use American military force against Germany in defense of his conception of the freedom of the seas has already been discussed. In late 1916 Wilson responded to House's theory that friction with Great Britain was caused by commercial rivalry by suggesting, "let us build a navy bigger than hers, and do what we please." At the same time, however, there is no doubt that Wilson conceived of himself as "speaking for liberals and friends of humanity in every nation" in a struggle for a new international system of peace, disarmament, and commercial freedom against entrenched reaction.

Only a supreme faith in the universal righteousness of their conception of America's national interests could have enabled House and Wilson to conceive of themselves as operating simultaneously as the wielders of traditional forms of national power and as the leaders of world liberalism. The point was, as has been shown, that Wilson's vision of a liberal world order of free trade and international harmony was not opposed to but rather served to complement his conception of the national interests of American liberal-capitalism. Wilsonian foreign policy in an era of war and revolution, then, can best be understood as a combination of liberal opposition to imperialism and of missionary nationalism, and this is the basic explanation of why, once the President accepted it, the concept of a war to make the world safe for democracy served to hold both the national and international elements of the Wilsonian world view in balance. Yet, if Wilson was able to maintain a balance between national considerations and liberal internationalism, his conservative and radical domestic critics were not.

The Republican opposition was unprepared to accept the image of America as the leader of liberal anti-imperialism, while the President's socialist and radical critics never fully accepted the use of American national power. On the international scene as well, the President faced challenges from the Left and the Right, which threatened to upset the precarious Wilsonian balance established between national considerations and liberal-internationalism. On the one hand, the use of American military power against the Central Powers tended to encourage militant imperialist elements in the Entente who were willing to collaborate with American power in the interests of victory, but who did not at all share Wilson's concern for the eventual reintegration of a liberalized Germany into a stable postwar community of powers. Ironically, the very weakness of German imperialism intensified Wilson's crusade against German imperialism, thereby unavoidably aiding Entente extremism at the same time. On the other hand, to the extent that he maintained even a limited and controlled revolutionary liberal posture, the President tended to encourage socialist forces on his Left, whose desire to use class politics to attain a new international system threatened both the President's goal of liberal-capitalist world order and his ultimate reliance on traditional diplomatic and military methods during war and peace negotiations. Even Wilson's calls during the war for democracy in Germany as a pre-condition of peace would help to cause the German Revolution of 1918, from which emerged a socialist threat to both capitalism and liberalism in Germany. In this connection, while ambivalent relations between Wilsonianism and democratic-socialism would be possible, Bolshevism would prove a more lasting challenge to the President's dream of liberal world order than would autocratic Germany.

Lenin's opposition to all efforts in the direction of a compromise peace of liberal reformism has already been discussed, but Lenin was no less opposed to any form of liberal or socialist rationale for participation on either side in the war. Since, after April 1917, it would be Wilson's role to give liberal legitimization to the Entente cause, some consideration of Lenin's approach to the issues of liberal war in general and the March Revolution in particular is essential to full comprehension of the ideological roots of the Wilson-Lenin conflict.

In Lenin's view, the world war was simply a conflict among capitalist-imperialist powers for the division of the underdeveloped areas of the world, and as such merited the unqualified opposition of all international-socialists. Since all wars on the part of the major powers after 1870 were essentially imperialist struggles for annexations and not defenses of homelands, and since both sides in the world conflict were equally predatory, it naturally followed for Lenin that it was wrong for socialists to support the war efforts of their respective countries either on the ground of national defense or by way of opposing the imperialism or social system of the enemy. For Lenin, the only socialist policy to follow in the face of imperialist war was that of a revolutionary attack on one's own government. Only such a policy of civil war could rescue socialism from what Lenin felt were the opportunistic and social patriotic attitudes of the majority socialist parties in the warring countries. As

Lenin saw it, the strong support given by these parties to their respective governments in the war resulted both from the fact that their working class leaders had become too dependent on parliamentary methods for political action and from the fact that a small group of privileged workers—the labor aristocracy—were benefitting from the profits of imperialism. In a larger sense, however, Lenin's contempt for democratic-socialism was rooted in his fundamental position that republican government did not mean the end of bourgeois rule over the workers and that, therefore, only opportunists and petty bourgeois democrats placed any faith in democratic procedures. We shall see that it was this Leninist dismissal of all the values of liberal democracy, which, as much as anything else, motivated Wilsonian hostility to Bolshevism. Also important in the context of the Wilson-Lenin conflict, however, was the fact that Lenin's rejection of traditional liberal values was coupled with an assault on all forms of war under capitalism in such a way as to form a position completely at odds with Wilson's projected war for a new liberal world order in league with Russian and Entente liberalism.

In his writings, Lenin totally rejected the notion that the war was a conflict between autocracy and democracy rather than a struggle for the division of the world among two capitalist coalitions, and he insisted as well that the liberal-capitalism of the Entente was not less imperialistic than the autocratic-capitalism of the Central Powers. In this connection, Lenin had already speculated prior to March 1917 as to whether or not, as many Russian social-democrats held, a republican revolution in Russia would legitimize socialist support for the Russian war effort. Lenin concluded, before the event, that under a republican form of government Russia would still be capitalist and therefore would still be waging an imperialist war. With the victory of the liberal revolutionaries over Tsarism in March 1917 it comes as no surprise to find Lenin opposing all liberal- and moderate-socialist efforts to arouse war enthusiasm in Russia and claiming that no change in war aims could alter the imperialist nature of the war. Lenin also indicted the Provisional Government as the servant of Entente imperialism to which, he held, Russia's liberal leadership was tied by the strings of financial indebtedness and secret treaties. Writing in *Izvestia* in June 1917, Trotsky supported Lenin by arguing that with the state apparatus of Russia still in the hands of the bourgeoisie, the revolution had not changed the character of the war in the slightest. Bolshevism demanded neither a liberal peace nor a liberal war, but called instead for socialist revolution throughout Europe. In so doing, it posed a total challenge to the Wilsonian world view.

In the chapters which follow, we shall be concerned with analyzing, in some detail, the ideological and diplomatic interaction which developed between Wilsonianism and Leninism during the 1917–19 period. In the broadest terms, it could be said that the challenge which Lenin posed for Wilson was related to the general question as to whether or not liberalism had a progressive role left to play in world history. For example, in countries such as Germany and Russia, where liberal-capitalism had not yet completed its historical task of defeating traditional reaction, Wilson would seek to revitalize the progressive potential of liberalism, whereas Lenin would seek to destroy both reaction and liberal-capitalism in one final socialist revolution. In a real sense, then, Wilsonianism represented liberalism's opportunity to regain its progressive dynamism and to end atavistic imperialism while, at the same time, containing revolutionary-socialism.

6. The Nineteen Twenties and the New Deal

The Corporate Ideology of American Labor Leaders from Gompers to Hillman RONALD RADOSH

Much of the opposition to socialism in America came from labor leaders rather than capitalists. At one end of the spectrum, Samuel Gompers, one of the founders of the American Federation of Labor, fought the Socialists in the name of non-ideological, "pure-and-simple" trade unionism that would leave the social order untouched but merely win for labor a larger share of the "take" within it. Gompers and the AFL succeeded in establishing a stable labor movement, but it was small and confined to skilled, nativeborn workingmen. These were the wage earners who least needed the protection of a trade union, and their gains were often at the expense of the rest.

Sidney Hillman was, at least superficially, a different sort of leader. His major interest was industrial unionism, and he wished to see the great mass of the semi-skilled and unskilled factory workers brought within the ranks of organized labor. Along with John L. Lewis of the United Mine Workers, Hillman, who was associated with the Amalgamated Clothing Workers, helped found the Congress of Industrial Organizations. This body eventually organized the bulk of the American industrial labor force. The CIO was also more active politically, and more socially conscious. But despite the differences, as Ronald Radosh shows below, both leaders at heart supported the social status quo and endorsed the domestic and foreign programs of corporate leadership. Though Radosh refrains from making the point explicitly, he demonstrates the continuity between the conservatism of early union leadership and that of the present.

FOR FURTHER READING:

Ronald Radosh, *American Labor and United States Foreign Policy*, (Random House, 1969); Melvyn Dubovsky, *When Workers Organize: New York City in the Progressive Era*, (Amherst, 1968); Melvyn Dubovsky, *We Shall Be All: The History of the IWW*, (Quadrangle, 1969); Norman Ware, *The Labor Movement in the United States 1860–1895: A Study in Democracy*,

Source: Ronald Radosh, "The Corporate Ideology of American Labor Leaders from Gompers to Hillman," *Studies on the Left*, vol. 6, no. 6 (Nov.-Dec. 1966), pp. 66–88.

(Peter Smith, 1959); Irving Bernstein, *The Lean Years: A History of the American Worker 1920–1933**, (Pelican Penguin Books, 1966); Matthew Josephson, *Sidney Hillman, Statesman of American Labor,* (Doubleday, 1952).

Asterisk denotes paperback edition.

Historians of American labor usually describe two strains in trade unionism: the "pure and simple" business unionism of Samuel Gompers, and the social unionism of Sidney Hillman or Walter Reuther. But beneath these avowed differences there is a fundamental concensus shared by both kinds of labor leaders—that a corporate society offers the best means of achieving industrial stability, order and social harmony.

Corporate thinkers view society as composed of various functional economic groups caused by the division of labor. Workers are defined as producers rather than as a social class. Therefore they hold an equal stake with management in developing efficient industrial production. The goal of such thinkers is peaceful industrial relations in which each sector of the economy has political representation and is coordinated by an impartial administration. Ideally, an economic congress should be created in which each functional group would be represented. Such a congress of economic groups would work more equitably than the system in which the different groups blindly scramble for power.

C. Wright Mills was perhaps the first social scientist to emphasize that labor leaders framed unions as instruments for integration into the existing political economy, not levers for changing it. It was the labor leader's desire to "join with owners and managers in running the corporate enterprise system and influencing decisively the political economy as a whole." The result, in Mills' words, was a "kind of 'procapitalist syndicalism from the top.' "

In this paper I hope to present some tentative but provocative suggestions as to the way in which Samuel Gompers in the 1920's, and Sidney Hillman in the 1930's, sought to find a place for labor within a corporate capitalist economic structure.

After defeats suffered by labor in the Homestead, Pullman and Coeur d'Alene strikes of the 1890's, Samuel Gompers concluded that unions could not beat the growing "trusts" in head-on collisions. Accepting the growth of the large corporations as natural and inevitable, Gompers sought to organize the workers within the system as an alternative to socialism. The problem was to find means whereby the employer and worker could function together harmoniously.

This problem was met by espousing labor participation in the National Civic Federation. Organized in 1900 by Ralph Easley, Mark Hanna and Samuel Gompers, the Federation sought to resolve class conflict and institute cooperative relations between capital and labor. The employer who led the Civic Federation hoped to establish a community of interest between previously warring groups and create one unified corporate body. Gompers' association with men like Hanna led him to believe that industrial peace would reign, since the "men who control wealth in this country are at bottom human and adaptable to the changed order of relations." Hanna signed a collective bargaining agreement with the AFL union in his steel plant, and worked to convince capitalists to concede "the rightful demands of labor."

From the birth of the Civic Federation to 1914, Gompers' idea about labor were molded by his association with those sophisticated employers who saw the AFL as a conservative and disciplined junior partner in a stable corporate order. It was Gompers' wartime experience, however, that led to maturation of his thought. The wartime need for an uninterrupted flow of goods and services, the participation of union leaders in the Administration and the growth of union membership impressed upon labor leaders the desirability of taking a new position. Before the war the AFL was indifferent to production and efficiency, scorned productivity theories and was hostile to the scientific management movement. The war years taught the AFL leaders the value of preaching cooperation and efficiency to increase production. It was then that Gompers began a close association with scientific engineers from the Taylor school.

During the war the Wilson Administration tried to institutionalize cooperative relations between labor, industry and government. The War Industries Board, Bernard Baruch reported, established price fixing, allocation and priorities policies under which the "manufacturing facilities of the Nation were almost as effectively transformed into governmental agencies as though the Government had absorbed them." Baruch's board worked with Gompers and sought to adjust disputes over wages, hours of labor and working conditions. Gompers was never "a class champion obstructionist," Board secretary Grosvenor B. Clarkson reported, and he proved a "strong believer in the scheme of close cooperation with industry and was one of the first to endorse the program of industrial group committees to facilitate government dealings with private business.

As the government developed a large cartelizing program that kept up prices and stabilized industry under administration tutelage, Gompers came into contact with leading corporate figures involved in this reorganization. Daniel Willard, President of the Baltimore and Ohio Railroad and the first head of the War Industries Board, was close to Gompers. As members of the Advisory Commission to the Council of National Defense in 1916, Willard noted that he and Gompers found themselves "in very full accord concerning most questions of fundamental importance."

After the war Gompers' contact with such sophisticated industrialists continued. The 1920's saw a revival of the National Civic Federation. Industrialists such as Edward A. Filene, of Filene and Sons, and former Secretary of Commerce William C. Redfield were among the luminaries active in trying to forge a new community of interest. Charles A. Coffin, chairman of the Board of General Electric, expressed the Civic Federation's position when he observed that the task of industry was to find methods by which the "best among labor and the best among the employers" could cooperate. Coffin branded employers who supported the open-shop movement as "oppressive." "Sympathetic, broad-minded employers," he said, should be ready to "discipline and denounce the radicals among the employers, and to meet on that ground men like Mr. Gompers and his associates who are combatting the radical movement in labor." The NCF position was also supported by former Assistant Secretary of the Navy Franklin D. Roosevelt, who sat on the Civic Federation Executive Committee. During the seven and one half years that he supervised a ship building industry of one hundred thousand, Roosevelt did not have "a single strike in a single trade in a single Navy yard." FDR attributed this stability to the agreement that if a dispute occurred, management and labor would "sit around the table and talk it over," a plan which always worked. Roosevelt criticized both the old-fashioned employer who refused to accept modern conditions and the radical worker who dreamt of far-off ideals. He urged labor-capital cooperation to meet domestic problems, and called for elimination of misleading socialist schemes such as those emanating from the Rand School in New York.

The man whose thought most affected Gompers was the prolabor Secretary of Commerce Herbert Clark Hoover. Hoover analyzed the American industrial system as composed of three basic units—capital, labor and government. His objective was to have these groups function together harmoniously. He therefore demanded a voice in labor policy in President Harding's Cabinet. Defining labor and management as producers, not as social classes, Hoover saw large areas of mutual interest that had to be cultivated. Once in office Hoover began the pattern of prolabor intervention by government that culminated in the New Deal. As coordinator of Woodrow Wilson's Second Industrial Conference, Hoover had favored collective bargaining, had criticized company unions and urged an end to child labor. E. D. Howard, the labor negotiator for the firm of Hart, Schaffner and Marx, was among those who in 1920 urged that "it would be a great step forward if Mr. Hoover were appointed Secretary of Labor." While there was evidence that many "reactionary employers" wanted to eliminate unions, there were "also a great number of more thoughtful and more liberal-minded employers who would like to carry on the work started by the President's conference," and "block the efforts of the reactionaries and also of the radical people on the other side" and "do something constructive."

In May of 1924 Hoover gave a speech before the United States Chamber of Commerce in which he presented his concept of self-determination in industry. Hoover pleaded that new regulations favoring human rights had to be developed out of the voluntary forces in the nation. Legislation entered the business world only when abuses existed, and remedies had to come "out of the conscience and organization of business itself; these restraints which will cure abuse . . . eliminate waste . . . that will march with larger social understanding." The United States, Hoover stated, was "in the midst of a great revolution," a transformation from a period of "extremely individualistic action into a period of associational activities." Through autonomous associational bodies, America was moving "towards some sort of industrial democracy."

After reading his speech Samuel Gompers wrote Hoover that he found "genuine inspiration" in the address; it was "the most valuable contribution to the understanding of industrial organizations" and would "without doubt further constructive progress for which I share your concern." Gompers proceeded to use the speech as a vehicle for a major statement. Writing that Hoover's views met and "match perfectly the policy and philosophy of the American Federation of Labor," Gompers agreed that those who sought "retention of our basic institutions" had to cure "the abuses which naturally" develop. Gompers endorsed the concept of self-government in industry, claiming that the legislative world lacked the informed intelligence necessary to deal with industrial problems. American labor "goes all the way with Mr. Hoover," Gompers wrote, "or Mr. Hoover goes all the way with Labor." Hoover had a "keen understanding of our industrial order, including Labor's part in the operation thereof—and that is all Labor asks of any man." Gompers departed from Hoover in only one respect; he emphasized the need to grant unions "greater participation in the impending changes."

Gompers' evolving corporatist outlook became clear in his evaluation of the wartime experience. 1924 saw Bernard Baruch argue for a new scheme to institute price fixing of all commodities and to reinstitute wartime type controls, when "wages had to be the same as were then prevailing in the industry." While labor was satisfied with that, Baruch wrote Gompers, he was concerned that Gompers was "opposed to . . . my plan for mobilizing industry." Baruch could not understand this because he knew that "neither you nor any of the men associated with me . . . during the war, could be opposed . . . because it is only what we were endeavoring to put into execution at that time."

Gompers assured Baruch that he was aware that many did not have "your sympathetic attitude towards labor." Moreover, labor had given its wholehearted support during the war because the War Industries Board recognized unions, and had arranged that "representation be provided for all elements concerned in producing including labor." Industrial policy of the future would have to be the result of decisions reached by "a thoroughly representative group" which would have the "confidence of industry."

Gompers believed that society moved not through the exercise of political power, but through the recognition that decision making power was concentrated directly in autonomous functional economic units. He emphasized that the WIB worked through "the organized agencies of industry and enforced decisions by economic means." The methods, machinery of operation and decisions were far different than any which could be secured through political means. In fact, Gompers recalled, "the complete collapse of political machinery during the war emergency has remained in my mind as a most significant feature. During the months of our intense activity we were scarcely aware of the existence of Congress."

Baruch was pleased to find that Gompers shared his conception. "It gave me great pleasure to receive your letter," he wrote, and to find that "your thoughts are exactly in accord with me on this whole subject." Baruch expressed his debt to Samuel Gompers. "My recommendations," he informed him, "were based on our mutual experience. None of my contacts in Washington were of more benefit or of greater pleasure to me than the one I had with you."

The attempt to organize, balance and coordinate functional economic groups took final shape in the demand that a new economic parliament be created. As AFL Vice-President Matthew Woll expressed it, the Federation hoped that there would "come into existence an economic and industrial chamber, in which all factors in industry will be fairly represented, and which will determine the rules and regulations that industries will impose upon themselves." The most explicit statement was to be made at the 1923 Convention in the Executive Board's statement "Industry's Manifest Duty." Here the AFL leadership revealed that it sought the "conscious organization of one of the most vital functional elements for enlightened participation in a democracy of industry." State regulation was undesirable because decisions that affected people's daily lives were made by men in autonomous economic groups. Functional elements in our national life had to work out their own problems without regulation. The mission of industrial groups was "to legislate in peace," and to develop an "industrial franchise comparable to our political franchise." It was Gompers' corporate conception that led him to respond positively to Benito Mussolini's attempt to build a corporate state in Italy. Despite differences in method, Gompers saw a set of common assumptions shared by Italian fascists and liberal American trade unionists.

Gompers' corporate overview, with its stress on functional democracy, efficiency and production, is often viewed as a pragmatic response to paternalism of open-shop employers. When confronted with benevolent employers, some argue, labor sought to prove that "it was industry's most able helpmeet." Others view the AFL's emphasis on efficiency as an admission that they were in a period of decline. By striving to improve output, the declining AFL hoped to gain the employer's acceptance. As one labor historian has written, the emphasis on production was "a kind of 'if you can't lick 'em, join 'em philosophy,'" to which most employers "did not want to be 'joined.'"

Writers taking this view contrast the AFL approach with that developed by CIO leaders in the 30's. The latter are praised for organizing unskilled workers, for their use of militant tactics and for purportedly developing a new labor ideology. But the corporate ideology of American labor leaders actually matured in the New Deal era. CIO leaders stressed efficiency and productivity, and favored a formal corporate state. The difference was that in the 30's they hoped that the CIO industrial unions would be the labor bodies given representation in the new industrial parliament.

In the 1930's labor leaders became involved with a new group of far-sighted industrialists who wanted to establish a place for unionism in the corporate capitalist economy. Gerard P. Swope, architect of his own plan for a corporate state—the Swope Plan—was one industrialist who wanted to integrate labor into the system. As early as 1926 Swope had sought to convince William Green to form a nationwide union of electrical workers organized on an industrial basis. Swope felt that having an industrial union might mean "the difference between an organization with which we could work on a business like basis and one that would be a source of endless difficulties."

William Green, maintaining his commitment to the craft union bloc in the AFL, rejected Swope's pleas. Swope preferred industrial organization for one simple reason; he saw his industry "intolerably handicapped if the bulk of our employees were organized into different and often competing craft unions." They could deal easily with one bargaining agent, but not with more than one dozen. When the CIO was organized and the left-led United Electrical Workers began to organize G.E., Swope rejoiced. He informed one of his vice-presidents that "if you can't get along with these fellows and settle matters, there's something wrong with you." The UE was praised by Swope as "well led, the discipline good." Julius Emspak, a top official of the union, recalled that Swope was an "enlightened" employer who told him that the time had come when "industry would have to recognize that" a union representative should sit on the company's board of directors.

Not only did Swope favor industrial organization, but he supported the Black Bill for a thirty-hour week and the minimum wage amendment introduced by Frances Perkins. While William Green opposed the amendment urging that it would reduce the hourly earning of skilled labor, Swope supported it because he claimed that the AFL did not cover all unskilled labor. It was a necessity since out of the "millions of men employed in industry, a very small proportion is in the American Federation of Labor." The legislation was on behalf of the unskilled worker "who needs protection . . . those who have no organization working for them." Congress, Swope said, had to act on behalf of the "millions of men who are not members" of the AFL and "for whom no one is talking."

The early New Deal was to be characterized by the introduction of planning techniques that had antecedents in the trade associations of the 1920's. The War Industries Board cartelization reached fruition in the National Recovery Administration. One of NRA's key architects was Donald Richberg, who had been chosen for his position because of his labor background. As a young Chicago lawyer, Richberg had written both the Railway Labor Act of 1926 and the Norris-La Guardia Act of 1932. In 1933 Richberg argued that industrial unions would have to be the prerequisite for an American corporatism. "If industrial workers were adequately organized," he wrote, "it would be entirely practical to create industrial councils composed of representatives of managers, investors and workers and then to create a national council composed of similar representatives of all essential industries." In the council "all producing and consuming interests would be so represented that one group could hardly obtain sanction for a policy clearly contrary to the general welfare." Richberg was critical of craft union leaders. He wished that they had "seized" labor's "great opportunity to organize the unemployed," and had ignored "the hampering tradition of craft unionism," simply organizing men and women "denied their inherent right to work." Labor should have demanded that "their government should no longer be controlled by rulers of commerce and finance who had failed to "meet their obligations." If such a movement had been built, if labor had created one "mighty arm and voice" of the "unemployed millions," Congress would have listened to the dispossessed.

Richberg also forecast the conservative role which industrial unions would play. "Let me warn those who desire to preserve the existing order," he cautioned, "but intend to do nothing to reform it, that if this depression continues much longer the unemployed will be organized and action of a revolutionary character will be demanded." To avoid this people had to be put back to work. The answer was to mobilize the nation "through the immediate creation of a national planning council, composed of representatives of major economic interests who recognize the necessity of a planned economy," or, in other words, the American corporate state—or the NRA.

NRA, as Eugene Golub has observed, revealed that "the basic idea of corporatism had been accepted as part of the American scene." Businessmen in each industry were given exemption from antitrust prosecution, and were granted permission to draw up codes of fair competition which the government would enforce as law. The codes also established minimum wages in each industry, and price and production quotas. Labor was to receive the protection offered in Section 7-a, which guaranteed its right to organize. Despite the obvious corporate origins and function of NRA, liberals and radicals ignored its conservative heritage because of what Arthur K. Ekirch called their "widespread confidence in the broad nature and humanitarian goals of the New Deal's planning." FDR's use of big business methods and wartime regimentation was forgotten because the goal was more jobs and better working conditions. The commitment to support reform if liberals would bypass criticism of the conservative nature of NRA was understood by Richberg himself. NRA would win the allegiance of liberals by providing Title II which offered a program of public works. In a draft prepared for the NRA planning committee Richberg suggested that "it would be at least a tactical error not to begin the bill with a public works program," with the provision for trade agreements following as further stimulation to stabilization of industry. "If this is not done," he explained, "the reaction of the host of people expecting, advocating and convinced of the value of public works will be antagonistic to the general program." If "industrial control leads off, with public works as a secondary, incidental part of the program, it will be difficult to avoid violent opposition from those now clamoring for public works who might swallow a somewhat 'fascist' proposal to get their 'democratic' measure of relief." In facetiously using the terms he expected critics to cite in the future, Richberg showed awareness that reformers would acquiesce in the corporate state if reform was part of its program.

The most significant success that the Roosevelt Administration had was the integration of organized labor into the corporate system. The old line craft unions were insufficiently structured to aid unskilled labor. Therefore unions that had a sudden revival under NRA were industrial outfits such as the United Mine Workers and the Amalgamated Clothing Workers. NRA turned unionism into a semi-public institution whose organization was part of the new government program. NRA officials understood that the AFL unions were not capable of fulfilling the NRA program for a rise in labor's condition. As Benjamin Stolberg wrote in 1933, "in short, the socialist unions, whose militancy has been kept alive these last few years by an inner left wing opposition, fitted very easily into the drift towards state capitalism, which characterizes the New Deal."

It is not surprising to find that Sidney Hillman, the Jewish immigrant who built the Amalgamated Clothing Workers, would emerge as a major exponent of a corporate state in which labor would be guaranteed a formal position. Hillman's contribution to corporate ideology is usually ignored. Hillman was originally a socialist and led a union whose rank and file was Marxist inclined. Moreover, he favored industrial unionism and his own Amalgamated was created in an internal rebellion against the AFL garment union in Chicago.

The truth about Hillman's attitude was carefully explained by William H. Johnston, the President of the AFL Machinists. Trying to reassure Baltimore and Ohio President Daniel Willard about the effect of radical workers on the B and O, Johnston urged that Willard disregard rhetoric and look at reality. "I believe it is a mistake to be too much disturbed by every unfortunate phrase or differing angle" some labor groups use, he wrote. What Willard had to realize is that "in labor circles discussion is free and often acrimonious, that labor people have their own traditions" and use their own terminology. It was essential "not to confuse phrases with the reality." Johnston's example was relations between the hat firm of Hart, Schaffner and Marx and Hillman's Amalgamated Clothing Workers, "no strikes having taken place in the plant and cooperative experiments having been developed to a high degree." Yet, Johnston commented, "the union itself is full of 'revolutionary' propaganda, and even its officers are far more outspoken in their radical political and industrial doctrines than the officers of any railroad unions." If the "well disposed employers had taken this sort of thing too seriously or had allowed themselves to be upset by everything that was said in the union, then friendly relations with their employees might have been broken off a hundred times." But these employers "were realistic and concentrated on the job in hand. They did not confuse realities with phrases."

The record indicates that the employers acted wisely in disregarding the Amalgamated's radical rhetoric. Hillman's role was that of champion of cooperative schemes in the garment industry. Like Gompers, Hillman received the aid of government during the First World War. In August of 1917 Secretary of War Newton

D. Baker had composed a directive assuring that sound industrial conditions would be in force in firms manufacturing army uniforms. A control board was established to see that standard wages, the eight hour day and union conditions were met. With this agreement the Amalgamated grew rapidly and organized most of the clothing industry. By 1919 Hillman was advocating stabilization of the industry by creation of one national organization of clothing manufacturers, a move opposed at the time by other union officers. As Hillman's biographer observed, his "intellectual approach . . . was sympathetic to 'statism,' an attitude formed during World War I, when a constructive policy toward organized labor had been adopted by the Federal Government."

When rank and file unionists opposed administration policy, such as American participation in the World War, the union moved to curb antiwar agitation. Amalgamated officer Frank Rosenblum wrote that the union's newspaper had "overdone itself in its criticism of the government." While Rosenblum agreed that the war was unjust, he felt that attacks on it should not be given "the space and prominence it has until now," and that the union should "not do anything which will antagonize any one." To Rosenblum it was "a question of expediency." To criticize the war meant an opening for those who wanted to harm the union, since there were "enough forces in and out of the labor movement seeking to destroy the Amalgamated without getting the U.S. Government on the job to assist them." If it kept up an antiwar stance, the union would "lose friends which it might need in the future."

The union did not lose its friends. By the 1920's Hillman was the leading advocate of "the new unionism," whose supporters put their stress on efficiency. They argued that an industry which was not productive could not be prosperous, and that industry would yield benefits to all groups if it was efficiently administered. Hillman introduced what were called standards of production into the clothing trade, in which a specified shop production was agreed to by representatives of both sides, and was guaranteed by the union.

For this attitude Hillman won praise from important figures. Ray Stannard Baker saw the Amalgamated representing "in the labor question what the League of Nations represents in international relations," substituting in place of militancy "a system for the prevention of war and conflicts between employers and employees." The result of Hillman's program would be that workers would not be "compelled in despair to turn to radical movements in the hope of securing what they consider their right—a joint voice with the employer in the determination of conditions of labor." Since the Amalgamated was supposedly a radical union, this was a substantial achievement.

Most satisfied with the work of the Amalgamated were employers. Joseph Schaffner had signed the first binding agreement with the union. The result, he stated in 1915, was that "in our own business, employing thousands of persons . . . many of them in opposition to the wage system and hostile to employers as a class, we have observed astonishing changes in their attitude during the four years under the influence of our labor arrangement." Workers knew that "justice will be done them" once the company gave the union a voice. Another employer explained that before the union entered his New York firm the workers often simply refused to produce. After he signed with the union the Amalgamated gave its permission to dismiss hostile workers, "and with their sanction we discharged every man in the shop, and are now building up a new force." Years ago, the employer explained, such discharges would have meant a "general strike," but now his firm "had the disciplinary power of the union behind us." The union's worth was also demonstrated by E. Strouse, a leading Baltimore clothing manufacturer. Writing to Hillman in October of 1919, Strouse complained that the local leader in Baltimore was so loaded down with work that he was unable to be reached "when we need him most." Asking that the union representative meet with him once a day, Strouse noted that "I have been trying to get more production for weeks and have been unable to do so." Could you "not do something that we might have him oftener," Strouse asked, "because I feel that with his finesse he is able to get for us what we want, better than we can ourselves and it is urgent from many angles that we get our production."

By 1919 Hillman had called for "the organization of every industry, beginning from the raw materials, completing with the agencies for distribution, and providing representation from all the factors in industry, and placing upon all of them the responsibility of running the industry." The result, Robert W. Bruere wrote, was that continuity of production was guaranteed, and strikes and lockouts did not occur. Hillman had proved the "ability of rightminded employers and trade union leaders to sublimate class conflict into integral class concert." Labor's concern shifted from the haggles or getting more to the joint concern for achieving "efficient production." Like Samuel Gompers, Hillman's approach led him into the camp of Herbert Hoover. After Hoover was elected to the Presidency Hillman termed his efforts the "first definite national move to carry out the plans favored by the Amalgamated for the last fifteen years."

By 1931 Hillman actively called for creation a formal corporate state structure. Speaking at a conference held in March with leading progressive Senators, Hillman demanded that government step in to alleviate bread lines and the plight of the poor, which he attributed to the lack of "planning in industry." Hillman called for creation of an "economic council for industry" similar to the one Bernard Baruch operated during the First World War. The council should have "representatives of all the parts that make up industry management, capital, labor and government representing the public," and should be empowered to make recommendations to both industrial leaders and Congress.

From 1931 on Hillman became the main labor advocate of a corporate society. Gerard Swope and other industrialists favored mobilization of industries into trade associations that would regulate and stabilize prices and production. Hillman's model differed only in that it demanded labor representation as an equal factor in industry. "Planless production for uncoordinated distribution" was attacked by Hillman as the "core of our individualistic social system." Instead of a *laissez-faire* one had to substitute "purposive intervention in social processes," and begin to think "in terms of economic planning" by creating a national economic council. Hillman made it clear that he did not favor socialist planning in which capitalists would play no role. Rather, he envisioned a corporate state in which authority would rest in a "national house of industrial representatives" on which both management and labor leaders sat.

Hillman had come to sound like Hoover in the 1920's, since he emphasized a joint employer-worker attack on instability by "increasing individual productivity, reducing cost, eliminating waste . . . and taking advantage of the new technical advances in industry." Unions would assume greatly increased responsibility for the quantity and quality of output, which meant "a revolutionary change in the attitude of the worker toward his job." But for this to work nationally, a government "instrumentality" was needed to "guide a national economic plan." The national program that would gain Hillman's favor was the NRA, and Hillman became its most ardent champion. NRA, he wrote, provided "for a measure of national economic planning, in business enterprise and productive activity." It could be used by labor to throw open union doors, and hence "unorganized industries and areas must be invaded by union organizers. Existing and functioning organizations," Hillman warned, "must abandon the narrow craft outlook. Labor must think of itself in terms of the whole working class."

Speaking to the 1934 Amalgamated convention, Hillman told delegates that NRA was "a new constitution for both labor and industry." By eliminating the sweatshop employer it provided "a basis of equality for labor." Hillman predicted that NRA would "remain a permanent part of our industrial life," because it recognized the "need for planning" and because the codes of fair competition made "further development possible." NRA gave labor "representation in the governing of industry and it assigns to the government the place of an umpire." Roosevelt had seen the need to create an organization representing "all elements in industry." NRA, Hillman asserted, proved that a social organization could be changed within its own shell. It aimed at a coordinated balance of production, and saw the "fundamental necessity for government regulation and supervision of industrial processes and of economic forces." It was "the beginning of national economic planning," and those who wanted "to ride into the land of promise" had to first "lay the road." Moreover, employers through NRA were "becoming accustomed to consider the demands of labor an integral part of the industrial situation."

In March of 1935 Hillman cited NRA as proof that "we have come to maturity as a nation in our understanding and in our handling of the problems arising out of a complex economic system." Workers knew that they had "an economic interest with employers in the successful operation of the establishment." That is why they favored increased productivity, and denied the autocratic employer who held that business was their own exclusive affair. It was to NRA's credit that it recognized the social "nature of industry." It truly forecast "a new birth in industrial relations," and the "responsible labor leaders" had learned "the lessons of cooperative relations under the New Deal." They knew that "the source of our prosperity is increased production," and Hillman guaranteed that labor thought in these terms whenever it strived to gain a just share of the product. As he put it, "organized labor, with the full feeling that it 'belongs' and that everyone recognizes it is an essential part in industry, will cooperate to make it more efficient, more productive, more humane."

Hillman's support of NRA was unique in that he backed its extension long after the majority of organized labor had concluded that NRA was resulting in the spread of company unions. Attacking those Congressional liberals who blamed NRA for monopolistic price-fixing, Hillman compared them with those who favored ending unions because they were not perfect. Asking radicals "not to hurry things beyond their natural course," Hillman asked that labor support NRA and demand increased authority to "impose a code on every industry."

Hillman then worked in Washington to affect a rapproachement between dissident labor leaders and the administration. The labor leaders agreed to stop attacking

NRA, Philip Murray was appointed to the National Industrial Recovery Board and the administration began to show a sympathetic attitude to the pending Wagner labor disputes bill. More important, Hillman's close associate Robert Soule revealed that Hillman began "discussions which may lead to the evolution of a labor organization which can cooperate with the government in place of the American Federation of Labor." Labor, adopting this path, would "have ready access to the White House."

Hillman had begun to take steps that would lead to representation for industrial unions in the corporate state. The industrial unions, he assured all, would function responsibly. In a 1937 interview Hillman stressed that the CIO emphasized "that industry is based on three factors of equal importance," and that the "labor factor" was entitled to a fair share. The CIO was "not a movement to change the competitive system," but was, rather, trying "to make the system workable." It asked only a "proportionate share of the progress of industry" in which labor was one of the three "vital and participating elements." Commenting accurately that Hillman subscribed to the "principle enunciated by the late Samuel Gompers," the interviewer quoted Hillman as advising that after a contract was signed, "every employee should lend himself to complete cooperation with the employer in the interest of efficient management of industry." Responsible labor shared a set of common economic goals with the employer. Hillman stressed that the CIO objected in principle to sitdown strikes. He "chuckled" as he told the press that "Wall Street is beginning to recognize the CIO."

Hillman always stressed that if studied, industry would see that the CIO recognized the need for a prosperous industry. In fact, the CIO had contributed to this end "in choosing the form of industrial organization." It had rejected craft unionism precisely because "it permits of no responsibility in the relationship between labor and management." Sounding like Gerard Swope, Hillman pointed out that no employer could enter into seventeen agreements with seventeen unions, and be sure of avoiding jurisdictional strikes "which make it impossible to have responsible leadership." By 1933 Hillman was explaining that "efficiency in the men's clothing industry" had reached its highest point. The union had "helped many manufacturers to introduce efficiency methods because" at the same time they helped their members by enabling the employers to stay in business. Hillman added, *"Industry-wide union organization is, of course, essential if cooperation and efficiency are to be brought to this degree."*

While Sidney Hillman was leading the industrial workers into absorption in the corporate capitalist system and towards political commitment to the Roosevelt Administration, some criticism was beginning to emerge from labor's ranks. It came, however, from the remaining descendants of the Gompers machine in the AFL. Men trained by Gompers, such as Matthew Woll, president of the Photo-Engravers and an AFL vice-President, and the old pro-war socialist William English Walling, were two who quickly became disenchanted with NRA and became outspoken critics of the New Deal. Originally both had hoped that NRA would lead to a new partnership between equal factors in industry. As it turned out, workers were not given equal protection, and no guarantee existed that labor was to be organized as efficiently as the employers were in trade associations. Woll and Walling dissented from Hugh Johnson's belief that strikes were economic sabotage against the government. They defended the right to strike as the sole assurance workers had as a preventative to compulsory labor. As for the plea of Johnson that labor be subject to government control, Woll and Walling viewed that demand as one pointing "in the direction of Fascism" and as the "opposite of self-government in industry."

In 1935 Woll emerged as a full-scale critic of the New Deal. While he favored an economic congress that would represent functional groups, Woll wanted it to be voluntary and labor to be afforded equal representation. NRA gave only a "semblance of recognition" to all factors. It worked not to create unity, but to accentuate differences and to "undermine every vestige of concord in the functional groups in industry." Industry was functioning under a form of "capitalistic syndicalism" in which labor had no direct voice. Under NRA codes monopoly had grown, cartelization of the economy had been encouraged and "corporate control had been permitted to strengthen its grip upon the economic life of the nation." Woll felt that while NRA held out the promise of a corporate society, the goal had been subverted by its actual practice. Labor "might well assert," he wrote, "that the seed of Fascism had been transplanted" and that political government reigned supreme. The NRA's system of "compulsory trade association, of code membership, and of code observance borders closely upon the corporate or syndicalist form of organization characterized by Fascism in Italy." Labor might "well be concerned regarding its future hope and policy to deal effectually with such a strongly entrenched and cartelized system of industry."

Rather than urge compliance with code authorities, Woll suggested that labor should remove its support from the concept of NRA itself. "Not anywhere this side of Fascism, or complete control by the Government," Woll wrote, "could code provisions be adequately enforced." Woll worried that the unions might become the equivalent of Fascist labor groups, in which industries were organized "along lines somewhat akin to what has taken place in each of our major industries operating under a code." In Italy labor was subordinate to the state in the guise of governmentally controlled unions. Woll explained that "the cartelization of American industry which has gone on under codes is a familiar story in the early history of Fascist Italy." "Are we," Woll queried, "heading toward a business Fascism?"

Another aspect of New Deal policy questioned by Woll was American foreign policy. Woll argued that an economic surplus was being invested abroad instead of being put to use at home. While the internationalist view was "put before the world as a form of idealism," it was sustained "mainly by private international banking and trading interests." Implying that internationalism actually meant interventionism, Woll saw no relation between "the internationalist idea of free trade and peace." On the contrary, "economic activities of private interest outside of national boundaries were likely to "carry us toward war than toward peace." Many plans for economic ties were meant to "cover growing economic conflicts" due to foreign investments.

Commenting that many saw the "chief cure for the present depression and for unemployment . . . in the development of the export market," Woll dissented from Cordell Hull's path of gaining security through increase of reciprocal trade treaties. "The arguments of those who made possible" that legislation, Woll wrote, "are precisely the same as have been used by all those who see the solution of our present economic problem not in the increase of American purchasing power, but in plunging our nation into the mad and illusory race for foreign markets." While Woll's vision of creating a viable home market for existing surpluses was marred by the faulty argument that the export trade was unimportant for the economy, he did not hesitate to demand creation of an order that did not have to seek its prosperity through foreign expansion. "To attempt any radical extension of our foreign trade through 'reciprocal tariffs,' " he stressed, "is not only likely to get us into economic conflict with the nations excluded . . . but involves us in difficulties due to 'most favored nation' provisions." The only solution was at home. Woll hoped that capitalism would prove itself by developing full employment through a highly developed home market. Rising surpluses had to be absorbed by the home market "through increasing the income of wage-earners."

The 1930's revealed the apparently strange picture of conservative craft union leaders developing a fairly rigorous critique of the direction taken by the leaders of corporate capitalism. They urged that problems be solved at home, and opposed the expansionist course of the New Deal abroad and its corporatism at home. During these years industrial unions were flourishing under a New Deal aegis. Their leaders renounced a critical approach, and urged the absorption of labor into the very mechanism of the corporate state. Although the AFL leaders began to criticize, their reliance on craft organization made their critique irrelevant and allowed it to go virtually unnoticed. Most misread their views as the desperate pleading of old-line conservatives. Liberals and radicals forgot that the militant tactics of the CIO soon ended, and as William A. Williams has explained, the "labor movement rather rapidly settled down into the syndicalist pattern that was by then clearly emerging from the excitement and flux of the New Deal."

The labor movement and its leadership chose to align itself with American business and its path of foreign expansion. In exchange labor received government protection as it entered a stage of rapid growth. The labor leaders developed an ideological view of reality in which they asserted that the old capitalist system with its manifold problems had basically changed. In failing to point out the fallacies of this view, and by failing to explain that labor's victories were byproducts of continued expansion abroad, American radicals quietly forfeited their responsibility of providing a radical alternative.

While radicals worked hard to organize workers into industrial unions and at times won the leadership of CIO branches, they unwittingly became the allies of those whose concern was to fit labor into the corporate structure. John L. Lewis explained in December of 1935 that the "dangerous state of affairs" might very well have led to " 'class consciousness' " and "revolution as well." Lewis hoped that it could "be avoided," and he pledged that his own industrial union was "doing everything in their power to make the system work and thereby avoid it." The CIO leaders gained the aid of the left in the attempt to make the system work. Once it was on its feet the services of the left were no longer appreciated, and radicals were purged from the labor movement with only a ripple of protest emanating from the rank and file. Labor's post-war position of acquiescence in the policies of different conservative administrations had been assured, and the corporate ideology of American labor leaders remained dominant and unchallenged.

The "Industrial–Military Complex" in Historical Perspective: The Inter War Years PAUL A. C. KOISTINEN

One of the most effective New Left indictments of recent America emphasizes the existence of a military-industrial complex, with an immense stake in continual international crises and wars. The complex is composed, as its name suggests, of high military officers and industrial leaders. In the case of the military men, advancement, power, and prestige depend on the maintenance of a large military establishment. The industrialists need large military orders to make profits for their firms and to please stockholders.

When stated in this way, this hypothesis sounds very much like the native notion that wars are the interventions of the munitions maker, "merchants of death," whose greed sends thousands to their destruction. Actually, however, the proposition is a great deal more sophisticated than it appears. It is now clear that many thousands of Americans have a stake in continuing international crises. The defense industries today include more than the makers of old-fashioned "munitions." A large proportion of the aviation and electronics industries are directly subsidized by Defense Department contracts. Much federally sponsored "basic research" in the physical and social sciences is also justified by military needs. Universities have committed vast resources to solving "defense" problems. All this means that thousands of technicians, scientists, and factory workers, besides the many who serve them, are dependent on continued federal outlays for military purposes. In some communities almost every one is locked into a continuation of war, either cold or hot, and the possibility of peace is a frightening threat. The result, so the argument runs, is that we cannot have peace because powerful interests, including thousands of ordinary citizens, oppose it.

While the "merchants of death" idea is venerable, the present statement of the power of the military-industrial complex dates from the mid–nineteen fifties. It was given enormous prestige by President Dwight Eisenhower in 1961 in his now classic statement of the dangers of America's continuing economic stake in war. In the selection below, Paul Koistinen demonstrates that the roots of the present problem go back at least to the 1920s.

FOR FURTHER READING:

Seymour Melman, *Our Depleted Society**, (Delta, 1966); Seymour Melman, *Inspection for Disarmament*, (Colorado University Press, 1958) James L. Clayton (editor) *The Economic Impact of the Cold War**, (Harcourt, Brace and World, 1970); Ralph Lapp, *The Weapons Culture*, (Norton, 1968); Paul A. C. Koistinen, "The Industrial Military Complex in Historical Perspective: World War I," *Business History Review* (Winter, 1967).

Asterisk denotes paperback edition.

Source: Paul A. C. Koistinen, "The 'Industrial-Military Complex' in Historical Perspective: The Inter War Years," *Journal of American History*, vol. 56, no. 4 (March 1970), pp. 819–839.

Scholars and journalists have limited their analyses of the "industrial military complex" to the years of World War II and the Cold War. This focus is quite natural, for it is during this period that the multibillion-dollar war and defense budgets have had the most dramatic effects upon the nation's institutional structure. Nevertheless, to neglect the years prior to 1940 greatly limits an understanding of the "complex" which has resulted from the military's expanded role in the federal government and its elaborate ties with the industrial community.

The "industrial-military complex" of World War II and after is an outgrowth of economic mobilization for World War I, of interwar planning by the armed forces and the business community for future emergencies, and of defense spending during the 1920s and 1930s. Almost all practices currently ascribed to the "complex" arose before 1940.

During World War I, as during World War II, federal agencies, largely controlled by industry and the military, regulated the economy. World War I differed from World War II, however, in that the army, the largest wartime military service, was a reluctant participant in the civilian mobilization agencies. Relatively isolated within the federal government and the nation before hostilities, the army was suspicious of, and hostile toward, civilian institutions. It was also unprepared for the enormous wartime responsibilities. Congress and the Wilson administration had to force the army to integrate its personnel into the War Industries Board (WIB). This integration was essential for coordinating army procurement with the Board's regulatory functions in order to maintain a stable economy.

After the war, Congress authorized the army to plan for procurement and economic mobilization in order to insure its preparation for future hostilities. The navy also joined the planning process. The interwar planning was guided by thousands of industrialists, and by the late 1930s the armed services were not only prepared for wartime operations but also in full agreement with prominent industrial elements on plans for economic mobilization. Those plans, based on World War I mobilization, provided the guidelines for regulating the World War II economy.

Interwar planning was inseparable from defense spending. Many of the businessmen who participated in the planning were associated with firms that were actual or potential military contractors. Despite the relatively small defense budgets of the 1920s and 1930s, the pattern of industrial-military relations during those years foreshadows in many striking ways what developed after World War II.

The American economy was mobilized for World War I by federal agencies devised and staffed primarily by businessmen. In the Army Appropriations Act of August 1916, Congress provided for a Council of National Defense, which consisted of six cabinet members, to serve as the President's advisory body on industrial mobilization. It was assisted by a National Defense Advisory Commission (NDAC), composed largely of businessmen serving for a dollar-a-year or without compensation; most of the members surrendered neither their positions nor incomes as private citizens. When the nation declared war, NDAC assumed responsibility for mobilizing the economy. In July 1917 a more effective mobilization agency, WIB, took over NDAC functions; the former agency, like the latter, was controlled by business elements. Until March 1918, neither NDAC nor WIB had legal authority to enforce its decisions; both were subordinate to the Council of National Defense, and it could only advise the President.

During 1917, businessmen perfected the mobilization agencies and devised the means for curtailing civilian production and converting industry to meet governmental needs. In addition, they developed price, priority, allocation, and other economic controls. By the end of the year, WIB had created the organization and the controls essential for regulating a wartime economy.

Through WIB, industry largely regulated itself during World War I. Key to WIB's operations were major subdivisions called commodity committees, which served under the chairman and his lieutenants. These committees, which made policy for and administered the various industries, were staffed by businessmen who often came from the industries they directed. Assisting the commodity committees were war service committees which were trade associations or councils elected by the national industries. Since the war service committees were neither organized nor financed by the government, they officially only "advised" the commodity committees. But in practice the commodity committees relied heavily upon industry representatives to formulate and execute all policy decisions.

Even without legal authority to enforce its decisions, WIB had industry's cooperation because businessmen dominated it. Industry's cooperation, however, was not enough to maintain a stable wartime economy. WIB required some control over procurement by the war and navy departments and other agencies. Throughout 1917 it attempted to coordinate procurement with its own operations in order to prevent the various departments and agencies from competing among themselves and to insure uniform prices and the distribution of contracts according to availability of facilities, resources, and transportation. Economic stability depended upon such coordination, since wartime demand always exceeded supply. With only advisory powers, WIB relied upon the procurement agencies' voluntary cooperation. While most of these proved to be reasonably cooperative, the war department—the largest, most powerful procurement agency—undermined WIB's regulatory efforts by acting independently and purchasing billions of dollars worth of munitions. As a result, industrial plants in the Northeast were overloaded with contracts; prices skyrocketed; critical shortages of fuel, power, and raw materials developed; and the railway and shipping systems became hopelessly congested.

The war department was both unwilling and unable to cooperate with WIB—unwilling, because it feared that the civilian agency would try to take over army procurement functions; unable, because the department could not control its own supply operations, let alone coordinate them with WIB. As many as eight supply bureaus, such as the Quartermaster Corps and the Ordnance Department, purchased independently for the army. Competing with one another and other purchasing agencies, the bureaus let contracts indiscriminately, commandeered facilities without plan, and hoarded supplies. Cooperation between WIB and the war department was also thwarted by the fact that WIB was organized along commodity lines while the army's supply network was structured by function (such as ordnance and quartermaster). Before army procurement could be coordinated with WIB, the war department had first to accept the need for cooperating with the civilian mobilization agency and then to centralize its supply network along commodity lines. For months, the department would do neither, not only because it was suspicious of WIB but also because it was torn by internal dissension.

In theory, the war department was under the centralized control of the chief of staff, aided by the General Staff. Serving as the secretary of war's principal military adviser, the chief of staff supervised the entire army, including the supply bureaus as well as the combat troops. This system never worked in practice. The bureaus resisted control by the chief of staff. Conflict between the General Staff and the bureaus rent the war department before the war; it paralyzed the department during hostilities.

Unable to regulate the economy without war department cooperation, WIB during 1917 sought the authority to impose its will on the department. But Secretary of War Newton D. Baker, reflecting army suspicion of the Board, squelched the efforts to give it more than advisory powers. He managed to do so because he served as chairman of the Council of National Defense, under which WIB functioned, and as Woodrow Wilson's chief adviser on industrial mobilization.

By the winter of 1917–1918, with WIB stalemated by the war department and the latter virtually collapsing under burgeoning munitions requirements, the economy had become critically dislocated. The business community and Congress demanded that the crisis should be resolved by placing military procurement under a civilian munitions ministry. Adamantly opposed to such a drastic remedy, Wilson headed off the critics in March 1918 by separating WIB from the Council of National Defense and placing it directly under his control. He granted it broad powers for regulating the economy, including a measure of authority over the procurement agencies. To avoid losing control of procurement and to facilitate coordination with WIB, the war department also began reforming its supply system. In December 1917, the department began to consolidate the bureaus into one agency under General Staff control. The new organization was structured to match WIB's commodity committee system.

From March 1918, the strengthened WIB, under the chairmanship of Bernard M. Baruch, effectively used the organization and economic controls developed over the past year to regulate the economy. Procurement was coordinated with WIB activities by integrating war department representatives and those of the other purchasing agencies into WIB. Once the department reorganized its system and adopted a cooperative attitude, members of the army commodity committees joined WIB committees and shared equally in making decisions. Working together, industrial and military personnel learned that WIB could function for their mutual interests. Through WIB's operations, the foundations for the "industrial-military complex" was laid.

The collaboration of industry and the military continued during the 1920s and 1930s and took the form of procurement and economic planning for future wars. This planning was authorized by Congress in the National Defense Act of 1920, which reorganized the war department's system of supply and procurement. To insure that the army did not disrupt economic mobilization in a future emergency, the act placed the supply bureaus under an assistant secretary of war. It was assumed that he would be an industrialist. The assistant secretary would supervise the bureaus and, through planning, prepare them for wartime procurement. Since the assistant secretary was made the chief of staff's equal, the secretary of war had two principal advisers instead of one, as had been the case before 1920.

Congress based the legislation upon the recommendations of Assistant Secretary of War Benedict Crowell, various industrial consultants, several bureau chiefs, and other military personnel. Crowell, a Cleveland businessman who had been involved in military procurement since 1916, believed that World War I demonstrated that industrial production was as important to military success as were tactics and strategy. He felt that supply and procurement must receive the same emphasis in war department affairs as did the traditional military functions. That would not take place, he maintained, under the old system in which the chief of staff, aided by the General Staff, served as the secretary of war's principal adviser. The General Staff would neglect supply and procurement because it knew little about those subjects. Only by placing the bureaus under a qualified civilian who was equal to the chief of staff, he argued, would the army be prepared for future hostilities. Crowell and his associates intended that the assistant secretary of war should plan only for army procurement. Congress went further. The National Defense Act empowered the assistant secretary, though in an ambiguous way, to plan for an entire wartime economy. Why Congress authorized the more comprehensive planning is obscure.

J. Mayhew Wainwright, the first assistant secretary of war under the act, set up an Office of the Asssistant Secretary of War (OASW) with personnel drawn from the bureaus. In 1922 an Army-Navy Munitions Board was created in order to include the navy in the planning and to coordinate the supply systems of the two services. And, in 1924 the war department supply planners organized an Army Industrial College to facilitate their work.

At first, OASW concentrated upon wartime military procurement, but it soon became obvious that this planning was futile without also planning for economic mobilization. Though authorized to draft such plans, war department officials, civilian and military alike, hesitated to assume what they considered to be civilian responsibilities. It took the influence of Baruch to convince the war department that economic planning was not exclusively a civilian matter. After World War I, he and other architects of wartime mobilization insisted that the nation's security depended upon constant preparation for war. They favored joint industry-military planning for economic mobilization in order to avoid confusion and delay. Baruch pleaded with the department to draw up full-scale plans for mobilization based on World War I. After years of hesitation, OASW began to plan for economic mobilization as well as procurement. Under Baruch's critical eye, the supply planners between 1929 and 1931 drafted the first official economic blueprint for war—the "Industrial Mobilization Plan" of 1930.

This plan amounted to little more than a proposal for using the methods of World War I to regulate a wartime economy. The key to OASW's blueprint was a War Resources Administration. Comparable to the War Industries Board, the War Resources Administration would rely upon a commodity committee-war service committee system for economic control. The military services would also organize their procurement networks along commodity lines and integrate their personnel into the War Resources Administration. In a future war, the economy would be mobilized by new federal agencies largely dominated by industrial and military personnel. In 1933, 1936, and 1939, the war department published revised editions of the plan. With each revision, the proposed mobilization apparatus was simplified and patterned more explicitly after the World War I model.

The fact that the war department wrote the 1930 plan is of the greatest significance. After ten years of planning, OASW recognized that modern warfare required a totally planned economy; the armed services would have to adapt themselves to the civilian mobilization agencies during hostilities. The Industrial Mobilization Plan did not mean, however, that the army as a whole had accepted the new conditions of warfare. Before that could take place, the supply planners had to convert the chief of staff and the General Staff to their point of view. Throughout the 1920s and into the 1930s, the army's command structure refused to recognize that supply and procurement set limits for tactics and strategy; and the General Staff's war plans provided for raising and fielding an army at rates that exceeded the economy's capacity. The General Staff insisted that supply had to adjust to strategy. OASW and the supply bureaus adamantly opposed such thinking. Both the economy and the military mission, they argued, would be threatened. The admonition went unheeded for years.

The General Staff turned a deaf ear to OASW because, knowing little about procurement, it could not gauge the effects of industrialized warfare on the army or the economy and, therefore, continued to view civilian and military responsibilities as if they were unrelated. In addition, the General Staff and OASW were rivals for power. The General Staff resented the 1920 reorganization which deprived it of control of the bureaus. It was intent upon keeping the supply side of the department subordinate to itself. If the General Staff granted the importance of supply and procurement in military affairs, it would strengthen the hand of its rival. Relations between the two groups in the war department became so embittered in the 1920s that communication broke down almost completely. In the 1930s, however, the strife began to wane. As relations improved, the General Staff gradually became more receptive to OASW ideas.

A major turning point occurred in 1935–1936, when General Malin Craig became chief of staff and Harry W. Woodring, secretary of war. Woodring, who had served as assistant secretary of war from 1933 to 1936, was convinced of the need for practical war plans. Craig agreed. Under their combined influence, the General Staff's Mobilization Plan of 1933 was scrapped and the Protective Mobilization Plan drawn up and perfected between 1936 and 1939. It was the first war plan based on the nation's industrial potential. A radical change had taken place in the thinking of the army's command structure. It had finally accepted army dependence on the civilian economy in order to fulfill the military mission. Woodring observed: "I believe the reduction of our mobilization program to sensible workable proportions to be one of the highest attainments of the War Department since the World War."

OASW planning naturally led to numerous war department contacts with the business community. Thousands of industrialists, most of whom had participated in wartime mobilization, guided and assisted the department's efforts in various ways. When the Army Industrial College was organized, it had an Advisory Board graced with such prominent business figures as Baruch, Elbert H. Gary, and Walter Gifford. The various procurement districts also set up civilian advisory boards composed of army contractors to review the department's supply operations. In 1925 the department organized a Business Council, which included members from the nation's largest corporations, to help introduce modern business techniques into army operations and to familiarize the industrialists with army procurement and planning methods.

Most contacts between the war department and the industry involved representatives from trade associations and interested corporation executives. Often these men were or became reserve officers assigned to OASW. By 1931 about 14,000 individuals served in such a capacity. They aided in the drafting of procurement and mobilization plans and sought to further cooperative relations between the military and business.

Mixed motives explain industry's participation in war department planning. Firms contracting with the army obviously welcomed the opportunity of working closely with OASW in order to secure or advance their special interests. Some business elements assisted the army so that they could identify their products or materials with national defense in order to enhance their chances for tariff protection, government assistance, or other special privileges. Also their firms received free publicity of a "patriotic" nature. But reasons other than immediate economic concerns must be considered in assessing industry's role in army planning. Industrial preparedness became almost an ideological crusade for some business executives after the war. That was the case with Baruch and his coterie; with Howard E. Coffin, a prominent industrialist and leading participant in wartime mobilization; and with businessmen associated with the American Legion. They participated in army planning as a means of preparing the nation for war. The business community in general was not so disposed. Without being committed to industrial preparedness *per se,* many businessmen were willing to assist in the planning at the war department's request because it helped the department to adjust its structure and thinking to modern warfare.

The general trend of the interwar political economy is also significant for measuring the response of business to army planning. World War I greatly strengthened the cooperative ethic within the business community and between it and the government. Before World War II, both business and the government experimented with official and unofficial attempts at economic control through industrial cooperation. The National Recovery Administration was only the most formal example. The army's economic planning accurately reflected this cooperative trend.[1] For that reason, among others, the planning received the endorsement of interested businessmen.

OASW did not confine itself simply to planning for industrial mobilization. It also sought legislative authority for implementing the "Industrial Mobilization Plan" in an emergency.

During the 1920s the department's drive for industrial preparedness was carried on in conjunction with the American Legion. The Legion rank and file seethed with resentment about alleged wartime profiteering and the unequal burden shouldered by the fighting forces. In order to remove the promise of riches as an inducement to war and to distribute the burdens of warfare more equitably, the returning veterans demanded a total draft of manpower and capital in any future emergency. Ironically, the Legion's peace movement, which originated in dissent over the economics of World War I, was ultimately converted into support for the "Industrial Mobilization Plan" based on the wartime model. Legion leadership and its special relationship with the war department explains why. Substantial business elements and former military officers dominated Legion affairs; throughout the 1920s the secretaries and assistant secretaries of war were usually active Legionnaires. When acting on the proposal for a total draft that was favored by the rank and file, the Legion leaders turned to the war department for assistance. In 1922, OASW drafted for the Legion a bill that in general terms would have granted the President almost unlimited authority over the nation's human and economic resources in the event of war. The Legion consistently referred to the bill as a "universal draft," as a measure for promoting peace, and as a proposal for "equalizing wartime burdens." That was scarcely the case. The bill was so vague that it could be used for many different purposes. Its grant of authority was so great and its power so general that it could sanction a presidential dictatorship. Once the economic planning of OASW was fully underway, the war department and the Legion leadership clearly intended the bill to be a general grant of authority for implementing the "Industrial Mobilization Plan."

Beginning in 1922, the Legion-sponsored bill was repeatedly introduced in Congress. Despite Legion lobbying and war department support, each Congress sidetracked the proposed legislation. Unable to get its bill through Congress, the Legion asked for a bipartisan commission to study and recommend policies for industrial mobilization. An active campaign by congressmen who were also Legionnaires soon led to action. By a joint resolution in June 1930, Congress created the War Policies Commission (WPC), which consisted of eight congressmen and six cabinet members. Six of the fourteen commissioners were Legionnaires. The Commission was to study and make recommendations for equalizing war burdens and preventing war profiteering, and it was to formulate "policies to be pursued in event of war."

WPC, like the Legion's drive for a "universal draft," quickly became a means for furthering military preparation. Because the war department dominated the proceedings, WPC emphasized how to mobilize the economy for war and not how to equalize war burdens and eliminate war profits. Secretary of War Patrick J. Hurley, an active Legionnaire, served as WPC's chairman. WPC's staff came almost exclusively from the war department. The department's presentation of its 1930 "Industrial Mobilization Plan" and Baruch's testimony on the economics of World War I were the highlights of WPC's public hearings. After extended deliberations, WPC, with only one dissenting vote, directly endorsed the department's planning and indirectly endorsed the "Industrial Mobilization Plan." WPC efforts were more impressive as an attempt to popularize and legitimize department planning than as a serious study of wartime economics.

Despite a friendly Commission, the department was unable to drum up much overt support for its plans. In addition to the department itself, the principal advocates of the planning before WPC were the American Legion and some wartime mobilization leaders like Baruch, Gifford, and Coffin. The business community in general was either unconcerned about or unwilling to commit itself publicly on issues involving economic mobilization. Of the thousands of businessmen participating in the army planning, only a few came forward to testify.

Although support for department planning was weak, the opposition was vociferous. Witnesses like Norman Thomas, several congressmen, and spokesmen for some peace societies and humanitarian groups were hostile to WPC and the department's plans. Some advocates of peace detected inherent dangers in the department's work. According to their analyses, the promise of wartime riches, while not a major cause of war, was a contributing one that had to be eliminated. The army's plans would not do this. Moreover, the opponents feared that the industrial-military ties resulting from department planning could endanger the nation's future. But the critics—among them a member of WPC, Representative Ross A. Collins of Mississippi—were weak on analysis. Their critique of the department's plans and planning was often nebulous, contradictory, or incomplete. Seymour Waldman, a journalist covering the hearings, articulated more clearly and precisely what appeared to alarm Collins and some witnesses before WPC:

> The hearings revealed a gigantic machine, whose intricate parts touch the entire nation, which is being constructed by the War Department and industrial magnates

for use in the event of war. . . . They reveal the dangers inherent in a militarization of industry, and industrialization of the military forces, or a combination of the two. . . .

I would feel rewarded and gratified if this book should be the precursor of a much needed diagnosis of the whole problem, a study of the interlocking of our war mechanism and our economic system. . . . Such a work . . . is imperative if we are to be effective in preventing more national and international bloodshed.

Opposition to the department's plans and proposed legislation for implementing them increased after WPC's hearings as the peace and isolationist movement gained in strength. The most formidable challenge came from the Senate's so-called Nye Committee. In addition to the munitions makers, the Nye Committee's purview included economic mobilization for World War I, interwar military procurement policies, and the "Industrial Mobilization Plan." In a fragmentary manner, the Committee disclosed the dynamics of an emerging "industrial-military complex." The elements were presented in the Committee hearings and reports, but they were not fitted together. Senator Gerald P. Nye and his colleagues still saw only through a glass darkly.[2]

The Nye Committee clearly perceived that industrialized warfare created qualitatively new and ominous problems for the nation. To fight a modern war, even to prepare for one, eroded the barriers between private and public, civilian and military institutions. The Committee observed that during hostilities "[p]ractically every important industry in the country is necessary for the supply of the armed forces." "[E]ven in time of peace," the Committee reported, "the line of demarkation between the munitions industry and other industries is not clear and fixed."

From its investigation of interwar defense spending, the Committee established that various industries depended upon military contracts for profitable operations and that the military services depended upon them for developing and producing weapons. There were many prime examples. Shipbuilding indirectly included "the steel companies, the electrical manufacturing groups, the boiler producers, the instrument people," and "the biggest banking interests in the Nation." Du Pont and other munitions producers were virtual adjuncts of the war department. Industrialists and military leaders regarded their interests as mutual. Industry favored and worked for increased military appropriations; the armed services granted industry special favors, encouraged monopoly where it served their interests, financed research, and, despite legislation to the contrary, displayed little concern about profit restraints. Committee members were shocked to find that the war and navy departments, and even the commerce and state departments at times, cooperated with munitions firms in a manner that compromised national policies for disarmament, arms limitation, arms sales, and arms embargoes. The fact that Public Works Administration funds, intended to stimulate industrial recovery, went to the armed services and that some businessmen favored defense spending as an antidote to the depression also disturbed Nye and his colleagues.

The Nye Committee found a web of personal as well as contractual ties binding industrial-military elements. Retired army and navy officers often joined firms contracting with the services. Frequently, officials of corporations supplying the armed services became reserve officers. A society like the Army Ordnance Association, organized in 1919, combined in its membership actual or potential military contractors and retired and active army officers. The Association lobbied for the army, participated in the industrial mobilization planning, and attempted to influence war department policies and the selection and promotion of personnel.[3]

The Nye Committee carefully avoided charges of conspiracy. It pointed out that plausible reasons existed for what was done and stated that it was not drawing a one-to-one correlation between expenditures for defense and the causation of war. Nevertheless, argued the Committee,

> any close associations between munitions and supply companies . . . and the service departments . . . , of the kind that existed in Germany before the World War, constitutes an unhealthy alliance in that it brings into being a self-interested political power which operates in the name of patriotism and satisfies interests which are, in large part, purely selfish, and that such associations are an inevitable part of militarism, and are to be avoided in peacetime at all costs.

In order to check the growth of an "unhealthy alliance," a majority of the Committee favored nationalizing the munitions facilities. Congress never seriously considered the proposal. Upon the advice of the Roosevelt administration, Congress even refused to strengthen regulations governing military procurement as the Committee minority recommended.

The army's economic planning for war also disturbed the Nye Committee. The planning, argued the Committee, assured that industry and the military would function more effectively as a team than they had in World War I; but, because the "Industrial Mobilization Plan" was patterned after wartime methods, it would not eliminate the "economic evils of war." According to the Committee's analysis, World War I mobilization was accompanied by "shameless profiteering" and extravagant waste. The war left a legacy of inflation, debt, and increased concentration of economic power. Similar results would occur in a future war if industry, in conjunction with the armed services, virtually regulated itself.[4]

In order to secure the nation's economic future and to remove the promise of riches as an inducement to war, the Nye Committee maintained that wartime "economic evils" had to be eliminated. That required radical changes in the economic system during hostilities, not the preservation of the status quo as proposed by the "Industrial Mobilization Plan." The profit motive and the prerogatives of private property would have to be modified. To accomplish that purpose, the Committee supported legislation drafted under the direction of John T. Flynn. In an emergency, profits would be limited to 3 per cent and personal annual income to $10,000. No individual with direct or indirect interests in an industry could serve in a government capacity involving that industry. Moreover, the President would be granted vast authority over the economy to the point of conscripting capital and management if necessary. Although vague at many points, the Flynn legislation amounted to a proposal for state capitalism during wartime with the industrial managers removed from the seats of power.

The war department opposed the Committee's major recommendations. It viewed with alarm any taxation proposals that threatened production. It maintained that conscripting management would not work and insisted that economic mobilization was impossible without the assistance of managers of the industries to be regulated. Baruch responded to the proposed bill with undisguised hostility. Attempting to change the economic system during a war, he argued, was an invitation to disaster.

In its most impressive reports, the Nye Committee curiously agreed with both the war department and Baruch. The Committe's support of the Flynn proposals ignored its own findings. Without constitutional amendments that could be "far worse than the situation of profiteering in a national emergency," the Flynn legislation could not be enforced. The Committee recognized that, even if the bill and the necessary amendments were adopted, they would probably be repealed or ignored in an emergency. The only men qualified to administer a wartime economy were industrialists themselves. It was inconceivable that they would attempt to enforce laws they considered detrimental to the economy and to the war effort.

The Flynn bill was introduced into Congress in 1935. For a time, Franklin D. Roosevelt seemed disposed toward the bill. Ultimately, he joined Baruch, the war department, and, with reservations, the Legion in backing competing legislation that would have granted the President authority for mobilizing the economy, but with few safeguards against abuse. That bill would have sanctioned what the "Industrial Mobilization Plan" proposed. The administration let it be known that it, too, believed that curtailing the profit motive during a war would jeopardize any mobilization program. No legislation was passed.

After the Nye Committee investigation, the nation knew more about the political economy of warfare; but short of avoiding war and excessive spending for defense, there was no viable way to prevent close and compromising relations between business and the armed services. Military spending in the American industrial system inevitably drew industrial and military elements together, and the threat of an "unhealthy alliance" was always present.

War department planning entered its final and most important phase after the Nye Committee investigation. With the approach of war and the growing American preparedness movement, the department launched a drive for the appointment of a joint industry-military board to review and ultimately to implement the "Industrial Mobilization Plan."

The proposal for a joint board originated with civilians who were concerned about a major flaw in the "Industrial Mobilization Plan." Because of a continuing distrust of civilian institutions, the army determined to dominate the wartime mobilization agencies. To insure that OASW plans were realistic and to keep the nation ready for war, Baruch and others repeatedly recommended that industrialists officially meet each year with the war department. They would review the department's plans and prepare themselves for the eventuality of official duty.

The war department resisted suggestions for officially sharing its planning authority with industrialists until Louis Johnson, a past American Legion commander, became assistant secretary of war in June 1937. With international relations deteriorating, Johnson was determined to prepare both the army and the nation for war. He arranged for Baruch, some former WIB members, and younger talent to serve as an advisory board to OASW. For Johnson, that was the first essential step for instituting the "Industrial Mobilization Plan." But the President refused to sanction the scheme. Despite the setback, Johnson was determined to create an advisory board. He was stealthily maneuvering to achieve that end in mid-1939, when Roosevelt, fearing that war was imminent and that the nation might become involved, authorized Johnson to set up a mobilization advisory group called the War Resources Board (WRB). Roosevelt chose Edward R. Stettinius, Jr., of United States Steel Corporation as chairman and left the selection of other members to the war department. With Stettinius serving as an intermediary, Johnson, Acting Secretary of the Navy Charles Edison, Army Chief of Staff George Marshall, and two senior members of OASW selected the others. In addition to Stettinius, WRB included Gifford, president of American Telephone and Telegraph; John Lee Pratt of General Motors Corporation; Robert E. Wood, chairman of Sears, Roebuck, and Company; Karl T. Compton of the Massachusetts Institute of Technology; and Harold G. Moulton, president of the Brookings Institute. The membership was cleared with the President. Why Baruch was excluded is still unclear. He was described as being "sore as hell" about being passed over. WRB did not get his blessing until his close associate, John Hancock, was appointed to it in September. Hancock played a prominent role in WRB proceedings.

Assistant Secretary of War Johnson announced to the nation that WRB would review the "Industrial Mobilization Plan" of 1939, revise it if necessary, and implement it in an emergency. Key to the plan was the War Resources Administration, organized along commodity committee-war service committee lines with military representatives integrated into it. Unlike earlier plans, the 1939 edition moderated proposed military influence in the civilian agencies.

Working hand in hand with the armed services, WRB, while still reviewing the "Industrial Mobilization Plan," began preparing to institute it. In sharp contrast to its attitude toward WPC, the business community was eager to cooperate with WRB. The National Association of Manufacturers and the United States Chamber of Commerce rushed forward to volunteer their services. Through conferences with these organizations, former WIB members, the commerce department, and other private and public sources, WRB drew up an industrial who's who to staff the War Resources Administration and also made provisions for the use of war service committees. The most daring move was a memorandum drafted for the President's signature that would have granted the WRB and the Army-Navy Munitions Board authority to mobilize the economy and that instructed all government agencies to cooperate with those two boards.

Roosevelt suddenly cut the ground from under WRB shortly after its creation because the war scare had waned and because of widespread opposition within the administration and the nation to it. Liberal Democrats were aghast at the dominant position held by the major banking and industrial interests in WRB. They identified Stettinius, Gifford, and Pratt with J. P. Morgan. The anti-Morgan banking elements on Wall Street who were sympathetic to the administration were bitterly disappointed. Labor and agriculture were irate over their exclusion.

The President waited until WRB had completed reviewing the "Industrial Mobilization Plan" and had submitted a final report in November 1939 before dismissing it. In its final report, WRB indirectly endorsed the war department plan and fully accepted its basic assumptions. A wartime economy should be regulated by federal agencies largely controlled by industry and the military services. In circumscribed terms, WRB recommended the suspension of the antitrust laws and also suggested that domestic reform would be a casualty of a mobilized economy. It further proposed that the Army-Navy Munitions Board, through consultation with industry, continue to explore the yet unresolved issues of industrial mobilization. It concluded by offering its advisory services for the future.[5] Roosevelt thanked WRB members and never called on them again.

WRB's fate did not negate the years of planning. Because of this planning, the war department adjusted to emergency conditions during World War II with relative ease. In the late 1930s the department began a gradual transition from planning for, to participating in, a mobilization program. Starting in 1937–1938, Congress, after years of departmental advocacy, authorized educational orders and the stock-piling of essential and strategic raw materials and slowly modified peacetime restraints on military contracting.[6] As the army and military budgets grew, OASW expanded its staff and activities proportionately until the mobilization stage was reached in 1940–1941. Whiting in mid-1940, Assistant Secretary of War Johnson observed: "Without the benefit of plans perfected by 20 years of study the successful and timely execution of this [expanded munitions] program would have been virtually impossible."

When the war department began the transition to mobilization in 1937–1938, it also launched the drive for implementing the "Industrial Mobilization Plan"; it had been convinced by the years of planning that civilian mobilization agencies were essential for fulfilling the military mission. During 1940–1941, the Army-Navy Munitions Board played a more active role in mobilizing the economy than the army plans had envisaged. But that was the case principally because the civilian agencies were weak. After WRB's demise, the Roosevelt administration relied upon the resuscitated NDAC and other agencies that were totally inadequate for mobilization. War department officials were in the vanguard of those working for more effective civilian agencies until the creation in early 1942 of the War Production Board.

Throughout the years 1940–1941, the war department, and the navy department as well, sided with industry on most major policies involving economic mobilization. After war was declared, the nation's largest corporations and the armed forced ultimately dominated the War Production Board through an alliance of mutual interests. Though officially rejected in 1939, the principal proposals concurred in by WRB and the military were adopted during World War II. As foreseen by the Nye Committee and others, relations between the business community and the armed services during World War I and the interwar period prepared the way for the full-blown "industrial-military complex" of World War II and the Cold War years.

NOTES

1. The War Department's participation in NRA resulted directly from OASW planning.
2. The Nye Committee findings although not all of its recommendations, received the unanimous endorsement of all members.
3. "Preliminary Report . . . on Investigation of the Munitions Industry," No. 944, Part 1, pp. 220–21; "Report . . . on Investigation of the Munitions Industry," No. 944, Part 3, pp. 10–11, 159–217; Senate, *Hearings Before the Special Committee Investigating the Munitions Industry,* Part 36, pp. 11972–12043; Part 37, pp. 12399–443, 12501–28, 12766. Concern existed about military contractors employing retired officers before World War I. "To Increase the Efficiency of the Military Establishment of the United States," House, *Hearings before the Committee on Military Affairs,* 64 Cong., 1 Sess., 1916, pp. 540–42, 1147–48, 1153–55; "Army Appropriations Bill, [Fiscal] 1917," House, *Hearings before the Committee on Military Affairs,* 64 Cong., 1 Sess., 1916, pp. 848–50.
4. "Preliminary Report . . . on Investigation of the Munitions Industry," No. 944, Part 1, pp. 345–89; "Report on War Department Bills S.1716-S.1722 . . . ," 74 Cong., 2 Sess., No. 944, Part 4, p. 1–46 (direct quotations, 7, 11), 57–61; "Report on Government Manufacture of Munitions . . . ," No. 944, Part 7, pp. 3–64; "To Prevent Profiteering in War," *Senate Report,* 74 Cong., 1 Sess., No. 577 (Serial 9879), 9–20. See also Senate, *Hearings Before the Special Committee Investigating the Munitions Industry,* Parts 13, 14, 15, 16, 17, 21, 22, 24, 36, 37. The Nye Committee was less critical of World War I military procurement practices than an earlier investigation by the so-called Graham Committee. See "War Expenditures," House, *Hearings before the Select Committee on Expenditure in the War Department,* 66 Cong., 1

Sess., Vol. 3, 1921 (Serial 1), [Reports of Committee]; *ibid.*, Vol. 1, 1921 (Serial 1); *ibid.*, 1920 (Serial 3).

5. "Report of the War Resources Board," Oct. 13, 1939, File No. 334.117.3, PB ASW Office of the Secretary of War. The Army-Navy Munitions Board (ANMB) was reorganized and strengthened in 1931–1932, and the "IMP" was published by ANMB even though OASW continued to do most of the work.

6. Educational orders were intended to help industry and the army through the transitional phase from planning to mobilizing for war. Without the restrictions of competitive bidding, the army could award contracts to selected firms for the limited production of various munitions items. In that way, industry accumulated the tools and worked out the techniques for quantity production and the army tested its munitions designs and procurement plans. Educational orders were first introduced before World War I at the instigation of business-men and public officials striving to prepare the nation for hostilities. For years after the war, Congress rejected bills authorizing educational orders. Before such legislation was passed in the late 1930s, however, the army interpreted the laws and regulations governing procurement in a way that allowed it to grant some educational orders to selected firms. During the 1930s, the businessmen in the Army Ordance Association launched a drive for educational orders to help stimulate industrial recovery.

Origins of a Welfare State   PAUL CONKIN

The Old Left was divided over the New Deal. Many Socialists considered it a sham or at best a palliative for the serious ills of capitalism. Much of the Progressive Left supported it, seeing it as the fulfillment of the Progressive impulse of the period before the First World War. The Communists blew first cold, then hot, as Soviet foreign policy switched from support for international revolution to the "Popular Front" of Liberals and Marxists against Fascism.

The historians of the New Deal have overwhelmingly been intense partisans of the movement they have described. They may have reservations about Roosevelt's opportunism, his deceptiveness, his lack of imagination, and his inconsistency. As late as the eve of World War II, they generally acknowledge the failure of New Deal recovery efforts. But they have nothing but praise for the reform program that constituted the Welfare State. Given the realities of America during the 1930s, and given the strong tradition of laissez-faire, they find the New Deal's achievements little short of revolutionary. Of all the reform movements that have left their mark on the country, the New Deal seems to have made the most difference in the lives of the average man.

The New Left, at the very least, is impatient with the New Deal. So much of what modern America is, was started in the New Deal years, and much of the New Left's disaffection from our own era permeates their thinking about the 1930s. At least as important is the extent to which Roosevelt and his supporters blunted the edge of real institutional change. The sick nation got a pain-killer rather than a cure and the opportunity for structural innovation was lost. The following selection by Paul Conkin is a harsh critique of Roosevelt and the movement he led. The author is a man of the Left who is unmoved by the liberal pieties of most New Deal historians.

Source: Paul Conkin, *The New Deal* (New York: Thomas Y. Crowell Company, 1967), chap. iii, "Origins of a Welfare State," pp. 53–82.

FOR FURTHER READING:

William E. Leuchtenberg, *Franklin Roosevelt and the New Deal**, (Harper Torchbooks, 1963); Arthur Schlesinger, Jr., *The Coming of the New Deal,* (Houghton Mifflin, 1959); Arthur Schlesinger, Jr., *The Politics of Upheaval,* (Houghton Mifflin, 1960); Howard Zinn, (editor) *New Deal Thought**, (Bobbs Merrill, 1966); Barton Bernstein, "The New Deal: The Conservative Achievements of Liberal Reform," in Barton Bernstein (editor) *Towards a New Past: Dissenting Essays in American History**, (Pantheon, 1969); Jerold S. Auerbach, "New Deal, Old Deal or Raw Deal: Some Thoughts on New Left Historiography," *Journal of Southern History,* (February, 1969).

Asterisk denotes paperback edition.

The misery of depression multiplied the need for public welfare. The Democratic sweep in the election of 1934 created a favorable political climate for new federal action. Several New Deal agency heads had already worked out ambitious programs and waited hopefully for funds. Mounting public pressure, often fanned by nostrum-peddling demagogues, helped mute established inhibitions. The Court deathblow to the N.R.A. in 1935, plus congressional pressures, forced Roosevelt to seek a new labor policy, while bitter attacks from a majority of businessmen so angered him that he gladly turned to the working classes for political support. Finally, a growing number of his advisers accepted a monetary, budgetary approach to a still elusive recovery and thus welcomed the deficits involved in large relief programs. These pressures all converged on Congress in 1935, producing a new body of legislation that, with almost unbelievable speed, launched the American welfare state, a brand new, large, ungainly infant, destined to survive all the hazards of childhood and a maladjusted adolescence, eventually to mature in the Great Society, still ugly but increasingly popular.

The term "welfare state" has many connotations, accompanied by degrees of emotional approval or distaste. To a few Americans it is an antonym of freedom, a synonym of socialism, a repudiation of responsibility, a catalyst of character decline and civilization's rot. To others it connotes halfway, palliative measures, mere sops to the exploited in behalf of preserving privilege and unfair advantage. Rooted in the conservatism of a Bismarck, it is the complete antithesis of socialism. To a much larger group, it is an imperfect but necessary compromise between various contending forces and is thus the middle way, the moderate answer. Despite all the bitterness of the thirties, or even of the sixties, a type of welfare capitalism has become the established system in America, approved by a substantial majority of the voters. It is now conventional and orthodox, however much bolstered by an effective political appeal that still makes it sound progressive and daring, which it really never was.

In a loose way, everyone favors enhancing the general welfare. The problem is one of means. In the American past the key term was always opportunity, with a type of disciplined freedom closely connected. Governments had a crucial role— protecting and extending opportunity. In this sense, every good state was a welfare state. In a free society, with beckoning opportunities, with no special privileges, each individual or cooperative effort to take advantage of existing opportunities was conceived as a lesson in responsibility, as an inducement to good character, and as a fulfilling experience. Such a simple but profound faith lay at the moralistic heart of American politics. Private property, meaning the actual means of production, and free enterprise, meaning the private right to manage these means, were indispensable elements in this faith. In fact, they were at the heart of a moral society. Everyone should have an opportunity to own and manage, or at least to share in the owning and management, of productive property. But, to repeat a truism, the faith survived but not the sustaining environment. There was never as much opportunity as the faith presumed. By 1930 only a few people could own and manage property. In this sense opportunity disappeared. But an ersatz type of opportunity —to work for other men, to sell one's labor to those who did own and manage property—replaced an earlier dream of farm or shop, along with an ersatz type of property—common stock, or claims on profits but no real role in management. In the depression even these poor substitutes paled. Up to fifteen million family heads could find no market for their labor and had to turn either to private or public charity.

This simplified analysis helps clarify the welfare state under Roosevelt and the mixed reception to it. Some welfare measures directed at better opportunity, such as education, had been urged by Jefferson and long since provided by state governments, although Emerson first asked the vital question—opportunity for what, for ownership and enterprise, for responsibility, involvement, and fulfilment, or just opportunity for productive employment. In the New Deal, some legislation, typified by the Farm Tenancy Act of 1937, was directed, realistically or not, at the old Jeffersonian idea of true property and true enterprise, at restored opportunity in the most sweeping sense. This was paralleled by what seemed a considerable, even devastating attack on entrenched privilege, on monopolistic wealth, on concentrated economic power, on unfair rules in the market place. At this point the New Deal was most traditional, not only reechoing the rhetoric of progressivism but of Puritanism. The idea of broad opportunity, the sense of moral responsibility, was an older and deeper orthodoxy than *laissez faire*, as such a conventional American, such an able politician, as Roosevelt always sensed. But much of the welfare legislation of the thirties was of a different sort. Simply, it was a "take-care-of" type of welfare. The federal government undertook numerous programs to succor the unemployed, the elderly, and the exploited, by direct relief, by work programs, and by regulative laws that forced employers to be more generous.

The most penetrating criticism of government charity came from Jeffersonians and socialists. To such an old Jeffersonian liberal as Herbert Hoover, the assumption of direct responsibility for the individual by any government, and particularly by a distant federal government, endangered the whole idea of personal responsibility and misconstrued the area of responsibility rightly reserved for government. Sustained gifts from governments would create a passive, alienated group of men, without a real stake in society, with no compelling involvement, and with a dangerous political tendency to march in step with any demagogue promising more welfare. He always insisted that the long-range welfare of the individual could only be served by his active, creative participation in our private economy, and not by accepting some dole, concealed or not. Thus welfare was a dangerous answer to depression; recovery and restored opportunity the only legitimate, long-term answer.

On the socialist left, the most astute critics agreed. But, unlike Hoover they did not expect to solve the problems of depression by restoring the business society of the twenties. They felt that welfare measures obscured the continued injustices of capitalism, thus allaying the rightful demands for economic justice. Welfare, by stilling the voice of dissent, and by stimulating consumption and higher profits, represented a type of government insurance for a capitalist economy. Even if there were some leveling of wealth, some truly progressive taxes, there could be no true opportunity. Instead of aid to the unemployed, the existing economic system should be replaced by one that not only guaranteed employment but that gave to all citizens some sense of personal involvement and some share in ownership and management. These socialists, whether Christians, Marxists, or pragmatists, still had the vision of a co-operative commonwealth.

But the battle over welfare legislation, then or now, usually did not revolve around fundamental issues. On one level the advocacy or opposition was framed in light of immediate economic interest. This included both those who asked "What can I get?" as well as those who cried "What will it cost me?" The battle of interests was clothed in the folklore of our society, in the myths accepted by millions of people. Thus, the verbal icons of Jefferson were wrapped tightly around the most unpalatable injustices and the most transparent privileges. The old clichés of populism and progressivism, stripped of their real meanings, were used to oversimplify the very complexities that demanded thought and laborious action.

The welfare legislation of 1935, or the second hundred days, has occasioned critical divergence among historians. Raymond Moley first condemned Roosevelt for deserting a true concert of interests and for discontinuing early co-operative overtures to business. To him, the new welfare measures, joined with the class appeals in the campaign of 1936, represented a demagogic radicalism and a betrayal of all Roosevelt's early promises. In a loose way, most other historians, including textbook authors, have accepted Moley's contention that Roosevelt moved to the "left" in 1935, but, often reflecting a lingering progressive bias, they have usually approved of the shift. Tugwell reversed the judgment, as had contemporary socialist critics. He agreed with Moley that Roosevelt had gone progressive, probably for political rather than ideological reasons. But he denied that it was a legitimate turn to the left, condemning it as a conservative (i.e., progressive) betrayal of the concert of interests, which he defined in terms of planning rather than of Moley's partnership with business. For Tugwell, the old progressive rhetoric, however radical it sounded, was only political nonsense employed to disguise tthe return of America to private manipulators. Schlesinger, with some sympathy for Tugwell's position, sympathized with the more practical expedients pursued by Roosevelt and his new, Brandeisian advisers. He thus described the New Deal as moving to the left politically, economically to the right of Tugwell's planning concepts, but not necessarily to the right of early New Deal programs.

The largest welfare program of the New Deal, and of American history, began in 1935. A newly elected, exceedingly generous Congress approved a $4,880,000,-000 Emergency Relief Appropriation, to be spent as Roosevelt saw fit. This was, up until this time, the largest appropriation in American history and the largest accretion to the national debt. It was used to consolidate and expand numerous early, temporary relief programs, which had served up to thirty million people. About $1,500,000,000, the largest single block, went to Harry Hopkins and to a new relief organization created by executive order, the huge Works Progress Administration (W.P.A.). In turn, the W.P.A. used most of its share, plus endless new appropriations, for work programs for the unemployed. At times its projects resembled those of the more reputable P.W.A., even as a favored Hopkins cut into what Ickes believed should have been his share of the appropriation. Against the wishes of congressional liberals, W.P.A. wages were generally scaled below those of private industry, and anyone offered private employment became ineligible for W.P.A. work. Burdened by a lack of developed plans for massive public works, by an oversupply of unskilled laborers, and by rigid rules, the W.P.A. was inefficient by any private standard. Nonetheless, the completed projects in part compensated for the money spent and represented a great gain over direct doles. Despite vigorous efforts to maintain high morale, and despite the sincere appreciation of most workers, the W.P.A. could not escape some of the stigma of relief. In fact, derisive opponents would not let it. Also, the W.P.A. could only employ about a third of those who needed work, leaving millions to the care or neglect of states. Many had to remain on a dole, often supplemented by free food distributed by a Federal Surplus Commodities Corporation.

Less expensive and more daring were the several white collar programs set up by the W.P.A., drawing upon earlier experiences of the C.W.A. and some State Relief Administrations. For the first time in American history, the federal government gave a vast subsidy to some of the fine arts and to scholarship (Federal Theater, Federal Writers', and Federal Art projects). Much of the art, particularly plays, sculpture, and painting, reflected the social concern of the thirties. The most rewarding aspect of these programs was the degree of participation. Music, painting, and the theater, usually frivolous sideshows of the wealthy, centered in a few large cities and priced beyond the common people, were now merged with daily life, in murals on public buildings, in local symphonies, in amateur theaters. Just as important, thousands of people were able to participate in creative endeavors, including handicrafts. Another subagency, the National Youth Administration, directed by Hopkins' assistant, Aubrey Williams, inaugurated a vast scholarship program under the guise of student work, and set up work projects for school dropouts.

A second large block of the relief appropriation went to Rexford G. Tugwell, who headed another new agency, the Resettlement Administration (R.A.). It absorbed the rural relief and rehabilitation programs of the old F.E.R.A. and the uncompleted communities of the Division of Subsistence Homesteads. Tugwell had more plans than funds. As the title suggests, he wanted to resettle urban slum dwellers in autonomous garden cities and submarginal farmers in new, productive farm villages, with co-operation a guiding concern of both groups. His greatest monuments were three suburban greenbelt cities and a few dozen new farm communities. The largest share of his funds had to be used to continue a rural relief program. One of the liberals disillusioned with the failure of the A.A.A. to become an instrument of rural reform, and long contemptuous of the Extension Service, Tugwell set up a duplicate farm organization, with its own agents, but dedicated only to the exploited and underprivileged.

The R.A. would not compromise with existing evils. Almost alone, it fought for equal benefits for Negroes. It was the only New Deal agency to set up group medical plans. Contrary to the idols of Congress and to the ruling commitment of the Department of Agriculture, R.A. leaders questioned fee simple ownership and experimented both with long-term leases and co-operative farms. Concerned with farm labor, it set up migratory camps and tried to alleviate the plight of the "Okies." But in most cases it loaned funds to small farmers for needed equipment or vital necessities and then supervised their farm program, protected them from exploitation, and took a percentage of their crops as repayment. The R.A. became a new, solicitous bank for small landowners and a second, protective landlord for tenants. It was not only one of the most honest but probably the most class-conscious of New Deal agencies. Soon it antagonized practically every vested interest, a good mark of its relative effectiveness. Yet its funds permitted it only to touch the problems of rural areas, particularly in the South. With restricted prerogatives, plus a tenant-purchase program at odds with its earlier orientation, the R.A. moved into the Department of Agriculture in 1937 and became the Farm Security Administration (F.S.A.). Congress gleefully destroyed it during the war, replacing it with an attenuated Farmers' Home Administration.

The Social Security Act of 1935 became the supreme symbol of a welfare state. As enacted, it hardly deserved the honor or opprobrium. At most, it set some enduring precedents and established a new area of federal responsibility. As shown by Edwin E. Witte [*Development of the Social Security Act* (Madison, 1962)], the bill was tremendously complex, compromising many divergent plans and establishing an array of welfare programs. Although not responsible for the details of the act, Roosevelt had worked for better old age benefits and for unemployment insurance while governor of New York. As early as 1934 he signed a Railroad Retirement Act. In the same year, he witnessed the growing frustration of the under-privileged classes, who had so far reaped a bitter pill in New Deal recovery programs. With unfulfilled expectations, revolutionary feelings grew even faster than in 1932. Various movements, often roughly but arbitrarily classed to the right and left, gained vast public support. Two of these, led by Huey Long and Francis E. Townsend, focused on the extremes of wealth in America and proffered schemes for either sharing the wealth (Long) or providing elaborate pensions for the elderly (Townsend). Naive or oversimplified, their platforms revivified the old problem of Henry George—great wealth and great poverty. Roosevelt, as a good politician, saw the tremendous political appeal of legislation directed at the elderly and unemployed and thus joined his support to that of congressional authors. Even most Republicans, with apprehensive glances over their left shoulders and aware of the mildness of the final version, supported the bill.

The Social Security Act set up the present compulsory tax for retirement benefits, a tax assessed in equal parts on employer and employee. About half of the people were excluded by the original act, including farmers, domestics, and the elderly. The employee tax represented a significant drain from already low payrolls and thus a further obstacle to recovery. The original act did not protect against accidents and illness before retirement, provided no medical insurance, and paid benefits on the basis of past earning instead of present needs. Thus, it was close to a compulsory insurance system, paid for largely by those who benefited. The unemployment insurance provision delegated most responsibility to the states and invited chaotic variations in always inadequate payments. Since the retirement coverage was so limited, the act provided matching federal funds for traditional state pensions for the aged and funds for dependent mothers, children, and the crippled and blind. The present public welfare system, although administered locally and almost always inadequate, is closely tied to this federal assistance.

In housing, as in retirement, the New Deal made a modest, even parsimonious, beginning. The P.W.A. could loan funds to local, limited-dividend housing corporations, for both housing projects and slum clearance. Under Ickes' watchful eyes, only a few projects were approved (less than 25,000 housing units by 1937).

The several community programs involved only limited numbers but, in the case of the greenbelt towns of the Resettlement Administration, quite imaginative experiments, not only in housing, but in community planning. But there was no follow-up. Instead, beginning in 1934 the government tried to stimulate private construction, aid home buyers, and protect mortgage bankers through a loan insurance program administered by a Federal Housing Administration (F.H.A.). Since the F.H.A. assumed final responsibility for repayment (a service paid for by a tax on borrowers) and required certain standards in construction, this program helped many middle-income families buy homes at a low rate of interest. In no sense was it a federal housing program. In the thirties it did not appreciably stimulate private home building and thus failed as a recovery measure. Finally, in 1937, after years of effort by housing and urban renewal proponents, and particularly by Senator Robert F. Wagner of New York, Roosevelt agreed to support a small housing and slum-clearance program. The Wagner-Steagall Act established the United States Housing Authority as a government corporation. It had $500,000,000 to lend to state or local housing authorities. The terms were generous, with low interest and extended (sixty years) repayments. When housing projects replaced slums, annual contributions by the U.S.H.A. further subsidized the program. Federal rules required rents well below competitive rates and limited residency to low-income families. The first results, under local direction, were almost universally ugly and depressing developments, segregated, stigmatized by origin and by residency requirements, resented by local citizens, and located in the worst sections of town.

Relief, unemployment insurance, and low-income housing all represented tangible, if limited, benefits for the working class. Roosevelt wanted to help farmers and laborers gain minimal economic security as part of their American birthright. He did not easily move beyond this commitment. Paternal business, if paternal enough, seemed adequate. Early in his Presidency, he easily co-operated with businessmen who shared his humane concern and in several cases sided with business in labor-management disputes. Thus, until 1935 he was clearly pro-agriculture, even pro-labor, but not pro-union. But events pushed him into the camp of the labor unions. Section 7 (a) of the N.I.R.A., if liberally interpreted, was indeed the long-awaited Magna Carta of organized labor. In part frustrated by company unions, never given adequate protection by the N.R.A. staff, the American Federation of Labor nonetheless acted as if it were a Magna Carta and began large organizational drives. In 1934, strikes erupted throughout the country, often directed by labor radicals rather than by the conservative A.F.L. From the impetus of the strikes came the revolutionary rise of industrial unions, the schism of 1935, and the vitality and political effectiveness of the new Congress of Industrial Organizations. Militant unionism had its golden age in the thirties. As a whole, union workers loved and supported Roosevelt, while business leaders reviled him. With the death of N.R.A., Roosevelt had to choose a new labor policy. He belatedly chose the side of the unions. They had votes and loved a Roosevelt willing to show some interest in their problems.

If 7(a) was the Magna Carta, the National Labor Relations Act of 1935 (Wagner Act) was the bill of rights for unions. It involved an almost unbelievable capitulation by the government. The architect of the bill, Senator Wagner, served as chairman of the National Labor Board under the N.R.A. Frustrated by the business-oriented leadership of Hugh Johnson, the Board has limited success in protecting workers. In 1934 Roosevelt established a National Labor Relations Board (N.L.R.B.) as a separate, but rather futile, agency which still had to utilize the statutory provisions of the N.I.R.A. As a result, Wagner fought, without Roosevelt's blessings, for new statutory authority and a new, more powerful N.L.R.B. His bill passed the Senate without Administration support, and then with it breezed through the House. The bill guaranteed the right of collective bargaining by a union chosen by a majority of employees, legalized collective action (strikes, boycotts), and by a code of fair practices outlawed such traditional weapons as the company union, blacklist, and yellow-dog contract. The act empowered a new N.L.R.B. to conduct representation elections and hear any complaints from unions. Big labor, in one sweep, almost gained equality with big business. But for the majority of workers, as yet unorganized, the Wagner Act was less important than Social Security. Tied to the interstate commerce clause, it did not protect the bargaining rights of public employees, service and agricultural workers, and workers in strictly intrastate commerce.

The welfare legislation, large in hopes generated, often pitifully small in actual benefits, hardly represented a social revolution. Except for relief, only a small burden had been added to the national budget, and none of the welfare programs significantly redistributed the wealth of the country. Not only Huey Long, but politicians of varied persuasions wanted to lessen disparities of income and accumulated wealth. Some progressives, led by Brandeis and like foes of centralized power, also wanted to help restore competition by placing a tax burden on bigness. Roosevelt, enraged by hostile newspapers and by business criticism, increasingly advised by Felix Frankfurter (then at the Harvard Law School and a Brandeis disciple), and always thirsting for a good fight, presented Congress with a new and biting tax proposal in the spring of 1935. It had two purposes: a fairer sharing of the tax burden and penalities on large enterprise. The bill, soon labeled a "soak-the-rich" measure, provoked an embittered controversy. It marked the most decisive turn by Roosevelt from consensus politics to a clear appeal to the disinherited. The tax message rested on the depressing fact that, so far, New Deal policies had created a more regressive tax system, with greater burdens on consumption and low incomes than on large incomes. Large corporations had used the depression to reduce debts and to increase their liquid capital, even while suffering operating losses, suspending dividends, and thus avoiding taxes. Also, then as now, large incomes escaped existing tax schedules by loopholes and avoidance.

Roosevelt asked for a graduated corporate income tax, a separate intercorporate dividend tax to prevent an escape via subsidiary companies, an inheritance and gift tax, and a more sharply graduated income tax. His message to Congress was loaded with encomium for small enterprise and diatribes against business concentration and large accumulations of wealth. In Congress, Roosevelt, who never pushed the tax bill as strenuously as the other legislation, suffered a mild defeat. Only a token corporate income tax passed. The inheritance tax was dropped. In all, small tax increases produced only $250,000,000 in annual revenue. The bill neither soaked the rich, penalized bigness, or significantly helped balance the budget. A later (1936) tax on undistributed dividends and excess profits was likewise attentuated and subsequently repealed. Thus, tax policy was not to play an important role in New Deal economic policy, at least beyond the realm of rhetoric and psychological warfare.

But the battle against bigness became a standard New Deal brand. Not that it ever achieved significant results. That was impossible. The emphasis shifted only after the demise of the N.R.A. In crucial industries like coal, petroleum, and the retail trades, with many small producers, the federal government almost of necessity continued an N.R.A. type of detailed regulation and protection under new, more carefully drafted legislation. In industries dominated by a few large producers, the collusion and accommodation once again became a private, in part clandestine operation, while Roosevelt's avowed policy was free competition, the prosecution of monopoly, and concessions to small business. Under Thurman Arnold, beginning in 1938, the Antitrust Division of the Department of Justice expanded its operations to the highest level in history, perhaps as much for punitive reasons as for restored competition or, as even Arnold suggested, as a type of folk ritual that at least pointed to the ultimate superiority of government over the corporations.

The most vulnerable area of chaotic and wasteful bigness was in the electrical utilities, where operating companies were often controlled by pyramiding holding companies. In the wake of the T.V.A. battles, here were identified political devils. With some glee, Roosevelt asked Congress to pass a Public Utilities Holding Company Act, which would empower the S.E.C. to simplify and rationalize the holding companies to make geographic and economic sense and to abolish those without economic justification (the "death sentence"). It also authorized the Federal Power Commission to integrate, under federal controls, operating companies into regional systems. All hell broke loose. Led by able apologists like Wendell Willkie, and by less ethical lobbyists by the hundreds, the utility companies spent a billion dollars to defeat or emasculate the bill. As its first direct slap at Roosevelt, Congress amended the death sentence amid turbulent accusations of unfair lobbying and unfair Administration pressure, both true.

The private utilities won a minor battle, not a war. They still faced severe regulation. Also, in line with T.V.A., the Administration added vast public power projects at Grand Coulee and Hoover dams and tried for years to get additional valley authorities. In 1935, under the Emergency Relief Appropriation, Roosevelt set up a Rural Electrification Administration (R.E.A.), which could not construct rural power facilities but which used low-interest loans in an unsuccessful attempt to encourage private companies to serve rural areas. In 1936 Congress made the R.E.A. into an independent lending agency, against a last, vengeful outpouring of vituperation from private power companies. The R.E.A. provided low-interest loans to rural co-operatives, which built their own lines and either manufactured or purchased their own power. It became one of the most successful of New Deal agencies, providing not only low-cost power to remote areas but valuable lessons in co-operation and local democracy.

The welfare measures and the battle against bigness were also related to the old problem of recovery. Since the largest welfare expenditures came from the borrowed appropriation of 1935, they provided a direct stimulus to increased consumption. But this stimulus was at least in part balanced by the insecurity of businessmen, who saw terrible apostasy in most relief measures and apocalyptic doom in the holding company and tax proposals. Roosevelt still yearned for a balanced budget but justified deficits on humane grounds. Several new advisers, such as Thomas Corcoran, a boyish but intellectually quick protégé of Frankfurter, seemed more concerned with penalizing big business than in achieving recovery. But one New

Deal official, Marriner Eccles, a competent Utah economist and banker, viewed the depression very much as Keynes and worked assiduously for banking and spending policies conducive to recovery (which necessitated, among other things, an increase in business activity). More than anyone except Tugwell (who left the New Deal at the end of 1936), Eccles offered economic advice that, though much more pro-business, was logical and coherent. As new head of the Federal Reserve System, Eccles drafted the Banking Act of 1935 in order to give the Federal Reserve complete control over credit.

The original Federal Reserve Act set up a dual banking system, in part centralized, in part local, in part federal, in part private. Early New Deal legislation made private banking more ethical, protected depositors, but did not change the basic system or fully rescue central banking from private and local control. Before 1933 the Federal Reserve Board had no real control over credit. The one technique, the rediscount rate, was controlled by the twelve regional banks. The rediscount rate, or interest charged member banks for discounting eligible securities, in large part determined the over-all interest rate, and therefore the cost of enlarging the monetary supply. Rediscounting at Federal Reserve banks is simply a way of creating new credit (or new money), limited only by canons of eligibility, minimal reserve requirements, and, subject to statutory change, the government reserve of gold. The Thomas Amendment to the A.A.A., which authorized the gold experiments, also gave the Federal Reserve Board, in times of declared emergencies, control over the reserve requirements of member banks (the percentage of total deposits that have to be held in liquid assets). Eccles wanted to complete this trend.

The main section of his bill, as eventually passed, reorganized the Federal Reserve System and gave the new board of governors (still headed by Eccles) control over an Open Market Committee, which could buy and sell government securities as a direct, quick stimulant to credit expansion or retraction, a function, formerly performed only by the New York Reserve Bank. It broadened the classification of eligible paper and gave the board a veto over rediscount rates, power to veto the selection of presidents and vice presidents of the twelve reserve banks, and, within set limits, permanent control over reserve requirements. Except in detail, these changes conformed to Eccles' desires [see *Beckoning Frontiers, Public and Private Recollections* (New York, 1951)], but represented many face-saving amendments engineered by old Carter Glass, one of the architects of the Federal Reserve System. What Congress conspicuously deleted was a statement of policy Eccles had attached to the bill. In it he argued that the Federal Reserve Board should adopt policies to maintain business stability and to mitigate unstabilizing influences on production, trade, prices, and employment by monetary action and credit administration. This looked toward the Employment Act of 1946 and toward avowed policy today. In actual practice the Board, by open market operations, shifts in the rediscount rate, and rare changes in reserve requirements, did just this, finally bringing the supply of money and the cost of credit almost completely into the area of public policy.

By credit control the government can do a great deal to halt inflationary spirals and by lowering interest rates can even promote consumer buying in periods of mild recession. But in such deep depressions as in the thirties, central banking policies are almost useless unless supported by budgetary and tax measures or by direct controls. There simply was no demand for easy credit. Absurdly low interest rates could not induce enough buying or investment for recovery. The new Federal Reserve controls, added to the sustained incomes provided by Social Security, were good tools for fighting against another severe depression but impotent for recovery. Eccles realized this and advocated continued deficit spending, preferably on large public works projects. He lectured fellow bankers on the archaic and misinformed idea that anything but small, balanced governmental budgets would lead to inflation and eventual economic collapse. In the thirties, with surplus production and low demand, there was no real inflationary situation. Except for managed prices under the early N.R.A. and A.A.A., there was no serious price inflation in the thirties, apart from a brief, artificial spurt just before the recession of 1937. It came at the one time when government budgets were in balance.

Beginning in 1935 there was a steady upturn in almost all economic indexes. The valley of depression began to rise slowly toward the foothills of recovery, a recovery which was too often conceived in the terms of 1929, as if continued growth was unthinkable. The weaknesses were obvious. Unemployment, after declining from the peak of 1933 (twelve to fifteen million), sunk to approximately eight million and stuck there. Consumer buying remained well below 1929. The construction industries were pitifully depressed at only one-fourth the high level of 1929. The economy had achieved an equilibrium of slow growth, sustained largely by relief expenditures. Yet the old idea of a mature economy persisted. Many New Dealers, including Roosevelt, were happy with the rising charts. In the campaign of 1936 he promised to battle against the remaining ills of the economy and against the selfish men who prevented full victory, and proudly took credit for having lifted America from depression.

By 1936 the depression should have been over. "Ifs" abound: *If* businessmen in particular had understood New Deal policies and had responded in confidence rather than unreasonable fear. *If* Roosevelt had not, by 1936, turned in devastating fury upon business and thus fanned resentment and increased confusion. *If* Roosevelt, rather than using business leaders as scapegoats and merely badgering the corporations with diversionary but essentially harmless policies, had really turned toward increased federal direction and ownership. Or *if* the government, in spite of early promises of economy, had pumped such enormous sums of borrowed money into the economy that it had to respond.

By 1936 the last strategy was the going fad among intellectuals. Keynes had just published his epochal *General Theory of Employment, Interest and Money,* in which he plotted in mathematical exactitude the multiplying effects of central banking, tax, and budgetary policies on a market economy. But even large government investments were only stimulants. They could be resisted by countervailing factors that inhibited private spending. It seemed that between 1933 and 1937 the New Deal floundered between ever more daring banking and budgetary measures on one hand and ever more uncertain and stubborn business leaders on the other. Every new economic stimulant acted as a depressant on the minds of the affluent. This was aggravated by the almost total lack of dialogue between the government and business.

By 1936 the New Deal was submerged in irony. To understand this is to get at the heart of the history of the thirties and to get a much better perspective on the welfare state. At the national level, Roosevelt emerged in the clothing of a great progressive reformer. From his early attempts to understand the economic issues, from the tutelage of the brain trust, or even of the gold faddists, he moved to a firm posture—against bigness, against unearned privileges, against economic selfishness;

and for the little man, for the exploited, for good and unselfish people everywhere. To Raymond Moley, this class appeal represented a damaging radicalism. To Tugwell, it represented a false smoke screen, or a political sideshow, for concealing a turn to a very conservative economic philosophy, and with it a permanent rejection of real planning.

Both were correct. Roosevelt did move away from economic realities and into the lair of the demagogue. Of course most leaders of large businesses were selfish. But small businessmen were also selfish and by all odds more so than large ones. So were labor leaders, and, believe it or not, even farmers. The label is meaningless. Of course many selfish and shortsighted businessmen, particularly small business-men, did what they could without punishment in the pursuit of profits, even in some cases where the law forbade. So do most men. They even did it with full assurance that it was right, that the whole country gained from their daring enterprise. Not only did they do it, they would continue to do it, unless stripped of the power to do it or converted to a whole new world view that prevented it (an unlikely answer in spite of Roosevelt's sermons). But Roosevelt kept preaching his denunciatory ser-mons. He fanned the resentment of good, as well as of selfish and jealous, Americans without power and of farsighted or politically loyal ones with power. He stimulated righteous indignation and the atmosphere of a moral crusade. But the crusade could do nothing except take punitive action: divide a holding company, threaten but never collect progressive taxes, or use welfare measures to uplift the downtrodden victims of evil men.

The crusade almost always ended in some degree of futility. The battle for the "people" had to eventuate in legislation, had to pass through Roosevelt and the Congress, and then stand up in the courts. In Roosevelt's terms, every New Deal "reform" was a generous act by good men of power against bad men of power. In fact, it was usually a confused compromise by an indistinguishable mixture of good and bad men of power, with Roosevelt (abetted by many his-torians) generally finding most Republican politicians, conservative Southern Democrats, and at least four Supreme Court judges to be bad men of power, allied to numerous bad men throughout the country. But neither bad men nor good men saw much beyond the evident selfishness of their opponents. Thus, instead of recognizing real devils, or contemplating major but almost impossible changes in American institutions or in the real power structure (not the party structure), the good men either tried some mild detergent in futile efforts to clean up the existing system or tried to appease and care for those who were suffering because of its inadequacies. The good men of power were as much a part of the system as the bad men of power. They could not see that monopoly was a natural and not always harmful end result of a private market system, that negative regulation in behalf of competition would not, could not, and probably should not work, and that more biting, more stringent positive controls would be truly revolutionary, that is, would force a shift of economic and political control, and thus often threaten their own privileged positions. Even when Roosevelt, conventional in beliefs but pleasingly archaic in his gentlemanly *noblesse oblige*, or his academic advisers (presumably good men without power) framed legis-lation that had some bite, such as a pure food and drugs act or a tax reform bill, it rarely survived Congress. When an ambiguous, potentially radical program did survive, or was sneaked in by executive order, it was usually neutralized by administrators, nullified by the courts, endlessly frustrated in its day-by-day operations, or eventually destroyed or emasculated for political reasons.

The story of most New Deal frustration remains untold. The thirties was indeed a reform decade, a period when sensitivity to injustice, to vast structures of privilege, to the terribly empty life of most people, prevailed as never before. Much of the concern remained outside government, in critics of the New Deal, in radical political movements, in artists of varied mediums, in a few philosophers. But many reformers worked in or with New Deal agencies, particularly the relief agencies. They were always in the minority and had to fight an unending battle within their own agencies. But the outside battle was the main one. As they struggled to carry out their programs, dealing directly with the exploited people who loved Roosevelt, they often found their task impossible. The economic and social institutions of a Democratic South, as an example, presented one tremendous source of frustration. Blocked at every turn, they learned anew the ever-relevant lesson of Lincoln Steffens. Those who effectively frustrated their efforts also loved Roosevelt and were on the side of the angels. They were also powerful. The devils could be dealt with, but not the angels. Mrs. Roosevelt knew their plight, and they loved her for knowing. On occasion, F.D.R. knew also and, when political realities permitted, tried to help his loyal good men without power. But there was nothing in his leadership capable of transforming the desires of these loyal reformers into a new structure of political power. It may have been impossible, even had he tried. Master of politics, he was also captive to politics. Thus the story of the New Deal is a sad story, the ever recurring story of what might have been. Perhaps only Tugwell among major historians has shown a vague appreciation of this sadness, but even he quickly returned to the charisma of an adored leader.

Since the New Deal failed to fulfill even the minimal dream of most reformers, why did all the evil men of power, plus millions of Republican dupes, oppose it? To Roosevelt, the answer was simple: they were evil. Economic royalists, with a monopoly of power, they were not content with a repaired and honest capitalism. Instead, they wanted to drive on with their plutocracy and bring down upon the heads of the good men of power the inevitable revolution. Then good bankers would suffer and good businessmen might lose the management of their corporations. But this answer, although in part true, was too simple. The opponents of Roosevelt misconstrued the direction of the New Deal. Many believed Roosevelt's class rhetoric. They really thought America was losing its "free" capitalist soul to some type of socialism. In their praise of freedom lurked some valuable criticism of the New Deal. Also, many Americans, perhaps particularly the monied classes, never trusted Roosevelt, much less some of his advisers. The New Deal was indeed a mixed company, a type of political bohemia, frequented by many of the better sort, but still dangerous. Roosevelt was a puzzling creature. Even when he served conservative causes, he preached an alien gospel. Let us have anything but a righteous gentleman in Washington. Even a Marxist would have made more sense to them. Finally, almost no one thought in terms of vast economic expansion, and thus no one could see welfare as other than a permanent liability, somehow drawn from the ledger of profits or high incomes, either directly by taxes or indirectly by government deficits and inflation. The threat to earnings, the inhibition to investment, seemed the central issue, more important than declining fears of revolution, humane concern, or an occasional recognition of the importance of purchasing power.

But the supreme irony is here. The enemies of the New Deal were wrong. They should have been friends. Security was a prime concern of the insecure thirties. It cut across all classes. Businessmen, by their policies, desperately sought it in lowered corporate debts and tried to get the government to practice the same austerity. Even when ragged and ill-housed, workers opened savings accounts. The New Deal, by its policies, underwrote a vast apparatus of security. But the meager benefits of Social Security were insignificant in comparison to the building system of security for large, established businesses. But like stingy laborers, the frightened businessmen did not use and enjoy this security and thus increase it. The New Deal tried to frame institutions to protect capitalism from major business cycles and began in an unclear sort of way to underwrite continuous economic growth and sustained profits. Although some tax bills were aimed at high profits, there was no attack on fair profits or even on large profits. During the thirties, as all the way up to the sixties, there was no significant leveling by taxes. The proportionate distribution of wealth remained. Because of tax policies, even relief expenditures were disguised subsidies to corporations, since they were in large part paid by future taxes on individual salaries or on consumer goods. Thus, instead of higher wages creating a market, at the short-term expense of profits, the government subsidized the businessman, without taking the cost out of his hide as he expected and feared.

Even at the local level there was no significant shift of the economic and social structure. Negroes, politically purchased by relief or by the occasional concern of bureaucrats or Mrs. Roosevelt, remained a submerged and neglected caste. Service and farm labor, including migratory, received slight succor. Millions continued in desultory enslavement to immediate needs. Thus the people of power gained added security and lost only two commodities: undisciplined freedom and a degree of popular respect. The last they regained quickly. Most of all, the individual farmer lost some entrepreneurial freedom and accepted a degree of central planning, albeit through democratic procedures. Even manufacturing industries had to accept new procedural limitations—labor laws, added regulatory agencies, new taxes, and minimum wage and maximum hours. But these were necessary for security and for ordered growth. Even without government action, many restraints were developing within large corporations, even in the twenties, and some were simply part of a rationalizing process in business. Security demanded procedural rules, a degree of uniformity in practice, and even a formalized relationship with organized labor. Only small, aggressive adventurers or promoters suffered from the new procedural limitations. The only leveling, and the only real bite, hit the middle income groups and some small businesses. Perhaps the Chambers of Commerce were correct in condemning Roosevelt in 1935. The National Association of Manufacturers was not.

Government spending in behalf of multiplied private spending, the strongest weapon of Eccles and Keynes, was to be the final and most complete insurance policy for American capitalism. After 1937, even Roosevelt reluctantly swallowed this pill. Keynes was the last great classical economist, in the tradition of Adam Smith, Ricardo, the Mills, Marx, and Marshall. A British Liberal, formal, analytical, he tried to devise the minimal government devices necessary to maintain most of the free aspects of a market system. At the beginning of this greatest economic tradition, Adam Smith tried to get the freedom. At the end, Keynes tried to keep as much as possible. He wanted to set up safeguards to prevent serious depressions, to maintain full employment, and at the same time provide all the welfare measures required by human concern. He wanted to avoid socialist ownership and bureaucratic management on one hand and the severe controls of a corporate state on the other. His complex arguments had small influence on the New Deal, but his general prescription eventually prevailed.

The magic in Keynes, at least for an interval, was the magic of growth itself, which springs from new knowledge but is implemented through political economy. Growth can raise a whole society, with rising profits matching rising wages and rising government income supporting rising welfare measures. Business, so fearful of new welfare, never realized that it could be paid for by government credit and that public debts could be maintained (or repaid) without extra tax rates and without a significant redistribution of income or wealth. Roosevelt wanted some redistribution. Like Keynes, he had social as well as economic goals. But he rarely achieved these—witness again the congressional compromises and the frustrated bureaucrats on the moral battlefield. During World War II, when massive spending purchased unbelievable growth, Roosevelt had to suspend social goals and let the public subsidize plant expansion, profits, and, above all, future profits. By then he had no political alternative. Full employment, plus overtime, reduced the welfare burden, while growth and temporarily high taxes helped pay the cost of war. Some temporary leveling actually occurred. After the war the large government subsidy to business continued—in huge defense purchases, in contracts awarded in behalf of corporate survival, in research, in tax relief, in a flexible use of antitrust laws, in enough welfare increases to soothe the discontented, in a tacit acceptance of administered prices, and increasingly even in an unwillingness to antagonize the business community (even Democrats learned the old Hoover bit about confidence).

The battle between economic leaders and the New Deal was never complete. Some businessmen and many large farmers (historians generally call them enlightened) supported Roosevelt throughout the thirties. Many more, if they had understood Roosevelt's purposes, would surely have backed him. In the same sense, Roosevelt, considering his objectives, his willingness to retain and strengthen a private economy, should have worked more at understanding and communicating with businessmen, for their choices had more to do with the success of the New Deal than anything else. Yet, there was a real issue dividing the two. Simply, it was a matter of power. Roosevelt was powerful and could not be controlled by anyone or by any group. In this sense he was incorruptible, perhaps as much so as any President in American history. For two years even intense lobbying could not block his control over the legislative process. As Tugwell always believed, there was the potentiality of a major shift in the government of the country, with Roosevelt responding to academic advisers and effecting policies which would seriously invade the managerial prerogatives of major private interests. Instead of a limited socialization of product via welfare, Roosevelt could have socialized management or even the plant. He never did this; seemingly, he never wanted to, but until 1937 he seemed to have the political power and never gave enough

assurances to convince businessmen that he might not. For a while, normal channels of power in the federal government were circumvented, particularly in 1933–34.
This is why the courts became the heroes of conservative groups. But even as
Roosevelt secured great political power, and thus potential economic power, the
power of economic decision making remained perilously in private hands, less
secure and less potent than ever before. The tense situation could not endure.

The shift to welfare policies and then to Keynesian recovery policies took away
most of the threat and left private interests shaken but more secure than ever.
Nationalization and economic planning became dead issues. Through banking
and budgetary policies the government's resources were to be used to protect,
support, and occasionally discipline private producers. This meant a helping hand
for private industry, but with too many obligations, too many secure guarantees,
and too many restrictions for many old-fashioned industrialists. Security does
reduce freedom.

But the government had, more clearly than ever in the past, committed itself
to national economic goals. This was one of the enduring achievements of the
New Deal. Since it rejected planning (except to a degree in agriculture) and
refused to do its own producing, it had no alternative but to rely on the major
corporations and to subsidize them if necessary to insure its goals of rapid growth,
high levels of employment, and low welfare needs. Even a slight increase in
private economic activity can do more to benefit the country than vast welfare
programs. Precluded from direct economic action, the government had to use
indirect controls and incentives, plus persuasion, bribes, or, if politically possible,
threats and punitive measures. In this situation, high profits rightfully became
desirable public policy, since they increased the total economic activity and the
level of national prosperity. In spite of all the ridicule, nothing was now truer
than the quip: "What is good for General Motors is good for the country."
Under the emerging system, the welfare of both were inseparable.

The dependence was mutual. The large corporations, protected by a generous
government against the insecurity of the past (when politicians could safely allow
depressions) and also against their own worst mistakes and abuses, were tied
to government policies. The national budget was almost as important as their
corporate budgets. The action of the Federal Reserve Board, or even random
pronouncements by government officials, could wreck their best-laid plans. Welfare spending became a small but marginally vital part of the total market for
goods, forcing some business acquiescence even here. In a few areas, such as
low-rent housing, welfare programs became the major support for very profitable
businesses. Later, defense spending would completely support large companies
and provide the margin of profit for hundreds. Increasingly, business and government were linked in more subtle ways, particularly by a common economic
orthodoxy and a common need for certain skills. Bureaucrats moved from Ivy
League campuses to corporations and on to Washington. The situation invited,
in fact necessitated, co-operation, or a truly joint enterprise. Roosevelt cleared
the way for such co-operation, but he never desired it or achieved it and probably
never perceived its inescapable logic. Unlike most politicians, he was never a
good businessman, nor could he share power easily.

The old, individualistic capitalist did not fit the new picture. Mavericks were
taboo. But neither did reformers fit. The new partnership, with greater government

participation and greater benefits (the welfare state for business), left room for tension, even bitter conflict, as between mutually dependent husband and wife. Always, one or the other partner could try to gain too much power and upset the partnership. There was an overlapping but never identical constituency. Generally, with time and enough advice from Keynesian counselors, the two settled into almost blissful matrimony. Lyndon Johnson finally illustrated what a beautiful and happy home is possible when both sides can sit down and reason together. What about the constituency? For business, the shareholders have profited. Dividends have been large and capital accumulation even larger. For government, the larger constituency presents a much more variegated pattern. But most able and fortunate people, if they have been loyal, have received well in material returns and have profited from the general benevolence and good will of both the private and government bureaucrats who look out for them.

But the economic magic of sustained growth and the political magic of welfare can be irrelevant to moral and religious vision, which may also demand a just community. For the more sensitive New Dealers, or outside critics, Keynes provided a technique for priming the economic pump but no means of purifying the water. They thirsted after the pure product. Growth could simply intoxicate the affluent minority (or majority), blunt their sensitivity, and leave them in satiated lethargy, full but unfulfilled. Welfare could do the same for the poor. Growth could lead to vast production, to an enormous gross national product, but also to ugliness and spiritual poverty everywhere. It might even lead to full employment and undreamed-of security (goals not attained because of too small a government investment), yet to a society bereft of meaningful work, of personal involvement, even of democratic participation. It might suggest the blessing of leisure but bring only the curse of idleness. Finally, it would surely conceal injustice and leave the exploited to the tender and prejudiced mercy of local conscience. During the war the disturbing reformers dropped from view and did not emerge again until the sixties. Then, to the profound surprise of all good men of power, the one-third ill-fed and ill-housed, and the two-thirds alienated and desperate, still existed. In spite of the New Deal and in spite of all that welfare!

From New Deal to New Frontiers   LLOYD GARDNER

The New Left is not only skeptical of Roosevelt's domestic policies; they disapprove even more of his foreign policy. As they can trace much of the modern overblown welfare state to the New Deal, they can also trace America's present international involvements to Roosevelt's interventionist policies during the decade 1935–1945.

Source: Lloyd Gardner, *Economic Aspects of New Deal Diplomacy* (Madison, Wisc.: University of Wisconsin Press, 1964), chapt. viii, "From New Deal to New Frontiers," pp. 152–174.

Many liberals, and a few men of the Left also, find this criticism disturbing. Of all the wars America has fought, they are apt to find most tolerable the confrontation with Hitler and fascism. Here was no imperialist struggle for markets or for spheres of influence. This was a battle for civilization itself, with defeat certain to plunge the world into barbarity and a reign of total brutality and force. For the many Marxist sympathizers with the Soviet Union, it is clear that the war helped save the last best hope of socialism.

The New Left is skeptical of Roosevelt's foreign policy, and is unwilling to accept its idealist, anti-Fascist rationale at full face value. In the following selection, Lloyd Gardner suggests that Roosevelt's increasing fear of Hitler and Mussolini in part grew out of concern for American trade in a world dominated by fascism. Shortly after the war itself, Charles Beard had made a similar point, but in a much cruder and more acerbic way. Gardner's thesis owes something to Beard, and also something to William Appleman Williams' view that Americans have always turned outward in order to avoid seriously considering solving major social and economic problems by drastic structural change. On the other hand, he does not deny that the American people had good reason to fear for their safety in a world controlled by Hitler and his friends, and he rejects the crude notion that Roosevelt involved the country in an international holocaust to save his faltering party from defeat.

FOR FURTHER READING:

Lloyd Gardner, *Economic Aspects of New Deal Diplomacy*, (University of Wisconsin Press, 1964); Robert Divine, *Illusion of Neutrality**, (Quadrangle, 1968); Robert Divine, *The Reluctant Belligerent: American Entry into the Second World War**, (Wiley, 1965); Manfred Jonas, *Isolationism in America 1935–1941*, (Cornell University Press, 1966); Warren J. Cohen, *The American Revisionists: Lessons of Intervention in World War I*, (University of Chicago Press, 1967); Charles A. Beard, *American Foreign Policy 1932–1940: A Study in Responsibilities*, (Archon, Shoe String, 1968); Charles C. Tansill, *Backdoor to War: The Roosevelt Foreign Policy, 1933–1941*, (Charles Regnery, 1952); Robert Freeman Smith, "American Foreign Relations 1920–1942," in Barton Bernstein (editor) *Towards a New Past: Dissenting Essays in American History**, (Pantheon, 1969).

Asterisk denotes paperback edition.

Unwilling to see Germany and Italy establish a joint hegemony in Europe, the United States finally plunged into the very fields of political involvement it had hoped to avoid through neutrality.

Hitler's military challenge forced the issue. The strain of finding a way to meet it cracked and shattered domestic political alliances, especially after the Administration called for serious rearmament in 1938. The Progressive-Northern Democrat front fell into many fragments. Although not all Progressives refused to follow the Administration, many did, including some of Roosevelt's strongest allies on social legislation.

Undoubtedly many former opponents of the New Deal found the growing emphasis on foreign affairs to their liking. The militancy of Southern conservative Democrats has long been a feature of American politics. The isolationist wing of Progressivism in the Republican party, on the other hand, was much less happy at sharing a bed with the *Chicago Tribune* and the Hearst Press.

Thoughtful interventionists had concluded, perhaps reluctantly, that America could not work out its destiny in the same world with the Axis—the world could not endure, Stimson had said in a radio address, half-slave and half-free. Some isolationists admitted the force of this argument, but replied that even if the country could lead a crusade against the Axis, it would surely lose its soul in the process. A few conservative isolationists, however, did not hesitate to advocate a Fortress America that would have imitated fascist economic—and perhaps later on political—methods in the Western Hemisphere. Socialists had a vision of the Western Hemisphere, too. But whatever their disagreement on the future, both believed the interventionists exaggerated the threat and that a strong America need not fear for its existence as a free nation.

This brings one to the question of New Deal shortcomings and specific failures in the recession of 1937–38. The recurrent specter of unemployment and low prices did hover over the New Dealers well into the period when the Administration was aiding the Allies with "everything short of war," but to blame this spirit's influence, at least in the narrow sense, or to call it the demon which drove Roosevelt into the war, simply is not warranted.

One of Roosevelt's ablest defenders, Basil Rauch, quite rightly pointed out that although domestic economic problems sharpened many issues, they did not make the Axis challenge "either more or less minatory." Rauch goes on, however: "Besides Roosevelt had made it clear from the beginning of his administration that the danger was real to him." Now whether one agrees with Rauch that this was the role Roosevelt essayed or not, he has raised an important question: When and for what reasons did the New Deal undertake political involvement in Europe? To answer simply in order to stop Hitler's military thrust is right but only the first cut in a probe that should go much deeper. The Anglo-American conservative poet-intellectual T. S. Eliot had some scathing words for contemporaries which represented a thoughtful corrective to the growing emotionalism of the times, but far more importantly, to the idealization of the Anglo-American Alliance after the war. He said in his *Idea of a Christian Society* (1940): "Sometimes we are almost persuaded that we are getting along very nicely, with a reform here and a reform there, and would have been getting along still better, if only foreign governments did not insist upon breaking all the rules and playing what is really a different game." [1]

Whether one agrees even partially with Eliot, there is another point to be made, the years before and after. World War II demonstrated that the United States regarded the defense of its liberal trade system as central to the conduct of its foreign policy and the stem of that policy's ideology. This is not to say that Americans did not regard Germany as primarily a military threat, especially after the violation of the Munich promise, but when the United States looked to the postwar world, it planned for one that was liberal economically and politically.

And of course Cordell Hull always led the Administration in linking foreign and domestic matters under the umbrella of his reciprocal trade agreements program. He remarked to Henry Stimson in 1938 that he had truly hoped to force Germany back into line through the creation of a trading bloc of twenty or thirty nations, but national economic difficulties stemming from the recession were choking both the domestic economy and his foreign economic policy.

But the Secretary's troubles in pre-war years more generally resulted from an inability to sustain neutrality, matched with a reluctance to involve the United

States, and though Sumner Welles and William Bullitt criticized Hull for wanting his cake and eating it too, the Secretary's attitude better typified the country as a whole.

The gold problem and the question of the Spanish Civil War were good examples of the American predicament. These were two issues among many which led American leaders to the conclusion that intervention was the only way out of the world of the 1930's, for it was impossible to accept the possibility of an Axis victory. Committed to defeating the Axis, the United States at once began postwar planning for a better world. The State Department was determined that the economic reorganization of the peace should follow the broad outlines of the Reciprocal Trade Agreements Act, and there should be no political deals between other members of the Grand Alliance to mar the vision of an open world.

Neutrality Becomes a Dead-End Street

Opened to their cores, the relatively peripheral gold problem and the Spanish Civil War question both display the failure of American neutrality, and therefore are representative of the kind of developments and situations that led the United States towards intervention. The former directed attention to shortcomings in the Hull program; in fact, some thought that if the gold situation was any real indication of the direction of future events, the trade program was heading nowhere. The Spanish Civil War and the key question that rose out of it, recognition of Francisco Franco's regime, created both an economic and a political issue. The Administration wanted to protect American interests in Spain and it wanted to keep Madrid separated as much as possible from Berlin and Rome, but it found it could do neither very successfully.

In an encouraging letter to the President at the end of 1937, the State Department pointed out its gains for the country as a result of significant increases in trade with Agreement countries. About the time he read this report, Roosevelt was asking Treasury Secretary Morgenthau what would become of American foreign trade if other nations followed Germany's example and left the gold standard entirely. The Secretary had no satisfactory reply.

Fortune magazine had an unhappy one: "The Hull trade agreements have been a useful step in the right direction. But to open up real frontiers, under a general policy of raising the standard of living of other countries, we shall have to go much further."

Treasury purchases of gold, like the Export-Import Bank, had become an adjunct to the trade agreements program. It was international pump-priming of the most obvious kind. First used in 1933 to reinflate the dollar, the Treasury's continued buying of gold put dollars into the world economy, and as Treasury expert Alvin Hansen explained, it was "a form of intensified protectionism, and, on the other hand, tend[ed] to force exports through what is known as 'exchange dumping!' "

But as *Fortune* suggested, the water supply from such wells was not unlimited. Gold purchases were at best only a temporary palliative, albeit a most effective one in the 1937 recession when American exports fell only 7 per cent despite a drop in imports of over 36 per cent. The preservation of this "favorable balance of trade" owed much to the billion and a half dollars the Treasury sent into the world economy in exchange for gold.

But the more gold that the United States drew off in this way, loaded into truck caravans, and carted off to Federal Reserve banks or Fort Knox, the less other nations had to sell. South African mines were pressed to keep up with the demand. By the end of the 1930's America owned more than 60 per cent of the world's gold. "Here we are," quipped Tom Lamont, "sitting on top of this heap of gold with nowhere to go with it, unless we can encourage foreign trade." But, and almost as an afterthought, he added, "There are no frontiers to the mind and genius of the American people." Yet the practical question of how to increase world trade in an Axis-dominated situation, which was at the base of Roosevelt's question to Morgenthau, remained to be answered. Nor could it be until American political involvement opened new frontiers.

Perched on top of this less and less valuable and more and more exposed heap of gold, the Administration was also an open target for critics of its Spanish policy. Liberal malcontents scornfully referred to it as an intervention by nonintervention. And Herbert Feis later agreed: "The governments of the Allies came, in the midst of war, to rue their consent to Franco's victory."

Before the Spanish dictator's victory, the United States had followed England and France in their efforts to keep the Spanish Civil War just that and not the beginning of a final showdown with Germany and Italy. After the Republic was crushed, the State Department was chagrined at its inability to restore satisfactory relations with Madrid. Once again German and Italian influence seemed to stand in the way politically and to encourage Franco to imitate fascist autarchy. This was especially galling because the Department had allowed commercial agents from Franco's forces to come to American ports "for the purpose of validating shipping documents and hence helping our trade. . . ."

A number of businessmen had very badly wanted renewed trade relations with Spain even before Franco's victory had become assured. Representatives of the National Foreign Trade Council called at the Department to make a final plea that the Administration get in "on the ground floor after Franco wins."

A special conference considered such pleas on March 24, 1939. Department officials decided that the right thing to do would be to recognize Franco in "two or three days, partly because our business interests demand it, partly because it is vital to all to maintain American control over all communications between Europe and Latin America which center in Spain; [and] partly because we and Soviet Russia alone have not recognized the inevitable—an embarrassing partnership."

As soon as recognition had been granted, the National Foreign Trade Council's spokesmen were right back with suggestions for an Export-Import Bank loan to Spain—based, significantly, upon the example of new loans to Brazil. These businessmen thought that such a loan would not only stimulate a resurrection of Spanish-American trade but also release blocked American credits. State Department officers were somewhat piqued at learning that they had already contacted the Commerce Department and the Export-Import Bank. Moreover, the Agriculture Department also seemed to be out in front of the State Department (despite its leadership by the "liberal" Henry Wallace) because it wished to dispose of surplus cotton and keep in touch with Spanish markets for the future. The State Department wanted to achieve political results before making any such loan.

Sumner Welles was able to use the potential Export-Import Bank credit as a lever to pry out of the Spanish ambassador promises concerning the release of Americans who had been imprisoned during the Civil War for serving in the Republican army, the return of International Telephone and Telegraph officials to Spain, and a "firm guarantee," which the ambassador personally initialed, that "American business would be treated in Spain on the basis of equality and in accordance with the principles of international law."

But once again, without American participation in a more direct fashion, relations between a European nation and Washington never became satisfactory. The attempt to bribe Franco away from Hitler and Mussolini only partially succeeded, though he did stay out of the war. International Telephone and Telegraph quarreled with the Franco government over the terms of its future participation in that country, and it took a good deal of State Department pressure to solve that question. Indeed, a retiring Spanish Ambassador thanked the Department for making it plain that return of American properties "was the central and vital issue."

The Administration Accepts the Challenge

The central and vital domestic issue, said a group of experts for the Brookings Institution, was the evidence they found to demonstrate that the New Deal had actually destroyed the confidence necessary to promote expansion. America's economic malaise could not be overcome so long as the "combined savings made by insurance companies and savings institutions . . . were more than three times the value of corporate bond and note issues" as had happened in the 1937–38 recession.

Practically all conservatives shared or sympathized with the Brookings Institution findings. It was plain enough to them that the New Deal had undermined the venturesome spirit of American capitalism. Roosevelt admitted the difficulties, but he and the New Dealers considered that the monopolists and malefactors of great wealth were pursuing deliberately restrictive policies in an attempt to regain control of the Government. On March 4, 1938, the President described the situation in straight and simple language: "We have fifteen or twenty million Americans in this country who today have no purchasing power. There are fifteen or twenty million Americans falling into that category."

A month later the President formally launched the Second New Deal (some call it the Third) as his counterattack against the recession and his enemies of the Left and the Right. Led by Solicitor Robert Jackson and Harry Hopkins, it was designed to be a two-pronged maneuver. Jackson was to join the Temporary National Economic Committee's fight against monopolists, while Hopkins officially introduced Keynesian deficit spending as Administration policy.

Even as they initiated this attack on the country's domestic economic problems, Roosevelt's advisers were becoming more and more disturbed by the external threat and both consciously and unconsciously comparing and sometimes linking the two in ways that Cordell Hull had done in his discussion with Henry Stimson. One can speculate forever on this matter and never reach solid ground, but the methods a few of these advisers used to bring the problem into focus can be set forth in some detail.

We begin with Harry Hopkins. Hopkins was given a new job in the fall of 1938. As a possible successor, Roosevelt wanted him to dispel notions of his radicalism by accepting and serving well in the position of Secretary of Commerce. Secretary Hopkins did make a good impression, though illness kept his actual participation in

Department matters at a below-normal level. Later, as a trusted lieutenant in the fight against the Axis, Hopkins further succeeded in obtaining the backing and confidence of the Dollar-a-year Men as well as many others in the business community.

In the Congressional hearing on his nomination to the Commerce Department post, the former relief administrator defended the PWA and the WPA appropriations by pointing out that during the 1937 recession the nation had suffered the sharpest drop in employment in any "period of time that has ever occurred in our history." But as befitted his new assignment, Hopkins declared that "business must succeed and must be able to work with Government, if our economic system is to be preserved." The New Deal was already on the statute books, he told newsmen on March 8, 1939, and if the low 62 billion dollar gross national product were to grow into a prosperous 80 or 90 billion, the Government was going to have to aid business on "101 fronts." "With 12 million unemployed we are socially bankrupt and politically unstable."

Speaking in his home state of Iowa, the Commerce Secretary pledged himself to business recovery: "This country cannot continue as a democracy with 10,000,000 or 12,000,000 unemployed. It just can't be done. We have got to find a way of living in America in which every person in it shares in the national income, in such a way, that poverty in America is abolished."

From the Commerce Department's Business Advisory Council, Hopkins received reports and recommendations on domestic affairs which served also to focus attention on new trade outlets in Latin America and other world markets. He attended White House Conferences where he and these men, as he told newsmen, had "some very considerable discussion of foreign trade. . . ."

When fused with his own ideas on the Nazi menace, these influences found their way into speech drafts and remarks such as the following:

> We must also recognize that today foreign trade is being used by some countries as a vehicle to support political and cultural penetration. Unless we acquiesce in such penetration, we must be prepared through the adoption and use of national powers to meet quality, quantity and price on such a basis as to get the business.

For Hopkins, the Axis challenge was a very real threat no matter what sort of ideology spawned it.

Adolf Berle had rebelled against resurgent trust-busting, yet his opposition to this "hole in the program" came at a time when domestic differences in the Administration were being subordinated to the international question. One should not neglect Berle's criticisms of the Second New Deal and their revelation about his worried state of mind because they contrasted so sharply with his views once the United States had chosen to oppose the Axis. Testifying before the TNEC, the former Brain Truster said that if the country had truly come to the point where creation of wealth was demanded as "a function of the government . . . the choice should be the considered choice of the country and not the result of a policy of drift." Even more pointedly he wrote Roosevelt: "The paramount necessity now is to do some thinking at least one lap ahead of the obvious financial and industrial crisis, which is plainly indicated within the next few years."

Like Hopkins, Berle had great fears for the future in these months, and also like Hopkins he was familiar with the external threat. When he prepared a speech for the President after the Munich Conference in September, 1938, the adviser described darkly the dangers of a world dominated by fear and the sword; then he justified "the need for rearmament unless there were honest disarmament." Roosevelt looked at this draft and put in a strengthening paragraph to dramatize Berle's points "in a way which left little doubt that the line of demarcation between democracy and Nazism was one which could not be bridged or marked by a high wall with each side keeping his ideas to himself without interference from the other."

In sober discussions with the President and Sumner Welles during these months, as it became more and more obvious that appeasement had failed, Berle prophesied gloomily that an Axis victory would isolate America in "the unfortunate position of an old-fashioned general store in a town full of hard-bitten chains." The only alternative would soon be all-out aid to the democracies to prevent a total Axis victory.

When the war did come, Berle wondered if there were another choice, wondered if it would be possible to prepare a Fortress America against a Russo-German Europe. Such plans ran against the "process of men's minds," but eventually, in years, this domination would break up. "But they will be ghastly years."

So Berle concluded that a Fortress America was not really a possibility to be preferred to a dramatic showdown with the Axis. "I could wish," he then impatiently wrote Stimson, "that the country were a little more interested in preparedness than it appears to be." An associate in the State Department recorded Berle's "lurid picture" of the British fleet being driven out of Gibraltar even back as far as Canada, and behind it Hitler menacing the whole Western Hemisphere. Against this dark vision, Berle tried to build up a crusading spirit, said the observer.

J. P. Moffat feared that this spirit had too great a hold on another colleague, Assistant Secretary of State George Messersmith. He had allowed his anti-Hitlerism to fill his thinking about American foreign trade. Messersmith had first tied these two up, it will be recalled, back in 1933. Now he pointed to Hitlerism as a time-bomb not only in Europe, but also in America. "How futile it is to believe and to argue, as some still do," he declared before the National Foreign Trade Convention in 1938, "that a value of trade such as this [six billion dollars] does not have a vital bearing upon our internal life and upon the standard of living of our population." The year before, he had advised this export-minded group: "There is practically no phase of the relationship between states in this day in which economic factors do not enter. . . ." Every day, the Department worked on problems intimately concerned "with our whole economic structure. . . ."

Messersmith opposed any sort of deal with Germany which might compromise American trade principles and/or allow Berlin to obtain money for armaments. He, Francis Sayre, and Cordell Hull thought alike on this problem. On February 18, 1938, Hull forwarded one of his memorandums to Roosevelt. After outlining the difficulties the United States would come up against if England and France fell before Germany, he continued: "our troubles" will "come a little later" and that thought "does not give me any comfort." Already Germany's advancing forces had left little "prospect for our progress in Southeastern Europe." And to give the aggressor a free hand there would be to give him one everywhere.

Secretary Hull had also spoken to the 1938 Foreign Trade Convention, and his words complemented Messersmith's message. When nations like Germany and Japan reject orderly trade practices and patterns, first comes regimentation, then preparation for war. The Secretary brought a new aide into the Department at this time, the well-known author and publicist George Fort Milton, to help older aides in the public campaign for the reciprocal trade agreements program as the best protection against domestic regimentation and foreign trade aggression. "We are confronted with a choice," read one of Milton's letters to a former president of the United States Chamber of Commerce, "between a healthy competitive economy linked to a freely functioning international market, and a regimented economy operating on the basis of federal subsidies and quotas, in accordance with the principles of self-containment."

Other advisers were convinced, along with *Fortune,* that the trade agreements program could never do the job without American leadership in the Grand Alliance. Always among the first to make the leap from thought to action, Henry Wallace spoke for stronger action in his new book, *The American Choice* (1940): If the nation were to prevent intolerable increases in unemployment, it had to invest monies and export goods totaling at least four billion dollars each year. "I think we ought to face the fact that with a Hitler controlling the exports, imports and exchanges, it is impossible to get an adequate outflow of exports from the United States, and that an increase of governmental intervention is inevitable."

To Roosevelt's quickening interest in the task of stopping Hitler's advances, Hull's methodical presentations and cautious maneuvers appeared inadequate (even though the Secretary seemed to have a pretty free hand in Asia); yet the Secretary sensed a more sympathetic interest in his work and goals emanating from the White House at this very time. He was confirmed in this belief when the President ordered Cabinet officers to become familiar with a speech Hull had delivered before the Farm Bureau Federation on December 5, 1939. Looking ahead for a moment, the spirit and even the letter of the President's declaration of a national emergency on May 27, 1941, were in perfect accord with Hull's general view. There were alternatives to a showdown with the Axis, Roosevelt said, but:

> Tariff walls—Chinese walls of isolation—would be futile. Freedom to trade is essential to our economic life. We do not eat all the food we can produce; and we do not burn all the oil we can pump; we do not use all the goods we can manufacture. It would not be an American wall to keep Nazi goods out; it would be a Nazi wall to keep us in.

Although this quotation is typical of his speech, it should be pointed out that Roosevelt obviously tried to pick out arguments that would demonstrate American self-interest in the fight against Hitlerism. They were not necessarily his own views, though other evidence would indicate they were. Even if they were not, it is significant to see what kinds of arguments he used to make his point.

Growing Support for Intervention Outside the Administration

American public opinion on foreign affairs had separated into an antipodal structure by the time of this speech. The extremes were defined in the Committee to Defend America by Aiding the Allies, and by its opposite, the America First Committee.

Among the leading interventionist voices was that of the *New York Times,* which editorialized on the Hull trade agreements in even better style than the Secretary himself. The RTA program had become the best protection against "some form of totalitarianism" erupting in America. It had been Germany's loss of foreign markets which had forced that unhappy country to Nazism—and (significantly enough) had been the key factor in forcing the United States to try the NRA and AAA experiments, concluded the editor. The lesson was obvious.

During the war, *Times* publisher Arthur H. Sulzberger looked back on the immediate prewar years and stated his belief that the United States had consciously chosen war "because we knew that our future could not be as bad as we had mapped it unless we halted the aggressor as quickly as we could."

Sulzberger was reviewing a complex and emotional era but *Fortune's* 1940 poll of executive opinion revealed at that time how divided and uncertain American business leaders were over the advisability of trading with the German economic bloc, and also how sure over 60 per cent of them were that America had to maintain and expand its foreign trade. Nearly half predicted a totalitarian reorganization of business if Hitler were to win the war. This magazine had recently reported a sudden shift in business opinion after the outbreak of war in Europe and the November, 1939, repeal of the arms embargo of the Neutrality Act. "For a time the easy-chair conversations in the Union League Club sounded like a conference of Administration whips. Indeed, the broad shift in business's attitude toward Roosevelt was almost as phenomenal as the get-together of Nazis and Soviets." Itself an able molder of public opinion, this magazine had several times gone on record in favor of "Mr. Hull's trade policy" both in editorials and in letters by the editor to President Roosevelt. Thirty-two of fifty newspapers polled in one survey and eighty-eight out of 120 in another favored a repeal of the arms embargo.

Another Hull booster and sometime participant in New Deal diplomacy was Tom Lamont, who observed that the editors of the more cautious *Collier's* had the greatest respect for the trade program; and Lamont early offered his services to help repeal the arms embargo, as did other like-minded economic leaders. They felt as Bernard Baruch did, who later recalled that his differences with the New Deal were "submerged in my growing awareness of an imminent danger as the troubled thirties drew to a close"; or as W. Averell Harriman did, who wrote Roosevelt of his personal admiration and that of "my friends in industry and finance upon your masterful handling of our foreign policy"; or, finally, as did Wendell Willkie, who warned the Indiana Bankers Association that a German victory in Europe would endanger the American "system of free enterprise."

Congress reflected this growing desire for an interventionist foreign policy, concluded an observer from the State Department who watched President Roosevelt issue a call for an end to the arms embargo. The applause at every place where the President declared his intention to keep out of war was equaled every time he mentioned the "cash and carry" amendment, which, said this officer of the Department sardonically, was "immensely popular with the Congressmen who had just returned from their districts." Senator Key Pittman could not have given a more direct explanation of this feeling: "The condition with regard to industry and labor in this country today is so deplorable that further obstructions to our exports would bankrupt large sections of our country."

And Secretary Stimson could affirm from his new position in the War Department that "cash and carry" was successful in the period before Lend-Lease. Between 1938 and 1940, he noted in his War Diary, $1,400,000,000 were spent in the

United States for war materials. "The vast majority of people and of Congress saw the need for these orders, financed by foreign capital and developing American industry, and believed the United States safeguarded from war by the Neutrality Act."

This was what had become of the neutrality debate of the 1930's: Americans deceived themselves into thinking that they were protected from war and were able to gather up the profits from the belligerents. Other Americans were so convinced that their country had to enter the war either for self-protection or for self-interest, or for a combination of both and morality, that they went along with or even encouraged the deception. The Business Advisory Council was sure of one thing: "An enlargement of our opportunities for trade and investment in foreign countries *is now essential* to maximum national prosperity" (emphasis in original). Self-containment with its regulations and controls would destroy "free enterprise and . . . the democratic processes which we prize so highly."

Another semi-official business group, the newly formed Committee for Economic Development, pointed out to Undersecretary of Commerce Jesse Jones that the "importance of foreign trade" had to be considered of fundamental interest to the nation. On the other hand, many businessmen, while desiring foreign trade, thought Roosevelt's foreign policies were as bad as his domestic ones. But the isolationist Senator Burton K. Wheeler was dismayed to find in his travels around the country that so "many of the Chambers of Commerce, and Lions Clubs, and other organizations are for doing everything short of war."

An Administration complaint in late 1940—that the "business people of the country," though enjoying the benefits of cash and carry, were still slumbering and unaware of their responsibilities for the Defense Program and the sacrifices they would be called upon to make—was probably only too accurate. Ironically, the defense effort had temporarily reversed the basic economic problem of the 1930's. Instead of overproduction, the Administration found itself trying to pull more out of the American economy. Alarmed by the slow reaction of American productive machinery to this crisis, Roosevelt concerned himself as late as August, 1941, with the task of getting the meaning of the defense program "down to the little man of America."

Rousing American economic leaders to meet this production problem was difficult in part because of the President's own soothing assurances that America was not going into any foreign wars unless attacked. As Stimson had explained, cash and carry was supposed to free the country instead of involving it. Then, too, there was a well-justified fear abroad in the nation that the surpluses would come back as soon as the war was over. Roosevelt was thinking "about this matter" and informed an adviser that he was determined that "there shall be no depression of prices after the war." But this kind of assurance did not dispel the doubts about the defense boom. "The defense effort," wrote Bruce Catton in *War Lords of Washington,* "was rather like a brand new baby, which—for all anybody could predict—might grow up to be either a horse thief or a clergyman."

Isolationists argued that it would be worse than a horse thief. They contended that the United States did not have to participate in a foreign war to preserve political democrary and free enterprise. Sears Roebuck's forceful leader, General Robert Woods, spoke for the America First Committee before the Council on Foreign Relations and offered their views:

Americans like myself feel that our true mission is in North and South America. We stand today in an unrivaled position. With our resources and organizing ability we can develop, with our Canadian friends, an only partially developed continent like South America. . . . I think we should also make it clearly understood that no government in Mexico, Central America and the Carribbean South American countries will be tolerated unless it is friendly to the United States and that if necessary we are prepared to use force to attain that object.

The first real test between these two points of view came when the Administration called upon Congress in January, 1938, for a two-ocean navy. Thus began the debate which lasted until the passage of Lend-Lease.

The Last Great Debate Begins—American Naval Policy

Three days before the end of 1937, President Roosevelt sent an open letter to the chairman of the Senate Subcommittee on Naval Appropriations. He began with a reference to the European arms buildup. "I have used every conceivable effort to stop this trend, and to work toward a decrease of armaments. Facts, nevertheless, are facts, and the United States must recognize them." It was likely, therefore, that he would soon request new ship construction.

Within the month came the expected request for authorizing the construction of six new battleships and stand-by authorization of an additional twelve. When completed, this program would provide a two-ocean navy. Admiral Leahy's testimony has already been cited in another place, but to present the framework once more, Leahy had said that United States policy was designed to support the Monroe Doctrine, to protect American nationals abroad, to protect American shipping, and to protect American territory, including island possessions, against invasion. He had also said: "At the present time it is the national policy to protect our commerce."

When the floor debate began, several unhappy congressmen demanded to know just how far the Administration would go to support these national policies, and to what extent was America's rearmament tied to Great Britain's foreign policy.

Senator Robert Reynolds had joined the issue on January 6, 1938, insisting that "the time has come when the American people should interest themselves in America first, last, and all the time." The nation should seek foreign markets in Latin America and stop fooling around in the Orient and in Europe. Senator Harry S. Truman rose to give the answer: China's troubles with Japan came from the "very policy which the Senator is now advocating for America, that is, to live within themselves, and not have communications with the rest of the world. . . ." Truman's rejoinder seems all the more significant if it be kept in mind that Reynolds had not called for total isolation.

Two western senators returned to the attack with a different maneuver; they cited Roosevelt and Hull for the prosecution of the noninterventionist case. Colorado's Edwin Johnson quoted a 1928 speech by Roosevelt which had raised the "pertinent question" why Congress was being called upon to authorize ships to be built "next year and the year after, and the year after that." "This brings the naval question," Johnson continued, quoting from Roosevelt, "out of the realm of our immediate naval needs and into the realm of diplomatic juggling."

Homer T. Bone of Washington scored Hull's notion of "our interests" in the Far East as the Secretary had enumerated them in an address to the National Press Club.

"When there are ten or twelve million idle people in this country," charged the Senator, "to prate about 'our interests' in China is both dangerous and useless."

Administration spokesman Senator David Walsh of Massachusetts replied simply that America no less than Great Britain had interests in all parts of the world. "It is estimated by our experts that unless we are able to keep open certain trade routes the United States of America could not maintain itself for more than 2 years without being defeated by a powerful enemy."

Walsh went on: "The Federal Government may give up everything else, but it cannot give up the lives of its people and its property. It must have a navy! And it is only a question of what kind of a navy and what size navy we must have. The navy is our police force. It is our fire department. It is our protection. It is our life."

Though the Administration won this point easily enough, the isolationists rose up again in the 1941 Lend-Lease debate. Before moving to that, however, the concomitant reconstruction of the merchant marine should be described, since it has gone pretty much unnoticed—a circumstance that is particularly unfortunate, for the basic arguments and logic were the same as for military or naval rearmament: the necessity to maintain trade routes against any Axis attempts to dominate the seas.

As far back as the fall of 1936, Roosevelt had informed Michigan Senator James Couzens of the plight of the American merchant marine; it had suffered a series of ups and downs since the 1840's: "What I need and what the country needs is a fearless Chairman of the Maritime Commission, who will take the responsibility in setting up and putting through a new and permanent Mercantile Marine policy."

He soon found his man in Admiral Emory S. Land. Reviewing his first years as Chairman of the Commission since 1937, Land said that the United States had by 1941 come a long way in building merchant shipping so that "the productivity of American farms and factories" would not again "lapse into the inactivity which followed the last World War and plunged our nation into economic distress." To that end the government had by 1941 committed $1,750,000,000 to the Maritime Commission, and it expected to receive still another $1,250,000,000 for the construction of "two ships a day for each of the next two years." In 1944 a Congressional Committee on Post-War Policies asked Land why the merchant marine had once been so weak. Land's reply said much about the intellectual development of American foreign policy: "Primarily Horace Greeley's maxim, 'Go West, young man.' We cannot go West anymore."

Senator Royal Copeland defended a Maritime Commission appropriation in 1938 by arguing that even if the merchant marine was not self-supporting and even if the Treasury had to keep pouring funds into it, ". . . who can question that it is part of wisdom for the United States of America, having a surplus of American products and a surplus of manufactured products to create services in South America which would eventually lead to increased exports?"

Land and Copeland had developed a theme which was taken over with only a minor variation by an interventionist speaker at a rally in May, 1941: "It is a corner stone of American destiny that the seas be free . . . ; they will not be free under Hitler's domination. The lifeline of our country is the sea routes leading variously throughout the world. They must be preserved so that the productivity of American genius may further enrich the world and inspire all friendly nations to the greater effort in the ways of better living." And for a coda there was Admiral Land's exuberant declaration: "Does Hitler really think he can stop us?"

The Last Great Debate Ends—Lend-Lease

The State Department first greeted the Munich Pact with a "sigh of relief and pleasure," though only a few in that department thought that a chance would now arise for "real appeasment on sound economic foundations."

But, *pro forma*, the Department kept up its pressure to bring Germany back into line, and goods from the Sudeten area were separated from those coming from the rest of Czechoslovakia. A few months later, countervailing duties were reimposed on all German goods. The German chargé told Sumner Welles that the duties would upset his government. "To this I made no reply," Welles recorded coldly. The German diplomat then reported to Berlin that Secretary Hull believed that all political problems were capable of an economic solution. "The preponderance of the economic over the political is the result of the involvement of American commerce with the whole world," cabled the German. "Hence the national interest of America is in the greatest possible encouragement of international trade and in the maintenance of peace. She feels that both are threatened by the totalitarian powers."

As 1939 began, the Administration was indeed responding to this dual threat. Rearmament continued, of course, and the President launched a campaign, not successful until November, to repeal the arms embargo; he also took personal responsibility for selling military airplanes to the French government. When a public storm arose over this issue, Roosevelt called the Senate Foreign Relations Committee to a White House conference, where he tried to satisfy his critics among them and in the nation. He discussed the world in geopolitical terms: If "one nation dominates Europe, that nation will be able to turn the world sphere." The current struggle was one "between different kinds of economies"—between the have nations and the have-nots.

"Why dammit," exclaimed Secretary Hull about this time, "these nations have told us again and again what they mean to do. . . . If they succeed, we will have to transact our business with the rest of the world through Tokyo and Berlin."

In March, Hitler moved his legions all the way into Czechoslovakia. The American President asked Hitler and Mussolini to guarantee the rest of Europe that there would be no more territorial rearrangements. If Berlin and Rome would do that, then "the United States would be prepared to take part in discussions looking towards the most practical manner of opening up avenues of international trade to the end that every nation of the earth may be enabled to buy and sell on equal terms in the world market as well as to possess assurance of obtaining the materials and products of peaceful economic life." Hitler laughed; Mussolini sarcastically called it "a result of progressive paralysis."

On September 1, German armies rolled into Poland and the war began. Within three months, Congress had repealed the arms embargo and the United States was selling war goods and munitions to the Allies. If only to keep the record straight, the President sent Sumner Welles to Europe the following spring to see if there was any basis at all for a negotiated peace. Welles found none.

Traveling to the capitals of each belligerent, Welles repeated the President's long-standing economic offers. In Berlin the German Foreign Minister reasserted his country's claim to close economic and political ties with Central Europe, but more ominous was the dark declaration which stayed in Welle's mind that the United States should not "forget that one thousand years ago German Emperors had been crowned in Prague."

Without doubt the Lend-Lease discussion and debate climaxed the Great Debate over foreign policy in the 1930's. It was Welles's answer to the German foreign minister, and it was the nation's decision to oppose the Axis—and to make a commitment to that goal. At the end of 1940 Great Britain declared that its dollar supplies had fallen too low to permit further purchases on the cash and carry plan. Even if there were some differences of opinion about this claim, and some downright skepticism, everyone in the Administration accepted the broad conclusion that if aid to Britain was essential to victory over the Axis, then it had to be given. On December 18, 1940, the British government was told to go ahead and place orders totaling over three billion dollars; a way would be found to pay for them.

House Resolution 1776 was introduced in January, 1941, to provide that way. Administration spokesmen explained that this Lend-Lease idea and its fulfillment was fully as vital to American security as the creation of the army and navy at the time of independence. Navy Secretary Knox referred also to another historic time and act—the Monroe Doctrine of 1823—and he said that for 118 years that Doctrine had prevented non-American military and political intervention in the Western Hemisphere. It had been "enunciated for preserving the territorial, economic, and social integrity of the United States." Germany threatened that integrity and had to be stopped.

Secretary of War Stimson described Lend-Lease as a "skillful Yankee bargain." To begin with, Great Britain had already spent over 605 million dollars in cash and had thereby provided "our manufacturers working capital with which to build factories and take care of her orders." Consequently, England had contributed "vitally" to our productive capacity. And finally, since management of the new aid program would always be in American hands, it would make for a coordinated and effective war effort.

Before workers in the offices of the War Department, the Secretary called it unprecedented and magnificent realism. Furthermore, if anyone asked them if Congress' war-making power had been bypassed, his personal reply would be, "Congress has declared war to this extent at least." And the President reportedly told the Polish Ambassador on March 6, 1941: "We Americans will have to buy this war as such. Let us hope at the price of Lend-Lease only. But who can say what price we may ultimately have to pay?"

Acting partly upon the momentum supplied by the passage of Lend-Lease, President Roosevelt now began that last series of "complicated maneuvers" which revisionist-minded historians have so belabored. And it is noteworthy that even Secretary Stimson considered the April, 1941, decision to order the navy to report German ship movements to the world a "disingenuous" means of supporting British convoys: "I wanted him to be honest with himself. To me it seems a clearly hostile act to the Germans and I am prepared to take the responsibility of it." Roosevelt may have assumed that Hitler still did not want to risk a shooting war with the United States even after this "clearly hostile act." Nonetheless, Stimson was justly worried about the President's haphazard approach to such an important matter of peace and war. This sterile debate on Roosevelt's personal morality, though barely relevant, has thus taken precedence over the political economy of American foreign policy.

Incidents did occur on the Atlantic between German and American ships, but war came from the other direction. On September 11 the President told the American people in a "fireside chat" about the decision to convoy Lend-Lease ships to

England. For if the Axis won, he said, the "Atlantic Ocean which has been, and which should always be, a free and friendly highway for us would then become a deadly menace to the commerce of the United States, to the coasts of the United States and even to the inland cities of the United States."

Turning the Challenge into Opportunity

Planning for the postwar period had already begun; the Atlantic Conference between Roosevelt and Churchill, for example, was divided into strategy sessions on how to deal with Germany and forestall Japan and sessions devoted to more long-range matters, such as the disarmament of the aggressors and prospects for continuing the Anglo-American alliance.

A letter from former President Herbert Hoover to Secretary Hull in March, 1941, typified the American mood in approaching these problems. Though discredited by the New Dealers and turned down by the voters, Hoover's summary of the alternatives before the United States, like his earlier one in 1933, ably outlined the situation: "The passage of the Lend-Lease Act obviously involves us deeply in the consequences of the war. But it also gives our government a measure of responsibility to see that the policies pursued by the British are in the interest of both winning the war and winning a peace, and in the interests of the United States." Hoover was particularly worried that the British food blockade "negatived" all the principles England had advanced in war propaganda against fascism. These were exactly the same arguments Mr. Hoover had advanced to Woodrow Wilson just after World War I when he described how Central Europe was "rumbling with social explosion" and on the verge of "total collapse." Then, as in 1941, Hoover sought to "use food control to aid in winning the war and the peace and in the special interests of the United States."

Great Britain would have to follow policies not incompatible with American plans, it was contended: "No help to Germany," one State Department official said in September, 1939, "but no dominion status for ourselves." Most of the officers in the Department suspected that London wanted to organize a huge trading orbit after the war, to the exclusion of American interests.

Compared to the protests and sanctions against Germany before the United States entered the war, those sent to Great Britain were mild and they could have been simply for the record, but past experience with British trade policies made them more important than that. Indeed, they were like Woodrow Wilson's protests against British naval policies before American entrance into World War I, which he tried to eliminate in the Fourteen Points. "This Government has made it clear," read a typical protest against restrictions on American exports to British Africa, "that it attaches the highest importance to the sanctity of treaties and that violations of treaty rights wherever they occur tend to spread still further the forces of disorder."

In plainer language still, Secretary of Commerce Hopkins reported to the Cabinet on April 4, 1940: "There is no doubt that relative to our pre-September position we stand to increase our net exports because of the war." Since the British were being forced to buy more from the United States, "We are, of course, in a position to exercise considerable influence upon [them] in decisions of policy which affect us."

Lend-Lease was the best lever to use to achieve this goal, and from the beginning the State Department wanted to use it to pry open the Ottawa Agreements. These developments will be considered in a later chapter; suffice it here to indicate that President Roosevelt thought a framework agreement on Lend-Lease repayment should be made first, while the details could be left to continuing negotiations.

Sumner Welles tried to establish such a framework at the Atlantic Conference, and he and Roosevelt spent much time on their way to meet Churchill discussing the problem of opening trade so that underdeveloped countries could help themselves and increase their standards of living. The more prosperous nations would then enjoy the reciprocal benefit of larger foreign markets for their goods. Without the cooperation of the British Empire this was useless talk, and Welles realized it clearly. Lord Halifax, the British Ambassador to the United States, confirmed that Roosevelt had spoken "earnestly" to Churchill about economic matters and noted that the President and Welles seemed worried already about a possible rebirth of isolationism in America. Halifax gave it as his opinion that the two American leaders were determined to have a share in "moulding and running the world" after the war.

A key example of this determination was Washington's flat opposition to Anglo-Russian preliminary attempts to define possible spheres of influence in Europe. This question was touched on at the Atlantic Conference, but the very urge to join with the British in making a generalized postwar statement like the Atlantic Chapter had come partly from Roosevelt's concern about Churchill's unilateral pronouncements on the postwar world. On July 14, for instance, the President had sent a message to the Prime Minister disclosing his interest in "rumors regarding trades or deals" in Anglo-Russian talks. He asked for a public statement from London, which he would then back up, reassuring the world that "no postwar peace commitments as to territories, populations or economics have been given." The Atlantic Charter was just such a statement.

American leaders decided from 1938 to 1941 that the country could not achieve its destiny in a closed world dominated by the Axis. Having gone that far with its assumptions, the Administration had to accept political commitments, not only for the war period but also in order to restore an open world society. The doubts and uncertainties since 1933 in European policy were gone; World War II provided a new chance to reshuffle for another "deal" both in domestic and in foreign policy.

In this changed world and in a changed mood, Adolf Berle felt exhilarated about the future: "There is no need to fear. Rather, we shall have an opportunity to create the most brilliant economic epoch the U.S. has yet seen. It is entirely feasible to make the country at once more prosperous and more free than it has ever been. And . . . without sacrificing any of the essential freedoms."

Berle's new optimism presupposed (perhaps unconsciously) the extension of American commitments far beyond anything in American diplomacy before 1941. Were Americans up to that challenge as well as to the lesser, immediate one?

NOTE

1. The hostile reception given to A. J. P. Taylor's *Origins of the Second World War,* despite his disclaimers, which are borne out in the book, of pro-Hitlerism are evidence not only of a desire to point out his specific errors of fact and judgment, but perhaps a dangerous desire to see only the villainy of one man behind the war and to seek no more.

7. World War Two and the Cold War

America in War and Peace: The Test of Liberalism BARTON BERNSTEIN

The domestic failures of the New Deal, particularly the elusiveness of recovery, were partly redeemed by World War Two. Unemployment melted away as millions were drawn off into the armed forces and into booming war industries. With the stagnant mass of the jobless gone, the income distribution of the nation inevitably improved. Prosperity returned, and despite wartime shortages, most civilians enjoyed a much higher standard of living than before. Equality was further enhanced by rationing and price controls, which prevented the rich from engrossing the limited supply of civilian goods. High income taxes also helped equalize living standards, while a Fair Employment Practices Act reduced discrimination against blacks, so that they too were able to participate in many of the gains other Americans experienced.

This is the picture of the War as painted by liberal historians. But is it accurate? As Barton Bernstein shows below, it is at best only a small part of the total reality. Nor are the liberal views of the postwar domestic scene any more valid. Leaving McCarthyism aside, we find the Truman years marked by a recession from even the limited social gains of the war period. The Taft-Hartley Act represented a retreat from the support organized labor had received from the federal government. The Fair Employment Practices Act was allowed to lapse, and blacks found that with the end of the labor shortage, they were once more the first to be fired. Truman often talked "liberal," but as Bernstein notes, he was generally ineffectual, and his rhetoric may well have prevented the enactment of actual liberal legislation. In a word, neither the War nor the Truman Fair Deal, Bernstein says, can be considered milestones on the road to social and economic justice in America.

FOR FURTHER READING:

Eric Goldman, *The Crucial Decade and After: America 1945–1960**, (Vintage, 1960); Barton Bernstein (editor) *Politics and Policies of the Truman Administration**, (Quadrangle, 1970); Richard Kirkendall (editor) *The Truman Period as a Research Field*, (University of Missouri Press, 1967); Louis W. Koenig, *The Truman Administration: Its Principles and Prac-*

Source: Barton Bernstein, "America in War and Peace: The Test of Liberalism," in *Towards a New Past: Dissenting Essays in American History*, ed. Barton Bernstein (New York: Pantheon Books, 1968), pp. 289–308.

tice, (New York University Press, 1956); Cabell Phillips, *The Truman Presidency: The History of a Triumphant Succession**, (Pelican Penguin, 1966).

Asterisk denotes paperback edition.

The domestic events of the war and postwar years have failed to attract as much scholarly effort as have the few years of the New Deal. The reforms of the thirties and the struggle against depression have captured the enthusiasm of many liberal historians and have constituted the major themes shaping their interpretations. Compared with the excitement of the New Deal years, the events at home during the next decade seem less interesting, certainly less dramatic.

The issues of these years also seem less clear, perhaps because the period lacks the restrictive unity imposed upon the New Deal. Despite the fragmentary scholarship, however, the major issues are definable: economic policies, civil rights, civil liberties, and social welfare policies. The continued dominance by big business, the consolidation of other groups within the economy, the challenge of racial inequality—these are the themes of the wartime Roosevelt administration. Toward the end of Roosevelt's years, they are joined by another concern, the quest for social reform, and in Truman's years by such themes as economic readjustment, the renewed struggle against inflation, and the fear of disloyalty and communism. These problems are largely the legacy of the New Deal: the extension of its limited achievements, the response to its shortcomings, the criticism of its liberalism.

It was during the war years that the nation climbed out of depression, that big business regained admiration and increased its power, and that other interests became effective partners in the political economy of large-scale corporate capitalism. While the major interests focused on foreign policy and on domestic economic problems—on mobilization and stabilization, later on reconversion and inflation—liberal democracy was revealing serious weaknesses. Opposing fascism abroad as a threat to democratic values, the nation remained generally insensitive to the plight of its citizens who suffered indignity or injury because of their color. Violating liberal values in the process of saving American democracy, Roosevelt's government, swept along by a wave of racism, victimized Japanese-Americans. Uncommitted to advancing the Negroes' cause, the war government resisted their demands for full participation in democracy and prosperity, and grudgingly extended to them only limited rights.

Though the New Deal had gone intellectually bankrupt long before Pearl Harbor and reform energies were submerged during most of the war, they reappeared in the last years of the conflict. Reviving the reform spirit in 1944, Roosevelt called for an "Economic Bill of Rights" for postwar America. In this last year, however, he was unable to achieve his goals, and Truman's efforts were usually too weak to overcome the conservative coalition blocking his expanded reform program. Mobilized by apprehension, liberals wrongly believed that the conservative bloc wished to destroy unions, to reorganize the corporate economy, and to leave the nation without protection from depression. But as unions endured and the economy grew, the fears and energies of liberals waned. Exaggerating the accomplishments of past reforms and believing that widespread prosperity had been achieved, they lost much of their social vision: they came to praise big business, to celebrate pluralism, to ignore poverty. Yet to their surprise they fell under vigorous attack from the right, in a new assault on civil liberties. In viewing McCarthyism as an attack upon the reform tradition, however, liberals failed to understand that they and the Democratic administration, as zealous anticommunists, also shared responsibility for the "red scare."

I

During the war and postwar years, big business regained national admiration and received lavish praise for contributing to victory over fascism. Yet few realized that business had not initially been an enthusiastic participant in the "arsenal of democracy." Such firms as Standard Oil of New Jersey, Dow Chemical, United States Steel, Dupont, General Motors, and the Aluminum Company of America had assisted the growth of Nazi industry and delayed America's preparation for war. Even after most Americans had come to condemn fascism, these corporations had collaborated with German business, sharing patents and often blocking production of defense materials in America. The general ideology of these firms was probably best expressed by Alfred Sloan, Jr., the chairman of the General Motors board, when he replied to a stockholder: ". . . an international business operating throughout the world should conduct its operations in strictly business terms without regard to the political beliefs in its management, or the political beliefs of the country in which it is operating."

In the two years before Pearl Harbor, major industries were also reluctant to prepare for defense. Though the aircraft industry ended its "sit-down" strike after the government had relaxed profit restrictions and improved terms for amortization, other industries continued to resist expansion and production for defense. Sharing the common opinion that American intervention was unlikely, and painfully recalling the glutted markets of the depression decade, the steel industry and the aluminum monopoly (Alcoa) opposed growth, which might endanger profits. Nor were the automobile makers and larger producers of consumer durables willing to take defense contracts which would convert assembly lines from profitable, peacetime goods to preparation for a war that many believed, and President Roosevelt seemed to promise, America would never enter.

Fearful of bad publicity, the leaders of these industries never challenged the administration nor demanded a clear statement of their responsibility. They avoided a dialogue on the basic issues. Still suffering from the opprobrium of the depression, industrialists would not deny corporate responsibility to the nation. Though privately concerned about the welfare of their companies, industrialists never argued that they owed primary responsibility to their stockbearers. Fearful of jeopardizing their firms' well-being, company officials did not publicly express their doubts. Yet they could have objected publicly to executive suasion and contended that the issues were so grave that a Congressional mandate was necessary. Instead, they publicly accepted their obligation to risk profits for American defense, but in practice they continued to avoid such risks. Often they made promises they did not fulfill, and when they resisted administration policy, they took refuge in evasion. They restricted the dialogue to matters of feasibility and tactics—that expansion in steel and aluminum was unnecessary, that partial conversion was impossible, and that available tools could not produce defense goods.

The government also avoided opening the dialogue. The prewar mobilization agencies, administered largely by dollar-a-year men, did not seek to embarrass or coerce recalcitrant industries. Protecting business from public censure, the directors of mobilization—such men as William Knudsen of General Motors and Edward Stettinius of United States Steel—resisted the efforts of other government officials to force prompt expansion and conversion. In effect, Knudsen, Stettinius, and their cohorts acted as protectors of "business as usual." Despite the protests of the service secretaries, Roosevelt permitted the businessmen in government to move slowly. Though he encouraged some assistants to prod business, and occasionally spurred the dollar-a-year men, he avoided exerting direct pressure on big business.

The President was following the strategy of caution. Reluctant to encourage public criticism of, or even debate on, his foreign policy, he maneuvered to avoid conflict or challenge. Because the nation respected big businessmen, he chose them to direct mobilization. He too had faith in their ability, and he hoped to win cooperation from the suspicious business community by selecting its leaders as his agents.

While many liberals criticized Roosevelt's reliance upon big business, the most direct, public challenge to business power came from Walter Reuther, vice-president of the recently formed United Automobile Workers, and from Philip Murray, president of the CIO and the United Steel Workers. Criticizing "business as usual" policies, they proposed a labor-management council to guide industry during war. The plan shocked industrialists. It was radicalism, an invasion of management's prerogatives, a threat to private enterprise, asserted business leaders. They would not share power or sanction a redefinition of private property. Having grudgingly recognized industrial unions shortly before the war, they remained suspicious of organized labor and were unwilling to invite its leaders into the industrial councils of decision making.

Despite these suspicions, the administration called upon labor leaders and their organizations for cooperation in the war effort. Needing their support, Roosevelt appointed union chiefs to positions in the stabilization and mobilization agencies, and thus bestowed prestige upon organized labor. Calling for a labor-management partnership, he secured a wartime no-strike pledge. As junior partners in the controlled economy, labor leaders generally kept the pledge.[1] Cooperating with business leaders in the defense effort, union representatives, by their actions, convinced many businessmen that organized labor did not threaten large-scale corporate capitalism.[2] By encouraging labor-management cooperation, the war years, then, provided a necessary respite between the industrial violence of the thirties and sustained collective bargaining and speeded the consolidation of the new organization of the American economy.

It was within a government-controlled economy (dominated by business) that the major interests struggled for economic advantages. Farmers, rescued from the depression by enlarged demand, initially battled price controls but soon acceded to them and tried simply to use political power to increase their benefits. Also reaping the gains of war, workers received higher incomes but bitterly criticized the tight restraints on hourly wage increases. Business, also recovering from the depression, complained about price controls, which indirectly limited profits. Though all interests chafed under the restraints, none disputed in principle the need for government-imposed restraints on wages and prices: all agreed that a free price system during war, when civilian demand greatly outstripped consumer goods, would have created inequity and chaos.

Despite price restrictions and the excess-profits tax, the major corporations prospered, benefitting from cost-plus contracts and the five-year amortization plan (which made the new plants partial gifts from the government). As dollar-a-year men poured into Washington, big firms gained influence and contracts. Smaller businessmen, unable to match the influence and mistrusted by procurement officers declined in importance. In a nation that prized the large corporation, few had confidence in small business. Even the creation of a government agency to protect small business failed to increase significantly its share in the war economy.

The interests of big business were defended and advanced by the dollar-a-year men, and particularly by those on the War Production Board (WPB), the agency controlling resources. In many wartime Washington agencies, and especially on the WPB, the leaders of big business and the military served together and learned to cooperate. Burying earlier differences about preparation for war, they developed similar views of the national interest and identified it with the goals of their own groups. The reconversion controversy of 1944, which C. Wright Mills views as the beginning of the military-industrial alliance, is the outstanding example of this coalition of interests.

In early 1944, big business was experiencing large military cutbacks and withdrawing subcontracts from smaller firms, often leaving them idle. Temporarily proponents of strong controls, most of the WPB executives from industry and finance would not allow these smaller firms to return to consumer goods. They collaborated with representatives of the military to block the reconversion program. Desiring control of the wartime economy, such military leaders as Robert P. Patterson, Under Secretary of War, James Forrestal, Under Secretary of the Navy, and Major General Lucius Clay, Assistant Chief of Staff for Matériel, feared that reconversion would siphon off scarce labor and disrupt vital production. Joining them were such WPB executives as Charles E. Wilson, president of General Electric, Lemuel Boulware, a Celotex executive and later a General Electric vice-president, and financiers Arthur H. Bunker of Lehman Brothers and Sidney Weinberg of Goldman, Sachs. Sympathetic to military demands, they were also afraid that the earlier return of small producers to consumer markets would injure big business. While some may have acted to protect their own companies, most were simply operating in a value system that could not accept a policy which seemed to threaten big business. Through cunning maneuvering, these military and industrial leaders acted to protect the prewar oligopolistic structure of the American economy.

The war, while creating the limited prosperity that the New Deal had failed to create, did not disrupt the economic distribution of power. Nor did the extension of the wartime income tax significantly reallocate income and wealth, for the Congress even rebuffed Roosevelt's effort to limit the war incomes of the wealthy. Though the wartime measures and not the New Deal increased the tax burden on the upper-income groups, "the major weight," emphasizes Gabriel Kolko, "fell on income groups that had never before been subjected to the income tax."

II

Failing to limit business power or to reallocate wealth, the wartime government was more active in other areas. Yielding to pressures, Roosevelt slightly advanced the welfare of the Negro, but the President also bowed to illiberal pressures and dealt a terrible blow to civil liberties when he authorized the forced evacuation of 110,000 loyal Americans of Japanese descent.

It was the "worst single wholesale violation of civil rights" in American history, judged the American Civil Liberties Union. Succumbing to the anti-Japanese hysteria of Westerners (including the pleas of California Attorney-General Earl Warren and the Pacific coast congressional delegation under Senator Hiram Johnson) and the demands of the military commander on the coast, the President empowered the Army to remove the Japanese-Americans.[3] ("He was never theoretical about things. What must be done to defend the country must be done," Roosevelt believed, later wrote Francis Biddle, his Attorney-General.) "Japanese raids on the west coast seemed not only possible but probable in the first months of war, and it was quite impossible to be sure that the raiders would not receive important help from individuals of Japanese origin," was the explanation later endorsed by Secretary of War Henry Stimson.[4]

Privately Stimson called the episode a "tragedy," but he supported it as War Department policy. Opposing the decision, Biddle could not weaken the resolve of Roosevelt. Though liberals protested the action, the Supreme Court later upheld Roosevelt and the War Department.[5] "The meaning of the decision," concludes Arthur Link, "was clear and foreboding: in future emergencies no American citizen would have any rights that the President and the army were bound to respect when, *in their judgment,* the emergency justified drastic denial of civil rights."

Though anti-Japanese feeling was most virulent on the Pacific coast, racism was not restricted to any part of America. In most of America, Negroes had long been the victims of hatred. Frequently lacking effective legal protection in the South, Negroes also encountered prejudice, fear, and hatred in the North. During the war there were racial clashes in Northern cities. New York narrowly averted a major riot. In Los Angeles whites attacked Negroes and Mexicans, and in Detroit whites invaded the Negro sector and pillaged and killed.[6]

Despite the evidence of deep racism, liberal historians have usually avoided focusing upon the hatred in white America and the resort to violence.[7] Curiously, though emphasizing the disorganization of the Negro community, they have also neglected the scattered protests by organized Negroes—boycotts of white-owned stores in Negro areas of Memphis and Houston when they would not hire Negroes, a sit-in in a public library in Alexandria, Virginia, a Harlem boycott of a bus line to compel the hiring of Negro drivers.

Condemned to inferiority in nearly all sectors of American life, Negroes did not share in the benefits of the early defense economy. Denied jobs in many industries, they also met discrimination by the military. The Air Corps barred them, the Navy segregated them to the mess corps, and the Army held them to a small quota, generally restricting them to menial tasks. During the 1940 campaign, Negro leaders attacked the administration for permitting segregation and discrimination, and demanded the broadening of opportunity in the military. It is not "a fight merely to wear a uniform," explained *Crisis* (the NAACP publication). "This is a struggle for status, a struggle to take democracy off a parchment and give it life."

Negroes gained admission to the Air Corps when it yielded under White House pressure, but they failed to gain congressional support for wider participation in the military. At Roosevelt's direction the War Department did raise its quota of Negroes—to their proportion in the population. But the Army remained segregated. Though unwilling to challenge segregation, the administration still courted Negro leaders and the black vote. Rather than bestowing benefits upon the masses, Roosevelt maintained their allegiance by offering symbolic recognition: Colonel Benjamin O. Davis, the Army's highest ranking Negro, was promoted to Brigadier General, and some prominent Negroes were appointed as advisers to the Secretary of War and the Director of Selective Service. ("We asked Mr. Roosevelt to change the rules of the game and he countered by giving us some new uniforms," complained the editors of the *Baltimore Afro-American*. "That is what it amounts to and we have called it appeasement.")

As the nation headed toward war, Negroes struggled to wring other concessions from a president who never enlisted in their cause and would not risk antagonizing powerful Southerners. Discriminated against by federal agencies during the depression and denied an equal share of defense prosperity, Negroes were unwilling to acquiesce before continued injustice. In some industrial areas the NAACP and *ad hoc* groups organized local protests. After numerous unsuccessful appeals to the President, Negro leaders planned more dramatic action—a march on Washington.

Demanding "the right to work and fight for our country," the leaders of the March on Washington Movement—A. Philip Randolph, head of the Brotherhood of Sleeping Car Porters, Walter White, executive secretary of the NAACP, and Lester Granger, executive secretary of the Urban League—publicly requested executive orders ending racial discrimination in federal agencies, the military and defense employment. In private correspondence with the President they sought more: the end of segregation in these areas. So bold were their goals that some still have not been enforced by the government, and it is unlikely that Negro leaders expected to secure them.

Refusing to give up the march for the promise of negotiations, Negro leaders escaped the politics of accommodation. Though white liberals urged Randolph and his cohorts to call off the march, they would not yield. Applying pressure on an uncomfortable administration, they ultimately settled for less than they had requested (and perhaps less than they had anticipated)—an executive order barring discrimination in defense work and creating a Federal Employment Practices Committee (FEPC). Meagers as the order was, it was the greatest achievement in American history for organized Negro action.[8]

FEPC did not contribute significantly to the wartime advancement of the Negro. His gains were less the results of federal efforts than of the labor shortage. Undoubtedly, the committee would have been more effective if Roosevelt had provided it with a larger budget, but the Negro's cause never commanded the President's enthusiasm. Yet he did protect FEPC from its enemies, and by maintaining the agency, stressed its symbolic importance.

It affirmed the rights of Negroes to jobs and focused attention on the power of the federal government to advance the interests of its black citizens. It did not smash the walls of prejudices; it only removed a few bricks. FEPC, concludes Louis Ruchames, "brought hope and a new confidence into their [Negro] lives. It gave them cause to believe in democracy and in America. It made them feel that in answering the call to their country's colors, they were defending, not the oppression and degradation, to which they were accustomed, but democracy, equality of opportunity, and a better world for themselves and their children."

Still relegated to second-class citizenship, Negroes had found new dignity and new opportunity during the war. Loyal followers of Roosevelt, loving him for the few benefits his government had extended, black Americans had become important members of the shifting Democratic coalition. By their presence in Northern cities, they would also become a new political force. For the Democratic party and the nation, their expectations and needs would constitute a moral and political challenge. By its response, white America would test the promise of liberal democracy.

III

When the nation joined the Allies, Roosevelt had explained that "Dr. Win-the-War" was taking over from "Dr. New Deal," and there were few liberal legislative achievements during the war years. Those benefits that disadvantaged groups did receive were usually a direct result of the labor shortage and the flourishing economy, not of liberal politics. By 1944, however, Roosevelt was prepared to revive the reform spirit, and he revealed his liberal vision for the postwar years. Announcing an "Economic Bill of Rights," he outlined "a new basis for security and prosperity": the right to a job, adequate food, clothing, and recreation, a decent home, a good education, adequate medical care, and protection against sickness and unemployment.[9]

Noble as was his vision of the future society, Roosevelt was still unprepared to move far beyond rhetoric, and the Congress was unsympathetic to his program. While approving the GI Bill of Rights,[10] including educational benefits and extended unemployment pay, Congress resisted most liberal programs during the war. Asserting its independence of the executive, the war Congress also thwarted Roosevelt in other ways—by rejecting a large tax bill designed to spread the cost of war and to reduce inflationary pressures, and by liquidating the National Resources Planning Board, which had originated the "second bill of rights" and also studied postwar economic planning.

By its opposition to planning and social reform, Congress increased the anxieties of labor and liberals about the postwar years and left the new Truman administration poorly prepared for the difficult transition to a peacetime economy when the war suddenly ended. Fearing the depression that most economists forecast, the administration did, however, propose a tax cut of $5 billion. While removing many low-income recipients from the tax rolls, the law was also of great benefit to large corporations. Charging inequity, organized labor found little support in Congress or the executive, for the government was relying upon business activity, rather than on consumer purchasing power, to soften the economic decline. Significantly, despite the anticipated $30 billion deficit (plus the $5 billion tax), no congressman expressed any fear of an unbalanced budget. Clearly fiscal orthodoxy did not occupy a very high place in the scale of values of congressional conservatives, and they accepted in practice the necessity of an unbalanced budget.

Before the tax bill passed, the wartime harmony of the major interest groups had crumbled: each struggled to consolidate its gains and advance its welfare before the anticipated economic collapse. Chafing under the no-strike pledge and restrictions on wage raises, organized labor compelled the administration to relax its policy and free unions to bargain collectively. Farmers, fearful of depression, demanded the withdrawal of subsidies which artificially depressed prices. Big business, despite anticipated shortages, secured the removal of most controls on the allocation of resources.

As the economic forecasts shifted in late autumn, the administration discovered belatedly that inflation, not depression, was the immediate economic danger. The President acted sporadically to restrain inflationary pressures, but his efforts were too occasional, often misguided, and too weak to resist the demands of interest groups and actions of his own subordinates.

Beset by factionalism and staffed often by men of limited ability, Truman's early government floundered. By adopting the practice of cabinet responsibility and delegating excessive authority to department chiefs, Truman created a structure that left him uninformed: problems frequently developed unnoticed until they had swelled to crises, and the choice then was often between undesirable alternatives. Operating in a new politics, in the politics of inflation, he confronted problems requiring greater tactical skill than those Roosevelt had confronted. Seeking to maintain economic controls, and compelled to deny the rising expectations of major interest groups, his administration found it difficult to avoid antagonizing the rival groups. In the politics of depression, the Roosevelt administration could frequently maintain political support by bestowing specific advantages on groups, but in the politics of inflation the major interest groups came to seek freedom from restrictive federal controls.

So difficult were the problems facing Truman that even a more experienced and skilled president would have encountered great difficulty. Inheriting the hostile Congress that had resisted occasional wartime attempts at social reform, Truman lacked the skill or leverage to guide a legislature seeking to assert its independence of the executive. Unable to halt fragmentation of the Democratic coalition, and incapable of ending dissension in his government, he also found that conservative subordinates undercut his occasional liberalism. Though he had gone on record early in endorsing a reform program ("a declaration of independence" from congressional conservatives, he called it),[11] he had been unsuccessful in securing most of the legislation—a higher minimum wage, public housing, expanded unemployment benefits, and FEPC. Even the employment act was little more, as one congressman said, than a license to look for a job. The President, through ineptitude or lack of commitment, often chose not to struggle for his program. Unable to dramatize the issues or to command enthusiasm, he was an ineffectual leader.[12]

So unsuccessful was his government that voters began jibing, "To err is Truman." Despairing of a resurgence of liberalism under Truman, New Dealers left the government in droves. By the fall of 1946, none of Roosevelt's associates was left in a prominent position. So disgruntled were many liberals about Truman and his advisers, about his unwillingness to fight for price controls, housing, benefits for labor, and civil rights, that some turned briefly to serious consideration of a new party.[13]

IV

Achieving few reforms during his White House years, Truman, with the notable exception of civil rights, never moved significantly beyond Roosevelt. The Fair Deal was largely an extension of earlier Democratic liberalism, but Truman's new vigor and fierce partisanship ultimately made him more attractive to liberals who despairingly watched the GOP-dominated Eightieth Congress and feared a repeal of the New Deal.

Their fears were unwarranted, as was their enthusiasm for the Fair Deal program. In practice it proved very limited—the housing program only provided for 810,000 units in six years of which only 60,000 were constructed;[14] social security benefits were extended to ten million[15] and increased by about 75 per cent, and the minimum wage was increased to 75 cents, but coverage was reduced by nearly a million. But even had all of the Fair Deal been enacted, liberal reform would have left many millions beyond the benefits of government. The very poor, the marginal men, those neglected but acknowledged by the New Deal, went ultimately unnoticed by the Fair Deal.[16]

While liberals frequently chafed under Truman's leadership and questioned his commitment, they failed generally to recognize how shallow were his reforms. As the nation escaped a postwar depression, American liberals gained new faith in the American economy. Expressing their enthusiasm, they came to extoll big business for its contributions. Believing firmly in the success of progressive taxation, they exaggerated its effects, and congratulated themselves on the redistribution of income and the virtual abolition of poverty. Praising the economic system, they accepted big agriculture and big labor as evidence of healthy pluralism that protected freedom and guaranteed an equitable distribution of resources.

Despite the haggling over details and the liberals' occasional dismay at Truman's style, he expressed many of their values. Like Roosevelt, Truman never challenged big business, never endangered large-scale capitalism. Indeed, his efforts as well as theirs were directed largely to maintaining and adjusting the powers of the major economic groups.

Fearing that organized labor was threatened with destruction, Truman, along with the liberals, had been sincerely frightened by the postwar rancor toward labor. What they failed to understand was that most Americans had accepted unions as part of the political economy. Certainly most major industrialists had accepted organized labor, though smaller businessmen were often hostile. Despite the overwrought rhetoric of debates, Congress did not actually menace labor. It was not seeking to destroy labor, only to restrict its power.

Many Americans did believe that the Wagner Act had unduly favored labor and was creating unions indifferent to the public welfare and hostile to corporate power. Capitalizing on this exaggerated fear of excessive union power, and the resentment from the postwar strikes, businessmen secured the Taft-Hartley Act. Designed to weaken organized labor, it tried but failed to protect the membership from leaders; it did not effectively challenge the power of established unions. However, labor chiefs, recalling the bitter industrial warfare of the thirties, were still uneasy in their new positions. Condemning the legislation as a "slave-labor" act, they responded with fear, assailed the Congress, and declared that Taft-Hartley was the major political issue.

Within a few years, when unions discovered that they were safe, Taft-Hartley faded as an issue. But in 1948 it served Truman well by establishing the GOP's hostility to labor and casting it back into the Democratic ranks. Both the President and union chiefs conveniently neglected his own kindling of antilabor passions (as when he had tried to draft strikers). Exploiting Taft-Hartley as part of his strategy of patching the tattered Democratic coalition, Truman tied repeal of the "slave-labor" law to price controls, farm benefits, anticommunism, and civil rights in the campaign which won his election in his own right.

V

In courting the Negro the Truman administration in 1948 made greater promises to black citizens than had any previous federal government in American history. Yet, like many Americans, Truman as a senator had regarded the Negro's plight as peripheral to his interests, and with many of his generation he believed that equality was compatible with segregation. As President, however, he found himself slowly prodded by conscience and pushed by politics. He moved cautiously at first and endorsed only measures affirming legal equality and protecting Negroes from violence.

Reluctant to fragment the crumbling Democratic coalition, Truman, in his first year, had seemed to avoid taking positions on civil rights which might upset the delicate balance between Northern and Southern Democrats. While he endorsed legislation for a statutory FEPC that the Congress would not grant, his efforts on behalf of the temporary FEPC (created by Roosevelt's executive order) were weaker. Having already weakened the power of the temporary agency, he also acquiesced in the legislative decision to kill it. Despite the fears of Negro leaders that the death of FEPC would leave Negroes virtually unprotected from discrimination in the postwar job market, Truman would not even issue an order requiring nondiscrimination in the federal service and by government contractors.

Though Truman was unwilling to use the prestige or power of his great office significantly on behalf of Negroes, he did assist their cause. While sidestepping political conflict, he occasionally supported FEPC and abolition of the poll tax. When Negroes were attacked, he did condemn the racial violence. Though generally reluctant to move beyond rhetoric during his early years, Truman, shortly before the 1946 election, found conscience and politics demanding more. So distressed was he by racial violence that when Walter White of the NAACP and a group of white liberals urged him to assist the Negro, he promised to create a committee to study civil rights.

The promise of a committee could have been a device to resist pressures, to delay the matter until after the election. And Truman could have appointed a group of politically safe men of limited reputation—men he could control. But instead, after the election, perhaps in an effort to mobilize the liberals for 1948, he appointed a committee of prominent men sympathetic to civil rights. They were men he could not control and did not seek to control.

The committee's report, undoubtedly far bolder than Truman's expectations, confirmed charges that America treated its Negroes as second-class citizens. It called for FEPC, an antilynching law, an anti-poll tax measure, abolition of segregation in interstate transportation, and the end of discrimination and segregation in federal agencies and the military. By attacking Jim Crow, the committee had moved to a redefinition of equality and interpreted segregation as incompatible with equality.

Forced by the report to take a position, he no longer could easily remain an ally of Southern Democrats and maintain the wary allegiance of Negro leaders and urban liberals. Compelled earlier to yield to demands for advancement of the Negro, pressures which he did not wish fully to resist, Truman had encouraged these forces and they were moving beyond his control. On his decision, his political future might precariously rest. Threatened by Henry Wallace's candidacy on a third-party ticket, Truman had to take a bold position on civil rights or risk losing the important votes of urban Negroes. Though he might antagonize Southern voters, he foresaw no risk of losing Southern Democrats, no possibility of a bolt by dissidents, and the mild Southern response to the Civil Rights Report seemed to confirm this judgment.

On February 2, 1948, Truman asked the Congress to enact most of the recommendations of his Civil Rights Committee (except most of those attacking segregation). Rather than using his executive powers, as the committee had urged, to end segregation in federal employment or to abolish segregation and discrimination in the military, he *promised* only to issue orders ending discrimination (but not specifying segregation) in the military and in federal agencies. Retreating to moderation, the administration did not submit any of the legislation, nor did Truman issue the promised executive orders. "The strategy," an assistant later explained, "was to start with a bold measure and then temporize to pick up the right-wing forces. Simply stated, backtrack after the bang."

Truman sought to ease Southern doubts by inserting in the 1948 platform the party's moderate 1944 plank on civil rights. Most Negro leaders, fearing the taint of Wallace and unwilling to return to the GOP, appeared stuck with Truman and they praised him. Though they desired a stronger plank, they would not abandon him at the convention, for his advocacy of rights for Negroes was unmatched by any twentieth-century president. To turn their backs on him in this time of need, most Negroes feared, would be injuring their own cause. But others were prepared to struggle for a stronger plank. Urban bosses, persuaded that Truman would lose, hoped to save their local tickets, and prominent white liberals sought power and principle. Triumphing at the convention, they secured a stronger plank, but it did not promise social equality. By promising equality when it was still regarded as compatible with segregation, they were offering far less than the "walk forthrightly into the bright sunshine of human rights," which Hubert Humphrey, then mayor of Minneapolis, has pledged in leading the liberal effort.

When some of the Southerners bolted and formed the States Rights party, Truman was freed of any need for tender courtship of the South. He had to capture the Northern vote. Quickly he issued the long-delayed executive orders, which established a federal antidiscrimination board, declared a policy of equal opportunity in the armed forces, and established a committee to end military discrimination and segregation. (In doing so, Truman courted Negro voters and halted the efforts of A. Philip Randolph to lead a Negro revolt against the draft unless the military was integrated.) Playing politics carefully during the campaign, Truman generally stayed away from civil rights and concentrated on inflation, public housing, and Taft-Hartley.

In the new Democratic Congress Truman could not secure the civil rights program, and a coalition of Southern Democrats and Northern Republicans blocked his efforts. Though liberals were unhappy with his leadership, they did not question his proposed legislation. All agreed on the emphasis on social change through legislation and judicial decisions. The liberal way was the legal way, and it seldom acknowledged the depth of American racism or even considered the possibility of bold new tactics. Only occasionally—in the threatened March on Washington in 1941, in some ride-ins in 1947, and in the campaign of civil disobedience against the draft in 1948—had there been bolder means. In each case Negroes had devised and carried out these tactics. But generally they relied upon more traditional means: they expected white America to yield to political pressure and subscribe to the dictates of American democracy. By relying upon legal change, however, and by emphasizing measures to restore a *modicum* of human dignity, Negroes and whites did not confront the deeper problems of race relations which they failed to understand.[17]

Struggling for moderate institutional changes, liberals were disappointed by Truman's frequent unwillingness to use his executive powers in behalf of the cause he claimed to espouse. Only after considerable pressure did he create a FEPC-type agency during the Korean War. His loyalty-and-security program, in its operation, discriminated against Negroes, and federal investigators, despite protests to Truman, apparently continued to inquire into attitudes of interracial sympathy as evidence relevant to a determination of disloyalty. He was also slow to require the Federal Housing Administration to stop issuing mortgages on property with restrictive covenants, and it continued, by its policies, to protect residential segregation.

Yet his government was not without significant achievements in civil rights. His special committee had quietly acted to integrate the armed forces, and even the recalcitrant Army had abolished racial quotas when the President secretly promised their restoration if the racial imbalance became severe. And the Department of Justice, despite Truman's apparent indifference, had been an active warrior in the battle against Jim Crow. Entering cases as an *amicus curiae,* Justice had submitted briefs arguing the unconstitutionality of enforcing restrictive covenants and of requiring separate-but-equal facilities in interstate transportation and in higher education. During the summer of 1952, the Solicitor-General's office even won the administration's approval for a brief directly challenging segregated primary education.

The accomplishments of the Truman years were moderate, and the shortcomings left the nation with a great burden of unresolved problems. Viewed from the perspective of today, Truman's own views seem unduly mild and his government excessively cautious; viewed even by his own time he was a reluctant liberal, troubled by terror and eager to establish limited equality. He was ahead of public opinion in his legislative requests, but not usually in his actions. By his occasional advocacy, he educated the nation and held high the promise of equality. By kindling hope, he also may have prevented rebellion and restrained or delayed impulses to work outside of the system. But he also unleashed expectations he could not foresee, and forces which future governments would not be able to restrain.

NOTES

1. Joel Seidman, *American Labor from Defense to Reconversion* (Chicago, 1953), pp. 131–51. It was in response to the coal strikes led by John Lewis that Congress passed the Smith-Connally Act.
2. "With few exceptions, throughout the war years labor, not management, made the sacrifices when sacrifices were necessary," concludes Paul A. C. Koistinen, "The Hammer and the Sword: Labor, the Military, and Industrial Mobilization" (unpublished Ph.D. dissertation, University of California at Berkeley, 1965), p. 143.
3. Stetson Conn *et al., Guarding the United States and Its Outposts,* in *United States Army in World War II: The Western Hemisphere* (Washington, 1964), pp. 115–49. The Canadian government also moved Japanese away from the coast.
4. Quoted from Henry L. Stimson and McGeorge Bundy, *On Active Service* (New York, 1948, p. 406. The prose is presumably Bundy's, but Stimson apparently endorsed the thought (p. xi). Also see War Department, *Final Report: Japanese Evacuation from the West Coast* (Washington, 1943), pp. 9–10.
5. *Korematsu* v. *U.S.,* 323 US 214, at 219. The Court split and Justice Black wrote the opinion. Justices Roberts, Murphy and Jackson dissented. Also see *Hirabayshi* v. *U.S.,* 320 US 81.
6. Apparently Roosevelt refused to condemn the riots. Vito Marcantonio to Roosevelt, June 16, 1943, and reply, July 14, 1943, Vito Marcantonio Papers, New York Public Library. Also see Roosevelt's Proclamation No. 2588, in Samuel Rosenman, ed., *The Public Papers of Franklin D. Roosevelt,* (13 vols.; New York, 1938–50), XII, 258–59.
7. "This was the dark side of an otherwise bright picture," concludes Link, *American Epoch,* p. 529. Also see Frank Freidel, *American in the Twentieth Century* (New York, 1960), p. 405. Oscar Handlin, *The American People in the Twentieth Century* (Cambridge, Mass., 1954), p. 215; Everett C. Hughes, "Race Relations and the Sociological Imagination," *American Sociological Review,* XXVIII (December 1963), 879–90.
8. For the notion that the events of the war years constitute the beginnings of the civil rights revolution, see Dalfiume, "Desegregation of the Armed Forces," pp. 177–89.
9. Message on the State of the Union, January 11, 1944, in Rosenman, ed., *Public Papers of Roosevelt,* XIII, p. 41. For some evidence that Roosevelt was at least talking about a new alignment of politics, see Samuel Rosenman, *Working with Roosevelt* (London, 1952), pp. 423–29. Probably this was a tactical maneuver.
10. President's statement on signing the GI Bill of Rights, June 22, 1944, in Rosenman, ed., *Public Papers on Roosevelt,* XIII, 180–82, and Rosenman's notes, pp. 183–84. The GI Bill has generally been neglected as an antidepression measure.
11. Quoted in Jonathan Daniels, *The Man of Independence* (Philadelphia, 1950), p. 288. For evidence that Truman was trying to head off a bolt by liberals, see *New York Times,* August 12, 1945; Harold Smith Daily Record, August 13, 1945, Bureau of the Budget Library, Washington, D.C.
12. Lubell, *The Future of American Politics,* pp. 8–27, while emphasizing the continuation of the prewar executive-legislative stalemate and the strength of conservative forces in the postwar years, has also been critical of Truman. "All his skills and energies . . . were directed to standing still. . . . When he took vigorous action in one direction it was axiomatic that he would contrive soon afterward to move in the conflicting direction" (p. 10). Cf. Richard Neustadt, "Congress and the Fair Deal: A Legislative Balance Sheet," in Carl Friedrich and John Galbraith, eds., *Public Policy,* V, 351–81.
13. Curtis MacDougall, *Gideon's Army* (3 vols.; New York, 1965–66), I, 102–27. The National Educational Committee for a New Party, which would be explicitly anticommunist, included John Dewey, A. Philip Randolph, Daniel Bell and Lewis Corey.
14. Richard O. Davis, *Housing Reform during the Truman Administration* (Columbia, Mo.) p. 136. The original measure aimed for 1,050,000 units in seven years, at a time when the nation needed more than 12,000,000 units to replace inadequate housing. During the Truman years, the government constructed 60,000 units of public housing (pp. 105–38). Rather than creating programs to keep pace with urban needs, the government in these years fell further behind. In contrast, private industry was more active, and it was assisted by non-constroversial federal aid. Under Truman's government, then, the greatest achieve-

ment in housing was that private capital, protected by the government, built houses for the higher-income market.

15. Under the old law, the maximum benefit for families was $85 a month and the minimum was $15, depending on prior earnings. The new minimum was $25 and the maximum $150. (*Social Security Bulletin,* September 1950, p. 3). Unless couples also had other sources of income, even maximum benefits ($1,800 a year) placed them $616 under the BLS "maintenance" standard of living and $109 above the WPA-based "emergency" standard of living —the poverty level. (Calculations based on Kolko, *Wealth and Power,* pp. 96–98.) Since the payments were based on earnings, lower-income groups would receive even fewer benefits. They were the people generally without substantial savings or significant supplementary sources of income, and therefore they needed even more, not less, assistance.

16. Bernstein, "Economic Policies of the Truman Administration." Truman had achieved very little: improved unemployment benefits, some public power and conservation projects, agricultural assistance, and a National Science Foundation. He failed to secure the ill-conceived Brannan Plan and two programs suggested by Roosevelt: federal aid to education and health insurance. For his health insurance programs, see his messages of November 19, 1945, in *Public Papers of Truman* (1945), pp. 485–90, and of May 19, 1947, in *ibid.,* (1947), pp. 250–52. In 1951, when the BLS calculated that a family of four needed $4,166 to reach the "maintenance" level, 55.6 percent of the nation's families had incomes beneath that level (Bureau of the Census, *Income Distribution in the United States,* p. 16.).

17. There was no urging of special programs to assist Negroes left unemployed (at roughly double the white rate) in the mild recession of 1949–1950, nor was there open acknowledgement of race hatred.

The Cold War Begins   DAVID HOROWITZ

From a New Left perspective the greatest catastrophe of the Truman years was the advent of the Cold War. That event radical scholars lay at the door of the United States.

As the New Left sees it, by 1945 the Soviet Union was exhausted by its gigantic military effort in World War Two. Though the Communists had succeeded in destroying Hitler's war machine, the four-year struggle against the Nazis had produced vast human and physical devastation in Russia itself. The United States, on the other hand, emerged from the War unscathed, and was in a position to be generous to her former ally, who, in any case, could not afford to antagonize a nation armed with that most terrifying instrument of destruction ever devised, the Atom Bomb. Instead of recognizing her obligations to world peace, however, the United States chose to use its power to its own advantage. The wartime alliance with the Soviet Union did not long survive. Indeed, even before Hitler's surrender, it had begun to dissolve, and the use of the Atom Bomb on Japan had been designed to intimidate the Soviet leaders and force them to make concessions to the Anglo-American position on the future of Eastern Europe. Thereafter, the United States acted as if the Soviet Union was a serious threat to the "free world" and moved on every front to block her legitimate aspirations and to frustrate her natural desire for security.

Few of the New Left scholars have any illusions about the repressive and undemocratic nature of Soviet society. Yet they would deny that Russia at any time

Source: David Horowitz, *The Free World Colossus: A Critique of American Foreign Policy in the Cold War* (New York: Hill and Wang, 1965), chap. v, "The Cold War Begins," pp. 69–85.

endangered the safety of the United States, and they would insist that the obviously hostile intentions of the United States pushed the Russians into some of their more truculent responses. The earliest moves in what came to be called the Cold War, including the Marshall Plan, are described below by David Horowitz, in a chapter from his larger critique of post–World War Two American foreign relations.

FOR FURTHER READING:

Denna F. Fleming, *The Cold War and Its Origins 1917–1960,* (Doubleday, 1961); William Appleman Williams, *The Tragedy of American Diplomacy*,* (Delta, 1962); Ronald Steel, *Pax Americana,* (Viking, 1968); Walter LaFeber, *America, Russia and the Cold War 1945–1966*,* (Wiley, 1967); Herbert Feis, *The Atomic Bomb and the End of World War II,* (Princeton University Press, 1966); Gar Alperovitz, *Atomic Diplomacy: Cold War Essays,* (Doubleday, 1969); Arthur Schlesinger Jr., "Origins of the Cold War," *Foreign Affairs* (October, 1967).

Asterisk denotes paperback edition.

After the dissolution of the wartime alliance, there remained only one possible bulwark against the imminence of a dangerous "world split"; that bulwark was the nascent United Nations. The destructions of the war had left an extraordinary imbalance in the world's industrial power structure. Three-quarters of the world's invested capital and two-thirds of its industrial capacity were concentrated inside one country, the United States; the rest was shared over the other 95 per cent of the earth's inhabited surface. "One nation had acquired a near monopoly on [the] all-important factor for sustaining life." It was the United States, therefore, that was faced with the decision which it alone could make: whether to use its industrial capacity to promote international reconstruction through an international agency, thus laying the groundwork for a stable world order—or whether to use its capacity as an instrument of power-politics, that is, to establish an American hegemony over the existing international power structure, to reconstruct one power center at the expense of others and in that way to promote American political and economic ends. This decision had already been taken by 1946.

The United Nations Relief and Rehabilitation Administration had been set up in 1943 to provide aid in food and goods to populations which might otherwise have starved. It was financed by the United States and administered through the United Nations. Fiorello La Guardia, former New Deal mayor of New York who administered the program, told the United Nations General Assembly in 1946 that unless relief of this kind continued, there would be widespread starvation. He proposed to set up a Food Fund to carry on the work of UNRRA (which had been scheduled for completion by 1947—though its work proved to be far from done) and this was warmly supported by the other representatives, except the American and British delegations.

To the dismay of the Assembly, the British and Americans recommended instead that individual governments and international organizations give assistance to those countries which they saw fit to help. America and Britain turned down every amended proposal which was suggested and announced that they would refuse to accept any majority vote on the subject that did not meet their point of view. In other words, any further relief was to be given under conditions of strict political discrimination.

La Guardia was horrified. "Does the Government of the United States," he exclaimed, "intend to adopt a policy which will make innocent men and women suffer because of the political situation which makes their Government unacceptable to the United States? . . . Each rich nation will choose the recipient and make its own conditions. That's plain, ordinary, old-time power politics that has produced war after war."

The UNRRA case illustrates how ready the new United States leadership was to abandon far-sighted wartime policies. Had the new Administration, in fact, continued to pursue the Roosevelt course of treating nations as equals, of seeking to create and strengthen truly international agencies, they might have had a more credible case in disclaiming, as they did, all responsibility for the failure to lay the foundations for international order in the post-war world. But this UNRRA case proved to be only the beginning of a consistent United States pattern of by-passing international agencies and orienting key global programs from the standpoint of its own narrow national interest.

The Soviet veto has long been held up as the force that singlehandedly rendered the United Nations ineffective in these years, but this is not borne out by the record. Of forty uses of the veto by the Russians through 1949, twenty-two were on membership applications, an aftermath of the Argentine affair and the decision of the United States to marshal bloc majorities instead of working towards compromise in terms of existing relations of power. The Soviet veto only "was effective in excluding a committee of inquiry into the change of régime in Czechoslovakia. In all other cases it was bypassed in one way or another, so far as practical results are concerned."

Unlike the Soviet Union, the United States controlled the voting majority in the United Nations and thus could be confident in the basic direction of its policies. The United States' failure to transfer some of the vast power that it had accumulated to the authority of the United Nations can have only one explanation. In the classic manner of strong nation states America wanted that power, to exercise it by means and for purposes as she saw fit. Thus when it was within her ability to strengthen and effectively create a sorely needed international machinery, the United States chose to preserve the traditional power structure of nation states, and to enjoy her newly achieved predominance (supplanting Britain, Germany and Japan) even if it meant aborting or rendering ineffectual the United Nations.

In the Fall of 1946, there had been some hopeful signs that the growing breach between East and West might still be healed. The peace treaties with the Nazi satellites (Italy, Bulgaria, Finland, Hungary and Rumania) had been agreed upon and signed, and for a few weeks the feeling of "peace" was really in the air. The United States had ended a bone of contention by returning six hundred Danubian barges and ships to their Danubian owners (they had been impounded in Germany) while Bulgarian and Rumanian officials made statements welcoming American friendship and capital, and the United States and Czechoslovakia patched up their recently strained relations. "The sun of peace is rising at last," commented British Foreign Secretary Bevin in New York.

Then, in the last days of January 1947, the worst snowstorm since 1894 descended on Britain and paralyzed her. Within four months, it was demonstrated to the world that where once the seat of mighty empire had stood, only a gaping power vacuum remained, so financially ruined as to be incapable of supporting army or navy, the necessary instruments of her will. As a result, India, Burma, Palestine were cast loose from British rule (Palestine to United Nations administration); South Africa, Guatemala, Argentina, Iraq and Egypt challenged the shell of English power in one way or another without suffering reprisal.

This crisis led Britain to inform the United States on February 24, that she could no longer pay for her troops in Greece or continue aid to Turkey. On March 12, 1947, Truman went before Congress to announce the Truman Doctrine and to seek military and economic aid for the two countries, especially Greece where civil war was still raging. However, instead of proposing to assist in solving the genuine social and economic crisis of Greece, President Truman used the occasion of Britain's withdrawal to launch an ideological crusade against totalitarian régimes. Truman declared that every nation was faced with a choice between alternative ways of life.

> One way of life is based upon the will of the majority, and is distinguished by free institutions, representative government, free elections, guarantees of individual liberty, freedom of speech and religion and freedom from political repression.
> The second way of life is based upon the will of a minority forcibly imposed upon the majority. It relies upon terror and oppression, a controlled press and radio, fixed elections, and the suppression of personal freedom. . . .

Taken in the abstract the conflict of values expressed here is one of the most critical that political man has to face. In the context of the world of 1947, however, the statement was a vast oversimplification of a very complex set of choices in a very complex world system. In the context of the specific situation in Greece, the best that could be said of Truman's antithesis was that it was irrelevant. Greece under Tsaldaris was quite obviously a totalitarian régime, and United States economic and military aid was clearly aid to totalitarian forces.

This widely noted gap between Truman's rhetoric and the concrete reality at hand was hardly surprising since the Doctrine had been in Truman's mind a long time before it was announced. As early as the London Conference of Foreign Ministers in September 1945, he had decided to proclaim the existence of a world division and the United States' determination to crusade against one of the two parties. "He made up his mind then that, when a fitting opportunity arose and one which Congress and the people would recognize as such, he would proclaim the new doctrine," wrote Arthur Krock, the informed Washington columnist of the New York *Times*. "On several occasions he thought the time had come, but some of his important advisors talked him out of it." When the British informed the United States that they were withdrawing from Greece, a situation arrived which Truman found suited to his "long held purpose", and Clark Clifford was set to drafting "the global anti-Communist policy."

Such was the genesis of perhaps the major document in America's cold war offensive: an ideology waiting for a set of facts (and as it happened, the wrong facts) to confirm it. Small wonder that the scholarly Kennan was distraught at this version of containment.

The Truman Doctrine, of course, was more than mere rhetoric; it also postulated a *modus operandi* which embodied an important policy decision, namely, *to by-pass the United Nations.*

Four months earlier, the Food and Agriculture Organization (FAO) of the United Nation's Economic and Social Council had produced a complete plan for Greek reconstruction, which would not have been subject to any veto, because no veto existed in the Council. Moreover, the plan would not have precluded the sending of military aid to the country while it was still unable to stabilize itself under the reconstruction program.

But the Truman Administration was not interested in the United Nations at this point. Instead of transferring what had been a British sphere of influence into the hands of the United Nations, thereby extending the authority of the organization and acting to establish a new order in international affairs, the United States chose to *replace* Britain as a national power in that area.

The repercussions of this action were immediate and profound. On March 10, the Moscow Conference of Foreign Ministers had opened negotiations on the major problems confronting the two great powers. According to W. W. Rostow, Director of the State Department's Policy Planning Staff in the Kennedy and Johnson Administrations and from 1947 to 1949 special assistant to the Executive Secretary of the Economic Commission for Europe, the failure of this conference was the irreversible turning point in postwar relations with the Soviet Union. Wrote Rostow:

> The United States went to the Moscow meetings prepared with a range of clear detailed negotiating positions in order to establish whether Soviet objectives were compatible with American interests on the questions of German unity, German disarmament, and the end of the Austrian occupation.

The delegation went "prepared to stretch to the limit to meet legitimate Russian security interests in the structure of Germany and Europe" in a mood "of searching flexibility" and "mature realization of the consequence of failure in Moscow: a split Germany and Europe the reunification of which was difficult if not impossible to perceive through the mists of a dangerous and tense future."

Here then was the key post-war moment, an effort by the United States to go all out in a spirit of compromise to reach an accord with the Soviets. Here, if at any time, the "split" was preventable. But, alas, "the position taken by the Soviet negotiators was thoroughly unambiguous: Stalin refused to move toward a definitive settlement in Europe." Thus defeated in their carefully planned move to prevent the tragic inception of the cold war, "the Americans came home from Moscow firm in the conclusion that the United States should never again negotiate from a base of weakness." Reports of Europe's benighted economic condition then converged "with the conclusions about Stalin's attitude and intentions drawn from the Moscow Conference [to] set the stage for the Marshall Plan."

The Marshall Plan, then, was conceived as a "counter-offensive" (Rostow's term) to the Soviet Union's moves in East Europe and as a reaction to Stalin's decision, registered at the Moscow Conference, to rebuff all gestures of compromise looking toward settlement of the problem dividing Europe. In line with this partisan conception, the Marshall Plan by-passed the United Nations Economic Commission for Europe which was composed of every European state and gave no veto right to its members:

> . . . there was even in being an organization dedicated to European economic co-operation—the Economic Commission for Europe—*The ECE was, however, an organization of the United Nations, with Soviet and Eastern European countries as members. Its very existence posed a basic question. Should an effort be made to embrace all of Europe in a new enterprise of reconstruction, or should the lesson of the Moscow Conference be read as indicating that the only realistic*

alternative for the West was to accept the split and to strengthen the area still outside Stalin's grasp? [Emphasis added.]

The decision, of course, was to "accept the split" and in effect to intensify it. Central to Rostow's argument in placing the onus for this split on the Soviet Union, was his contention that at the Moscow Conference a serious and well planned United States gesture of compromise was met with intransigence. The United States response to this Soviet attitude was to adopt a cold war posture and launch a counter-offensive.

Given the circumstances in which Rostow's book was written, his thesis reflects apparently the then prevailing view within the State Department. The difficulty with this version of events is that it fails to take into account the fact that *it was precisely two days after the start of the Moscow Conference that Truman "shouted" his "war-cry" of March 12!* Howard K. Smith's eyewitness report records the catastrophic effect of the Truman Doctrine speech on the negotiations:

> Still in the glow of the settlement on the satellite peace treaties in New York two months before [the Russians] were determined to be charming, amiable hosts. Vishinsky, the official welcomer, wrung the hand of John Foster Dulles before photographers as though he were a visiting delegate to the League of Proletarian Advocates and not a Wall Street Fascist Beast. . . .
>
> In the first days of the conference Soviet press reports on it were thorough and free from their customary acid asides on Western motives. Molotov proved uncommonly conciliatory in the opening discussion on rules of procedure and yielded his own suggestions first to those of Marshall, then to those of Bevin.
>
> The Russians undoubtedly assumed that all was well and that things would go according to prescription. They had learned the formula for procedure from the satellite negotiations and were prepared to follow it; but this time with more ease, for they knew the ropes: two years of haggling and pressuring until deadlock was reached, then settlement on that basis.

Stalin even told Marshall in the course of the conference that "these were only the first skirmishes and brushes of reconnaissance forces. . . . After people exhausted themselves in dispute, they then recognized the necessity of compromise. . . . That compromises were possible on all main questions. . . . It was necessary to have patience and not become pessimistic. . . ." But patience was given no chance to do its work.

> Right on top of the conference, two days after it opened, burst the bombshell of the Truman Doctrine. President Truman said, "nearly every nation must choose between" the two worlds; it sounded like an ultimatum to the rest of Europe to be with us or to be counted against us. That wiped the smiles off the Russians' faces. While America prepared to move into Greece, Russia proceeded to button up Hungary, arresting democratic leaders to the accompaniment of angry diplomatic protests from the West.
>
> . . . the four men sat down in a world in turmoil and tried to carry on as though it all had nothing to do with their conference. It was impossible.

From this impasse Marshall returned to America with plans for strengthening the Western bargaining position, since, in the words of Rostow, "it was useless to test Soviet intentions before self-evident Western strength and the development of alternatives to Soviet agreement had narrowed the realistic choices open to Moscow to a range of solutions compatible with the American interest."

In fact, however, there remained a "schism" in the State Department "in attitudes toward Eastern European and Soviet participation" in the projected Marshall Plan. Partly as a result of this schism, no official decision was taken to exclude the Communist and other East European states. Special care, moreover, was taken to provide the plan with a rhetoric which did not betray the more partisan intentions reflected in its structure. In his famous June 5 speech announcing the initiative, Secretary of State Marshall declared: "Our policy is directed not against any country or doctrine but against hunger, poverty, desperation and chaos."

For their part, the Soviets took a wait-and-see attitude and went so far as to allow Czechoslovakia, Poland and Yugoslavia to reach out "toward Marshall's initiative and to the West."

Under the terms of the Marshall proposal, the European powers were to draw up their own program for European recovery, which the United States (a Republican Congress willing) would then finance. For the purpose of drawing up such a plan, the European powers met in the summer of 1947 in Paris. The Soviets were invited by the British but according to Rostow, "Bevin and the British Foreign Office [as well as some American officials] were fearful that Stalin would agree and took no pains to create a hospitable atmosphere at Paris for Molotov."

Molotov arrived at the conference with a contingent of 89 economic experts and advisers. The Soviets, whose repeated three year request for a $6 billion credit from the United States had been "lost" in Washington, were cautious in their pre-conference statement to the British representative in Moscow.

In the fateful two days that Molotov remained in Paris, he was presented with a plan drawn up by Bevin and Bidault based on the principle of integrating national economies. But "integration in a single plan means that each nation must produce what it produces best. To Mr. Molotov this looked like asking the Eastern countries to jettison their various national 'plans' to industrialize, and to become instead the agricultural granary of the West; that would be the ideal integration. Tied to an industrial nation, an agricultural nation always becomes the weak dependent sister."

Molotov rejected the plan and walked out of the conference in a gesture of open hostility which stunned those who had seen the Marshall proposal, however, mistakenly, as a step toward the restoration of European unity. The manner and nature of his rejection were characteristic of Soviet diplomacy in the period that followed:

> . . . —breaking off talks in a peeve, giving no explanation save an acid, jargon-ridden attack on America that made little sense, leaping to the fantastic conclusion that the plan was a pattern for aggressive war against Russia and ordering Communists everywhere to sabotage the plan to the point of subverting their government— . . .

From the Soviet point of view, the challenge which the Marshall "counter-offensive" presented to their interests was serious. It must be remembered that "Eastern Europe in the early summer of 1947 had by no means reached full satellite status. A democratic government existed in Prague; in Warsaw all manner of Polish nationalists, inside and outside the Communist Party, had not yet been brought to heel; in Yugoslavia, unknown to the West, Tito . . . was stirring the Bulgarian and Hungarian Communists with ideas about a Balkan Communist alliance, quasi-independent of Moscow." The Soviet leaders had only to review the events of the previous spring in Western Europe to grasp the full meaning of Rostow's use of the adjective "offensive" in connection with the Marshall initiative. For against the background of Europe's economic crisis, United States failure to channel its aid through international organizations had carried obvious implications. The crisis was "above all a dollar crisis. The goods and supplies the world most wanted—wheat, meat, coal, steel, machinery—were only to be found in the Western Hemisphere and as the nations bought them eagerly, their dollars drained away . . . by the middle of the summer it was clear that either the United States would have to provide more dollars or the Western European nations would cease to be able to buy at all."

In France, the socialist Premier Ramadier warned the country that the time would come when "each credit will be dictated by political realities. A little of our independence is departing from us with each loan we obtain." He proceeded to appeal to America for another credit. In May 1947 Ramadier dismissed the Communists from his cabinet. The same thing happened in Italy. Soviet stategists would have been quick to note that an offer of Marshall Aid might tempt the non-Communist members of the ruling coalition in Czechoslovakia, for instance, to follow the French and Italian examples (although this was unlikely). In any case, the political significance of American economic power could not be ignored.

On July 2, Molotov left the Paris Conference; on July 10, a trade agreement was concluded between the Soviet Union and Bulgaria, on July 11 with Czechoslovakia, on July 14 with Hungary, on July 25 with Yugoslavia, on August 4 with Poland and on August 26 with Rumania. This was an important step in the direction of the economic consolidation of East Europe; the political division of the continent came next.

In November, the newly activated Cominform, consisting of the Communist Parties of East Europe, Italy and France, issued a statement which in less veiled terms reiterated the substance of the Truman Doctrine, albeit from the other side of the curtain:

> . . . Two opposite political lines have formed: On the one side the policy of the USSR and democratic countries directed toward undermining imperialism and strengthening democracy, on the other side is the policy of the USA and England directed toward strengthening imperialism and strangling democracy. . . .
>
> The Truman-Marshall plan is only a constituent part, the European section of the general plan of world expansionist policy carried on by the United States in all parts of the world. . . .

With the issuance of the Cominform statement, the lines for the cold war were clearly drawn. The Communist parties of Europe began a campaign to oppose the Marshall Plan by all means available to them. The effect was to lend substance to fears of sabotage and subversion, to oppose a plan on which the economic revival of West Europe depended and thus to help thrust political power into the hands of the right wing everywhere. The decisive expression of these changes in the state of affairs and the shape of power was the Czechoslovakian *coup* in February 1948.

The very bloodlessness of this *coup*—performed without an execution, and with only a few arrests, and actively opposed neither by Foreign Minister Masyryk nor President Benes, the two most respected and powerful democrats in the country—ought to have indicated to the West that the *coup* was not necessarily a pattern for the rest of Europe, since no takeover there could have been carried out without a civil war. This consideration did not prevail, however, and the Communist seizure of power served to congeal those fears and attitudes which have dominated thinking in the West ever since. For the source of this reaction in Europe one has only to turn to the power vacuum created by the defeat of Germany and the collapse of the United Kingdom.

For the first time since the rise of the Bolsheviks, the Russians had emerged into Europe. "Russian troops were garrisoned at the outskirts of Hamburg, once the greatest continental port, not a long cannon-shot from the Western seas."

> No nation ever held such extensive sway over Europe with the consent of the other great powers. Russia had directly annexed an area in Europe of about 250,000 square miles—an area larger than that of France, Switzerland, Holland, Belgium and Denmark together. Eight other Eastern European countries and parts of two more had become her satellites.

This was not any Russia, which had extended itself so greatly, moreover, it was Stalinist Russia, Russia of the purges and the forced labor camps, Russia which had absorbed the Baltic states.

Thus poised over a prostrate continent with no other counter-balancing European power in sight, in the wake of massive strikes led by native Communist parties in France and Italy, the Soviets subverted the democratically elected, pro-Soviet Government of the one central European state which had become the symbol of the whole disastrous slide into World War II.

If ever a symbol of appeasement existed, it was the sellout of Czechoslovakia by the Western powers at the Munich Conference in 1938. If ever there could be a psychological rallying point for the creation of a new European Army in the post-war years, it was a new blow against that unfortunate people. No extenuations, no careful analysis of the falseness of analogies between 1948 and ten years before, could erase, in the minds of the public, the seemingly incontrovertible image of history repeating itself.

The power of this event can perhaps be gauged by the reaction in Scandinavia. There, a formidable movement towards unification and neutralism had been growing. Denmark, Norway and Sweden had joined the Marshall Plan for compelling economic reasons. But when a "Western Union" conference was held in Brussels (the plan had been announced in January 1948 by Bevin) they demurred, publicly declaring that they would not participate in a scheme condemned by Russia.

In Sweden, Dr. Ernst Wigforss, the Minister of Finance, shocked Americans by a public statement saying that the danger in the cold war was not a Russian act of aggression so much as a possible forestalling attack by the United States. Then came the Czech *coup*.

> The event sent a shudder through all Scandinavia. Almost overnight the mood of amicability toward Russia collapsed in all three countries. Laborite Prime Minister Gerhardsen of Norway—once considered a rabid Red himself—launched a bitter attack on Norwegian Communists in the Storting. On May Day 1948, the Swedish Socialist Premier, Erlander, followed this up. 'The *coup* in Czechoslovakia,' he said, 'was a testing time not only for Prague, but also for Stockholm.' It is a sign of the changing pressures of the times that the Danish upper house of Parliament, the Landsting, which had not held a foreign-policy debate for over a hundred years, held one after the Czech *coup*. A Copenhagen radio broadcast

actually instructed citizens to report to the nearest police station any suspicious moves that might indicate an attempted seizure of power.

Despite long-standing policies of pacifism and neutrality, "a bill before the Swedish parliament to reduce military estimates was replaced by one asking for a fifty per cent increase in planes and a one hundred per cent increase in personnel for the air force." Norway and Denmark followed suit, and in addition joined Nato when it was formed (Sweden maintaining her neutrality to give Russia no excuse for Sovietizing Finland).

Thus appearing as a verification of the most apocalyptic prophecies of those who feared and hated Soviet power, the *coup* in Czechoslovakia strengthened the hand of every die-hard anti-Bolshevik and extreme nationalist in the Western camp. In the wake of this event, the liberal-left entered into an alliance with the reactionary right from which neither it, nor the Western World has yet recovered. Russian aggression, though in areas behind the Iron Curtain, served to underwrite every catastrophic step taken in the West toward massive rearmament and to make possible the ascendancy of political figures like Dulles and Adenauer.

With the sides now clearly formed, the cleavage into armed military camps was merely a question of time, since the Soviets had accomplished for the West its chief and most difficult task: the marshalling of public opinion. Even so, rearmament in countries like Britain proved a difficult and economically straining proposition. In the East, without the enormous over-productive capacity of the United States, it was disastrous. Forced to support a 1.6 million man army for Stalin's defenses, the hitherto impressive economic advance of East Europe was halted and a period of intense hardship and Stalinist construction began, resulting in the revolts of 1956.

Before Nato, and before the rearming of East Europe, however, an event occurred which stripped the veil from some of the pretenses under which this more intensified phase of the cold war was to be waged. In June 1948, the great schism between Tito and Stalin occurred, and was followed by a vast purging of Titoist heretics in the Communist Parties of East Europe.

For the East, these events refuted Moscow's claims that its actions were purely defensive in the interests of world socialism. The purging of men like Gomulka and the hundreds of thousands of Communist Party members accused of Titoism was nothing more than a purging of all politically effective nationalist elements in the now satellite nations. If the Soviets had been willing to tolerate a measure of independence and national development during the less hostile times of 1945–8, their answer to Western toughness was to put the defense of Russia above all other ends, even if it meant the brutal subjection of their own Communist allies.

On the other hand, the Titoist heresy and the responses it elicited, undercut, at the outset, the main justification for the Western military build-up, the creation of Nato and the rearming of the German war machine. For the failure of the Red Army or of any of the satellite armies to invade the renegade state ("I will shake my little finger—there will be no more Tito. Tito will fall." Stalin had said) could mean only one of two things. Either the Soviets were not willing to invade a country presenting a strong national front—or, *already existing American military power,* was sufficient to deter Stalin from any armed aggression in Europe.

Thus *before* Nato, *before* Western and West German rearmament, *before* the spiralling and debilitating arms race had seized hold of Europe, Communist power was adequately and effectively "contained" by the greater and more vastly extended power of the USA. And this, it may be noted, was fully realized by American strategists, indeed by the very man who was the foremost proponent of a rearmed and re-militarized world, who went so far as to attempt to revive the military will of atom-blasted Japan. In March 1949, John Foster Dulles declared:

> So far as it is humanly possible to judge, the Soviet Government, under conditions now prevailing does not contemplate the use of war as an instrument of its national policy. I do not know any responsible official, military or civilian, in this Government or any Government who believes that the Soviet Government now plans conquest by open military aggression.

The Rhetoric of Politics: Foreign Policy, Internal Security, and Domestic Politics in the Truman Era, 1945-1950 ATHAN THEOHARIS

The New Left and the liberals disagree over the origins and significance of McCarthyism. To the liberals, Senator Joseph R. McCarthy of Wisconsin was an unprincipled demagogue who sought to use virulent anti-communism to discredit his liberal Democratic opponents for political reasons. He himself was a weapon of the right against the moderate left, but much of his support came from groups that had been a part of the old New Deal coalition. McCarthy, in this view, did not appeal primarily to old-fashioned conservatives, but to "ethnics," workingmen, and rural and small-town folk who wished to discredit the liberal intellectuals who had flirted with the Left during the 1930s. His supporters were much like the Populists, and both the rabid anti-Communists of the post–World War Two period and the Populists shared many of the same notions about the betrayal of the American people by the elite. All told, the liberals, and the liberal intellectuals in particular, were the victims of the quasi-Fascist potential that resided in the masses and that had periodically flourished in times of confusion and frustration.

The New Left rejects the idea that McCarthy had anything in common with the reformist forces of earlier America. Michael Rogin has attempted to demonstrate that there was little continuity between traditional areas of populism and those of McCarthyism. The latter movement, he believes, drew on conservative Republican support. In the article below, Athan Theoharis blames McCarthyism on the liberals themselves. In initiating the Cold War they created a climate of rabid anti-communism. The Truman administration itself was active in witch-hunting and weeding out subversives. It was the ironic fate of Fair Deal liberals that they fell victim to the Frankenstein monster that they themselves had helped to create.

Source: Athan Theoharis, "The Rhetoric of Politics: Foreign Policy, Internal Security, and Domestic Politics in the Truman Era, 1945–1950," in *Politics and Policies of the Truman Administration,* ed. Barton Bernstein (Chicago: Quadrangle Books, 1970), pp. 196–202, 219–235.

FOR FURTHER READING:

Michael Rogin, *The Intellectuals and McCarthy: The Radical Specter,* (M.I.T. Press, 1967); Richard Rovere, *Senator Joe McCarthy*,* (Meridian World, 1959); William F. Buckley, Jr. and L. Brent Bozell, *McCarthy and His Enemies*,* (Charles Regnery, 1954); Allen Guttman, *Korea and the Theory of Limited War*,* (Heath, 1967); John Steinke and James Weinstein, "McCarthy and the Liberals," *Studies on the Left* (Summer, 1962).

Asterisk denotes paperback edition.

American politics after World War II poses an intriguing problem for the historian of the Cold War: the emergence of McCarthyism and the effectiveness after 1950 of the senator and his cohorts, the McCarthyites. How does one explain the different political objectives of McCarthy's principal exponents (political conservatives) and a major source of his popular support (small businessmen, professionals, urban workers, and members of ethnic groups)? While the exponents of McCarthyism were anti-progressive and sought to undercut reform, these other supporters rejected attacks that simply disparaged the New Deal. Furthermore each group had very different reasons for supporting the senator's concern with national security.

How did McCarthy successfully exploit tactics which earlier had failed for other conservatives? Since 1934 conservative congressmen (primarily Republicans) had accused the New Deal of being alien, subversive, and communistic. During World War II, and more openly from 1945 through 1948, these congressmen had extended their assault to the foreign policy decisions of the Roosevelt-Truman administrations. But their charges of "softness toward communism," whether aimed at domestic or international policy, were not credible to a public that had come to revere the New Deal and support internationalism.

The success of the McCarthyites' attacks after 1950 poses another paradox in view of their earlier opposition to the Truman administration's foreign policy. Although their rhetoric was militantly anti-communist, most McCarthyites from 1946 through 1949 denounced such containment policies as foreign aid, the Truman Doctrine, the commitment of U.S. troops overseas and NATO. They considered these military-economic responses too aggressive, an unwarranted overextension of American commitments. They saw the "communist threat" as primarily domestic, not international. After World War II they pressed for retrenchment; their conception of the proper national defense was not collective security but unilateral preparedness. Despite their militant posture, in their position on legislation the McCarthyites were cautious and restrained. They opposed the administration's policy of confrontation, preferring to conserve national resources and to deal with internal problems of subversion (by which they meant the New Deal outlook).

The Truman administration's militant anti-Soviet policy from 1945 through 1950 (including the loyalty program, prosecution of the American Communist party leadership, and development of the containment policy) contrasted sharply with the

I wish to express my appreciation to the Truman Institute for National and International Affairs and to Wayne State University for their support of my research, and to the University of Iowa, particularly Mrs. Emily Hartnell, for assistance in typing the manuscript. I am grateful for the editorial assistance and criticisms of Stanley Shapiro, Walter LaFeber, Richard Kirkendal, David Shannon, Otis Graham, Michael Rogin, and Ivan Dee.

McCarthyites' negativism. One might have expected the Truman administration, because it pursued an anti-communist course (in both international and internal security), to have been invulnerable to charges of vacillation, indecisiveness, laxity, or "softness toward communism." And one might have expected that, when confronted by the McCarthyite assault, the Truman administration could have reviewed the McCarthyites' own record on foreign policy from 1945 to 1950 to discredit such accusations. In fact, the administration adopted this tactic. Its failure poses the paradox in explaining the effectiveness of McCarthyism.

Another problem for the historian lies in the conflicting positions of liberals (whether inside the Truman administration or among its supporters) and conservative McCarthyites on democratic procedures and the right to dissent. More often after 1948 the liberals, not the McCarthyites, sought to restrict the political dialogue, to define certain subjects as beyond the pale of responsible discussion. Asserting that they were protecting the national security, administration supporters dismissed criticism as dangerous and subversive. They based their position on the separation of powers and the need to protect individual rights, and affirmed the President's right to refuse congressional requests for confidential information (loyalty reports or international agreements). In contrast, the McCarthyites demanded an open, searching appraisal of foreign policy decisions and the internal security program. Their democratic posture, limited to national security considerations, did not imply a tolerance of all dissent but was restricted to legislative-executive relations. Thus they demanded an end to executive secrecy, affirmed Congress' right of access to all privileged information secured by the administration, and asserted their right to share in decision-making, to review administration policy decisions, and to investigate federal personnel. Formally, the McCarthyites adopted a democratic stance and rejected the doctrine of executive privilege or expertise.

These contradictions and apparent inconsistencies make it difficult to explain even the phenomenon of McCarthy, much less his impact. The negative, irresponsible nature of the McCarthyite critique and the hysterical, conspiratorial tone of the post–1950 policy debate have provided the basis for the currently accepted view, advanced by Daniel Bell, Richard Hofstader, *et al.,* of "status politics." The "status" theorists see McCarthyism as an emotional, demagogic, backward-looking movement. According to this view, the McCarthyites, by resorting to conspiratorial explanations, were able to capitalize on the disaffection of those Americans who were frustrated over their loss of status and incapable of understanding the complexities of the modern world.

Undeniably, popular anti-communism was often emotional, oversimplified, and took the conspiratorial view. But these features were not unique or consistent. More important, a shifting, aimless, nonideological quality characterized popular anti-communism. The shifts reflect not a definite set of principles but a response to specific events—or to the public perception of the meaning of those events. Americans in the immediate postwar period were, for the most part, anti-communist and anti-Soviet, despite memories of the wartime alliance. Postwar international developments and domestic differences, such as the conflict between communists and noncommunists within the labor and progressive movements, added to this distrust. Anti-communism did assume an ideological form among many American Catholics, a phenomenon due in great part to the Vatican's reaction to the atheistic materialism of communism and to communist restrictions on the Catholic Church in postwar Eastern Europe. But the emotional anti-communism of most Catholics and non-Catholics resulted from the tensions of the Cold War.

In 1945 and 1946 there had been distinct tolerance toward the Soviet Union and American Communists, a tolerance that was not to last in succeeding years. In March (55 per cent to 31 per cent) and September (54 per cent to 30 per cent) 1945, the public remained confident that U.S.-Soviet cooperation could be sustained. This trust fluctuated in 1946 and 1947 but remained, as did public support for summit diplomacy or the United Nations as instruments for preserving the peace. Even the initial public assessment of the Truman Doctrine (March 1947) focused on nonmilitary (economic or political) policy options. Most Americans approved of the Truman Doctrine (57 per cent to 32 per cent, 12 per cent no opinion), supported sending civilian experts to Greece to supervise the handling of aid (83 per cent to 14 per cent, 3 per cent no opinion), yet opposed sending military experts to assist the Greek armed forces (54 per cent to 37 per cent, 9 per cent no opinion). Similarly, while suspicious of American Communists, the public was less rigid than in later years: in 1945 it advocated surveillance or was either indifferent or tolerant. Moreover, the public distinguished between communists and radicals. As late as October 1947, 36 per cent supported and 41 per cent opposed legislation prohibiting communist sympathizers from holding public office.

This ambivalence reflects the pragmatic character of popular anti-communism as it was shaped by certain crises. From 1945 through 1947 the tone of presidential statements and news stories about U.S.-Soviet relations was conciliatory and reasonably tolerant. The Yalta, Potsdam, and Moscow conferences and the Sino-Soviet treaty of August 1945 were reported with great enthusiasm. Even *Time* magazine extolled Yalta as "the most important conference of the century," praised its spirit of cooperation as providing the basis for a lasting peace, and claimed that no citizen of the United States, the Soviet Union, or Great Britain could charge that his nation's interests had been "sold down the river."

This tolerance was an early victim of the Cold War. The information presented to the public after 1947, which in turn shaped the public's perception of the Soviet Union and American Communists, became increasingly anti-communist. This shift in perception and the dominant anti-communist rhetoric contributed to the McCarthyite impact after 1950.

The Bell-Hofstadter analysis is deficient, on the one hand, because it is ahistorical in ignoring the peculiar characteristics of the McCarthyites (the timing of their impact) and, on the other, because it fails to examine the direction of the postwar policy debate. The aim of this essay is to offer another evaluation, to view McCarthyism not as an aberration but as a development consistent with the rhetoric of the postwar political debate.

One of my basic assumptions is that President Truman's manner of defining the objectives of American policy radically altered the rhetoric of American politics; that Truman's statements and decisions structured the national security debate, affecting the understanding of the American public and thus their expectations and fears. It is true that public attitudes, already anti-communist, were altered by the events around which controversy sharpened—Soviet foreign policy and subversion. But the emotional anti-communism of the postwar years was shaped by Truman's depiction of Soviet motives and U.S. policy options, his portrayal of U.S. actions as wholly altruistic, and his preference for military power over accommodation.

Second, I contend that McCarthyism was made possible by the intensification of the Cold War. A heightened concern over national security matters transformed domestic priorities and radically changed many of the basic tenets of American politics. And McCarthyism derived its impact from these new tenets—which provided the rationale for containment and the loyalty program. The nature of these policies—because they conceived of radicalism, whether at home or abroad, as potentially subversive, because they denied the legitimacy of Soviet power and strategic objectives, and because they saw communism as monolithic, alien, and unpopular—served to legitimize conservative, status quo politics.

Third, McCarthyism was consistent with this new Cold War rhetoric. Administration policy, both domestic and foreign, reacted against disruptive change. Administration policy statements sought scapegoats, not solutions, attempted to preclude, not adapt to, change, and were vague in defining terms like "subversion," "disloyalty," and "aggression." Moreover, the *ad hoc* nature of administration policy responses, and the reversal of Franklin Roosevelt's priorities, demanded that public support be secured. To arouse the public to accept a more interventionist role in the immediate postwar years required that the administration resort to the use of anti-communist symbols in almost a reflex fashion. At the same time, the administration failed to delineate the limits of American power or the specific nature of the communist threat.

As one result, the interests of the American public gradually shifted during the postwar years from a concern over socio-economic reform to an obsession with the communist threat to national security. With the passage of time, and the fears of a catastrophic nuclear war or an endless Cold War, rigidity and intolerance became characteristic of the American polity. A policy of firmness, of seeking to negotiate from positions of strength, may have been at first restrained and realistic, but it was soon transformed into a rhetoric wherein all disagreements became tests of American will or courage. Self-esteem became self-righteous arrogance. And political conservatives, by centering their protest on the administration's inability to safeguard national security (instead of attacking New Deal reforms), acquired new respectability and influence.

Finally, the timing of McCarthy's attack was propitious—immediately after the trials of Alger Hiss and Judith Coplon, the Soviet explosion of an atomic bomb, the success of the Chinese Communists, the arrest of the Rosenbergs, and the outbreak of the Korean War. These events seemingly confirmed the existence of an internal security threat. Through misleading specific charges, McCarthy was able to capitalize on this malaise and concern.

*   *   *

II

As with its foreign policy, the Truman administration's manner of defining, as well as its response to criticism of, its internal security policy contributed to the development of a distinctly repressive domestic climate. In 1947 Truman had instituted a federal employee loyalty program, ostensibly for national security reasons. At that time and subsequently he did not clearly define the program's limited objectives. Specifically, he did not distinguish between individual disloyalty and political radicalism (whether belief or act). This imprecision, by blurring distinctions, helped reshape the public view about political activism and its conception that past or current radicalism confirmed an individual's subversive proclivities. Investigations of the political activities and beliefs of government personnel became justified as a legitimate security concern and eventually led to a shift in the standard for dismissal. Presumption of doubt as to the loyalty of a prospective or incumbent employee became sufficient justification for a denial of clearance.

The administration had defined the loyalty program's principal objective as the exclusion of *all* potentially disloyal individuals from federal employment. The program's rationale was outlined in the recommendations of a Temporary Commission (established by the President in November 1946 to determine the adequacy of existing loyalty procedures). The commission agreed that a loyalty program was needed, and noted:

> The *presence* within the government of *any* disloyal or subversive persons, or the attempt by *any* such persons to *obtain* government employment, presents a problem of *such importance* that it must be dealt with *vigorously and effectively.*

This was a grave "threat" to the national security, the commission said, though it did not enumerate, document or specifically define its nature. Concerned with insuring effective surveillance procedures, vague in its standards and fears, the commission argued:

> While the Commission believes that the employment of disloyal or subversive persons presents *more than a speculative* threat to our system of government, it is *unable*, based on the *facts* presented to it, to state with any degree of certainty *how far reaching* that threat is. Certainly, the recent Canadian Espionage exposé, the *Communist Party line activities* of *some* of the members of a government employee organization, and current disclosures of disloyal employees provide *sufficient* evidence to convince a fair-minded person that a threat exists.

The attempt to achieve absolute security by averting potential subversion implied that security could not be achieved by traditional surveillance methods or by dismissing an employee after proving his disloyalty. Suspect persons, who might engage in "subversive" activities, were security risks. The program therefore rested on the premise that disloyalty and subversive tendencies must be determined in advance to preclude a threat to the national security. By this standard, subsequent disclosures of "spying" activities (Alger Hiss, Judith Coplon, Ethel and Julius Rosenberg, John Stewart Service, William Remington) highlighted the inadequacies of the President's loyalty program. The administration's subsequent denial that any threat existed, following these developments and contradicting its earlier rhetoric, pointed apparently to negligence or culpability. To have suggested, moreover, that "even one disloyal person constitutes [a serious threat] to the security" of the United States served to strengthen Joe McCarthy's number charges. If one disloyal person was a serious threat, didn't 205, 81, 57, or 3 demand urgent action, not apology?

In another sense, the Truman administration's response to Henry Wallace's presidential candidacy also contributed to the development of a more intolerant political climate. In the 1948 presidential campaign, Truman, the Democratic National Committee, and the Americans for Democratic Action resorted to red-baiting in order to discredit Wallace. In an address on St. Patrick's Day, Truman rejected the support of "Wallace and his communists." The President further emphasized the "communists'" efforts to defeat him by supporting a third party. And the Democratic National Committee published a series of pamphlets and advertisements labeling the Progressive party as communist-influenced. Both Truman and the National Committee stressed the administration's anti-communist foreign policy and internal security record. They contrasted this record to Republican obstructionism and the GOP's seeming indifference to the communist threat posed by the Progressive party at home (as reflected in its complicity with Progressive efforts to get on the ballot) and Soviet expansionism abroad (its opposition to foreign aid policies).

To discredit the Progressive party, the ADA paid for advertisements in major urban newpapers listing the names of the party's principal contributors and the organizations on the Attorney General's list to which these contributors belonged or had belonged. Ironically, the McCarthyites later resorted to this same presumption of guilt by association when attacking personnel of the Truman administration and the ADA. (During the 1950 congressional campaign the Democratic State Central Committee of Pennsylvania sought to use this tactic against certain Republican congressional incumbents. The committee contrasted the similarity of these Republicans' voting records on key foreign policy issues to that of Congressman Vito Marcantonio.)

This rhetoric heightened public fears about communism. The administration's attempt to impugn the motives of its right-wing critics added another aspect—a loss of credibility. The partisan, anti-congressional manner of Truman's response to the House Committee on Un-American Activities allowed the McCarthyites to adopt an anti-executive stance. In the form of congressional authority, on the premise of the need for restraints on executive powers, and in the guise of a national security concern, the McCarthyites were able to capitalize on Truman's resort to censorship of the investigative records of loyalty proceedings. Moreover, the President's tactic of dismissing criticisms of the loyalty program as partisan in motivation increased public doubts about his priorities. The public came to interpret administration prosecution of "disloyal" federal employees as evidence not of administration vigilance but as a partisan response to pressure from the McCarthyites.

This view of administration priorities became the norm in 1950 but had not been the original basis for the Truman-McCarthyite confrontation. In 1945–1948 Truman could conveniently ignore or dismiss right-wing accusations that a serious communist threat existed. In part the administration's tactic succeeded because the public viewed the charges of the House Committee on Un-American Activities as having a specific conservative purpose, directed less at internal subversion than against the New Deal. And during this period the public was relatively unconcerned about internal security matters.

In 1947 and 1948 HUAC's investigation had concentrated on domestic attitudes, specifically whether communists had infiltrated the New Deal and the motion picture industry. These initial investigations were concerned not so much with "espionage" in the sense of sabotage or foreign subversion, but with ideas and associations. The implication was that communists, by infiltrating the Roosevelt administration, or Hollywood, had created an un-American climate (reformist New Deal or sympathetic to the Soviet Union). Only after the disclosure of the "pumpkin papers" by Whittaker Chambers in December 1948 did the committee emphasize espionage activities. And Chambers, during this preliminary phase, had echoed the charge that communists, by infiltrating the New Deal, had successfully influenced policy-making. In testimony and public statements prior to November, Chambers had denied that Alger Hiss had engaged in espionage and insisted that Hiss's sole activity as a Communist party member had been to promote communist infiltration of the New Deal.

In view of the obvious partisanship of the House Committee and the still tolerant public attitude toward radicalism—distinguishing between radicalism and communism in 1947 and 1948—Truman then had the opportunity to develop a climate conducive to civil liberties. Instead, he only emphasized the committee's excessive, publicity-seeking procedures. His partisan responses were effective, not because they were articulate and well-reasoned but primarily because the committee had overreacted and had not been able to prove its grave accusations. When faced with the committee's "communists-in-government" charges, Truman dismissed them as a "red herring" devised by anti-New Deal Republicans to cover up for the 80th Congress' reactionary record. He challenged the committee to turn over to the Attorney General evidence of wrongdoing. At the same time the President and his Attorney General, Tom Clark, cited the administration's effective anti-communist record and particularly its actions dismissing disloyal federal employees and prosecuting the leaders of the U.S. Communist party. Clark contrasted this "positive" record to that of the 80th Congress, expressing his frustration over Congress' indifference to legislation proposed by the Justice Department that had been designed to "strengthen" existing security procedures (authorizing wiretapping, extending registration requirements, and increasing surveillance).

In response to a subpoena of the House Committee for the loyalty records of certain federal employees, Truman on March 14, 1948, directed federal agencies to ignore future congressional requests or subpoenas for confidential information without his express approval. This reversed earlier procedures and widened the rift between Congress and the President. Truman justified his refusal by citing three arguments: (1) the constitutional separation of the executive and legislative branches; (2) the importance of secrecy to protect innocent employees from publicity of unfounded charges; and (3) the need to preserve the confidentiality of FBI sources to expedite future investigations.

But Truman did not use this opportunity to explain that much of the information contained in these reports was clearly unreliable and unsubstantiated. He made no distinction between researched and confirmed information of FBI agents, on the one hand, and the hearsay testimony of paid informants, personal interviews, or unsolicited letters, on the other. By failing to make this distinction, Truman helped to create the impression that all the information in these reports had been secured through accurate, thorough investigations. Later, McCarthy would cite excerpts from these reports as "evidence" that security risks were still found in the federal service, thereby confirming the need for further exposure. And McCarthy could say that administration censorship was designed to cover up its laxity, and thus endangered the national security.

The decision (in March 1948) to bar HUAC from access to the loyalty reports was surprising. Just two months earlier, the House Appropriations Committee had secured permission to examine the State Department loyalty reports. The committee's access to these reports had hardly undermined the national security. And, considering McCarthy's principal sources of information—State and Justice Department personnel—the administration's reiteration of the argument that disclosure to Congress would cripple the FBI's investigations had little impact. Instead, it appeared to the public that this administration decision was less a concern for the national interest than a desire to cover up administration culpability. McCarthy could adopt the posture of a disinterested, loyal public servant deeply concerned about the national security and desiring solely to inform the public of the real internal security problem covered up by the administration.

As a pronounced anti-communist, Truman did not, in 1948, 1949, or early 1950, take these charges seriously. Indeed, he called the 1948 election results a confirmation of public support for his handling of internal security, and a repudiation of the charges and tactics of the House Committee on Un-American Activities. Because he had been able during the 1948 campaign to dismiss the HUAC members as partisan publicity seekers, Truman maintained this stance and relied on the belief that he had public support. Thus, when charges of an internal security problem were repeated in 1949, Truman simply castigated these congressmen and other critics of his loyalty program as headline hunters.

At the same time Truman asserted that no one "who believes in the destruction of our form of government" should teach children. This kind of vague, emotion-laden statement contributed to insecurity and fear and precluded a realistic understanding of what constituted a threat to the national security. Truman never clearly defined the nature of this threat or what constituted "destruction of our form of government." This vagueness created a tension which the administration intensified by its earlier uncritical commitment to instituting more "effective" internal security procedures.

Indeed, from 1946 through 1948 the Department of Justice had operated with few executive restraints in its efforts to insure the passage of internal security legislation. Specifically, in 1946 Attorney General Clark had successfully secured additional investigative authority for the FBI by capitalizing on Truman's distress over the Canadian Royal Commission's disclosure of Soviet wartime espionage. By distorting an earlier (1940) Roosevelt directive authorizing the FBI to wiretap in well-defined circumstances, Clark obtained Truman's assent to a new directive extending the authorization to include investigations of "subversion" and "criminal activities." Concurrently, in 1947 and 1948, Justice (unsuccessfully) pressed the Congress to enact legislation broadly extending its authority in matters affecting the "national security." The effect of these actions was to heighten public fears about the communist threat and contribute to a vastly changed climate in which McCarthyism flourished .

In addition, the excessive independence of the department during these earlier years served to distinguish its actions in the public mind from those of the President. This distinction was strengthened as the result of efforts by White House staff members after 1949 to curb the department's legislative efforts. In effect, this rift tended to contradict administration protestations of anti-communism: it was seemingly less concerned about the communist threat than the department. White House efforts to restrain Justice failed because of the outbreak of the Korean War.

The Korean War made internal security legislation politically popular. And whereas earlier measures (Mundt-Nixon, Ferguson-Johnston) had been stymied, by 1950 the combination of the war and public obsession with "subversion" increased the prospect that some form of "internal security" legislation would be enacted. Although Truman acted to avert the passage of repressive legislation and accordingly introduced a measure far less restrictive of civil liberties, the nature and quality of the administration's leadership against Senator McCarran's proposed bill was neither principled nor courageous. In fact, the administration's equivocation served only to increase public fears.

In its proposal the administration had accepted the premise that the American Communist party posed a serious threat to the national security, requiring that its activities and those of its alleged fronts should be curbed, and that existing security procedures were inadequate to deal with the threat. In essence this position provided the rationale for Senator McCarran's bill, a bill that was more restrictive of civil liberties and vaguer in its definition of subversive activities. The administration thereby lost whatever leverage it might have commanded to defeat the McCarran bill. It could not simultaneously argue that the national security was seriously threatened and that civil liberties should not be transgressed. Traditionally, in times of serious crisis or war, individual liberties had been sacrificed (suspension of the writ of habeas corpus, internment of the Japanese). The administration's protests against excessive restrictions on civil liberties appeared less than realistic.

Truman's strategy of stopping the McCarthyites by proposing an alternate bill failed. The President's decision to veto the omnibus measure introduced by Senator McCarran did not contribute to a more tolerant political climate, but, like his proposed measure, intensified the public obsession with communism. In his veto message, Truman said:

> It has been claimed over and over again that this [the McCarran bill] is an "anti-communist" bill—a "communist control" bill. But in actual operation the bill would . . . actually weaken our existing internal security measures and would seriously hamper the Federal Bureau of Investigation and other security agencies. . . .
>
> No consideration of expediency can justify the enactment of such a bill as this, a bill which would so greatly weaken our liberties and give aid and comfort to those who would destroy us.

Truman's denunciation, on anti-communist grounds, of the McCarran bill changed the mind of no one who felt that the nation needed more effective internal security legislation. The act might be unconstitutional (subsequent Supreme Court decisions confirmed this), and it did circumscribe individual liberties. But its purpose was to hamper recruitment and the secrecy of the Communist party and communist-front organizations. Conceding the gravity of the threat, that effort was desirable and realistic. To suggest, as Truman did, that the measure would aid the communists was incredible and reflected on the administration's partisanship or "softness toward communism."

Truman's primary concern was not to safeguard civil liberties but to establish his anti-communist credentials and thus refute his critics. This commitment is revealed in the timing and nature of the President's reaction to McCarthy's charges of communist infiltration of the State Department. When the Senate decided to investigate these charges, Truman seemed indifferent. Confident that the public was convinced of the effectiveness of his internal security program, Truman, in a March 30, 1950, press conference, summarily dismissed McCarthy as "the greatest asset that the Kremlin has." In support of his own solid anti-communist credentials, Truman cited his policy decisions—the loyalty program and various military-economic policies to contain Soviet expansion. Focusing on McCarthy's motives, Truman argued that

> there are a certain number of members of the Republican Party who are trying to dig up that old malodorous horse called "isolationism." And in order to do that, they are perfectly willing to sabotage the bipartisan foreign policy of the United States. And this fiasco which has been going on in the Senate is the very best asset that the Kremlin could have in the operation of the cold war.

As in his earlier response to the House Committee, Truman again challenged his critics to turn over any evidence they had to the proper authorities so that prosecution could be initiated. This criticism was not only groundless but treasonous, Truman implied, and he denounced criticisms of his foreign policy decisions as an effort to "sabotage the foreign policy of the United States [which] is just as bad in this cold war as it would be to shoot our soldiers in the back in a hot war."

In two major responses to McCarthyism, Truman revealed his estimate of the senator's politicial effectiveness and underscored his own ambivalent commitment to civil liberties. Specifically, Truman failed to take an unequivocal stand on the question of the confidentiality of loyalty records; instead he vacillated, responding to public pressure. At first he agreed to cooperate fully with the Tydings Committee which was investigating McCarthy's charges. At the same time he refused, on national security grounds, to permit committee access to State Department files; instead he offered to have the Loyalty Review Board examine the cases under investigation and submit its recommendations to the President. Then Truman reversed himself and ordered the board to report directly to the committee. And, in a still more dramatic reversal, he later agreed to release the loyalty files of the State Department, but not those of the FBI, to the Tydings Committee. Truman's indecision and vacillation reflected the partisan priorities underlying his decisions—when a principled stand became unpopular, pressure was relieved by gradual concessions.

Because he did not at first view McCarthyism—at least the senator's charges of February-April 1950—as a major political threat, Truman rejected proposals by White House staff members and Democratic congressmen (such as Representative Helen Douglas and Senators Tydings and McMahon) that might have restored public confidence in the administration's loyalty program and procedures. Again, in May 1950, these staff members and congressmen urged Truman to reestablish this confidence by appointing a special presidential commission to investigate the loyalty program. It would determine what procedures might be needed to protect the national security yet provide safeguards to individual rights. These advocates argued that the Tydings Committee had failed to rebut McCarthy's charges because the American public considered the committee's report incomplete, partisan, or biased. In contrast, a bipartisan blue-ribbon commission, they maintained, could effectively repudiate McCarthy's charges. This proposal was seriously considered in early June 1950 but was temporarily sidetracked with the outbreak of the Korean War.

Members of the White House staff, nonetheless, continued to press for a commission. The Korean War, they argued, created a climate that made possible the enactment of proposed internal security bills (by Senators Karl Mundt, Homer Ferguson, and Pat McCarran, and Representatives John Wood and Richard Nixon) that threatened civil liberties. Staff members doubted that the President could exercise the impartial leadership necessary to defeat these measures but thought a presidential commission could. After the enactment of the McCarran Act and McCarthyism's demonstrated effectiveness in the 1950 congressional elections—and only then—Truman reconsidered the proposal and in January 1951 formally appointed a special commission headed by Admiral Chester Nimitz.

Ostensibly, the commission was established to review existing internal security procedures. Based on that investigation, the commission was to recommend improvements to protect individual rights and the national security. This balanced objective did not constitute the basic thrust of the commission's operation or concern. When it did function, the commission at first did nothing more than consider a proposed amendment of the loyalty program's standard for dismissal. Suggested by the Department of Justice and the Loyalty Review Board as early as 1949, the revision was seriously considered within the administration in early 1951. The appointment of the Nimitz Commission only delayed presidential action on this recommendation. Because the effective operation of the commission was stymied, Truman decided to act without awaiting the commission's decision. On April 21, 1951, he issued Executive Order 10241, implementing this new standard.

The new standard for dismissal impinged upon individual rights and indirectly affirmed McCarthyite charges that the existing loyalty program had been ineffective. As one result, cases once cleared—the most notable being that of John Stewart Service—were reviewed again. Under the new provision, Service was denied loyalty clearance in 1951. This reversal of earlier departmental and board decisions clearing him was not based on evidence of Service's disloyalty but on his former personal associations and some of the reports he had made criticizing Chiang Kai-shek's Nationalist government while stationed in China as a foreign service officer during the war.

III

Although he differed in both principle and objective from Senator McCarthy, Truman in his own right was a militant anti-communist. Initially confident that his internal security and foreign policy record rendered him invulnerable to charges of "softness toward communism," Truman dismissed the McCarthyite attacks as partisan while he reiterated his own anti-communism. When he was confronted by a loss of public confidence, Truman essentially complied with the McCarthyites' demands while simultaneously denying that existing loyalty procedures were inadequate. In addition, he sought to discredit the McCarthyites by suggesting that their attack undermined the national security. These tactics—self-righteous anti-communism and attempts to discredit dissent—were ineffective, primarily because of the crisis in public confidence created by the Korean War and the "spy" scandals of 1949–1950. The partisan nature of Truman's response to attacks on his internal security program and his conduct of foreign policy, moreover, increased this loss of public confidence.

The Korean War and the communist victory in China, following the Soviet explosion of an atomic bomb and the Hiss, Coplon, and Rosenberg "espionage" cases, increased public demands for effective internal security safeguards. The Cold War threatened imminently to become a hot war; it seemed that a real internal threat to the national security existed. Particularly after 1950, the Soviet threat, both external and internal, became a major and frightening concern to the American public. In addition, the administration had earlier oversold its policies. Hoping to undermine prevailing fears of war, the administration prior to 1950 had adopted a confident, predictive tone over the prospects for success. Truman then sought to quiet public fears about containment by proclaiming boldly that his policies would avert war and insure an American peace. The Korean War thus had a psychologically devastating impact upon the public by undercutting these hopes. At the same time, by contradicting earlier administration assurances, the war undermined Truman's credibility.

Judged in light of the kind of leadership Truman offered, and the options and rhetoric he presented, the public response to McCarthyism was neither irrational nor frenzied. McCarthy's slogans and solutions might seem simplistic, but since 1945 Truman had defined foreign and domestic issues in equally simplistic terms. Not only the issues, but the solutions to foreign policy and internal security problems were presented as obvious and clear-cut. International change and revolution were simply Soviet subversion which threatened the national security. Each crisis was a confrontation, or potential one, with the Soviet Union. Revolutionary movements were foreign subversion, not national radicalism. With these definitions, the Truman administration failed to provide a realistic assessment of the nature of the Cold War conflict. Confrontation was described in moralistic terms; there was no concession that Soviet actions were strategic or the result of power-political or geographic factors. Instead, the administration usually described the Soviets as not worthy of diplomatic concession, as a numerically small leadership group without popular support (thus politically fragile), and as untrustworthy except if confronted by superior power. This exaggerated moralistic description ignored the limits of American influence, the international political situation, legitimate Soviet security fears, and the inevitable counter-response inherent in confrontation. Truman's overreliance on power, the confident predictions of containment, and the premises of the "domino theory" strengthened a peculiar perception of national security.

Given this definition of United States altruism and omnipotence, the American people might well ask why our postwar foreign policy had failed to secure the peace, failed to "liberate" Eastern Europe, failed to "save" China or preclude the Korean War and Chinese Communist intervention in that war. How had the Soviet Union acquired knowledge to produce the atomic bomb and thus directly threaten American security? A ready explanation to these questions was subversion—for the existence of "even one" disloyal person in the administration posed a grave threat to the national security. It was in this context that the public came to see the major threat to the national security as "communists in government." Had not Alger Hiss attended the Yalta Conference where China and Eastern Europe were "lost"? Had not the Rosenbergs passed on *the* "secret" of the atomic bomb to Soviet agents? Were not these cases symptomatic? And had not the McCarthyites consistently warned the public about the political unreliability of the New Dealers and about the naiveté or stupidity of Roosevelt's Soviet policy, as at Yalta?

The Korean War contributed to this reassessment and directed public attention to the primacy of internal security and domestic subversion. An effective loyalty-security program was needed; a strong military already existed but had not been effectively used by the Truman administration. If the public sought scapegoats and easy answers to complex problems, its response was consistent with the prevailing rhetoric which the President had used to define international and domestic security problems since 1945. Necessarily, this rhetoric and Truman's policies affected the domestic political climate. In creating new standards for judgment and response, President Truman, unwittingly created the basis for McCarthyism's later effectiveness—a repressive political climate and an erroneous conception of Soviet weakness, the nature of subversion, and American omnipotence.

8. Recent America

The United States in Vietnam, 1944-66 GABRIEL KOLKO

No other event in our recent history has divided the United States so profoundly as the intervention in Vietnam. That vexatious and disturbing involvement has very complex roots, a fact that helps to explain why it has been so easy to misconceive the nature of the problem that confronts the United States in that remote land.

At the end of World War II, the French, who had first occupied parts of Indo-China in the mid-nineteenth century, restored their full authority in the land, following five years of Japanese occupation. They found that the weakening of French power had permitted the rise of a strong independence movement under the leadership of Communist-trained Ho Chi Minh and his party, the Viet Minh. The first French response to Ho and his demands was acquiescence. In 1946, the French recognized the Democratic Republic of Vietnam as an autonomous state, though under French protection. Soon after, they changed their mind, and attempted to overthrow Ho and his party. The war that ensued, instigated by the French, dragged on for six bitter years.

This war was primarily a struggle for independence, but it was also a social revolution greatly complicated by the victory of the Communists over the National-ists in mainland China. This event tipped the balance in Asia and affected the Indo-China struggle by putting a powerful Communist state adjacent to the Vietnam Republic, and by pushing the non-Communists out of the Viet Minh party. The Americans and British reacted to this development by recognizing the French puppet in Vietnam, the Emperor Bao Dai. This was followed by substantial military assistance to the French, much of it in the guise of aid to the Bao Dai regime.

In 1954, after the ignominious defeat of French arms at Dienbienphu, a drained and exhausted France agreed to a cease-fire and negotiations with the Viet Minh and Ho over the future status of the Indo-China area. At Geneva a series of accords were reached between the French and the Ho government that attempted to settle the future of the whole region. Besides the French and the Viet Minh, Great Britain, the Soviet Union, Communist China, the United States, the autonomous Indo-China kingdoms of Laos and Cambodia, and the French puppet regime, the State of Vietnam, participated. The agreement provided for a cease-fire and a line of

Source: Gabriel Kolko, *The Roots of American Foreign Policy: An Analysis of Power and Purpose* (Boston: Beacon Press, 1969), chap. 1v, "The United States in Vietnam, 1944–66," pp. 109–132.

demarcation at the 17th parallel between the Viet Minh controlled areas and those still under Bao Dai. The demarcation line was to be temporary and the two Vietnams were to be united in July, 1955, following a general election that would determine which regime would control the united country.

In the selection below, Gabriel Kolko describes what followed as the United States threw its support behind the conservative regime of Ngo Dinh Diem, who superseded Bao Dai as leader in South Vietnam. As Kolko tells it, it is a tale that reflects America's determination to prevent threatening social change everywhere in the world and to preserve American international hegemony wherever possible.

FOR FURTHER READING:

Bernard B. Fall, *The Laos Crisis of 1961,* (Doubleday, 1969); Bernard B. Fall, *Hell is a Very Small Place: The Siege of Dien Bien Phu*,* (Vintage, 1968); David Halberstam, *Making of a Quagmire,* (Random House, 1965); Marvin E. Gettleman (editor) *Vietnam: History, Documents and Opinions on a Major World Crisis*,* (Fawcett Crest, 1965); Theodore Draper, *Abuse of Power*,* (Viking, 1967); Carl Oglesby and Richard Shaull, *Containment and Change*,* (Macmillan, 1967); Howard Zinn, *Vietnam: The Logic of Withdrawal*,* (Beacon, 1967); Noam Chomsky, *American Power and the New Mandarins,* (Pantheon, 1969).

Asterisk denotes paperback edition.

The Aftermath of Geneva: The U.S. Entrenchment, 1955–59

The United States attached such grave reservations because it never had any intention of implementing the Geneva Accords, and this was clear from all the initial public statements. The *Wall Street Journal* was entirely correct when on July 23rd it reported that "The U.S. is in no hurry for elections to unite Viet Nam; we fear Red leader Ho Chi Minh would win. So Dulles plans first to make the southern half a showplace—with American aid."

While various United States missions began moving into the area Diem controlled, Dulles addressed himself to the task of creating a SEATO organization which, as Eisenhower informed the Senate, was ". . . for defense against both open armed attack and internal subversion." To Dulles from this time onward, the SEATO treaty would cover Vietnam, Cambodia, and Laos, even though they failed to sign the Treaty and in fact the Geneva Agreement forbade them to do so. Article IV of the SEATO treaty extended beyond the signatories and threatened intervention by the organization in case of aggression "against any State or territory" in the region, or if there was a threat to the "political independence . . . of any other State or territory. . . ." Under such an umbrella the United States might rationalize almost any intervention for any reason.

The general pattern of United States economic and military aid to the Diem regime between 1955 and 1959, which totaled $2.92 billion in that period, indicates the magnitude of the American commitment, $1.71 billion of which was advanced under military programs, including well over a half-billion dollars before the final Geneva-scheduled election date.

That elections would never be held was a foregone conclusion, despite the efforts of the North Vietnamese, who on the first of January 1955 reminded the French of their obligations to see the provision respected. Given the internecine condition of the local opposition and its own vast strength among the people, the Democratic Republic of Vietnam had every reason to comply with the Geneva provisos on elections. During February 1955 Hanoi proposed establishing normal relations between the two zones preparatory to elections, and Pham Van Dong in April issued a joint statement with Nehru urging steps to hold elections to reunify the country. By this time Diem was busy repressing and liquidating internal opposition of every political hue, and when it received no positive answer to its June 6th pleas for elections, the D.R.V. again formally reiterated its opposition to the partition of one nation and the need to hold elections on schedule. During June the world turned its attention to Diem's and Dulles' response prior to the July 20th deadline for consultations. Diem's response was painfully vague, and the first real statement came from Dulles on June 28th when he stated neither the United States nor the regime in the south had signed the Agreement at Geneva or was bound to it, a point that Washington often repeated and which was, in the case of the south, patently false. Nevertheless, Dulles admitted that in principle the United States favored ". . . the unification of countries which have historic unity," the myth of two Vietnams and two nations not yet being a part of the American case. "The Communists have never yet won any free election. I don't think they ever will. Therefore, we are not afraid at all of elections, provided they are held under conditions of genuine freedom which the Geneva armistice agreement calls for." But the United States, it was clear from this statement, was not bound to call for the implementation of the agreement via prior consultations which Diem and Washington had refused until that time, nor did Dulles say he would now urge Diem to take such a course.

Diem at the end of April 1955 announced he would hold a "national referendum" in the south to convoke a new national assembly, and on July 16th he categorically rejected truly national elections under the terms of Geneva until ". . . proof is . . . given that they put the superior interests of the national community above those of Communism. . . ." "We certainly agree," Dulles stated shortly thereafter, "that conditions are not ripe for free elections." The response of the D.R.V. was as it had always been: Geneva obligated the Conference members to assume responsibility for its implementation, including consultations preparatory to actual elections, and in this regard Diem was by no means the responsible party. But the English favored partition, and the French were not about to thwart the United States Government. The fraudulent referendum of October 23rd which Diem organized in the south gave Diem 98 percent of the votes for the Presidency of the new "Government of Vietnam." Three days later Washington replied to the news by recognizing the legitimacy of the regime.

In reality, using a regime almost entirely financed with its funds, and incapable of surviving without its aid, the United States partitioned Vietnam.

To the D.R.V., the United States and the Diem Administrations' refusal to conform to the Geneva Accords was a question for the members of the Geneva Conference and the I.C.C. to confront, and while it had often made such demands—during June and again November 1955, and directly to Diem on July 19th—in September and again on November 17, 1955, Pham and Ho publicly elaborated their ideas on the structure of an election along entirely democratic lines. All citizens above eighteen could vote and all above twenty-one could run for office. They proposed free campaigning in both zones and secret and direct balloting. The I.C.C. could supervise. On February 25, 1956, Ho again reiterated this position.

On February 14, 1956, Pham Van Dong directed a letter to the Geneva co-chairmen pointing to the repression in the south, its de facto involvement in an alliance with the United States, and the French responsibility for rectifying the situation. He now proposed that the Geneva Conference reconvene to settle peacefully the problem of Vietnam. The British refused, and again on April 6th the Diem government announced that "it does not consider itself bound by their provisions." On May 8th the Geneva co-chairmen sent to the north and south as well as to the French, a demand to open consultations on elections with a view to unifying the country under the Geneva Accords. Three days later the D.R.V. expressed readiness to begin direct talks in early June at a time set by the Diem authorities. Diem refused. The D.R.V. continued to demand consultations to organize elections, submitting notes to this effect to the Geneva co-chairmen and the Diem government in June and July 1957, March and December 1958, July 1959 and July 1960, and later, for arms reduction, resumption of trade, and other steps necessary to end the artificial partition of Vietnam. These proposals failed, for neither Diem nor the United States could survive their successful implementation.

Washington's policy during this period was clear and publicly stated. On June 1, 1956, after visiting Diem with Dulles the prior March, Walter S. Robertson, Assistant Secretary of State, attacked the Geneva Accords, which ". . . partitioned [Vietnam] by fiat of the great powers against the will of the Vietnamese people." He lauded Diem's rigged "free election of last March" and stated the American determination "To support a friendly non-Communist government in Viet-Nam and to help it diminish and eventually eradicate Communist subversion and influence. . . . Our efforts are directed first of all toward helping to sustain the internal security forces consisting of a regular army of about 150,000 men, a mobile civil guard of some 45,000, and local defense units. . . . We are also helping to organize, train, and equip the Vietnamese police force." Such policies were, of course, in violation of the Geneva Accords forbidding military expansion.

The term "eradicate" was an apt description of the policy which the United States urged upon the more-than-willing Diem, who persecuted former Vietminh supporters, dissident religious sects, and others. An estimated 40,000 Vietnamese were in jail for political reasons by the end of 1958, almost four times that number by the end of 1961. Such policies were possible because the United States financed over 70 per cent of Diem's budget, and the main United States emphasis was on the use of force and repression. There were an estimated minimum of 16,600 political liquidations between 1955–59, perhaps much higher. Suffice it to say, every objective observer has accepted *Life* magazine's description in May 1957 as a fair estimate:

> Behind a facade of photographs, flags and slogans there is a grim structure of decrees, "re-education centers," secret police. Presidential "Ordinance No. 6" signed and issued by Diem in January, 1956, provides that "individuals considered dangerous to national defense and common security may be confined on executive order" in a "concentration camp." . . . Only known or suspected Communists . . . are supposed to be arrested and "re-educated" under these decrees. But many non-Communists have also been detained . . . The whole machinery of security has been used to discourage active opposition of any kind from any source.

The International Control Commission's teams complained of these violations in the south, and in the north they claimed that the only significant group to have its civil liberties infringed was the Catholic minority, approximately one-tenth of the nation. The cooperation of the D.R.V. with the I.C.C. was a critical index of its intentions, and an example of its naïve persistence in the belief Geneva had not in reality deprived them of its hard-fought victory. The vast military build-up in the south made real cooperation with the I.C.C. impossible, and its complaints, especially in regard to the airfields and reprisals against civilians, were very common. In certain cases the Diem regime permitted I.C.C. teams to move in the south, but it imposed time limits, especially after 1959. Although there is no precise way of making a count of what figures both Diem and the United States were attempting to hide, by July 1958 the D.R.V.'s estimate that Diem had 450,000 men under arms was probably correct in light of Robertson's earlier estimate of United States plans and the $1.7 billion in military expenditures for Diem through 1959.

Although the large bulk of American aid to Diem went to military purposes, the section devoted to economic ends further rooted an entirely dependent regime to the United States. That economic aid was a total disaster, exacerbated a moribund economy, ripped apart the urban society already tottering from the first decade of war, and enriched Diem, his family, and clique. Yet certain germane aspects of the condition of the southern economy are essential to understand the next phase of the revolution in Vietnam and further American intervention, a revolution the Americans had frozen for a time but could not stop.

The Vietminh controlled well over one-half the land south of the 18th parallel prior to the Geneva Conference, and since 1941 they had managed to introduce far-reaching land reform into an agrarian economy of grossly inequitable holdings. When Diem took over this area, with the advice of United States experts he introduced a "land reform" program which in fact was a regressive "modernization" of the concentrated land control system that had already been wiped out in many regions. Saigon reduced rents by as much as 50 percent from pre-Vietminh times, but in fact it represented a reimposition of tolls that had ceased to exist in wide areas. In cases of outright expropriation, landlords received compensation for property that they had already lost. In brief, the Diem regime's return to power meant a reimposition of a new form of the prewar 1940 land distribution system in which 72 percent of the population owned 13 percent of the land and two-thirds of the agricultural population consisted of tenants ground down by high rents and exorbitant interest rates. For this reason, it was the landlords rather than the peasantry who supported "agrarian reform."

Various plans for resettling peasants in former Vietminh strongholds, abortive steps which finally culminated in the strategic hamlet movement of 1962, simply helped to keep the countryside in seething discontent. These *agrovilles* uprooted traditional villages and became famous as sources of discontent against the regime, one which was ripping apart the existing social structure. In brief, Diem and the United States never established control over the larger part of south Vietnam and the Vietminh's impregnable peasant base, and given the decentralization and the corruption of Diem's authority, there was no effective basis for their doing so. The repression Diem exercised only rekindled resistance.

In the cities the dislocations in the urban population, constantly augmented by a flow of Catholic refugees from the north, led to a conservative estimate in 1956 of 413,000 unemployed out of the Saigon population of two million. The $1.2 billion in nonmilitary aid given to the Diem regime during 1955–59 went in large part to pay for its vast import deficit which permitted vast quantities of American-made luxury goods to be brought into the country's inflationary economy for the use of the new *comprador* class and Diem's bureaucracy.

The United States endorsed and encouraged the military build-up and repression, but it did not like the strange mélange of mandarin anti-capitalism and Catholic feudalism which Diem jumbled together in his philosophy of personalism. Diem was a puppet, but a not perfectly tractable one. The United States did not appreciate the high margin of personal graft, nor did it like Diem's hostility toward accelerated economic development, nor his belief in state-owned companies. Ngo Dinh Nhu, his brother, regarded economic aid as a cynical means of dumping American surpluses, and the United States had to fight, though successfully, for the relaxation of restrictions on foreign investments and protection against the threat of nationalization. Ultimately Diem was content to complain and to hoard aid funds for purposes the United States thought dubious.

The U.S. thought of Vietnam as a capitalist state in Southeast Asia. This course condemned it to failure, but in April 1959, when Eisenhower publicly discussed Vietnam, ". . . a country divided into two parts," and not two distinct nations, he stressed Vietnam's need to develop economically, and the way ". . . to get the necessary capital is through private investments from the outside and through government loans," the latter, insofar as the United States was concerned, going to local capitalists.

1959–64: The Resistance Is Rekindled

Every credible historical account of the origins of the armed struggle south of the 17th parallel treats it as if it were on a continuum from the war with the French of 1945–54, and as the effect rather than the cause of the Diem regime's frightful repression and accumulated internal economic and social problems. The resistance to Diem's officials had begun among the peasantry in a spontaneous manner, by growing numbers of persecuted political figures of every persuasion, augmented by Buddhists and Vietminh who returned to the villages to escape, and, like every successful guerrilla movement, it was based on the support of the peasantry for its erratic but ultimately irresistible momentum. On May 6, 1959, Diem passed his famous Law 10/59 which applied the sentence of death to anyone committing murder, destroying to any extent houses, farms, or buildings of any kind, means of transport, and a whole list of similar offenses. "Whoever belongs to an organization designed to help to prepare or perpetuate crimes . . . or takes pledges to do so, will be subject to the sentences provided. . . ." The regime especially persecuted former members of the Vietminh, but all opposition came under the sweeping authority of Diem's new law, and the number of political prisoners between 1958 and the end of 1961 quadrupled. The resistance that spread did not originate from the north, and former Vietminh members joined the spontaneous local resistance groups well before the D.R.V. indicated any support for them. Only in 1960 did significant fighting spread throughout the country.

At the end of 1960 the United States claimed to have only 773 troops stationed there. By December 1965 there were at least fourteen major United States airbases in Vietnam, 166,000 troops, and the manpower was to more than double over the following year. This build-up violated the Geneva Accords, but that infraction is a fine point in light of the fact that the United States always had utter contempt for that agreement. In reality, the United States was now compelled to save what little it controlled of the south of Vietnam from the inevitable failure of its own policies.

It is largely pointless to deal with the subsequent events in the same detail, for they were merely a logical extension of the global policies of the United States before 1960. One has merely to juxtapose the newspaper accounts in the United States press against the official rationalizations cited in Washington to realize how very distant from the truth Washington was willing to wander to seek justification for a barbaric war against a small nation quite unprecedented in the history of modern times. To understand this war one must always place it in its contextual relationship and recall that the issues in Vietnam were really those of the future of United States power not only in Southeast Asia but throughout the entire developing world. In Vietnam the United States Government has vainly attempted to make vast power relevant to international social and political realities that had bypassed the functional conservatism of a nation seeking to save an old order with liberal rhetoric and, above all, with every form of military power available in its nonnuclear arsenal.

By 1960 it was apparent that Diem would not survive very long, a point that an abortive palace revolt of his own paratroop battalions emphasized on November 11th. When Kennedy came to office amidst great debates over military credibility and the need to build a limited-war capability, Vietnam inevitably became the central challenge to the intellectual strategists he brought to Washington. In May 1961, Kennedy and Dean Rusk denounced what they called D.R.V. responsibility for the growth of guerrilla activity in the south, a decision Rusk claimed the Communist Party of the D.R.V. made in May 1959 and reaffirmed in September of the following year. This tendentious reasoning, of course, ignored the fact that the prior September, Pham Van Dong again urged negotiations on the basis of reciprocal concessions in order to achieve unity without recourse to "war and force." By the fall two missions headed by Eugene Staley and the leading limited-war theorist, General Maxwell Taylor, went to Vietnam to study the situation. On October 18th Diem declared a state of emergency, and on November 16th Kennedy pledged a sharp increase in aid to the regime, which newspapers predicted would also involve large United States troop increases. During November the *Wall Street Journal,* for example, admitted that aid would be going to a regime characterized by "corruption and favoritism," and described the "authoritarian nature of the country" which allowed the National Liberation Front, formed at the end of December 1960, to build up a mass base among ". . . the farmers who welcome an alternative to corrupt and ineffective appointees of the regime."

The United States Government could hardly admit that the problem in southern Vietnam was the people's revolt against the corruption of an oppressive regime that survived only with American guns and dollars, and not very well at that, and so it was necessary, while once again violating the Geneva Accords, to build up the myth of intervention from the D.R.V. At this time the United States Government effected a curious shift in its attitude toward the Geneva Accords, from denouncing or ignoring it to insisting that it bound the other side and, implicitly, that the United States had endorsed it. When asked about how a vast increase in United States military aid affected the agreement, Washington from this time on insisted, in Rusk's words, that ". . . the primary question about the Geneva Accords is not how those Accords relate to, say, our military assistance program to South Vietnam. They relate to the specific, persistent, substantial, and openly proclaimed violations of those accords by the north Vietnamese. . . . The first question is, what does the north do about those accords?" "If the North Vietnamese bring themselves into full compliance with the Geneva Accords," Rusk stated on December 8th as he released the so-called White Paper, "there will be no problem on the part of South Vietnam or any one supporting South Vietnam." Only the prior month Ho publicly called for the peaceful reunification of the country via the terms of Geneva. Not surprisingly, Rusk never referred to the question of elections.

The United States White Paper of December 1961 was inept, and an excellent source of information for disproving nearly all the American claims of the time. It consisted of a mélange of data, case histories, and quotes from D.R.V. statements, most obviously out of context. As for China or Russia supplying the N.L.F. with arms, the White Paper admitted "The weapons of the VC are largely French- or U.S.-made, or handmade on primitive forges in the jungle." Evidence ranged from South Vietnamese interrogation records to reproductions of human anatomy from a Chinese text book to photos of medical equipment made in China and the cover of a private diary. The White Paper exhibited no military equipment and the long extracts from various D.R.V. congresses and publications revealed merely that the D.R.V. was officially committed to ". . . struggle tenaciously for the implementation of the Geneva agreements" and "peaceful reunification of the fatherland." The State Department's incompetent case was less consequential than the renewed and frank exposition of the "domino" theory: if all of Vietnam chose the leadership of Ho and his party, the rest of Asia would "fall." Above all, as the American press acknowledged, if the United States did not intervene the shabby Diem regime would collapse without anything acceptable replacing it.

During early 1962 the United States announced and began the Staley Plan— Operation Sunrise—for razing existing villages and regrouping entire populations against their will; and in February created a formal command in Vietnam. Officially, to meet I.C.C. complaints, the United States reported 685 American soldiers were in Vietnam, but in fact reporters described the truth more accurately, and Washington intensified a long pattern of official deception of the American public. Yet the United States position was unenviable, for on February 27th Diem's own planes bombed his palace. This phase of the story need not be surveyed here—more pliable and equally corrupt men were to replace Diem. As one American officer in April 1962 reported of growing N.L.F. power, "When I arrived last September, the Vietcong were rarely encountered in groups exceeding four or five. Now they are frequently met in bands of forty to sixty."

On March 1st, while alleging D.R.V. responsibility for the war, Rusk declared its ". . . all in gross violation of the Geneva Accords." The problem, he argued over the following years, came from the north. As for the D.R.V.'s appeal that the Geneva Conference be reconvened, he suggested "There is no problem in South Vietnam if the other side would stay its hand. . . . I don't at the moment envisage any particular form of discussion. . . ." No later than March, American forces in Vietnam were actively locked in combat.

Despite propaganda of the lowest calibre which the State Department and White House issued, more authoritative statements from various Government agencies indicated reluctance to base planning on the fiction that the D.R.V. started the war in Vietnam. The Senate Committee on Foreign Relations report of January 1963 admitted that the N.L.F., ". . . is equipped largely with primitive, antiquated, and captured weapons." Despite the weakness of the N.L.F. in this regard against a regular army of well over 150,000, plus police, etc., "By 1961 it was apparent that the prospects for a total collapse in south Vietnam had begun to come dangerously close." American intervention had stayed that event. Speaking to the Senate Armed Services Committee in early March, General David Shoup, Commandant of the Marine Corps, freely admitted there was no correlation between the size of the N.L.F. and the alleged infiltrators from the north: "I don't agree that they come in there in the numbers that are down there. . . ." Not until July 1963 did the United States publicly and unequivocally claim that, for the first time, it had captured N.L.F. arms manufactured in Communist countries after 1954.

By the summer of 1963 it was obvious that the American Government and its ally Diem were headed toward military defeat in Vietnam and new and unprecedented political resistance at home. Diem's oppression of all political elements, his active persecution of the Buddhists, the failure of the strategic hamlet program, the utter incompetence of his drafted troops against far weaker N.L.F. forces the American press described in detail. At the beginning of September Washington was apparently bent on pressuring Diem but preserving him against mounting Buddhist protests, but as Kennedy admitted on September 9th as audible stirrings from senators were heard for the first time, "What I am concerned about is that Americans will get impatient and say, because they don't like events in Southeast Asia or they don't like the Government in Saigon, that we should withdraw." Quite simply, he stated four days later, "If it helps to win the war, we support it. What interferes with the war effort we oppose." The Americans would not sink with Diem.

On October 21st, after some weeks of similar actions on forms of economic aid, the United States Embassy in Saigon announced that it would terminate the pay for Diem's own special political army unless they went into the field. On October 30th this private guard was sent out of Saigon. The next day a military coup brought Diem's long rule to an end.

The United States recognized the new Minh coup on November 4th, amid disturbing reports of continued squabbling within its ranks. On the 8th Rusk confirmed that the mood in Washington was now tending toward winning military victory by rejecting a neutralist solution for Vietnam south of the 17th parallel, linking it to "far-reaching changes in North Vietnam," again insisting that the north was responsible for aggression. "The other side was fully committed—fully committed —in the original Geneva settlement of 1954 to the arrangements which provided for South Vietnam as an independent entity, and we see no reason to modify those in the direction of a larger influence of North Vietnam or Hanoi in South Vietnam." The creation of this deliberate fiction of two Vietnams—North and South—as being the result of the Geneva Accords now indicated that the United States Government would seek military victory.

The new regimes were as unsatisfactory as the old one, and by mid-December the American press reported dissatisfaction in Washington over the dismal drift of the war. In his important dispatches in the *New York Times* at the end of 1963, David Halberstam described the failure of the strategic hamlet program, the corruption of Diem, the paralysis of Minh in these terms: "The outlook is that the situation will deteriorate unless the Government can wrest the initiative from the guerrillas.

Unless it can, there appears to be only two likely alternatives. One is a neutralist settlement. The other is the use of United States combat troops to prop up the Government."

The drift toward a neutralist solution at the beginning of 1964 was so great that Washington sought to nip it in the bud. In his New Year's Message to the Minh Regime, President Johnson made it clear that ". . . neutralization of South Vietnam would only be another name for a Communist take-over. Peace will return to your country just as soon as the authorities in Hanoi cease and desist from their terrorist aggression." Peace would be acceptable to the Americans after total victory. To alter their losing course, they would escalate.

At the end of January, as the Khanh coup took over, one of the new ruler's grievances against his former allies was that some had surreptitiously used the French Government to seek a neutral political solution. During February, the *New York Times* reported that Washington was planning an attack on the north, with divided counsels on its extent or even its relevance to internal political-economic problems. The United States preferred air bombing and/or a blockade, because as Hanson Baldwin wrote on March 6th, "The waging of guerrilla war by the South Vietnamese in North Vietnam has, in fact, been tried on a small scale, but so far it has been completely ineffective."

On March 15th Johnson again endorsed the "domino" theory and avowed his resolution not to tolerate defeat. On March 26th McNamara in a major address stressed the "great strategic significance" of the issue, and Vietnam as ". . . a major test case of communism's new strategy" of local revolution, one that might extend to all the world unless foiled in Vietnam. Behind the D.R.V., the Secretary of Defense alleged, stood China. The Americans rejected neutralism for Vietnam, reaffirmed aid to the Khanh regime, and darkly hinted at escalation toward the north. During these same days, for the first time in two decades key members of the Senate voiced significant opposition to a major foreign policy. It had become a tradition in the Cold War for Presidents to marshal support from Congress by creating crises, thereby defining the tone of American foreign policy via a sequence of sudden challenges which, at least to some, vindicated their diabolical explanations. A "crisis" was in the making.

All of the dangers of the Vietnamese internal situation persisted throughout spring 1964. On July 24th the *New York Times* reported that Khanh was exerting tremendous pressures on the United States to take the war to the north, even by "liberating" it. During these same days both the French, Soviet, and N.L.F. leaders joined U Thant in a new diplomatic drive to seek an end to the war by negotiations. Washington, for its part, resisted these pacific solutions.

On August 4th Johnson announced that North Vietnamese torpedo boats had wantonly attacked the U.S. destroyer *Maddox* in the Bay of Tonkin and in international waters, and as a result of repeated skirmishes since the 2nd he had ordered the bombardment of North Vietnamese installations supporting the boats. The following day he asked Congress to pass a resolution authorizing him to take all action necessary "to protect our Armed Forces." It was maudlin, fictional, and successful.

It was known—and immediately documented in *Le Monde*—that the United States had been sending espionage missions to the north since 1957—as Baldwin alluded the prior February—and that on July 30th South Vietnamese and United

States ships raided and bombarded D.R.V. islands. It was too farfetched that D.R.V. torpedo boats would have searched out on the high seas the ships of the most powerful fleet in the world, without scoring any hits which the United States might show the skeptical world. On August 5th the press asked McNamara for his explanation of the events. "I can't explain them. They were unprovoked. . . . our vessels were clearly in international waters. . . . roughly 60 miles off the North Vietnamese coast." When asked whether reports of South Vietnamese attacks in the area during the prior days were relevant, McNamara demurred! "No, to the best of my knowledge, there were no operations during the period. . . ." In testimony before the Senate during the same days it emerged that United States warships were not sixty miles but three to eleven miles off D.R.V. territory, even though, like many states, the D.R.V. claimed a twelve-mile territorial limit. Over subsequent days more and more information leaked out so that the essential points of the D.R.V. case were confirmed, the long history of raids on the north revealed. By the end of September the entire fantasy was so implausible that the *New York Times* reported that the Defense Department was sending a team to Vietnam to deal with what were euphemistically described as "contradictory reports." They did not subsequently provide further details, for ". . . contributing to the Defense Department's reticence was the secret mission of the two destroyers," a mission the *New York Times* described as espionage of various sorts.

The United States escalated in the hope that it could mobilize a Congress at home and sustain the Khanh regime in Vietnam, which nevertheless fell the following month. During these days the United States Government admitted that the war was now grinding to a total halt as the Vietnamese politicians in the south devoted all their energy to byzantine intrigues. With or without war against the D.R.V., the United States was even further from victory. In assessing the condition in the south a year after the downfall of Diem, the *New York Times* reported from Saigon that three years after the massive increase of the American commitment, and a year after Diem's demise, ". . . the weakness of the Government [has] . . . once again brought the country to the brink of collapse. . . . Once again many American and Vietnamese officials are thinking of new, enlarged commitments—this time to carry the conflict beyond the frontier of South Vietnam."

The Bombing of the D.R.V.

On December 20, 1964, there was yet another coup in Saigon, and during the subsequent weeks the difficulties for the United States resulting from the court maneuvers among generals who refused to fight were compounded by the growing militancy of the Buddhist forces. By January of 1965 the desertion rate within the South Vietnamese Army reached 30 percent among draftees within six weeks of induction, and a very large proportion of the remainder would not fight. It was perfectly apparent that if anyone was to continue the war the United States would have to supply not only money, arms, and 23,000 supporting troops as of the end of 1964, but fight the entire war itself. During January, as well, a Soviet-led effort to end the war through negotiations was gathering momentum, and at the beginning of February Soviet Premier Kosygin, amidst American press reports that Washington in its pessimism was planning decisive new military moves, arrived in Hanoi.

On the morning of February 7th, while Kosygin was in Hanoi, American aircraft bombed the D.R.V., allegedly in response to a N.L.F. mortar attack on the Pleiku base in the south which cost eight American lives. There was nothing unusual in the N.L.F. attack, and every serious observer immediately rejected the official United States explanation, for the Government refused to state that the D.R.V. ordered the Pleiku action, but only claimed the D.R.V. was generally responsible for the war. The United States attack had been prepared in advance, Arthur Krock revealed on February 10th, and the *New York Times* reported that Washington had told several governments of the planned escalation before the 7th. The action was political, not military in purpose, a response to growing dissatisfaction at home and pressures abroad. It was already known that De Gaulle was contemplating a move to reconvene the Geneva Conference—which he attempted on the 10th, after D.R.V. urgings—and during the subsequent weeks, as the United States threatened additional air strikes against the D.R.V., both Kosygin and U Thant vainly attempted to drag the United States Government to the peace table. In response, the Americans now prepared for vast new troop commitments.

On February 26th, the day before the State Department released its second White Paper, Rusk indicated willingness to consider negotiations only if the D.R.V. agreed to stop the war in the south for which he held it responsible. Hence there was no possibility of negotiating on premises which so cynically distorted the facts, and which even Washington understood to be false. ". . . they doubt that Hanoi would be able to call off the guerrilla war," the *New York Times* reported of dominant opinion in Washington barely a week before the Rusk statement. The D.R.V. could not negotiate a war it did not start nor was in a position to end. The United States determined to intervene to save a condition in the south on the verge of utter collapse.

In its own perverse manner, the new White Paper made precisely these points. It ascribed the origins of the war, the "hard core" of the N.L.F., "many" of the weapons to the D.R.V. The actual evidence the Paper gave showed that 179 weapons, or less than 3 percent of the total captured from the N.L.F. in three years, were not definitely French, American, or homemade in origin and modification. Of the small number of actual case studies of captured N.L.F. members offered, the large majority were born south of the 17th parallel and had gone to the north after Geneva, a point that was readily admitted, and which disproved even a case based on the fiction—by now a permanent American premise—that Vietnam was two countries and that those north of an arbitrarily imposed line had no right to define the destiny of one nation. The tendentious case only proved total American responsibility for the vast new increase in the aggression.

Despite the growing pressure for negotiations from many sources, and because of them, by March the United States decided to implement the so-called "McNamara-Bundy Plan" to bring about an "honorable" peace by increasing the war. On March 2nd air strikes against the D.R.V. were initiated once more, but this time they were sustained down to this very day. There were incredulously received rumors of vast increases in troop commitments to as high as 350,000. Washington made an accurate assessment in March 1965 when it realized it could not expect to save Vietnam for its sphere of influence, and that peace was incompatible with its larger global objectives of stopping guerilla and revolutionary upheavals everywhere in the world. Both McNamara and Taylor during March harked back to the constant theme that the United States was fighting in Vietnam "to halt Communist expansion in Asia." Peace would come, Johnson stated on March 13th, when "Hanoi is prepared or willing or ready to stop doing what it is doing to its neighbors." Twelve days later the President expressed willingness to grant a vast development plan to the region—which soon turned out to be Eugene Black's formula for increasingly specialized raw-materials output for the use of the industrialized world—should the Vietnamese be ready to accept the fiction of D.R.V. responsibility for the war.

It made no difference to the United States Government that on March 22nd the N.L.F., and on April 8th the D.R.V., again called for negotiations on terms which in fact were within the spirit of a Geneva Accords the United States had always rejected. It was less consequential that on April 6th the official Japanese Matsumoto Mission mustered sufficient courage to reject formally the thesis of D.R.V. responsibility for the war in the south and its ability, therefore, to stop the Vietnamese there from resisting the United States and its intriguing puppets. More significant was the fact that, as it announced April 2nd, the Administration had finally decided to send as many as 350,000 troops to Vietnam to attain for the United States what the armies of Diem, Khanh, and others could not—victory. The official position called for "peace," but in his famous Johns Hopkins speech on April 7th Johnson made it clear that "We will not withdraw, either openly or under the cloak of a meaningless agreement." Though he agreed to "unconditional discussions," he made it explicit that these would exclude the N.L.F. and would be with an end to securing ". . . an independent South Vietnam," which is to say permanent partition and a violation of the Geneva Accords. From this time onward the United States persisted in distorting the negotiating position of the D.R.V.'s four-point declaration and effectively ignored the demand of the N.L.F. for "an independent state, democratic, peaceful and neutral." It refused, and has to this day, a voice for the N.L.F. in any negotiations, and insisted that the N.L.F. and D.R.V. had attached certain preconditions to negotiations which in fact did not exist and which on August 3rd the N.L.F. again attempted to clarify—to no avail.

Experience over subsequent years has shown again and again that the words "peace" and "negotiations" from official United States sources were from 1964 onward always preludes to new and more intensive military escalation.

To the United States Government the point of Vietnam is not peace but victory, not just in Vietnam but for a global strategy which it has expressed first of all in Vietnam but at various times on every other continent as well. Johnson's own words in July 1965 stressed this global perspective while attributing the origins of the war to the D.R.V. and, ultimately, China.

> Its goal is to conquer the south, to defeat American power and to extend the Asiatic dominion of Communism.
> And there are great stakes in the balance. . . .
> Our power, therefore, is a very vital shield. If we are driven from the field in Vietnam, then no nation can ever again have the same confidence in American promise or American protection. . . . We did not choose to be guardians at the gate, but there is no one else.

One does not have to approve of this vision to accept it as an accurate explanation of why the United States Government is willing to violate every norm of civilized behavior to sustain the successive corrupt puppet governments in the south. But any careful reading of the declarations of Rusk and McNamara in the months preceding and following this statement reveals that it was not the Geneva Accords but rather SEATO and, more critically, the survival of United States power in a world it can less and less control that has defined the basis of United States policy in Vietnam. This official policy, as Rusk expounded it again in March 1966, is that Vietnam is "the testing ground" for wars of liberation that, if successful in one place, can spread throughout the world. When, as in January 1966, Undersecretary of State George Ball explained Vietnam ". . . is part of a continuing struggle to prevent the Communists from upsetting the fragile balance of power through force or the threat of force," in effect he meant the ability of the United States to contain revolutionary nationalist movements, Communist and noncommunist alike, unwilling to accept United States hegemony and dedicated to writing their own history for their own people.

★

Any objective and carefully prepared account of the history of Vietnam must conclude with the fact that the United States must bear the responsibility for the torture of an entire nation since the end of the Second World War. The return of France to Vietnam, and its ability to fight for the restoration of a colony, was due to critical political decisions made in Washington in 1945, and the later repression depended on financial and military aid given to France by the United States. First as a passive senior partner, and then as the primary party, the United States made Vietnam an international arena for the Cold War, and it is a serious error to regard the war in Vietnam as a civil conflict, or even secondarily as a by-product of one—for in that form it would hardly have lasted very long against a national and radical movement that the vast majority of the Vietnamese people always have sustained.

The United States Government responded to its chronic inability to find a viable internal alternative to the Vietminh and the N.L.F. by escalating the war against virtually the entire nation. To escape certain defeat time and time again, it violated formal and customary international law by increasing the scale of military activity. The United States met each overture to negotiate, whether it came from the Vietnamese, the French, or the Russians, by accelerated warfare in the hope of attaining its unique ends through military means rather than diplomacy.

Ultimately, the United States has fought in Vietnam with increasing intensity to extend its hegemony over the world community and to stop every form of revolutionary movement which refuses to accept the predominant role of the United States in the direction of the affairs of its nation or region. Repeatedly defeated in Vietnam in the attainment of its impossible objective, the United States Government, having alienated most of its European allies and a growing sector of its own nation, is attempting to prove to itself and the world that it remains indeed strong enough to define the course of global politics despite the opposition of a small, poor nation of peasants. On the outcome of this epic contest rests the future of peace and social progress in the world for the remainder of the twentieth century, not just for those who struggle to overcome the legacy of colonialism and oppression to build new lives, but for the people of the United States themselves.

The New Abolitionists   HOWARD ZINN

The Vietnam War was one source of the restlessness and disaffection that has afflicted the United States in the past decade. Another was the continued repression of the nation's black minority. In the 1950s, this oppression seemed most serious and intractable in the South. There, legal segregation, as well as an elaborate system of social and economic caste, degraded blacks and kept them in a position of permanent economic inferiority.

The system by this time was already under severe attack. Beginning in the 1940s, the courts, bit by bit, had struck down state and local ordinances that separated the races and confined blacks to inferior facilities. In 1954, in the momentous decision *Brown v. Board of Education of Topeka,* the edifice of school segregation was declared legally null and void. By the 60s, the movement for tearing down the whole of the Southern caste system was well under way with blacks serving not only as objects of radical white benevolence, but also as active fighters on their own behalf.

As Howard Zinn notes in the piece below, the young activists of such organizations as the Student Nonviolent Coordinating Committee (SNCC) succeeded not only in further eroding the walls of segregation but also in helping to radicalize much of the black community and inspiring radicalism among young whites as well. Their role, he suggests, was much like that of the pre-Civil War abolitionists.

FOR FURTHER READING:

Jack Newfield, *A Prophetic Minority**, (Signet, 1966); Louis Lomax, *The Negro Revolt**, (Signet, 1963); Arthur Waskow, *From Race Riot to Sit In: 1919 and the 1960's**, (Doubleday, 1966); Pat Watters and Reese Cleghorn, *Climbing Jacob's Ladder: The Arrival of Negroes in Southern Politics,* (Harcourt, Brace and World, 1967); Allen J. Matusow, "From Civil Rights to Black Power: The Case of SNCC, 1960–1966," in Barton Bernstein and Allen J. Matusow (editors) *Twentieth Century America: Recent Interpretations**, (Harcourt, Brace and World, 1969).

Asterisk denotes paperback edition.

For the first time in our history a major social movement, shaking the nation to its bones, is being led by youngsters. This is not to deny the inspirational leadership of a handful of adults (Martin Luther King and James Farmer), the organizational direction by veterans in the struggle (Roy Wilkins and A. Philip Randolph), or the participation of hundreds of thousands of older people in the current Negro revolt. But that revolt, a long time marching out of the American past, its way suddenly lit up by the Supreme Court decision, and beginning to rumble in earnest when thousands of people took to the streets of Montgomery in the bus boycott, first flared into a national excitement with the sit-ins by college students that started the decade of the 1960's.

Source: Howard Zinn, *SNCC: The New Abolitionists* (Boston: Beacon Press, 1965), chap. i, "The New Abolitionists," pp. 1–15.

And since then, those same youngsters, hardened by countless jailings and beatings, now out of school and living in ramshackle headquarters all over the Deep South, have been striking the sparks, again and again, for that fire of change spreading through the South and searing the whole country.

These young rebels call themselves the Student Nonviolent Coordinating Committee, but they are more a movement than an organization, for no bureaucratized structure can contain their spirit, no printed program capture the fierce and elusive quality of their thinking. And while they have no famous leaders, very little money, no inner access to the seats of national authority, they are clearly the front line of the Negro assault on the moral comfort of white America.

To be with them, walking a picket line in the rain in Hattiesburg, Mississippi or sleeping on a cot in a cramped "office" in Greenville, Mississippi; to watch them walk out of the stone jailhouse in Albany, Georgia; to see them jabbed by electric prod poles and flung into paddy wagons in Selma, Alabama, or link arms and sing at the close of a church meeting in the Delta—is to feel the presence of greatness. It is a greatness that comes from their relationship to history, and it does not diminish when they are discovered to be human: to make mistakes or feel fear, to act with envy, or hostility or even violence.

All Americans owe them a debt for—if nothing else—releasing the idealism locked so long inside a nation that has not recently tasted the drama of a social upheaval. And for making us look on the young people of the country with a new respect. Theirs was the silent generation until they spoke, the complacent generation until they marched and sang, the money-seeking generation until they renounced comfort and security to fight for justice in the dank and dangerous hamlets of the Black Belt.

Princeton philosopher Walter Kaufmann, writing in *The Faith of a Heretic*, called the young people born during World War II the "uncommitted generation." He said: "What distinguishes them is that they are not committed to any cause." But this was written in 1960. And in that year, out of that same generation which Kaufmann described, there emerged the first rebels of the decade. They came out of unexpected places: they were mostly black and therefore unseen until they suddenly became the most visible people in America; they came out of Greensboro, North Carolina and Nashville, Tennessee and Rock Hill, South Carolina and Atlanta, Georgia. And they were committed. To the point of jail, which is a large commitment. And to the point of death, which hovers always near a heretic in a police state and which turns to stare a Deep South Negro directly in the face at that moment when he utters that word so long taboo for Negroes in America, *"No."*

How do you measure commitment? Is it the willingness to take a day out of life and sacrifice it to history, to plunge for one morning or one afternoon into the unknown, to engage in one solitary act of defiance against all the arrayed power of established society? Then tens of thousands of young people, mostly black, some white, have committed themselves these past four years, by the simple act of joining a demonstration. Is commitment more than that—the willingness to wrench yourself out of your environment and begin anew, almost alone, in a social jungle which the most powerful forces in the nation have not dared to penetrate? Then the number is reduced to sixteen: those sixteen college youngsters who, in the fall of 1961, decided to drop everything—school and family and approved ambition—and move into the Deep South to become the first guerilla fighters of the Student Nonviolent Coordinating Committee.

By early 1964, the number was up to 150. In the most heated days of abolitionism before the Civil War, there were never that many dedicated people who turned their backs on ordinary pursuits and gave their lives wholly to the movement. There were William Lloyd Garrison and Wendell Phillips and Theodore Weld and Frederick Douglass and Sojourner Truth and a handful of others, and there were hundreds of part-time abolitionists and thousands of followers. But for 150 youngsters today to turn on their pasts, to decide to live and work twenty-four hours a day in the most dangerous region of the United States, is cause for wonder. And wherever they have come from—the Negro colleges of the South, the Ivy League universities of the North, the small and medium colleges all over the country—they have left ripples of astonishment behind. This college generation as a whole is not committed, by any means. But it has been shaken.

These 150—who next year will be 250 or more, because the excitement grows daily on the college campuses—are the new abolitionists. It is not fanciful to invest them with a name that has the ring of history; we are always shy about recognizing the historic worth of events when they take place before our eyes, about recognizing heroes when they are still flesh and blood and not yet transfixed in marble. But there is no doubt about it: we have in this country today a movement which will take its place alongside that of the abolitionists, the Populists, the Progressives—and may outdo them all.

Their youth makes us hestitant to recognize their depth. But the great social upsurge of post-war America is the Negro revolt, and this revolt has gotten its most powerful impetus from young people, who gave it a new turn in 1960 and today, as anonymous as infantrymen everywhere, form the first rank in a nonviolent but ferocious war against the old order.

It would be easy to romanticize them, but they are too young, too vulnerable, too humanly frail to fit the stereotype of heroes. They don't match the storybook martyrs who face death with silent stoicism; the young fellows sometimes cry out when they are beaten; the girls may weep when abused in prison. Most often, however, they sing. This was true of the farmer and labor movements in this country, and of all the wars; but there has never been a singing movement like this one. Perhaps it is because most of them were brought up on the gospel songs and hymns of the Negro church in the South, perhaps also because they are young, probably most of all because what they are doing inspires song. They have created a new gospel music out of the old, made up of songs adapted or written in jail or on the picket line. Every battle station in the Deep South now has its Freedom Chorus, and the mass meetings there end with everyone standing, led by the youngsters of SNCC, linking arms, and singing "We Shall Overcome."

The mood of these young people, which they convey to everyone around them in the midst of poverty, violence, terror, and centuries of bitter memories, is joy, confidence, the vision of victory: "We'll walk hand in hand . . . we are not afraid. . . ." Occasionally there is sadness, as in "I Been 'Buked and I Been Scorned." But most often there is an exuberant defiance: "Ain't Gonna Let Chief Pritchett Turn Me Round. . . ." They are happy warriors, a refreshing contrast to the revolutionaries of old. They smile and wave while being taken off in paddy wagons; they laugh and sing behind bars.

Yet they are the most serious social force in the nation today. They are not playing; it is no casual act of defiance, no irresponsible whim of adolescence, when young people of sixteen or twenty or twenty-five turn away from school, job, family, all the tokens of success in modern America, to take up new lives, hungry and hunted, in the hinterland of the Deep South. Jim Forman was a teacher in Chicago before he joined the SNCC, and an aspiring novelist; Bob Moses was a graduate of Harvard, teaching in New York; Charles Sherrod was a divinity school graduate in Virginia; Mendy Samstein, a graduate of Brandeis University, was on the faculty of a Negro college, working for his Ph.D. in history at the University of Chicago. Others found it easier—and harder—for they came right out of the Black Belt and, even though they tasted college, they had nowhere to go but back towards danger and freedom: John Lewis, Sam Block, Willie Peacock, Lafayette Surney, MacArthur Cotton, Lawrence Guyot and too many more to name.

In his study *Young Man Luther,* the psychologist Erik Erikson ponders the "identity crisis" which young people face. "It occurs in that period of the life cycle when each youth must forge for himself some central perspective and direction, some working unity, out of the effective remnants of his childhood and the hopes of his anticipated adulthood; he must detect some meaningful resemblance between what he has come to see in himself and what his sharpened awareness tells him others judge and expect him to be." It would be hard to imagine a more startling contrast than that between the young Negro as the old South saw him (or rather half-saw him, blurred and not quite human) and the vision of himself he suddenly perceived in the glare of the 1960's.

The entire nation, caught suddenly in the intersection of two images where it always thought there was only one, has begun slowly to refocus its own vision. So that what started as an identity crisis for Negroes turned out to be an identity crisis for the nation. And we are still resolving it. It is one of the conditions of effective psychotherapy that the patient must begin to see himself as he really is, and the United States, now forced by the young Negro to see itself through *his* eyes (an ironic reversal, for the Negro was always compelled to see himself through the eyes of the white man), is coming closer to a realistic appraisal of its national personality.

All young people, in their late teens or early twenties, face this "identity crisis" which Erik Erikson describes. As Erikson points out: "Some young individuals will succumb to this crisis in all manner of neurotic, psychotic, or delinquent behavior; others will resolve it through participation in ideological movements passionately concerned with religion or politics, nature or art." We have seen the delinquent responses, or simply the responses of non-commitment, on the part of millions of young people of this generation who have not been able to find their way. Young Negroes were among these, were perhaps even the most delinquent, the most crisis-ridden of all. But today, by the handful, or the hundreds, or perhaps the thousands, they are making their way through this crisis with a firm grip on themselves, aided immeasurably by the fact that they are anchored to a great social movement.

We ought to note, however, that this "participation in ideological movements" today has a different quality than that of earlier American student movements— the radical movements of the thirties, for instance. The young people in the

Student Nonviolent Coordinating Committee have not become followers of any dogma, have not pledged themselves to any rigid ideological system. Unswerving as they are in moving towards certain basic goals, they wheel freely in their thinking about society and how it needs to be changed. Erikson writes of a very few young people who, making their way through their identity crisis, "eventually come to contribute an original bit to an emerging style of life; the very danger which they have sensed has forced them to mobilize capacities to see and say, to dream and plan, to design and construct, in new ways." And this is true of those in the SNCC. They are radical, but not dogmatic; thoughtful, but not ideological. Their thinking is undisciplined; it is fresh, and it is new.

One must listen to Jane Stembridge speaking, a white girl from Virginia, part of that little band of black and white students who organized SNCC out of the turmoil of the 1960 sit-ins:

> . . . finally it all boils down to human relationships. It has nothing to do finally with governments. It is the question of whether we . . . whether *I* shall go on living in isolation or whether there shall be a we. The student movement is not a cause . . . it is a collision between this one person and that one person. It is a *I am going to sit beside you* . . . Love alone is radical. Political statements are not; programs are not; even going to jail is not. . . .

These new abolitionists are different from the earlier ones. The movement of the 1830's and 1840's was led by white New Englanders, bombarding the South and the nation with words. The present movement is planted firmly in the deepest furrows of the Deep South, and it consists mostly of Negroes who make their pleas to the nation more by physical acts of sacrifice than by verbal declamation. Their task is made easier by modern mass communication, for the nation, indeed the whole world, can *see* them, on the television screen or in newspaper photos—marching, praying, singing, *demonstrating* their message. The white people of America, to whom Negroes were always a dark, amorphous mass, are forced to see them for the first time sharply etched as individuals, their features—both physical and moral—stark, clear, and troubling.

But in one important way these young people are very much like the abolitionists of old: they have a healthy disrespect for respectability; they are not ashamed of being agitators and trouble-makers; they see it as the essence of democracy. In defense of William Lloyd Garrison, against the accusation that he was too harsh, a friend replied that the nation was in a sleep so deep "nothing but a rude and almost ruffian-like shake could rouse her." The same deliberate harshness lies behind the activities of James Forman, John Lewis, Bob Moses, and other leaders of SNCC. What Samuel May once said of Garrison and slavery might be said today of each of these people and segregation: "He will shake our nation to its center, but he will shake slavery out of it."

When SNCC leader Gloria Richardson in Cambridge, Maryland, refused, under a rain of criticism, to subject the issue of segregation to popular vote, one was reminded of the words of Wendell Phillips, explaining the apparent strange behavior of the abolitionists: "The reformer is careless of numbers, disregards popularity, and deals only with ideas, conscience, and common sense. . . . He neither expects, nor is overanxious for immediate success." Phillips contrasted the reformer with the politician, who "dwells in an everlasting now. . . ." In a similar mood, poet James Russell Lowell wrote: "The Reformer must expect comparative isolation, and he must be strong enough to bear it."

Yet the staff member of the Student Nonviolent Coordinating Committee can never be isolated as was the New England abolitionist of the 1830's, who was far from slave territory, and surrounded by whites unconcerned for the slave. The SNCC youngster is in the midst of his people, surrounded by them, protected by them. To be cut off, by harsh criticism of his "extremism," from Northern white intellectuals or from those in national political power is a minor blow, cushioned by a popularity based on the poor and the powerless, but perhaps even more comforting because of that.

Oddly enough—or perhaps naturally enough—the student movement has left the campuses where it began in those sit-ins of early 1960. The sit-in leaders have either graduated from or left college, and the fact that they call themselves the *Student* Nonviolent Coordinating Committee is primarily a reflection of their backgrounds, their youth, and perhaps their hope to return one day and bring a new dynamism to college education. Some go back to college after a year or two with the movement; others find a less formal but more genuine intellectual satisfaction in the movement. All live in a state of tension: there is the recognition that academic life is too far removed from the social struggle, alongside the frustration that exists for any intellectually aroused youngster separated from books and concentrated learning. At the same time, having exchanged college attire and the tree-lined campus for overalls and the dusty back roads of the rural South, they are getting the kind of education that no one else in the nation is getting.

There is another striking contrast to Garrison and Phillips, Lewis Tappan and Theodore Weld: these young people are not middle-class reformers who became somehow concerned about others. They come themselves from the ranks of victims, not just because they are mostly Negroes, but because for the most part their fathers are janitors and laborers, their mothers maids and factory workers.

In late 1963 I checked the backgrounds of forty-one field workers for SNCC in Mississippi (roughly one-third of the total SNCC force in the Deep South). Thirty-five of them were Negro, and twenty-five of them came from the Deep South. Of the six white staff members two were from the Deep South. The white youngsters and most of the Northern Negroes came from middle-class homes; their fathers were ministers or teachers or civil service workers. All of the Southern Negroes, and some of the Northern Negroes (twenty-one out of thirty-five) came from homes where the mothers were maids or domestics, the fathers factory workers, truck drivers, farmers, bricklayers, carpenters. Twenty-nine (about three-fourths) of the total SNCC Mississippi staff were between fifteen and twenty-two years old. There were twelve between twenty-two and twenty-nine, and one person each in his thirties, forties, and fifties. Twenty-six, or about two-thirds, of the Mississippi SNCC staff were either college graduates or had some college education. Ten had finished high school or had some high school education and two had no more than part of an elementary school education. If one were to generalize roughly about the SNCC staff in the Deep South, one would say they are young, they are Negro, they come from the South, their families are poor and of the working class, but they have been to college. Northern middle-class whites and Negroes are a minority.

As of mid-1964, about 150 people worked full-time for SNCC, roughly 80 percent of them Negro. Of the whites, most were Northerners, but the few white Southerners played important roles (Jane Stembridge, the first office secretary in Atlanta; Bob Zellner and Sam Shirah, assigned to white college campuses; Sandra Hayden, in the Jackson, Mississippi office). Of the Negro staff people, most were Southern born; more and more, young Negroes were being recruited out of Deep South towns to become SNCC field secretaries right there at home.

By 1963, the annual budget of SNCC was about $250,000, almost all of this coming from the contributions of individuals and organizations (churches, colleges, foundations). About one-fourth of this income was being used to pay the salaries of field secretaries, $10 a week for most of them, with a few married people in the Atlanta office receiving $50 or $60 a week. Most of the remaining income went to pay for field operations in Mississippi, southwest Georgia, and the other areas of concentration.

The two chief officers of SNCC are the Chairman (John Lewis) and the Executive Secretary (James Forman). One of the field secretaries in each major geographical area is known as a Project Director. An Executive Committee of twenty-one members, including two older "advisors," is the top policy-making body, and is elected at an annual conference in the spring.

Where do the 150 or so SNCC workers operate? Perhaps a dozen man the central office in Atlanta, a buzzing jumble of rooms above a tailor shop in the Negro section of Atlanta, not far from the Negro college campuses. Long-distance phone connections keep Jim Forman and John Lewis, the two top officers of SNCC, in day-to-day, sometimes hour-to-hour touch with crisis situations in those parts of the Deep South where SNCC maintains headquarters and "field secretaries" (as its staff members are called).

One of the two main areas of concentration is Mississippi, where SNCC's first penetration of the Deep South was made by Bob Moses and a few Negro youngsters from the Delta. A half-dozen spots in Mississippi have had varying degrees of attention: Greenwood, Hattiesburg, Jackson, Liberty, Greenville, Clarksdale. The other major focus of activity is southwest Georgia, where Charles Sherrod, a divinity school student from Virginia, came in the fall of 1961 and stayed to become a legend. Albany has been the center there, and, radiating from it, SNCC workers have moved into the terror-ridden towns of the old Cotton Kingdom: Americus, Dawson, Camilla, Sasser. Outside of Mississippi and Southwest Georgia, SNCC groups function in Selma, Alabama; Danville, Virginia; Cambridge, Maryland; Pine Bluff, Arkansas; and other places; they register voters, distribute food and clothing, lead demonstrations, conduct classes, vitalize long-dormant communities.

To visit SNCC field headquarters in these rural outposts of the Deep South is like visiting a combat station in wartime. Living conditions are crude. Sometimes there is a "Freedom House," an old frame dwelling with cots and blankets for the field secretaries and whoever else is staying over for the night. At other times, field people stay in homes in the Negro community. It may take weeks or months to dispel the initial fear on the part of local Negroes now aware of impending change and trouble. Negro women in town often become mothers to the SNCC youngsters far from home and family; they put them up, make meals for them, tend them when they are sick, go out on the line with them in demonstrations.

One thinks of Mrs. Boynton in Selma, Mrs. Woods in Hattiesburg, and Mrs. Daniels in Dawson. (Sheriff Jim Clark in Selma, hoping to arrest SNCC leader Prathia Hall, went straight to the home of Mrs. Boynton to find her.)

Over every one of these headquarters in the field, whether a "Freedom House" rented by SNCC, or a home or office donated by a local supporter, there hangs the constant threat of violence. The first SNCC headquarters in Selma was burned down; in Greenwood, two SNCC workers found themselves under siege by a mob or armed men and had to make their way over rooftops to safety; in Danville, police simply marched into the SNCC office and arrested everyone in sight.

"These are beautiful people down here," Sandra Hayden wrote to me from Mississippi shortly after she arrived there to work for SNCC. She was speaking about the Negroes of the Delta, aroused to take their first steps out of the past—but she was not speaking of color or that ordered set of physical characteristics which American society has characterized as "beauty." She was speaking of the souls of black folk—and of white folk too. She was speaking of a beauty of spirit, of a courage beyond comprehension, which pervades the ranks of the new abolitionists in the Deep South. It is expressed in Sandra Hayden herself tall, blonde, slender, a Texas girl who moved from the University of Texas into the student movement; it is expressed in the rugged, black, smiling face of Chuck McDew, peering through the bars of Baton Rouge jail; or the tawny, delicate features of Peggy Day in Terrell County; or the agonized, shining eyes of Mrs. Fannie Hamer, a middle-aged woman thrown off her land in Ruleville, Mississippi, who has gone to work for SNCC.

Those who join the SNCC staff agree to work for subsistence wages; this usually means $10.00 a week ($9.64 after deductions), and often weeks going by with no checks coming from Atlanta. It may mean knocking on doors for food, scrounging around for a pair of shoes, riding a mule along a country road because the car donated by some sympathizer has broken down. A typical SNCC automobile has always just run out of gas, and the driver has no money left to buy more. "You know it's like they're in another world," a college girl said after visiting SNCC headquarters in Greenwood, Mississippi.

These are young radicals; the word "revolution" occurs again and again in their speech. Yet they have no party, no ideology, no creed. They have no clear idea of a blueprint for a future society. But they do know clearly that the values of present American society—and this goes beyond racism to class distinction, to commercialism, to profit-seeking, to the setting of religious or national barriers against human contact—are not for them.

They are prepared to use revolutionary means against the old order. They believe in civil disobedience. They are reluctant to rely completely on the niceties of negotiation and conciliation, distrustful of those who hold political and economic power. They have a tremendous respect for the potency of the demonstration, an eagerness to move out of the political maze of normal parliamentary procedure and to confront policy-makers directly with a power beyond orthodox politics—the power of people in the streets and on the picket line.

They are nonviolent in that they suffer beatings with folded arms and will not strike back. There have been one or two rare exceptions of discipline being broken, yet this must be laid against hundreds of instances of astounding self-control in the face of unspeakable brutality.

Next to the phrase "nonviolence," however, what you hear most often among SNCC workers is "direct action." They believe, without inflicting violence, and while opening themselves to attack, in confronting a community boldly with the sounds and sights of protest. When it is argued that this will inevitably bring trouble, even violence, the answer is likely to be that given by James Bevel, who in his activity with the Southern Christian Leadership Conference works closely with SNCC in Alabama and Mississippi: "Maybe the Devil has got to come out of these people before we will have peace. . . ."

They have no closed vision of the ideal community. They are fed up with what has been; they are open to anything new and are willing to start from scratch. Erik Erikson talks about young rebels with a "rock-bottom" attitude, who "want to be reborn in identity and to have another chance at becoming once-born, but this time on their own terms." Nineteen-year-old SNCC veteran Cordell Reagan, brown-skinned, slender, explains himself this way:

It's not hard to interpret what our parents mean by a better world. You know, go to school, son, and get a good education. And what do you do with this? You get a degree, you move out into some little community housing project, you get married, five kids and two cars, and you don't care what's happening. . . . So I think when we talk about growing up in a better world, a new world, we mean changing the world to a different place.

Is it any wonder that Cordell Reagan and so many other SNCC workers have been put in jail again and again by Deep-South sheriffs for "contributing to the delinquency of minors"?

A young white student, explaining why he wanted to join SNCC, wrote about his new-found view of life:

I have never felt so intense, alive, such a sense of well-being, which is not to be confused with the illusion of "happiness" equated to "having fun." I have chosen to be outside of society after having been very much inside. I intend to fight that society which lied to and smothered me for so long, and continues to do so to vast numbers of people. . . . My plans are unstructured in regards to anything but the immediate future. I believe in freedom, and must take the jump; I must take the chance of action.

The nation has suddenly become aware that the initiative today is in the hands of these 150 young people who have moved into the Deep South to transform it. Everyone waits on their next action: the local police, the state officials, the national government, the mass media of the country, Negroes and whites sitting at their radios and television sets across the land. Meanwhile, these people are living, hour by hour, the very ideals which this country has often thought about, but not yet managed to practice: they are courageous, though afraid; they live and work together in a brotherhood of black and white, Southerner and Northerner, Jew and Christian and agnostic, the likes of which this country has not yet seen. They are creating new definitions of success of happiness, of democracy.

It is just possible that the momentum created by their enormous energy—now directed against racial separation—may surge, before it can be contained, against other barriers which keep people apart in the world: poverty, and nationalism, and all tyranny over the minds and bodies of men. If so, the United States may

truly be on the verge of a revolution—nonviolent, but sweeping in its consequences—and led by those who, perhaps, are most dependable in a revolution:
the young.

The Movement's Themes; The Movement's Origins PAUL JACOBS AND SAUL LANDAU

"The Movement" is the label that the New Left applies to that complicated
collection of leaders, organizations, and programs, that are directed toward changing
American society in fundamental ways. It is not a movement easily categorized
politically, nor is it defined by politics alone. Some Movement people are Socialists,
others are anarchists. Some believe in nonviolence, others are willing to use
guns and bombs to attack the oppressors and exploiters. Some are committed
only to black liberation, some largely to women's liberation, and others are
dedicated to world revolution. Some focus on altering men's lifestyles, others
are concerned primarily with issues of power and wealth.

Almost invariably, whatever their approach or particular ideological emphasis,
the Movement people are young. Most are in their twenties and thirties and are
concentrated in our colleges and universities. This is an obvious reason for the
widespread campus ferment, though the question of the central role of universities
in our modern technological society is another. In the selection below, Paul Jacobs
and Saul Landau attempt to summarize both the "themes" and the origins of the
enormously important new wave of dissent in American life. Their statement
was composed in 1966. In the years since then, much has happened to the
Movement. It has become both larger and more militant. Nevertheless, their
description constitutes a good introduction to the first years of the group whose
scholarly endeavors form the theme of this anthology.

FOR FURTHER READING:

Lewis Feuer, *Conflict of Generations*, (Basic Books, 1969); Kenneth Keniston, *Young Radicals: Notes on Committed Youth**, (Harcourt, Brace and World, 1968); Howard Zinn, "Marxism and the New Left," in Alfred F. Young (editor) *Dissent: Explorations in the History of American Radicalism*, (Northern Illinois University Press, 1968); Andre Schiffrin, "The Student Movement in the 1950's: A Reminiscence," *Radical America*, (May–June, 1968); James Kunen, *The Strawberry Statement: Notes of a College Revolutionary**, (Avon, 1970); Jack Newfield, *A Prophetic Minority**, (Signet, 1966).

Asterisk denotes paperback edition.

The Movement is a mélange of people, mostly young; organizations, mostly
new; and ideals, mostly American. In 1960 and 1961 the Freedom Riders and
Negro college students who sat-in in the South were acting in the spirit of The
Movement. Most of those who protested against President Kennedy's Cuban

Source: Paul Jacobs and Saul Landau, *The New Radicals: A Report with Documents* (New York: Vintage Books, 1966), chaps. i and ii, "The Movement's Themes," and "The Movement's Origins," pp. 3–14.

policy in 1962 were responding to the impulse of The Movement. That same impulse took them south for the Student Nonviolent Coordinating Committee (SNCC) in 1963, got them arrested in Sproul Hall at the University of California in 1964, and marched them to Washington in 1965 to demonstrate their opposition to the war. Movement youth can be found today in the San Joaquin Valley of California, helping striking farm workers; some will become organizers in the slum communities of Northern cities; others will try to change the university system in America.

These young people believe that they must make something happen, that they are part of a movement stirring just below the surface of life hitherto accepted all over the world. So they identify with the Zengakuren students whose snake-dance demonstrations prevented President Eisenhower from visiting Japan, and wince at the photos of the young rebel shot by a policeman in Santo Domingo. They empathize with the young Soviet poets who read their poetry at the statue of Mayakovsky in Moscow until the police break up the meeting.

How many people are in the American Movement? Certainly, it is possible to count those who are members of the organizations within The Movement, but that would be to misunderstand one of the basic facts of its nature: The Movement is organizations plus unaffiliated supporters, who outnumber by the thousands, and perhaps even hundreds of thousands, those committed to specific groups. The Movement's basic strength rests on those unaffiliated reserves, who are just as much a part of it as the organization youth.

The leitmotifs that dominate The Movement extend far beyond politics. The Movement is much more than anti-Vietnam marches, civil rights demonstrations, and student sit-ins. To be in The Movement is to search for a psychic community, in which one's own identity can be defined, social and personal relationships based on love can be established and can grow, unfettered by the cramping pressures of the careers and life styles so characteristic of America today.

The Movement rejects the careers and life styles of the American liberal, too, for to The Movement it is the liberal way of life and frame of mind that represent the evil of America. Those in The Movement feel that modern American liberals have substituted empty rhetoric for significant content, obscured the principles of justice by administrative bureaucracy, sacrificed human values for efficiency, and hypocritically justified a brutal attempt to establish American hegemony over the world with sterile anti-Communism. The Movement sees the liberals righteously proclaiming faith in American democracy from their comfortable suburban homes or offices, while the United States Air Force drops napalm on villages and poisons the rice paddies.

So, those in The Movement see not only the openly authoritarian or totalitarian society as an enemy but the administered, bureaucratic, dehumanized, rhetorical-liberal one as well. They reject liberal authority. They were stirred, momentarily, by President Kennedy's call for a commitment of freedom, but were so disappointed by his actions in Cuba and Vietnam that they turned on him with bitterness. And the Johnson Administration's foreign policy reinforces their view that America flouts, in action, the traditions of freedom and justifies the use of military instruments associated with the Nazis.

The new movement is also a revolt against the postwar "overdeveloped society," with its large bureaucracies in government, corporations, trade unions, and universities. To those in The Movement the new technologies of automation and cybernation, with their computers and memory-bank machines, are instruments of alienation, depersonalizing human relations to a frightening degree. The brain machines and the translation of human qualities into holes punched into a card are viewed as devices that break down communication and destroy community in the interests of efficiency. Technology's emphasis on routine efficiency has created a set of values, rationalized by its supporters as representing "the facts of modern life." But The Movement sees these values as false, imposed on the whole society without "the consent of the governed." Even worse, the decision-making over which the governed no longer have control extends far beyond politics: in the technological order every aspect of the people's lives is under the control of administrators far removed from responsibility to the governed. And the elders of those in The Movement have exchanged their decision-making right for the comforts of American affluence. All that remains is nineteenth-century rhetoric about democracy and freedom, and technology has drained the words of their content.

In their personal life style, their aesthetic sense, many in The Movement reject affluence and its associated symbols. The ambition to escape from poverty is no spur to action in their lives, for many are children of America's post-Depression *nouveau* middle class. Their parents are the once-poor scholars who head rich academic institutes; the ex-union organizers who run their own large businesses; the former slum dwellers who develop segregated real-estate tracts; the families once on the WPA who live in suburbia—all those who have made it. But their parents' desire to own, to accumulate, to achieve the status and prestige which go with material wealth, are meaningless goals to the children. To them television is not a wonder but a commonplace, and they see the $5,000 a year their parents spend on the analyst as too high a price to pay for the loss of human values.

The marvels of the space age are commonplace to them, too, and the voices to which they listen are not those of the orbiting astronauts exchanging banalities. They respond instead to the sense and sound of friendship and community, to the exultation they feel when thousands of people link hands and sing "We Shall Overcome." And to achieve that feeling of community, of life, they have been willing to sacrifice most middle-class comforts.

They are willing to do this, for until they enter The Movement their inability to affect the quality of their own lives disturbs them profoundly. Those of the upper middle class were trapped, protected to the point of coddling through their childhood and early teens, sated with *nouveau* affluence by the time they were twenty. They knew they could achieve a place in the society of their parents, but it was not a society in which they wanted a place; it offered little beyond physical comfort. They believed the ideals they were taught, and felt miserable when the ideals were exposed as empty words. Their awareness that Negroes and millions of poor have been left out of the society moved them to act rather than depend on the persuasion techniques advocated by their elders.

Many of them were born in the year of The Bomb, and so their history begins with the history of nuclear destruction. The twenties and even the thirties are almost prehistory to them, and the burning issues which agitated the older generation's radicals and liberals are devoid of meaning. Some know of the mid-fifties' McCarthyism and the House Un-American Activities Committee (HUAC), but the internecine wars of the thirties have little personal significance for them.

In some measure, too, the modes of extreme personal behavior adopted by this group—their permissive view of marijuana or hallucinogenics like LSD, their matter-of-fact acceptance of sexual freedom and their habitual profanity—are part of their search for identity. That search assumes a rejection of everything connected with their old identity and of the technological, bureaucratic values they see as dominant in American life. It is also possible that their difficulties in finding personal meaning in the routine politics of the civil rights struggle and their anguish in seeing the country carry out a foreign policy they believe to be totally bad force these young people into seeking meaning in experiences. They think the ivory-towered men of ideas have cheated them, lied to them, and that action and spontaneous experience will show them truth.

Above all, those in The Movement now restlessly seek to find a new politics and a new ideology that will permit them to link existential humanism with morally acceptable modes of achieving radical social change.

The Movement's origins are elusive and have many strands. In the 1930s and 1940s the radical movement encompassed a broad spectrum of organizations and political beliefs: the Communists and their front groups; the socialists, Trotskyists, and other anti-Stalinist organizations; sections of the CIO and a few other unions. The Communist groups, drawing worldwide support, dominated American radicalism, since their size and prestige were greater than any of the other political tendencies. And although the American Communist Party was shaken in 1939 by the Stalin-Hitler nonaggression pact, the Nazi attack on the Soviet Union returned them to political acceptability.

But by the mid-fifties the old movement was nearly dead. The Communist Party had declined badly in the postwar period, because of government persecution and its own internal weaknesses. The trade unions were no longer crusading, many once radical anti-Communists had become supporters of the Establishment, and the socialists were barely distinguishable from the liberal Democrats.

Then, when today's young radicals were still in junior high school, the entire Communist world was shaken by the revelations about Stalin made at the 20th Party Congress. The Communist movement soon suffered further blows from the uprisings in Hungary and Poland. The Labor Youth League (LYL), the Communist Party youth group, was disbanded shortly after the shock of 1956, but it would have declined from internal stress anyway. At the very time the American Marxists were being disillusioned by the actions of Soviet socialism, England, France, and Israel joined in an invasion of Egypt. A few intellectuals, faced with Western imperialism and brutal Soviet Marxism, began seeking a fresh way out of the crisis, developing what C. Wright Mills described as The New Left.

It started in England, where in 1957 a group of university intellectuals published two new journals, *Universities and Left Review* and *The New Reasoner*. In 1959 they merged into the *New Left Review*. Many of the editors had been members of or had been close to the Communist Party at Oxford. For them the failure of Marxism was more a failure of the vulgar Communist Marxists than of the theory. In the new journals the ideals of socialism were rediscovered, and the kind of humanist analysis that had been forgotten through purges, war, and Cold War was revived. Often, too, *New Left Review* debated ideas that could not comfortably be talked about within the framework of Soviet Marxism: alienation and humanism.

New Left political clubs of college and working-class youth followed the magazine's formation, and through 1959 this small group lit a new spark under dormant

English radicalism—Aldermaston marches in support of peace and against nuclear testing grew larger each year, and the Labour Party swung to the New Left position on nuclear weapons, for one year.

By the end of the fifties concern for racial justice was developing among American students. A strong reaction to the indignities of fear and anxiety heaped on the country by McCarthy and a general rejection of the symbols of American affluence were growing. Some youth responded with the "beat" mood; others developed an interest in the new British intellectual radicalism; still others rejected the style of life practiced by J. D. Salinger's characters.

Simultaneously, a group in the American pacifist movement, strongly influenced by pacifist leader A. J. Muste, was developing a "third camp" position, which rejected both the American and Soviet Cold War positions, concentrating instead on attempting to create a third force to resist all militarism. Many "third camp" pacifists had been involved in the civil rights struggle, to which they had brought the non-violent techniques that they had been studying and practicing since the outbreak of World War II. And although their original interest and commitment had an informal religious base, they moved over easily to politics.

As McCarthyism waned in the late fifties a group of university intellectuals, much like the British New Left although less vigorous and certain, began to develop around the universities of Wisconsin, California at Berkeley, and Chicago. At Wisconsin the Socialist Club was formed by ex-LYLers and younger undergraduates who had never experienced Communist Party schooling; at Berkeley a similar group called SLATE formed a student political party; at Chicago a student political party founded in the early fifties was revived.

At Wisconsin the success of the Socialist Club and the inspiration of the British New Left were combined with the teaching of William Appleman Williams, the historian, who attempted to use Marxism creatively to understand American history. The result was the publication of *Studies on the Left*, "a journal of research, social theory and review." Several months later at the University of Chicago a group of graduate students began to publish *New University Thought*.

The difference between the magazines was essentially over the use of the word "left." At a meeting held in Madison, Wisconsin, in 1960 to discuss merging the two magazines, the Chicago group, most of whom had had some experience with Communist youth groups as had the Wisconsin editors', argued that the word "left" and certainly the word "socialism" was so discredited as to be useless. The *Studies* editors argued that since they were socialists and Marxists, they should say so. One of their regrets was that during the McCarthy period they had been forced to mask their true political beliefs.

The advent of *Studies* and *New University Thought* marked the transition from old left Marxist dogma to a new period, even though most of the editors were Marxists who retained some loyalty to the Soviet Union, at least as a force for peace and reason. But the editors were also deeply concerned with scholarship, and saw themselves not so much as professional Movement people but as a new breed of university professor.

Meanwhile new journals appeared at Columbia, at Harvard, at campuses all over the country, reflecting the increased activity among intellectual radicals. These publications and the discussions over their contents were not limited to politics but covered every aspect of life from sexual freedom and pornography to civil rights and peace issues. Another generation graduated from high school, and the colleges and universities became breeding grounds for campus political activity and the civil rights drive. Some of the young people in The Movement began to exhibit an inclination for activism and a spirit of anti-intellectualism, in part a rejection of the very university system in which they were involved. "The University" came to be regarded as part of the Establishment, and as the point of immediate contact, the most oppressive part.

Unlike their immediate predecessors, who had published magazines like *Studies* and *New University Thought,* this new group of youth activists knew little about the debates of the thirties. They learned about Stalinism, Trotskyism, and Social Democracy only in an academic context. Outside the classroom they referred with a sneer to the "old days"—the thirties, forties, and now the fifties. Like the rest of American society, the old left, they believed, had in some way "betrayed" them: they had "sold out" or else were "hung up" on old and dead battles. To most of these young people Marx, Lenin, and Trotsky had little relevance for what they understood to be America's problems. They simultaneously refused to identify with the Soviet Union or to be greatly concerned about injustice in any of the Communist societies. Their enemy was the American society and its Establishment.

Many of the young people in this activist generation were the children of parents who had been the radicals and left liberals of the thirties and the forties. At home they had heard the discussions about civil rights, and they knew of the political pall that hung over the country during the McCarthy era. They had learned a set of ideals from their parents and now, much to their parents' discomfiture, they were trying to put those ideals into practice.

And so by 1960 this new generation was throwing itself against American society, literally and figuratively. They found a new hero in Castro, the man of action, the man without an ideology, whose only interest seemed to be bettering the life of the Cuban people. They responded to the youthful Castro with enthusiasm and demanded "fair play" for the Cuban Revolution.

In May 1960 they were ready for an action of their own, and the opportunity was provided by the House Un-American Activities Committee. Hundreds of students from the campuses of the University of California at Berkeley and San Francisco State College, joined by some of the people who were moving away from the inactivity of the "beat" coffee houses, demonstrated physically against the Committee's San Francisco hearing. And after the demonstration, which received enormous publicity, they scorned the allegation that they had been led or inspired by the Communists. That charge, which they knew to be untrue, only reinforced their feelings of distrust for the celebrants of American society.

They identified, too, with the Freedom Riders who went South in 1960 and 1961; for this again meant taking direct action with their own bodies against segregation. They were not interested in theory, and so the long historical articles even in such left journals as *Studies* were not seen by them as being relevant.

This new activist Movement influenced even those who thought of themselves as being outside of society. As the apolitical "beats"—almost alone as symbols of protest in the fifties—turned their concern to concrete issues of racial equality and peace, their style, dress, and decor affected the activists. Arguments about politics began to include discussions of sexual freedom and marijuana. The language of the Negro poet-hipster permeated analyses of the Cuban Revolution. Protests over the execution of Caryl Chessman ultimately brought together students and some Bo-hemians—the loose and overlapping segments of what was to become known as The Movement.

President Kennedy gauged accurately the need of many youth to participate in programs for justice, and a few of the new activists were attracted to the Peace Corps. The Peace Corps stressed, at least in its appeal, a non-paternalistic, activist program in which people would be helped to help themselves, but most activists rejected the Peace Corps or any other government program. They felt American society supported racism, oppressive institutions, capital punishment, and wars against popular movements in underdeveloped countries. "Alienation" was used to describe the society's effects on its citizens, and American society was seen as the source of injustice and suffering everywhere. While opposed to injustice and sup-pression of liberty in general, the activists did not feel the same outrage against Castro or Mao or Khrushchev that they could against their own rulers. It was "our" fault. Brought up and nutured on the United Nations and liberal political values, hearing them articulated so well by President Kennedy and Adlai Stevenson, they demanded purity at home first, and when it was not forthcoming, quickly became convinced that it was impossible, that there was something rotten at the core of American society.

This dashing of hopes, the feeling that they had succumbed to what turned out to be only rhetoric on the part of Kennedy and Stevenson, was an important part of their turning so bitterly against the Establishment.

And while the older ones among them had been able to articulate their views in a speech or a pamphlet, some of the younger ones, those who came into The Move-ment later and rejected politics—a small but growing number of middle-class youth —made a virtue of their inability to articulate and analyze coherently. They talked "from the gut," stumblingly, haltingly, using the language of the new folksingers, deliberately adopting a style that was the antithesis of what they had heard from their professors.

In their revulsion against the liberal intellectuals who were celebrating America and the end of ideology, the young activists rejected all ideology and traditional party politics, turning instead to where the action was, to SNCC, formed in 1960 by Negroes and whites, Southern and Northern. SNCC wasn't political; it was con-cerned with right and wrong, with people. The SNCC ideal of morality in action also provided the spur for the Students for a Democratic Society (SDS) and its community and campus programs: the decision to act was reinforced by the role of the liberal intellectuals in the 1961 Bay of Pigs episode and the 1962 missile crisis.

What began perhaps as a rebellion against affluence and liberal hypocrisy grew in a few years into a radical activism that protested injustice at the very core of the so-ciety. But when even this was tolerated by the structures that were under attack, some of the young radicals began to think about something beyond rebellion or radi-cal protest. The Movement now is struggling to develop an ideology that will guide them toward building an organization that can compete for political power.

9. Black Nationalism in America

Black Nationalism   ROBERT L. ALLEN

Almost any oppressed minority tends to become ambivalent toward the society that oppresses it. On the one hand, it is apt to take its cues from that society and in some way accept its values. This may lead to strenuous efforts to conform to these patterns in the hope of being allowed to merge as equals with the larger group. When the rewards of conforming are not forthcoming, as has so often been true for black Americans, this may in turn lead to severe frustration and self-contempt. The minority may also totally reject the majority's values and turn inward to develop its own "counterculture." Less common at the outset, particularly for a group like the transplanted Africans deprived of much of their heritage, this response is apt to grow with increasing self-awareness and with increasing frustration. Unable to enter the larger culture as a full equal, or unable to do so at the speed he desires, the outsider will often make a virtue of necessity and devote his talents and energies to creating a successful group life and culture of his own.

Black nationalism is one manifestation of heightened group consciousness among blacks. It represents a turning away from the ideal of the total assimilation of blacks into American life, cherished by many white liberals. In recent years black separatism has taken the form of embracing the African cultural and historical past and rejecting the values of modern white America. It has also meant serious efforts to establish totally black enclaves. These would not be mere ghettoes, however, but prosperous, viable, autonomous communities in which all aspects of social, economic, and political life would be controlled by their black inhabitants. In its most extreme version, this approach has led to the demand for a whole section of this country to be set aside for a black nation.

In whatever form, black nationalism is problematical to men of the Socialist left. The Socialist ideal has always been internationalist and universalist. In the United States, the Socialists have generally advocated total integration, though in the 1930s, the Communists briefly supported a southern black nation. In the selection that follows, a black Socialist examines the periodic waves of black nationalist sentiment that have erupted in our past and indicates their inadequacy as a solution to the plight of the black masses in the United States.

Source: Robert L. Allen, *Black Awakening in Capitalist America: An Analytic History* (Garden City, N.Y.: Doubleday and Company, 1969), chap. iii, "Black Nationalism," pp. 75–97.

FOR FURTHER READING:

Stokely S. Carmichael and Charles V. Hamilton, *Black Power: The Politics of Liberation in America**, (Vintage Books, 1968); C. Eric Lincoln, *Martin Luther King, Jr.: A Profile**, (Hill and Wang, 1969); John H. Clarke, *Malcolm X: The Man and His Time**, (Macmillan, 1969); Stokely S. Carmichael, "What We Want," *New York Review of Books,* (September 22, 1966); Andrew Kopkind, "The Future of Black Power," *New Republic,* (January 7, 1967); Vincent Harding, "Black Radicalism: The Road from Montgomery," in Alfred F. Young (editor) *Dissent: Explorations in the History of American Radicalism,* (Northern Illinois University Press, 1968).

Asterisk denotes paperback edition.

Black power as a variant form of black nationalism has roots that reach deep into the history and social fabric of black America. Like an unsatisfied need or a nagging conscience, black nationalism is an insistent motif that wends its way through black history, particularly of the last 150 years. One writer has called nationalism the rejected strain, implying that assimilationism—the desire to be fully incorporated into the surrounding white society—is the dominant, and the only significant, sentiment among black people.

A glance at history suggests that it would be more correct to say that nationalism, and overt separatism, are ever-present undercurrents in the collective black psyche which constantly interact with the assimilationist tendency and, in times of crisis, rise to the surface to become major themes.

Both nationalism and assimilation spring from black people's wish to be an integral part of a jargon society. This, after all, is what is meant by saying that man is a social animal. Nationalism, however, is rooted in the Afro-American's experience of being forcibly excluded from and rejected by a society which is usually overtly, and always covertly, racist and exploitative. In periods of social crisis—that is, when repression and terror are rampant or hopes of progress have been dashed—the resulting suspicion that equal participation is impossible becomes a certainty. Nationalist leaders and intellectuals come to the fore and assert that not only is racial integration not possible, it is not even *desirable*. Such an eventuality, they contend, would destroy the group's distinctive culture and its sense of ethnic identity.

Thus in the decade prior to the Civil War, a period of increasing despair for blacks, emigration movements were in vogue. The Fugitive Slave Act was passed by Congress as part of the Compromise of 1850, and thousands of fugitive slaves were forced to flee to Canada if they were to secure their freedom. In 1854 the Kansas-Nebraska Act opened northern territory to slavery and, in the infamous Dred Scott decision of 1857, the U. S. Supreme Court sanctioned the notion that black people were not citizens. These were indeed grim years for the nearly 4½ million blacks then living in this country.

Many free blacks, such as Frederick Douglass, became active in the abolitionist movement, but others sought some other way out of an increasingly oppressive situation. Martin R. Delaney was one of the latter. In 1852 Delaney advocated that black people emigrate to the east coast of Africa to set up a nation of their own. "We are a nation within a nation," he argued, sounding a now familiar note, "as the Poles in Russia, the Hungarians in Austria; the Welsh, Irish, and Scotch in the British dominion." [1] Delaney called for a convention of the best black intellects—"a true representation of the intelligence and wisdom of the colored freemen"—to lay plans for his colonial expedition. A convention to thrash out the question of emigration was actually held in 1854. Three proposals were presented to this convention. In addition to Delaney's, there were proposals that blacks emigrate to Central America or to Haiti. Envoys were dispatched to these proposed areas of colonization to investigate conditions and sound out local governments.

The emigrationists were not without their critics. Many free blacks opposed the idea of emigration. Douglass, for example, expressed the fear that the emigration effort would encourage the best educated of the race to depart the country, leaving behind those least qualified to press forward with the emancipation struggle. But this was not the only reason that blacks were critical of colonization schemes.

One of the earliest colonization attempts was undertaken in 1815 by Paul Cuffee, a relatively wealthy New England black sailor. Cuffee arranged for a small group of black colorists to travel to Africa. This action is believed to have inspired the formation of the white-controlled American Colonization Society in 1816. By and large, however, blacks were hostile to the Society's colonization plans. Their opposition stemmed not so much from any lack of desire to separate from whites but rather because they strenuously objected to the racist reasoning whites used in justifying emigration. The Society, which counted a number of slaveholders among its founders, had as its express purpose the removal of free blacks to Africa on the grounds that they were a "dangerous and useless part of the community." [2] This slur incensed most free blacks and turned them irreversibly against any thought of colonizing Africa. Only a few wanted so desperately to escape the torture that was America that they would solicit aid even from racists. Abraham Camp, a free black from Illinois, wrote a letter in 1818 to the Society accepting its offer of aid in traveling to Africa, "or some other place." "We love this country and its liberties, if we could share an equal right in them," Camp wrote, "but our freedom is partial, and we have no hope that it will ever be otherwise here; therefore we had rather be gone. . . ." [3]

The Civil War and its aftermath put an end to talk of emigration. The Emancipation Proclamation formally ended slavery, and black people were officially granted citizenship. Hopes were high among blacks that equality and the good life were just over the horizon. Blacks sought in every conceivable way to participate fully in the nation's life, to become just ordinary Americans. It truly seemed that Douglass's faith, the faith that white America could change and accommodate itself to blacks, was justified.

Black men were elected to serve in every southern legislature. South Carolina could even boast of a black majority in its legislative chambers. Some twenty blacks served in the U. S. House of Representatives, and the state of Mississippi sent two black senators to Washington. These were the years of Reconstruction, and even the Ku Klux Klan and its campaign of terrorism seemed for the moment insufficient to stem the rising tide of black hope.

But what the Klan and southern terrorists alone could not bring about, a tacit alliance of southern reactionaries with northern business interests and an uneasy northern white populace could indeed accomplish. Historian Lerone Bennett, Jr., has noted that

> Throughout this period, Northern reporters and Northern opinion-makers were shrewdly and effectively cultivated by Southerners who dangled the bait of profit,

telling Northern industrialists that nothing stood between them and maximum exploitation of the rich resources of the South except "Negro governments."[4]

The northern industrialists, being businessmen, fell for the bait of promised profits and began clamoring for a "settlement" of the troubles which had developed in the South as a result of terrorist violence and the Depression of 1873. Meanwhile, nervous whites in the North, more concerned with maintaining domestic tranquillity than insuring justice for all, were nearly panicked into a stampede by the seemingly indecisive Hayes-Tilden presidential election of 1876 which brought with it the threat of a new civil war.

Hayes, a Republican, was bitterly opposed in the South, but it appeared that he had won a majority of the electoral votes. The southerners staged a filibuster, which disrupted the orderly counting of the electoral votes in the House of Representatives. An ominously threatening atmosphere developed as it became clear that inauguration day would come and pass without a President having been chosen. With pressure mounting from both industrialists and the general northern public, a "settlement" was reached in the form of the Hayes-Tilden compromise of 1877. Hayes promised the white Southerners "the right to control their own affairs in their own way." In return for an end to the filibuster, he also said he would withdraw the federal troops remaining in the South.

These federal troops had been practically the only thing standing between black people and their tormentors. True, there were some black militia units organized, but with the return of state power to the hands of white racists, these black men didn't stand much of a chance. The "settlement" was climaxed when the U. S. Supreme Court, in another infamous decision, declared the Civil Rights Act of 1875 unconstitutional. Southern states rewrote their constitutions to disenfranchise black people, and any blacks who still showed an interest in the ballot were terrorized and murdered by the Klan. Segregation replaced slavery as the accepted mode of black subjugation.

This was a bitter experience for blacks, who realized that as far as their supposed white friends were concerned, when self-interest conflicted with anti-slavery idealism, the latter proved dispensable.

Thousands of blacks were lynched in the South between 1880 and 1900. Hundreds of thousands of others soon began the great northward trek in a vain search for some nonexistent promised land. They were met by hatred and violence little different from what they had known in the South. There were anti-black riots in New York in 1900; in Springfield, Ohio, in 1904; in Greensburg, Indiana, in 1906, and another massive riot in Springfield in 1908.

It was this crisis which thrust forward both Booker T. Washington and W. E. B. DuBois as spokesmen. These men were ideological antagonists and, while neither is usually regarded today as being a black nationalist, the thinking of both exhibited curiously nationalist undertones. Washington is frequently described as an Uncle Tom accommodationist while DuBois is thought of as the father of the civil rights protest movement. Both leaders were trying to force a viable response to the imposition of segregation and growing anti-black violence.

Social critic Harold Cruse has argued that "Washington actually laid the basic economic foundation and motivation for Negro Nationalism in America even though he, himself, was no militant Nationalist."[5] The reason for this, according to Cruse, is that Washington was "the Negro bourgeois prophet par excellence" and black nationalism "is usually bourgeois in its origins in its earliest inceptions." Washington advocated the uplifting of the black masses through industrial education and economic self-help projects. He founded Tuskegee Institute as a school to train black workers in agricultural and industrial vocations, and among his economic enterprises was the African Union Company, which he organized to promote trade between American blacks and the Gold Coast of Africa. At the turn of the century, to provide an institutional base for his idea that in the building of a black capitalist class lay the way to racial economic advancement, Washington founded the Negro Business League. Washington was willing to forgo black participation in politics and to accept segregation as the price to be paid for white financial support of his educational and economic efforts. But he thought that this was only a temporary concession and honestly believed that the black man who succeeded in business would be "treated with the highest respect by the members of the white race."

Unconsciously, Washington was playing a part analogous to the classic role assumed by a national bourgeoisie in an underdeveloped, colonial country. He was trying to create a native (black) capitalist class and appealed to the latent nationalist sentiment of the native (black) masses in urging them to support this new class. At the Eleventh Annual Conference of the Negro Business League in 1910, Washington, in a keynote address, urged his hearers to leave "determined that each individual shall be a missionary in his community—a missionary in teaching the masses to get property, to be more thrifty, more economical, and resolve to establish an industrial enterprise wherever a possibility presents itself." [6] Washington believed that the masses would follow this course out of a sense of racial pride and solidarity (what would be called "black consciousness" today). Those who took his advice, however, probably did so for other reasons. Abram L. Harris, in his book *The Negro as Capitalist,* contends that, "Although ostensibly sponsored as the means of self-help or racial cooperation, as it was sometimes called, through which the masses were to be economically emancipated, Negro business enterprise was motivated primarily by the desire for private profit and looked toward the establishment of a Negro capitalist employer class." [7] Leaving aside the question of personal motivations, the projected social consequence of Washington's action was to create an economic class among Negroes which could compete with white capitalists for the Negro market. This is exactly the same task assumed by a young national bourgeoisie in a colonial country. Since neither the embryonic black capitalist class, nor its colonial counterpart, have sufficient economic strength in their early years to offset the power of entrenched white business interests, they must whip up nationalist feeling among the masses if their struggle is to be successful. Calls to "support your own kind" became weapons in a fierce battle for economic hegemony. It is in this sense that Washington is to be viewed as a spokesman for bourgeois nationalism. The difficulty with Washington's program was that he failed to see that American capitalism had by then left the stage of free competition and entered that of monopoly (in the industrial and corporate areas), with bank loans and credits, not a businessman's own small capital, determining his success. Blacks had no capital to speak of, and financiers, who after all are capable of recognizing a threat to their own interests, saw no reason to provide them any. As a result, black businesses down to the present day have been largely confined to small-scale marginal operations. There is no substantial black capitalist class, only a handful of black capitalists.

DuBois was an archcritic of Washington. He accused Washington of shifting the burden for black oppression from the nation as a whole to the shoulders of black people. He attacked Washington for counseling submission to oppression. DuBois helped organize the Niagara Movement in 1905 to counter the program of the Washingtonians. Following in the tradition of Frederick Douglass and basing themselves on the tenet that "Persistent manly agitation is the way to liberty," the black intellectuals who formed the Niagara Movement drafted a statement of principles calling for, among other things, male suffrage, full civil rights, economic opportunity, and education of black youths according to ability. These were the militants of the day, and they would brook no talk of the black man meekly accepting his assigned lowly place in the order of things. "We refuse to allow the impression to remain," they thundered, "that the Negro-American assents to inferiority, is submissive under oppression and apologetic before insults. Through helplessness we may submit, but the voice of protest of ten million Americans must never cease to assail the ears of their fellows, so long as America is unjust." [8] The order must be changed, protested the Niagara activists.

Unfortunately, the Niagara Movement seldom got beyond oratorical protest, and eventually it was absorbed into the newly formed National Association for the Advancement of Colored People. The NAACP, established in 1910, soon became the major-based organization demanding Negro admission into the mainstream of American life.

But there was another aspect to DuBois' character during this period: his cultural nationalism. DuBois expressed an almost mystical faith in the dignity and innate sense of justice found in the souls of black folk. He felt that a strong cultural and psychological bond existed between American blacks and Africans, and he suggested that the communalism of the African clan might readily be transferred to black America. DuBois gave verbal form to his faith in a "Credo" written in 1904:

> Especially do I believe in the Negro Race; in the beauty of its genius, the sweetness of its soul, and its strength in that meekness which shall inherit this turbulent earth.
> I believe in pride of race and lineage itself; in pride of self so deep as to scorn injustice to other selves; in pride of lineage so great as to despise no man's father; in pride of race so chivalrous as neither to offer bastardy to the weak nor beg wedlock of the strong. . . .[9]

DuBois' fight for the word "Negro" as against small-n "negro" or "colored," was as militant and significant for its day as the recent fight for the word "black," now that "Negro" has come to represent the mentality of an NAACP very much changed from the time when DuBois was its guiding figure.

Soon DuBois developed an interest in Pan-Africanism, and he organized Pan-African Congresses in 1911, 1918, 1923, 1927, and 1945.[10] Pan-Africanism was anti-colonial, anti-imperialist in conception and purpose, and no mere cultural movement. DuBois and the African George Padmore are the acknowledged fathers of African nationalism, and DuBois could hardly be that without having been, in some measure, himself a black nationalist.

DuBois' nationalism was so insistent that at times it completely overwhelmed his fervor for Marxism. For a short period, very early in his life, he had been influenced by Marxism, but in 1933 he wrote an article for *Crisis* magazine entitled "Marxism and the Negro Problem," in which he asserted that both the white capitalist and the white proletariat participate in the exploitation of black people. When it comes to racial oppression, DuBois the nationalist argued, whites are all the same. But within a very few years, the activity of some Marxists, specifically the Communist Party, for admission of blacks into unions, for food for the hungry in the Great Depression and against blatant expressions of racism as was seen in the Scottsboro case, began the process that closed with DuBois joining the Communist Party in the last decade of his life.

If the crisis theory being outlined here is correct in explaining outbursts of nationalist feeling, then the question arises why DuBois and Washington were not more overt black nationalists? In the case of DuBois, it was probably his early affinity for the Marxism of the Socialist party, with its color blindness, that held him back from becoming an outspoken black nationalist. Throughout his life DuBois seemed to be trying with limited success to reconcile nationalism with Marxism. As for Washington, his close ties with prominent white benefactors insured that he could not safely utter any militant statements and required that he couch his nationalism in very cautious terms. The thesis of Washington's 1895 Atlanta Exposition Address, for example, when stripped of its timorous formulations and apologies, can be boldly restated in terms which would satisfy even the most ardent nationalist. Without altering basic meaning, "Cast down your buckets where you are" can become "We must build an independent economy in the black community." Or, "In all things that are purely social we can be as separate as the fingers" could have been, "We have no desire for social intercourse with a cold and soulless race." [11]

An essential feature of black nationalism is that the nationalist makes a virtue of the fact of black separateness from the bulk of American society. The only difference in the formulations above is that one set of statements does so in a halfhearted manner and the other set asserts separateness as a positive good.

Incidentally, both Washington and DuBois are excellent examples of the ambivalence which afflicts middle-class black leaders. DuBois once wrote that "The Negro group has long been internally divided by dilemmas as to whether its striving upwards should be aimed at strengthening inner cultural and group bonds, both for intrinsic progress and for offensive power against caste; or whether it should seek escape wherever and however possible into the surrounding American culture." [12] The middle-class black leader, particularly in times of social stress, personifies this dilemma. This is because, as will be examined in later pages, the black middle class as a whole vacillates between the two approaches posited by DuBois.

Another major crisis for the Negro occurred at the time of World War I. When the war was declared, white leaders plied black people with promises of equality. President Woodrow Wilson assured blacks that "With thousands of your sons in the camps and in France, out of this conflict you must expect nothing less than the enjoyment of full citizenship rights—the same as are enjoyed by every other citizen." [13] More than 350,000 black men served in the U. S. Armed Forces, and most of these were sent to France. But the promises proved to be empty. The Klan was reorganized in Georgia in 1915 and spread rapidly across the country. Within ten years it had an estimated membership of four million. In July 1917 a white mob ran wild in East St. Louis, wrecking some three hundred homes of blacks and killing 125 black men, women, and children. In the first year after the war, seventy blacks were lynched. Many of these were black soldiers, some still wearing their uniforms.

Black soldiers who had fought bravely in France, many of them winning citations for heroism, were not even permitted to march in the Paris Victory Parade of 1919.

During the same period, from 1915 to 1919, the black exodus from the South reached flood proportions. Some 750,000 black refugees migrated to the North searching for jobs and seeking to escape the legal and illegal barriers to progress which had been thrown up in the southern states.

It was in this setting that black nationalism again found expression, this time in the person of Marcus Garvey. Garvey took Washington's economic program, clothed it in militant nationalist rhetoric, and built an organization which in its heyday enjoyed the active support of millions of black people. Garvey, a Jamaican by birth, "identified the problem of American Negroes with the problem of colonialism in Africa. He believed that until Africa was liberated, there was no hope for black people anywhere." [14] He founded his Universal Negro Improvement Association in 1914 in Jamaica with the motto: "One God! One Aim! One Destiny!" But it was not until Garvey established his group in New York's Harlem in 1917 that it began to assume notable proportions. Within two months the UNIA had fifteen hundred members.

The African student of American black nationalism, E. U. Essien-Udom, outlined Garvey's beliefs:

Garvey's ideology was both nationalist and radical. His nationalist objective was the redemption of Africa for "Africans abroad and at home." He advocated racial purity, racial integrity, and racial hegemony. He sought to organize Negroes in the United States into a vanguard for Africa's redemption from colonialism and hoped eventually to lead them back to Africa. The major instrument for the achievement of these objectives was economic cooperation through racial solidarity. He believed that if the Negroes were economically strong in the United States, they would be able to redeem Africa and establish a world wide confraternity of black people. Above all, he believed that the Negroes of the world, united together by the consciousness of race and nationality, could become a great and powerful people. [15]

Garvey believed that economic power through ownership of businesses could lay a solid foundation for eventual black salvation. He established the Black Star Steamship Company, the Negro Factory Corporation, and sent a commercial and industrial mission to Liberia. All of these undertakings turned out to be complete failures because of incompetence, mismanagement, and other difficulties. [16]

Garvey was a charismatic leader, and his movement had a certain theatrical quality and flamboyance which made it appealing to the black masses. Colorful parades, uniforms, and marching songs were distinctive traits of the UNIA. At an ostentatious convention in 1920, Garvey himself was named Provisional President of Africa and President-General and Administrator of the UNIA. A "provisional government" was formed, and Garvey conferred knighthood upon the members of his "High Executive Council."

In 1925, Garvey was convicted of using the mails to defraud. The sentence was commuted by President Calvin Coolidge in 1927, and Garvey was deported as an undesirable alien. He died in London in 1940. After Garvey was deported, his movement split into factions and degenerated. Thousands of hopeful blacks lost the precious savings which they had invested in the UNIA.

Black bourgeois nationalism was in decline from 1930 through 1945. The

Depression struck Negroes with disproportionate severity, but the New Deal, created partly in response to pressure from the left, eased the situation. Blacks were admitted to federal work projects and Civilian Conservation Corps camps.

It was during this period that the Communist Party succeeded in establishing itself for a time as the leading advocate of equal rights for black people. Politically, the Communists recognized the Negroes in the Black Belt to be a nation, and in the northern ghettos to be a national minority suffering special discrimination, unlike the older Socialist party, which regarded blacks simply as dark-skinned poor workers and farmers without special problems.[17] The Communists, however, did not press their program of self-determination of the Black Belt and instead concentrated on trade union work and antidiscrimination struggles. They organized the American Negro Labor Congress, while their interracial Trade Union Unity League fought "to wipe out discrimination against Negro workers in the industries and in the unions," and demanded "equal pay for equal work, especially for Negroes. . . ."[18] In 1930 the ANLC was succeeded by the League of Struggle for Negro Rights, with Langston Hughes as president. On May 8, 1933, it led a march of thirty-five hundred to Washington to present President Roosevelt the "Bill of Civil Rights for the Negro People" which it had drafted.

In the South, the Communist organized the Sharecroppers Union in 1931 which attained six thousand members by 1934 in Alabama, Florida, Georgia, and the Carolinas. It defended farmers against foreclosures even to the use of guns. Five were killed in such encounters.

In March 1930, the Communist Party claimed a total of about fifteen hundred black members, but by 1938 this figure had risen to ten thousand, or 14 percent of total Party membership.[19] Adam Clayton Powell praised the Communists, and said that "Today there is no group in America, including the Christian Churches, that practice racial brotherhood one-tenth as much as the Communist Party."[20]

The Unemployed Councils founded by the Communists were the largest and most militant interracial organizations this country has known. A nineteen-year-old black Communist organizer, Angelo Herndon, led an interracial march for welfare in Atlanta, Georgia, in 1932. Sentenced to eighteen to twenty years on the chain gang for "attempting to incite to insurrection," he was freed by an immense national campaign which brought into the Communist movement his lawyer, Benjamin Davis, who later became, as a Communist, the second black city councilman in New York (succeeding Adam Clayton Powell on the latter's election to Congress).

Davis was recruited by the remarkable William L. Patterson, son of a slave, who was more responsible for the successful defense of the Scottsboro boys, nine black youths accused in 1931 of raping two white women, than any other individual. Patterson's organization of mass-demonstration defenses in legal cases continued until 1951, when he led several hundred people to the South in an unsuccessful attempt to save the Martinsville seven, charged with rape, from execution. This was the last movement-size undertaking of the American Communist Party in its twenty years as the most influential radical force in the black community, but Patterson, now seventy-five years old and still a Communist, continues to be effective. His 1951 book-length petition to the United Nations, *We Charge Genocide,* is presently on the reading list of the Black Panther party. It was on his advice that the Panthers engaged a white attorney prepared to conduct a militant defense, Charles Garry, as lawyer for Huey P. Newton. It was also on his advice that the Panthers conducted the mass-demonstration "Free Huey" campaign in defense of Newton.

The creation in 1935 of the Congress of Industrial Organizations under militant Communist prodding had the consequence that black and white workers fought side by side for their mutual benefit in the rubber, auto, steel, and mining industries, as well as in the National Maritime Union and the West Coast International Longshoremen's and Warehousemen's Union. Black economic boycotts were organized. "Don't buy where you can't work!" the organizers shouted.

With the advent of World War II, black men once again came to the defense of the country. At first there was some hesitancy because of discrimination and segregation in the defense program. A. Philip Randolph threatened a massive black March on Washington in 1941 unless President Franklin D. Roosevelt brought a halt to discrimination in defense plants. Executive Order 8802, establishing the federal Fair Employment Practices Commission, did just that. It prohibited racial and religious discrimination in war industries, government training programs, and government industries. The planned march was called off.

Over a million black men served in the Armed Forces during the war. They served in all capacities. Black pilots were trained at an Army flying school in Tuskegee, Alabama, and in 1942, the *Booker T. Washington,* the first U.S. merchant ship to be commanded by a black captain, was launched. On the home front, black workers, taking advantage of the defense jobs which were now open to them, began to improve their economic status. The income gap between black and white families closed appreciably during the period of World War II and the Korean War. After this period the gap began to widen again, partly because pressure for hiring and upgrading of black workers fell off as the government successfully destroyed the Communist Party.

A. Philip Randolph, a master strategist, used the wartime period of international turmoil to advance the Negro cause. In 1948 he proclaimed to a Senate committee that he would advise black youths to refuse military induction unless segregation and discrimination were banned in the armed forces. Once more a President yielded to Randolph's threat, and Harry Truman directed that the armed forces provide "equal treatment and equal opportunity" to all personnel.

But executive orders were not sufficient to combat the virus of racism which afflicted white America. At the height of the war in 1943, a bloody race riot occurred in Detroit, Michigan, and thirty-four persons died. Earlier in the same year troops had to be called in when a riot broke out in Mobile, Alabama, following the upgrading of black workers at a shipyard. After the war there was a resurgence of Klan activity and southern terrorism. More ominously, automation was by then clearly the wave of the future, raising the specter of widespread technological unemployment.

Large numbers of blacks, by that time, were firmly lodged in northern cities and the activities of the Communists and later of men like Randolph had made them aware, if only vaguely, of the latent power which they possessed. Important gains had been made during the war, but these were now threatened by postwar developments. For ordinary black people, particularly those in the northern cities, the question was how best to safeguard their newly achieved economic and social status. Two forms of black leadership projected programs designed to answer this question.

The first was represented by the NAACP and the Congress of Racial Equality, which was organized in 1942. As early as 1945 NAACP lawyers had begun making plans for a massive legal assault on the edifice of segregation. CORE activists favored the nonviolent, direct action approach. In 1947, CORE in conjunction with the Fellowship of Reconciliation organized the first freedom ride, then called a "Journey of Reconciliation." Its purpose was to test the enforcement of a U. S. Supreme Court decision outlawing segregation on interstate buses. Although the NAACP and CORE differed in their tactics, they were in agreement on the ultimate objective: to fight for racial integration as the means for insuring black equality.

While these two organizations went about their work, increasing numbers of blacks were turning to another organization—the Nation of Islam, sometimes known as the Black Muslims. The Muslims had been around since the early 1930s, but their membership had never climbed much above 10,000 in prewar years. In fact, by 1945, their ranks had dwindled to about one thousand in four temples. After the war, however, there was a steady growth both in the number of members and in the number of Muslim temples scattered in cities across the country. The NAACP and integrationism were boosted to national prominence in 1954 when the U. S. Supreme Court handed down its famous public school desegregation decision. Some people thought the struggle was close to reaching a successful conclusion. But this decision had little effect on the steady growth of the Muslim organization. In 1955 there were fifteen temples. This number rose to thirty temples in twenty-eight cities by March of 1959. With the insight gained by the passage of time, it is now clear that the Muslim appeal was not diminished by the 1954 decision because their base was fundamentally different from that of the NAACP and CORE. Both CORE and the NAACP were middle-class organizations which directed their attention to attacking the legal forms of segregation which were prevalent in the South. The Muslims were strongest among working-class blacks who resided in the urban areas of the North. Court decisions and southern freedom rides had little or no effect on the concrete economic status of these blacks.

It was in the summer of 1930 that a mysterious "prophet," W. D. Fard, appeared in Detroit peddling raincoats and silks, and dispensing strange teachings about Africa, the white man, the Christian Church, and Islam. Soon he organized the first Temple of Islam, and by 1934, when Fard mysteriously disappeared, the movement had grown to eight thousand members. It was then that Elijah Muhammad came into power. Muhammad was Minister of Islam under Fard. Born Elijah Poole in Georgia, his family migrated to Detroit where he joined the new movement and was given his "original" Islamic name. His "slave name," Poole, was then dropped.

Under Muhammad's guidance Fard was deified and identified with Allah, and the Muslim movement grew into a dedicated, tightly disciplined bloc with a membership estimated in the early 1960s at between sixty-five thousand and one hundred thousand. Muhammad set himself up in a mansion in Chicago, where Temple No. 2, the Muslim headquarters, is located. The Muslims established a "University of Islam"; their temples are found in practically every major American city, and they are collectively engaged in far-flung business and real estate activities.

The Muslim ideology is compounded of a fantastic mythology coupled with elements of orthodox Islamic doctrine. The Muslims reject Christianity, which they regard as the "white man's religion," and instead have constructed their own version of Islam. Allah is seen as the "Supreme Black Man," and it is asserted that the first men were black men. C. Eric Lincoln, in his classic study of the Muslims, described their beliefs:

> The "originality" of the Black Nation and the creation of the white race by Yakub, "a black scientist in rebellion against Allah"—this is the central myth of the Black Muslim Movement. It is the fundamental premise upon which rests the whole theory of black supremacy and white degradation. . . .
>
> These devils [white men] were given six thousand years to rule. The allotted span of their rule was ended in 1914, and their "years of grace" will last no longer than is necessary for the chosen of Allah to be resurrected from the mental death imposed upon them by the white man. This resurrection is the task of Muhammad himself, Messenger of Allah and Spiritual Leader of the Lost-Found Nation in the West.[21]

With this resurrection the white slavemasters are to be destroyed in a catastrophic "Battle of Armageddon."

The Muslim program calls for racial separation and a complete economic withdrawal from white society; this is to culminate in the establishment of a separate black state. On the back page of each issue of *Muhammad Speaks,* the weekly Muslim newspaper, are detailed the Muslim demands.

> We want our people in America whose parents or grandparents were descendants from slaves, to be allowed to establish a separate state or territory of their own— either on this continent or elsewhere. We believe that our former slave masters are obligated to provide such a land and that the area must be fertile and minerally rich. We believe that our former slave masters are obligated to maintain and supply our needs in this separate territory for the next 20 to 25 years—until we are able to produce and supply our own needs.
>
> Since we cannot get along with them in peace and equality, after giving them 400 years of our sweat and blood and receiving in return some of the worst treatment human beings have ever experienced, we believe our contributions to this land and the suffering forced upon us by white America, justifies our demand for complete separation in a state or territory of our own.

These obviously are long-term demands. In the interim the Muslims want equality of legal treatment, employment, and educational opportunities, although in the latter they want schools which are segregated by sex.

The Muslim organization grew in response to a perceived threat to the economic security of a certain class of black people. Black workers made significant occupational advances after 1940 in intermediate-level jobs such as operatives and kindred workers. But this category of workers was hard hit by technological unemployment due to automation. In 1960, for example, the unemployment rate in this category was 6.4 percent for males and 9.9 percent for females—a higher rate of unemployment than among any other category of workers except laborers.[22] At the same time that some black workers were moving into this new category, the demand for unskilled and semiskilled labor, categories in which blacks are traditionally overrepresented, was declining faster than black workers could be retrained for other lines of work.[23] Economic self-sufficiency of the race as a whole, the Muslims proposed, following a by now well-worn path, is the only solution to this problem. Racial integration is no answer, they contended, because it can't work.

The effectiveness of the Muslims was limited, however, by their religious mysticism, which alienated many blacks and obscured the question of how to change power relations in America, and by the fact that their organization served in large part as simply an alternative route to middle-class status for some blacks, rather than actively attacking the problem of general black oppression.

Nonetheless, the nationalist position was measurably strengthened in the middle 1960s when it became obvious to many observers that the integrationist civil rights movement had reached its peak and was in decline, having only minimally affected the lives of ordinary black people. This failure compounded the crisis which was precipitated at the close of the war years.

The next phase of nationalist expression followed the demise of the civil rights movement. The modern civil rights movement was launched by one of those little incidents which happen all the time, but which in a revolutionary epoch can assume awesome proportions. In December 1955, Mrs. Rosa Parks, a black woman weary from work, refused to give up her seat on a Montgomery, Alabama, city bus to a white man. The irate white bus driver had her arrested for this open affront to the unwritten, but, nonetheless, real southern behavioral code. The driver did not know, could not know, that southern blacks were like a coiled spring and that tension had reached the breaking point. Mrs. Parks was arrested little more than a year after the 1954 Supreme Court school decision, a decision which many southern blacks thought spelled the end of segregation. But the white South had responded in classic style and openly defied the Court ruling. The formation of the first White Citizens Council, in Indianola, Mississippi, just two months after the Court decision presaged the bitter struggle which was to come. Blacks, however, were in no mood for more procrastination. This was it. If talk of integration meant anything, now was time for the struggle to be joined and fought to its conclusion, whatever that might be.

Within two days the black people of Montgomery had begun organizing a massive boycott of the municipal buses. A young Baptist minister, Martin Luther King, Jr., who had arrived in town only months earlier, was named to head up the boycott. King was given the job probably because he was new and not identified with any of the factions which splintered the black community. It took more than a year for the bus boycott to succeed in finally forcing desegregation of public transportation facilities in Montgomery, but this struggle represented a clear victory for the non-violent, direct action tactics advocated by the newcomer from Atlanta. The tactic of court struggle stressed by the NAACP was cast in a shadow, and King became a national leader.

King moved on to new battles. As he wrote in his account of the Montgomery drama, *Stride Toward Freedom,* the problem in that city was "merely symptomatic of the larger national problem," and he decided to go wherever necessary to attack this problem.[24] Nonviolent change for the better was possible, King believed, if only the federal government and liberal whites would back the Negro struggle.

It was this belief which, as the crisis of black America deepened, converted King into what some regard as a reluctant accomplice of the white power structure. As the years passed, the liberal establishment tried to use King to restrain the threatening rebelliousness of the black masses and the young militants. Thus one of the admitted purposes of his poor people's campaign, for example, was to channel that rebelliousness into a movement he thought could be as effective as Gandhi's had been. In the press his calls for nonviolence were frequently contrasted with the "rabble rousing" of black militants.

King could not repudiate this role because he was convinced that the establishment could be pushed and pressured to implement his program, provided that he did not move so far and so fast as to lose his white liberal support.

In 1957, King organized his Southern Christian Leadership Conference, composed then mostly of black ministers from ten states. With SCLS as a base, King led numerous economic boycotts and desegregation and voter registration campaigns in cities such as Albany, Georgia; Birmingham, Alabama; St. Augustine, Florida; and Selma, Alabama. Jailed and beaten frequently, he was nearly killed in 1958, when he was stabbed in the chest by a black woman, while he was autographing books in Harlem. In his wanderings, King seemed to be in search of a "new Montgomery"—the right confrontation or combination of demonstrations which would wake up white America and result in the granting of full equality to black people.

By 1963 and the March on Washington, King's dream was no closer to being realized. Already, even among some of those who demonstrated in support of it, there was the gnawing suspicion that the civil rights bill, if passed, would not be effectively enforced, that it was only another palliative. Critics sprang up where none had been before. King himself was accused of being opportunistic in his campaigns and of not seeing them through to the finish. A new breed of leaders, drawn from the northern ghettos or the fierce rural civil rights drives in the South, was growing into maturity. Black Muslim Minister Malcolm X challenged King's espousal of integration and nonviolence. Later, after he left the Muslims, Malcolm, a cogent and persuasive speaker, advocated the need for radical change—and many listened. Young, skeptical leaders were also being tempered in King's stepchild organization, the Student Nonviolent Coordinating Committee. These activists, mostly college students or ex-students, were beginning to examine political and economic exploitation, and the American government's perpetration of injustice not only at home but in foreign countries. In January 1966, SNCC left the fold of traditional civil rights activity by taking a stand in opposition to the Vietnam war and the military draft. The SNCC radicals felt they were involved in a movement of worldwide dimensions.

With the advent of the era of urban rebellions in 1964, it became painfully obvious that the civil rights movement had not altered significantly the plight of the black masses. The cry of "black power" articulated this awareness and presented a new departure for the freedom movement. Black control of black organizations and communities was demanded, and militants turned their backs on the goal of racial integration. The liberal reform strategy advocated by King and others came under suspicious scrutiny. Revolution replaced integration as the most used word of the day.

King had secured a leadership position in the top ranks of the civil rights movement by adapting the thrust of his actions and campaigns to the shifting sentiment and conditions within the movement. He trailed the militants, but often managed to bring along large numbers of ordinary black people, particularly in the South, to the new positions he adopted. His initial efforts were aimed at legal rights, such as the right to vote and desegregation of public facilities. As early as 1965, however,

King urged President Lyndon B. Johnson to issue "unconditional and unambiguous" pleas for peace talks, but it was not until 1967 that he came out clearly against the Vietnam war, basing his opposition on his adherence to nonviolence and the fact that the war was draining funds from social welfare programs at home and thereby adding to urban unrest.

The Chicago open housing campaign in 1966 was King's first effort to deal with more basic internal issues. It ended without reaching its goal, but King regrouped his forces and late in 1967 began planning for a massive poor people's campaign in Washington. This new campaign was not to focus on civil rights but was to demand jobs and housing. Not only were blacks to be the beneficiaries, if it were successful, but also poor whites, Indians, and Spanish-speaking people. King sensed that he had to attack the economic problem because political rights were meaningless to a people held in economic bondage. When the Memphis garbage men went on strike and called on King to aid them, he readily accepted. The significance of that strike by black workers was pointed out by Norman Pearlstine, writing in the *Wall Street Journal* of March 8, 1968: "Negroes here [in Memphis] have found a weapon in the sanitation strike that may be picked up elsewhere by civil rights militants. In many communities, particularly in the South, sanitation departments are predominantly Negro." Pearlstine termed the alliance of black workers with civil rights groups a powerful coalition. The hope that such a coalition might give a new lease on life to a sinking civil rights movement was shattered, however, by an assassin's bullet.

Writing in *Look* magazine in the same month that he was killed, King once again articulated his basic philosophy and his continuing hope: "We have, through massive nonviolent action, an opportunity to avoid a national disaster and create a new spirit of class and racial harmony. . . . And all of us are on trial in this troubled hour, but time still permits us to meet the future with a clear conscience." Time, however, ran out, and the verdict of guilty which history first passed on white America in 1619 was once again confirmed.

With the apparent failure of the integration movement in the middle 1960s, black nationalism again became a visible force on the American scene. White journalists started quoting the same nationalist spokesmen whom they dismissed as madmen before. Malcolm X was still called a firebrand and an agitator, but the journalists realized now that he spoke for many black people. This was confirmed in 1966 when both SNCC and CORE openly embraced nationalism. The subsequent Black Power Conference in Newark and the revelation that the undeniably white Ford Foundation was financing CORE completely stilled any lingering doubts that black nationalism was nothing more than a fringe phenomenon. One could be for it or against it, but it was no longer possible to ignore nationalist sentiment.

NOTES

1. Herbert Aptheker (ed.), *A Documentary History of the Negro People in the United States,* Vol. I (New York: Citadel Press, 1951), pp. 327–28. It took an additional century, however, for black people's *consciousness* of their nationhood to become fairly widespread.
2. *Ibid.,* p. 71.
3. *Ibid.,* p. 72.
4. Benett, *Black Power U.S.A.* (Chicago: Johnson Publishing Co., 1967), p. 348.
5. *Liberator,* August 1964.

6. Quoted in E. Franklin Frazier, *Black Bourgeoisie* (New York: Collier Books, 1957), p. 134.
7. Quoted in Frazier, pp. 129–30.
8. Aptheker, *Documentary History,* Vol. II, p. 902.
9. *Ibid.,* p. 899.
10. William Z. Foster, *The Negro People in American History* (New York: International Publishers Company, Inc., 1954), p. 468. Foster contends that the importance of the Pan-African conference held during the peace talks after World War I was that "it emphasized the solidarity of American Negroes with the oppressed colonial peoples, and especially that it expressed the national sentiments of the American Negro people." (p. 435).
11. This is no fanciful stretching of the imagination. A "militant" restatement of Washington's thesis was expressed by Nathan Wright in *Black Power and Urban Unrest,* p. 20.
12. Quoted in E. U. Essien-Udom, *Black Nationalism* (New York: Dell, 1962), p. 43.
13. Quoted in Herbert Aptheker, *Toward Negro Freedom* (New York: New Century Publishers, 1956), p. 114.
14. Essien-Udom, p. 48.
15. *Ibid.,* p. 50.
16. *Ibid.,* p. 51.
17. In 1928 the Communist Party adopted a resolution which declared: "While continuing and intensifying the struggle under the slogan of full social and political equality for the Negroes, which must remain the central slogan of our Party for work among the masses, the Party must come out openly and unreservedly for the right of Negroes to self-determination in the Southern states, where the Negroes form a majority of the population. . . . The Negro question in the United States must be treated in its relation to the Negro question and struggles in other parts of the world. The Negro race everywhere is an oppressed race. Whether it is a minority (U.S.A., etc.), majority (South Africa), or inhabits a so-called independent state (Liberia, etc.), the Negroes are oppressed by imperialism. Thus, a common tie of interest is established for the revolutionary struggle of race and national liberation from imperialist domination of the Negroes in various parts of the world." (Foster, p. 461).
18. *Labor Fact Book* (New York: International Publishers, 1931), pp. 136–37.
19. Foster, pp. 458, 504.
20. *Ibid.,* p. 457.
21. C. Eric Lincoln, *The Black Muslims in America* (Boston: Beacon, 1961), pp. 76–77.
22. Leonard Broom and Norval Glenn, *Transformation of the Negro American* (New York: Harper & Row, 1965), p. 118.
23. *Ibid.*
24. *Stride Toward Freedom* (New York: Harper & Brothers, 1958), p. 189.

10. Women's Liberation in Perspective

Problems of Nineteenth-Century Feminism CELLESTINE WARE

Feminism has had a curious history in the United States. In some ways American women have been the freest in the world. The pioneer woman occupied a uniquely important place in her family, and in pioneer communities women were accorded rights that went beyond what was usual for the time. Some of our western states were among the first political units in the world to allow women to vote. Women in the United States also entered the professions early. In the 1840s, Elizabeth Blackwell succeeded in qualifying for a medical degree and in practicing medicine; other women followed. Women came to dominate the teaching profession, virtually displacing men except at the college level. Before the Civil War, American women were active in a wide variety of reform causes, ranging from abolitionism and temperance to prison reform and improved care of the insane. During these years, moreover, many of the legal disabilities women had suffered under, disabilities that limited their control over their property and over their children, were lifted.

On the other hand, conservative opinion disapproved of strong-minded women, and most men treated women with a combination of condescension and exaggerated, belittling gallantry. Most women who worked for a living were neither doctors nor professional reformers, but ill-paid seamstresses, house servants, and factory girls. If middle-class women were pampered and petted, working-class women drudged and slaved to keep large families clean and fed without any of the mechanical help that modern women expect.

The women's rights movement in the United States was primarily a middle-class crusade dedicated to giving educated and ambitious women access to all the political and professional opportunities and rights of adult males. It also had another side, however. This aspect of feminism called for a radical restructuring of society, and particularly the family, to end once and for all the traditional sexual division of labor. It implied so drastic a shift in values and practices that it frightened and repelled all but the most radical feminists of the nineteenth and early twentieth centuries. Cellestine Ware notes below how the conservative women's rights advocates all too often sacrificed the well-being of women to the well-being of other oppressed groups. Even when feminists fought for women alone, they frequently

Source: Cellestine Ware, *Woman Power: The Movement for Women's Liberation* (New York: Tower Publications, Inc., 1970), chap. iv, "Problems of Nineteenth-Century Feminism," pp. 142–164.

accepted sex distinctions, though arguing that these made women superior to men. In the end, this approach—by the standards of today's Women's Liberation militants —left women everywhere still in chains to men.

FOR FURTHER READING:

William O'Neill, *Everyone Was Brave: The Rise and Fall of Feminism in America,* (Quadrangle, 1969); William O'Neill, *Woman Movement: Feminism in the United States and England,* (Barnes and Noble, 1969); William O'Neill, "Feminism as a Radical Ideology," in Alfred F. Young, (editor) *Dissent: Explorations in the History of American Radicalism* (Northern Illinois University Press, 1968); Eleanor Flexner, *Century of Struggle*,* (Atheneum, 1968); Aileen Kraditor, *The Ideas of the Woman Suffrage Movement 1890–1920,* (Columbia University Press, 1965); Aileen Kraditor, (editor) *Up From the Pedestal: Selected Writings in the History of American Feminism,* (Quadrangle, 1968); Edith DeRham, *Love Fraud: A Direct Attack on the Staggering Waste of Education and Talent Among American Women*,* (Pegasus, 1965); Barbara Welter, "The Cult of True Womanhood: 1820–1860," *American Quarterly* (Summer 1966).

Asterisk denotes paperback edition.

The struggle for women's emancipation has always been inspirited by the dialectic of whichever evolutionary and radical ideas were current. American feminism has linked itself with each protest against inequities and found in the struggle the material for its own movement. This self-discovery through working for others, this borrowing of ideas, tactics, and philosophical underpinnings from the male movements of the time has prevented the steady application of radical analysis to the question of women's oppression. In the end, women have found that the causes in which they fought so valiantly have each in their turn left women without the means of achieving full equality. Women never achieved the right to do and be whatever they pleased because even their protest movements evolved through working for others, through self-effacement in the drive to achieve human rights for whatever group was then considered most downtrodden. The attempts to operate from a mode radically individualistic and self-centered in its concentration on women's rights were fragmentary and never perceived as the *sine qua non* for female emancipation.

It was the churches that first taught women a dynamic for freeing themselves by teaching them to protest. "Protestantism, by its very nature, cannot set limits to the protests of its believers. The United States was both Protestant and republican and Michel Chevalier noticed: 'Protestantism, republicanism, and individuality are all one.' This ideal was bound to inspire women to protest, once they had learned not to organize against the fact of their inequality."

When Northern American women in the 1830's began to organize to free the slaves, they learned the politics of agitation for human rights. The Grimke sisters were Southern abolitionists who came North to preach and lecture about the sufferings of the slaves. They were the first women to speak in public before male and female audiences. No one reform can occur by itself. In the process of speaking out against slavery the Grimke sisters had to fight for women's right to address the public. The Grimke sisters declared that "whatsoever it is morally right for a man to do it is morally right for a woman to do."

"The famous Pastoral Letter of the Congregational Churches of Massachusetts against the Grimkes was remarkable in its failure. It stirred up ten feminists such as Lucy Stone, for each one that it deterred . . . The Letter may have deplored the mistaken 'conduct of those who encourage females to bear an obtrusive and ostentatious part in measures of reform'; but that conduct had been the conduct of many Congregational Ministers, who were grateful enough for the funds and free work from women in their churches . . . It was revivalist preachers who had borrowed many of the shock tactics of the old Puritans and had taught women how to use them."

"In seeking to free the slaves radical women became conscious of their own lack of freedom. Through helping others, they learned to help themselves. The destiny of American women and American Negroes has been interacting, and still is."

The dangers of learning how to struggle for oneself in the course of struggling for others is that one may not develop the independent analysis which is the only way that women will ever effect the radical changes necessary for their emancipation. At some point women must learn to distinguish their interest and politics from those of the causes in which they are enlisted. They must comprehend the solitary nature of their oppression. The abolitionists in fighting for the rights of slaves did not realize that all women were united as an oppressed class. The analogy they did form between marriage and slavery was helpful for giving them insight into their oppression but it did not equip them with the political analysis and the strategy to free themselves. "In an extreme or moderate form, the arguments over the equality of the slaves were applied by some educated women in their marriages . . . The white man could be matched by his wife or his slave; the mother was the equal of the father; no human being should be the master of another. Those women who wanted to become equal with white men found themselves in the struggle for the slaves' equality with white men. The support of him became the support of themselves." History was to prove that the support of the slave was not the support of the woman. True radicalism inheres in seeking the causes of one's own oppression and rooting these out. When the female suffragists saw that black men had got the vote while they were still disenfranchised, many of them turned their backs on the racial inequities in America. The fact was that there had been two separate struggles all along. If American feminists had kept an awareness of the distinctive character of their own oppression, they would not later have proved such untrustworthy supporters of racial equality.

It was their sense of betrayal at the admittance of the black man to suffrage that led feminists to make the split in their movement that was eventually to narrow the struggle for the emancipation to the single issue of woman's suffrage. This narrowing of the focus of feminism, with its eventual rejection of a radical analysis of the position of women, meant that feminism could never get to the root causes of women's oppression. The result was that the full emancipation of women has yet to be achieved.

*   *   *

Throughout the decades of struggle for women's rights, feminists changed their demands from higher education to access to the professions to the vote, but the underlying demand was always for autonomy. From the Seneca Falls Convention in 1848 on, women demanded the right to engage in public affairs. Elizabeth Cady Stanton, one of the organizers of the Convention, and Lucy Stone at that time espoused a radical form of feminism which if carried through would probably have led to the full emancipation of women. Both Lucy Stone and Elizabeth Cady Stanton were impelled into feminist activities by their anger at the wrongs that women suffered in marriage.

*   *   *

Both Lucy Stone and Elizabeth Cady Stanton would have been comfortable in a women's liberation gathering because they insisted that the woman's body was under her own control whatever rights the law gave her husband in marriage. "Beginning in 1848, it was possible for women who rebelled against the circumstances of their lives, to know that they were not alone." The feminists who launched the movement from Seneca Falls were strong in their belief that women were the equal and likeness of men except for their sexual differences.

As feminists gradually acquired the right to education and access to the professions, they focused on suffrage as a means of obliterating discrimination against women. All the early women's welfare programs were part of the fight for women's rights. Women needed special protection because they didn't exist as citizens. They were under the complete dominance of their fathers before marriage, and after marriage, they suffered a civil and political death. The law no longer regarded them as beings distinct from their husbands. The Temperance Union arose to safeguard women who had no legal redress against the abuses of alcoholic husbands. Feminist tracts moved from the expression of generalized unhappiness with the artificial limitations on women's activities to the demand for specific changes in customs and laws.

In half a century anti-feminist arguments against women suffrage moved from the preservation of femininity and the home to the state's right to decide which of its citizens could vote. The anti-suffragist arguments shifted because the feminists themselves "increasingly emphasized those grievances and demands that pertained to women's relations to the government. At last the chief stress was on securing married women's property laws and other attempts to wipe out legal inequities." More and more the strategies for the protection of women centered on the vote.

Unfortunately the feminist argument for woman suffrage changed over the years. In the beginning feminists argued that women had the right to vote as citizens and human beings. Later they asked for the right to vote so that they could bring their moral influence on the affairs of the nation. Demand for autonomy had always been consistent with the distinction between men's and women's worlds, but the pre-Civil War feminists always argued against the sexual division of life.

Once the argument for suffrage was based on the superior faculties of women, feminists had actually accepted such a distinction. Feminists hoped to get the vote by using the Victorian belief that ladies were the angels in a human world, but they thereby engaged themselves to appear publicly only within the guise of traditional femininity.

One reason for this major strategical error of accepting a world divided into men's and women's spheres was the anger and fear of the feminists on discovering that post-Civil War America was far from ready to enfranchise women. Women were shocked to discover that they had so miscalculated the tolerance of the nation.

The Fourteenth Amendment to the Constitution which federalized the exclusion of women from the vote was a traumatic blow which rigidified feminist thinking and made the women willing to make compromises that would have been unacceptable to them until then. The opinion throughout the North among their former allies, the abolitionists, was that the black man's suffrage would be endangered if accompanied by a request for woman suffrage. This was unacceptable to the radical feminists even though it was a correct reading of the nation's political temper. The republican state of Kansas rejected in 1867 a referendum that would have given the vote to women as well as blacks.

The sentiment of the country was completely intolerant of the vote for women. "The anti-suffrage cohorts went on conjuring hideous visions of an Amazonian sex pitted against 'man' . . . The basic argument on which the philosophy was grounded was that women *should* not vote or hold office because they *could* not. Here, too, the living record to the contrary in the growing total of suffrage states was either ignored or willfully distorted."

Lucy Stone was able to reconcile herself because she accepted the abolitionists' claim that black men had suffered more than white women and that their cause must come first. She and Stanton and Susan Anthony joined the Equal Rights Association, a coalition of abolitionists, Boston intellectuals, and feminists. Stanton and Anthony became increasingly embittered after the passage of the Fifteenth Amendment. They ascribed the failure of the Equal Rights Association to back immediate woman suffrage to the preponderance of men in the organization. In May, 1869, they broke off from the men and women in the Association to found the National Woman's Suffrage Association which was absolute in its quest for immediate woman suffrage along with other social reforms. The Stanton-Anthony feminists were ready to ally themselves with anyone who was in favor of woman suffrage.

The weekly paper that they put out was a reflection of the broad reforms that the women demanded. NWSA (The National Woman's Suffrage Association) declared that marriage reform "is of more vital consequence to woman's welfare, reaches down to a deeper depth in woman's heart and more thoroughly constitutes the core of the woman's movement, than any such superficial and fragmentary question as woman's suffrage." At the same time Susan Anthony asserted that disenfranchisement was the major block to female emancipation. This dual stand on the nature of needed reforms confused other women. If marriage reform and the burden of domesticity was the heart of the woman question (which history has indeed shown to be the case) why need Stanton-Anthony secede from the Equal Rights Association over the question of immediate woman suffrage? *Revolution*, which was edited by Stanton and managed by Anthony, did give the movement a forum and direction, but the problem was that it pointed in all directions at once.

The NWSA acquired the habit of using quite contradictory arguments if both supported woman suffrage. *Revolution* is to be praised for keeping alive the radical tradition of feminism when the general trend was toward a more conservative approach.

In November, 1869, AWSA (The American Woman Suffrage Association) was formed in Cleveland and headed by Lucy Stone. It spoke for the growing population of women entering the professions and interested in getting more social freedom. These women were not yet ready to speak out for woman suffrage, nor did they make any radical analysis of the social structure. The schism between the National and the American was one between radical and conservative. The National regarded women's rights as a broad cause extending from political to social to sexual restructuring of women's identity. The American, unlike Susan Anthony, was interested in organizing working women and avoided issues that it considered might alienate the influential sectors of the community. Significantly *The Woman's Journal,* organ of the American, was a success in the decade that lay ahead while *Revolution* failed. This was indicative of the increasing conservatism of American society. By 1875 Susan Anthony had regressed to the Victorian issue of women's morality in arguing for woman suffrage in her article *Social Purity*.

The National had made another error by cutting itself off from the labor unions. In her anxiety to get work for women printers, Anthony sent them in as strike-breakers to union shops. After that she was no longer welcome at labor conventions.

The decade from 1880–1890 saw the suffrage movement turn conservative as a reflection of the lessening of social tolerance for militance. "The middle class was learning to identify organized labor with social turmoil." The strikes during the depression 1873–1878 "did not help to reassure women taught by press and pulpit to identify any kind of militancy with radicalism." By 1890, the radical and conservative wings of the feminist movement had become reconciled. The National and the American merged to become the National American Woman Suffrage League which became the League of Women Voters in 1920.

In a period that saw the ascendancy of middle-class values, and in which feminism was cut off from labor, feminists ceased to ask radical questions. With the exception of Stanton, Charlotte Perkins Gilman and a few others, the movement chose to see the basis for female emancipation in systematic and legal attempts to convince the nation to give women the vote. The social makeup of the suffrage leadership was changing perceptibly. "There were fewer housewives or women who did the greater part of their own work and more professionals, writers, and women of substantial means." "The kind of day-to-day contact that had enabled Miss Anthony to organize Working Women's Associations and had sent her to conventions of the National Labor Unions had vanished." Feminism turned respectable and middle class in its ideas and goals as well as in its membership. "Another generation of women leaders was developing in this new atmosphere even while veterans like Miss Anthony, Mrs. Stone and Mrs. Stanton were still on the scene. The younger women were not, for the most part, distinguished by the breadth of their social views."

Sympathy and rapport with the working woman were missing from Rachel Foster Avery, Carrie Chapman Catt or Harriet Taylor Upton who led the later stages of the fight for suffrage.

"Around 1900 the promise of the American Revolution in terms of human equality and liberty were forgotten in the effort to win the vote for a limited number of white Anglo-Saxon women."

Unfortunately the women who did go among the poor did not apply a radical analysis to the causes of the oppression they found there. The women active in the social reform movement were also articulate suffragists but their orientation was very different from that of the early radical feminists. At the beginning of the 20th century, many of the worst disabilities of American women had been eliminated and others, greatly reduced. "While many of the changes which had taken place had been the outcome of sharply fought legislative battles, in general, they reflected the continuing expansion of women's interests and their activities in industry, in business, and in the professions . . . the 1890 census listed 4,005,532 (women) as gainfully employed . . . in 1910 7,444,787." It should have been evident to thoughtful feminists that the basic oppression of women was domestic, not legal or political, and that it was marriage and the family itself that generated their inequities. But many things militated against this understanding.

Society had changed its consciousness of social evils and how to deal with them. Whereas an earlier generation had been abolitionists, the society from 1880 on became social reformers. Institutional arteriosclerosis set in in post-Civil War America and radical change was discredited. Rapid industrialization had made some men rich and had made desperate the lives of their employees. As people became aware of increased social tension due to the acute contrasts between the rich and the poor, they institutionalized philanthropy and social reforms to help the poor. Feminists, rather than establishing their own ethics and inventing an analysis that would be productive of equality for them, went with the tide, and divided their energies between social reform and the suffrage movement. If women thought that suffrage would emancipate them they were only in agreement with their times.

Increased leisure had given the conscientious middle and upper class the time to idealize progress. Men and women came to believe that an educated public, if given the vote, could cure all social ills. Society was infinitely perfectable. To women, suffrage was a symbol of the equality necessary to effect reforms; this was the link between the feminists and the progressives.

* * *

In an age committed to reform through the system, the feminists did not think of making radical changes in their milieu itself. Feminists no longer asked radical questions because America would not tolerate them. The age one lies in determines the questions one asks and the forms of change one thinks possible. "The chief feature of social feminism was that it created roles for women that militated against their emancipation. Their benevolent enterprises met women's desires for useful and satisfying work without touching the sources of their inequality." Social reform accommodated women's need to act without requiring them to move outside the prevailing definition of a woman's nature. All the arguments of the anti-feminists were based on the idea of the lady. Once suffragists urged female enfranchisement on the grounds of woman's peculiar spirituality and probity, they had moved back inside the enclosure of womanly concerns. It was possible to see social reform and philanthropy as pure extensions of the duties of the good housewife.

* * *

The founding of the National Women's Trade Union League in 1903 fused educated middle-class women and working women for a common effort on behalf of working women. Settlement housework met the subjective needs of middle-class women because it showed that the social concerns of free women would not disrupt the existing order. American women never succeeded in thinking themselves out of the stereotype of marriage and children. Margaret D. Robins was perhaps the most important woman in establishing a contract between working women and the suffragists. She later broke with feminists over the Equal-Rights Amendment to the Constitution because even though it would (if passed) make women eligible for the higher-paying jobs reserved for men, it would repeal many of the protective laws for women workers that Mrs. Robins had helped to institute. Mrs. Robins, though recognizing a link between feminism and social reform, was more concerned with protecting the poor than with the achievements of full equality for women.

* * *

The failure of feminism was the failure of American society to institute forms or analysis that would realize the promise of democracy for all Americans. The Declaration of Independence would never have been signed by any of the legislators in America from the Civil War to the present. All efforts for the emancipation of women have coalesced in periods of intense social ferment and public debate. While this is probably true of all movements for equality, it has been the bane of the feminist movement precisely because women are in the habit of adopting the attitudes, with only a few alterations for fit, of the predominant male culture. As a result, feminists have always eventually accepted philosophical and politicial ideas and demonstrations that have not been germane to their own emancipation. Women have not been self-centered enough to effect their emancipation.

* * *

The resulting social feminists felt that the issue of woman suffrage would wait or did not think it essential to their high moral cause. The hard-core feminists, almost as far from true emancipation, believed that woman suffrage was essential to the success of all other reforms. Florence Kelley was a lifelong socialist but she had largely rejected the formulas of socialism for the Progressive doctrines that were the mainstream of the American ethos before the war. "Her whole strategy seems to have been based on the assumption that by organizing women and inspiring them with a higher social consciousness before they gained the vote, it would be possible to lead them to final victory afterward."

In this strategy she was a woman of her time—a Progressive social feminist. Her failure was the failure of the era to redefine society, politics and psychology to devise a strategy for female emancipation and working-class liberation.

The cyclical nature of the problem of the feminist movement is perhaps the most frightening conclusion that can be drawn from an examination of feminism in America. The suggestion that housework be professionalized and the same supporting arguments were presented at the recent New York Congress to Unite Women. Contemporary feminist literature repeats often Engel's dictum that within the family the husband is the bourgeois and the wife, the proletariat. The necessity of repeating the same arguments over and over again suggests the intractable, irrational nature of the opposition to feminism. Men remain the humans, women, their female creatures only capable of continuing in the never-diminishing round of domestic duties to which they have been relegated.

Charlotte Perkins Gilman was one of the few feminists to attack the cult of domesticity. William O'Neill, author of a book on the decline of feminism, criticizes Charlotte Gilman and Florence Kelley for not embracing socialism as the only system that could emancipate women through removing the burden of housework and child-rearing to the public domain. Yet at the turn of the century socialism seemed a long-range ideal, rather than a pragmatic means of redressing social ills. There was not then, as there is now, the example of successful socialism in other countries. Gilman wanted to lift the burden of domesticity from women but her failure to provide the social context in which this could be achieved is simply the measure of resistance in America to any collective solution to the problems of family life.

* * *

Many tracts written between the Civil War and World War I either called for or predicted the machinization and professionalization of homemaking chores . . . They assumed that once women had won the right to work beyond the domestic sphere they would automatically do so, if only they could be freed from household drudgery. Cooperative kitchens and other such arrangements would give them the freedom and enable them to find remunerative careers suited to their individual tastes, while those women (and men) with talent and liking for housework would become skilled, well-paid professionals doing jobs hitherto done by housewives who, in many cases, had neither talent nor liking for the work.

* * *

Charlotte Gilman knew that it was the popular conception of the family that was the obstacle to full sexual equality. Our present economy is dependent on women as a reserve for cheap labor. The labor of women is cheap because they do not believe their work is important to the economy. They have accepted the popular idea that women only work to get luxuries for their families.

* * *

To succeed, feminism must obliterate this cherished and carefully nurtured media-image.

The mistakes of Anna Shaw, who replaced Susan Anthony as leader of the movement upon Anthony's death, should be learned by every contemporary feminist. Anna Shaw was limited by her geographical and sociological background from making the alliances that would have given feminism some much needed strength. Anna Shaw "remained too much the rural Westerner to understand the need of combining with urban progressive and labor forces to win over the Eastern cities. She could only understand the need of working with the evangelical churches and temperance women of the small Western towns, and here woman suffrage was successful." Shaw failed to broaden the base for the movement because she limited herself to the public with which she was most comfortable. There is some danger of this deliberate delimitation of membership in the new feminism. The WLM is presently urban or college-centered in its program and in its attempts to reach the public precisely because that is the expected basis of its membership. To succeed, feminism must engage the sympathies of the small-town woman and of the churchgoing housewife. The WLM must not remain an organization of professionals, intellectuals, and radical students.

During Shaw's leadership of the movement, Southern delegates had gained a remarkable ascendancy. She alienated the Easterners raised in the anti-slavery tradition by accepting Southern vice-presidents in the organization. "As one Negro leader wrote to another about the suffragists, 'All of them are mortally afraid of the South, and if they could get the Suffrage Amendment through without enfranchising coloured women, they would do it in a moment.' "

The final stages of the suffrage movement are tarnished by the compromises that suffragists made to win backing for the vote. In the North much of the resistance to the vote was based on the idea that the new immigrant women voters would provide natural material for the corrupt machine vote in the large cities. The race question in the North actually meant prejudice against the Irish, Italian and Jewish immigrants. To manipulate this racial fear to the advantage of woman suffrage, Northern suffrage leaders began to urge the advantages of the "educated vote." Even Elizabeth Cady Stanton declared in 1902 that "suffragists would be willing to restrict the vote to educated women provided only that the insurmountable qualification of sex be forever removed."

*   *   *

The Woman's Party was a coalition of Harriet Stanton Blatch, daughter of Elizabeth Cady Stanton, and Alice Paul, both of whom had lived in England and realized the effectiveness of the militant feminists there. The period from 1896 to 1910 is generally considered least active in the history of the early feminist movement. Harriet Stanton Blatch returned from England in 1910 to find no effort being made to persuade Congress to vote in woman suffrage and a complete lack of political knowledge in the movement. The by-law of feminism at that time was to educate the public, but there was no active work going on. Blatch formed the Equality League, which initiated the practice of suffragist parades. These parades riveted public attention on the feminist cause.

Alice Paul formed the Congressional Union, which utilized militant tactics to push for a Federal amendment on woman suffrage. She revitalized the feminist movement, but she was excluded from leadership and replaced by Carrie Chapman Catt, who had the political finesse and deviousness to organize the final drive for woman suffrage. The amalgamation of the Equality League with the Congressional Union was called the Woman's Party.

Led by the indomitable Alice Paul, the Woman's Party continued the fight for female emancipation long after it was a dead issue to the rest of America. It was the Woman's Party that initiated the drive in 1923 for an Equal-Rights Amendment to the Constitution. Forty-seven years have gone and the Amendment is still not passed. It is presently supported by NOW and was introduced in this session of Congress by Senator Eugene McCarthy and Senator John Tower, Representatives Catherine May and Martha Griffiths. The amendment reads: "Equality of rights under the law shall not be denied or abridged by the United States or by any state on account of sex." The Amendment has been held up in every Congress by the Senate subcommittee on Constitutional Amendments. After Congressional approval the Amendment would require approval by three-fourths of the state legislatures.

*   *   *

Lillian Wald, Margaret D. Robins, and Jane Adams went into the slums to persuade working women of their need for suffrage. Andrew Sinclair sees the support of the working women for suffrage as crucial to its attainment. Ella Bloor, a middle-class labor organizer, made better working conditions her priority; suffragists made the vote theirs. Bloor said: "For many of the secure middle-class ladies, the suffrage movement was a mere feminist fad. I tried to make them see the really vital importance of suffrage to the working women, as a weapon against economic insecurity. And I tried to make them see that not the vote alone was important, but its proper use in building a better society.

"Once women did get the vote, political differences split the labor leaders from the middle-class suffragists." In Ella Bloor's opinion, the splendid and militant Woman's Party degenerated to a 'narrow, anti-labor sect.' In fact, most of its members had nearly reverted to the American middle-class idea of what freedom and equality meant, the opportunity to become a lady.

For a brief period before WW I, feminism was quite a stylish movement, but with the death of progressivism, it was no longer popular. When Roosevelt and the Republican Party disassociated themselves from the idea of progressive reform, the ideals of social reform were discredited. This early demise suggests that pre-WW I feminism was indeed a fad and that the women were for the most part only inspired by the ideas and politics of the men then in control.

Political and legal reforms did not bring women economic equality. "After the war, employers avoided equal pay laws by simply refusing to give women men's jobs." The women who had earned their Ph.D's before the war discovered in the 20's that they could not advance in their careers. Fewer women went on to graduate schools and women lost interest in careers as opposed to mere jobs.

The flappers of the 20's thought of self-fulfillment through exploration of the new social and sexual mores. They looked to marriage and domesticity rather than to economic independence for their major satisfaction in life. The identity of women in America was basically unchanged. Women made no demands for an enlarged social role.

Those women in the 30's who did pursue careers did so at the conscious expense of their private lives. A constellation of authorities from Havelock Ellis, Freud, and God told women and men a woman's happiness was in her home and family life. Women stopped asking who they were and what they wanted. They accepted the old Victorian redefinitions of womanhood.

"The double standard of morals did not mean simply that men enjoyed sexual advantages denied to women, but also that masculine activities were self-justifying while women had always to identify themselves with the highest moral and social good to excuse even relatively modest enterprises." The practical result of this was that two generations of mothers told their daughters that the most important thing in a woman's life before her marriage is her chastity, after her marriage, it is her husband and children.

The reverberations of these teachings may be seen in the uneasiness that women radicals feel at concentrating on women's issues and at calling themselves feminists. An evaluation of the problems of American feminism makes evident that women must engage in a self-initiated radical analysis of their social identities and the options that our society and polity offer them. Women must create their cultural tradition and rediscover the myths of the female. Our culture now is entirely male in its symbols and in the priority it gives them, in its determination of what is and is not natural.

Western society has mechanisms for utilizing the expression of male alienation—the academic and criminal worlds—but no institutions exist that will unequivocally foster the talents of an eccentric woman or provide emotional support for the needs of a free woman. A girl growing up has no models for womanhood. Womanhood is an unknown, a hole in space. Men are the humans, women, the aliens, an afterthought of creation.

The creation of a vital feminist movement depends on women's revival of self-knowledge, unqualified by men. They must create a female principle in order to create a politics. Politics is the expression of the needs of the recognized self, and women have been denied self-knowledge for thousands of years.

In order to do this the women will have to fight.

*   *   *

The new domesticity and demure womanhood—black women get behind your man—both physically and psychologically, is cited as undeniable example of the way that the feminine role has been constructed by men to support the male identity. This has required millenniums of self-denial. The black male's reassertion of female submission is a clear indication of the basis of manhood in our society. The men are black and proud; the women are black and pregnant. This is simply a less subtle statement of the usual relationship that obtains between men and women in our society.

It's time for women to reject the masculine definition of themselves. Women have just got to learn how to be free.

11. The Uses of Violence in America

Violence and Social Change in American History HOWARD ZINN

Americans are ambivalent about violence. Radicals denounce all forms of violence employed in the name of official purposes, whether domestic or international. The brutal methods of the police at home and of the armed forces abroad repel them. On the other hand, though there is a pacifist wing of the Left, certain radical groups believe that violence directed against the existing racial and political order is often justified and indeed necessary. Conservatives reverse the order. America can impose its will forcibly on other nations for the sake of its own values, but at home the discontented must not allow the law's delays to push them into using force to get redress. What seems to be at stake on both conservative and radical sides is the object of the violence. Both groups will endorse violence in a good cause; both deplore it when employed by its opponents.

As a historical question, violence has interested students of America for some time. Part of the consensus hypothesis is that the United States has largely avoided violent episodes. The Civil War excepted, we solved our major social and economic problems through peaceful parliamentary processes. No doubt there were exceptions to this generality, but we can ascribe most of those to our frontier heritage, and somehow frontier-inspired violence was relatively innocent. Howard Zinn, in the selection below, attempts to analyze the nature of violence in the American past. He acknowledges that large areas of our national life have been free of serious disorder. But he also insists that we have always used violence against outsiders, both foreigners and those who were not within the inner circle of the middle classes.

FOR FURTHER READING:

Report of the National Advisory Commission on Civil Disorders (Bantam Books, 1968); Tom Hayden, *Rebellion in Newark: Official Violence and Ghetto Response**, (Vintage, 1969); Thomas Rose (editor) *Violence in America: A Historical and Contemporary Reader**, (Vintage, 1970); Arthur Waskow, *From Race Riot to Sit In: 1919 and the 1960's**, (Doubleday, 1966); Staughton Lynd (editor) *Non-Violence in America: A Documentary History** (Bobbs-Merrill, 1966); St. Clare Drake, "Urban Violence and American Social Movements" in *Urban Riots: Violence and Social Change**, (Vintage, 1969).

Asterisk denotes paperback edition.

Source: Howard Zinn, "Violence and Social Change in American History," in *Violence in America: A Historical and Contemporary Reader,* ed. Thomas Rose (New York: Vintage Books, 1970), pp. 70–80.

There is a basic misconception about the United States, I am going to argue, which goes something like this: that the United States is a peculiarly nonviolent nation, with a special dispensation for achieving social change through peaceful parliamentary reform. My thesis is that this idea is based on two failures of vision; one is a failure to recognize how much overt violence has characterized our behavior toward nationalities and races other than our own; the other is a failure to recognize the place of violence—both overt and hidden—in American social progress. This misconception brings about a double standard: there is, on the one hand, a national tendency to absolutize the value of social change at the expense of human life when the violence required for this change is directed at other nations or other races; and on the other hand, a tendency to absolutize the value of peace at the expense of social change *within* the national framework.

With these preliminary statements, I would like to discuss violence and social change in the history of the United States, not pretending to do more than a brief, impressionistic survey. And then I want to suggest a number of propositions about violence which may be worthy of thought.

Our first great social upheaval was the expulsion of the British and their local officialdom in the establishment of an independent nation. A new privileged class was created, based on the overthrow of the royal and proprietary colonial governments and the redistribution of land after the confiscation of royal, proprietary and Loyalist estates. There were accompanying changes: the diminution of property requirements for political participation in the new state constitutions; the abolition of primogeniture and entail; the disestablishment of the Anglican Church; and the freeing of slaves in the Northern states. This was accomplished by seven years of warfare in which 25,000 in the Continental Army were killed, about one out of every eight men who served. To judge the extent of this violence, one would have to consider that the same ratio of dead in our present population would amount to a death list of 1,500,000.

The next great social change was the pacification of the continent and the creation of a vast common market, from ocean to ocean, 1,500 miles deep, through which labor, capital, raw materials, and finished goods could move freely. This was a vital prerequisite for the development of that industrial colossus which in the twentieth century would produce half the world's goods with six percent of the world's people. And the creation of this common market involved a series of violent acts which we have conveniently put out of memory.

The first of these acts was the expulsion and extermination of the Indians, who at the time of Columbus numbered 1,000,000 in what is now the United States, and who number about 400,000 today. Violence certainly is frequent *within* groups, but it seems to be invoked most easily when directed at strangers. The outsider is either physically odd, linguistically or culturally distinct, or is invested with strangeness because of distance. He becomes an invisible victim, an object of sorts, toward whom enmity can multiply without qualm. In the early nineteenth century, a French traveler noted this in American treatment of the Indian:

> In the heart of this society, so policed, so prudish, so sententiously moral and virtuous, one encounters a complete insensibility, a sort of cold and implacable egoism when it's a question of the American indigines. . . . it's the same pitiless instinct which animates the European race here as everywhere else.

According to John Collier, Commissioner of Indian Affairs in the Roosevelt

Administration and one of the world's leading authorities on the Indians, there were 600 distinct Indian societies at the time the white man arrived in North America, and there was not one square mile of the continent unoccupied or unused. "These societies existed in perfect ecological balance with the forest, the plain, the desert, the waters, and the animal life." Their warfare with one another was controlled, moderate, cautious; their ambitions were small.

Then the white man came, and not one white conqueror, as in the area south of the Rio Grande, but various powers: Spanish, Dutch, French, and English, battling with one another and drawing Indians into their battles. Still, the Indian societies were kept whole, and rule was indirect, as a calculated policy of the competing European powers, and then codified by the new United States as the basic law of Indian relations.

But when the Spanish, Dutch, French, and English were gone from the continent, Collier says, "there remained only one expanding empire, race-prejudiced and with a boundless land hunger, The former policies toward Indian societies and Indian-hood became reversed; a policy at first implicit and sporadic, then explicit, elaborately rationalized and complexly implemented, of the extermination of Indian societies and of every Indian trait, of the eventual liquidation of the Indians, became the formalized policy, law and practice."

The record is hard to read without flinching, because it is the shadowed underside of the most cherished events in American history. We romanticize the early Virginian adventurers, but they settled on the territory of the Powhatten Confederacy and destroyed its members in bloody warfare. We are proud of the Puritans, but that great Puritan divine, Cotton Mather, a leading intellectual of the colony, said, when disease decimated the Indians after the Mayflower landing: "The woods were almost cleared of those pernicious creatures, to make room for a better growth." When the New England settlers burned the wigwams of the Pequots and massacred them as they fled, Cotton Mather recorded it coolly: "It was supposed that no less than six hundred Pequot souls were brought down to hell that day." Andrew Jackson, often heralded as a kind of early New Dealer, sent General Winfield Scott after the Cherokees of Georgia, driving fourteen thousand of them westward in the "trail of tears," in which four thousand died on the way. After the Civil War, the Plains Indians were hunted down, harassed, and killed, the remaining ones squeezed into the Indian Territory of Oklahoma and finally driven out of there, too.

The United States Army crushed the Indian in a series of wars and battles: the Chivington Massacre of 1864 in Colorado, the Black Kettle Massacre by Custer in 1868 in Texas, the driving of the Cheyennes south in 1878, and the Massacre of Wounded Knee in 1890. There were the Cheyenne-Arapaho War and the Sioux Wars of the 1860's. In the 1870's came the Red River War, the Nez Percé War, the Apache War, and more Sioux Wars.

In the record of violence, we might note a phenomenon different than either the quick destruction of the body, or the slow destruction of the spirit, and that is the elimination of the means of life—land, shelter, clothing, food. In the case of the Plains Indian this was accomplished by the slaughter of his most essential raw material: the buffalo. First the railroads split the great herds in two parts; then professional hunters with repeating rifles made the plains a slaughterhouse; by 1870 a million a year were being killed. By 1875 the southern herd was practically exterminated, and ten years later, the northern herd.

Collier says: "It was among the Plains Indians that the policy of annihilation of the societies and then of the individual Indian personality was carried to the farthest extreme." This statement is important because it is a recognition of violence beyond the physical: the destruction of culture and personality. It sounds strangely familiar to us these days, because we have lately become aware that lynching was not the worst thing that happened to the Negro in this country. In Stanley Elkins' comparison of the Nazi concentration camps with the American slave plantations (in his book, *Slavery*), his concern is not the whippings and beatings, but the assaults on the psyche, the warping of the self, the crippling of identity. And of course this did not end with the outlawing of slavery, because the violence done to the Negro person continues on the Southern plantation, in the Southern town, and in the Northern ghettos. Again and again, the young Negro uses the term "concentration camp" or "prison" to describe the ghetto.

The evacuation of the Indian was one necessary step in the forcible clearing of that national area which would house the most productive economy in world history. Piece by piece, what is now the United States was assembled: some acquisitions were made through clever diplomacy, such as the Louisiana Purchase and the Oregon Territory; others were made through violence, such as East Florida after a campaign of harassment by Andrew Jackson, and the Southwestern states (from New Mexico to California) as a result of the Mexican War. By the time of the Civil War, the United States extended from ocean to ocean. By 1890, Frederick Jackson Turner could use the Census Bureau's finding that the frontier was gone to start a train of discussion on its meaning. That Turner saw the frontier as a benign influence on American democracy was still another sign of the national tendency to test our benevolence by how we behave toward one another, and not toward those— whether Indians, Negroes, Mexicans, or Spaniards—*beyond* the frontier.

The Civil War, with all its complexities, is very much a part of the same process described above, a violent and successful effort on the part of the national government to maintain its control over a great agrarian hinterland whose raw materials and markets were needed for the burst of economic development that would take place in the late nineteenth century. President Lincoln said plainly that the retention of the South in the Union, and not slavery, was his main concern. My point is that the presumed peaceful constitutional and economic development of this great territory of the United States required a war that took 600,000 lives. Out of a population of 33,000,000, some 2,300,000 young men went to fight, and one out of four died. If applied to our present population, it would be 3,500,000 died in war. Edmund Wilson, in his biting introduction to *Patriotic Gore,* takes some of the romantic nonsense out of not only the Civil War Centennials, but all adulatory treatments of American territorial growth.

In the course of the war, slavery was abolished. Whether it was the prime cause of the war or not (and we would have to distinguish between its economic-political aspects and its human aspects to discuss that), its abolition was one of the great social changes in American history, and was a consequence of the most concentrated burst of violence this nation has ever experienced. It is hard to see how slavery could have been ended when it was, without *either* a series of revolts such as those planned by John Brown, or finally a devastating war waged, ironically, two years later by the very government that condemned John Brown to death for seeking a *less* costly means of emancipating the slave.

If the position of the Negro in this country is any test of the thesis that our free institutions have developed on the basis of peaceful parliamentary change, that thesis could hardly be advanced with any seriousness. That it can be advanced is testimony to how small a part the Negro plays in the national consciousness. He is always an exception, to be noted and then shoved aside, so that the state of the nation can be calculated without his troublesome presence. (When one sixth of the nation consisted of black slaves, this was known as "the peculiar institution.") The violence done *to* the Negro in his state of slavery, beyond the physical violence, divesting him of property, of wife and children, of education, of African culture, of his own identity —the process of total alienation—was never properly counted, even by our more humane scholars, who often limited their concern to wondering how many Negroes were really whipped by the plantation owner. And the violence done to his spirit in contemporary society is only beginning to enter our consciousness.

With independence from European control secured, with the continent united and pacified (and here, as with the American Revolution, there were bonuses: a National Bank, and Tariff, Railroad, and Homestead Acts, no longer opposed by the South), the next great social change was the industrialization and urbanization of an agrarian nation. This can be considered a peaceful development only if violence is limited to overt, intense physical harm. Those who worked on the railroads, in the mines, in the factories and mills were subjected to a kind of servitude destructive of both body and spirit. The hours were long, the wages low, and often there was a serflike incarceration in company towns. George Fitzhugh, in *Cannibals All,* had, just before the Civil War, castigated Northerners who criticized slavery while holding on to their industrial system. "You, with the command over labor which your capital gives you, are a slave owner—a master, without the obligations of a master. They who work for you, who create your income, are slaves, without the rights of slaves."

The depressions of the 1870's and the 1890's brought great distress. During the first three months of 1874, for instance, about 90,000 homeless workers, many of them women, lodged in New York City's police station houses, huddled together on benches. They were turned out at daybreak, hungry, to make room for the next batch. The Granger, Greenback, and Populist Movements rose in response to the distress of farmers in those years. The depressions eased and the movement declined, but the point is that the nation's industrial progress was made at great human cost to millions of people, a cost that must be reckoned in any expanded definition of violence. Barrington Moore's new book, *Social Origins of Dictatorship and Democracy,* illustrates, in his words, "the contributions of violence to gradualism" in the chapter in which he discusses the enclosure movement in England, another country with supposedly peaceful parliamentary development.

Another of the important social changes in American history was the development of what we call the "welfare state," the establishment of acceptable living standards for two thirds of the nation, limiting poverty and distress to those parts of the population which cannot easily combine (farm and service workers) or which lack a territorial base (migrant workers) or which are set off racially from the rest of the population. The welfare state began slowly in the Progressive Era with the legislation of the Wilson Administration and reached its height with the New Deal. What is often overlooked is the part played by violence of an overt kind in bringing about what is called the Age of Reform, which started in the twentieth century.

The Progressivism of Roosevelt-Taft-Wilson followed a period of the most violent labor struggles any country has ever seen: the railroad strikes of 1877, which brought troops and workers into armed clashes; the Haymarket events of 1886; the Homestead Strike of 1892; the Lawrence Textile Strike of 1892; the Pullman Strike of 1894; the Colorado Coal Strike of 1913–14, culminating in the Ludlow Massacre. This was the period of Big Bill Haywood, Mother Jones, and the Industrial Workers of the World. As for the New Deal era, it was accompanied by violent strikes, sit-down and regular; the mayhem documented in the La Follette Committee hearings is startling to anyone who thinks that the quiet politicking and the eloquence of FDR tells the story of the New Deal reforms.

The most important social change of recent years is the *de jure,* although not the *de facto,* end of segregation in the South and the awakening of the nation to the outcry of the Negro, for the first time since Reconstruction. Whatever the inadequacies, the lack of enforcement, of the various Civil Rights Bills passed since 1957, however empty are many of the passionate statements on racial equality from the White House, it seems quite clear that ten years of turbulence in the Negro community, from the Montgomery boycott of 1955 to the Selma march of 1965, had a great deal to do with these small gains.

To turn to a quick overview, American society, I believe, does show a growing consensus over time. What we have, however, is not one long consensus, but a series of steps toward consensus, each accompanied by violence which either destroyed, expelled, or incorporated a dissident group. The Revolution established a new consensus based on independence, expelling the British and their Loyalist supporters. Those not satisfied with the new privileged classes (Shays' rebels in Massachusetts, the Whisky rebels in Pennsylvania) were suppressed by force of arms to create an outwardly peaceful consensus under the new Constitution. Those left out of the new arrangement—the black people—were repressed with the entire paraphernalia of the slave system. Organized labor, after the 1877–1939 period of violent strikes, was brought into the consensus with New Deal legislation. And recently, the middle-class Negro has been pacified with the promise of incorporation into white middle-class life, leaving his brethren (represented by the Stokely Carmichaels and others like him) outside the consensus.

More and more elements of American life have been invited into the dominant in-group of American society, usually after overt violence of various kinds; each accretion solidifies the group, which can then continue, or even increase, the violence directed toward those outside the consensus (respectable Negro leaders will be more and more welcome at the White House, while the police will be more and more used to break up Negro rebellions in the cities or on college campuses). The creation of a substantial consensus at home seems to create the possibility of using even greater amounts of violence against out-groups abroad. (I have not spoken of the rapid increase in the means of violence and the use of violence by the United States abroad in this century, because this is too well known; I would single out as dramatic points of significance the fire-bombing of Dresden, the atom-bombing of Hiroshima, and the napalm-bombing of Vietnam.)

Our much-praised peaceful constitutional development, in other words, is based on a system which keeps peace on the national level, while violating it on two other levels of human existence. That is, the system permits disturbing the inner peace of millions of Americans who are too poor, or too colored, or too different in one way or another to be treated with respect by government and society. And in the field of foreign policy it permits an absolutism in decision-making which acts against what both Hobbes and Locke recognized as a basic law of human nature—the preservation of life.

This brings me back to my thesis: that we have a double standard for the judgment of violence within and without the national-racial group, in which we place a supreme value on peace within the society that has already incorporated us, and a supreme value on violence directed at those outside the corporation. A striking example of this is the general alarm with which the government and the public have greeted militant Negroes' talk of self-defense, or any departure from absolute nonviolence, along with the general willingness of the government and the public to use the most fearsome weapons of violence in Asia.

Let me try now to state in conclusion what some of the elements of a single-standard ethic of violence might be:

1. All forms of pain and abuse—whether overt, concentrated, and physical, or psychological, hidden, and attenuated—should be placed on the same scale of destructive actions. This creates great problems in weighing some forms of violence against others, but is preferable to solving problems too easily by assigning *no* weight to types of violence beyond the standard definition. The common ingredients, the molecular elements of all kinds of violence, need to be isolated. (For instance, we need to recognize the identity of the violence in both crime and punishment.)

2. It follows from this that we pay a price for superficial social peace which represses and hides subsurface violence. The price is not only the maintenance of that infraviolence, but the eventual explosion into overt violence. The much-lauded compromises of 1820 and 1850 which smoothed over the slavery question may have made inevitable the Civil War. The Depression of the 1930's may have been a price paid for glossing over the distress of the 1920's. Grievances saved pay compound interest.

3. Official violence should be granted no special privileges over private violence. John Brown was hanged for attempting, by rather small-scale act of violence, to free the Negro slave; but the United States government draws little opprobrium for a war in which 600,000 were killed in the same cause. A police murder, however unjustified, is privileged in a way that a private citizen's act of murder is not.

4. Violence done by others should be weighed equally with violence done by ourselves; we were horrified when Hitler killed several thousand people by dropping bombs on Rotterdam, but easily accepted the killing of over 100,000 people in the bombing of Dresden. We count the Viet Cong killing of a village chief as more terrible than the American bombing of the population of the village. Pearl Harbor is infinitely more condemned than Hiroshima. We are more troubled by a rock thrown by a Negro at a white policeman than by the policeman's shooting of another Negro. We would be shocked if Negroes decided to bomb the state of Alabama to get rid of its oppressive regime—but in international affairs we accept such reasoning.

5. We should assume that all victims are created equal, that violence done to men of other races or other political beliefs is not thereby given special dispensation: a dead Communist is a dead man, as is a dead anti-Communist. George Orwell, in *Homage to Catalonia,* wrote of holding his fire in the Spanish Civil War when a Fascist soldier, running past, had trouble keeping his pants up. "How can you kill a man," he wrote, "who is having trouble holding up his pants?"

6. Violence to property should not be equated with violence to people. When I was living in Atlanta, a policeman there shot and killed a Negro teenager who was running away from a store where a vending machine had been robbed of two dollars. Such scenes can be multiplied by the hundreds; many of those killed in urban riots in recent years were doing nothing but looting stores.

7. We should be constantly aware of our disposition to accept violence on the basis of symbolic arguments: animals commit violence for immediate and visible purposes, but humans can be driven to violence by a word, a slogan, a Pavlovian conditioning process in which we are so far removed from what the symbol stands for that we cannot rationally weigh the human costs and gains of our own acts. The word "nigger" or "imperialist" or "Communist" has driven, and still drives a rational judgment from the minds even of intellectuals.

8. Finally we should be aware of Jeremy Bentham's criterion, in his utilitarian scheme, of fecundity: that not only should we measure immediate results of actions, but that we should also consider the proliferating effects—of excessive action in the dispensation of overt violence, and of inaction in the toleration of subsurface violence. Insensitivity in either case may lead to unexpected and terrible consequences.